The National Register of Historic Places in New York State

Compiled for the Preservation League of New York State
by Peter D. Shaver

Foreword by Gov. Mario M. Cuomo

Introduction by Joan K. Davidson

Furthermore Press Edition

Preservation
League
of
New York
State

The Preservation League of New York State, founded in 1974, is the only statewide, not-for-profit membership organization dedicated to preserving New York's incomparable architectural heritage. The Preservation League implements this charge by providing technical and legal assistance, serving as a resource center, granting funds, issuing publications, sponsoring conferences and workshops, offering awards, producing and distributing films and videotapes, and maintaining a presence in the state legislature in Albany. Support for the Preservation League comes from foundations, corporations, government grants and contracts, and from a dedicated membership. For more information, write Preservation League of New York State, 44 Central Avenue, Albany, New York 12206, or call (518) 462-5658.

The Preservation League of New York State gratefully acknowledges funding for this publication from The J. M. Kaplan Fund, the Arthur Ross Foundation, and a federal grant from the New York State Office of Parks, Recreation and Historic Preservation.

First published in the United States of America in 1993 by
Rizzoli International Publications, Inc.
300 Park Avenue South, New York, New York 10010

LC: 93-86031
ISBN: 0-8478-1789-X   0-8478-1788-1 (paperback)

The activity that is the subject of this book has been financed in part with federal funds from the National Park Service, Department of the Interior. However, the contents and opinions do not necessarily reflect the views or policies of the Department of the Interior, nor does the mention of trade names or commercial products constitute endorsement or recommendation by the Department of the Interior. The activity has been administered by the New York State Office of Parks, Recreation and Historic Preservation. Regulations of the Department of the Interior strictly prohibit unlawful discrimination in federally assisted programs on the basis of race, color, national origin, age, or handicap. Any person who believes he or she has been discriminated against in any program, activity, or facility operated by a recipient of federal assistance should write to: Director, Equal Opportunity Program, U.S. Department of the Interior, National Park Service, P.O. 37127, Washington, D.C. 20013-7127.

Designed by Frank Benedict Design Incorporated.
Printed and bound in the United States of America.

Frontispiece: North tower and pier, Kingston–Port Ewen Suspension Bridge, Esopus (Ulster County).

PHOTO CREDITS

All photographs are reproduced from prints in the files of the Preservation League of New York State excepting those on pages: 176 from the Gannett Company; 43, 55, 181 Historic American Building Survey; 28 Landmark Society of Western New York; 80 Madison County Historical Society; 70, 87, 100, 106 National Park Service; 24, 57, 79, 84, 93, 111, 145, 146, 147, 152 New York State Council on the Arts; 36 New York State Historical Association; 107 Rockefeller Group; 142 Scenic Hudson; 155 Society for the Preservation of Long Island Antiquities; 2, 52, 62, 68, 73, 82, 85, 86, 88, 89, 90, 91, 102, 113, 119, 120, 124, 126, 131, 139, 143, 150, 151, 157, 167, 169, 172, 173, 175, 180, 182 State Historic Preservation Office; 54 SUNY at Buffalo; 118 Syracuse Area Landmark Theatre; 116 Syracuse University.

Photographers are identified for pictures on pages: 90, 91 Joseph Adams; 145 Joe Alper; 111, 152 Gil Amiaga; 88 Robert Y. Arthurs; 136 Gene Baxter; 55, 87, 106, 124, 139, 181 Jack E. Boucher; 126 Helen Breitbeck; 173 S. Brillon; 95 Burns Brothers; 54 Phyllis Christopher; 133 Lisa Clifford; 24 Emily de Rham; 84 Bruce Davidson; 52 Peter deVries; 82 Linn Duncan; 182 L. Dunforth; 39 Alan S. Everest; 64 Mary E. Fenner; 16 Bernd Foerster; 40 Michael Fredericks; 22, 23, 112 Jeffrey Gibbs; 121 Cornelia Brooke Gilder; 165 Karen Glazener; 2, 131 Larry E. Gobrecht; 169 V. Guariglia; 44 Walter Hanchett; 154 Kellogg Studio; 31 Lynn Kozuboski; 57 Richard J. Linke; 180 N. Lionni; 70 Jet Lowe; 61 Paul Malo; 138 Mark Nelson; 85 Hans Padelt; 175 Ann Parks; 113 Gerda Peterich; 79, 147 David Plowden; 142 Michael P. Rebic; 43, 97 Cervin Robinson; 125 Laura Rosen; 168 Matthew Seaman; 172 R. Smith; 35, 36, 128 Milo V. Stewart; 162 Harry Thayer; 146, 157 Sheldon Toomer; 48 Tania G. Werbizky; 89 Terry Winters; 123 Eugene Wright; 100 Steven Zane; 62 Mark Zeek.

CONTENTS

This publication celebrates 25 years of the National Register of Historic Places program in New York State. I congratulate the New York State Office of Parks, Recreation and Historic Preservation on its outstanding administration of the program which, largely under the direction of former commissioner Orin Lehman, has achieved official recognition for nearly 3,000 of our state's most significant structures and landscapes.

New York State has always been at the forefront of recognizing and protecting our heritage. In July of 1966, even before President Johnson signed the National Historic Preservation Act into law, New York emerged as a national leader by creating the New York State Historic Trust to operate our own system of historic sites and to establish the National Register of Historic Places that had been enacted by Congress. The duties of the Trust were later assumed by the Office of Parks and Recreation, which in 1981 formally added "Historic Preservation" to its name.

The Preservation League of New York State has captured one slice of New York's heritage with this publication, which will stand as a tribute to those who have endeavored to pass that heritage on to future generations. The League; the New York State Office of Parks, Recreation and Historic Preservation; and all New Yorkers who have participated in the National Register program deserve our thanks for protecting the architectural and historic heritage of our great Empire State. Excelsior!

Mario M. Cuomo
Governor, New York State

New York State Capitol, Albany.

The National Register of Historic Places was established under the National Historic Preservation Act of 1966 authorizing the Secretary of the Interior to maintain a roster of "districts, sites, structures, and objects significant in American history, architecture, archeology, and culture." Forged in response to concern for the erosion of the visible record of our past, the act extended federal recognition beyond properties designated as National Historic Landmarks to those of significance to states and localities, and it gave rise to an unusual partnership of federal and state agencies and private preservationists. Although the National Register is maintained by the National Park Service, the nomination process and the ultimate protection of listed properties are assigned to the states.

Listing in the National Register confirms that a property is worthy of preserving, offers protection through change-impact analysis, and opens the door to grants and tax incentives for rehabilitation and restoration. In New York State the nomination of properties is delegated to the Office of Parks, Recreation and Historic Preservation which, as the State Historic Preservation Office, reviews nominees for inclusion in the New York State Register of Historic Places and forwards eligible candidates to the National Register. Due to minor differences in the two programs, properties on the New York State Register are not necessarily listed in the National Register.

At the end of 1991, when this book was being compiled, there were 2,926 New York State properties listed in the National Register and comprising almost 60,000 buildings, sites, structures, and objects. This book provides a brief description of each of these properties. They are arranged alphabetically by county, locality (city, town, or village) within the county, and the property name of record in the National Register. The descriptions include address, some (but not all) alternative property names, and date of National Register listing. Some addresses, mainly those of archeological sites, have been withheld for property protection; others are amplified with hamlet identification for better access.

Several features of the descriptions may require explanation:

– All National Historic Landmarks are National Register properties and have been identified by the letters NHL followed by the date of landmark designation (which is also the date of National Register listing for those postdating 1966; those predating the National Historic Preservation Act are listed in the National Register as of October 15, 1966).

– Most properties demolished after National Register listing remain on the roster and are shown as demolished in the description.

– Areas with contiguous properties of historical or esthetic significance may be nominated to the National Register as historic districts. Noncontiguous properties that are recognized as components of significant groups may also be nominated collectively within multiple property submissions. Such groups are identified in the descriptions as Multiple Resource Areas (comprising noncontiguous but geographically linked properties) and Thematic Resources (comprising noncontiguous but thematically linked properties).

The descriptions are based mainly on National Register nomination forms prepared by different people in different parts of the state over a span of 25 years. It is only reasonable that variation in terminology will occur under such circumstances; while regularization has been attempted, some confusion in stylistic identifications is inevitable. The index attempts to help the reader through such confusion by means of cross-reference between or among ambiguous style designations.

Eastlake cottage in Thousand Island Park Historic District, Orleans (Jefferson County).

The Preservation League is indebted to many individuals and institutions for their hard work and generosity. Chief among the benefactors of this book has been Joan K. Davidson, president of The J. M. Kaplan Fund, who not only opened her purse but from the very beginning offered her support and guidance. The introduction to this book is testament to her commitment. Generous support has been received from the Arthur Ross Foundation, whose president Arthur Ross has sustained an ongoing interest in the project. The project was begun with a federal grant from the New York State Office of Parks, Recreation and Historic Preservation, whose Deputy Commissioner for Historic Preservation Julia S. Stokes and former Commissioner Orin Lehman have been consistent in their support.

The lion's share of the work was undertaken by Peter D. Shaver as both consultant to and staff member of the Preservation League. It was his task to read and interpret 25 years of National Register submissions written by scores of authors working under the guidance of a variety of state and federal administrations. In many cases he had to reduce a submission form of more than 50 pages to a paragraph of fewer than 50 words. It is no small achievement of his that the nearly 2,900 entries in this book have been translated into homogeneous stylistic and descriptive terminology. Also many entries have been updated with information learned or corrected since original National Register forms were written.

Early on the production of the book was assigned to Mike Gladstone. Working first as an individual consultant and later within the framework of Furthermore Press, he suggested the format and guided the editing, indexing, and design. Frank Benedict elegantly assembled a mass of disparate information and images of New York State architecture into a visual whole. Julie Hurst and Maria Clark assisted in his studio. Kate Norment as copy editor resolved innumerable questions arising from omission and inconsistency in the original submission forms and more recent changes in organization. The printing format was made possible by the generosity of Mohawk Paper Mills, Cohoes, New York.

Kindly reading parts or all of the manuscript along the way were: J. Winthrop Aldrich, Constance B. Barone, Douglas G. Bucher, John Clarke, Randall T. Crawford, the late Richard Crowley, Andrew S. Dolkart, Roger G. Gerry, Karen S. Hartgen, Roger Haydon, Cynthia Howk, William B. Johnston, Karen Morey Kennedy, Francis R. Kowsky, Robert B. MacKay, Stephanie W. Mauri, Kathleen Burton Maxwell, Jean S. Olton, Edward K. Pratt, Daniel D. Reiff, Barbara F. Van Liew, Diana S. Waite, and Judith Wellman.

The idea to publish the National Register in New York State originated in conversation with David S. Gillespie and Lawrence Gobrecht of the Office of Parks, Recreation and Historic Preservation. Members of their staff have been helpful as the work progressed, among them: Lucy Breyer, Robert Englert, Merrill Hesch, Andy Hope, Tony Opalka, Mark Peckham, and Nancy Todd. At the National Park Service, Patty Henry, Carolyn Pitts, and Beth Savage have done much to aid this project. Brenda Brown of the New York State Council on the Arts helped with photography research. Suzanne Davis of The J. M. Kaplan Fund was especially helpful in the early stages. The Board of Trustees and the Trustees Council of the Preservation League, under the leadership of Linda Gillies and Cynthia C. Wainwright, have been unfailing in their support of this book.

Finally, it was the staff of the Preservation League who brought this highly complex project to completion. Over a three-year period these have included: Clark J. Strickland, Frederick D. Cawley, Patricia V. Hunziker, Carol G. Walther, and Tania G. Werbizky.

*John Schoolcraft House, Guilderland
(Albany County).*

Joan K. Davidson

For a full quarter century now, I have been invoking the National Register of Historic Places as an architectural seal of approval, and as an ardent member of the Preservation League of New York State — the sponsor of this illuminating publication — have even fancied myself a bit player in the historic property designation business. Yet I find that to read this book is to be astonished. The National Register of the 1990s turns out to be something quite different, indeed something vastly more consequential, than I had assumed. It has become a document of social history, an encyclopedia of material culture, a revelation of the nature of community — even, possibly, a guide for planning the future of the built environment in our state. From the opening shot of an Esopus bridge pier to the final Arcade and Attica locomotive, this second compilation of National Register listings in New York State brings to light a regional heritage that is both complex and cohesive.

The first and until now only New York publication on the National Register was produced in 1976 as the pioneer state response to the great 1966 legislation that brought the National Register of Historic Places into being. That early book described some 300 New York properties that had achieved National Register status by 1973. (It also listed 100 or so properties in New York that had automatically entered the newly created Register as National Historic Landmarks.) By contrast with the 1976 publication, this new one deals with almost 3,000 New York State listings (of which only 225 are national landmarks).

There is something endearingly quirky about the early Register nominations. In New York County, to use one of our well-known counties as an example, the 1976 listings included one commercial skyscraper (Woolworth), one Upper East Side mansion (Carnegie), and one club (Players). All of these were among the automatically listed National Historic Landmarks, whereas the 47 state-nominated listings included two firehouses, six churches, two synagogues, and three (abandoned) hospitals. The sole state-nominated theater listing was the newly restored and converted Astor Library. Geographic distribution was spotty. Seven of the 47 state-nominated properties in New York County were located on Welfare (now Roosevelt) Island and another five were on Governors Island. Elsewhere, ten of a total 18 Dutchess County listings were in Poughkeepsie and 11 of 13 Monroe County listings in Rochester.

With justifiable apprehension, the 1976 book identified four New York State nominations that had been destroyed before they could be listed and another five that were destroyed despite listing. The fear of destruction coupled with heightened appreciation of vernacular architecture may help to explain early nominations that, while delightfully various, were individually unrepresentative of many of New York's 62 counties and together failed to reflect the state as a whole.

Erratic eruption of preservation interest in different parts of the state accounts for much of the uneven geographic representation of 1976. That unevenness persists today, but the tenfold growth of listings veils it. Remaining inconsistencies are cushioned by the historic districts that comprise many sites and structures and encompass large chunks of regional history. There were 41 such historic districts among the New York State listings of 1976 and there are over 400 today. These are now augmented by other multiple nominations that think big. Some recognize diverse resources clustered in geographic proximity and others focus on properties that may be scattered but are alike in theme — the Olmsted parks and parkways of Buffalo, the tide and windmills of Long Island, movie palaces, Quaker meetinghouses, sidewalk clocks, and the settings of women's rights history. By virtue of these collective additions, the total number of entities included in National Register listings for New York State — buildings, structures, sites, and objects — is now close to 60,000.

Why not approach this book backwards? Its heart and soul is the generous index that reveals the depth of learning inherent in such a bonanza of fact. We discover, for example, a network of New York State canals (10); theaters and Dutch barns (over 20 each); and octagonal buildings, mills, hotels, and bridges (40 or more each). We can pinpoint more than 300 Gothic Revival buildings, 450 Federal examples, and 500 Greek Revival

Clock at 1501 Third Avenue, one of the Sidewalk Clocks of New York City Thematic Resources (New York County).

ones. We find 20 listings of work by Alexander Jackson Davis; almost 50 for McKim, Mead & White. An appendix points the way to no fewer than 948 other architects, land scape architects, builders, and engineers, and the index locates specific New York State examples of their work. What becomes apparent through the index, in fact, is that the documentation underlying the National Register abounds in unanticipated information that unlocks the essence of our history and culture.

Because of this abundance we come to sense the special character of our state — observing stone buildings with origins in the Netherlands; rustic cottages and landscapes dependent on Downing; octagons inspired by Fowler; Hudson villas designed by Vaux; and the imposing Beaux-Arts residences of New York City, Westchester, and Long Island that owe their elegance and grandeur to McKim, Mead & White. Here is New York emerging as a leader of national architectural style — as it proclaims itself the Empire State. Here are the massive Greek Revival and Gothic Revival residential and civic build ings that gave the New York State streetscape its unique flavor at a time when energy and wealth were heading west and a vast system of roads and canals, railways and bridges united agriculture with rapidly advancing commerce and industry. Here are the barns, silos, hamlets, and scenic roads of New York's rich working landscape. And here are the Great Camps of the Adirondacks — unique in all the world — that signify not only tycoon privilege but New York's abiding devotion to wilderness and the outdoor life. Prehistory and evidence of native America are represented, and the experience of later immigrants is recognized alongside the sites of early settlement and of the American Revolution. The architecture of the major urban centers — Albany, Buffalo, New York City, Rochester, and Syracuse — has been captured, and the stylistic originality that engenders chauvinistic pride in some counties is balanced by the predictable (and infinitely lovable) expression of others.

Above all, the interweaving of environmental elements that support life is manifest. The connecting web of singular structures, congeries of structures, objects, sites, and the varied and glorious landscapes of our state is affirmed as worth saving. The roster bespeaks patterns of human habitation — of transportation, commerce, labor on land and water, and domestic arrangement — that have taken hold over time. It affirms that change, incremental and logical, is at the heart of our communal experience but that the age-old verities endure: the inspiration of nature's beauty and the reassurance of neighborhoods.

Through the careful amassing of data about what we have made, New Yorkers — and Americans — will remember what, deep down, they may always have known: that the cherished places of the mind's eye are at the core of our being. This is the yeast with which the modern preservation movement has risen in a scant generation to become a force in America's public life. May it grow more forceful still! May the National Register of Historic Places that you hold in your hand and the preservation movement of which it is a shining emblem lead us to secure the communities we love, communities that build strength upon strength because they are redolent of what has gone before.

These standards are used to determine the significance of properties nominated for listing in the National Register of Historic Places.

The quality of significance in American history, architecture, archeology, engineering, and culture is present in districts, sites, buildings, structures, and objects that possess integrity of location, design, setting, materials, workmanship, feeling, and association and

– that are associated with events that have made a significant contribution to the broad patterns of our history; or

– that are associated with the lives of persons significant in our past; or

– that embody the distinctive characteristics of a type, period, or method of construction, or that represent the work of a master, or that possess high artistic values, or that represent a significant distinguishable entity whose components may lack individual distinction; or

– that have yielded, or may be likely to yield, information important in prehistory or history.

Ordinarily cemeteries, birthplaces or graves of historical figures, properties owned by religious institutions or used for religious purposes, structures that have been moved from their original locations, reconstructed historic buildings, properties primarily commemorative in nature, and properties that have achieved significance within the past 50 years shall not be considered eligible for the National Register. However, such properties will qualify if they are integral parts of districts that do meet the criteria or if they fall within the following categories:

– a religious property deriving primary significance from architectural or artistic distinction or historical importance; or

– a building or structure removed from its original location but which is significant primarily for architectural value, or which is the surviving structure most importantly associated with a historic person or event; or

– a birthplace or grave of a historical figure of outstanding importance if there is no other appropriate site or building directly associated with his productive life; or

– a cemetery that derives its primary significance from graves of persons of transcendent importance, from age, from distinctive design features, or from association with historic events; or

– a reconstructed building when accurately executed in a suitable environment and presented in a dignified manner as part of a restoration master plan, and when no other building or structure with the same association has survived; or

– a property primarily commemorative in intent if design, age, tradition, or symbolic value has invested it with its own historical significance; or

– a property achieving significance within the past 50 years if it is of exceptional importance.

COUNTY LOCATIONS

These small maps showing the position of
each of the 62 New York counties in
alphabetical sequence will help the reader
determine relative county location.

CHAUTAUQUA COUNTY

DUTCHESS COUNTY

ALBANY COUNTY

CHEMUNG COUNTY

ERIE COUNTY

ALLEGANY COUNTY

CHENANGO COUNTY

ESSEX COUNTY

BRONX COUNTY

CLINTON COUNTY

FRANKLIN COUNTY

BROOME COUNTY

COLUMBIA COUNTY

FULTON COUNTY

CATTARAUGUS COUNTY

CORTLAND COUNTY

GENESEE COUNTY

CAYUGA COUNTY

DELAWARE COUNTY

GREENE COUNTY

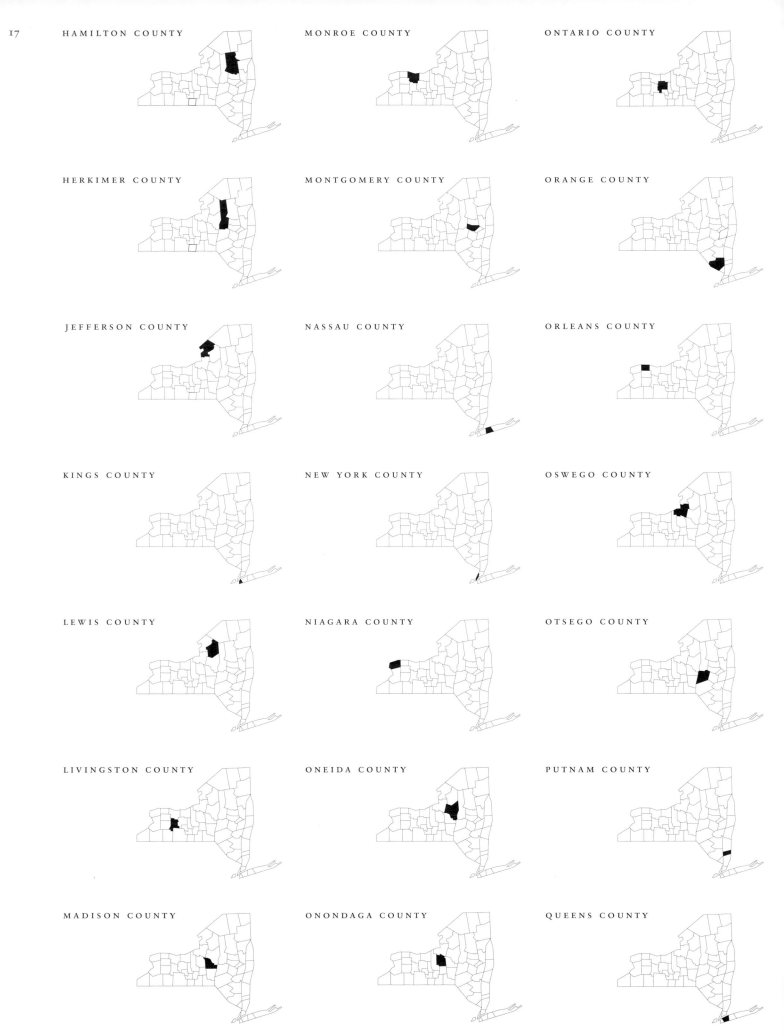

HAMILTON COUNTY

MONROE COUNTY

ONTARIO COUNTY

HERKIMER COUNTY

MONTGOMERY COUNTY

ORANGE COUNTY

JEFFERSON COUNTY

NASSAU COUNTY

ORLEANS COUNTY

KINGS COUNTY

NEW YORK COUNTY

OSWEGO COUNTY

LEWIS COUNTY

NIAGARA COUNTY

OTSEGO COUNTY

LIVINGSTON COUNTY

ONEIDA COUNTY

PUTNAM COUNTY

MADISON COUNTY

ONONDAGA COUNTY

QUEENS COUNTY

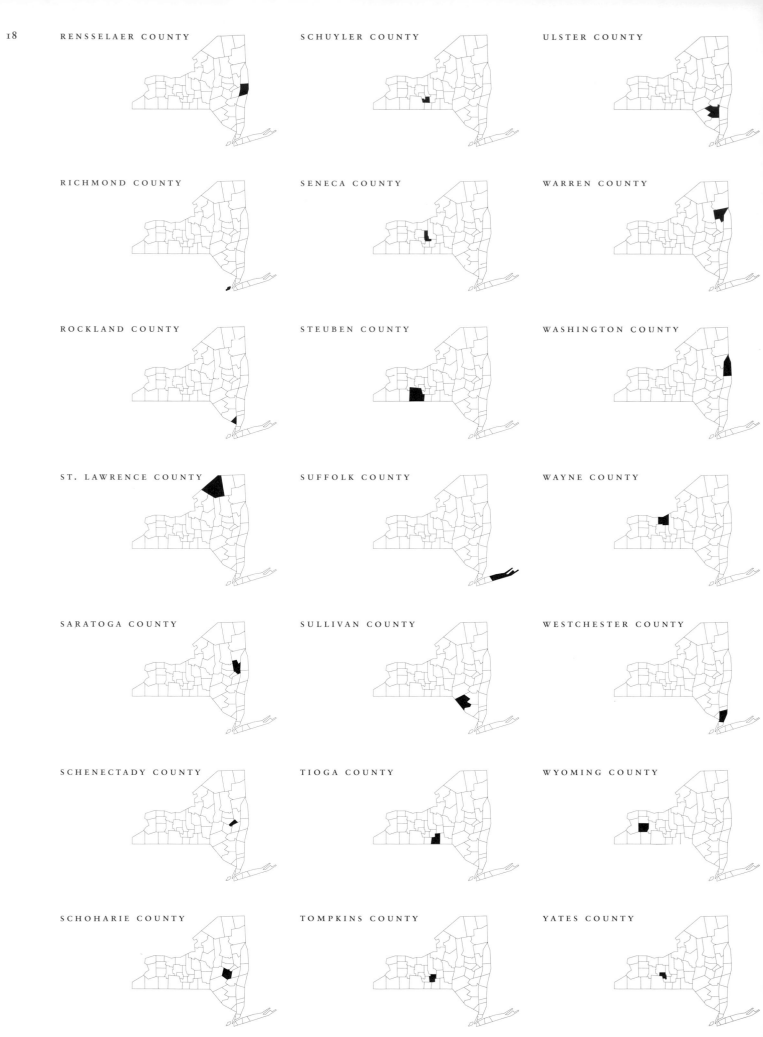

RENSSELAER COUNTY

SCHUYLER COUNTY

ULSTER COUNTY

RICHMOND COUNTY

SENECA COUNTY

WARREN COUNTY

ROCKLAND COUNTY

STEUBEN COUNTY

WASHINGTON COUNTY

ST. LAWRENCE COUNTY

SUFFOLK COUNTY

WAYNE COUNTY

SARATOGA COUNTY

SULLIVAN COUNTY

WESTCHESTER COUNTY

SCHENECTADY COUNTY

TIOGA COUNTY

WYOMING COUNTY

SCHOHARIE COUNTY

TOMPKINS COUNTY

YATES COUNTY

Albany

Abrams Building
55-57 South Pearl Street. A 4-story Roman-esque Revival brick commercial building built 1885.   02.14.1980; DEMOLISHED

Albany Academy (Joseph Henry Memorial)
Academy Park. Federal brownstone school with monumental interior chapel; designed by Philip Hooker; built 1815-17. Rehabilitated 1935 by Marcus T. Reynolds.   02.18.1971

Albany City Hall
Eagle Street at Maiden Lane. Richardsonian Romanesque stone building designed by Henry Hobson Richardson; completed 1883. Interior designed by Ogden & Gander (1917-19). 09.04.1972

Albany Institute of History and Art
135 Washington Avenue. Classical Revival brick museum designed 1907 by Fuller & Pitcher. Adjacent Classical Revival brick library designed by R. H. Hunt; built 1894-95 as residence.   07.12.1976

Albany Union Station (Peter D. Kiernan Plaza)
East side of Broadway between Columbia and Steuben streets. Monumental Beaux-Arts stone former New York Central Railroad passenger station designed by Shepley, Rutan & Coolidge; built 1898-1900.   02.18.1971

Arbor Hill Historic District– Ten Broeck Triangle
Irregular pattern along Ten Broeck Street from Clinton Avenue to Livingston Avenue; also roughly includes Ten Broeck Place and First, Second, and North Swan streets. Mid-19th-century residential neighborhood with large 3-story brick townhouses, detached modest frame dwellings, Gothic Revival St. Joseph's Catholic Church (1856-60, Patrick Keeley), and triangular park.   01.25.1979; BOUNDARY INCREASE 09.29.1984

Benjamin Walworth Arnold House and Carriage House
465 State Street and 307 Washington Avenue. Colonial Revival brick townhouse; designed by Stanford White; completed 1904.   07.26.1982

Broadway–Livingston Avenue Historic District
788-812 Broadway and 67-74 Livingston Avenue. Early to late 19th-century residential and commercial neighborhood.   01.07.1988

Buildings at 744, 746, 748, 750 Broadway
Four brick townhouses built c.1830-73. 12.17.1987

Great Western Staircase, New York State Capitol, Albany (p. 22).

Cathedral of All Saints
East side of South Swan Street, between Washington Avenue and Elk Street. Gothic Revival sandstone church designed by Robert W. Gibson; begun 1883.   07.25.1974

Cathedral of the Immaculate Conception
125 Eagle Street. Monumental Gothic Revival sandstone church designed by Patrick C. Keeley; built 1848-52; expanded and tower completed 1889-92 by Frederick C. Withers. 06.08.1976

Center Square–Hudson Park Historic District
Roughly bounded by Park Avenue and State, Lark, and South Swan streets. Large residential neighborhood with approximately 1,000 buildings, mostly 19th- and early 20th-century townhouses and rowhouses in broad range of styles. Also includes several religious and commercial buildings.   03.18.1980

Cherry Hill
South Pearl Street, between First and McCarty avenues. Large Georgian frame residence with gambrel roof; built 1787 for Colonel Philip Van Rensselaer and occupied until 1963 by his descendants; operated since 1964 as house museum.   02.18.1971

Church of the Holy Innocents
(Church of the Nativity of Our Virgin Lady) 275 North Pearl Street. Gothic Revival stone church designed 1850 by Frank Wills; stained-glass windows by John Bolton.   01.31.1978

Clinton Avenue Historic District
Irregular pattern along Clinton Avenue be-tween North Pearl and Quail streets, including some properties on cross streets. Large con-centration of over 500 brick and frame rowhouses and townhouses constructed as speculative housing c.1820-1920. Includes several churches and commercial buildings, and Palace Theatre (individually listed). 09.01.1988

Delaware and Hudson (D&H) Railroad Company Building
(State University of New York Headquarters) State University of New York Plaza. Monu-mental Flemish Revival limestone and cast-stone building with elaborate ornamentation; designed by Marcus T. Reynolds; built 1914-18.   03.16.1972 ILLUS. P. 23

Downtown Albany Historic District
Broadway and State, Pine, Lodge, and Colum-bia streets. Principal banking, retail, transpor-tation, and political district of Albany, containing many of the city's most important historic buildings designed by its leading architects. Buildings vary significantly in style and scale; the majority built 1880-1930. Individually listed buildings include St. Mary's Church, St. Peter's Church, D&H Railroad Company, First Trust Company, United Traction Company, Young Men's Christian Association, Old Post Office, and Albany Union Station. Other notable buildings include Renaissance Revival/Queen Anne former Kenmore Hotel (1878 with 1891 addition, Ogden & Wright), High Victorian former

Albany Business College (1889, Edward Ogden), Italian Renaissance style Masonic Temple (1895, Albert W. Fuller), Romanesque Revival Centennial Hall (1898, Albert W. Fuller), Dutch Colonial Revival R. B. Wing Building (1913 renovation by Walter Van Guysling), Dutch Colonial Revival former Hudson River Day Line Office (1907, Walter Van Guysling), Richardsonian Romanesque Hampton Plaza (built 1887 as National Commercial Bank, Robert W. Gibson), Victorian Gothic Manufacturers Bank (built 1874-75 as Farmers and Mechanics Bank, Russell Sturgis), Federal-period State Bank of Albany (1803, Philip Hooker; facade incorporated into office building designed 1927 by Henry Ives Cobb), Art Deco Home Savings Bank (1927, Dennison & Hirons), Beaux-Arts City & County Savings Bank (1902 with 1924 addition, Marcus T. Reynolds), Neoclassical Niagara-Mohawk Building (1915, Marcus T. Reynolds), Neoclassical National Savings Bank (1904, Marcus T. Reynolds), Moderne Main Post Office and Courthouse (1933-36, Gander, Gander & Gander with Electus D. Litchfield). 01.31.1980

First Reformed Church (North Dutch Church)
56 Orange Street. Large Federal brick church with paired towers; designed by Philip Hooker; built 1798; 1830 expansion and 1858 alterations.   01.21.1974

First Trust Company Building
Broadway and State Street. Beaux-Arts brick and stone building with rounded corner and dome; designed by Marcus T. Reynolds; built 1904-08.   01.18.1973

James Hall Office
Lincoln Park. Italianate brick villa built c.1852; attributed to Andrew Jackson Downing and Calvert Vaux. Former office of James Hall, paleontologist and geologist. NHL 12.08.1976

Dr. Hun House
149 Washington Avenue. Federal brick town-house built c.1805 for Elkanah Watson; design attributed to Philip Hooker; attached early 20th-century townhouse. Later owned by prominent local physician.   09.19.1972; DEMOLISHED 1972

Knickerbocker and Arnink Garages
72-74 Hudson Avenue. Early 20th-century commercial automobile garages with Gothic-style cast-stone facades; designed by J. Walter Montross.   11.28.1980; DEMOLISHED 1989

Lafayette Park Historic District
Roughly bounded by State, Swan, Elk, Spruce, Chapel, and Eagle streets. Small group of 19th-century brick townhouses facing historic park that contains Albany Academy (individu-ally listed) and is surrounded by the city's most important civic buildings, including Neoclassi-cal Albany County Courthouse (1916, Hoppin & Koen), and individually listed New York State Capitol, New York State Court of Appeals Building, New York State Education Building, and Albany City Hall. 11.15.1978

Mansion Historic District
Roughly bounded by Park Avenue and Pearl, Eagle, and Hamilton streets. A 16-block residential neighborhood with approximately 475 19th-century townhouses, several commercial buildings, 2 schools, 2 churches (1 designed by James Renwick, Jr.), and 3 small parks. 09.30.1982

New York Executive Mansion
138 Eagle Street. Mid-19th-century brick residence remodeled 1887 by Isaac G. Perry into present large Queen Anne brick mansion. Official governor's residence since 1883. 02.18.1971

New York State Education Building, Albany.

Opposite: Delaware and Hudson Railroad Company Building, Albany (p. 21).

New York State Capitol
Capitol Park. Monumental granite building with characteristics of Second Renaissance Revival, Richardsonian Romanesque, and Chateauesque styles; designed by Thomas Fuller, Leopold Eidlitz, Henry Hobson Richardson, and Isaac G. Perry; built 1867-99. One of the last massive all-masonry buildings constructed in 19th-century America. 02.18.1971; NHL 01.29.1979 ILLUS. P. 20

New York State Court of Appeals Building
(State Hall)
Eagle Street between Pine and Columbia streets. Large Greek Revival building with Ionic portico and dome; designed by Henry Rector; built 1842; later alterations including marble cladding. Used since 1916 by Court of Appeals. Contains relocated courtroom designed 1886 by Henry Hobson Richardson for New York State Capitol. 02.18.1971

New York State Education Building
Washington Avenue between Hawk and Swan streets. Monumental Beaux-Arts building dominated by colonnade of 36 marble columns with terra-cotta capitals; designed by Henry Hornbostel; built 1908-12. Notable interior spaces include 94-foot-high domed rotunda, former library reading room with Guastavino vault ceiling, and interior and exterior decora-

tion by muralist Will H. Low and sculptor Charles Keck. 03.18.1971

Nut Grove (William Walsh House)
McCarty Avenue. Greek Revival brick country house designed 1845 by Alexander Jackson Davis. 07.30.1974; DEMOLISHED 1980

Old Post Office
Broadway at State Street. Renaissance Revival stone-clad building designed by James G. Hill; built 1879-83. 01.20.1972

Palace Theatre
19 Clinton Avenue. Vaudeville and movie house designed by John Eberson; built 1930-31; Baroque-style interior. Now concert hall and civic auditorium. Movie Palaces of the Tri-Cities Thematic Resources. 10.04.1979

Pastures Historic District
Bounded by Madison Avenue, Green Street, Dongan Avenue, South Ferry Street, and South Pearl Street. A 13-block residential neighborhood with approximately 105 buildings, mostly 2- to 3-story brick townhouses built 1815-55. Notable buildings include Federal Governor Yates Residence (1811, Philip Hooker). 03.16.1972

Quackenbush House
683 Broadway. Dutch Colonial brick gable-end residence built c.1736. Earliest known example of Dutch urban architecture in Albany. Now a restaurant. 06.19.1972

Quackenbush Pumping Station, Albany Water Works
Quackenbush Square. Victorian brick waterworks facility built in 2 sections in 1852 and 1873; 1895-97 additions designed by Edward Ogden. 06.30.1983

St. Mary's Church
10 Lodge Street. Romanesque Revival brick church with stone trim; designed 1867 by Nichols & Brown; 175-foot tower added 1894. 07.14.1977

St. Peter's Church
107 State Street. Gothic Revival stone church designed by Richard Upjohn and Richard M. Upjohn; built 1859-60; 180-foot tower completed 1876. Weaver stained-glass window designed by Edward Burne-Jones and executed by Morris & Company of London. 03.16.1972; NHL 01.16.1980

Philip Schuyler Mansion
(Schuyler Mansion State Historic Site)
Clinton and Schuyler streets. Large Georgian brick residence built 1761-62 by John Gaborial, master carpenter, for General Philip Schuyler, prominent 18th-century political and military leader. Alexander Hamilton married Schuyler's daughter, Elizabeth, in house in 1780. Federal vestibule designed c.1815 by Philip Hooker. NHL 12.24.1967

South End–Groesbeckville Historic District
Roughly bounded by Elizabeth Street, Second and Morton avenues, and Pearl and Franklin streets. Mid-19th-century working-class neighborhood with approximately six hundred 2- and 3-story rowhouses and townhouses, several churches, and public buildings. Includes Philip Schuyler Mansion (individually listed). 09.13.1984

Ten Broeck Mansion
9 Ten Broeck Place. Federal brick residence built 1797-98 for Abraham Ten Broeck, prominent Albanian, delegate to Continental Congress, mayor of Albany, and brigadier general in American Revolution; design attributed to Philip Hooker. Operated as house museum by Albany County Historical Association. 08.12.1971

United Traction Company Building
598 Broadway. A 3-story Italian Renaissance style brick building with elaborate terra-cotta ornamentation; designed by Marcus T. Reynolds; built 1899. Mass transit headquarters in Albany for 50 years. 05.24.1976

Washington Park Historic District
Washington Park and surrounding properties Large late 19th-century landscaped park surrounded by brick and brownstone townhouses mostly constructed late 19th to early 20th centuries. Notable houses include Benjamin Walworth Arnold House (individually listed) and Richardsonian Romanesque Sard House (designed by Henry Hobson Richardson). 06.19.1972

Whipple Cast and Wrought Iron Bowstring Truss Bridge
1000 Delaware Avenue. A 110-foot single-span bridge built 1867 by Simon DeGraft. One of the earliest iron bridges of its type remaining in the United States. 03.18.1971

Young Men's Christian Association Building
(Steuben Health Club)
60-64 North Pearl Street. Romanesque Revival stone and brick building designed 1886 by Fuller & Wheeler; enlarged 1924; annex built c. 1880 and later incorporated into complex. 11.02.1978

Altamont

Altamont Historic District
Main Street between Thacher Drive and railroad station. Concentration of approximately 38 mostly frame 19th-century residences. Also includes Delaware and Hudson Railroad Passenger Station (individually listed). Guilderland Town Multiple Resource Area. 11.10.1982

Delaware and Hudson Railroad Passenger Station
Main Street and the Delaware and Hudson Railroad tracks. Stick Style frame station built 1887. 08.12.1971

Hayes House
104 Fairview Avenue. Large Colonial Revival frame residence with elaborate decoration; built 1910 for prosperous mill owner. Now a museum. 01.17.1973

Bethlehem

Bethlehem House (Rensselaer Nicholl House)
Off NY 144, east of Bethlehem. Colonial brick residence with gambrel roof; original section built 1736; additions 1796, 1810, and 1830. 04.11.1973

Onesquethaw Valley Historic District
(see New Scotland)

United States Post Office–Delmar
357 Delaware Avenue, Delmar. Colonial Revival brick post office built 1939-40. Interior mural (1940) by Sol Wilson. United States Post Offices in New York State, 1858-1943, Thematic Resources. 11.17.1988

Coeymans

Alcove Historic District
NY 11 and Alcove Road, Alcove. Small 19th-century rural hamlet on Hannacrois Creek; flourished in mid-19th century as mill center. 07.24.1980

Ariaantje Coeymans House
Stone House Road. Imposing Dutch Colonial stone residence built c.1716, with earlier attached wing; c.1790 alterations include gambrel roof and window sash. Adjacent 17th- and 18th-century archeological sites of mills and Native American and military encampments. 10.18.1972

Coeymans School
(Acton Civill Polytechnic Institute)
Southwest corner of Westerlo Street and Civill Avenue. Large Second Empire brick school with elaborate decoration; built c.1873; design attributed to Gilbert B. Croff. 12.29.1970

Onesquethaw Valley Historic District
(see New Scotland)

Cohoes

Downtown Cohoes Historic District.
Roughly bounded by Oneida, Van Rensselaer, Columbia, Main, and Olmstead streets. Concentration of approximately 165 properties, including principal civic and commercial buildings of city, 3 mills, 6 churches, and numerous residences. Most buildings constructed mid- to late 19th century at height of city's importance as textile mill and canal center. Includes individually listed Music Hall and Silliman Memorial Presbyterian Church.

Other notable buildings include monumental Romanesque Revival stone City Hall (1895, J. C. Holland).   09.13.1984

Harmony Mill Historic District

Between Mohawk River and New York Central Railroad tracks. Largest extant 19th-century mill complex in New York State. Includes 5 massive brick mills (Harmony Mill No. 3 individually listed), part of Erie Canal and power canals, several hundred factory workers' houses, mill manager's house, and the Cohoes Falls of the Mohawk River.   01.12.1978

Harmony Mill No. 3 (Mastodon Mill)

100 North Mohawk Street. Massive 2,400-foot-long, 5-story Second Empire brick mill designed by D. H. Van Auken; built in stages, 1866-72.   02.18.1971

Lock 18 of Enlarged Erie Canal

West of 252 North Mohawk Street, east of Reservoir Street, near Manor Avenue. Cut-stone double lock built 1837-42.   02.18.1971

Music Hall

Northwest corner of Remsen and Oneida streets. A 4-story Second Empire brick commercial building with 1,000-seat music hall on upper floors; designed by Charles B. Nichols and J. B. Halcott; built 1874. Restored and now used as theater.   02.18.1971

Olmstead Street Historic District

Olmstead Street between Ontario and Cayuga streets. Commercial and industrial district with large 4 1/2-story, mid-19th-century textile mill and 2 blocks of brick mill workers' rowhouses adjacent to former Erie Canal. Textile mill has been converted to housing.   06.19.1973

Silliman Memorial Presbyterian Church

Mohawk and Seneca streets. Large sandstone building complex consisting of church, church house, and manse; designed by Fuller & Wheeler in eclectic blend of early English Gothic and Romanesque Revival styles; built 1897. Deteriorated condition in 1991.   08.01.1979

Van Schaick House

Van Schaick Avenue, Van Schaick Island. Dutch Colonial brick residence with gambrel roof; built c.1735 by Wessel Van Schaick. Used as military headquarters during French and Indian Wars and American Revolution.   03.18.1971

Colonie

Bacon-Stickney House

441 Loudon Road, Loudonville. Victorian frame suburban cottage designed 1874 by William M. Woollett. Colonie Town Multiple Resource Area.   10.03.1985

Harmony Mill No. 3, Cohoes.

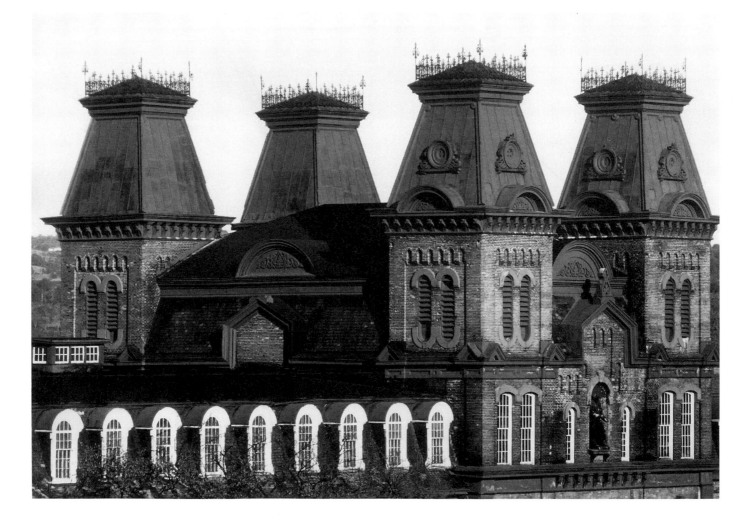

Bryan's Store
435 Loudon Road, Loudonville. A 19th-century 2-story frame building built as saloon and moved to present site c.1863. Later operated as post office and general store. Historic Resources of U.S. Route 9, Town of Colonie. 10.04.1979

Senator William T. Byrne House
463 Loudon Road, Loudonville. Late 19th-century frame residence with Colonial Revival additions and alterations in 1916 by architect Walter Van Guysling for Congressman and State Senator William T. Byrne. Colonie Town Multiple Resource Area. 10.03.1985

Frederick Cramer House
410 Albany-Shaker Road, Loudonville. Eastlake-style brick farmhouse designed by Ernest Hoffman; built 1877. Retains outbuildings. Colonie Town Multiple Resource Area. 10.03.1985

Martin Dunsbach House
140 Dunsbach Ferry Road, Dunsbach Ferry. Greek Revival brick farmhouse built c.1840. Colonie Town Multiple Resource Area. 10.03.1985

Royal K. Fuller House
294 Loudon Road, Loudonville. Norman-style brick residence built 1926-27 for New York State Commissioner of Canals and Waterways. Colonie Town Multiple Resource Area. 10.03.1985

Godfrey Farmhouse (Elm Tree Farm)
1313 Loudon Road. Greek Revival frame farmhouse with Doric portico; built c.1836. Historic Resources of U.S. Route 9, Town of Colonie. 10.04.1979

Gorham House
347 Loudon Road, Loudonville. Colonial Revival brick residence designed 1926 by Norman Sturgis with reused brick, structural members, doorways, and mantels from early 19th-century residence in Vischer's Ferry, Saratoga County. Historic Resources of U.S. Route 9, Town of Colonie. 10.04.1979

Isaac M. Haswell House
67 Haswell Road, Latham. Large Victorian frame farmhouse built 1880. Colonie Town Multiple Resource Area. 10.03.1985

Hedge Lawn (Jermain House)
592 Broadway. Imposing Greek Revival frame residence with Doric portico; built c.1840 for Jermain family; major Second Empire and later alterations. Onetime residence of General William Jenkins Worth. Brick carriage house designed 1908 by Ernest Hoffman. Colonie Town Multiple Resource Area. 10.03.1985

Henry-Remsen House
34 Spring Street, Newtonville. Modest vernacular frame farmhouse built c.1830; large Greek Revival addition c.1860. Dismantled and moved out of area. Colonie Town Multiple Resource Area. 10.03.1985

Ebenezer Hills, Jr. Farmhouse
1010 Troy-Schenectady Road. Large Federal frame farmhouse built c.1785; used as tavern after 1802; retains outbuildings. Deteriorated condition in 1991. Colonie Town Multiple Resource Area. 10.03.1985

Hughson Mansion
374 Loudon Road, Loudonville. Large Second Empire frame residence built c.1875 for Albany lumber merchant. Now part of modern church complex. Historic Resources of U.S. Route 9, Town of Colonie. 10.04.1979

Friend Humphrey House
372 Albany-Shaker Road, Loudonville. Late Federal frame farmhouse built c.1841 for Albany mayor. Colonie Town Multiple Resource Area. 10.03.1985

John Wolf Kemp House
216 Wolf Road. Federal brick farmhouse built c.1810 for tenant on Manor of Rensselaerswyck. Colonie Town Multiple Resource Area. 10.03.1985

John V. A. Lansing Farmhouse, Billsen Cemetery, and Archeological Site
219, 225, 237 Consaul Road. Greek Revival frame farmhouse built c.1840 incorporating part of an 18th-century structure. Early 19th-century cemetery and prehistoric archeological site on property. Colonie Town Multiple Resource Area. 10.03.1985

George H. Lawton House
27 Maxwell Road. Gothic Revival frame cottage built c.1854 for Albany merchant. Colonie Town Multiple Resource Area. 10.03.1985

Loudon Road Historic District
Loudon Road from Crumite Road to Menands Road, Loudonville. Residential district with approximately 22 residences on large lots, including early 19th-century former farmhouses, large Victorian summer houses, and early 20th-century suburban residences. Historic Resources of U.S. Route 9, Town of Colonie. 10.04.1979

D. D. T. Moore Farmhouse
352 Loudon Road, Loudonville. Mid-19th-century farmhouse with Colonial Revival alterations. Known as Middlebrook State Premium Farm in 1854. Originally on tract of 2,500 acres. Historic Resources of U.S. Route 9, Town of Colonie. 10.04.1979

Newtonville Post Office (First Baptist Church)
534 Loudonville Road, Newtonville. Simple vernacular brick building built 1852 as church. 03.14.1973

Casparus F. Pruyn House
207 Old Niskayuna Road, Newtonville. Late Federal/Greek Revival brick residence built c.1835 for business agent of Stephen Van Rensselaer III, last patroon of Manor of Rensselaerswyck. Operated as museum and community center by Friends of Pruyn House. Colonie Town Multiple Resource Area. 10.03.1985

Reformed Dutch Church of Rensselaer in Watervliet
210 Old Loudon Road, Latham. Greek Revival frame church built 1847; Henry H. Runkle, builder. Colonie Town Multiple Resource Area. 10.03.1985

Alfred H. Renshaw House
33 Fiddlers Lane, Newtonville. Imposing Tudor Revival brick residence designed by Norman Sturgis; built 1926-27 for general manager of Trojan Car Coupler Co. in Green Island. Formal gardens and landscape designed by Louise Payson. Colonie Town Multiple Resource Area. 10.03.1985

Schuyler Flatts
Address restricted. A 100-acre property with prehistoric archeological sites of Native American encampments and 1672 house of Philip Pieterson Schuyler, whose son Peter was early colonial governor, first mayor of Albany, and Indian agent. Major camping ground in 18th century for troops during military campaigns. House burned 1962. 01.21.1974

Simmons Stone House
554 Boght Road, Boght Corners. Vernacular stone residence built c.1848 for Daniel Simmons, proprietor of Simmons Axe and Edge Tool Co. in Cohoes. Colonie Town Multiple Resource Area. 10.03.1985

Springwood Manor
498 Loudon Road, Loudonville. Late 19th-century residence altered and enlarged 1912-13 in Colonial Revival style by architect Henry D. Klinger for John A. Manning, owner of Manning Paper Mills. Historic Resources of U.S. Route 9, Town of Colonie. 10.04.1979

Jedediah Strong House
379 Vly Road. Federal frame farmhouse built c.1795 for tenant on Manor of Rensselaerswyck. Colonie Town Multiple Resource Area. 10.03.1985

Treemont Manor
71 Old Niskayuna Road, Loudonville. Large Georgian Revival brick residence designed by Adams & Prentice; built 1929. Colonie Town Multiple Resource Area. 10.03.1985

George Trimble House
158 Spring Street. Arts and Crafts stucco and half-timbered residence built 1909-10. Colonie Town Multiple Resource Area. 10.03.1985

Van Denbergh-Simmons House
537 Boght Road, Boght Corners. Modest early 18th-century Dutch Colonial frame farmhouse; Federal-period addition c.1790 and Italianate addition c.1847. Colonie Town Multiple Resource Area. 10.03.1985

Verdoy School
957 Troy-Schenectady Road, Verdoy. Vernacular frame 1-room school built 1910. Colonie Town Multiple Resource Area. 10.03.1985

Watervliet Shaker Historic District
Watervliet-Shaker Road, near Albany County Airport. A 500-acre property of first Shaker

settlement in United States, started 1774 by Mother Ann Lee and disciples. Includes 20 19th-century buildings of 3 of the 4 original "family" compounds and large cemetery. Church Family Meeting House (1848) operated as museum by Shaker Heritage Society. 02.20.1973; BOUNDARY INCREASE 09.20.1973

Wheeler Home
485 Loudon Road, Loudonville. Large Georgian Revival brick residence built c.1920. Notable landscaped grounds. Historic Resources of U.S. Route 9, Town of Colonie. 10.04.1979

Whitney Mansion
489 Loudon Road, Loudonville. Federal brick residence built c.1825; once owned by inventor Christian Weeber; Colonial Revival alterations c.1906 for W. A. Whitney, Albany department store owner. Historic Resources of U.S. Route 9, Town of Colonic. 10.04.1979

Green Island

Green Island Car Shops
(Rensselaer and Saratoga Railroad Car Shops) James and Tibbits streets and the Delaware and Hudson Railroad tracks. Brick complex built 1871 for Rensselaer and Saratoga Railroad but used by Delaware and Hudson Railroad for maintenance of engines and rolling stock. Includes car-shop building, roundhouse, and water tower. 05.24.1973

St. Mark's Episcopal Church
69-75 Hudson Avenue. Gothic Revival stone church and chapel designed by Emlen T. Littell; built 1866-67. Adjacent Queen Anne rectory built 1883-84. Complex now used as community center. 11.07.1978

Guilderland

Albany Glassworks Site
Address restricted. Archeological site of Albany Glassworks, which operated 1785-1815. 07.22.1980

Apple Tavern
4450 Altamont Road. Large Colonial frame farmhouse built c.1760; major alterations c.1900 in Colonial Revival style. Operated as tavern by Hendrick Apple when first town meeting was held there in 1803. Includes 19th-century barn complex. Guilderland Town Multiple Resource Area. 11.10.1982

Aumic House
Leesome Lane. Large Queen Anne frame residence built 1887 as summer house on escarpment overlooking Altamont. Guilderland Town Multiple Resource Area. 11.10.1982

Chapel House
Western Avenue. Arts and Crafts stuccoed and half-timbered residence built c.1910. Guilderland Town Multiple Resource Area. 11.10.1982

Coppola House
Leesome Lane. Large Colonial Revival frame residence built c.1910 as summer house on escarpment overlooking Altamont. Guilderland Town Multiple Resource Area. 11.10.1982

Frederick Crounse House
3960 Altamont Road. Federal frame farmhouse built c.1802; earlier rear wings include small stone section built c.1760 and frame section built c.1780. Guilderland Town Multiple Resource Area. 11.10.1982

Jacob Crounse Inn
3933 Altamont Road. Large vernacular frame building constructed c.1833 as inn; enlarged c.1870. Guilderland Town Multiple Resource Area. 11.10.1982

John and Henry Crounse Farm Complex
3970 Altamont Road. Modest vernacular frame farmhouse built c.1790; large front wing built c.1860. Adjacent barn and tannery. Guilderland Town Multiple Resource Area. 11.10.1982

Freeman House
136 Main Street, Guilderland Center. Colonial frame residence built 1734; 1750 and 1800 additions. Guilderland Town Multiple Resource Area. 11.10.1982

Fuller's Tavern
6861 Western Turnpike, Fullers. Large vernacular frame residence with saltbox profile; built c.1795. Operated in early 19th century as tavern by John Fuller, local politician. Guilderland Town Multiple Resource Area. 11.10.1982

Gardner House
5661 Gardner Road. Second Empire frame farmhouse built c.1875 for local judge. Guilderland Town Multiple Resource Area. 11.10.1982

Gifford Grange Hall
Western Turnpike, Dunnsville. Vernacular frame building built c.1866 as store and post office. Guilderland Town Multiple Resource Area. 11.10.1982

Gillespie House
2554 Western Turnpike. Modest Greek Revival frame farmhouse built c.1840. Guilderland Town Multiple Resource Area. 11.10.1982

Guilderland Cemetery Vault
NY 158. Small cobblestone cemetery vault built c.1872. Guilderland Town Multiple Resource Area. 11.10.1982

Hamilton Union Church Rectory
2267 Western Turnpike. Greek Revival frame residence built 1857. Guilderland Town Multiple Resource Area. 11.10.1982

Hamilton Union Presbyterian Church
2291 Western Turnpike. Stick Style frame church with buttresses and large open bell tower; designed by August Howe; built 1886. Guilderland Town Multiple Resource Area 11.10.1982

Helderberg Reformed Church
Main Street, Guilderland Center. Victorian Gothic vernacular frame church built 1895. Guilderland Town Multiple Resource Area. 11.10.1982; DEMOLISHED

Adam Hilton House
6073 Leesome Lane. Substantial vernacular stone farmhouse built c.1800; porticoes added c.1860 to north and main facades. Guilderland Town Multiple Resource Area. 11.10.1982

Houck Farmhouse
6156 Ostrander Road. Greek Revival frame farmhouse built c.1850. Guilderland Town Multiple Resource Area. 11.10.1982

Knower House
3921 Altamont Road. Federal frame residence with Palladian window; built c.1800 for Benjamin Knower, hatter. Governor William L. Marcy married Cornelia Knower in house in 1824. Guilderland Town Multiple Resource Area. 11.10.1982

McNiven Farm Complex
4178 Altamont Road. Vernacular frame residence built c.1860 incorporating late 18th-century residence as rear wing. Guilderland Town Multiple Resource Area. 11.10.1982

Mynderse-Frederick House
152 Main Street, Guilderland Center. Vernacular frame residence built c.1800; Greek Revival modifications in 1840s, when house was adapted for use as tavern. Guilderland Town Multiple Resource Area. 11.10.1982

Stephen Pangburn House
2357 Old State Road, Parkers Corners. Frame farmhouse with simple Italianate and Gothic features; built 1861. Guilderland Town Multiple Resource Area. 11.10.1982

Charles Parker House
2273 Old State Road, Parkers Corners. Large Greek Revival frame residence built c.1844 as summer residence for New York City business man; later Italianate decorative trim and cupola. Guilderland Town Multiple Resource Area. 11.10.1982

Prospect Hill Cemetery Building
Western Turnpike. Cobblestone receiving vault built 1863. Guilderland Town Multiple Resource Area. 11.10.1982

Rose Hill
2259 Western Turnpike. Federal frame residence built c.1800 for Volkert Veeder, agent for Stephen Van Rensselaer III. Guilderland Town Multiple Resource Area. 11.10.1982

St. Mark's Lutheran Church
Main Street, Guilderland Center. Victorian frame church built 1872. Guilderland Town Multiple Resource Area. 11.10.1982

John Schoolcraft House
2299 Western Turnpike. Gothic Revival frame villa built c.1845 with elaborate decorative features including crockets, lancet windows,

and battlements. Guilderland Town Multiple Resource Area.   11.10.1982

Schoolhouse No. 6
206 Main Street, Guilderland Center. A 1-room cobblestone schoolhouse built 1860. Guilderland Town Multiple Resource Area. 11.10.1982

Sharp Brothers House
4382 Western Turnpike. Large Queen Anne frame farmhouse built c.1880 incorporating parts of c.1850 building. Includes large barn complex. Guilderland Town Multiple Resource Area.   11.10.1982

Sharp Farmhouse
4379 Western Turnpike. Stick Style frame farmhouse built c.1875. Adjacent large barn. Guilderland Town Multiple Resource Area. 11.10.1982

Van Patten Barn Complex
4773 Western Turnpike. Dutch barn built c.1790 and 2 early 19th-century English barns. Guilderland Town Multiple Resource Area. 11.10.1982; DISMANTLED 1990

Vanderpool Farm Complex
3647 Settles Hill Road. Vernacular frame farmhouse with simple Italianate trim; built 1855. Barn complex with Dutch barn built c.1800. Guilderland Town Multiple Resource Area. 11.10.1982

Veeder Farmhouse No. 1
3770 Western Turnpike. Large Federal farmhouse built c.1830 with fully developed decorative details. Identical house adjacent to east. Guilderland Town Multiple Resource Area. 11.10.1982

Veeder Farmhouse No. 2
3858 Western Turnpike. See Veeder House No. 1 Guilderland Town Multiple Resource Area. 11.10.1982

Menands

Albany Rural Cemetery
Cemetery Avenue. A 467-acre rural cemetery founded 1844. Contains large collection of tombs and monuments by well-known sculptors; graves of prominent local, state, and national figures including President Chester A. Arthur; and remains from 18th-century graveyards removed from downtown Albany. Lodge (now office building) and chapel designed 1882 and 1884 by Robert W. Gibson; superintendent's house designed 1899 by Marcus T. Reynolds. 10.25.1979

Louis Menand House
40 Cemetery Avenue. Queen Anne frame farmhouse incorporating earlier building; built 1881 for horticulturist Louis Menand, Jr. Colonie Town Multiple Resource Area 10.03.1985

Menand Park Historic District
Roughly bounded by Menand Road, Broadway, and Tillinghast Avenue. A 2-block area of 13 Arts and Crafts bungalows built 1913-25 as part of suburban development. Colonie Town Multiple Resource Area. 10.03.1985

Menands Manor (Home for Aged Men)
272 Broadway. Federal brick residence built c.1820; major additions and alterations in Stick Style by architect William M. Woollett and builder Richard Wickham when house was converted in 1877 to old-age home. Colonie Town Multiple Resource Area.   10.03.1985

Henry M. Sage Estate (Fernbrook)
One Sage Road. A 56-acre former estate of State Senator and Mrs. Henry M. Sage; main house built c.1890; extensively remodeled into Georgian Revival mansion c.1920 by architect Marcus T. Reynolds. Shingle Style secondary buildings and formal gardens. 07.04.1980

New Scotland

Onesquethaw Valley Historic District
Off NY 443 and 32 (also in towns of Bethlehem and Coeymans). Rural area of approximately 3,400 acres along Onesquethaw Creek. Includes 25 farms, related archeological sites, eight 18th-century stone houses, and wooded areas. Part of Onesquethaw Patent of 1687. 01.17.1974

Rensselaerville

Rensselaerville Historic District
Old Albany, Pond Hill, and Methodist Hill roads and Main Street. Intact early 19th-century rural hamlet with approximately 90 residences, churches, inns, commercial buildings, and cemeteries. Includes numerous fine Federal and Greek Revival frame buildings. Served as summer retreat community during late 19th and early 20th centuries. 09.15.1983

Watervliet

Watervliet Arsenal
South Broadway. Oldest operating federal arsenal in United States; founded 1813. Notable buildings include Quarters One (1841-42), Benet Weapons Laboratory (1865), Big Gun Shop (1888-1941), former Powder Magazine (1828), Ammunitions Storehouse (1849), Iron Building (1859, fabricated by Architectural Iron Works, New York City), and numerous other 19th-century barracks, shops, and factory buildings. NHL 11.13.1966

Watervliet Side Cut Locks
23rd Street at Hudson River. Remaining stonework of double locks constructed mid-19th century to connect Erie Canal with Hudson River at West Troy (Watervliet). 08.12.1971

Alfred

Alfred Village Historic District
Sections of North and South Main, Church, Ford, Glenn, Park, Sayles, Terrace, and West University streets. Rural village of approximately 133 properties, including individually listed Terra Cotta Building and Fireman's Hall, and concentration of 19th- and early 20th-century residential, commercial, civic, and religious buildings. Regional importance as cultural and educational center. Broad range of architectural styles; many buildings have terracotta roofs and features reflecting development of ceramic industry in village. 09.11.1985

Alumni Hall (Chapel Hall)
Alfred University. Large 3 1/2-story Greek Revival frame building designed by Maxson Stillman, Jr., master builder; built c.1851-52. Used as community meeting hall, worship center, and educational center on campus. 09.12.1985

Fireman's Hall (Alfred Village Hall)
7 West University Street. Late Victorian building with central bell/clock tower, constructed of brick made by Alfred Clay Brick Company; built 1890-91 by volunteer firemen as first home of A. E. Crandell Hook & Ladder Company. 03.18.1980

Allen Steinheim Museum
Alfred University. Gothic Revival mock castle built 1876-80 for Jonathan Allen, using variety of native rock specimens on exterior, and local and exotic woods on interior. 06.04.1973

Terra Cotta Building
North Main Street at Pine Street. A 1-story building built 1892 by Celadon Terra Cotta Company, Ltd., of Alfred, as office and product display case; all materials (brick, tiles) manufactured by company. 03.16.1972

Amity

Christ Episcopal Church
Gibson Hill Road, Belvidere. Modest rural Gothic Revival parish church with board-and-batten siding; designed by John Dudley; built 1860. 05.17.1974

Angelica (Town)

Belvidere
NY 408, Belmont. Imposing Federal brick and stone residence built 1804 for John B. Church, son-in-law of Philip Schuyler and brother-in-law of Alexander Hamilton. Property includes 2-story hexagonal teahouse. 03.16.1972
ILLUS P. 28

Angelica (Village)

Angelica Park Circle Historic District

Main and White streets and Allegany County Fairgrounds. Group of 19th-century public and religious buildings sited around octagonal village green, small residential district, and adjacent county fairgrounds. Includes Old Allegany County Courthouse (individually listed). 01.31.1978

Old Allegany County Courthouse

(Angelica Town Hall)
Park Circle. A 2-story Federal brick building with cupola; built 1819; used as county courthouse until 1892; Victorian modifications. 08.21.1972

Cuba

South Street Historic District

17 and 19-89 South Street. Tree-lined street adjacent to commercial core of village. Contains concentration of 40 mid-19th- to early 20th-century residential and religious buildings in broad range of architectural styles. 05.26.1988

Friendship

Wellman House

Main Street. Large Greek Revival frame residence built 1835 for Colonel Abijah Wellman, prominent local merchant; Victorian alterations and later additions by his son. Located on 3 acres of formal landscaped grounds in center of village. 06.20.1974

Wellsville

United States Post Office–Wellsville

40 East Pearl Street. Large Classical Revival limestone and brick post office designed by Walter B. Olmsted and Frederick V. Murphy; built 1931-33. Art Deco lobby with bas-reliefs (c.1932) by H. K. Bush-Brown and Fred Cowles. United States Post Offices in New York State, 1858-1943, Thematic Resources. 05.11.1989.

Wellsville Erie Depot

Depot Street. Large Queen Anne/Romanesque Revival brick former railroad passenger station built 1911. 08.27.1987

Belvidere, Town of Angelica (p. 27).

Bronx

Bartow-Pell Mansion and Carriage House
Pelham Bay Park, Shore Road. Large Greek
Revival stone residence and carriage house;
built 1836-42 for Robert Bartow, descendant
of Sir John Pell, second Lord of Manor of
Pelham; restored early 20th century by Delano
& Aldrich. Summer "White House" of Mayor
Fiorella LaGuardia. Operated as museum by
International Garden Club.   12.30.1974;
NHL 12.08.1976

House at 175 Belden Street
Picturesque Victorian Gothic frame cottage
built c.1850 on City Island overlooking Long
Island Sound.   06.03.1982

Bronx Borough Courthouse
East 161st Avenue, Third and Brook avenues
A 4-story Beaux-Arts granite building designed
by Oscar Bluemiser and Michael J. Garvin;
built 1905-15. Vacant since 1978.
02.25.1982

**Bronx Central Annex–United States
Post Office**
558 Grand Concourse. Monumental Moderne
gray brick post office with stylized classical
decorative features; designed 1935 by Thomas
Harlan Ellett. Interior mural series by Ben
Shahn and his wife, Bernarda Bryson.
05.6.1980

Bronx County Courthouse
851 Grand Concourse. Monumental 9-story
limestone-clad building of Moderne scale and
massing, embellished with classically derived
sculptural elements; designed by Joseph H.
Freedlander and Max Hausle; built 1931-34.
Frieze by Charles Keck. Sculptural groups by
Adolf A. Weiman, Edward F. Sandford, George
H. Snowden, and Joseph Kiselewski.
09.08.1983

Christ Church Complex, Riverdale
5030 Riverdale Avenue. Gothic Revival stone
parish church designed by Richard M. Upjohn;
built 1866. Adjacent parish house designed by
Dwight James Baum in similar style; built
1923.   09.08.1983

Robert Colgate House (Stonehurst)
5225 Sycamore Avenue. Italianate picturesque
stone villa built early 1860s for New York City
merchant and philanthropist.   09.08.1983

William E. Dodge House
(Greyston Conference Center)
690 West 247th Street. Large Gothic Revival
stone residence with Tudor-style features; built
1863-64 as summer home for philanthropist
William Earl Dodge, Jr.; enlarged 1892. Original design and enlargement attributed to James
Renwick, Jr.   08.28.1977

Edgehill Church of Spuyten Duyvil
(Riverdale Presbyterian Church)
2550 Independence Avenue. Tudor Revival
stone and half-timbered chapel designed 1888
by Francis H. Kimball.   10.29.1982

Eighth Regiment Armory
(Kingsbridge Armory)
29 West Kingsbridge Road. One of the world's
largest armories, with exterior appearance of
medieval Romanesque fortress and vast interior drill hall; designed by Pilcher & Tachau;
built 1912-17.   12.21.1982

52nd Police Precinct Station House and Stable
3016 Webster Avenue. Italian Renaissance style
brick buildings designed by Stoughton &
Stoughton; built 1904-06.
10.29.1982

**Fonthill Castle and the Administration
Building of the College of Mount St. Vincent**
West 261st Street and Riverdale Avenue. Fonthill Castle: Gothic Revival stone castle completed 1852 as country residence for actor
Edwin Forrest. Administration Building: monumental Early Romanesque Revival brick
building built in several stages 1857-1908;
modern wing. Original section designed by
Henry Engelbert.   07.11.1980

Fort Schuyler (State University of New York
Maritime College)
Throgs Neck at East River and Long Island
Sound. United States military fortification built
under direction of Captain I. L. Smith 1833-56
to defend New York City; granite construction
in shape of irregular pentagon. Converted
1974 for use as college.   06.29.1976

48th Police Precinct Station
1925 Bathgate Avenue. A 3-story Italian
Renaissance style building of yellow brick with
stone trim; designed 1900 by Horgan & Slattery; completed 1901.   05.06.1983

Grand Concourse Historic District
730-1000, 1100-1520, 1560, and 851-1675
Grand Concourse. Mile-long concentration of
early 20th-century apartment houses and institutional buildings along planned boulevard
connecting Manhattan to north Bronx. Many
buildings designed by local Bronx architects,
including Jacob M. Felson and Horace Ginsbern.   08.24.1987

Hall of Fame Complex
Bronx Community College Hall of Fame Terrace. Planned group of 4 Beaux-Arts buildings
designed 1892-94 by Stanford White for New
York University; built 1894-1912. Hall of
Fame building has 630-foot-long semicircular
colonnade containing 98 busts of great Americans by well-known sculptors.   09.07.1979
ILLUS P. 30

High Bridge Aqueduct and Water Tower
(see New York County)

High Pumping Station
Jerome Avenue, south of Mosholu Parkway.
Romanesque Revival building built 1901-06 to
pump water from Jerome Park Reservoir to

Bronx consumers; George W. Birdsall, Supervising Architect.   11.10.1983

Longwood Historic District
Roughly bounded by Beck Street, and Longwood, Leggett, and Prospect avenues. Small
residential neighborhood developed 1898-
1906 by George Johnson with mostly 2 1/2-
story semidetached houses in the Renaissance
and Romanesque Revival styles; many
designed by Warren C. Dickenson.
09.26.1983

Lorillard Snuff Mill (Old Snuff Mill)
New York Botanical Garden. A 2 1/2-story
fieldstone mill built c.1840 by P. Lorillard
Company on Bronx River; oldest extant
tobacco factory building in United States.
Restored 1954 and used as restaurant.
NHL 12.22.1977

Morris High School Historic District
Roughly bounded by Boston Road, Jackson
and Forrest avenues, and East 166th and
Home streets. Small district containing Morris
High School (1904, C. B. J. Snyder), 2 streets
of Classical Revival brick rowhouses (1900-
04), and Victorian Gothic Trinity Episcopal
Church of Morrisania (1874; enlarged 1906).
09.15.1983

Mott Avenue Control House
149th Street and Grand Concourse. One of
4 remaining ornamental entrances from New
York City's first subway system; designed by
Heins & LaFarge; built 1908. Interborough
Rapid Transit Control House Thematic
Resources.   05.06.1980

Mott Haven Historic District
Roughly bounded by Third and Brook avenues, and East 137th and East 142nd streets.
A 10-block residential area in 2 sections with
Renaissance Revival rowhouses, 5-story late
19th-century apartment houses, 2 churches,
library, and police station.   03.25.1980

New York Botanical Garden
200th Street and Southern Boulevard. One of
the world's leading botanical gardens, founded
1891 on 250-acre site straddling Bronx River.
Museum building designed 1896 by Robert W.
Gibson; massive Conservatory Range designed
1898 by William R. Cobb of Lord & Burnham
(restored 1970s and renamed Enid A. Haupt
Conservatory). First director Nathaniel Lord
Britton.   NHL 05.28.1967

**New York, Westchester and Boston Railroad
Administration Building**
(180th Street IRT Station)
481 Morris Park Avenue. Italian Renaissance
style building designed by Fellheimer & Long
with Allen H. Stem; completed 1912. Built for
"The Westchester" electric commuter railway.
04.23.1980

Park Plaza Apartments
1005 Jerome Avenue. An 8-story Art Deco
building with polychromatic terra-cotta decoration; designed by Marvin Fine of Horace
Ginsbern office; built 1928-31.   06.03.1982

Hall of Fame Complex, Bronx (p. 29).

Opposite: Binghamton City Hall.

Poe Cottage
2640 Grand Concourse. Modest early 19th-century frame farmhouse. Home of writer Edgar Allan Poe for two years late in his life. Purchased 1913 by City of New York and moved to present location in Poe Park. Operated as museum by Bronx County Historical Society.   08.19.1980

Public School 11
1257 Ogden Avenue. Romanesque Revival stone and brick school designed 1889 by George W. Debevoise, Superintendent; wing designed 1905 by C. B. J. Snyder.   09.08.1983

Public School 15
4010 Dyre Avenue. Victorian Gothic schoolhouse designed by Simon Williams, school principal; built 1877.   12.10.1981

Public School 17 (City Island Community Center and Historical Nautical Museum)
190 Fordham Street. Georgian Revival school designed by C. B. J. Snyder; built 1897-98.
09.27.1984

Rainey Memorial Gates
New York Zoological Park. Monumental bronze entrance gates with elaborate stylized plant and animal forms; designed 1926-31 by sculptor Paul Manship; dedicated 1934.
03.16.1972

Riverdale Presbyterian Church Complex
4761-4765 Henry Hudson Parkway. Gothic

Revival fieldstone church designed 1863 by James Renwick, Jr.; additions and alterations in 1936 in same style by Dwight James Baum. Complex includes manse and cottage.
10.14.1982

St. Ann's Church Complex
295 St. Ann's Avenue. Gothic Revival stone church built 1840; oldest surviving church building in the Bronx. Erected by Morris family, who made significant contributions to success of American Revolution and to direction of early republic. Family members buried in church crypt.   04.16.1980

St. James' Episcopal Church and Parish House
2500 Jerome Avenue. Gothic Revival stone church designed 1864 by Henry Dudley; parish house in similar style designed 1891 by Henry F. Kilburn.   09.30.1982

St. Peter's Church, Chapel, and Cemetery Complex
2500 Westchester Avenue. Gothic Revival stone church designed 1853 by Leopold Eidlitz; destroyed and reconstructed 1879 largely to original design with modifications by Cyrus L. W. Eidlitz. Mortuary chapel designed by Leopold Eidlitz; built 1867-68. Cemetery with gravestones dating from 1702.   09.26.1983

Henry F. Spaulding Coachman's House
4970 Independence Avenue. Stick Style frame cottage designed 1880 by Charles W. Clinton; once part of Spaulding estate.   11.04.1982

Sunnyslope
812 Faile Street. Gothic Revival stone residence in manner of Calvert Vaux; built c.1860 for businessman Peter S. Hoe on 14-acre suburban estate. Now used as church in urban area. 09.15.1983

United States Post Office–Morrisania
442 East 167th Street. Colonial Revival brick post office designed by William Dewey Foster; built 1936. United States Post Offices in New York State, 1858-1943, Thematic Resources. 11.17.1988

United Workers' Cooperatives
(Allerton Coops)
2700-2870 Bronx Park East. Two groups of 5- and 6-story apartment houses built 1926-29 as not-for-profit cooperative for secular Jewish, Communist, and garment worker families. Design elements of Tudor Revival and Dutch Expressionist styles. 09.11.1986

Valentine-Varian House
3266 Bainbridge Avenue. Georgian stone residence built 1758 for Isaac Valentine; sold 1791 to Isaac Varian; moved 1965 to become headquarters of Bronx Historical Society. 03.21.1978

Frederick Van Cortlandt House
Van Cortlandt Park at 242nd Street. Large Georgian stone residence with hipped roof and notable interior woodwork; built 1748-49. Operated as museum by National Society of Colonial Dames in the State of New York. NHL 12.24.1976

Washington Bridge
Harlem River, between West 181st Street, Manhattan, and University Avenue (also in New York County). Steel and iron arch bridge with arched masonry approaches; designed by Charles C. Schneider and Wilhelm Hildenbrand with modifications by Union Bridge Company; built 1886-89. First American bridge to use steel-plate girders for arch ribs. 09.22.1983

Wave Hill
675 West 252nd Street. A 20-acre estate overlooking Hudson River that evolved from early 19th-century manor into turn-of-the-century summer estate, to present use as public park and environmental center. Original residence built 1843 for William Lewis Morris; later significant renovations. Other buildings include Glyndor II, a Georgian Revival brick house built 1927; underground recreation building (1909); and numerous outbuildings. Significant landscape features. Much of estate developed by conservationist George W. Perkins. Past occupants of estate: Theodore Roosevelt, Samuel L. Clemens, and Arturo Toscanini. 09.09.1983

Binghamton

Binghamton City Hall (Hotel de Ville)
Collier Street between Court and Hawley streets. Beaux-Arts stone building designed 1897 by Raymond F. Almirall; completed 1898. Now part of a hotel complex. 03.18.1971

Broome County Courthouse
Court Street. Neoclassical stone building with Baroque-style octagonal dome and Ionic portico; designed by Isaac G. Perry; built 1897-98. 05.22.1973

Christ Church
Corner of Washington and Henry streets. Gothic Revival stone church designed by Richard Upjohn; built 1853-55; spire added 1903. 12.02.1974

Court Street Historic District
Roughly bounded by Chenango River and Carroll, Henry, and Hawley streets. Historic core of downtown Binghamton with concentration of 104 buildings, mostly commercial, in variety of architectural styles. Notable buildings include individually listed former City Hall and Broome County Courthouse, cast-iron Perry Block (1876, Isaac G. Perry), 12-story Beaux-Arts Press Building (1904, Arthur T. Lacey), and Art Deco Broome County Justice Building (1939, Walter Whitlack). Local architects represented in district also include Truman I. Lacey, and S. O. and H. A. Lacey. 09.07.1984

Alfred Dunk House (Brinker House)
4 Pine Street. Gothic Revival frame cottage built c.1853-54 for local businessman. 03.21.1985

Phelps Mansion (Monday Afternoon Club)
191 Court Street. Second Empire brick residence designed by Isaac G. Perry; built 1870. 06.04.1973

Railroad Terminal Historic District
Chenango Street at Erie-Lackawanna Railroad tracks. Concentration of 19 railroad structures, warehouses, and commercial buildings built 1876-1910. Includes monumental Italian Renaissance style Lackawanna Railroad Station (1901, Samuel Huckel, Jr.). 03.20.1986

Roberson Mansion
(Roberson Center for the Arts and Sciences)
30 Front Street. Imposing Italian Renaissance style residence designed by C. Edward Vosbury; built 1904-09 for lumber merchant Alonzo Roberson; large 1968 addition for Roberson Center. Landscape designed by Townsend & Fleming. Significant prehistoric archeological site on property. 03.25.1980

Robert H. Rose House
3 Riverside Drive. Large Queen Anne brick residence designed by C. Edward Vosbury; built c.1896. 08.26.1980; DEMOLISHED

South Washington Street Parabolic Bridge
Susquehanna River. A 484-foot 3-span lenticular metal-truss bridge manufactured by Berlin Iron Bridge Co. of Connecticut; erected 1886-87. Incorporates "parabolic" truss design patented by William O. Douglas. 01.30.1978

State Street–Henry Street Historic District
Roughly bounded by Water, Washington, State, and Lewis streets, Prospect Avenue, and Henry Street. A 2-block concentration of commercial, industrial, and institutional buildings mostly built late 19th and early 20th centuries. Includes Classical Revival/Moderne Federal Building (1935, Conrad & Cummings). 06.25.1986

John T. Whitmore House
111 Murray Street. Queen Anne brick and stuccoed residence built 1888. 08.14.1986

Deposit

State Theatre (Deposit Community Theatre and Performing Arts Center)
148 Front Street. Small Art Deco movie house designed 1937 by H. L. Beebe for Kallet-Comerford Co. 07.21.1988

Endicott

United States Post Office–Endicott
200 Washington Avenue. Classical Revival brick post office designed by Walter Whitlack; built 1937. Interior mural (1938) by Douglass Crockwell. United States Post Offices in New York State, 1858-1943, Thematic Resources. 11.17.1988

Johnson City

United States Post Office–Johnson City
307 Main Street. Colonial Revival brick post office built 1934-35. Interior mural series (1937) by Frederick Knight. United States Post Offices in New York State, 1858-1943, Thematic Resources. 05.11.1989

Windsor

Jedediah Hotchkiss House (Old Stone House)
10 Chestnut Street. Vernacular stone farmhouse built c.1823 by Hotchkiss family, founders of Village of Windsor. Birthplace of Jedediah Hotchkiss, hero of Confederate Army during Civil War. 06.03.1982

Windsor Village Historic District
College Avenue, Academy, Chapel, Church, Dewey, Elm, and Main streets. Principal historic area of rural village on Susquehanna River, developed in early 19th century as lumbering and agricultural community. Contains approximately 80 buildings, mostly mid-19th-century residential and commercial structures. 07.30.1980

Allegany Indian Reservation

Zawatski Site
Address restricted. Multicomponent archeological site with prehistoric Woodland and Archaic features and historic 19th-century settlement features. 06.11.1974

Ellicottville

Ellicottville Historic District
Washington, West Washington, Jefferson, and Monroe streets. Historic core of small village, with approximately 63 buildings and large public square. Includes Ellicottville Town Hall (individually listed), Gothic Revival St. John's Episcopal Church (1836) and other churches, Queen Anne Ellicottville School (1887), late 19th-century brick commercial blocks, and residences in Federal, Greek Revival, Victorian, and Colonial Revival styles. 08.22.1991

Ellicottville Town Hall
Village Square, corner of Washington and Jefferson streets. A 2-story Federal brick building built 1829 as Cattaraugus County Courthouse. 04.03.1973

Franklinville

Park Square Historic District
Bounded by North Main, Pine, Chestnut, South Main, Elm, and Church streets. Commercial core of village, developed in early 19th century as farm market town. Contains approximately 20 mostly late 19th-century commercial buildings situated around landscaped village green. Key buildings include Queen Anne style Morgan Hall (1885) and Blount Library (1914, Otis Dockstader). 09.22.1986

Gowanda

Gowanda Historic District
37-53 West Main Street. Row of 5 Neoclassical brick commercial buildings in central business district; built 1925-26. 09.22.1986

Little Valley

United States Post Office–Little Valley
115 Main Street. Colonial Revival brick post office built 1941-42. United States Post Offices in New York State, 1858-1943, Thematic Resources. 05.11.1989

Napoli

Gladden Windmill (Milks Windmill)
Pigeon Valley Road (original location). A 4-story frame windmill built 1890 by local farmer George Gladden; now dismantled and in storage in Glovers Mill, East Randolph. 07.16.1973

Olean

Olean Public Library
116 South Union Street. Beaux-Arts stone building designed by Edward L. Tilton; built 1909 with Andrew Carnegie endowment; rehabilitated 1985 for use as restaurant. 07.11.1985

United States Post Office–Olean
102 South Union Street. Italian Renaissance style brick post office designed by James Knox Taylor; built 1910-12. United States Post Offices in New York State, 1858-1943, Thematic Resources. 05.11.1989

Portville

Portville Free Library
2 North Main Street. Greek Revival frame residence with stepped-back 2nd story and decorative parapets; built 1847 for merchant Smith Parish; converted 1909 for use as library and later enlarged. 11.07.1991

Auburn

Case Memorial–Seymour Library
176 Genesee Street. Beaux-Arts brick and stone building designed by Carrère & Hastings; built 1898-1903; land and building donated by William E. Case. 05.06.1980

Cayuga County Courthouse and Clerk's Office
152-154 Genesee Street. Large 2-story Greek Revival stone courthouse with monumental Doric portico; designed by John I. Hagaman; built 1835-36; reconstructed and 3rd story added 1922-24 after fire (architects Carl Tallman and Samuel Hillger). Adjacent Queen Anne brick County Clerk's Office designed by Green & Wicks; built 1882. 06.21.1991

Flatiron Building
1-3 Genesee Street. A 3-story limestone commercial building built 1829. 03.05.1970; DEMOLISHED

Former United States Post Office and Federal Courthouse
151-157 Genesee Street. Richardsonian Romanesque brick and limestone building with corner tower and elaborate ornamentation; designed by Mifflen E. Bell; built 1888-90; expanded 1913-14 and 1937. Acquired 1984 for county offices. 06.11.1991

William H. Seward House
33 South Street. Early 19th-century Federal residence enlarged 1847 and 1870. Home of statesman William H. Seward from 1824 until his death in 1872. Museum. NHL 01.29.1964

South Street Area Historic District
South Street and sections of cross streets between Metcalf Drive and Lincoln Street. A 19th- and early 20th-century neighborhood with approximately 125 buildings, mostly large residences on large lots. Includes Federal, Greek Revival, Italianate, Queen Anne, Eastlake, Stick Style, Shingle Style, and Colonial Revival residences, many with carriage barns and outbuildings. Also includes several churches, institutional buildings, apartments, monuments, fences, and William H. Seward House (individually listed). 03.09.1991

Harriet Tubman Home for the Aged (Harriet Tubman Museum)
180-182 South Street. Home for aged and destitute African-Americans established 1908 by Harriet Tubman, former slave, slave rescuer, and humanitarian. NHL 05.30.1974

Willard Memorial Chapel–Welch Memorial Building
17-19 Nelson Street. Romanesque Revival stone buildings built 1892-94 as part of Auburn Theological Seminary; designed by

Andrew J. Warner; chapel interior by Tiffany Glass & Decoration Co. with wall mosaics by J. A. Holzer. 06.08.1989

Dr. Sylvester Willard Mansion
203 West Genesee Street. Monumental Greek Revival brick residence with 2-story Ionic portico; completed 1843 for prominent physician, entrepreneur, and philanthropist; late 19th-century Victorian alterations and additions. Property includes greenhouse and carriage house converted early 20th-century for use as science lab and experimental movie studio by Theodore Case. Now Cayuga County Museum of History and Art. 11.13.1989

Aurora

Aurora Steam Gristmill
Main Street. A 3 1/2-story stone mill on shore of Cayuga Lake; built 1817 for local inventor Roswell Tousley. One of first steam-powered gristmills west of Hudson River. Deteriorated condition. 07.30.1976

Aurora Village–Wells College Historic District
NY90. Entire historic area of village on Cayuga Lake, with over 1,000 Federal and Greek Revival residential and commercial buildings, numerous later 19th-century buildings, and 2 cemeteries. Includes Aurora Steam Gristmill (individually listed); Wells College, founded 1870, one of first liberal arts colleges for women; Glen Park (1852), Italianate villa designed by Alexander Jackson Davis with grounds by Andrew Jackson Downing, home of Henry Wells, founder of Wells College; and Gothic Revival A. C. Boyer Cottage (1838, William H. Ranlett; moved after 1980 out of district). 11.19.1980

Fleming

Sand Beach Church
NY38, south of Auburn. Early Romanesque Revival brick church built 1854-55, during ministry of Samuel Robbins Brown, well-known missionary to the Orient and founder of Elmira College. 06.10.1975

Ledyard

Jethro Wood House
NY34B. Vernacular frame farmhouse built c.1800. Home of Jethro Wood, whose 1819 patent for an improved cast-iron plow revolutionized farming methods. NHL 07.19.1964

Owasco

Lakeside Park
NY34A. A 25-acre portion of recreational park on Owasco Lake; designed 1895 and built by Auburn & Syracuse Electric Railroad Co. Structures include Colonial Revival pavilion (1912, Merrick & Randall), carousel shelter, and refreshment stand. 10.30.1989

Busti

Busti Mill (The Old Mill)
Lawson Road. Small-scale frame gristmill built c.1820-50; operated until 1948. 07.23.1976

Dr. John Lord House
Forest Road Extension. Gothic Revival frame residence built 1867 for local physician. 03.02.1991

Lewis Miller Cottage, Chautauqua (p. 34).

Chautauqua

Chautauqua Institution Historic District
Bounded by Chautauqua Lake, North and Lowell avenues, and NY394. Religious and educational summer community begun 1874 by Lewis Miller and H. J. Vincent. Includes 207 acres with several hundred residences, public buildings, planned streets, parks, and open spaces; many residences in Victorian Gothic style. Key buildings include Lewis Miller Cottage (individually listed), Amphitheater (1893, Lewis Miller), Second Empire Athe-

naeum Hotel (1881), and Hall of Christ (1899, Paul Peltz). 06.19.1973; NHL 06.29.1989

Lewis Miller Cottage (Chautauqua Institution)
NY394. A 2-story frame Victorian cottage built 1875; residence of founder of Chautauqua Institution. NHL 12.21.1965 ILLUS P. 33

Dunkirk

Point Gratiot Lighthouse Complex
(Dunkirk Light)
Dunkirk Harbor. A 61-foot-tall square stone lighthouse and attached Victorian Gothic brick keeper's house; built 1875 overlooking Dunkirk Harbor on Lake Erie. United States Coast Guard Lighthouses and Light Stations of the Great Lakes Thematic Resources. 12.18.1979

United States Post Office–Dunkirk
410 Central Avenue. Colonial Revival brick post office built 1928-29. United States Post Offices in New York State, 1858-1943, Thematic Resources. 11.17.1988

Fredonia

Fredonia Commons Historic District
Main, Temple, Church, Day, and Center streets. Nucleus of village, with twenty-five 19th- and early 20th-century civic buildings, churches, and commercial buildings sited around landscaped village green containing 2 cast-iron Victorian fountains. 10.19.1988

United States Post Office–Fredonia
21 Day Street. Colonial Revival brick post office built 1935-36. Interior mural (1937) by Arnold Blanch. United States Post Offices in New York State, 1858-1943, Thematic Resources. 11.17.1988

Jamestown

Euclid Avenue School
28 Euclid Avenue. Large 2-story brick school designed 1911 by C. C. Pederson in eclectic combination of Neoclassical and Mission styles; matching enlargement 1920 by Pederson. 03.21.1985

Walnut Grove
(Governor Reuben Fenton Mansion)
68 South Main Street. Large Italianate brick villa with 4-story corner tower and elaborate exterior and interior decoration; designed by Aaron Hall; built 1863 for Reuben Eaton Fenton, Governor of New York 1865-69. Owned since 1919 by City of Jamestown. 10.18.1972

North Harmony

Smith Bly House
4 North Maple Street, Ashville. Greek Revival frame residence with exuberant decorative features; built 1835. 10.01.1974

Westfield (Town)

Barcelona Lighthouse and Keeper's Cottage
East Lake Road, Barcelona. A 40-foot-tall circular stone lighthouse and stone cottage; built 1829. Early use of natural gas for illumination (1829). 04.13.1972

Westfield (Village)

Atwater-Stone House
29 Water Street. A 1 1/2-story vernacular frame residence built c.1812. Westfield Village Multiple Resource Area. 12.16.1983

L. Bliss House
90 West Main Street. Italianate frame house built c.1853 for local brewer. Westfield Village Multiple Resource Area. 09.26.1983

Harriet Campbell-Taylor House
145 South Portage Street. Greek Revival Italianate residence built 1851 for daughter of locally prominent judge. Westfield Village Multiple Resource Area. 09.26.1983

East Main Street Historic District
East Main Street. Area just west of village center, with 20 buildings, mostly large-scale residences built from 1830s to early 20th century. Includes village cemetery. Westfield Village Multiple Resource Area. 12.16.1983

Fay-Usborne Mill
48 Pearl Street. A 2-story frame former feed mill built 1899. Westfield Village Multiple Resource Area. 09.26.1983

French Portage Road Historic District
East Main and Portage streets. The 19th- and early 20th-century core of village, with 104 buildings. Includes village common, row of 1860s-70s brick commercial buildings, numerous residences, theater, hotel, museum, library, and municipal building. Westfield Village Multiple Resource Area. 12.16.1983

Frank A. Hall House
34 Washington Street. Mid-19th-century Italianate stuccoed villa owned after 1873 by owner of local newspaper. Westfield Village Multiple Resource Area. 09.26.1983

Lake Shore & Michigan Southern Freight Depot
English Street. A 1 1/2-story brick building with overhanging gable roof; built 1904. Westfield Village Multiple Resource Area. 09.26.1983

Lake Shore & Michigan Southern Railroad Station
English Street. Romanesque Revival brick former passenger station with terra-cotta and sandstone trim; built 1904. Westfield Village Multiple Resource Area. 12.16.1983

Gerald Mack House
79 North Portage Street. Italianate brick residence with elaborate cast-iron ornamentation; built c.1850. Westfield Village Multiple Resource Area. 09.26.1983

McMahan Homestead (Landmark Acres)
232 West Main Road. Federal frame residence built c.1820 for Colonel James McMahan, first settler in county. One of earliest extant residences in county. Early 20th-century alterations. Westfield Village Multiple Resource Area. 09.26.1983

Nixon Homestead
119 West Main Street. Queen Anne frame residence built 1890 for Samuel F. Nixon, politician and businessman. Westfield Village Multiple Resource Area. 09.26.1983

Rorig Bridge
Water Street at Chautauqua Creek. Cast- and wrought-iron single-span Pratt truss bridge manufactured 1890 by Groton Bridge Co., Groton, New York. Westfield Village Multiple Resource Area. 09.26.1983; DEMOLISHED 1989

Henry Dwight Thompson House
29 Wood Street. Victorian frame residence built 1869 for prominent local grape grower. Westfield Village Multiple Resource Area. 09.26.1983

Ward House
118 West Main Street. Italianate brick residence built late 1860s. Once part of 26-acre estate. Westfield Village Multiple Resource Area. 09.26.1983

Welch Factory Building No. 1
101 North Portage Street. A 3-story brick factory built 1897 for production of Welch's grape juice, one of major industries in area; 1899 and 1903 additions. Converted for use by local newspaper publisher. Westfield Village Multiple Resource Area. 09.26.1983

Reuben Gridley Wright Farm Complex
233 East Main Street. A 72-acre working farm with original outbuildings and tenant houses. Queen Anne main residence designed by Enoch Curtis; built 1884 for local grape grower. Westfield Village Multiple Resource Area. 09.26.1983

Reuben Wright House
309 East Main Street. A 2-story brick building built c.1830 as residence; enlarged mid-19th century for use as tavern. Westfield Village Multiple Resource Area. 09.26.1983

York-Skinner House
31 Union Street. Gothic Revival frame cottage built c.1866 incorporating original pre-1833 house. Westfield Village Multiple Resource Area. 09.26.1983

Ashland

Newtown Battlefield

(Newtown Battlefield Reservation State Park)
NY 17, 6 miles southeast of Elmira (also in
towns of Chemung and Elmira). Site of Revolutionary War Battle of Newtown on August 29,
1779, between Sullivan Expedition, under
command of Major General John Sullivan, and
Iroquois Nations.   NHL 11.28.1972

Chemung

Newtown Battlefield (see Ashland)

Elmira (Town)

Newtown Battlefield (see Ashland)

Quarry Farm

Crane Road. The 255-acre summer residence
of Samuel L. Clemens (a.k.a. Mark Twain)
during 1870s and 1880s, and home of his wife
Olivia's sister, Mrs. Theodore Crane. Picturesque frame farmhouse with late 19th-century
additions and alterations. Location where
Twain wrote *The Adventures of Tom Sawyer,
The Prince and the Pauper, A Tramp Abroad,*
and most of *The Adventures of Huckleberry
Finn.* 03.13.1975

Elmira (City)

Chemung Canal Bank Building

415 East Water Street. Greek Revival brick
commercial building built 1833 as bank; Italianate and Beaux-Arts features from enlargements and alterations in 1868, 1880s, and
1903. Adapted for use as Chemung County
Historical Society Museum and Library.
06.23.1978

Chemung County Courthouse Complex

210-228 Lake Street, between Market and East
Church streets. Complex of 4 buildings: Early
Romanesque Revival courthouse (1861-62,
Horatio Nelson White); county clerk's office
(1875) and annex (1895); and Greek Revival
district attorney's and treasurer's building
(1836; Classical Revival portico designed 1899
by Pierce & Bickford). 08.12.1971

Elmira Civic Historic District

East Church, Lake, East Market, Baldwin, Carroll, and State streets. Concentration of 38
19th- and early 20th-century civic, commercial,
and educational buildings. Notable buildings
include Chemung County Courthouse Complex (individually listed), monumental Beaux-
Arts City Hall (1895, Pierce & Bickford), Italian Renaissance style Young Men's Christian
Association (1924), Beaux-Arts former United

States Post Office (1902, James Knox Taylor),
Neoclassical Steel Memorial Library (1921-
23), and Greek Revival Arnot Art Museum
(c.1835; private art gallery added 1880; extensive alterations 1911-12 by Pierce & Bickford
for conversion to museum). 07.30.1980

Elmira College Old Campus

Roughly bounded by College and West Wash-
ington avenues, North Main Street, and Park
Place. Historic core of old campus, founded
1855 as Elmira Female College. Notable build-
ings include monumental Early Romanesque
Revival Cowles Hall (1855, E. L. Barber),
Hamilton House (1870), Mark Twain's study
(1874, moved to college 1952 from Quarry
Farm), Romanesque Revival Gillett Hall (1892,
Otis Dockstader of Dockstader & Considine),
Neoclassical Carnegie Science Hall (1911,
Edward L. Tilton), Romanesque Revival Fas-
sett Commons (1917, Pierce & Bickford), and
Collegiate Gothic Tompkins and Hamilton
halls (1927 and 1926; Coolidge, Shepley,
Bulfinch & Abbot). 08.23.1984

*Chemung County Courthouse Complex,
City of Elmira.*

Fire Station No. 4
301 Maxwell Place. Flemish Revival brick building with terra-cotta decoration; designed by Pierce & Bickford; built 1897-98.
03.24.1988

F. M. Howell and Company
50 and 79-105 Pennsylvania Avenue. Complex of 5 brick industrial buildings built 1890-1910 for box manufacturer and label maker. Building 3 designed by Pierce & Bickford. Buildings 1 and 2 designed by Joseph Considine.
08.27.1984

Near Westside Historic District
Roughly bounded by Chemung River, College Avenue, and Second and Hoffman streets. A 25-block concentration of approximately 450 19th- and early 20th-century residential properties with small number of commercial and religious buildings; mostly single-family mid-size residences in variety of styles including Second Empire, Eastlake, Queen Anne, Colonial Revival, and Arts and Crafts.   12.22.1983

Park Church
208 West Gray Street. Eclectic Gothic-inspired stone church with mansard roof; designed by Horatio Nelson White; built 1874-76 during ministry of reformer Thomas Beecher. Early example of institutional church complex, containing library, gym, and kitchen.
05.25.1977

Elmira Heights

Elmira Heights Village Hall
268 East 14th Street. Eclectic yellow brick building in blend of Northern Renaissance Revival and Chateauesque styles; designed by Pierce & Bickford; built 1896 and used as village hall until 1979.   05.06.1982

Horseheads

Hanover Square Historic District
Junction of East Franklin, West Franklin, North Main, and South Main streets. A 19th-century business district with 21 commercial buildings, mostly Renaissance Revival attached brick buildings built 1860s-70s.
10.29.1982

Horseheads 1855 Extension Historic District
Grand Central Avenue, and Fletcher, Sayre, West Mill, and Center streets. Residential neighborhood developed in mid- to late 19th-century with approximately 28 Gothic Revival, Italianate, and Queen Anne residences and bungalows on large lots along tree-lined streets. 07.30.1980

Teal Park
Steuben, Pine, and West Main streets. A 3/4-acre village park with whimsical bandstand designed 1910 by Eugene Zimmerman, nationally known cartoonist for *Puck* and *Judge*. Zim Thematic Resources.   10.07.1983

Zimmerman House
601 Pine Street. Queen Anne residence designed and built 1890 by Eugene Zimmerman (see Teal Park). Zim Thematic Resources.
10.07.1983

Rosekrans Building, Village of Greene.

Afton

Main Street Historic District
169-191 and 158-180 Main Street. Group of
11 Romanesque Revival brick commercial
buildings built late 19th century as result of
village's development as regional transportation center. 06.30.1983

Bainbridge

Bainbridge Historic District
East Main, Juliand, North Main, Pearl, South
Main, and West Main streets, Park Place, and
Railroad Avenue. Central core of 19th-century
village, with approximately 100 properties,
including large village green with Victorian
bandstand, 2 churches, small commercial
district, and numerous residences.
11.09.1982

Columbus

Columbus Community Church
NY 80. Greek Revival frame church built 1844;
Victorian modifications added 1879.
03.20.1986

Earlville

Earlville Historic District
(also in Madison County)
Fayette, North, South, East, and West Main
streets. Historic core of small rural village,
with approximately 165 properties, mostly
commercial and residential buildings built
1880-1920. Includes Earlville Opera House
(individually listed). 10.29.1982

Earlville Opera House
(Douglass Opera House)
12-20 East Main Street. A 3-story Queen Anne
brick commercial building built 1890; opera
house on upper floors. 01.22.1973

Greene (Town)

Bates Round Barn
NY 12. A 60-foot-diameter round barn con-
structed of clay tile and light wood framing;
central silo and domical roof; built 1928.
Central Plan Dairy Barns of New York State
Thematic Resources. 09.29.1984

Young Round Barn
NY 12. An 80-foot-diameter round barn with
light framing, central silo, pressed-iron exterior, and double hipped gambrel roof with
cupola; built 1914-16. Central Plan Dairy
Barns of New York State Thematic Resources.
09.29.1984

Greene (Village)

Greene Historic District
Chenango, Genesee, and Jackson streets. Historic core of 19th-century village, with approximately 130 properties, including main
commercial area, oldest residential neighborhoods, and public buildings. Notable buildings
include Rosekrans Building (individually
listed), Beaux-Arts Moore Memorial Library
(1903), Gothic Revival Zion Episcopal Church
(1886, Henry M. Cogden), and Colonial
Revival Sherwood Hotel (1913). District contains several exceptional examples of Federal,
Greek Revival, Gothic Revival, and Colonial
Revival residences. 09.09.1982

Rosekrans Building
62 Genesee Street. A 2-story commercial building with ornate sheet-iron facade manufactured
by Mesker Brothers Iron Co., St. Louis, Mis-
souri; built 1892. 07.27.1979

New Berlin

New Berlin Historic District
Roughly along Main, West, and Genesee
streets. Concentration of 122 properties in
19th-century core of village, including main
commercial area, oldest residential area,
railroad-related buildings, and public and
religious buildings. Includes Preferred Manor
(individually listed). 08.12.1982

Preferred Manor (Horace O. Moss House)
45 South Main Street. Imposing late Federal/
Greek Revival stone residence built 1831 for
one of the county's leading citizens. Stair hall
with original scenic wallpaper entitled "Chasse
de Compiegne," printed c.1830 in Paris.
05.17.1974

Norwich

Chenango County Courthouse District
(Broad Street–Main Street Historic District)
North Broad, South Broad, East Main, and
West Main streets, and Park Place. Group
of approximately 45 commercial, public, and
religious buildings and 2 parks in central part
of village. Notable buildings include Greek
Revival Chenango County Courthouse (1837),
Masonic Temple (1878), Congregational
Church (1861), City Hall (1903-06), and Erie-
Lackawanna Railroad Station (1902).
06.10.1975

North Broad Street Historic District
North Broad Street between Newton Avenue
and Mitchell Street. A 3-block concentration
of 41 residences with outstanding examples of
Greek Revival, Italianate, Queen Anne, and
Stick styles. 11.21.1978

United States Post Office–Norwich
20-22 East Main Street. Colonial Revival brick
post office designed by George Ketcham; built
1932-33. United States Post Offices in New
York State, 1858-1943, Thematic Resources.
05.11.1989

Otselic

Newton Homestead (Gladding International
Sport Fishing Museum)
Ridge Road, South Otselic. A 2-story octagonal brick residence with cupola; built c.1860
by Leroy and Courtland Newton. 06.03.1982

South Otselic Historic District
Gladding, North and South Main streets, Clarence Church and Plank roads, and Potter and
South Otselic avenues. Area encompassing
most of small rural hamlet, with 60 residential,
commercial, industrial, and religious buildings.
Residences mostly built mid-19th century;
commercial buildings mostly built late 19th-
century. Headquarters since 1816 of Gladding
Corporation, fishing-line manufacturers.
09.08.1983

Oxford

Theodore Burr House
(Oxford Memorial Library)
Fort Hill Square. Federal frame residence with
Victorian alterations; built 1810-12 for found-
ing settler of Oxford and pioneer American
bridge designer and builder. 09.11.1981

Oxford Village Historic District
Roughly Washington Avenue, State Street,
Chenango River, Merchant and Green streets,
Washington Park, and Albany and Pleasant
streets. Large district encompassing entire
village core, with approximately two hundred
19th-century residential, commercial, and
institutional buildings; 2 village parks; and
railroad-associated buildings. Notable buildings include Theodore Burr House (individually listed), St. Paul's Church (1856-57, Henry
Dudley), several buildings built by local builders Elihu Cooley and David and James Sherwood, and National Bank of Oxford (1894,
Isaac G. Perry). 09.17.1985

United States Post Office–Oxford
South Washington Avenue. Colonial Revival
brick post office built 1939-40. Interior mural
(1941) by Mordi Gassner. United States Post
Offices in New York State, 1858-1943, Thematic Resources. 05.11.1989

Sherburne

Sherburne High School
16 Chapel Street. Collegiate Gothic brick
building with terra-cotta trim; designed by
J. Mills Platt; built 1924-25; 1935 addition
designed by Raymond Freeburg. 11.03.1988

Sherburne Historic District
North and South Main, East and West State,
Classic, Summit, and Church streets, and Park
Avenue. Concentration of 119 properties
encompassing most of historic village core.
Includes numerous frame Federal, Greek
Revival, and Victorian residences; several early
19th-century churches, frame and brick commercial buildings, 3 mills, and buildings
associated with Chenango Canal.
10.29.1982

Adirondack State Forest Preserve
Located in Clinton, Essex, Franklin, Fulton, Hamilton, Herkimer, St. Lawrence, and Warren counties. First state forest preserve in the United States; established 1885 to preserve several million acres of forest land.
NHL 05.23.1963

Champlain

Fort Montgomery
Richelieu River. A 3-acre site with ruins of pentagonal stone fort built 1843-70 by federal government on site of earlier fortification that guarded approach to Lake Champlain from British invasion.   08.22.1977

Dannemora

Church of St. Dismas, The Good Thief
Clinton Correctional Facility. Large Gothic Revival stone church designed by Frederick Vernon Murphy and Thomas Lorcroft; built 1939-41 by and for inmates of state prison. Stained glass, ironwork, and woodwork crafted by inmates under supervision of Rambush Decorating Co.   11.21.1991

Keeseville (see also Keeseville, Essex County)

Double-Span Metal Pratt Truss Bridge
Ausable Street (also in Essex County). Wrought-iron truss bridge built 1877 by Murray Dougal & Co., Milton, Pennsylvania; William H. Law, engineer. Earliest extant example of its type in state. Keeseville Village Multiple Resource Area.   05.20.1983

Keeseville Historic District
Roughly bounded by Vine, Chesterfield, Clinton, Hill, Pleasant, Front, and Beech streets. Historic core of 19th-century milling community on Ausable River, with 142 industrial and commercial buildings, working-class houses, stylish entrepreneurs' residences, Victorian churches, and 2 bridges spanning river. Bridges include 240-foot-span steel suspension footbridge built 1888 by Berlin Iron Bridge Co. of Connecticut and 110-foot-span stone-arch bridge designed 1842 by Silas Arnold. Keeseville Village Multiple Resource Area.
05.20.1983

Peru

Valcour Bay
Four miles south of Plattsburgh on west shore of Lake Champlain (also in town of Plattsburgh). Site of naval engagement on October 11, 1776, between American fleet, under command of Benedict Arnold, and British fleet,

under command of General Sir Guy Carleton, which delayed British invasion of northern colonies. Includes site on western half of Valcour Island and bay between island and mainland.
NHL 01.01.1961

Plattsburgh (Town)

Plattsburgh Bay (see city of Plattsburgh)

Valcour Bay (see Peru)

Plattsburgh (City)

William Bailey House
176 Cornelia Street. Small vernacular stone residence built c.1825. Plattsburgh City Multiple Resource Area.   11.12.1982

Brinkerhoff Street Historic District
Brinkerhoff Street between Oak and North Catherine streets. A 1-block residential district with 13 properties, mostly brick and frame residences built in variety of styles 1845-90. Plattsburgh City Multiple Resource Area.   11.12.1982

John B. Carpenter House
42 Prospect Avenue. Modest vernacular stone residence built c.1845. Plattsburgh City Multiple Resource Area.   11.12.1982

City Hall
City Hall Place. A 2-story Neoclassical limestone-clad building with pedimented portico and copper-clad dome; designed by John Russell Pope; built 1917.   12.12.1973

Clinton County Courthouse Complex
135 Margaret Street. Monumental Richardsonian Romanesque brick and stone building with square central tower; designed by Marcus F. Cummings; built 1889. Adjacent Italianate brick Chamber of Commerce (1885; attributed to Marcus F. Cummings). Plattsburgh City Multiple Resource Area.   11.12.1982

House at 56 Cornelia Street
Greek Revival residence built c.1850. Plattsburgh City Multiple Resource Area.
11.12.1982

Court Street Historic District
Court Street between Oak and Beekman streets. A 4-block residential neighborhood with 54 buildings built mostly in late 19th and early 20th centuries. Includes many large Queen Anne and Colonial Revival residences. Plattsburgh City Multiple Resource Area.
02.24.1983

Delaware & Hudson Railroad Complex
Bridge Street. Queen Anne/eclectic brick railroad passenger station with elaborate decoration; designed by Albert W. Fuller; built 1886 by David Van Schaick. Also includes repair shop and switching building built 1893 by James Ackroyd. Plattsburgh City Multiple Resource Area.   11.12.1982

D'Youville Academy
100 Cornelia Street. Large 2 1/2-story Second Empire brick building built c.1878 as school and nunnery by Gray Nuns of Ottawa, Canada. Plattsburgh City Multiple Resource Area.   11.12.1982

First Presbyterian Church
34 Brinkerhoff Street. Monumental Victorian Gothic limestone church designed by Frederick W. Brown; built 1868-73. Plattsburgh City Multiple Resource Area.   11.12.1982

Fort Brown Site
Northwest of junction of Elizabeth Street and NY9. One of 3 defensive redoubts constructed by American forces prior to September 1814 Battle of Plattsburgh during War of 1812. Now part of Plattsburgh Bay National Historic Landmark.   12.15.1978

W. W. Hartwell House & Dependencies
(Regina Maria Retreat House)
77 Brinkerhoff Street. Second Empire stone residence built c.1870 for prosperous merchant. Includes carriage house, groundskeeper's cottage, and landscaped grounds. Plattsburgh City Multiple Resource Area.
11.12.1982

Hawkins Hall
Beekman Street, State University of New York at Plattsburgh. Large 2-story Collegiate Gothic stone building designed by William E. Haugaard; built 1932 as State Normal School. Plattsburgh City Multiple Resource Area.
11.12.1982

Kent-Delord House
17 Cumberland Avenue. Federal frame residence built 1797 for Captain John Bailey, early settler in northern New York State; Nathan Averill, builder. Later home of James Kent, Justice of Supreme Court of New York and Henry Delord, leading citizen of Plattsburgh. Museum.   02.18.1971

Paul Marshall House
24-26 Cornelia Street. Federal stone and brick residence built c.1828. Plattsburgh City Multiple Resource Area.   11.12.1982

Old Stone Barracks
Rhode Island Avenue, Plattsburgh Air Force Base. Large 2-story stone barracks with full-width 2-story wood veranda; built 1838 as military housing.   02.18.1971

Charles C. Platt Homestead
96-98 Boynton Avenue. Federal brick residence built c.1802 by Charles C. Platt. Only remaining structure in Plattsburgh associated with Platt family, who were instrumental in development of city. Plattsburgh City Multiple Resource Area.   11.12.1982

Plattsburgh Bay
Cumberland Bay (also in town of Plattsburgh). Three sites related to naval and land engagement of September 11, 1814, between American forces, under command of General Alexander Macomb and Lieutenant Thomas Macdonough, and British forces, under com-

mand of General George Prevost, which drove British from Champlain Valley near end of War of 1812. Sites include Plattsburgh Bay, Fort Brown Site (individually listed), and Macdonough Monument (1926, John Russell Pope). NHL 12.19.1960

The Point Historic District
Roughly bounded by Jay, Hamilton, Peru, and Bridge streets. Residential district with 38 buildings, mostly built 1815-80. Includes earliest extant group of residences in Plattsburgh. Plattsburgh City Multiple Resource Area. 11.12.1982

Z. Ritchie House
26 South Catherine Street. Gothic Revival residence built c.1860. Plattsburgh City Multiple Resource Area. 11.12.1982

St. John the Baptist Roman Catholic Church and Rectory
20 Broad Street. Gothic Revival stone church with multi-spired tower and buttresses; designed by Victor Borgeau of Montreal; built 1874. Adjacent stone rectory with French-Canadian "Quebecquois" decorative elements;

built 1909-10. Plattsburgh City Multiple Resource Area. 11.12.1982

United States Oval Historic District
Plattsburgh Air Force Base. A 53-acre property with 26 late 19th- and early 20th-century Queen Anne and Colonial Revival barracks, officers' quarters, and associated buildings surrounding large parade ground; built 1893-1934 as component of Plattsburgh Barracks, United States Army Reservation. 08.30.1989

S. F. Vilas Home for Aged & Infirmed Ladies
Beekman and Cornelia streets. Large Queen Anne brick building designed by Marcus F. Cummings; built 1889. Plattsburgh City Multiple Resource Area. 11.12.1982

W. G. Wilcox House
45-51 Lorraine Street. Large Eastlake frame multiple dwelling built c.1888 by owner of local coal and wood business. Plattsburgh City Multiple Resource Area. 02.24.1983

Winslow-Turner Carriage House
210 Cornelia Street. Italianate brick building with hipped roof and cupola; built 1876. Main house demolished 1976. Plattsburgh City Multiple Resource Area. 11.12.1982

Fort Montgomery, Champlain.

Ancram

Simons General Store
Ancram Square. Italianate frame store built 1873-74 by Martin Luther Hills at center of small rural hamlet. 04.23.1973

Austerlitz

Spencertown Academy
NY203, Spencertown. A 2-story Greek Revival frame building with pedimented Ionic portico; built 1847 and used as school until 1970. 04.03.1973

Jacob Rutsen Van Rensselaer House, Claverack.

Steepletop (Edna St. Vincent Millay House)
East Hill Road. Late 19th-century frame farmhouse on approximately 800-acre rural estate that was retreat of poet Edna St. Vincent Millay 1925-50. NHL 11.11.1971

Canaan

Lace House (Uriah Edwards House)
NY22 and Miller Road. Federal frame residence built 1806 by New Englander Uriah Edwards. 02.21.1985

Chatham (Town)

Knollcroft
County 9, New Concord. Queen Anne brick and frame residence built 1880 as summer home of George Chesterman, New York City financier. Retains outbuildings and landscaped grounds. 08.14.1985

Spengler Bridge
Spengler Road over Kinderhook Creek. A 130-foot-long metal Pratt truss bridge built 1880 by Morse Bridge Co. of Youngstown, Ohio. 02.23.1973

Chatham (Village)

Union Station
NY66 and NY295. Richardsonian Romanesque stone railroad passenger station with bell-cast hipped roof; designed by Shepley, Rutan & Coolidge; built 1887. 05.01.1974

Claverack

Double-Span Whipple Bowstring Truss Bridge
Van Wyck Lane. A 162-foot-long metal bridge fabricated 1870 by John D. Hutchinson. Only known extant example of its type in New York State. 04.17.1980

Jan Van Hoesen House
NY66. Dutch Colonial brick residence built C.1720 for Hudson Valley freeholder. Initials of first owner monogrammed in black clinker headers on gable end. 08.01.1979

Jacob Rutsen Van Rensselaer House and Mill Complex
NY23. Group of 14 interrelated 19th-century structures, including main residence, commercial and industrial buildings, agricultural structures, and dwellings on landscaped grounds. Complex developed by prominent landowner and entrepreneur. Main residence is large Federal brick building with canted front corners; built C.1805; Greek Revival and Colonial Revival modifications. 09.09.1982

Clermont

Bouwerie
Buckwheat Bridge Road. A 60-acre farmstead with imposing Dutch Colonial brick residence with gambrel roof; built C.1762. Also includes 19th-century barn complex. Associated with Ten Broeck family, earliest and most prominent family in Clermont. Clermont Town Multiple Resource Area. 10.07.1983

Thomas Brodhead House
US9 and Buckwheat Bridge Road. Federal brick residence built C.1795 and brick smoke house. Clermont Town Multiple Resource Area. 10.07.1983

Clarkson Chapel
West side of NY9G. Modest Gothic Revival frame church built 1860. Clermont Town Multiple Resource Area. 10.07.1983

Clermont

Clermont State Historic Park. Large 2 1/2-story Georgian brick and stone residence built c.1730 on 13,000-acre landholding of Robert Livingston. Burned by British in 1777 during American Revolution and rebuilt soon after for his wife, Margaret Beekman Livingston, and son, Robert R. Livingston, first United States Minister of Foreign Affairs and Chancellor of New York State.   NHL 11.28.72

Clermont Academy

West side of US9. A 2-story, 5-bay Federal frame school with octagonal cupola; built 1834. Clermont Town Multiple Resource Area. 10.07.1983

Clermont Estates Historic District

South of Germantown. A 2-mile-long group of 7 estates on Hudson River developed mid- to late 19th century by children of Edward P. Livingston. Estates include Second Empire stuccoed Northwood (1856, William Baldwin Stewart), Second Empire brick Holcroft (1881), Second Empire brick Oak Lawn (1872), Second Empire frame Midwood (1885-87, Michael O'Connor and Robert L. Clarkson), Greek Revival stuccoed Southwood (1849; Victorian alterations), Second Empire brick Chiddingstone (c.1860), Second Empire brick Motherhouse (c.1852, late 19th-century alterations and 20th-century additions when converted to convent). Also includes 2 former tenant houses on Livingston manor: Federal frame Clermont Cottage (c.1800) and Colonial frame Sylvan Cottage (c.1778). 05.07.1979

Coons House

East side of NY9G. Greek Revival frame residence with pedimented portico; built c.1850. Adjacent barn and woodshed. Clermont Town Multiple Resource Area.   10.07.1983

Hickory Hill

Buckwheat Bridge Road. Greek Revival frame residence with 3-bay pedimented facade; built c.1859 by Hudson River ship captain E. L. Tinkelpaugh. Landscaped grounds. Clermont Town Multiple Resource Area.   10.07.1983

Hudson River Historic District

South of Germantown along Hudson River to south of Staatsburg (most properties located in Dutchess County). A 20-mile-long area along Hudson River encompassing individually listed Sixteen Mile District and Clermont Estates Historic District. Also includes hamlets of Annandale-on-Hudson, Barrytown, Rhinecliff, and Staatsburg in Dutchess County; village of Tivoli in Dutchess County; individually listed properties in hamlet of Rhinecliff; Margaret Lewis Norrie State Park; and large areas of agricultural lands east of Hudson River. NHL 12.14.1990

Old Parsonage

Buckwheat Bridge Road. A 2-story, 3-bay Picturesque frame cottage built c.1867. Clermont Town Multiple Resource Area. 10.07.1983

Sixteen Mile District

South of Clermont along Hudson River (most properties located in Dutchess County). Important collection of 30 contiguous Hudson River estates (all except Clermont are located in Dutchess County) associated with Livingston family and other prominent figures in New York and American history; many designed by America's foremost architects and landscape designers of the 19th and early 20th centuries. Also includes 18th-century Dutch and Palatine German farmhouses, sites of 18th-century houses, and riverfront portions of several hamlets including Annandale-on-Hudson, Barrytown, and Rhinecliff. District includes approximately 250 buildings and sites; most estates include numerous outbuildings. Estates include Clermont (individually listed), Gothic Revival Teviot (1843), Greek Revival Rose Hill (1843), Georgian The Pynes (1790-94; enlarged 19th century), Federal Callendar House (1794; 1830s Greek Revival veranda; south wing designed by Johnston Redmond c.1913; murals by Olin Dows), Italianate William R. Ham House (c.1860), Jacobean Revival Ward Manor House (1918; Hoppin & Koen; 1923 annex; now part of Bard College), Sands House (c.1865; now part of Bard College), Classical Revival Blithewood (c.1910, Francis L.V. Hoppin; now part of Bard College), Montgomery Place (individually listed), Massena (1886, William A. Potter), Roman Revival Edgewater (1820; 1852 hexagonal library and gatehouse designed by Alexander Jackson Davis), Classical Revival Sylvania (c.1904, Charles A. Platt), Rokeby (individually listed), Steen Valetje/Mandara (1849-51, Frank Wills; major alterations, including 1874-76 north wing by Sturgis & Brigham, 1890 south wing by William Sturgis, 1973 Georgian exterior), Orlot (1942, L. Bancel LaFarge), Georgian Revival Obolensky House (Mott B. Schmidt), Italianate Wilderstein (1853, John Warren Rich; 1887-89 additions by Arnout Cannon, Jr.; landscaped grounds by Calvert Vaux), Wildercliff (vernacular frame residence built 1799; 19th- and 20th-century alterations and additions), Norman-style Wyndclyffe. Linden Grove (1853; deteriorated condition), Mission-style Whispering Pines (1906), The Locusts (1941, John Churchill; 19th-century outbuildings), Classical Revival Mills Mansion State Historic Site (1832; complete rebuilding in 1895-96 by McKim, Mead & White), Victorian Gothic Hoyt House (1855, Calvert Vaux; interior remodeled in Georgian style by Robert Palmer Huntington). Estates with no longer extant main residences but with intact outbuildings and/or landscaping include Leacote, Ferncliff (casino designed 1902 by Stanford White), Ankony, Ellerslie, Linwood, and Hopeland. Other notable buildings include mid-19th-century residences in Annandale-on-Hudson designed by Alexander Jackson Davis as tenant houses for Montgomery Place, and several buildings on Bard College campus, including Victorian Gothic Stone Row (1885-91, Charles C. Haight), Gothic Revival Ludlow-Willink Hall (1865-66, Richard Upjohn), Gothic Revival Chapel (1856, Charles Babcock), and Gothic Revival Bartlett Tomb (1869, Frederick C. Withers).   03.07.1979

St. Luke's Church

West side of US9. Gothic Revival frame church designed by Richard M. Upjohn; built 1857-59. Clermont Town Multiple Resource Area. 10.07.1983

Stone Jug

NY9G and Jug Road. Modest vernacular stone and brick residence built 1752 by Konradt Lasher, a Palatine German. Also includes Greek Revival farmhouse (1846), mid-19th-century barn, and sites of two 18th-century houses, all built by Lasher family.   04.20.1978

Gallatin

Melius-Bentley House

(see Pine Plains, Dutchess County)

Germantown

German Reformed Sanctity Church of the East Camp Parsonage

Maple Avenue. Small vernacular stone residence built c.1746 for pastor of church in Palatine German settlement; enlarged c.1767. 01.30.1976

Greenport

Olana (Frederic E. Church House–Olana State Historic Site)

Church Hill, east end of Rip Van Winkle Bridge. The 250-acre hilltop estate of Hudson River School painter Frederic E. Church. Main residence designed by Church and Calvert Vaux in eclectic combination of Oriental and Moorish decorative elements on basic Italianate villa form; built in 2 stages (1870-72, 1888-89). Elaborate interior with original furnishings. Significant designed landscape and outbuildings.   NHL 06.22.1965   ILLUS. P. 43

Oliver Wiswall House

South of Hudson. Large Greek Revival residence; built c.1836 for business and civic leader in Hudson.   09.04.1980

Hudson

Dr. Oliver Bronson House and Stables

West side of US9. Federal frame residence built c.1819; significant 1839 and 1849 alterations designed by Alexander Jackson Davis. One of earliest examples of Picturesque or "bracketed" style. Threatened with demolition. 02.20.1973

Cornelius H. Evans House

414-416 Warren Street. Large Second Empire brick residence built 1861 for prominent local brewer.   11.01.1974

Front Street–Parade Hill–Lower Warren Street Historic District

Front and Warren streets. A 3-block area of original settlement of city by New Englanders in 1783. (See Hudson Historic District.) 03.05.1970; BOUNDARY DECREASE 07.03.1986

Hudson Historic District

Roughly bounded by Warren, Fourth, Sixth, Seventh, Eighth, Union, Allen, and Grant streets, and Penn Central Railroad. Commercial core and principal residential neighborhoods, with 750 buildings representing development of city from 1783 founding to last major building period in 1930s. Outstanding examples of Federal and Greek Revival urban residences and commercial buildings. Includes individually listed Cornelius H. Evans House and Front Street–Parade Hill–Lower Warren Street Historic District. Hudson Multiple Resource Area. 10.21.1985

Rossman-Prospect Avenue Historic District

Prospect and Rossman avenues. Group of 12 Colonial Revival and Tudor Revival residences and bungalows built 1887-1926 as part of planned suburban development known as Prospect Hill. Hudson Multiple Resource Area. 10.21.1985

United States Post Office–Hudson

402 Union Street. Neoclassical brick post office with marble Doric portico and trim; designed by James Knox Taylor; built 1909-11; enlarged 1938. Interior sculptural relief (1938) by Vincent Glinsky. United States Post Offices in New York State, 1858-1943, Thematic Resources. 11.17.1988

Kinderhook (Town)

Lindenwald

(Martin Van Buren National Historic Site) NY9H, east of Kinderhook. A 2 1/2-story Federal brick residence built 1797; enlarged and remodeled 1849 by Richard Upjohn. Home of President Martin Van Buren 1841-62. NHL 07.04.1961

Luycas Van Alen House

NY9H, east of Kinderhook. A 1 1/2-story Dutch Colonial brick residence with steeply pitched parapeted gable roof; built 1737; enlarged mid-18th century and restored 1960s. Museum. NHL 12.24.1967

Kinderhook (Village)

Kinderhook Village Historic District.

Both sides of US9. Approximately 250 buildings in heart of village, with several 18th-century residences; important group of Federal, Greek Revival, and Gothic Revival residences; and late 19th-century commercial buildings. Notable buildings include Federal James D. Vanderpoel House (c.1819, attributed to Barnabus Waterman; now operated as house museum). 07.24.1974

Livingston

The Hill

(Henry W. Livingston House–Linlithgo) US9 and NY82, north of Bell's Pond. Monumental 2-story Classical Revival stuccoed brick residence completed 1799 for Henry Walter Livingston; design attributed to Pierre Pharoux. 02.18.1971; BURNED 1972; DEMOLISHED 1983

Livingston Memorial Church and Burial Ground

County 10 and Wire Road. Modest Gothic Revival brick church built 1870 on site of 1721 church and above Livingston family burial crypt established 1727. Adjacent cemetery. 09.12.1985

Oak Hill

Oak Hill Road, north of Linlithgo. A 2 1/2-story, 5-bay Federal brick residence overlooking Hudson River; built 1795 for John Livingston, son of third and last manor lord; 19th-century alterations. Includes numerous estate buildings. 06.26.1979

Richmond Hill

County 31. A 269-acre early 19th-century farm complex with 2 1/2-story Federal brick residence built 1813-14 for Walter Tryon Livingston, earlier Dutch barn, and several out-buildings. 07.06.1988

Teviotdale

Wire Road. A 2 1/2-story Georgian stone and brick residence; built 1774 as country estate of Walter Livingston (design attributed to him); Federal-period alterations. 10.10.1979

New Lebanon

Elisha Gilbert House

US20, Lebanon Center. Large Federal frame residence with gambrel roof; built 1794; interior Masonic Lodge room outfitted in 1795. Adjacent family cemetery. 09.07.1984

Lebanon Springs Union Free School

NY22, Lebanon Springs. A 2-story Arts and Crafts stuccoed school designed by Fuller & Robinson; built 1913. 11.21.1991

Mount Lebanon Shaker Society

US20. The 270-acre property of former Shaker settlement that flourished in 19th century as central ministry of the religious sect. Includes approximately 34 buildings of the 5 groups or "families," built 1785-1876. NHL 06.23.1965

Stockport

Church of St. John the Evangelist

Chittenden Road. Gothic Revival frame church with tall central bell tower; built 1846-47. 04.13.1972

Stuyvesant

R. and W. Scott Ice Company Powerhouse and Ice House Site

River Road. Foundation of massive ice storage house and ruins of powerhouse; built 1885; once part of thriving ice-harvesting industry along Hudson River. Now part of state preserve. 02.21.1985

Stuyvesant Falls Mill District

New Street and NY22, Stuyvesant Falls. A 19th-century water-powered mill complex on Kinderhook Creek. Includes hydroelectric plant (1900), Waddell Cotton Mill (1827 and 1888) and dependencies (1845), Van Allen mill owner's residence (1847), 2 small dwellings, Upper Falls Dam (1827), steel-truss bridge (1899), and several mill sites. 09.15.1976

Johannis L. Van Alen Farm

School House Road. A 160-acre farmstead with Dutch Colonial residence with gambrel roof (c.1760), late 18th-century Dutch barn, corn crib, and small barn. 04.26.1973

Taghkanic

House at New Forge

128 New Forge Road, New Forge. Greek Revival residence built c.1850. Sole surviving building from former milling community of New Forge. Includes outbuildings and mill sites. 12.14.1987

Valatie

First Presbyterian Church

Church Street. Victorian Gothic brick church with structural polychromy and large open bell tower; designed by Ogden & Wright; built 1878. 09.07.1979

Nathan Wild House

3007 Main Street. Federal frame residence built 1826 for prominent mill owner; enlarged and remodeled 1830s-70s. 05.30.1991

Wild's Mill Complex

US9 and NY203. A 5-story brick textile mill and associated structures on west bank of Kinderhook Creek; built 1846; large 1890 addition. Main building demolished. 06.14.1982

Interior, Olana, Greenport (p. 41).

Cincinnatus

Cincinnatus Historic District
Main Street and Taylor Avenue. Group of 14
buildings in small rural hamlet on Otselic
River. Includes Federal frame Congregational
Church (1831-32), Georgian Revival brick
Kellogg Library (1930; Carl W. Clark), and 12
vernacular frame 19th-century residences.
09.07.1984

Cortland

Cortland County Courthouse
Courthouse Park. Monumental 3-story Neoclassical limestone building with high dome
supported by Corinthian columns; designed by
James Riley Gordon; built 1924.
10.09.1974

Cortland Fire Headquarters
21 Court Street. Flemish Revival/Arts and
Crafts yellow brick building with corner bell
tower and elaborate decorative stone trim;
designed by Sackett & Park; built 1914.
07.12.1974

*Tompkins Street–Main Street Historic
District, Cortland.*

Tompkins Street–Main Street Historic District
Tompkins Street and Main Street from Tompkins Street to Clinton Avenue. Concentration
of 109 properties, including 19th-century core
of city, 40 large late 19th- and early 20th-
century residences, and 50-acre rural cemetery.
Notable buildings include Federal Elisha Morgan House (c.1810, moved from Cherry
Valley, Otsego County), several Victorian
Gothic and Romanesque Revival commercial
buildings, Chateauesque Chester F. Wickwire
House (1889-90, Samuel Burrage Reed; now
1890 House Museum), and Georgian Revival

Charles C. Wickwire House (1912, Pierce &
Bickford). Encompasses previously listed
Tompkins Street Historic District (1975).
11.17.1982

United States Post Office–Cortland
88 Main Street. Neoclassical limestone post
office built 1913-15; enlarged 1940-41. Interior sculpture (1943) by Ryah Ludins. United
States Post Offices in New York State, 1858-
1943, Thematic Resources.   11.17.1988

Cortlandville

Cortland County Poor Farm
Off NY13, northeast of Cortland. A 112-acre
working farm on Tioughnioga River established 1836 as county poor farm. Includes
complex of thirteen 19th- and early 20th-
century residential and agricultural buildings
associated with the development of the institution.   10.29.1982

Homer

Old Homer Village Historic District
North, South, and Main streets, Central Park,
and Clinton, James, Cayuga, and Albany
streets. Principal core of small rural village settled in early 19th century, with approximately
175 residential, commercial, religious, and
public buildings. Includes fine examples of
Federal, Greek Revival, and Victorian styles.
10.02.1973

United States Post Office–Homer
2 South Main Street. Colonial Revival brick
post office built 1937-38. Interior mural
(1937) by Frank Romanelli. United States Post
Offices in New York State, 1858-1943, Thematic Resources.   05.11.1989

Water, Wall, and Pine Streets Lenticular Truss Bridges
Water, Wall, and Pine streets. Group of 3 iron
bridges over Tioughnioga River; built 1881 by
Corrugated Metal Co., East Berlin, Connecticut.   10.05.1977

McGraw

Main Street Historic District
Central core of small 19th-century rural hamlet, with 27 buildings, including Federal and
Greek Revival residences, early 20th-century
commercial buildings, 2 churches, and small
early 19th-century cemetery.
09.25.1986

Presbyterian Church of McGraw
Main Street. Modest Colonial Revival brick
church designed by Pierce & Bickford; built
1901. 09.11.1986

Preble

Little York Pavilion
Off NY281, south of Preble. A 2-story Stick
Style frame pavilion with 2-story open veran-

dah; built 1906 as part of Little York Amusement Park on Little York Lake.   07.27.1979

Solon

Hatheway Homestead

NY41. Large Greek Revival stone residence built 1844 as rural seat for local politician Samuel G. Hatheway.   01.20.1978

DELAWARE COUNTY

Andes

Andes Historic District
Delaware Avenue, Main and High streets, and Tremperskill Road. Central core of rural village, with 84 mid-19th- to early 20th-century residences, public and commercial buildings, and 2 farms. Notable buildings include Gothic Revival United Methodist Church, Greek Revival United Presbyterian Church, and Gothic Revival Corner Store (1858). 06.28.1984

Delhi (Town)

Judge Gideon Frisbee House
NY10, northeast of Delhi. A 2-story, 5-bay Federal frame residence and barn built c.1798 for lumber merchant and land developer. Headquarters of Delaware County Historical Association.   12.12.1976

MacDonald Farm (see Meredith)

Delhi (Village)

Delaware County Courthouse Square District
Roughly bounded by Second, Church, Main, and Court streets. Group of sixteen 19th-century civic, commercial, and religious buildings surrounding village green. Notable buildings include Second Empire Delaware County Courthouse (1868, Isaac G. Perry), Greek Revival Presbyterian Church (1831, Charles Hatheway), and Greek Revival Delaware National Bank (1838, Charles Hatheway). 07.16.1973

Murray Hill
Murray Hill Road. Large Italianate frame villa on 78-acre property; built 1867 for state Supreme Court Judge William Murray. Includes tenant house and carriage house. 06.03.1982

United States Post Office–Delhi
10 Court Street. Colonial Revival brick post office built 1938-39. Interior mural (1940)

by Mary Earley. United States Post Offices in New York State, 1858-1943, Thematic Resources.   11.17.1988

Franklin

Franklin Village Historic District
Wakeman and Institute avenues, and Main, Center, Maple, Water, Second, Third, and West streets. Concentration of approximately 165 buildings and structures in rural village settled in late 18th century along Ouleout Creek Valley. Includes numerous Federal, Greek Revival, and Victorian residences, small commercial district, public and institutional buildings, and 4 cemeteries. Notable properties include New Stone Hall (individually listed), Federal Isaac Platt House (1822), Greek Revival Baptist Church (1834), Gothic Revival Methodist Church (1834), Gothic Revival residence at 115 Main Street (c.1860), Gothic Revival St. Paul's Episcopal Church (1865, attributed to Richard and Richard M. Upjohn), and Ouleout Valley Rural Cemetery (established 1874).   09.07.1984

New Stone Hall
Center Street. A 3-story, 8-bay Greek Revival stone building built 1855-56 as main academic building for Delaware Literary Institute. 05.06.1980

Kortright

Hanford Mill (see Meredith)

McArthur-Martin Hexadecagon Barn
McArthur Hill Road. A 100-foot-diameter, 16-sided frame dairy barn built 1883. Largest central-plan barn known to have been built in New York State. Central Plan Dairy Barns of New York State Thematic Resources. 09.29.1984

MacDonald Farm (see Meredith)

Meredith

Hanford Mill
County 12, East Meredith (also in Kortright). A 50-acre 19th-century mill complex on Kortright Creek, with 4-story frame saw and gristmill (1820; later additions), several secondary buildings, mill raceway and pond, section of former New York Central Railroad, and 2 railroad bridges. Museum.   03.26.1973

MacDonald Farm
Elk Creek and Monroe roads (also in Kortright and Delhi). A 200-acre farmstead with Greek Revival farmhouse (1851), herb garden designed late 1930s by Catherine MacDonald Odell, late 19th-century tenant houses, mill, hop barn, and other agricultural buildings. 04.03.1973

Middletown

Kelly Round Barn
NY30, Halcottsville. A 90-foot-diameter round barn with balloon framing, central silo, and conical roof; built 1899; reconstructed 1988 for use as cultural center. Central Plan Dairy Barns of New York State Thematic Resources.   09.29.1984

Pakatakan Artist Colony Historic District
NY28 and Dry Brook Road, Arkville. Group of 16 Shingle Style cottages and studios, and hotel on 65-acre property. Informal art colony for Catskill School landscape artists 1886-1930.   02.21.1989

Roxbury

Main Street Historic District
Concentration of 49 properties in small rural hamlet on east branch of Delaware River. Includes mid-19th-century vernacular frame residences, 2 churches, cemetery, and school. Notable buildings include Greek Revival Methodist Church (1858), Gothic Revival Gould Memorial Church (1893), and Tudor Revival Roxbury Central School (1939). 02.29.1988

Woodchuck Lodge (John Burroughs Home)
Two miles from Roxbury on Burroughs Road. A 25-acre property with vernacular frame farmhouse built 1860-61 by Curtis Burroughs, brother of naturalist and author John Burroughs, who summered at lodge 1910-21. Now operated as seasonal museum. Small part of property operated as State Historic Site. NHL 12.29.1962

Stamford

Churchill Park Historic District
Western section of village, laid out and landscaped 1895 as resort community by Dr. Stephen Churchill. Includes monumental Second Empire Rexmere Hotel (1898), approximately 50 frame buildings built 1870-1920 as summer houses and boardinghouses, tree-lined streets, and artificial lakes. 11.17.1980

Walton

Gardiner Place Historic District
Group of 3 public buildings including Richardsonian Romanesque William B. Ogden Free Library (1896-97, Morris & Walker), Neoclassical Village Hall (1912-14, William Towner), and United States Post Office (individually listed).   05.24.1984

United States Post Office–Walton
Gardiner Place. Colonial Revival brick post office built 1936-37. United States Post Offices in New York State, 1858-1943, Thematic Resources. 05.11.1989

Amenia

Hendrik Winegar House
NY2 off NY343. A 2 1/2-story, 5-bay Colonial stone and brick residence built c.1761. 04.15.1975

Beacon

Madam Catharyna Brett Homestead
50 Van Nydeck Avenue. A 1 1/2-story, 5-bay Dutch Colonial frame residence built c.1715 as part of mill-farm complex on Fishkill Creek. 12.12.1976

Eustatia
12 Monell Avenue. A 1 1/2-story High Victorian Gothic brick cottage overlooking Hudson River; designed by Frederick C. Withers; built 1867 for John and Caroline Monell; partially landscaped 10-acre property. 02.26.1979

Howland Library
(Howland Center for Cultural Exchange) 477 Main Street. A 2-story Stick Style eclectic brick and frame building designed by Richard Morris Hunt; built 1871-72; interior alterations 1895 by Charles B. Van Slyck. 05.07.1973

Lower Main Street Historic District
142-192 and 131-221 Main Street. A 2-block neighborhood with 36 mostly 3-story late 19th-century Italianate brick attached commercial buildings. 01.07.1988

Mount Beacon Incline Railway and Power House
Howland Avenue and Wolcott Street (also in Fishkill), Mount Beacon. A 2,364-foot-long cable railway ascending Mount Beacon; designed 1901 by Otis Elevator Co.; operated until 1971 as part of recreational complex. Hudson Highlands Multiple Resource Area. 11.23.1982

Reformed Dutch Church of Fishkill Landing
44-50 Ferry Street. High Victorian Gothic brick church designed by Frederick C. Withers; built 1859; 1870s rear wings and tower. Adjacent cemetery established 1813. 08.31.1988

Tioronda Bridge
South Avenue over Fishkill Creek. Iron bowstring truss bridge built 1869-73 by Ohio Bridge Co. 10.08.1976

United States Post Office–Beacon
369 Main Street. Colonial Revival fieldstone post office designed by Gilbert Stanley Underwood; built 1935-37. Interior mural series (1937) by Charles Rosen. United States Post Offices in New York State, 1858-1943, Thematic Resources. 11.17.1988

Beekman

Sylvan Lake Rock Shelter
Address restricted. Prehistoric stratified site containing material from Archaic to Late Woodland occupations such as projectile points and tools. 07.12.1974

Clinton

Clinton Corners Friends Church
Salt Point Turnpike. A 1 1/2-story Shingle Style frame Quaker meetinghouse built 1890; enlarged 1915. Converted for use as residence. Dutchess County Quaker Meeting Houses Thematic Resources. 04.27.1989

Creek Meeting House and Friends' Cemetery
Salt Point Turnpike. A 2-story vernacular fieldstone Quaker meetinghouse built 1777-82; converted for use as grange hall. Adjacent cemetery. Dutchess County Quaker Meeting Houses Thematic Resources. 04.27.1989

Windswept Farm
Sunset Trail Road. An 80-acre farmstead with vernacular Federal frame farmhouse built 1823 by Amos Lyons, 2 barns, and cider mill. 09.07.1989

Dover

Tabor-Wing House
NY22 and Cemetery Road. A 2 1/2-story, 5-bay Federal frame residence with elaborate decorative detail; built c.1810 for Thomas Tabor. 06.03.1982

East Fishkill

Bykenhulle
21 Bykenhulle Road. A 2 1/2-story Greek Revival frame farmhouse built 1841 for Peter Adriance. Adjacent barn and poultry house. 12.30.1991

Fishkill (Town)

Bannerman's Island Arsenal
Pollepel Island (Hudson River). Ruins of castle and outbuildings designed by Francis Bannerman VI; built 1901-10 for storage of munitions and surplus war materials. Now part of Hudson Highlands State Park. Hudson Highlands Multiple Resource Area. 11.23.1982

Dutchess Manor
400 Breakneck Road. A 2 1/2-story Second Empire brick residence built 1889 for Francis Timoney, brickyard owner; now operated as restaurant. Adjacent carriage house and gatehouse. Hudson Highlands Multiple Resource Area. 11.23.1982

Fishkill Supply Depot Site
Northeast of Beacon. A 70-acre archeological site of major Quartermaster Company Commissary facility in 1777-79 during American Revolution; includes Van Wyck-Wharton House (individually listed). 01.21.1974

Mount Beacon Incline Railway and Power House (see Beacon)

Mount Gulian (Gulian Verplanck II House)
Off US1-84, north of Beacon. A 12-acre property with archeological deposits associated with Verplanck family, who settled there in early 18th century. Includes reconstructed c.1740 stone residence and c.1740 barn (moved to site). Operated as museum by Mount Gulian Society. 11.19.1982

Stony Kill Farm
NY9D, west of Fishkill (also in Wappinger). A 125-acre farm with 18th-century Colonial stone farmhouse (Washington House) built by Verplanck family, large Greek Revival/eclectic residence built 1843, 3 tenant houses, and large barn complex. Operated since 1973 by New York State Department of Environmental Conservation as Verplanck-Stony Kill Practice Farm and Environmental Education Center. 03.20.1980

Van Wyck-Wharton House
US9, south of Fishkill. A 1 1/2-story Dutch Colonial frame residence built c.1733 by Cornelius Van Wyck; large addition c.1756; functioned during American Revolution as part of Fishkill Supply Depot. Museum. 04.13.1972

Fishkill (Village)

Fishkill Village Historic District
Roughly along NY52 from Cary Street to Hopewell Street. Central portion of small village, with approximately 95 late 18th- to late 19th-century residential, commercial, public, and religious buildings. Notable buildings include Colonial Dutch Reformed Church (1725-36; rebuilt 1786) and Trinity Church (1768). 03.20.1973

Hyde Park

Bergh-Stoutenburgh House
US9. A 1 1/2-story, 5-bay Dutch Colonial stone residence with gambrel roof; built pre-1778; later frame additions. 09.27.1972

Crum Elbow Meeting House and Cemetery
Quaker Lane. A 2-story vernacular frame Quaker meetinghouse built 1797; enlarged c.1810. Adjacent cemetery. Dutchess County Quaker Meeting Houses Thematic Resources. 04.27.1989

John Hendricks House and Dutch Barn
Old Post Road, Staatsburg. Large Federal stone residence with 2-story front porch; built c.1785. Property includes late 18th-century Dutch barn. 09.07.1984

Hyde Park Railroad Station
River Road. A 1-story Mission-style brick passenger station designed by Warren & Wetmore; built 1914 for New York Central Railroad. 09.11.1981

Eleanor Roosevelt National Historic Site (Val-Kill)

Violet Avenue. A 180-acre property with fields, woods, wetlands, and 5 buildings. Refuge for Eleanor Roosevelt from 1924 until her death in 1962. Two principal buildings include Eleanor's House (built 1926 to house Val-Kill Industries) and Stone Cottage (1925-26, Henry Toombs). Property also includes prehistoric and historic archeological resources. 05.27.1977

Home of Franklin D. Roosevelt National Historic Site (Springwood)

US9, two miles south of Hyde Park. Birthplace and home of President Franklin D. Roosevelt. Main house built 1826 and enlarged several times. Property includes graves of Franklin D. and Eleanor Roosevelt and Franklin D. Roosevelt Library. 01.15.1944

Hudson River Historic District
(see Clermont, Columbia County)

Sixteen Mile District (see Clermont, Columbia County)

William Stoutenburgh House

US9G, East Park. A 1 1/2-story, 5-bay Colonial vernacular stone residence built c.1765 for prominent local family. 09.27.1972

United States Post Office–Hyde Park

East Market Street and US9. Colonial Revival stone post office designed by R. Stanley-Brown; design modeled after John Bard House with advice from President Franklin D. Roosevelt; built 1940. Interior mural series (1941) by Olin Dows. United States Post Offices in New York State, 1858-1943, Thematic Resources. 05.11.1989

Vanderbilt Mansion National Historic Site (Hyde Park)

US9, north edge of Hyde Park. The 212-acre Hudson River estate of Frederick W. Vanderbilt with massive Second Renaissance style limestone mansion designed by McKim, Mead & White; built 1896-98. Extensive gardens. 12.18.1940

LaGrange

Beekman Meeting House and Friends' Cemetery

Emans Road. A 1 1/2-story vernacular frame Quaker meetinghouse built 1838. Adjacent cemetery. Dutchess County Quaker Meeting Houses Thematic Resources. 04.27.1989

Millbrook

Nine Partners Meeting House and Cemetery

NY343 and Church Street. A 2-story vernacular brick Quaker meetinghouse built 1780. Adjacent cemetery. Dutchess County Quaker Meeting Houses Thematic Resources. 04.27.1989

Northeast

Ezra Clark House

Mill Road. Georgian brick farmhouse built c.1780. 02.21.1985

Hiddenhurst

Sheffield Hill Road. A 17-acre estate with Colonial Revival frame residence built 1903 as country retreat of Thomas B. Hidden, paint manufacturer and Manhattan real estate developer. 02.21.1991

Nine Partners Meeting House, Millbrook.

Pawling (Town)

Akin Free Library

97 Quaker Hill Road, Quaker Hill. A 2 1/2-story Victorian/eclectic stone library with ornate central tower; designed by John A. Wood; built 1898-1908 with funds provided by philanthropist Albert J. Akin. 11.21.1991

Oblong Friends Meetinghouse

Meetinghouse Road, Quaker Hill. A 2 1/2-story, 5-bay Colonial shingled meetinghouse built 1764-65 as nucleus of Quaker settlement. Largely intact interior. Operated as museum by Historical Society of Quaker Hill and Vicinity. 01.12.1973

Pawling (Village)

John Kane House

126 East Main Street. Modest Colonial farmhouse built 1740 by William Prendergast; large Federal main block added c.1810-20 by John Kane. Outbuildings include brick smokehouse, carriage barn, and woodshed. Served as Washington's Headquarters in 1778 during American Revolution. 10.20.1980

Pine Plains

Melius-Bentley House

Mount Ross Road (also in Gallatin, Columbia County). A 25-acre property with Colonial frame farmhouse built in 3 stages: 1-room-plan house built c.1717 by Johannes Jacob Melius, a Palatine German immigrant; 1-room- plan addition built c.1725; 2-story Federal section built c.1802. 08.11.1982

The Pines

Maple Street. Large Stick Style villa built 1878 for William S. Eno, prominent local attorney and banker. Includes 5 acres of landscaped grounds and several original outbuildings. 09.26.1983

Pleasant Valley

Bloomvale Historic District

Junction NY82, Route 13, and East Wappingers Creek (also in town of Washington). Large Federal frame residence built c.1801 for Isaac Bloom. Adjacent cider mill (1913), worker's house, and structures and sites associated with 18th- and 19th-century mills. 12.30.1991

Newcomb-Brown Estate

Brown Road at US 44. A 34-acre property with large 2 1/2-story, 5-bay Georgian brick farmhouse with gambrel roof and frame kitchen wing; built c.1770 for prosperous farmer and leaseholder. Includes seven 19th-century outbuildings.   10.07.1988

Poughkeepsie (Town)

Abraham Brower House

2 Water Street, New Hamburg. Modest 1 1/2-story, 3-bay Greek Revival brick residence built c.1845. Adjacent small shop building. New Hamburg Multiple Resource Area. 02.27.1987

Adolph Brower House

1 Water Street, New Hamburg. A 2 1/2-story, 3-bay Greek Revival brick residence with 2-story front porch; built c.1845. New Hamburg Multiple Resource Area.   02.27.1987

Hudson River State Hospital, Main Building

US 9. Massive High Victorian Gothic brick insane asylum with polychromatic exterior; designed by Frederick C. Withers; built 1867-70. Includes 10 acres of original grounds designed by Olmsted & Vaux.
NHL 06.30.1989

Locust Grove (Samuel F. B. Morse House)

370 South Road. A 100-acre estate overlooking Hudson River with large brick residence built early 19th century for Montgomery family; substantially enlarged and remodeled 1851-52 in Tuscan villa style with angled corners, porte cochere, 4-story tower, and stuccoed exterior; alterations designed by Alexander Jackson Davis with prominent inventor and artist Samuel F. B. Morse; early 20th-century addition. Museum.   NHL 01.29.1964

Entry, Hudson River State Hospital, Town of Poughkeepsie.

Main Street Historic District

New Hamburg. Group of 3 Greek Revival residences and 3 Victorian commercial buildings built c.1845-c.1876 at core of small Hudson River hamlet. New Hamburg Multiple Resource Area.   02.27.1987

Rosenlund Estate Buildings at Marist College

US 9. Victorian Gothic stone gatehouse, gardener's cottage, and carriage house designed by Detlef Lienau; built 1860s as part of estate of iron manufacturer Edward Bech; altered after 1908 for use by college.   05.14.1991

St. Nicholas-on-the-Hudson Church
(Zion Memorial Chapel)

37 Point Street, New Hamburg. Modest Victorian Gothic frame church designed by Edward Lansing Satterlee; built 1902. New Hamburg Multiple Resource Area.   02.27.1987

William Shay Double House

18 Point Street, New Hamburg. Italianate brick double house built c.1870. New Hamburg Multiple Resource Area.
02.27.1987

Shay's Warehouse and Stable

32 Point Street, New Hamburg. Italianate brick warehouse and attached stable built c.1865 for rag and cotton-waste dealer. New Hamburg Multiple Resource Area.
02.27.1987

Stone Street Historic District

New Hamburg. Group of 4 mid- to late 19th-century Greek Revival and Victorian residences. New Hamburg Multiple Resource Area.   02.27.1987

Union Free School

Academy Street, New Hamburg. A 2-story Italianate brick school built c.1875. New Hamburg Multiple Resource Area.
02.27.1987

Vassar College, Main Building

Raymond Avenue. Monumental 5-story Second Empire brick building covering approximately 4 acres; designed 1860 by James Renwick, Jr.; completed 1864.   09.19.1973;
NHL 06.24.1986

Vassar College Observatory

Raymond Avenue. Victorian brick observatory designed by Charles S. Farrar; built 1865 for Maria Mitchell, astronomer, professor, crusader for higher education for women, and first woman elected to both American Academy of Arts and Sciences and American Philosophical Society.   NHL 07.17.1991

Poughkeepsie (City)

Academy Street Historic District

Academy Street between Livingston and Montgomery streets. A 3-block area with approximately 45 buildings, mostly substantial mid- to late 19th-century frame or brick residences. Includes Gothic Revival church designed 1887 by William A. Potter. Poughkeepsie Multiple Resource Area.   11.26.1982

Adriance Memorial Library

93 Market Street. Large Neoclassical stone library with Corinthian portico and central dome; designed by Charles F. Rose; built 1896-98. Poughkeepsie Multiple Resource Area.   11.26.1982

Amrita Club

170 Church Street. Large 3-story Georgian Revival brick building built 1912. Poughkeepsie Multiple Resource Area.   11.26.1982

Balding Avenue Historic District

Balding Avenue between Mansion and Marshall streets. A 1-block residential area with 28 modest late-19th century frame residences. Poughkeepsie Multiple Resource Area.
11.26.1982

Barrett House
(Dutchess County Art Association)

55 Noxon Street. Greek Revival brick townhouse built c.1835. Poughkeepsie Multiple Resource Area.   11.26.1982

O. H. Booth Hose Company

532 Main Street. A 3-story Arts and Crafts eclectic brick firehouse designed by William J. Beardsley; built c.1908. Poughkeepsie Multiple Resource Area.   11.26.1982

Boughton-Haight House
(Schoonmaker Chapel)

73-75 South Hamilton Street. Italianate brick double townhouse built c.1875. Poughkeepsie Multiple Resource Area.   11.26.1982

Cedarcliff Gatehouse

66 Ferris Lane. Gothic Revival brick residence built c.1845 as gatehouse to James Winslow estate; possible design attribution to Andrew Jackson Downing. Poughkeepsie Multiple Resource Area.   11.26.1982

Church of the Holy Comforter

13 Davies Place. Gothic Revival stone church designed by Richard Upjohn; built 1860.
04.13.1972

Church Street Row

Church Street between Academy and Hamilton streets. Group of 9 brick or frame residences built 1855-95. Poughkeepsie Multiple Resource Area.   11.26.1982

Clark House

85 Cedar Avenue. Tudor Revival concrete block bungalow built c.1919 for factory foreman. Poughkeepsie Multiple Resource Area.
11.26.1982

Clinton House (State Historic Site)

547 Main Street. Large Georgian stone residence built c.1765 by Hugh Van Kleeck; rebuilt 1783; restored 20th century. Headquarters of Dutchess County Historical Society. Owned by New York State Office of Parks, Recreation and Historic Preservation. Poughkeepsie Multiple Resource Area.   11.26.1982

Collingwood Opera House
and Office Building (The Bardavon)

31-37 Market Street. A 5-story Italianate brick

commercial building built 1863; connected opera house built 1868-69; designed by James S. Post. Opera house interior remodeled 1923 by William J. Beardsley. Now operated as theater by Bardavon 1869 Opera House. 10.20.1977

Dixon House
49 North Clinton Street. Gothic Revival frame residence built c.1862. Poughkeepsie Multiple Resource Area. 11.26.1982

Dutchess County Court House
10 Market Street. A 4-story Neoclassical brick and stone building designed by William J. Beardsley; built 1902-03. Poughkeepsie Multiple Resource Area. 11.26.1982

Dwight Street–Hooker Avenue Historic District
Dwight Street between Hamilton Street and Hooker Avenue, and 79-85 Hooker Avenue. Group of 18 large frame residences built 1895-1915 in variety of eclectic styles as part of planned suburban development; overall plan designed by Horace Trumbauer. Architects of residences include Percival M. Lloyd and DuBois Carpenter. Poughkeepsie Multiple Resource Area. 11.26.1982

Eastman Terrace
1-10 Eastman Terrace. Row of 10 connected 3 1/2-story Second Empire brick townhouses designed by A. G. Thompson; built 1872. Poughkeepsie Multiple Resource Area. 11.26.1982

Ethol House
171 Hooker Avenue. A 1 1/2-story stone and frame bungalow designed 1910 by Andre Reid. Poughkeepsie Multiple Resource Area. 11.26.1982

Farmer's and Manufacturer's Bank
43 Market Street. A 2 1/2-story Greek Revival brick bank built 1834. Poughkeepsie Multiple Resource Area. 11.26.1982

First Presbyterian Church
25 South Hamilton Street. Monumental Romanesque Revival granite church designed by Percival M. Lloyd; built 1905-08. Poughkeepsie Multiple Resource Area. 11.26.1982

First Presbyterian Church Rectory
98 Cannon Street. Second Empire brick residence built c.1857. Poughkeepsie Multiple Resource Area. 11.26.1982

Freer House
70 Wilbur Boulevard. Modest Colonial stone farmhouse built c.1728. Poughkeepsie Multiple Resource Area. 11.26.1982

Garfield Place Historic District
Both sides of Garfield Place. A 3-block neighborhood of 25 properties, mostly large brick residences built 1850-75. 11.29.1972

Glebe House
635 Main Street. A 1 1/2-story, 5-bay Georgian brick residence built c.1767 as parsonage for Anglican church; operated as house museum by Dutchess County Historical Society. Poughkeepsie Multiple Resource Area. 11.26.1982

Gregory House
140 South Cherry Street. Second Empire frame residence built c.1869. Poughkeepsie Multiple Resource Area. 11.26.1982

Grey Hook
5 Ferris Lane. A 1 1/2-story bungalow designed and built 1911 by Raymond H. Bushnell; first concrete block house in Poughkeepsie. Poughkeepsie Multiple Resource Area. 11.26.1982

Harlow Row
100-106 Market Street. Row of 4 attached 3 1/2-story Second Empire brick townhouses built c.1874. Poughkeepsie Multiple Resource Area. 11.26.1982

Hasbrouck House
75-77 Market Street. Large Queen Anne brick residence designed by Frederick C. Withers; built 1885 for local judge/historian Frank Hasbrouck. Poughkeepsie Multiple Resource Area. 11.26.1982

Hershkind House
30 Hooker Avenue. Stick Style frame residence built c.1885. Poughkeepsie Multiple Resource Area. 11.26.1982

Italian Center
227 Mill Street. Large mid-19th-century brick residence with major alterations c.1890 in Queen Anne style. 04.19.1972

Lady Washington Hose Company
20 Academy Street. A 3-story Arts and Crafts eclectic firehouse designed by Percival M. Lloyd; built 1908. Poughkeepsie Multiple Resource Area. 11.26.1982

Luckey, Platt & Company Department Store
332-346 Main Mall. Group of 3 contiguous commercial buildings: 4-story Victorian brick building (c.1867), large 5-story Classical Revival brick building (1922-23, Edward C. Smith), and 3-story Classical Revival building (c.1910, Percival M. Lloyd). Poughkeepsie Multiple Resource Area. 11.26.1982

Mader House
101 Corlies Avenue. Stuccoed bungalow built c.1925. Poughkeepsie Multiple Resource Area. 11.26.1982

Main Mall Row
315 Main Mall to 11 Garden Street. Row of 8 connected 3- to 4-story Renaissance Revival brick and stone commercial buildings built 1871-c.1874. Poughkeepsie Multiple Resource Area. 11.26.1982

Market Street Row
88-94 Market Street. Row of 3 residences: Mott-Van Kleeck House (c.1786; 19th-century modifications), Eastlake residence

(c.1876), and Queen Anne brick residence (c.1890). Poughkeepsie Multiple Resource Area. 11.26.1982

Mill Street–North Clover Street Historic District
Mill, Main, Mansion, Vassar, North Bridge, North Clover, and Davies streets, and Lafayette Place. A 14-block residential area with approximately 130 buildings, mostly 2- and 3-story mid- to late 19th-century brick detached residences. Includes individually listed Vassar Institute, Vassar Home for Aged Men, Church of the Holy Comforter, Second Baptist Church, and Italian Center. 02.07.1972; BOUNDARY INCREASE 05.21.1987

Montgomery Street Meeting House
Montgomery Street. A 2-story Victorian brick Quaker meetinghouse built 1863; altered 1890. Dutchess County Quaker Meeting Houses Thematic Resources. 04.27.1989

Moore House
37 Adriance Avenue. Arts and Crafts residence designed by DuBois Carpenter following designs of Gustav Stickley; built 1910. Early use of hollow-tile construction in Poughkeepsie. Poughkeepsie Multiple Resource Area. 11.26.1982

Mulrien House
64 Montgomery Street. Modest Gothic Revival frame cottage built c.1862. Poughkeepsie Multiple Resource Area. 11.26.1982

New York State Armory
61-65 Market Street. Large Richardsonian Romanesque brick armory with towers and turrets; designed by Isaac G. Perry; built 1891. Poughkeepsie Multiple Resource Area. 11.26.1982

Niagara Engine House
8 North Hamilton Street. A 3-story brick firehouse with Gothic-style decorative detail; designed by Percival M. Lloyd; built 1909. Now used as ambulance service. Poughkeepsie Multiple Resource Area. 11.26.1982

Pelton Mill
110 Mill Street. A 4 1/2-story brick mill on Val Kill Creek; built c.1834; rebuilt 1854. Poughkeepsie Multiple Resource Area. 11.26.1982

Phillips House
18 Barclay Street. Queen Anne frame residence built c.1891 for hardware merchant. Poughkeepsie Multiple Resource Area. 11.26.1982

Post-Williams House
44 South Clinton Street. Second Empire frame residence with tower; design attributed to James S. Post; built c.1877. Poughkeepsie Multiple Resource Area. 11.26.1982

Poughkeepsie Almshouse and City Infirmary
20 Maple Street. A 7-acre property with large 3-story Italianate brick former almshouse (1868-69, J. A. Wood), Colonial Revival City Infirmary (1907, Percival M. Lloyd), and outbuildings. 12.04.1978

Poughkeepsie (Old) City Hall
(Mid-Hudson Arts and Science Center)
228 Main Street. A 2-story Greek Revival brick
building with cupola; built 1831 as village hall
and market. 01.20.1972

Poughkeepsie Meeting House
Hooker Avenue and Whittier Boulevard.
A 2-story Colonial Revival brick Quaker meet-
inghouse designed by Alfred Bussell; built
1928. Dutchess County Quaker Meeting
Houses Thematic Resources. 04.27.1989

Poughkeepsie Railroad Bridge
Spans Hudson River (also in Lloyd, Ulster
County). Monumental 6,767-foot-long steel-
truss railroad bridge built 1876-88 by Union
Bridge Co. No longer in use. 02.23.1979

Poughkeepsie Railroad Station
41 Main Street. Large 4-story Beaux-Arts brick
railroad station designed by Warren & Wetmore; built 1914-18. Waiting room with patterned brick walls and exposed wood rafters.
11.21.1976

Poughkeepsie Trust Company
236 Main Street. A 6-story Beaux-Arts stone
office building designed by Percival M. Lloyd;
built 1906. Now courthouse annex. Poughkeepsie Multiple Resource Area. 11.26.1982

Poughkeepsie Underwear Factory
6-14 North Cherry Street. A 3 1/2-story brick
factory built c.1874 as William S. Patten's
Live Oak Leather Manufactory; doubled in size
c.1887 for Dutchess Manufacturing Co.
Poughkeepsie Multiple Resource Area.
11.26.1982

Reynolds House
107 South Hamilton Street. Large Shingle Style
residence with cobblestone 1st story; designed
by DuBois Carpenter for owner of elevator
company; built c.1895. Poughkeepsie Multiple
Resource Area. 11.26.1982

Rombout House
Vassar Farms, New Hackensack Road. Large
Italianate frame farmhouse built c.1854.
Poughkeepsie Multiple Resource Area.
11.26.1982

Sague House
167 Hooker Avenue. Stone and frame
bungalow designed 1910 by Andre Reid.
Poughkeepsie Multiple Resource Area.
11.26.1982

St. Paul's Episcopal Church
161 Mansion Street. Gothic Revival stone
church designed by Emlen T. Littell; built 1873;
south transept and gallery added 1892 by Richard M. Upjohn; interior remodeled 1906 by
Tiffany Glass & Decoration Co. Poughkeepsie
Multiple Resource Area. 11.26.1982

Second Baptist Church (The Vassar Temple)
36 Vassar Street. Greek Revival frame building
with Doric portico; built c.1838.
01.20.1972

Smith Metropolitan A.M.E. Zion Church
Smith and Cottage streets. Gothic Revival
brick church designed by DuBois Carpenter;
built 1910 for local African-American community. Adjacent parsonage built 1914.
11.21.1991

South Hamilton Street Row
81-87 South Hamilton Street. Row of 4 large
Italianate and Second Empire frame residences
built 1871-72. Poughkeepsie Multiple
Resource Area. 11.26.1982

Thompson House
100 South Randolph Avenue. Large Second
Empire brick residence built c.1880. Landscaped property with brick carriage house and
octagonal privy. Poughkeepsie Multiple
Resource Area. 11.26.1982

Travis House
131 Cannon Street. A 3-bay Greek Revival
brick residence built c.1848. Poughkeepsie
Multiple Resource Area. 11.26.1982

**Trinity Methodist Episcopal Church
and Rectory**
1-3 Hooker Avenue. Romanesque Revival
brick church and Queen Anne brick rectory
designed by Corydon Wheeler; built 1892.
Poughkeepsie Multiple Resource Area.
11.26.1982

Union Street Historic District
Grand, South Bridge, Union, South Perry,
Delano, and South Clover streets. An 8-block
residential neighborhood with approximately
165 buildings, mostly modest 2-story brick
detached residences and rowhouses built
throughout 19th century. 12.09.1971

United States Post Office–Poughkeepsie
Mansion Street. Large Colonial Revival fieldstone post office designed by Eric Kebbon with
advice from President Franklin D. Roosevelt;
design based on Federal Dutchess County
Courthouse; built 1937-39. Notable 2-story
lobby with murals by Georgina Klitgaard,
Charles Rosen, and Gerald Foster. United
States Post Offices in New York State, 1858-
1943, Thematic Resources. 05.15.1989

Upper-Mill Street Historic District
Roughly Mill Street from Center Plaza to
Catherine Street. Group of approximately 30
brick or frame residences and several
double houses built 1830-1900 for factory
owners; includes Gothic Revival church and
Romanesque Revival First Congregational
Church (1860; John H. Dudley). Poughkeepsie
Multiple Resource Area. 11.26.1982

Vassar Home for Aged Men
(Cunneen-Hackett Cultural Center)
9 Vassar Street. Large 3-story Italianate brick
building completed 1880 on site of Matthew
Vassar townhouse. 04.13.1972

Vassar Institute
12 Vassar Street. A 2-story Second Empire
brick building designed by J. A. Wood; built
1882. Now part of Cunneen-Hackett Cultural
Center. 01.20.1972

Matthew Vassar Estate (Springside)
Academy Street. A 27-acre country estate with
landscaping and buildings designed 1850 for
Matthew Vassar by Andrew Jackson Downing.
Main house demolished and facade removed
to New York State Museum. NHL 08.11.196

Vassar-Warner Row
South Hamilton from Montgomery to 40
Hamilton Street. Group of 4 buildings, includ-
ing monumental Greek Revival brick Vassar-
Warner Home (built 1838 as Dutchess County
Academy; 1898 enlargement by Corydon
Wheeler) and 3 Queen Anne residences.
Poughkeepsie Multiple Resource Area.
11.26.1982

Young Men's Christian Association (Old)
58 Market Street. A 3-story Beaux-Arts/Italian
Renaissance style building with terra-cotta
facade; designed by Jackson & Rosencrans;
built 1908. Poughkeepsie Multiple Resource
Area. 11.26.1982

Red Hook (Town)

Heermance Farmhouse
Kerleys Corners Road. Dutch Colonial stone
farmhouse built c.1725-50; enlarged c.1772.
05.06.1980

Hudson River Historic District
(see Clermont, Columbia County)

Montgomery Place
River Road. A 425-acre Hudson River estate
with large Federal stuccoed stone residence
built 1804-05 for Janet Livingston Montgomery, widow of General Richard Montgomery,
hero of American Revolution; major Classical
Revival alterations 1843-44 and 1863-64 by
Alexander Jackson Davis. Property also
includes significant mid-19th-century landscape features and Picturesque dependencies,
and tenant houses in hamlet of Annandale.
05.02.1975

Rokeby (La Bergerie)
River Road. Large Hudson River estate with
Federal-period residence built 1811-15 for
soldier/diplomat John Armstrong and wife,
Alida Livingston; enlarged mid-19th century
for Margaret and William Backhouse Astor;
1895 alterations by Stanford White; landscaping c.1840 by Hans Jacob Ehlers and 1911 by
Olmsted Brothers; numerous dependencies.
03.26.1975

Sixteen Mile District
(see Clermont, Columbia County)

Red Hook (Village)

Elmendorph Inn
43-45 North Broadway. Large Colonial frame
building with modified gambrel roof; built
c.1750 as residence and tavern; enlarged
several times prior to 1830; served as meeting
place for town of Red Hook. Under restoration by Friends of Elmendorph.
09.20.1978

Halfway Diner (Village Diner)
39 North Broadway (US9). Silk City prefabricated metal diner manufactured 1925
by Paterson Vehicle Co. of Paterson, New
Jersey. 01.07.1988

Maizefield
75 West Market Street. Large Federal brick residence with fine classical details; built c.1797
for General David Van Ness, prominent public
and military figure during and after American
Revolution; enlarged 19th century.
11.26.1973

Rhinebeck (Town)

Barringer Farmhouse
US9. A 15-acre farmstead with Greek Revival
frame farmhouse built c.1835. Rhinebeck
Town Multiple Resource Area. 07.09.1987

Cox Farmhouse
Old Post Road, North. Colonial vernacular
stone farmhouse remodeled and enlarged 1842
in Greek Revival style. Rhinebeck Town Multiple Resource Area. 07.09.1987

Evangelical Lutheran Church of St. Peter
US9, north of Rhinebeck. Federal vernacular
stone church built 1786; present tower added
1823. Adjacent frame schoolhouse built
c.1833. 04.24.1975

Evergreen Lands
Delano Drive. Tudor Revival stone, stuccoed,
and half-timbered residence and caretaker's
lodge designed c.1932 by John Russell Pope
for estate of Laura Delano, cousin of Franklin
D. Roosevelt. Rhinebeck Town Multiple
Resource Area. 07.09.1987

Fredenburg House
Old Post Road. Modest 2-room-plan Colonial
stone farmhouse built c.1716 in German
vernacular tradition. Rhinebeck Town Multiple
Resource Area. 07.09.1987

Free Church Parsonage
William and Grinnell streets, Rhinecliff.
Gothic Revival frame cottage built c.1869.
Rhinebeck Town Multiple Resource Area.
07.09.1987

Grasmere
Mill Road. A 60-acre estate with brick main
house built in stages c.1824-1910, stone barn
and stable complex, tenant house, several outbuildings, and significant landscape features.
Original section of house built in Federal style
for Peter R. Livingston on site of earlier house.
Rhinebeck Town Multiple Resource Area.
07.09.1987

The Grove
Miller Road and NY308. A 21-acre estate
with large Federal main residence built c.1795
for Philip J. Schuyler, son of General Philip
Schuyler; remodeled by McKim, Mead &
White. Rhinebeck Town Multiple Resource
Area. 07.09.1987

Heermance House and Law Office
Rhinecliff and Long Dock roads, Rhinecliff.
Italianate frame residence built c.1858 and
adjacent modest Gothic Revival frame office
built c.1886. Rhinebeck Town Multiple
Resource Area. 07.09.1987

Hillside Methodist Church
US9. Modest rural Victorian stone church with
Picturesque features; built c.1855. Adjacent
early 20th-century parish hall. Rhinebeck
Town Multiple Resource Area.
07.09.1987

Hudson River Historic District
(see Clermont, Columbia County)

Kip-Beekman-Heermance Site
Address restricted, Rhinecliff. Archeological
site of Dutch Colonial residence built c.1700
and occupied by prominent local families for
210 years. Rhinebeck Town Multiple Resource
Area. 04.19.1989

Mansakenning
Ackert Hook Road. A 113-acre estate with
Georgian Revival stone residence built c.1903
for Eugene Tillotson Lynch. Includes guest
cottage, barns, carriage house, and sheds.
Rhinebeck Town Multiple Resource Area.
07.09.1987

Marquardt Farm
Wurtemburg Road, Wurtemburg. A 22-acre
farmstead with Federal frame farmhouse and
Dutch barn built c.1810. Includes intact group
of outbuildings and support structures.
Rhinebeck Town Multiple Resource Area.
07.09.1987

J. W. Moore House
Mill Road. Mid 19th-century farm complex
with Gothic Revival frame farmhouse, carriage
house, well house, barn, and corn crib.
Rhinebeck Town Multiple Resource Area.
07.09.1987

Morton Memorial Library
Kelly Street, Rhinecliff. Large Colonial Revival
brick library designed by Hoppin, Koen &
Huntington; built 1905. Rhinebeck Town
Multiple Resource Area. 07.09.1987

O'Brien General Store and Post Office
Schatzell Avenue and Charles Street, Rhinecliff.
A 3-story Italianate brick commercial/residen-
tial building built c.1860s; brick and frame
rear wings. Rhinebeck Town Multiple
Resource Area. 07.09.1987

Jan Pier House
NY308. Colonial vernacular stone farmhouse
built c.1761; major 1881 alterations in Second
Empire style. Late 19th-century outbuildings
including stone and brick smokehouse.
Rhinebeck Town Multiple Resource Area.
07.09.1987

Pilgrim's Progress Road Bridge
Miller Road, south of NY308. Triple-arch
stone vehicular bridge built c.1858 over Landsman Kill. Rhinebeck Town Multiple Resource
Area. 07.09.1987

Progue House
Primrose Hill Road. A 95-acre farmstead with
2-story stone farmhouse built c.1763 in German vernacular tradition and mid-19th-cen-
tury outbuildings. Rhinebeck Town Multiple
Resource Area. 07.09.1987

Pultz Farmhouse
Wurtemburg Road, Wurtemburg. Modest
vernacular frame farmhouse built c.1750;
enlarged c.1800. Rhinebeck Town Multiple
Resource Area. 07.09.1987

Rhinecliff Hotel
Schatzell Avenue, Rhinecliff. A 3-story Italianate frame hotel built c.1855 near ferry landing
and railroad on Hudson River. Rhinebeck
Town Multiple Resource Area. 07.09.1987

Riverside Methodist Church and Parsonage
Charles and Orchard streets, Rhinecliff. Small
Gothic Revival stone church built c.1859 and
Victorian frame parsonage built c.1888.
Rhinebeck Town Multiple Resource Area.
07.09.1987

Rock Ledge
Ackert Hook Road. A 400-acre estate with
Italian Renaissance style stone main residence
and 9 dependencies and support structures;
designed by Francis L. V. Hoppin and Whitney
Warren; built c.1904-06 for William Starr
Miller. Operated since 1987 as residential
treatment center. Rhinebeck Town Multiple
Resource Area. 11.28.1989

**St. Paul's Lutheran Church, Parsonage,
and Cemetery**
Wurtemburg Road, Wurtemburg. Federal
frame church built 1802; octagonal belfry
added 1832; remodeled 1861. Adjacent mid-
19th-century cemetery. Rhinebeck Town Multiple Resource Area. 07.09.1987

Salisbury Turnpike Bridge
Old Turnpike Road. Single-span stone-arch
vehicular bridge built 1858 over Landsman
Kill. Rhinebeck Town Multiple Resource Area.
07.09.1987

Robert Sands Estate (The Homestead)
NY9G and Miller Road, east of Rhinebeck.
Large Federal frame residence built c.1796 for
entrepreneur and merchant. Farm complex on
property includes Dutch barn. 02.24.1975

Sipperly-Lown Farmhouse
US9. A 27-acre farmstead with Victorian
frame farmhouse built c.1868, Dutch barn
built c.1800, and other outbuildings.
Rhinebeck Town Multiple Resource Area.
07.09.1987

Sixteen Mile District
(see Clermont, Columbia County)

Slate Quarry Road Dutch Barn
Slate Quarry Road. Large frame Dutch barn
built c.1790s. Rhinebeck Town Multiple
Resource Area. 07.09.1987

Steenburg Tavern
US9. Modest 1 1/2-story vernacular stone

residence built c.1750; used as tavern during American Revolution; enlarged 1790s. Rhinebeck Town Multiple Resource Area. 07.09.1987

Stonecrest

Old Post Road. Large Shingle Style frame and stone residence built 1905 as summer house for George D. Beatty of Brooklyn. Rhinebeck Town Multiple Resource Area.   07.09.1987

Strawberry Hill

Ackert Hook Road. A 21-acre farmstead with vernacular stone farmhouse built c.1762 (c.1900 wings), Dutch barn, and other outbuildings. Rhinebeck Town Multiple Resource Area.   07.09.1987

Traver House

Wynkoop Lane, Wurtemburg. Modest 1 1/2-story vernacular stone farmhouse built c.1730; frame wing c.1790. Rhinebeck Town Multiple Resource Area.   07.09.1987

J. E. Traver Farm

Violet Hill Road. A 14-acre farmstead with Greek Revival frame farmhouse built 1830s with mid-19th-century decoration, and massive mid-19th-century barn complex with Picturesque architectural details. Rhinebeck Town Multiple Resource Area.   07.09.1987

John H. Traver Farm

Wurtemburg Road. A 20-acre farmstead wit Italianate frame farmhouse built c.1876, Dutch barn built c.1800, and 19th-century outbuildings. Rhinebeck Town Multiple Resource Area. 07.09.1987

Van Vredenberg Farm

Cedar Heights Road. An 8-acre farmstead with Greek Revival frame farmhouse built c.1830 and 6 mid- to late 19th-century outbuildings. Rhinebeck Town Multiple Resourc Area. 07.09.1987

Williams Farm

Enterprise Road. A 109-acre farmstead with Greek Revival frame farmhouse built c.1835 and mid- to late 19th-century outbuildings. Rhinebeck Town Multiple Resource Area. 07.09.1987

Rhinebeck (Village)

Astor Home for Children

36 Mill Street. Large Jacobean Revival brick and stone institutional building designed by McKim, Mead & White; built 1914; non-his toric additions. Property includes historic guest cottage and modern outbuildings. Orig nally established by Morton and Astor famili

Henry Delamater House, Village of Rhinebeck.

as rest home for convalescent children. Rhinebeck Town Multiple Resource Area. 07.09.1987

Benner House
77 Mill Street. A 1-story, 1-room-plan Colonial stone residence built c.1739 in German vernacular tradition. Rhinebeck Town Multiple Resource Area. 07.09.1987

Henry Delamater House
44 Montgomery Street. Gothic Revival frame residence designed 1844 by Alexander Jackson Davis. Considered one of the finest examples of an American Gothic cottage. 05.07.1973

The Maples
108 Montgomery Street. Late Federal/Greek Revival frame residence built 1833; remodeled and enlarged 1860s in Picturesque style. Rhinebeck Town Multiple Resource Area. 07.09.1987

Rhinebeck Village Historic District
US9 and NY308. Large central portion of village, with approximately 340 residential, public, commercial, and religious buildings. Numerous examples of vernacular and high-style Colonial, Federal, Greek Revival, Gothic Revival, Victorian, and Colonial Revival styles. Includes Henry Delamater House (individually listed). 08.08.1979

United States Post Office–Rhinebeck
14 Mill Street. Colonial Revival stone post office designed by R. Stanley-Brown; designed as replica of Kip-Beekman-Heermance House with advice from President Franklin D. Roosevelt; built 1938-39. Interior mural series (1940) by Olin Dows. United States Post Offices in New York State, 1858-1943, Thematic Resources. 05.11.1989

Tivoli

Hudson River Historic District
(see Clermont, Columbia County)

Sixteen Mile District
(see Clermont, Columbia County)

Watts DePeyster Firehouse
86 Broadway at Pine Street. Romanesque Revival brick firehouse designed by Michael O'Connor; built 1898. 11.16.1989

Union Vale

Oswego Meeting House and Cemetery
Oswego and North Smith roads. A 1 1/2-story frame Quaker meetinghouse built 1790. Adjacent cemetery. Dutchess County Quaker Meeting Houses Thematic Resources. 04.27.1989

Wappinger

Cornelius Carman House
River Road South, Chelsea. A 1 1/2-story Federal frame residence with Doric portico; built c.1835 for local sloop builder; later additions. Chelsea Multiple Resource Area. 12.30.1987

Chelsea Grammar School
Liberty Street, Chelsea. A 1-room Italianate vernacular brick school built 1875. Chelsea Multiple Resource Area. 08.25.1987

Captain Moses W. Collyer House
(Driftwood)
River Road South, Chelsea. A 2 1/2-story Colonial Revival frame residence built 1899 for renowned Hudson River boat captain and author. Chelsea Multiple Resource Area. 08.25.1987

Joseph Horton House
NY376, New Hackensack. A 1 1/2-story Dutch Colonial frame farmhouse with flared gambrel roof; built 1752-55. 11.02.1988

St. Mark's Episcopal Church
Liberty Street, Chelsea. Modest Gothic Revival frame church built 1866. Chelsea Multiple Resource Area. 08.25.1987

Stony Kill Farm (see town of Fishkill)

Wheeler Hill Historic District
Wheeler Hill Road. Group of 6 estates and outbuildings overlooking Hudson River, including Italianate Obercreek (c.1850; remodeled 1920s), Second Empire Elmhurst (c.1867; remodeled c.1885), Greek Revival Edge Hill (c.1840; c.1855 additions), Federal Henry Suydam House (c.1835; remodeled c.1855), Federal William Crosby House (c.1800; enlarged c.1870), and Italianate Carnwath Farms (c.1850; enlarged c.1870). Also includes vernacular stone residence and frame store built mid-18th century. 06.14.1991

Wappingers Falls

Bain Commercial Building
59-61 West Main Street. Second Empire brick commercial residential building built c.1875. Wappingers Falls Multiple Resource Area. 09.29.1984

Duchess Company Superintendent's House
120 Market Street. Greek/Gothic Revival brick residence built c.1848 for print works superintendent. Wappingers Falls Multiple Resource Area. 09.29.1984

Mulhern House
14-16 Market Street. Federal vernacular frame double house built c.1815 for mill workers. Wappingers Falls Multiple Resource Area. 09.29.1984

United States Post Office–Wappingers Falls
2 South Avenue. Colonial Revival stone and brick post office designed by R. Stanley-Brown in regional vernacular 18th-century style with

advice from President Franklin D. Roosevelt; built 1939-40. Interior murals (1940) by Henry Billings. United States Post Offices in New York State, 1858-1943, Thematic Resources. 05.11.1989

Wappingers Falls Historic District
Roughly bounded by South Avenue, and Elm, Main, Park, Walker, Market, and McKinley streets. Concentration of approximately 100 mostly 19th-century buildings near Wappingers Creek, including Dutchess Bleachery complex, double mill worker's houses, mill manager's residences, 5 churches, a park, and 2 bridges. Significant buildings include Mesier Homestead (c.1741, with Gothic Revival alterations) and Queen Anne Grinnell Library (c.1887). Includes Wappingers Falls Post Office (individually listed). Wappingers Falls Multiple Resource Area. 09.29.1984

Washington

Bloomvale Historic District
(see Pleasant Valley)

Lynfeld (Milton Ham House)
South Road at Tyrell Road. A 23-acre property with large Italianate frame farmhouse built c.1871 and 2 late 19th-century barns. 03.19.1987

ERIE COUNTY

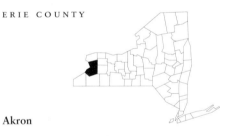

Akron

United States Post Office–Akron
118 Main Street. Colonial Revival brick post office built 1939-41. Interior mural (1941) by Elizabeth Logan. United States Post Offices in New York State, 1858-1943, Thematic Resources. 11.17.1988

Angola

United States Post Office–Angola
80 North Main Street. Colonial Revival brick post office built 1938-39. Interior mural (1940) by Leopold F. Scholz. United States Post Offices in New York State, 1858-1943, Thematic Resources. 11.17.1988

Buffalo

Albright-Knox Art Gallery
1285 Elmwood Avenue, in Delaware Park. Massive Neoclassical marble building designed by Edward B. Green; built 1900-05; facade dominated by Ionic porticoes and colonnades; caryatid figures by Augustus Saint-Gaudens; 1962 addition by Gordon Bunshaft of Skidmore, Owings & Merrill. 05.27.1971

Allentown Historic District

Off NY 384. Primarily residential neighborhood developed as streetcar suburb after Civil War. Contains approximately 750 buildings, mostly residences, in Italianate, Second Empire, Queen Anne, Eastlake, and Colonial Revival styles. Also includes apartment buildings, commercial buildings, churches, and parks. Notable properties include Kleinhans Music Hall (individually listed), Richardsonian Romanesque First Presbyterian Church (1889-91, Green & Wicks), Coit House (1818; oldest standing structure in city), Italianate former Quaker Meeting House (1869), Symphony Circle (1869, Frederick Law Olmsted), Birge Mansion (Little & Brown), apartments by Edward B. Green and George Cary, and residences by McKim, Mead & White. 04.21.1980

Berkeley Apartments (Graystone Hotel)
24 Johnson Park. A 6-story Italian Renaissance style building designed by architect Carlton T. Strong and engineer Ernest L. Ransome; built 1894-97. Early example of large-scale reinforced-concrete construction. 10.15.1987

Blessed Trinity Roman Catholic Church Buildings
317 LeRoy Avenue. Massive church in Lombard-Romanesque style designed by Chester Oakley and Albert Schallmo; built 1923-28 of unmolded medieval-style brick; terra-cotta interior decoration. Adjacent school building (1907) and parish house (1914). 08.03.1979

Buffalo and Erie County Historical Society
25 Nottingham Court. Large Neoclassical marble building designed by George Cary as New York State Pavilion of Pan-American Exposition of 1901; side wings designed 1929 by Cary; exterior sculpture by Edmond Romulus Amateis, Roland Hinton Perry, and Charles Henry Nichaus. 04.23.1980; NHL 02.27.1987

Buffalo Gas Light Company Works
(Jackson Plant, National Fuel Gas Company) 249 West Genesee Street. A 3-acre gas-manufacturing complex with main building designed by John H. Selkirk to resemble a fortress; built 1859. Also includes coal shed, retort house, stables, and office building. 09.01.1976

Buffalo Main Light
Buffalo River. A 68-foot-high octagonal limestone lighthouse built 1833-36; tower raised 1857. United States Coast Guard Lighthouses and Light Stations of the Great Lakes Thematic Resources. 07.19.1984

Buffalo North Breakwater South End Light
Buffalo Harbor. A 29-foot-high bottle-shaped cast-iron beacon built 1903. United States Coast Guard Lighthouses and Light Stations of the Great Lakes Thematic Resources. 08.04.1983

Buffalo State Hospital
400 Forest Avenue. Massive Romanesque Revival sandstone insane asylum designed 1870-72 by Henry Hobson Richardson with Andrew J. Warner, Supervising Architect; main building built 1872-90; siting and landscaping planned by Frederick Law Olmsted and Calvert Vaux. 01.12.1973; NHL 06.24.1986

Cazenovia Park–South Park System
South Buffalo (also in Lackawanna). Park and parkway system designed by Frederick Law Olmsted; built 1894-96. Components include 76-acre Cazenovia Park, 155-acre South Park, Heacock Place, McKinley Parkway, McClellan Circle, Red Jacket Parkway, and McKinley Circle. Notable structures include Cazenovia Park Casino (1912, Esenwein & Johnson) and South Park Botanical Gardens Conservatory (1889, Lord & Burnham; rebuilt 1930). Olmsted Parks and Parkways Thematic Resources. 03.30.1982

County and City Hall (Old County Hall)
95 Franklin Street. Massive High Victorian Gothic granite building with 270-foot-high clock and bell tower; designed by Andrew J. Warner; sculptural figures on tower by Giovanni F. Scala; built 1871-75. 05.24.1976

Delaware Avenue Historic District
West side of Delaware Avenue between North and Bryant streets. Series of 14 large-scale residences built for prosperous Buffalo families between 1891 and World War I. Architects include McKim, Mead & White; Charles P. H. Gilbert; Edward B. Green; and Esenwein & Johnson. 01.17.1974

Delaware Park–Front Park System
North Central Buffalo. Park and parkway system designed by Frederick Law Olmsted and Calvert Vaux; developed 1868-76. Components include 350-acre Delaware Park, Gates Circle, Chapin Parkway, Soldiers' Place, Lincoln Parkway, Bidwell Parkway, Colonial Circle, Richmond Avenue, Ferry Circle, Symphony Circle, Porter Avenue, Columbus Park, and Front Park. Notable structures in Delaware Park include Lincoln Parkway Bridge (1900, Green & Wicks), Stone Bridge (c.1887), and Art Deco Main Zoo Building (1935-40). Olmsted Parks and Parkways Thematic Resources. 03.30.1982

William Dorsheimer House
434 Delaware Avenue. Second Empire brick residence designed by Henry Hobson Richardson; built 1869-71 for prominent lawyer and politician. Reflects influence of French Neo-Gothic movement. 11.21.1980

Row at 17-21 Emerson Place
Row of 6 identical attached Second Empire frame residences in 2 sections; built 1900. Masten Neighborhood Rows Thematic Resources. 03.91.1986; DEMOLISHED 1987

Row at 33-61 Emerson Place
Two identical rows of 7 attached frame residences in eclectic blend of Colonial Revival, Shingle Style, and Eastlake styles; built 1893. Masten Neighborhood Rows Thematic Resources. 03.91.1986

Forest Lawn Cemetery
1411 Delaware Avenue. A 267-acre rural cemetery founded 1849, with naturalistic landscape designed by Charles E. Clarke and Joseph Earnshaw; large collection of tombs and monuments designed by well-known sculptors and architects; and graves of prominent local, state, and national figures. Notable structures include Neoclassical Administration Building (1907, George Cary), Colonial Revival Superintendent's Residence (1929, Bley & Lyman), Gothic Revival Chapel Complex (1882, enlarged early 20th century), Main Street Gate (1901, Henry Osgood Holland), and late 19th-century stone-arch bridges. 05.10.1990

Fosdick-Masten Park High School
(City Honors School)
Masten Avenue and East North Street. Large Italian Renaissance style school with terra-cotta exterior; designed by Esenwein & Johnson; built 1912-14. 06.30.1983

Guaranty Building (Prudential Building)
Church and Pearl streets. A 13-story office building with elaborate terra-cotta facades; designed by Louis Sullivan; built 1894-95.

Regarded as a milestone in modern skyscraper architecture.   03.20.1973; NHL 05.15.1975

Martin Luther King, Jr., Park
(The Parade, Humboldt Park)
A 56-acre park designed by Frederick Law Olmsted and Calvert Vaux as part of park and parkway system; redesigned 1896; later alterations. Major structures include Shelter House (1904, Robert Wallace), Art Deco Buffalo Museum of Science (1926-27, Esenwein & Johnson), Greenhouse (1907), and Humboldt Park Casino (1926). Olmsted Parks and Parkways Thematic Resources.
03.30.1982

Kleinhans Music Hall
Symphony Circle. International style music hall designed by Eliel and Eero Saarinen with F. J. and W. A. Kidd; built 1938-40.
NHL 06.30.1989

Lafayette High School
370 Lafayette Avenue. Large Beaux-Arts eclectic brick and sandstone school designed by Esenwein & Johnson; built 1901-03.
12.03.1980

Laurel and Michigan Avenues Row
1335-1345 Michigan Avenue. L-shaped row of 9 identical attached Italianate frame residences built 1880. Masten Neighborhood Rows Thematic Resources.   03.19.1986

Macedonia Baptist Church
511 Michigan Avenue. Modest brick church built 1845 for free African-American population of Buffalo; associated with Rev. Dr. J. Edward Nash and Mary B. Talbert, influential community leaders.   02.12.1974

Darwin D. Martin House
125 Jewett Parkway. Large, sprawling 2-story Prairie Style brick residence designed by Frank Lloyd Wright; built 1904 for local businessman.
NHL 02.24.1986

Darwin D. Martin House Complex
123 Jewett Parkway. Prairie Style family complex designed 1903-05 by Frank Lloyd Wright. Includes Darwin D. Martin House (individually listed), George Barton House, and Gardener's Cottage.   12.30.1975

New York Central Terminal
(Buffalo Central Terminal)
495 Paderewski Drive. Monumental Art Deco steel-frame and brick railroad station complex designed by Fellheimer & Wagner; built 1927-30; dominated by 271-foot-high octagonal office tower.   09.07.1984

Niagara Frontier Transit Buildings
(Buffalo East Side Railway Company Horse and Car Barn)
855 Main Street. Pair of large Italianate brick buildings built 1881-83 as horse and car barns.
05.14.1980; DEMOLISHED

Parkside East Historic District
Roughly bounded by Parkside, Colvin, and

Humboldt avenues, Amherst and Main streets, and New York Central Railroad. A 226-acre residential neighborhood with approximately 1,100 buildings, mostly detached single-family frame residences built late 19th to early 20th centuries. Curvilinear street plan and subdivision planned 1876-c.1886 by Frederick Law Olmsted. Notable buildings include Darwin D. Martin House Complex (individually listed), Romanesque Revival Church of the Good Shepherd (1888, Marling & Burdett), and Davidson House (1908, Frank Lloyd Wright). Olmsted Parks and Parkways Thematic Resources.   10.17.1986

Parkside West Historic District
Roughly bounded by Amherst Street, Nottingham Terrace, Middlesex Road, and

Guaranty Building, Buffalo.

Opposite: Darwin D. Martin House, Buffalo.

Delaware Avenue. A 53-acre residential neighborhood with approximately 82 large-scale residences on landscaped lots; designed 1876 by Frederick Law Olmsted; developed 1923-40. Many houses designed in Tudor Revival, Colonial Revival, and Chateauesque styles. Architects include Bley & Lyman, Shelgren & North, Frederick Backus, Edmund Gilchrist, Herbert C. Swain, and George Cary. Olmsted Parks and Parkways Thematic Resources. 12.10.1986

Pierce Arrow Factory Complex
Elmwood and Great Arrow avenues. A 34-acre automobile-manufacturing complex designed 1906-07 by Albert Kahn; Lockwood, Green & Co.; and Trussed Concrete Steel Co.; built 1906-22; closed 1938. 10.01.1974

Riverside Park
Niagara River. A 22-acre park designed 1898 by Olmsted Brothers; 17 additional acres acquired 1912. Olmsted Parks and Parkways Thematic Resources. 03.30.1982

Theodore Roosevelt Inaugural National Historic Site (Ansley Wilcox House)
641 Delaware Avenue. Greek Revival residence built 1838 with later alterations and additions. Theodore Roosevelt took oath of office as President of United States in front parlor on September 14, 1901, after assassination of William McKinley at Pan-American Exposition. 11.02.1966

St. Andrew's Evangelical Lutheran Church Complex
Sherman and Peckham streets. Gothic Revival/Romanesque Revival brick church designed by Louis Saenger; built 1884-85. Also includes original church (1859, remodeled into school) and Queen Anne parish house (1892). 09.08.1983

St. Luke's A.M.E. Zion Church
(Durham Memorial A.M.E. Zion Church)
174 East Eagle Street. Small Tudor Revival brick church designed by Louis Greenstein; built 1920-22; oldest surviving A.M.E. Zion church in Buffalo. 09.15.1983

St. Paul's Episcopal Cathedral
Pearl Street. Large Gothic Revival sandstone church designed by Richard Upjohn; built 1849-51; tower added 1870-71; interior and roof rebuilt by Robert W. Gibson with Cyrus K. Porter after 1888 fire. 03.01.1973; NHL 12.23.1987

Shea's Buffalo Theater
646 Main Street. Opulent movie palace with 4,000-seat auditorium; designed by C. W. and George L. Rapp for Michael Shea; built 1925. 05.06.1975

South Buffalo North Side Light
Buffalo Harbor. A 29-foot-high bottle-shaped cast-iron beacon built 1903. United States Coast Guard Lighthouses and Light Stations of the Great Lakes Thematic Resources. 08.04.1983

United States Post Office–Buffalo
121 Ellicott Street. Monumental Romanesque Revival/Chateauesque/French Gothic style building designed by Jeremiah O'Rourke, William Martin Aiken, and James Knox Taylor; built 1894-1901. Now Erie County Community College. 03.16.1972

USS *The Sullivans* (DD-537)
One Naval Cove Park. A 376-foot-long Fletcher class steel destroyer built 1943 by Bethlehem Steel Corp. in San Francisco, California, for United States Navy. Served with distinction in the Pacific during World War II.
NHL 01.14.1986

West Village Historic District
Roughly bounded by South Elmwood Avenue, and Chippewa, Georgia, Prospect, Carolina, and Tracy streets. Urban residential neighborhood with approximately 100 detached single-family residences and apartment buildings built 1854-1914 in Italianate, Second Empire, Queen Anne, Romanesque Revival, and Italian Renaissance styles. 05.06.1980

Woodlawn Avenue Row
75-81 Woodlawn Avenue. Row of 4 identical attached Stick Style frame residences built 1898. Masten Neighborhood Rows Thematic Resources. 03.19.1986

Young Men's Christian Association Central Building
45 West Mohawk Street. Large English/Flemish Renaissance style brick building with 10-story central tower; designed by Green & Wicks; built 1901-02. 09.08.1983

Cattaraugus Indian Reservation

Thomas Indian School
NY438. Rural school campus built 1900 by New York State as boarding school for Native Americans; buildings designed in Georgian Revival style by Barney & Chapman. School closed 1958. 01.25.1973

Cheektowaga

Chapel of Our Lady Help of Christians
(Maria Hilf Chapel)
4125 Union Road. Brick and limestone church built in 3 stages for local Alsatian immigrant community: sanctuary (1853), front half of nave (1871), back of nave and Classical Revival main facade (1926; Foit & Baschnagel); interior decoration derived from Alsatian heritage. 12.14.1978

Clarence

J. Eshelman & Company Store
6000 Goodrich Road. Large 3-story Italianate brick and cast-iron commercial building built 1872 by leader of local German immigrant community. 05.06.1982

Depew

United States Post Office–Depew
Warsaw Street. Colonial Revival brick post office built 1938-39. Interior mural (1941) by Anne Poor. United States Post Offices in New York State, 1858-1943, Thematic Resources. 11.17.1988

East Aurora

Millard Fillmore House
24 Shearer Avenue. Modest Federal frame residence built 1826 by Millard Fillmore, 13th President of the United States. Originally on Main Street; moved to present location 1930.
NHL 05.30.1974

Roycroft Campus
Main and South Grove streets. Complex of 9 stone and half-timbered buildings built 1896-1910 as artistic community of Arts and Craft movement under direction of Elbert Hubbard. 11.08.1974; NHL 02.24.1986

Hamburg

Kleis Site
Address restricted. Archeological site of early 17th-century Native American village. 04.20.1979

Kenmore

Eberhardt Mansion
2746 Delaware Avenue. Large Richardsonian Romanesque stone residence designed by Cyrus K. Porter; built 1893 for local land developers. 09.08.1983

Lackawanna

Cazenovia Park–South Park System
(see Buffalo)

Lancaster

United States Post Office–Lancaster
5064 Broadway. Colonial Revival brick post office built 1938-39. Interior mural (1940) by Arthur Getz. United States Post Offices in New York State, 1858-1943, Thematic Resources. 05.11.1989

North Collins

Gamel Hexadecagon Barn
Shirley Road. An 80-foot-diameter 16-sided dairy barn built c.1900. Central Plan Dairy Barns of New York State Thematic Resources. 09.29.1984

Orchard Park

Johnson-Jolls Complex
4287 South Buffalo Street. Italianate brick

residence built 1869-70 for local merchant Ambrose Johnson. Includes early 20th-century outbuildings.   05.06.1980

Springville

Buffalo, Rochester & Pittsburgh Railroad Station
227 West Main Street. A 1 1/2-story eclectic brick passenger station with terra-cotta roof; built 1910.   11.07.1991

United States Post Office–Springville
75 Franklin Street. Colonial Revival brick post office built 1936-37. Interior mural (1938) by Victoria H. Huntley. United States Post Offices in New York State, 1858-1943, Thematic Resources.   05.11.1989

Tonawanda

United States Post Office–Tonawanda
96 Seymour Street. Large-scale Colonial Revival brick post office built 1939-40. United States Post Offices in New York State, 1858-1943, Thematic Resources.   05.11.1989

West Seneca

Eaton Site
Address restricted. Large archeological site of prehistoric Iroquois village believed to date to mid-16th century.   04.03.1979

Williamsville

Williamsville Water Mill Complex
56 and 60 Spring Street. Early 19th-century 2 1/2 story frame water-powered mill and associated buildings and structures. Early commercial manufacturer of hydraulic cement. 09.22.1983

One-room schoolhouse on Harmon Noble property, Essex Village Historic District.

Adirondack State Forest Preserve
(see Clinton County)

Chesterfield

Elkanah Watson House
Port Kent. Unusual 2-story, 5-bay, Federal stone residence with 2-tiered portico overlooking Lake Champlain; designed by Philip Hooker; built 1827-28 for famed banker and agriculturalist.   NHL 07.19.1964

Crown Point

Fort Crown Point
Crown Point Reservation, near Lake Champlain Bridge. A 5-sided fort built 1760 by British army under direction of General Lord Jeffrey Amherst; lapsed into disrepair after explosion in 1773 and later played minor role in American Revolution. Now part of Crown Point Reservation State Historic Site. NHL 11.24.1968

Fort St. Frederic
Crown Point Reservation, near Lake Champlain Bridge. A 5-sided fort built 1730s by the French as stronghold in Champlain region; abandoned 1759 and leveled by the British. Now part of Crown Point Reservation State Historic Site.   NHL 10.09.1960

Ironville Historic District
Area surrounding Ironville, including Furnace Street and Penfield Pond. Small hamlet of approximately 12 buildings, several archeological sites, and cemetery remaining from iron industry center.   12.27.1974

Elizabethtown

Hand-Hale Historic District
River and Maple streets. Two adjoining 19th-century properties built for 2 prominent families of New York State jurists. Includes Greek Revival house (1849), law office, and outbuildings of Augustus C. Hand family; Federal house (1814; Victorian modifications), law office, and outbuildings of Robert S. Hale family.   03.05.1979

Essex

Church of the Nazarene (Bouquet Chapel)
NY22, west of Essex, Bouquet. Modest Gothic Revival frame rural chapel built 1855. 06.19.1973

Essex County Home and Farm
NY22, southwest of Whallonsburg. Rural almshouse complex of 7 late 19th-century brick

and frame institutional and farm buildings and cemetery on 24-acre property.   09.23.1982

Octagonal Schoolhouse
NY22, Bouquet. Vernacular stone 1-room octagonal schoolhouse built 1826 by Benjamin Gilbert for Daniel Ross.   01.17.1973

Essex Village Historic District
West bank of Lake Champlain. Hamlet of approximately 150 mostly early 19th-century residential, commercial, and religious buildings in Federal, Greek Revival, early Victorian, and other styles. Notable buildings include Federal Wright's Inn (c.1790), Greek Revival Greystone (c.1853), Greek Revival Essex Inn (c.1810.c.1835), Federal Hascall House (c.1800), Greek Revival John Gould House (1833), Federal Hickory Hill (1822), Greek Revival Cyrus Stafford House (1847), Federal Greystone Cottage (c.1815), and Federal/Greek Revival Harmon Noble House (c.1835). 05.28.1975

Keeseville

Double-Span Metal Pratt Truss Bridge
(see Clinton County)

Keeseville Historic District
(see Clinton County)

Rembrandt Hall
Clinton Street. Gothic Revival brick residence designed by Isaac G. Perry; built c.1851 for Emma Barton, daughter of Rembrandt Peale. Interior circular staircase built by Isaac G. and Seneca Perry. Keeseville Village Multiple Resource Area.   05.20.1983

Tomlinson House
Kent Street. Late Federal frame residence with Doric portico; built 1846 for prominent local attorney and politician. Keeseville Village Multiple Resource Area.   05.20.1983

Lake Placid

United States Post Office–Lake Placid
201 Main Street. Colonial Revival. Moderne brick post office built 1935-36. Interior mural (1937) by Henry Billings. United States Post Offices in New York State, 1858-1943, Thematic Resources.   11.17.1988

Moriah

Witherbee Memorial Hall
Broad Street, east of Office Road, Mineville. Large Shingle Style building built 1893 as social club for employees of local iron-mining industry.   04.22.1991

Newcomb

Adirondack Iron and Steel Company: Upper Works
North of Tahawus at Henderson Lake. A 400-acre archeological site and remains of mid-

19th-century ironworks complex and hamlet of Adirondack. Includes standing ruins of 60-foot blast furnace built 1854.   10.05.1977

Camp Santanoni
North of NY28N. Great Camp complex designed 1888-90 by Robert H. Robertson for Albany banker Robert C. Pruyn as part of 12,000-acre private preserve. Agricultural complex includes Shingle Style barn, stone dairy, and tenant houses. Entrance complex includes stone and wood gatehouse attributed to Delano & Aldrich. Complex on Newcomb Lake includes 5-mile entrance road, massive Rustic-style log main lodge, boathouse, and studio. Great Camps of the Adirondacks Thematic Resources.   04.03.1987

North Elba

John Brown Farm (State Historic Site)
John Brown Road, near Lake Placid. Home and grave of abolitionist John Brown, who settled the property in 1849.   06.19.1972

Port Henry

Van Ornam & Murdock Block
Main Street. Row of 4 attached Italianate brick commercial buildings built 1874-c.1880 as focal point of village.   11.14.1982

Saranac Lake

Will Rogers Memorial Hospital
NY86. Massive 3-story Tudor Revival building designed by William E. Scopes; built 1928-29 as tuberculosis hospital for vaudeville entertainers.   09.08.1983

Schroon

Samson Fried Estate (Birch Hill)
NY74, Severence. A 34-acre summer estate on Paradox Lake built for New York City businessman and amateur musician. Includes large Shingle Style Arts and Crafts main house (1902) and outbuildings.   02.27.1987

Ticonderoga (Town)

Fort Ticonderoga
(Fort Ticonderoga/Mount Independence)
NY22, south of Ticonderoga (also in Addison County, Vermont). A 2,200-acre site of strategic military importance for control of Champlain Valley by the French, British, and Americans in 18th century. Includes Fort Ticonderoga, built 1755 by the French, captured 1759 by the British, captured 1775 by Ethan Allen, restored early 20th century by Pell family (museum); archeological site of French village, King's Garden, and redoubts; The Pavilion, residence

Camp Santanoni, Newcomb.

built 1826 for William Ferris Pell; Mount Independence, site of American fortifications during American Revolution; Mount Defiance, site of British fortifications during American Revolution; and Mount Hope, site of American fortifications during American Revolution.
NHL 10.09.1960; BOUNDARY EXPANDED 1984

Ticonderoga (Village)

Amherst Avenue Historic District
322-340 Amherst Avenue. Group of 10 Colonial Revival and Arts and Crafts frame residences and bungalows built 1921-23 by builder William A. Gale for Ticonderoga Pulp & Paper Co. as company housing. Ticonderoga Multiple Resource Area.   06.16.1989

Black Watch Library
161 Montcalm Street. Small Jacobean Revival brick building designed by William Pitcher; built 1905. Ticonderoga Multiple Resource Area.   11.15.1988

H. G. Burleigh House
307 Champlain Avenue. Large Queen Anne concrete veneer and stone residence built in 2 sections in 1894 and 1905 for local businessman and politician. Stone section designed by C. G. Remington. Ticonderoga Multiple Resource Area.   11.15.1988

Central School
324 Champlain Avenue. Large Jacobean Revival brick school designed by Carpenter & Blair; built 1906-07. Ticonderoga Multiple Resource Area.   11.15.1988

Clark House
331 Montcalm Street. Arts and Crafts stone and shingled bungalow built 1921 by local mason Frank Clark. Ticonderoga Multiple Resource Area.   11.15.1988

Community Building
Montcalm and Champlain streets. Large Colonial Revival granite building built 1927 under auspices of local philanthropist Horace A. Moses; designed by M. H. Westhoff. Ticonderoga Multiple Resource Area.   11.15.1988

Clayton H. Delano House
25 Father Jogues Place. Large Italianate frame house built 1857; enlarged c.1890 in Queen Anne style for founder of Ticonderoga Pulp and Paper Co. Ticonderoga Multiple Resource Area.   11.15.1988

Ferris House
16 Carillon Road. Large Colonial Revival frame residence designed by William A. Gale for politician Mortimer Ferris; built 1911. Ticonderoga Multiple Resource Area.   11.15.1988

Gilligan and Stevens Block
115 Montcalm Street. A 3-story Italianate/ Queen Anne brick commercial block built 1882-84. Ticonderoga Multiple Resource Area.   11.15.1988

Hancock House
Montcalm and Wicker streets. Large Georgian Revival granite building built 1925-26 as first headquarters of New York State Historical Association; designed by M. H. Westhoff as replica of Hancock House in Boston. Now headquarters of Ticonderoga Historical Society. Ticonderoga Multiple Resource Area.   11.15.1988

Lake George Avenue Historic District
301-331 Lake George Avenue. Group of 12 Arts and Crafts frame bungalows built 1919-21 by builder William A. Gale for Ticonderoga Pulp & Paper Co. as company housing. Ticonderoga Multiple Resource Area.   06.16.1989

Liberty Monument
US9 at Montcalm Street. Large bronze and granite monument depicting "Liberty" and historical military figures from Ticonderoga's past; sculpted by Charles Keck; dedicated 1924. Ticonderoga Multiple Resource Area.   11.16.1989

Silas B. Moore Gristmill
218 Montcalm Street. A 2-story frame mill built 1879-80 on La Chute River. Ticonderoga Multiple Resource Area.   11.15.1988

New York State Armory
315 Champlain Avenue. A 2-story Jacobean/ Tudor Revival brick building designed by William E. Haugaard; built 1934-35. Ticonderoga Multiple Resource Area.   11.15.1988

The PAD Factory
109 Lake George Avenue. A 3-story brick factory building built 1893 by S. B. Remington for manufacture of blank books. Ticonderoga Multiple Resource Area.   11.15.1988

St. Mary's Church and Rectory
10-12 Father Jogues Place. Gothic Revival sandstone church built 1888-92; rectory built 1868 and remodeled in Colonial Revival style. Ticonderoga Multiple Resource Area.   11.15.1988; REMOVED FROM LISTING 05.25.1989

Ticonderoga High School
Calkins Place. Large 3-story Georgian Revival brick school designed by Tooker & Marsh; built 1928-30. Ticonderoga Multiple Resource Area.   11.15.1988

Ticonderoga National Bank
101 Montcalm Street. Granite building in eclectic Art Deco/Moderne style; designed by A. S. Miller; built 1927-29. Ticonderoga Multiple Resource Area.   11.15.1988

Ticonderoga Pulp and Paper Company Office
Montcalm Street. Modest 2-story Queen Anne brick building built 1888. Museum. Ticonderoga Multiple Resource Area.   11.15.1988

United States Post Office–Ticonderoga
123 Champlain Avenue. Colonial Revival brick building built 1936-37. Interior mural (1940) by Frederick Massa. United States Post Offices

in New York State, 1858-1943, Thematic Resources. 05.11.1989

Westport

First Congregational and Presbyterian Society Church of Westport
(United Christ Church of Wadhams)
Main Street (County 10), Wadhams. Small Federal frame church built 1836; moved 1866; late 19th-century alterations. Includes adjacent parish hall. 12.19.1988

Willsboro

Abraham Aiken House
NY22. A 4-acre property with large Federal brick farmhouse built 1807, late 18th-century barn, and mid-19th-century tenant house. 06.08.1989

Edgewater Farm
470 Point Road, Willsboro Point. A 20-acre farmstead with vernacular frame farmhouse built c.1796 by David Rowley, Sr.; 1820 addition and large Greek Revival addition c.1830. Property includes two 19th-century barns, creamery, and family cemetery. 02.17.1988

Willsboro Congregational Church
NY22. Small Gothic Revival stone church built 1834. 05.31.1984

Adirondack State Forest Preserve
(see Clinton County)

Brighton

Camp Topridge
Great Camp complex on 105-acre property on Upper St. Regis Lake. Includes 30 Rustic-style buildings, associated structures, and 2 ponds. Developed 1923-36 for General Foods magnate Marjorie Merriweather Post to designs of Theodore Blake of Carrère & Hastings. Great Camps of the Adirondacks Thematic Resources. 11.07.1986

Camp Wild Air
Great Camp complex on 19-acre property on Upper St. Regis Lake. Includes 10 Rustic-style buildings built c.1890-29 for family of publisher Whitelaw Reid. Rebuilding and enlargement of camp 1917-20 attributed to McKim, Mead & White; 1960s additions by Edward Larrabee Barnes. Great Camps of the Adirondacks Thematic Resources. 11.07.1986

Paul Smith's Hotel Store
Paul Smith's College campus, Paul Smiths. Colonial Revival frame commercial building built 1893 as part of resort hotel complex. 12.03.1980; DEMOLISHED 1982

Duane

Duane Methodist Episcopal Church
NY99. Modest Victorian vernacular frame church built 1883-85. 08.09.1991

Malone

First Congregational Church
2 Clay Street. Romanesque Revival limestone church with castellated tower and granite and terra-cotta ornamentation; designed by Tristram Griffin; built 1883. 06.06.1991

Horton Gristmill
Mill Street. A 2½-story stone gristmill built 1809 on east bank of Salmon River. 04.21.1975

Anselm Lincoln House
49 Duane Street. Late Federal vernacular stone residence built 1830 by early settler of village. 04.21.1975

Malone Freight Depot
99 Railroad Street. Large 1-story eclectic sandstone depot built c.1852 for Northern Railroad. 12.12.1976

Paddock Building
34 West Main Street. Large 3-story sandstone commercial building built 1848; oldest surviving stone commercial building in Franklin County. 11.07.1976

United States Post Office–Malone
East Main and Washington streets. Classical Revival brick and limestone post office built 1934. United States Post Offices in New York State, 1858-1943, Thematic Resources. 05.11.1989

Santa Clara

Eagle Island Camp
Great Camp complex on 32-acre island in Upper Saranac Lake. Includes 14 Rustic-style buildings and associated structures designed 1902 by William L. Coulter for statesman Levi P. Morton. Great Camps of the Adirondacks Thematic Resources. 04.03.1987

Moss Ledge
Great Camp complex on 31-acre property on Upper Saranac Lake. Includes 7 Rustic-style buildings and associated structures designed c.1898 by William L. Coulter for Isabel A. Ballantine. Great Camps of the Adirondacks Thematic Resources. 11.07.1986

Prospect Point Camp
Great Camp complex on 38-acre property on Upper Saranac Lake. Includes 27 Rustic-style buildings and associated structures mostly

designed 1902-05 by William L. Coulter for financier Adolph Lewisohn. Great Camps of the Adirondacks Thematic Resources. 11.07.1986

Saranac Lake

Berkeley Square Historic District
30-84 Main Street and 2-29 Broadway. Historic core of commercial area of village, with 22 mostly 3-story brick or stone buildings; some with cure porches for tubercular patients. Includes Georgian Revival Harrietstown Town Hall (1928, Scopes & Feustman) and buildings designed by William L. Coulter and William Distin, Jr. Saranac Lake Multiple Resource Area. 02.11.1988

Paul Smith's Electric Light and Power and Railroad Company Complex
2 Main Street. A 2-acre complex with large Neoclassical terra-cotta-clad office building (1927), brick powerhouse (1909), concrete bridge (c.1927), and Lake Flower Dam and Power Flume (1936-38). Saranac Lake Multiple Resource Area. 11.02.1987

Tupper Lake

Beth Joseph Synagogue
Corner of Lake and Mill streets. Modest frame synagogue built 1906 and adjacent rabbi's residence. Oldest synagogue in Adirondacks. 09.01.1988

Adirondack State Forest Preserve
(see Clinton County)

Dolgeville

Dolge Company Factory Complex
South Main Street (also in Herkimer County). A 17-acre complex on East Canada Creek developed in late 19th century by Alfred Dolge for manufacture of felt for piano sounding boards. Company noted for profit-sharing and community planning. Became David Green and Co. after 1894. Includes large limestone factory (1886), former horse barn, iron Pratt truss bridge (1887), and Dolge mansion (1895). 09.17.1974

Ephratah

Garoga Site
Address restricted. Prehistoric archeological site of late 16th-century Mohawk Iroquois village. 07.22.1980

Klock Site
Address restricted. Large prehistoric archeological site of late 16th-century Mohawk Iroquois village. 07.22.1980

Smith Pagerie Site
Address restricted. Large prehistoric archeological site of late 16th-century Mohawk Iroquois village. 04.22.1980

Gloversville

Downtown Gloversville Historic District
Roughly bounded by Spring, Prospect, East Fulton, South and North Main, and Elm streets. The 25-acre core of central business district of leather-processing and glove-making community, with approximately 78 mostly late 19th-century brick commercial buildings. Notable buildings include Gloversville Free Library (individually listed), Italianate Heacock Block (c.1869), Second Empire Kasson Opera House–Schine Building (1880), Art Deco Jewish Community Center (1929), Queen Anne Old City Hall (1885, Marcus F. Cummings), Richardsonian Romanesque First Baptist Church (1890, Henry F. Kilburn), Renaissance Revival Kingsborough Hotel (1902, Frederick L. Comstock), Renaissance Revival Gloversville High School (1906, Wilson Potter), Renaissance Revival Eccentric Club (1908, Frederick L. Comstock), Tudor Revival Masonic Temple (1919, R. Sluyter), and Classical Revival Glove Theater (1914). 09.12.1985

Gloversville Free Library
58 East Fulton Street. Beaux-Arts brick and stone Carnegie library designed 1902 by Albert Randolph Ross; built 1904. 05.24.1976

Kingsboro Historic District
Area surrounding Kingsboro Avenue Park. Early 19th-century residential neighborhood surrounding triangular park. Includes Greek Revival Kingsborough Church (1838), former school (1900, now Fulton County Historical Museum), 17 residences, and cemetery. 02.24.1975

Johnstown

Fulton County Courthouse
North William Street. A 1 1/2-story Georgian brick courthouse with octagonal cupola; built 1772-73; attributed to Samuel Fuller. Interior altered 1895 and 1931. 07.24.1972

Fulton County Jail (Tryon County Courthouse)
Perry and Montgomery streets. A 2-story vernacular stone jail built 1772 by Zephaniah Batcheller under direction of Sir William Johnson. Rebuilt after 1849 fire; large Georgian Revival addition in 1896 designed by Frederick Cummings. 10.19.1981

Johnson Hall (State Historic Site)
Hall Street. Large Georgian frame residence built 1763 for Sir William Johnson, Superintendent of Indian Affairs of the Northern Colonies. Includes 2 adjacent stone blockhouses (1 original, 1 rebuilt). NHL 10.09.1960

United States Post Office–Johnstown
14 North William Street. Neoclassical stone post office designed by James Knox Taylor; built 1912-14. United States Post Offices in New York State, 1858-1943, Thematic Resources. 05.11.1989

Camp Topridge, Upper St. Regis Lake, Brighton.

Alexander

Alexander Classical School
Buffalo Street. A 3-story late Federal cobblestone building with cupola; built 1837. Now Alexander Town Hall. 10.25.1973

Batavia

Batavia Club
Main and Bank streets. Federal brick building built 1831 as Bank of Genesee by Hezekiah Eldredge. Batavia Club since 1886.
06.19.1973

Genesee County Courthouse
Main and Ellicott streets. A 2-story Greek Revival limestone building with cupola; built 1841-43. 06.18.1973

Opposite: Pieter Bronck House, Town of Coxsackie.

Detail of Gifford-Walker Farm, Town of Bergen.

Genesee County Courthouse Historic District
Bounded by Porter and Jefferson avenues, and Main, Court, and Ellicott streets. Group of 5 civic buildings, including Neoclassical United States Post Office (1919), Italianate City Hall (built 1853 as residence, altered 1917 for use as city hall), Genesee County Courthouse (individually listed), Classical Revival County Building (1926-27, Bohacket & Brew), and Victorian Gothic Sheriff's Office and Jail (1902-03, William J. Beardsley). Also includes Soldier's Monument (1919). 12.10.1982

Holland Land Office
West Main Street. Federal limestone building built 1812-13 as office of Joseph Ellicott, agent for Holland Land Company. Museum.
NHL 10.09.1960

Richmond Memorial Library
19 Ross Street. Small Richardsonian Romanesque stone library designed by James G. Cutler; built 1889 as memorial to Dean Richmond, Jr. 07.24.1974

Bergen (Town)

Gifford-Walker Farm
7083 North Bergen Road, North Bergen (also in Clarendon, Orleans County). A 69-acre farmstead with elaborately decorated Gothic Revival frame residence built 1870 by Aaron Gifford. 01.10.1980

Bergen (Village)

Lake Street Historic District
10 and 12 South Lake Street and 11-27 North Lake Street. Group of 11 Renaissance Revival and early 20th-century brick commercial buildings built 1880-1921. 09.05.1985

LeRoy

Keeney House
13 West Main Street. Large Greek Revival frame residence built 1851 by Philo L. Pierson for local claim agent; renovated 1927 to designs of Bryant Fleming for Calvin N. Keeney, prominent businessman and horticulturist. Includes carriage house and grounds designed by Fleming. 09.11.1979

United States Post Office–LeRoy
2 Main Street. Colonial Revival limestone post office built 1936-38; design attributed to James B. Arnold. United States Post Offices in New York State, 1858-1943, Thematic Resources.
05.11.1989

Pembroke

Mount Pleasant
2032 Indian Falls Road, Corfu. A 31-acre farmstead with Italianate frame farmhouse built 1861-62 for Abram Mook. Includes several outbuildings. 08.09.1984

Stafford

Morganville Pottery Factory Site
Morganville Road off NY237, Morganville. Archeological site of 19th-century earthenware pottery factory and kilns. 02.15.1974

Stafford Village Four Corners Historic District
Junction of US5 and US237. Group of 6 buildings at main crossroads in rural hamlet, including eclectic Stafford Town Hall (c.1850; remodeled 1907-09), Federal Marvin-Radley-Diefendorf House (c.1809), Greek Revival Radley-Worthington House (c.1831), Gothic Revival St. Paul's Episcopal Church (1841), Greek Revival Stafford Seminary (1848), and eclectic Odd Fellows Hall (1890; enlarged 1915-17). 10.08.1976

Athens (Town)

Newkirk Homestead
Sandy Plains Road, northwest of Leeds. A 20-acre farmstead with frame main house and outbuildings. House built in 3 stages with 18th-century original section, Federal addition, and Greek Revival alterations.   07.22.1979

West Athens Hill Site
West of Athens. Prehistoric archeological site of Paleo-Indian quarry, workshop, and habitation.   03.20.1973

Athens (Village)

Athens Lower Village Historic District
Roughly bounded by Hudson River, NY385, Vernon and Market streets. Large portion of village on Hudson River, with approximately 270 19th- and early 20th-century residences, commercial buildings, and public buildings. Notable examples of Federal, Greek Revival, and Second Empire residences. Athens Village Multiple Resource Area.   11.28.1980

Brick Row Historic District
Off NY385. Group of 27 modest Greek Revival brick rowhouses built 1864 as housing for Saratoga & Hudson River Railroad. Athens Village Multiple Resource Area.   11.28.1980

Hudson-Athens Lighthouse
Hudson River, south of Middle Ground Flats. Second Empire brick building built 1874 on man-made pier. Hudson River Lighthouses Thematic Group.   05.29.1979

Stranahan-DelVecchio House
North Washington Street. Greek Revival brick residence built c.1852 for William P. A. Stranahan, real estate agent. Athens Village Multiple Resource Area.   11.28.1980

Albertus Van Loon House
North Washington Street. Dutch Colonial stone residence with gambrel roof; built 1724. Athens Village Multiple Resource Area.   11.28.1980

Zion Lutheran Church
North Washington Street. Greek Revival brick church built 1853. Athens Village Multiple Resource Area.   11.28.1980

Cairo

Susquehanna Turnpike (see village of Catskill)

Catskill (Town)

Salisbury Manor
NY145, northwest of Leeds. A 47-acre former farmstead with large vernacular fieldstone residence built 1730 for Abraham Salisbury. House enlarged 1760 and remodeled 1823.   06.19.1979

Susquehanna Turnpike (see village of Catskill)

Catskill (Village)

Thomas Cole House
218 Spring Street. Federal brick residence built 1815 as country seat for Thomas Thomson. Part-time residence and studio of Hudson River School artist Thomas Cole until his death in 1848. Museum.   NHL 06.23.1965

East Side Historic District
Roughly bounded by Catskill Creek, Hudson River, and River, Harrison, Day, and Gardner streets. Central business district and adjacent residential areas of village on Hudson River, with approximately 500 mostly 19th-century commercial, residential, and religious buildings. Includes Thomas Cole House (individually listed) and notable examples of Federal, Greek Revival, Italianate, and Second Empire buildings.   08.09.1982

Eleanor
Off Lower Main Street in Catskill Creek. A 36-foot-long gaff-rigged wood racing sloop designed by Clinton H. Crane and built c.1903 at B. F. Wood Shipyard, City Island, New York.   12.27.1982

Susquehanna Turnpike
Begins at Catskill and follows Mohican Trail (NY145) and County 20 and 22 northwest to Schoharie County line (also in towns of Catskill, Cairo, and Durham). A 25-mile-long route of early 19th-century turnpike between Catskill and West Durham. Includes 2 stone bridges and several original milestones.   01.02.1974

United States Post Office–Catskill
270 Main Street. Colonial Revival brick post office designed by E. P. Valkenburgh; built 1935-36. United States Post Offices in New York State, 1858-1943, Thematic Resources.   11.17.1988

Coxsackie (Town)

Bronck Farm 13-Sided Barn
Old Kings Road. A 70-foot-diameter barn built c.1832 for Leonard Bronck. Included in Pieter Bronck House NHL. Central Plan Dairy Barns of New York State Thematic Resources.   09.29.1984

Pieter Bronck House
US9W, two miles west of Coxsackie. Dutch Colonial fieldstone residence built 1663; rear wing added 1685; brick section added 1738. Museum.   NHL 12.24.1967

Flint Mine Hill Archeological District
Address restricted. Multicomponent prehistoric site with human activity since early postglacial times. Includes flint quarry sites, workshop sites, and campsites.   11.29.1978

Forestville Commonwealth
Off NY81, northwest of Earlton. The 200-acre archeological site of Forestville Commonwealth, a short-lived utopian community founded 1826 following the principles of Robert Owen.   11.20.1974

Coxsackie (Village)

Reed Street Historic District
Reed, Ely, Mansion, and River streets. Small central business district of village on Hudson River, with 32 mostly 3-story Italianate brick commercial buildings. Also includes 3 Federal residences.   05.06.1980

Durham

Susquehanna Turnpike (see village of Catskill)

Greenville

Greenville Presbyterian Church Complex
North Street, NY 32. Complex of 3 civic buildings, including Greek Revival frame church (1860), vernacular chapel (1885), Greenville Free Academy (1906), and adjacent village green.   03.28.1985

Prevost Manor House (Hush-Hush Farm)
Off NY 81, west of Greenville. Large vernacular frame residence built 1793-94 on 200-acre parcel. Once part of 7,000-acre tract granted to Major Augustine Prevost.   11.15.1972

Lexington

Lexington House
NY 42. Large 3-story Italianate frame building built c.1883 as resort hotel in Catskill Mountains. Includes several support buildings.
09.04.1986

New Baltimore

Peter Houghtaling Farm and Lime Kiln
Lime Kiln Road, West Coxsackie. A 154-acre farmstead with vernacular stone farmhouse built 1794, several domestic dependencies, 19th-century barn complex, family cemetery, and mid-19th-century lime kiln.
03.20.1986

Van Bergen House
US 9W at Schiller Park Road. Large 2-story Federal stone residence built c.1786 for Peter A. and Hester Van Bergen; doubled in size c. 1820. Adjacent stone smokehouse.
04.25.1991

Prattsville

Morss Homestead–Federal City Homestead
NY 23, Red Falls. Early 19th-century farm complex on 6-acre property. Includes Greek Revival frame residence built c.1830 for industrialist B. G. Morss and 4 outbuildings.
09.30.1983

Zadock Pratt House
Main Street. Federal frame residence built c.1828 for founder of Prattsville; mid-19th-century additions and alterations. Museum.
08.14.1986

Windham

Centre Presbyterian Church
Main and Church streets. Federal/Greek Revival frame church built 1834; interior remodeled 1886; later additions.
09.07.1979

Adirondack State Forest Preserve
(see Clinton County)

Indian Lake

Blue Mountain House Annex
NY 30, Blue Mountain Lake. Small log cottage built 1876 as part of large resort hotel complex overlooking Blue Mountain Lake. Now part of Adirondack Museum Complex.   12.07.1977

Church of the Transfiguration
NY 30, north of Blue Mountain Lake. Small log church on shore of Blue Mountain Lake; designed by Manly N. Cutter; built 1885.
07.26.1977

Long Lake

Camp Pine Knot
Great Camp complex on 10-acre property on Raquette Lake. Includes 20 Rustic-style buildings, mostly designed by owner William West Durant and built 1877-1900. Owned by Collis P. Huntington family 1895-1949. Great Camps of the Adirondacks Thematic Resources.   11.07.1986

Fort Herkimer Church, German Flatts.

Camp Uncas
Great Camp complex on 16-acre property on Mohegan Lake. Includes 18 Rustic-style buildings, mostly designed by William West Durant and built 1893-95. Owned by J. Pierpont Morgan family 1896-1917. Great Camps of the Adirondacks Thematic Resources.   04.03.1987

Echo Camp
Great Camp complex on 12-acre property on Raquette Lake. Includes 19 Rustic-style buildings built 1883-1925 for former Connecticut governor Phineas C. Lounsbury. Great Camps of the Adirondacks Thematic Resources.   11.07.1986

Sagamore
Off NY 28 at West end of Sagamore Lake. Great Camp complex on 18-acre property on Sagamore Lake. Includes 22 Rustic-style buildings mostly designed by owner William West Durant and built 1892-1901. Owned by Alfred G. Vanderbilt family 1901-54. Now operated as Sagamore Institute. Great Camps of the Adirondacks Thematic Resources.
01.11.1976

Whelan Camp
Mick Road. Large Shingle Style/Rustic camp complex on Raquette Lake; built 1915-18 for New York City cigar merchant George J. Whelan.   12.21.1989

Wells

Wells Baptist Church
Main Street. Small Greek Revival frame church built 1845.   09.01.1988

Adirondack State Forest Preserve
(see Clinton County)

Cold Brook

Cold Brook Feed Mill
NY 8. A 2 1/2-story frame mill built 1857; retains some original equipment.   10.09.1974

Danube

Herkimer House
(Herkimer Home State Historic Site)
Near NY 5 s. Georgian brick residence with gambrel roof; built c.1750 for Nicholas Herkimer, Revolutionary War general; remodeled 1820s; restored 1914-15 and 1960-67.   02.12.1971

Indian Castle Church
NY 5 s, Indian Castle. Small vernacular frame church built c.1769 as Indian mission church for Sir William Johnson, Superintendent of Indian Affairs; later alterations.   02.18.1971

Zoller-Frasier Round Barn
Fords Bush Road, Newville. An 80-foot-diameter frame barn with conical roof and round cupola; built c.1895. Central Plan Dairy Barns of New York State Thematic Resources.   09.29.1984

Dolgeville

Dolge Company Factory Complex
(see Dolgeville, Fulton County)

United States Post Office–Dolgeville
41 South Main Street. Colonial Revival brick post office built 1939-40. Interior mural (1941) by Michael Newell. United States Post Offices in New York State, 1858-1943, Thematic Resources.   11.17.1988

Frankfort

United States Post Office–Frankfort
East Main Street. Colonial Revival/Moderne brick post office built 1940-41. Interior mural (1942) by Albert Wein. United States Post Offices in New York State, 1858-1943, Thematic Resources.   05.11.1989

German Flatts

Fort Herkimer Church (Reformed Protestant Dutch Church of German Flatts)
NY 5 s, East Herkimer. Colonial limestone church built 1767 by Palatine German settlers; 2nd story added 1812.   07.24.1972

Herkimer

Herkimer County Courthouse
320 North Main Street. Large 3 1/2-story Second Empire brick courthouse designed by A. J. Lathrop; built 1873. Site of 1906 trial of Chester Gillette, the background of which formed the framework for Theodore Dreiser's *An American Tragedy*.   01.14.1972

Herkimer County Historical Society
(Dr. A. Walter Switer House)
400 North Main Street. Large Queen Anne brick residence built 1884.   04.13.1972

Herkimer County Jail
327 North Main Street. A 2 1/2-story Greek Revival limestone jail built 1835.   01.14.1972

The Reformed Church
405 North Main Street. Greek Revival brick church built 1835 on site of 1770 church. Interior redecorated 1912 by Tiffany Glass & Decoration Co.   03.16.1972

United States Post Office–Herkimer
135 Park Avenue. Colonial Revival brick post office with terra-cotta trim; designed by Ross Edgar Slayter; built 1933-34. United States Post Offices in New York State, 1858-1943, Thematic Resources.   05.11.1989

Ilion

Remington Stables
One Remington Avenue. Large Italianate brick former stables/carriage house built 1870 for Philo Remington, grandson of founder of Remington Arms Co.   10.29.1976

Thomas Richardson House
317 West Main Street. A 4 1/2-acre property with large Italianate brick residence built 1873 for local attorney. Includes original carriage house and landscape features.   09.07.1984

United States Post Office–Ilion
48 First Street. Colonial Revival brick post office built 1935-35. Interior sculpture (1937) by Edmund Amateis. United States Post Offices in New York State, 1858-1943, Thematic Resources.   05.11.1989

Little Falls

Herkimer County Trust Company Building
Corner of Ann and Albany streets. Greek Revival stone former bank with Doric portico; built 1833.   03.05.1970

United States Post Office–Little Falls
25 West Main Street. Beaux-Arts post office designed by James Knox Taylor; built 1907-09. United States Post Offices in New York State, 1858-1943, Thematic Resources.   05.11.1989

Salisbury

Salisbury Center Covered Bridge
Fairview Road over Spruce Creek, Salisbury Center. A 42-foot single-span Burr arch truss wooden covered bridge built 1875.   06.19.1972

Warren

Jordanville Public Library
Main Street, Jordanville. Small Neoclassical frame library with Tuscan portico; designed by Trowbridge & Livingston; built 1907-08.   05.24.1984

Adams

Talcott Falls Site
US 11 at Old Rome State Road (also in town of Watertown). A 125-acre property with vernacular stone inn built 1825 by Major Daniel Talcott, prehistoric archeological inhabitation site, and historic archeological mill sites.   06.05.1974

Alexandria

George C. Boldt Yacht House
Wellesley Island. Massive Shingle Style frame boathouse designed c.1899 by Hewitt & Hewitt as principal dependency to George C. Boldt Estate. Contains 4 large boat bays, office service wing with crenellated tower, and caretaker's residence.   04.26.1978

Densmore Methodist Church of the Thousand Islands
Route 100 at Densmore Bay, Wellesley Island. Small Shingle Style frame church built 1900.   05.19.1988

Ingleside
Cherry Island, St. Lawrence River. A 4-acre property with large Queen Anne/Shingle Style summer residence built c.1900 for New York City merchant Abraham Abraham. Property includes boathouse, pedestrian bridge, gazebo, and outbuildings.   04.16.1980

Longue Vue Island
St. Lawrence River. A half-acre landscaped artificial island with large Arts and Crafts stone residence and boathouse designed by Barney & Chapman; built 1904-05 as summer residence for New York City lumber dealer Hudson P. Rose.   11.04.1982

Alexandria Bay

Cornwall Brothers' Store
2 Howell Place. A 2-story Victorian commercial building built 1866 at edge of St. Lawrence River. Museum.   05.02.1975

Antwerp

Dr. Abner Benton House
Main Street, Oxbow. Federal brick residence
built 1819 for local doctor and community
leader. 08.23.1982

Brownville

William Archer House
112 Washington Street. Vernacular limestone
residence built c.1811. Stone Houses of
Brownville Thematic Resources. 11.19.1980

General Jacob Brown Mansion
Brown Boulevard. Imposing Federal limestone
residence built c.1811 for military hero of War
of 1812. Stone Houses of Brownville Thematic
Resources. 11.19.1980

Brownville Hotel
Brown Boulevard and West Main Street. A
3-story Federal limestone hotel built c.1820.
Stone Houses of Brownville Thematic
Resources. 11.19.1980

Vogt House
110 Main Street. Federal limestone residence
with stepped gable ends; built c.1826. Stone
Houses of Brownville Thematic Resources.
11.19.1980

Arthur Walrath House
114 Corner Pike. Vernacular limestone
residence built c.1811. Stone Houses of
Brownville Thematic Resources. 11.19.1980

Cape Vincent (Town)

Xavier Chevalier House
Gosier Road. A 53-acre farmstead with small
vernacular limestone farmhouse built 1852,
mid-19th-century barn, and limestone smoke
house. Cape Vincent Multiple Resource Area.
09.27.1985

Nicholas Cocaigne House
Favret Road. A 102-acre farmstead with
modest vernacular limestone farmhouse built
1839 for French émigré. Includes 4 outbuildings. Cape Vincent Multiple Resource Area.
09.27.1985

Remy Dezengremel House
Rosiere Road. A 228-acre farmstead with
vernacular limestone farmhouse built c.1850
and three 19th-century outbuildings. Cape
Vincent Multiple Resource Area. 09.27.1985

Joseph Docteur House
Rosiere Road. A 126-acre farmstead with
small vernacular limestone farmhouse built
1847, 19th-century barn, and 20th-century
sheds. Cape Vincent Multiple Resource Area.
09.27.1985

Reuter Dyer House
Rosiere Road. A 94-acre farmstead with modest
vernacular limestone farmhouse built c.1839

and 2 large 19th-century barns. Cape Vincent
Multiple Resource Area. 09.27.1985

Fort Haldimand Site
Address restricted. The 25-acre archeological
site of fort and defenses built 1778 by British on
Carleton Island as strategic stronghold against
Americans. 12.15.1978

Johnson House
Tibbetts Point Road. A 10-acre farmstead with
modest vernacular limestone farmhouse built
c.1840 and 4 outbuildings. Cape Vincent
Multiple Resource Area. 09.27.1985

Captain Louis Peugnet House
Tibbetts Point Road. Large vernacular
limestone residence built 1837-40 for French
émigré. Cape Vincent Multiple Resource Area.
09.27.1985

George Reynolds House
River Road. Modest vernacular limestone
farmhouse built 1837-43. Cape Vincent
Multiple Resource Area. 09.27.1985

Tibbetts Point Light
Tibbetts Point. A 60-foot stuccoed brick
lighthouse built 1854. Adjacent keeper's
dwelling, assistant keeper's dwelling, and steam
fog-signal building. United States Coast Guard
Lighthouses and Light Stations of the Great
Lakes Thematic Resources. 07.19.1984

Union Meeting House
Millens Bay Road. Vernacular frame church
built 1869. Cape Vincent Multiple Resource
Area. 09.27.1985

Claude Vautrin House
Mason Road. A 263-acre farmstead with
vernacular limestone farmhouse built 1855
and six 19th-century outbuildings. Cape
Vincent Multiple Resource Area. 09.27.1985

Warren Wilson House
Favret Road. A 185-acre farmstead with
modest vernacular limestone farmhouse built
c.1837 and associated outbuildings. Cape
Vincent Multiple Resource Area. 09.27.1985

Cape Vincent (Village)

Levi Anthony Building
Broadway. A 3-story Italianate brick commer-
cial building built 1884. Cape Vincent Multiple
Resource Area. 09.27.1985

Aubertine Building
Broadway. A 3-story Italianate frame commercial building built c.1880. Theater space on
2nd floor. Cape Vincent Multiple Resource
Area. 09.27.1985

John Borland House
Market Street. Federal frame residence built
1818-28. Vacant in 1991. Cape Vincent
Multiple Resource Area. 09.27.1985

Broadway Historic District
St. Lawrence River, west edge of village, on
Broadway and Tibbetts Point. A 22-acre district

with 3 estate properties built 1815-40 by
prominent French émigrés. Includes Vincent
LeRay House (individually listed), Greek
Revival Maple Grove (1838; built for
Theophilus Peugnet), Greek Revival Beech-
wood (1840; built for Henry and Annette
Crevolin), and several dependencies. Cape
Vincent Multiple Resource Area. 09.27.1985

James Buckley House
Joseph Street. Gothic Revival frame cottage
built c.1845. Cape Vincent Multiple Resource
Area. 09.27.1985

E. K. Burnham House
565 Broadway. Italianate brick residence with
cupola; built 1870 for local merchant. Property
includes boathouses and garage. Cape Vincent
Multiple Resource Area. 09.27.1985

Jean Philippe Galband du Fort House
James Street. Modest vernacular frame
residence; original section built 1818-21
for French émigré. Cape Vincent Multiple
Resource Area. 09.27.1985

Duvillard Mill
Broadway. Large 4 1/2-story limestone
industrial building built in 1856 as steam-
powered gristmill; late 19th-century Stick Style
exterior trim. Became fishery station 1895.
Cape Vincent Multiple Resource Area.
09.27.1985

Glen Building
Broadway. Small Italianate frame commercial
residential building built c.1887. Cape Vincent
Multiple Resource Area. 09.27.1985

Vincent LeRay House
Broadway. Imposing Federal limestone
residence built c.1815 for Vincent LeRay.
Includes landscaped grounds. 11.15.1973

Lewis House
Market Street. Modest Victorian frame
residence with 3-story tower; built c.1875.
Cape Vincent Multiple Resource Area.
09.27.1985

Roxy Hotel
310 Broadway. Large 3-story vernacular brick
hotel built 1894. Cape Vincent Multiple
Resource Area. 09.27.1985

Cornelius Sacket House
571 Broadway. Large Colonial Revival frame
residence with gambrel roof; built c.1900.
Formal sunken garden in front yard and
boathouse at rear on St. Lawrence River. Cape
Vincent Multiple Resource Area. 09.27.1985

General Sacket House
4407 James Street. A 3-acre property with large
Second Empire frame residence built 1872-75,
landscaped grounds, and carriage house. Cape
Vincent Multiple Resource Area. 09.27.1985

St. John's Episcopal Church
Market Street. Late Federal frame church
built 1841; late 19th-century modifications.
Adjacent cemetery. Cape Vincent Multiple
Resource Area. 09.27.1985

St. Vincent of Paul Catholic Church
Kanady Street. Gothic Revival limestone church built 1858 for local French immigrant community. Cape Vincent Multiple Resource Area. 09.27.1985

Otis Starkey House
Point Street. Federal frame residence with arcaded facade; built 1820 for local merchant. Cape Vincent Multiple Resource Area. 09.27.1985

Carthage

State Street Historic District
249-401 and 246-274 State Street, and 106-108 Mechanic Street. A 3-block section of commercial center of village, with 29 buildings, mostly attached 3- and 4-story brick rows built late 19th century. Notable buildings include Victorian First National Bank (1894). 09.22.1983

United States Post Office–Carthage
521 State Street. Colonial Revival brick post office built 1934-35. United States Post Offices in New York State, 1858-1943, Thematic Resources. 11.17.1988

Chaumont

Cedar Grove Cemetery
End of South Washington Street. Small rural cemetery with terraced lots overlooking Lake Ontario; established 1873. Lyme Multiple Resource Area. 09.06.1990

Chaumont Grange Hall and Dairymen's League Building
Main Street. A 2-story vernacular Victorian frame building built 1898 as grange and meeting hall. Lyme Multiple Resource Area. 09.06.1990

Chaumont Historic District
Main and Washington streets. Residential and commercial section of village with 31 properties, mostly Greek Revival, Gothic Revival, Italianate, Eastlake, and Queen Anne residences. Notable buildings include stamped-metal-clad Masonic Hall (c.1898), Gothic Revival Backus-Copley House (1860), and Victorian Gothic stone Copley Office Building (1872). Lyme Multiple Resource Area. 09.06.1990

Chaumont House
Main Street. Large 2 1/2-story Federal limestone residence begun 1806 and completed 1820 for landowner and developer James LeRay de Chaumont; later used as tavern and summer home. Lyme Multiple Resource Area. 09.06.1990

Chaumont Railroad Station
Main Street. A 1-story eclectic frame passenger station built c.1900 by New York Central Railroad. Destroyed by fire 1990. Lyme Multiple Resource Area. 09.06.1990

Evans-Gaige-Dillenback House
Evans Road (County 12E). A 2 1/2-story Federal limestone residence built c.1820 for Musgrove Evans, agent for land developer James LeRay de Chaumont. Lyme Multiple Resource Area. 09.06.1990

George Brothers Building
Mill Street. A 2-story Victorian commercial building clad with decorative stamped metal; built 1899. Lyme Multiple Resource Area. 09.06.1990

George House
Washington Street. Queen Anne stone and frame residence built 1895-1902. Adjacent carriage house. Lyme Multiple Resource Area. 09.06.1990

Clayton

Clayton Historic District
203-215 and 200-326 James Street, and 500-544 and 507-537 Riverside Drive. A 2-block section of commercial area of village, with 31 buildings, mostly commercial late 19th-century and early 20th-century masonry structures. Notable buildings include Italianate brick Barker Building (1854) and Captain Simon Johnston House (individually listed). 09.12.1985

Captain Simon Johnston House
507 Riverside Drive. Large Italianate frame villa built 1880-82 for local shipbuilder and ship captain. 06.17.1982

Ellisburg

Pierrepont Manor Complex
North of Mannsville on Ellisburg Street. A 9-acre complex of 5 buildings built for William Constable Pierrepont, landowner and developer. Includes Federal frame manor house and carriage barn (1826), Federal frame land office (1822), Zion Episcopal Church (1836), and parish hall (1856). 09.15.1977

Evans Mills

LeRay Hotel
Main and Noble streets. Federal brick tavern/hotel built 1827 by Captain John Hoover. 10.29.1982

Hounsfield

Bedford Creek Bridge
Campbell's Point Road, over Bedford Creek. Limestone semicircular arch bridge with 18-foot span; built c.1825. Hounsfield Multiple Resource Area. 10.18.1989

Conklin Farm
Evans Road. A 194-acre farmstead with Queen Anne frame double farmhouse, horse barn, and milk house built c.1905. Hounsfield Multiple Resource Area. 10.18.1989

District School No. 19
Sulphur Springs Road. A 1-room vernacular limestone schoolhouse built 1837. Hounsfield Multiple Resource Area. 10.18.1989

District School No. 20
NY 3, south of Purpura Corners. A 1-room vernacular limestone schoolhouse built c.1837. Hounsfield Multiple Resource Area. 10.18.1989

East Hounsfield Christian Church
NY 3, East Hounsfield. Greek Revival frame church built 1844. Hounsfield Multiple Resource Area. 10.18.1989

Galloo Island Light
Galloo Island. A 60-foot-high conical limestone lighthouse built 1867; attached keeper's house. United States Coast Guard Lighthouses and Light Stations of the Great Lakes Thematic Resources. 08.04.1983

Dr. Samuel Guthrie House
Military Road, west of Mill Creek. Federal brick residence built 1818 for American discoverer of chloroform and inventor of "percussion pills" for firearms; stone rear wing added 1822. Hounsfield Multiple Resource Area. 10.18.1989

Resseguie Farm
Parker Road, east of Resseguie Road. A 20-acre farmstead with Greek Revival brick farmhouse (c.1840) and 5 historic outbuildings, including cattle barn, granary, pig sty, chicken coop, and former carriage barn. Hounsfield Multiple Resource Area. 10.18.1989

Shore Farm
North of Old Military Road, east of Mill Creek. A 114-acre farmstead on Lake Ontario with stone farmhouse and 2 outbuildings built c.1822 for Joseph Luff; farmhouse substantially altered c.1895 in Colonial Revival style and farmstead converted to gentleman's farm for Nathaniel Wardwell. Hounsfield Multiple Resource Area. 10.18.1989

Stephen Simmons Farmhouse
Camps Mills Road, west of Salt Point Road. Federal limestone farmhouse built c.1818. Hounsfield Multiple Resource Area. 10.18.1989

Star Grange No. 9
Sulphur Springs Road opposite Jericho Road. A 2-story vernacular frame grange hall built 1931. Hounsfield Multiple Resource Area. 10.18.1989

Stephenson-Frink Farm
West of Salt Point Road, north of Mill Creek. A 200-acre farmstead with American 4-square stuccoed concrete block farmhouse built 1917-18, five 19th- and early 20th-century outbuildings, and site of original c.1833 farmhouse. Hounsfield Multiple Resource Area. 10.18.1989

Sulphur Springs Cemetery
Sulphur Springs Road, west of Waite Road.

A 2-acre settlement-era cemetery established c.1812; expanded c.1879 in Romantic landscape fashion. Hounsfield Multiple Resource Area.   10.18.1989

LeRay

LeRay Mansion
Fort Drum Military Reservation, northeast of Black River. Large 2-story Greek Revival stuccoed stone residence with Ionic portico and symmetrical flanking wings; originally built 1790s and rebuilt c.1825 for James LeRay de Chaumont. Property includes early 19th-century outbuildings and landscaped grounds. 07.11.1974

Old Stone Shop
Main Street, Three Mile Bay. A 1 1/2-story Greek Revival stone building built c.1838-39 as double blacksmith shop for Asa Wilcox and Aura Wilson. Lyme Multiple Resource Area. 09.06.1990

Point Salubrious Historic District
Point Salubrious Road. Group of 7 properties overlooking Lake Ontario, including early 19th-century farmhouse (converted 1904 to boardinghouse), late 19th-century farmhouse, and 5 bungalows built early 20th-century as summer cottages. Lyme Multiple Resource Area.   09.06.1990

Commandant's House, Sackets Harbor Battlefield, Sackets Harbor.

Lyme

District School No. 3
NY3 at County 57, Putnam Corners. Vernacular frame 1-room schoolhouse built c.1875. Lyme Multiple Resource Area.   09.06.1990

Getman Farmhouse
South Shore Road, Point Peninsula. A 29-acre farmstead with vernacular Greek Revival farmhouse built c.1860. Lyme Multiple Resource Area.   09.06.1990

Lance Farm
South Shore Road, Point Peninsula. A 189-acre farmstead with Queen Anne frame farmhouse built 1908 by local builder Gamble & Sons, 3 mid-19th-century outbuildings, and 3 early 20th-century outbuildings. Lyme Multiple Resource Area.   09.06.1990

The Row Historic District
Main Street, Three Mile Bay. Group of 3 modest vernacular Greek Revival frame residences and outbuildings built c.1845-50 by local ship carpenters and merchants. Lyme Multiple Resource Area.   09.06.1990

Taft House
Main Street, Three Mile Bay. Queen Anne frame residence and carriage house built 1908 by local builder Gamble & Sons from design published by Radford Architect and Co. of Chicago. Lyme Multiple Resource Area 09.06.1990

Taylor Boathouse
Main Street, Three Mile Bay. Large 2-story eclectic frame boathouse built c.1905 as part of estate on Lake Ontario. Lyme Multiple Resource Area.   09.06.1990

Three Mile Bay Historic District
Depot Street, Three Mile Bay. Group of
4 buildings, including Greek Revival frame
Three Mile Bay Baptist Church (1840) and
parsonage (1844, enlarged 1908), vernacular
frame Three Mile Bay Grange Hall (1874),
and Italianate frame Union Free School (1878).
Lyme Multiple Resource Area.   09.06.1990

United Methodist Church
South Shore Road, Point Peninsula. Victorian
Gothic frame church built 1882. Lyme Multiple
Resource Area.   09.06.1990

Menzo Wheeler House
Main and Depot streets, Three Mile Bay. Large
Gothic Revival frame residence built 1860 for
local merchant. Lyme Multiple Resource Area.
09.06.1990

Wilcox Farmhouse
Carrying Place Road. A 186-acre farmstead
on Lake Ontario with 2 1/2-story Greek Revival
stone farmhouse built C.1839 and adjacent
privy. Lyme Multiple Resource Area.
09.06.1990

Orleans

Irwin Brothers Store
NY 180, Stone Mills. Federal and Greek Revival
limestone store/tavern built in 3 stages 1823-50.
Adjacent carriage barn.   09.15.1983

Rock Island Light Station
Rock Island, north of Fishers Landing. Complex of 6 buildings on 4-acre island, including
lighthouse (1882), Shingle Style frame keeper's
house (1882), and outbuildings.
11.14.1978

Stone Mills Union Church
NY 180, Stone Mills. Late Federal limestone
church built 1837. Now operated as museum
by Northern New York Agricultural Society.
12.12.1976

Thousand Island Park Historic District
South tip of Wellesley Island. A 145-acre
property developed as religious campground.
Contains approximately 300 buildings, mostly
Gothic Revival, Queen Anne, Eastlake, and
eclectic frame cottages built 1875-1920.
11.14.1982

Sackets Harbor

Elisha Camp House
310 General Smith Drive. Large Federal brick
residence built 1808-15 for land agent; design
attributed to Barnabus Waterman. Noteworthy
interior finishes include original French scenic
wallpaper.   04.23.1973

Madison Barracks
Military Road. A 113-acre property on Lake
Ontario with approximately 40 buildings built
1816-1920s for major United States military
installation established to protect northern

boundary of the country. Notable buildings
include Stone Row (1816), limestone Hospital
(1816), and limestone Water Tower (1892).
Property abandoned after World War II and
redeveloped as housing in 1980s.   11.21.1974

Sackets Harbor Battlefield (State Historic Site)
Coastline and area from Sackets Harbor
west to include Horse Island (also in
Hounsfield). A 260-acre property on Lake
Ontario with archeological sites of 2 War of
1812 forts and naval station. Includes Greek
Revival Commandant's House (1847-48) and
Lieutenant's House (1849).   12.31.1974

Sackets Harbor Village Historic District
Main, Washington, Pike, Edmund, Hill,
Hamilton, Broad, and Ambrose streets. Central
core of village, with 156 buildings, including
19th-century residences, 2-block business
district, 2 churches, park, and 2 museums.
Notable buildings include Federal Augustus
Sacket House (1802-03), Elisha Camp House
(individually listed), Union Hotel (individually
listed), and numerous Federal and Greek
Revival frame and limestone residences and
commercial buildings.   09.15.1983

Union Hotel
Main and Ray streets. A 3 1/2-story Federal
limestone hotel built 1817-18. Now part of
Sackets Harbor Battlefield State Historic Site.
06.19.1972

Watertown (Town)

Talcott Falls Site (see Adams)

Watertown (City)

Roswell P. Flower Memorial Library
229 Washington Street. Large Neoclassical
marble library designed by Orchard, Lansing &
Joralemon as memorial to former governor of
New York State; built 1903. Lavish interior
with domed rotunda; designed by Lamb
Studios.   01.10.1980

Jefferson County Courthouse Complex
Arsenal and Sherman streets. Early Romanesque Revival brick courthouse with corner
tower; designed by Horatio Nelson White; built
1862. Adjacent Queen Anne brick County
Clerk's Office (1884, J. W. Griffing) and eclectic
stone Surrogate's Building (1905, Hose &
Kieff).   06.07.1974

Paddock Arcade
Washington Street. A 174-foot-long shopping
arcade built 1850-51 as part of 4-story Gothic
Revival commercial building; designed by Otis
L. Wheelock; altered in 20th century.
06.15.1976

Paddock Mansion
228 Washington Street. Large Eastlake brick
residence designed by John Hose; built 1876 for
prominent merchant-banker. Significant
original interior finishes. Headquarters of
Jefferson County Historical Society since 1922.
12.11.1979

Public Square Historic District
Roughly Court, Arsenal, Washington, Frank-
lin, and State streets. Central business district
of city with 64 buildings, public square, and
monuments. Buildings mostly 3- to 4-story
attached commercial buildings built 1850-
1930. Notable structures include cast-iron
fountain (1869) and Soldiers' and Sailors'
Monument (1890) in Public Square, Paddock
Arcade (individually listed), Richardsonian
Romanesque First Baptist Church (1891,
Charles H. Smith), Neoclassical United States
Post Office (1908-09), Roswell P. Flower
Monument (1902, Augustus Saint-Gaudens),
and Georgian Revival Black River Valley Club
(C.1906).   09.07.1984

Watertown Masonic Temple
240 Washington Street. Neoclassical terra-
cotta-clad building with Doric portico;
designed by Charles E. Dewey; built 1914-17.
01/23.1980

KINGS COUNTY

Brooklyn

Albemarle-Kenmore Terraces Historic District
Albemarle Terrace, Kenmore Terrace, and East
21st Street, Flatbush. Middle-class residential
courts with 32 rowhouses; designed by Slee
& Bryson; built 1916-19. Albemarle Terrace:
Colonial Revival dormered rowhouses.
Kenmore Terrace: brick rowhouses with
garages reflecting influence of Garden City
movement.   06.30.1983

Astral Apartments
184 Franklin Street, Greenpoint. Massive
6-story Romanesque Revival apartment house
designed by Lamb & Rich; built 1885-86 by
philanthropist Charles Pratt for working-class
families. Incorporated innovative safety and
comfort features.   10.29.1982

Atlantic Avenue Control House
Flatbush and Atlantic avenues. Brick- and
terra-cotta-clad control house designed by
Heins & LaFarge; built 1908 as ornamental
entrance to subway system. Interborough
Rapid Transit Control House Thematic
Resources.   05.06.1980

Atlantic Avenue Tunnel
Below Atlantic Avenue between Boerum
Place and Columbia Street. Half-mile-long
brick and stone elliptical, barrel-vaulted
railroad tunnel designed by architect Asa
Stebbins, engineer William Vibbert, and builder
William Beard; built 1844 by Long Island
Railroad to connect ferry and rail route
between New York Harbor and Boston. In
use until 1861; rediscovered 1980.
09.07.1989

Floyd Bennett Field Historic District
Flatbush Avenue, Jamaica Bay. A 328-acre
airport with original layout and several original
hangars and support buildings. First municipal
airport in New York City; built 1928-31.
Became noted as prime airport for experimental
fliers. Conveyed 1941 to United States Navy.
Now part of Gateway National Recreation
Area. 04.11.1980

**Boathouse on the Lullwater of the Lake
in Prospect Park**
Prospect Park. Neoclassical terra-cotta pavilion
designed by Helmle & Huberty; built 1904-05.
01.07.1972

Boerum Hill Historic District
Roughly bounded by Pacific, Wyckoff, Bergen,
Nevins, Bond and Hoyt streets. Residential
neighborhood with approximately 225
buildings, mostly 3-story Greek Revival and
Italianate brick rowhouses built mid-19th
century. 09.26.1983

Boys' High School
832 Marcy Avenue. Massive block-long
Romanesque Revival brick school with 10-
story corner tower; designed by James W.
Naughton; built 1891; addition designed by
C. B. J. Snyder; built 1911. 02.25.1982

Brooklyn Borough Hall
209 Joralemon Street. Massive Greek Revival
stone building with Ionic portico; designed by
Gamaliel King; built 1851 as city hall.
Significant interior features include 2-story
main entrance hall. Renovations in 1897 after
fire include Georgian Revival cupola and
Beaux-Arts courtroom. 01.10.1980

Brooklyn Bridge
Spans East River from Brooklyn to Manhattan
(also in New York County). Monumental
5,989-foot-long limestone, granite, and steel
bridge designed by John A. and Washington A.
Roebling; built 1869-83; for 20 years the
longest suspension bridge in the world. One of
the greatest engineering achievements of the
19th century. NHL 01.29.1964

Brooklyn Heights Historic District
Bounded by Atlantic Avenue, Court and Fulton
streets, and the East River. A 130-acre residential district with over 1,000 buildings,
mostly Federal, Greek Revival, Gothic Revival,
and Italianate brick rowhouses on fairly regular
street grid. Notable buildings include Packer
Collegiate Institute (1854, Minard Lafever),
Early Romanesque Revival Church of the
Pilgrims (1846, Richard Upjohn), High Vic-
torian Gothic St. Ann's Protestant Episcopal
Church (1869, Renwick & Sands), and indivi-
dually listed Church of St. Ann and the Holy
Trinity, Plymouth Church of the Pilgrims, and
Brooklyn Historical Society.
NHL 01.12.1965

Brooklyn Historical Society
(Long Island Historical Society)
128 Pierrepont Street. A 4-story Renaissance
Revival brick building wih terra-cotta ornamentation; designed by George B. Post; built
1878-81. First major building on the East
Coast to use locally made terra-cotta ornamentation. NHL 07.17.1991

Brooklyn Museum
Eastern Parkway and Washington Avenue.
Monumental Neoclassical limestone museum
designed by McKim, Mead & White; built
1895-1915; exterior statuary and decoration
by Daniel Chester French and other American
sculptors. 08.22.1977

Carroll Gardens Historic District
Carroll and President streets between Smith
and Hoyt streets. A 2-block residential area
with 160 buildings, mostly 2- and 3-story
Italianate brownstone rowhouses built
1860s-80s. 09.26.1983

Casemate Fort, Whiting Quadrangle
Off NY 27, Fort Hamilton. Rectangular stone
and brick fort designed 1819 by United States
Army and United States Navy to secure control
of New York Harbor; completed 1826.
08.07.1974

Church of St. Ann and the Holy Trinity
(Holy Trinity Protestant Episcopal Church)
157 Montague Street. Large Gothic Revival
brownstone church with elaborate exterior
and interior ornamentation; designed by
Minard Lafever; built 1844-47. Stained-glass
windows by John and William Jay Bolton,
first church glass designed in America.
NHL 12.23.1987

Clinton Hill Historic District
Roughly bounded by Willoughby and Grand
avenues, Fulton Street, and Vanderbilt Avenue.
A 32-block residential neighborhood with over
1,000 buildings built c.1840-1930, including
freestanding mansions, rowhouses, and
apartment buildings. Numerous Italianate,
Second Empire, Renaissance Revival, and
Romanesque Revival rowhouses, and Beaux-
Arts, Italian Renaissance style, and Colonial

Revival mansions designed by Montrose Morris, Mercein Thomas, William B. Tubby, Adam E. Fischer, Robert H. Robertson, Alfred J. Manning, Axel S. Hedman, Herts & Tallant, Slee & Bryson, and others. Several early 20th-century apartment buildings, including Romanesque Revival/Queen Anne Vendome (1887, Halstead P. Fowler) and 429 Clinton Avenue (1916, Slee & Bryson). Also includes 5 churches and numerous carriage house/stables. 06.19.1985

Clinton Hill South Historic District
Roughly Lefferts Place and Brevoort Place between Washington Avenue and Bedford Place. A 10-block residential neighborhood with approximately 240 buildings, mostly 3-story Italianate brick and brownstone row-houses built 1860s-80s. Architects include Amzi Hill, Robert Dixon, Parfitt Brothers, Mercein Thomas, George L. Morse, and Axel S. Hedman. 07.17.1986

Cobble Hill Historic District
Roughly bounded by Atlantic Avenue, Court, Degraw, and Hicks streets. A 22-block residential neighborhood with several hundred buildings, including numerous Greek Revival, Gothic Revival, Italianate, Second Empire, and Renaissance Revival brick and brownstone rowhouses, and several churches, apartment buildings, and schools. Notable buildings include Christ Church (1841-42, Richard Upjohn), Strong Place Baptist Church (1850-51, Minard Lafever), and Romanesque Revival Tower Buildings (1878-79, William Field & Son). 06.11.1976

Coney Island Fire Station Pumping Station
2301 Neptune Avenue. Moderne limestone water-pumping station designed by Irwin S. Chanin; built 1938. 12.08.1981

William B. Cronyn House
271 Ninth Street. Large Second Empire brick residence built 1856-57 for Wall Street merchant. 06.03.1981

Cyclone Roller Coaster
834 Surf Avenue, Coney Island. A 3,000-foot-long steel-framed roller coaster with wood track and railings; built 1927 for entrepreneurs Jack and Irving Rosenthal as part of one of America's premier amusement parks; altered 1939. 06.25.1991

Cypress Avenue West Historic District
(see Queens County)

Ditmas Park Historic District
Bounded by Marlborough Road, Dorchester, Ocean, and Newkirk avenues. A 10-block suburban neighborhood with 172 buildings, mostly freestanding Colonial Revival frame residences and several bungalows, built beginning 1902. Architects include Frank J. Helmle, Arlington D. Isham, John J. Petit, Benjamin Driesler, and Slee & Bryson. Includes Flatbush Congregational Church (1910, Allen & Collens). 09.30.1983

Eastern Parkway
From Grand Army Plaza to Ralph Avenue. A 3-mile-long parkway designed by Frederick Law Olmsted and Calvert Vaux as approach to Prospect Park; built 1870-74. Features 3 road-ways separated by 2 tree-lined pedestrian malls. 09.26.1983

83rd Precinct Police Station and Stable
179 Wilson Avenue, Bushwick. A 3-story Romanesque Revival polychromed brick police station and attached stable; designed by William B. Tubby; built 1894-95. 04.14.1982

Emmanuel Baptist Church
279 LaFayette Avenue. Large French Gothic style church designed by Francis H. Kimball; built 1886-87. Earlier chapel at rear of building designed by E. L. Roberts; built 1882-83. 12.16.1977

Erasmus Hall Academy
Between Flatbush, Bedford, Church, and Snyder avenues. Large 2 1/2-story Federal frame school built 1786. First secondary school chartered by Regents of New York State. 11.11.1975

Federal Building and Post Office
271 Cadman Plaza East. Massive Richard-sonian Romanesque granite building with corner tower; designed by Mifflen E. Bell; built 1885-91. Large addition completed 1933. 10.09.1974

Opposite: Brooklyn Bridge, looking toward Manhattan.

Brooklyn Museum.

Feuchtwanger Stable
159 Carlton Avenue. Romanesque Revival brick commercial stable with terra-cotta trim; designed by Marshall J. Morrill; built 1888. 03.20.1986

Flatbush Dutch Reformed Church Complex
890 Flatbush Avenue and 2101-2103 Kenmore Terrace, Flatbush. Federal stone church designed and built 1793-98 by Thomas Fardon. Adjacent Greek Revival/Italianate parsonage

(1853), Georgian Revival church house (1924, Meyer & Mathieu), and 18th-century cemetery. 09.08.1983

Buildings at 375-379 Flatbush Avenue and 185-187 Sterling Place
Prospect Heights. Group of 4 Italianate brownstone commercial/residential buildings with eclectic detailing; designed by William M. Cook; built 1885. 09.07.1984

Flatbush Town Hall
35 Snyder Avenue, Flatbush. High Victorian Gothic building with 3-story corner tower; designed by John Y. Cuyler; built 1874-75. 07.24.1972

Flatlands Dutch Reformed Church
Kings Highway and East 40th Street. Greek Revival frame church built 1848. Adjacent Classical Revival administration building (1904) and cemetery with burials dating from late 17th century on. 08.30.1979

Fort Greene Historic District
Roughly bounded by Ashland Place, Hanson Place, and Vanderbilt and Myrtle avenues. A 30-block residential neighborhood with several hundred buildings, mostly 3- and 4-story Italianate, Second Empire, and Neo-Grec rowhouses. Also includes apartment houses and commercial, religious, and institutional buildings. Notable properties include 33-acre Fort Greene Park (1868, Olmsted & Vaux), Prison Ship Martyrs' Monument in Fort Greene Park (1908, McKim, Mead & White), row of cast-iron commercial buildings on Fulton Street (1882, Charles A. Snedecker), Brooklyn Technical High School (1931-32), and Brooklyn Academy of Music (1907-08, Herts & Tallant). Architects include William B. Tubby, Lamb & Rich, Montrose Morris, Amzi Hill, Parfitt Brothers, Mundell & Teckritz, and Lord & Hewlett. 09.26.1983; BOUNDARY INCREASE 09.07.1984

Friends Meetinghouse and School
110 Schermerhorn Street, downtown. Small vernacular brick meetinghouse built 1857; design attributed to Charles T. Bunting. Attached Classical Revival school designed by William B. Tubby; built 1902. 11.04.1982

Fulton Ferry Historic District
Roughly bounded by East River and Washington, Water, Front, and Doughty streets. Several-block area on East River with 19th-century commercial/residential buildings. Includes former Brooklyn City and Newtown Railroad Co. building (1860-61), Empire Stores (several structures built 1869-85 as coffee and sugar warehouses), massive 7-story Romanesque Revival former Eagle Warehouse (1893), and Marine Fire-boathouse (early 20th century). 06.28.1974

Gage and Tollner Restaurant
372 Fulton Street, downtown. A 3-story late Italianate brownstone building with 1890s storefront and intact restaurant interior from 1892. 06.03.1982

Grecian Shelter
Prospect Park near Parkside Avenue. A 1-story Neoclassical pavilion with elaborate marble and terra-cotta decorative trim; designed by McKim, Mead & White; built 1905 as croquet shelter. 01.20.1972

Greenpoint Historic District
Roughly bounded by Kent, Calyer, Noble, and Franklin streets, Clifford Place, and Manhattan Avenue. An 11-block residential neighborhood with mostly 3-story Italianate, Second Empire, and Queen Anne brick rowhouses built late 19th century. Also includes walk-up apartment houses, commercial buildings, churches, and banks. Notable buildings include Greenpoint Savings Bank (1908, Helmle & Huberty), Church of the Ascension (1866, Henry Dudley), St. Anthony of Padua Church (1874, Patrick C. Keely), and Union Baptist Church (1863). 09.26.1983

Hanson Place Seventh Day Adventist Church
88 Hanson Place, downtown. Early Romanesque/Greek Revival brick church designed by George Penchard; built 1857-60 as Hanson Place Baptist Church. 04.23.1980

Houses on Hunterfly Road Historic District
1698-1708 Bergen Street, Bedford-Stuyvesant. Group of 4 small vernacular frame residences built c.1840-83 in early free African-American settlement of Weeksville. Restored 1980s as a museum by Society for the Preservation of Weeksville and Bedford-Stuyvesant History. 12.05.1972

Kings County Savings Bank
135 Broadway, Williamsburg. A 4-story Second Empire stone bank designed by King & Wilcox; built 1868. 04.16.1980

Knickerbocker Field Club
114 East 18th Street, Flatbush. Colonial Revival/Shingle Style frame clubhouse designed by Parfitt Brothers; built 1892-93 as part of suburban residential development known as Tennis Court. Destroyed by fire. 10.29.1982

Lefferts-Laidlaw House
136 Clinton Street, Wallabout. Greek Revival frame temple-fronted residence built c.1840. 09.12.1985

Lincoln Club (Independent United Order of Mechanics of the Western Hemisphere)
65 Putnam Avenue. A 4-story Queen Anne brick clubhouse with terra-cotta and brownstone trim; designed by Rudolph L. Daus; built 1889. 01.27.1983

Litchfield Villa
Prospect Park West and Fifth Street. Large Italianate brick villa with 3- and 4-story towers; designed by Alexander Jackson Davis; built 1854-57 for railroad pioneer Edwin C. Litchfield. 09.14.1977

Manhattan Bridge
Spans East River, between Front and Canal streets (also in Manhattan, New York County). Monumental 6,375-foot steel suspension bridge with long flexible steel towers and stone

approaches. Bridge designed by Gustav Lindenthal and O. F. Nichols; built 1901-09. Beaux-Arts entrance portals designed by Carrère & Hastings. 08.30.1983

Monsignor McGolrick Park and Shelter Pavilion
Bounded by Nassau and Driggs avenues, Russell and Monitor streets, Greenpoint. A 9-acre urban park with large crescent-shaped Neoclassical pavilion designed 1910 by Helmle & Huberty. Also includes statue of "Victory" by C. A. Heber erected 1922 as Greenpoint War Memorial, and bronze figure by Antonio de Filippo erected 1938 to commemorate Civil War battle between *Monitor* and *Merrimac*. 05.06.1980

New England Congregational Church and Rectory (Light of the World Church)
177-179 South Ninth Street, Williamsburg. Italianate brownstone and brick church designed by Thomas Little; built 1852-53. Adjacent Italianate rectory built 1868. 09.15.1983

New Lots Reformed Church and Cemetery
630 New Lots Avenue, Bushwick. Federal frame church with Gothic-style windows; built 1823-24. Adjoining cemetery established 1841. 05.19.1983

New Utrecht Reformed Church Complex
18th Avenue and 83rd Street, New Utrecht. Fieldstone church with Gothic-style windows and ornamentation; built 1828. Also includes Romanesque Revival brick church house (1892, Lawrence B. Valk) and Queen Anne parsonage (1885). 04.09.1980

Ocean Parkway
From Church Avenue to Seabreeze Avenue. A 6-mile-long parkway with central drive flanked by 2 tree-lined malls, 2 service roads, and sidewalks; designed 1866 by Frederick Law Olmsted and Calvert Vaux; built 1874-76 to link Prospect Park with Coney Island. 09.08.1983

Old Brooklyn Fire Headquarters
365-367 Jay Street. A 5-story Romanesque Revival brick, granite, and sandstone building with 7-story corner tower and terra-cotta decoration; designed by Frank Freeman; built 1892. 01.20.1972

Old Gravesend Cemetery
Gravesend Neck Road and MacDonald Avenue. A 16-acre cemetery established c.1658 in community of Gravesend, first English-speaking settlement in Dutch colony of New Netherlands. 09.17.1980

Parachute Jump
Coney Island. A 250-foot-tall steel-framed aerial amusement ride built 1939 for New York World's Fair by inventor Commander James H. Strong and engineering firm Elwyn E. Steelye & Co.; dismantled and reassembled 1940-41 in Steeplechase Park on Coney Island by architect Michael Mario and engineer Edwin W. Kleinert. 09.02.1980

Park Slope Historic District

Roughly bounded by Prospect Park West, Berkeley Place, 15th Street, and Sixth, Seventh, and Flatbush avenues. A 33-block residential neighborhood with tree-lined streets, wide avenues, and mostly 3-story Italianate, Second Empire, Victorian Gothic, Renaissance Revival, Queen Anne, Romanesque Revival, and Classical Revival rowhouses and townhouses. Notable buildings include Venetian Gothic style Montauk Club (1891, Francis H. Kimball), several Romanesque Revival residences designed by C. P. H. Gilbert, and Victorian Gothic St. John's Episcopal Church (1870 and 1885, Edward Tuckerman Potter and John R. Thomas).   11.21.1980

Plymouth Church of the Pilgrims

Orange Street between Henry and Hicks streets. Brick church built 1849. Under ministry of Henry Ward Beecher, church was major center for abolitionist movement between its founding in 1847 and outbreak of Civil War. Stained-glass windows (1907-09) designed by Frederick Lamb. Adjacent church home and gymnasium built 1913.   NHL 07.04.1961

Prospect Heights Historic District

Roughly bounded by Pacific and Bergen streets, Flatbush and Vanderbilt avenues, and Park Place. A 6-block residential neighborhood with approximately 300 buildings, mostly 3-story Italianate, Neo-Grec, and Romanesque Revival brick and brownstone rowhouses built late 19th century.   09.15.1983

Prospect Park

Bounded by Parkside, Ocean, and Flatbush avenues, Prospect Park West, and Prospect Park Southwest. A 526-acre urban park designed by Frederick Law Olmsted and Calvert Vaux; begun 1865. Contains network of roads, bridle paths, walks, bridges, lakes, naturalistic and formal elements, other landscape features and buildings as part of original design, and later additions. Notable features include several stone-arch bridges, 75-acre Long Meadow, Lullwater and 57-acre lake, Vale of Cashmere and Pools (1895), native and exotic tree specimens (including 100-year-old Camperdown Elm), Concert-Grove (1870-94), and numerous buildings and structures by well-known architects, including Soldiers' and Sailors' Memorial Arch (1889-92, John H. Duncan); entrance columns, entrance column pedestals, and buildings designed by McKim, Mead & White; pavilion and buildings designed by Helmle, Huberty & Hudswell; Dutch Colonial Lefferts Homestead (1777-83, moved to park in 1918); Quaker Cemetery (established 1840s); and sculptures by Frederick Mac-Monnies and others. Includes individually listed Grecian Shelter, Boathouse on the Lullwater, and Litchfield Villa.   09.17.1980

Prospect Park South Historic District

Roughly bounded by BMT Railroad tracks, Beverly Road, and Coney Island and Church avenues. A 15-block residential neighborhood with 203 large single-family, freestanding residences in wide variety of styles, including Colonial Revival, Queen Anne, Tudor Revival, Elizabethan Revival, and eclectic design elements derived from Japanese, Swiss Chalet, and Arts and Crafts tastes. Neighborhood developed 1899-1920 by real estate developer Dean Alvord; overall house specifications and many houses designed by John J. Petit.   07.21.1983

Polhemus Place, Park Slope Historic District, Brooklyn.

Public Bath No. 7

227-231 Fourth Avenue. Italian Renaissance style bathhouse with terra-cotta ornamentation; designed by Raymond F. Almirall; built 1906-10.   09.12.1985

Public School 7

131-143 York Street. A 3-story Victorian Gothic/Renaissance Revival school designed by James W. Naughton; built 1882; 1907 Neoclassical annex.   11.03.1983

Public School 39

417 Sixth Avenue, Park Slope. A 3-story Italianate/Second Empire brick school designed by Samuel B. Leonard; built 1876-77.   04.17.1980

Public School 65K

158 Richmond Street, Cypress Hills. A 2-story Victorian school; original section built 1870; 1889 Romanesque Revival extensions and facade designed by James W. Naughton.   12.10.1981

Public School 71K

119 Heyward Street, Williamsburg. A 3-story Second Empire brick school designed by James W. Naughton; built 1888-89.   11.04.1982

Public School 108

200 Lindwood Street, Cypress Hills. Large 3 1/2-story Romanesque Revival brick and sandstone school designed by James W. Naughton; built 1895.   12.10.1982

Public School 111 and Public School 9 Annex

249 and 251 Sterling Place, Prospect Heights.

A 2-story Early Romanesque Revival brick school designed by Samuel B. Leonard; built 1867; 1887 Romanesque Revival wings designed by James W. Naughton. A 3-story brick and sandstone annex designed by James W. Naughton; built 1895-96 across street from main building. 12.14.1981

Quarters A (Commander's Quarters; Matthew C. Perry House)
United States Naval Facility. Federal frame residence with notable exterior and interior detail; built 1805-06. Onetime residence of diplomat Commodore Matthew C. Perry. Includes carriage house and grounds. NHL 05.30.1974

John Rankin House
440 Clinton Street, South Brooklyn. Large Greek Revival brick residence built 1839 for local merchant. 11.16.1978

John Roosevelt "Jackie" Robinson Residence
5224 Tilden Street, Flatbush. A 2-family residence built c.1915. Home of the first African-American major league baseball player 1947-50. NHL 05.11.1976

Rockwood Chocolate Factory Historic District
54-88 Washington Avenue, 13-53 Waverly Avenue, and 255-275 Park Avenue, Wallabout. A 17-building factory complex built 1891-1928 in Romanesque Revival and Second Renaissance Revival styles. Architects for buildings include J. G. Glover, Parfitt Brothers, Ernest Flagg, and Lockwood, Green & Co. Occupied 1904-57 by Rockwood Co., one of the country's largest chocolate and cocoa producers. 10.06.1983

Russian Orthodox Cathedral of the Transfiguration
228 North 12th Street. Monumental 4-story church in Russian Byzantine style with yellow brick exterior, 5 onion-shaped domes, and lavishly ornamented interior; designed by Louis Allmendinger; built 1916-21. 04.16.1980

St. Bartholomew's Protestant Episcopal Church and Rectory
1227 Pacific Street, Crown Heights. Queen Anne brick church with stone trim and battered tower; designed by George P. Chappell; built 1886-90. 04.23.1980

St. George's Protestant Episcopal Church
800 Marcy Avenue, Bedford-Stuyvesant. Victorian Gothic polychromed brick church and Sunday school building designed by Richard M. Upjohn; built 1886-89. 09.08.1983

St. Luke's Protestant Episcopal Church
520 Clinton Avenue, Clinton Hill. Large Romanesque Revival stone church complex with Italian Romanesque style features; designed by John Welch; built 1888-91. Includes sanctuary, chapel, Sunday school, cloister, and church hall. 09.16.1982

St. Mary's Episcopal Church
230 Classon Avenue, Clinton Hill. Gothic Revival brownstone church in style of early English rural parish church; designed by Richard T. Auchmuty of Renwick & Auchmuty; built 1858-59. Adjacent rectory. 07.21.1983

St. Paul's Protestant Episcopal Church
199 Carroll Street. High Victorian Gothic bluestone church with sandstone trim; designed by Richard M. Upjohn; built 1866-69; early 20th-century interior modifications designed by Ralph Adams Cram; attached parish hall. Adjacent Venetian-inspired rectory designed 1911 by Kirby & Petit. 12.21.1989

68th Police Precinct Station House and Stable
4302 Fourth Avenue, Sunset Park. A 3-story Romanesque Revival brick police station and attached stable; designed by Emile M. Gruwe; built 1886. 06.03.1982

South Bushwick Reformed Protestant Dutch Church Complex
855-857 Bushwick Avenue, Bushwick. Greek Revival frame church with temple front; designed by Messrs. Morgan; built 1852-53. Attached Sunday school building designed by J. J. Buck; built 1880-81. 11.04.1982

South Congregational Church
President and Court streets, Carroll Gardens. Early Romanesque Revival brick church complex with 1851 chapel, 1857 church, ladies' chapel and Sunday school (1889, F. Charles Merry), and Gothic Revival rectory (1893, Woodruff Leeming). 11.04.1982

Houses at 291-299 and 290-324 State Street
Group of eighteen 3-story Italianate rowhouses built 1847-c.1875. Second group of five 3-story Italianate brownstone rowhouses built 1871. 01.17.1980

Stoothoff-Baxter-Kouwenhaven House
1640 East 48th Street, Flatlands. Small Colonial vernacular frame residence with Flemish features; built c.1747; large main section added 1811; kitchen wing added 1880. 11.14.1982

Stuyvesant Heights Historic District
Roughly bounded by Macon, Tompkins, Decatur, Lewis, Chauncey, and Stuyvesant streets. A 13-block residential neighborhood with 430 buildings on tree-lined streets and broad avenues, with mostly 2- and 3-story Italianate, Neo-Grec, Romanesque Revival, Neoclassical, and Italian Renaissance style brick and brownstone rowhouses and free-standing mansions built late 19th and early 20th centuries. Also includes several churches. 12.04.1975

Sunset Park Historic District
Roughly bounded by Fourth Avenue, 38th Street, Seventh Avenue, and 64th Street. A 71-block residential neighborhood with approximately 3,200 buildings, mostly 2-story Renaissance Revival brick and sandstone rowhouses built in late 19th and early 20th centuries. Also includes numerous mixed-use commercial/residential buildings, and several religious and civic buildings. 09.15.1988

23rd Regiment Armory
1322 Bedford Avenue. Massive Romanesque Revival brick armory with sandstone and terra cotta trim, dominated by 7-story castellated corner tower; designed by Fowler & Hough with Isaac G. Perry; built 1891-95. 05.06.1980

United States Army Military Ocean Terminal
58th-65th Street and Second Avenue. A 100-acre property on upper New York Bay. Original complex of 8 large-scale reinforced-concrete warehouses and piers designed by Cass Gilbert built 1918. Additional 2 buildings built 1942-44 and 1 built before terminal construction. Terminal played important role in mass movement of military goods and troops between World Wars I and II. 09.23.1983

United States Post Office–Flatbush Station
2273 Church Avenue. Colonial Revival brick post office designed by Lorimer Rich; built 1936. United States Post Offices in New York State, 1858-1943, Thematic Resources. 11.17.1988

United States Post Office–Kensington Station
421 McDonald Avenue. Colonial Revival brick post office designed by Lorimer Rich; built 1935-36. United States Post Offices in New York State, 1858-1943, Thematic Resources. 11.17.1988

United States Post Office–Metropolitan Station
47 Debevoise Street. Colonial Revival brick post office built 1936-37. United States Post Offices in New York State, 1858-1943, Thematic Resources. 11.17.1988

United States Post Office–Parkville Station
6618 20th Avenue. Colonial Revival brick post office designed by Carroll H. Pratt; built 1936-37. United States Post Offices in New York State, 1858-1943, Thematic Resources. 11.17.1988

Weir Greenhouse
750-751 Fifth Avenue. Frame commercial greenhouse with octagonal dome; built 1880; rebuilt 1895 to design of G. Curtis Gillespie. 05.10.1984

Williamsburgh Savings Bank
175 Broadway. A 4-story Classical Revival limestone bank with monumental cast-iron dome and elaborate interior decoration; designed by George B. Post; built 1875. 04.09.1980

Willoughby-Suydem Historic District
Suydem Street and Willoughby, St. Nicholas, and Wyckoff avenues. A 1 1/2-block residential neighborhood composed of fifty 3-story brick tenements with Romanesque, Renaissance, and Classical Revival style ornamentation in terra-cotta and stone; built 1904-06. Architect of several rows include Robert T. Rasmussen and Louis Berger & Co. Ridgewood Multiple Resource Area (see also Queens County). 09.30.1983

Pieter Claesen Wyckoff House
5902 Canarsie Lane. Dutch Colonial frame residence; original section built c.1652; main house built 1740 with addition in 1820; restored 1982. Museum.   NHL 12.24.1967

Wyckoff-Bennett Homestead
1669 East 22nd Street. A 1 1/2-story Dutch Colonial frame residence built c.1766.
12.24.1974; NHL 12.08.1976

Palladian windows in gable ends; built 1789. Includes small stone barn.   11.26.1973

Lowville

Franklin B. Hough House
Collins Street. Italianate brick villa built 1860–61. Home of Franklin B. Hough, known for his work in forest preservation and author of bill that enacted Adirondack Forest Preserve in 1885.   NHL 05.23.1963

Constable Hall, Constableville.

Constableville

Constable Hall
Off NY 26. Federal limestone residence built 1810-19 by William Constable, Jr., son of land speculator who helped open northern New York for settlement. Museum. 03.07.1973

Constableville Village Historic District
Roughly bounded by Sugar River, Main, North Main, West Main, Church, High, West, and James streets. Intact historic core of small village, with 112 commercial, residential, and institutional buildings built 1828-1928. Includes rural cemetery and bridge. 09.15.1983

Leyden

Edmund Wilson House
Off NY 12 on Talcottville Road, south of Port Leyden. Large Federal limestone residence with

Lyons Falls

Gould Mansion Complex
Main Street. Large Queen Anne stone and shingled residence, carriage and horse barn, and small office building designed by Fuller & Pitcher; built 1902-04 for Gorden Gould, major paper manufacturer. Headquarters of Lewis County Historical Society.
04.19.1978

Martinsburg

Methodist Episcopal Church of West Martinsburg
West Martinsburg Road. Small late Federal frame church built 1840. 09.15.1983

West Turin

Jonathan C. Collins House and Cemetery
West Road, near Constableville. Large Federal frame residence built 1797-1802 for early Lewis County political family. Adjacent cemetery.
11.09.1988

Avon

Avon Inn
55 East Main Street. A 2-story Greek Revival frame building with monumental Ionic portico and elaborate decorative features; built 1840s as residence; enlarged and remodeled 1882 as sanitarium and again in 1912 as inn. 04.16.1991

Barber-Mulligan Farm
5403 Barber Road, northeast of Avon (also in Rush, Monroe County). A 640-acre farm complex with 35 buildings, including Greek Revival main house (1850), numerous farm buildings, Federal Greek Revival cobblestone house (c.1835), and 2 frame Victorian tenant houses. 05.19.1980

Dansville

Dansville Library
200 Main Street. Large Federal frame building built 1824 as residence; enlarged 1924 as library by Claude F. Bragdon. 09.14.1977

Pioneer Farm (McCurdy House)
NY 36. Federal brick residence built c.1822. 12.18.1970; DEMOLISHED late 1970s

Black and White Farm Barn, Groveland.

United States Post Office–Dansville
100 Main Street. Colonial Revival brick post office designed by Charles A. Carpenter; built 1932-33. United States Post Offices in New York State, 1858-1943, Thematic Resources. 11.17.1988

Geneseo (Town)

Wadsworth Fort Site
South Geneseo. Prehistoric archeological site of fortified Iroquois village, c.1400-1500 A.D. 06.11.1975

Geneseo (Village)

The Homestead
NY 39 and US 20A. A 103-acre property with large frame residence begun 1804; continuously occupied by Wadsworth family and enlarged throughout 19th and 20th centuries. Outbuildings include barns, icehouse, garage, and herdsman's and gardener's cottages. 08.30.1974

Geneseo Historic District
(Main Street Historic District and Expansion) Main Street and residential streets on east side. Central core of village, with approximately 300 commercial, religious, civic, and residential buildings in Federal, Greek Revival, Gothic Revival, Italianate, Second Empire, Queen Anne, Eastlake, and Colonial Revival styles built early 19th to early 20th centuries. Notable properties include The Homestead (individually listed), 184-acre Hartford House estate (c.1836; built for Wadsworth

family after English Regency villa), Federal brick Big Tree Inn (c.1833), Georgian Revival brick Livingston County Courthouse (1898, Claude F. Bragdon), and Temple Hill Cemetery. Architects also include William J. Beardsley, Frederic Butler, C. N. Otis, Robert Sherlock, and Hugh McBride. 07.09.1977; BOUNDARY INCREASE 03.21.1985; NHL 07.17.1991

Groveland

Black and White Farm Barn
7420 Dansville–Mount Morris Road, near Sonyea. One of New York State's largest 19th-century frame barns; built 1884 with protected inner yard and continuous roof monitors for ventilation of hay. 02.08.1988

Claud No.1 Archeological Site
Address restricted. Prehistoric archeological site believed to represent seasonal camp occupied by Archaic period groups as early as 2500 B.C. and later by Susquehanna tradition groups and the historic Iroquois. 08.19.1975

Lima (Town)

Clark Farm Complex
7646 East Main Street. A 130-acre farmstead with main residence built early 1830s and numerous farm-related support structures from late 19th and early 20th centuries. Lima Town Multiple Resource Area. 08.31.1989

Ganoung Cobblestone Farmhouse
2798 Poplar Hill Road. A 94-acre farmstead with Federal cobblestone residence built c.1830, 19th-century shed, carriage barn, and well. Lima Town Multiple Resource Area. 08.31.1989

Godfrey House and Barn Complex
1325 Rochester Road. A 5-acre farmstead with Italianate frame residence built c.1850 and outbuildings, including 2 barns, chicken shed, milk house, silo, and garage. Lima Town Multiple Resource Area. 08.31.1989

Leech-Lloyd Farmhouse
1589 York Street. Federal frame farmhouse built c.1800 by one of the first settlers in the area. Lima Town Multiple Resource Area. 07.13.1989

Leech-Lloyd Farmhouse: Barn Complex
1589 York Street. A 19th-century barn, pigpen, shed, and machine shed associated with Leech-Lloyd farmhouse. Lima Town Multiple Resource Area. 08.31.1989; DEMOLISHED

Leech-Parker Farmhouse
1537 York Street. Federal frame farmhouse built c.1800. Lima Town Multiple Resource Area. 08.31.1989

Markham Cobblestone Farmhouse and Barn Complex
Heath Markham Road. A 198-acre farmstead with Federal cobblestone farmhouse built 1830s. Outbuildings include barns, sheds, silos, and well with pump house. Lima Town Multiple Resource Area. 08.31.1989

Martin Farm Complex
1301 Bragg Street. Vernacular frame farmhouse remodeled and expanded in late 19th century into Italianate villa. Includes milk house, privy, machine shed, smokehouse, carriage house, office, pergola, and dairy barns. Lima Town Multiple Resource Area. 08.31.1989

Morgan Cobblestone Farmhouse
6870 West Main Road. Federal cobblestone farmhouse built 1832. Lima Town Multiple Resource Area. 08.31.1989

Ogilvie Moses Farmhouse
2150 Clay Street. Greek Revival vernacular frame residence built c.1830. Includes small outbuildings. Lima Town Multiple Resource Area. 08.31.1989

Zebulon Moses Farmhouse
2770 Clay Road. Early 19th-century vernacular frame farmhouse remodeled 1860s and 1870s with Italianate and Gothic Revival ornamentation. Includes 3 barns, carriage barn, and machine shed. Lima Town Multiple Resource Area. 08.31.1989

North Bloomfield School
7840 Martin Road, North Bloomfield. Small 2-story Federal brick school built c.1827 as meetinghouse for First Universalist Society of Lima; used as school and community building beginning 1842; closed 1951. 05.28.1981

Thomas Peck Farmhouse
7955 East Main Street. Vernacular limestone farmhouse built c.1812; enlarged late 19th century. Outbuildings include Gothic Revival guest house, brick icehouse, and brick privy. Lima Town Multiple Resource Area. 08.31.1989

School No. 6
6679 Jenks Road. Small 1-story Greek Revival cobblestone schoolhouse built 1843. Lima Town Multiple Resource Area. 08.31.1989

Lima (Village)

Alverson-Copeland House
1612 Rochester Street. Greek Revival/Italianate brick residence with Egyptian Revival porch columns; built c.1853. Lima Town Multiple Resource Area. 08.30.1989

Barnard Cobblestone House
7192 West Main Street. Federal/Greek Revival cobblestone house built c.1830; interior alterations 1880s. Lima Town Multiple Resource Area. 08.31.1989

Bristol House
1950 Lake Avenue. Italianate frame residence built early 1870s. Lima Town Multiple Resource Area. 08.31.1989

Cargill House
1839 Rochester Street. Greek Revival brick residence built 1852. Lima Town Multiple Resource Area. 08.31.1989

Dayton House
7180 West Main Street. Gothic Revival frame house built c.1844; remodeled mid-1850s. Lima Town Multiple Resource Area. 08.31.1989

William DePuy House
1825 Genesee Street. Greek Revival frame residence built c.1851. Lima Town Multiple Resource Area. 08.31.1989

Draper House
1764 Rochester Street. Italianate frame house built c.1842; remodeled 1860s. Lima Town Multiple Resource Area. 08.31.1989

Genesee Wesleyan Seminary and Genesee College Hall
College Street. Massive 4 1/2-story Greek Revival brick and stone seminary built 1842. Adjacent Greek Revival brick and stone 2-story hall built 1851. 07.19.1976

Harden House
7343 East Main Street. Queen Anne frame house built c.1885. Lima Town Multiple Resource Area. 08.31.1989

William Harmon House
1847 Genesee Street. Gothic Revival board-and-batten house built c.1851. Lima Town Multiple Resource Area. 08.31.1989

Hillcrest
7242 West Main Street. Federal brick residence built 1838-40. Includes barn/carriage house and gazebo. 05.06.1980

Lima Village Historic District
Rochester and East Main streets. Historic core of village, with 21 commercial, religious, civic, and residential properties, including groups of late 19th-century 2- and 3-story brick commercial buildings, Romanesque Revival Presbyterian Church, former library, and 7 large frame residences built mid- to late 19th century. 11.20.1987

Franklin J. Peck House
7347 East Main Street. Greek Revival frame house built c.1853. Lima Town Multiple Resource Area. 08.31.1989

St. Rose Roman Catholic Church Complex
Lake Avenue. Brick church in basilica form with Romanesque Revival, Italianate, and Gothic Revival details; Queen Anne and Romanesque Revival school; church and school designed by Andrew J. Warner; built 1870-75. Also includes convent, rectory, and garage. 08.25.1988

Spencer House
7372 East Main Street. Federal/Greek Revival frame house built 1830s; enlarged twice in mid-19th century. Includes carriage house. Lima Town Multiple Resource Area. 08.31.1989

Stanley House
7364 East Main Street. Greek Revival
frame house built c.1857. Lima Town
Multiple Resource Area. 08.31.1989

William L. Vary House
7378 East Main Street. Queen Anne frame
residence built c.1885. Lima Town Multiple
Resource Area. 08.31.1989

Asahel Warner House
7136 West Main Street. Large vernacular
frame residence built c.1810; enlarged late
19th century with 3rd-floor Masonic Hall.
Lima Town Multiple Resource Area.
08.31.1989

Matthew Warner House
7449 East Main Street. Vernacular brick
residence built c.1806; enlarged c.1860
and c.1920. Lima Town Multiple Resource
Area. 08.31.1989

Livonia

Livonia Baptist Church
9 High Street. Greek Revival vernacular frame
church built 1870. 03.25.1977

Mount Morris

General William A. Mills House
14 Main Street. Federal/Greek Revival brick
residence built 1838; design attributed to
Colonel Walker Hinman. 12.19.1978

St. John's Episcopal Church
State Street at Stanley Street. Gothic Revival
brick church designed by W. Hamlin; built
1857 by W. Hinman. Adjacent Gothic Revival
parsonage built 1867 and grave site.
07.19.1991

Portage

Edgerley
9303 Creek Road, south of Oakland. A 19-acre
property with Tidewater-inspired Greek
Revival vernacular brick residence built 1828.
Includes sheds, barn, and gardener's cottage.
07.16.1980

West Sparta

R. P. Kemp No. 1 Site
West of West Sparta. Prehistoric archeological
site of Owasco-Late Woodland village.
08.22.1977

York

Westerly
Chandler Road, near Piffard. Greek Revival/
Italianate brick residence built 1850. Includes
barns, playhouse, and tenant cottage.
12.19.1974

Brookfield

Wheeler House Complex
NY8, Leonardsville. Large Italianate frame
residence and attached bank, 2-story frame
commercial building, and massive frame
carriage house; built 1874 for businessman
John Wheeler. 09.22.1983

Canastota

Canal Town Museum
122 Canal Street. Modest 1-story frame commercial building built 1874 adjacent to Erie
Canal. Canastota Multiple Resource Area.
05.23.1986

Canastota Methodist Church
Main and New Boston streets. Massive
Richardsonian Romanesque marble church
designed by Merrick & Randall; built 1909.
Canastota Multiple Resource Area.
05.23.1986

Canastota Public Library
102 West Center Street. Neoclassical stone
and brick library endowed by Andrew Carnegie
and designed by Archimedes Russell; built
1902. Canastota Multiple Resource Area.
05.23.1986

House at 233 James Street
Greek Revival frame residence built 1846.
Canastota Multiple Resource Area.
05.23.1986

House at 205 North Main Street
Modest Second Empire frame residence built
c.1870. Canastota Multiple Resource Area.
05.23.1986

House at 313 North Main Street
Greek Revival frame residence built c.1840;
remodeled 1880s with Eastlake features.
Includes carriage house. Canastota Multiple
Resource Area. 05.23.1986

House at 326 North Peterboro Street
Large Queen Anne frame residence with
Colonial Revival features; built c.1890.
Includes carriage house. Canastota Multiple
Resource Area. 05.23.1986

House at 328 North Peterboro Street
Large Queen Anne/Eastlake frame residence
built c.1870. Includes carriage house. Canastota Multiple Resource Area. 05.23.1986

Peterboro Street Elementary School
220 North Peterboro Street. Collegiate
Gothic brick and concrete school designed
by Earl Hallenbeck; built 1927 as high
school. Canastota Multiple Resource Area.
05.23.1986

Judge Nathan S. Roberts House
West Seneca Avenue. Federal frame residence
built c.1820 for Judge Roberts, one of the
founders of Canastota and instrumental in
directing Erie Canal through village. Outbuildings include barn, carriage house, and
smokehouse. Canastota Multiple Resource
Area. 05.23.1986

House at 115 South Main Street
Modest Victorian frame cottage built mid-
19th century; remodeled 1880s with Queen
Anne and Eastlake details. Canastota Multiple
Resource Area. 05.23.1986

**South Peterboro Street Commercial
Historic District**
Roughly bounded by NY76, Diamond and
Center streets, Penn Central Railroad, Depot
Street, and Commerce Avenue. Core of central
business district of village, with 25 buildings
built c.1870-1930, mostly 2- and 3-story brick
commercial buildings with upper residential
floors. Canastota Multiple Resource Area.
05.23.1986

**South Peterboro Street Residential
Historic District**
Roughly bounded by James, Terrace, South
Peterboro, Rasbach, and Hickory streets.
Residential neighborhood with 32 properties
built c.1850-1930, including Greek Revival,
Italianate, Eastlake, Queen Anne, and Colonial
Revival residences and associated outbuildings
and 2 churches. Canastota Multiple Resource
Area. 05.23.1986

House at 107 Stroud Street
Modest Italianate frame residence with
Eastlake porch details; built c.1875. Canastota
Multiple Resource Area. 05.23.1986

United Church of Canastota
144 West Center Street. Large eclectic brick
and stone church with multigabled roof and
towers, and Arts and Crafts interior; designed
by Melvin H. Hubbard; built 1903. Canastota
Multiple Resource Area. 05.23.1986

United States Post Office–Canastota
118 South Peterboro Street. Colonial Revival
brick post office built 1940-41. Interior mural
(1942) by Alison M. Kingsbury. United States
Post Offices in New York State, 1858-1943,
Thematic Resources. 11.17.1988

Cazenovia (Town)

Abell Farmhouse and Barn
Ballina Road. A 95-acre farmstead with
Italianate frame residence and barn built
c.1870. Cazenovia Town Multiple Resource
Area. 11.02.1987

Annas Farmhouse
4812 Ridge Road. Late Federal/early Greek
Revival farmhouse built c.1832. Cazenovia
Town Multiple Resource Area. 02.18.1988

Beckwith Farmhouse
4652 Syracuse Road. A 27-acre farmstead
with Federal frame farmhouse built 1810.

Cazenovia Town Multiple Resource Area. 11.02.1987

Brick House
3318 Rippleton Road. Large Italianate/eclectic brick farmhouse built c.1870; notable interior. Cazenovia Town Multiple Resource Area. 02.18.1988

Cedar Cove
East Lake Road. Large Stick Style/Queen Anne frame residence, boathouse, carriage house, and gardener's cottage designed by George B. Post; built 1884-88 on Cazenovia Lake as summer estate of New York City merchant Joseph Dodridge Peet. Cazenovia Town Multiple Resource Area. 07.15.1991

Chappell Farmhouse
Ridge Road, south of Hoffman Road. Late Federal/early Greek Revival frame farmhouse with substantially intact interior; built 1835. Includes 19th-century frame barn. Cazenovia Town Multiple Resource Area. 11.02.1987

Cobblestone House
Syracuse Road, south of Woodfield Road. Greek Revival cobblestone farmhouse built c.1840. Includes 19th-century carriage house. Cazenovia Town Multiple Resource Area. 11.02.1987

Zephinia Comstock Farmhouse
2363 Nelson Street (US20). Federal vernacular frame farmhouse built c.1830. Includes 19th-century barn. Cazenovia Town Multiple Resource Area. 11.02.1987

Crandall Farm Complex
2450 Ballina Road. A 124-acre farmstead with Italianate frame residence built c.1870. Outbuildings include 2 frame barns, privy, carriage barn, and cobblestone well house. Cazenovia Town Multiple Resource Area. 11.02.1987

Evergreen Acres
Syracuse Road, north of US20. A 28-acre property with large Federal frame farmhouse built c.1814; enlarged c.1860 and early 20th century. Includes historic stone walls, barns, carriage house, and other farm-related structures. Cazenovia Town Multiple Resource Area. 11.02.1987

Hillcrest
Ridge Road. An 8-acre property on Cazenovia Lake with large Queen Anne frame residence and 3 outbuildings; built 1903-05 as summer estate of Robert Benson Davis; Colonial Revival modifications c.1920. Cazenovia Town Multiple Resource Area. 07.15.1991

The Maples
2420 Nelson Street (US20). A 24-acre property with Greek Revival frame farmhouse with Doric portico; built c.1835. Notable interior. Includes 2 barns. Cazenovia Town Multiple Resource Area. 11.02.1987

The Meadows Farm Complex
Rippleton Road. Farmstead with Picturesque frame farmhouse built c.1900, Federal farmhouse built c.1810, large dairy barn complex, and 5 dependencies built late 19th to early 20th centuries. Cazenovia Town Multiple Resource Area. 11.02.1987

Middle Farmhouse
4875 West Lake Road. Modest Federal frame farmhouse built c.1820. Cazenovia Town Multiple Resource Area. 11.02.1987

Niles Farmhouse
Rippleton Road, opposite Rippleton Cross Road. Federal frame farmhouse built c.1807. Cazenovia Town Multiple Resource Area. 11.02.1987

Notleymere
4641 East Lake Road. Large Queen Anne/Shingle Style frame residence and boathouse designed by Robert W. Gibson; built 1885-89 on Cazenovia Lake as summer house of Reverend Frank Norton, Bishop of Albany diocese. Cazenovia Town Multiple Resource Area. 07.15.1991

Old Trees
Rippleton Road. A 168-acre property with Rustic-style frame residence built 1917 as summer house of Frederick R. Hazard, founder of Solvay Process Co.; remodeled 1937 in Georgian Revival style by architects Bley & Lyman. Adjacent outbuildings. Cazenovia Town Multiple Resource Area. 07.15.1991

Ormonde
East Lake Road at Ormonde Road. Large Shingle Style/Colonial Revival frame residence and boathouse designed by Frank Furness; built 1885-88 on Cazenovia Lake as summer estate of Philadelphia banker George R. Preston. Cazenovia Town Multiple Resource Area. 07.15.1991

Parker Farmhouse
3981 East Road, south of Number Nine Road. A 44-acre farmstead with Federal frame farmhouse built c.1820; saltbox addition at rear and Gothic Revival front porch. Includes barns and outbuildings. Cazenovia Town Multiple Resource Area. 11.02.1987

Rolling Ridge Farm
3937 Number Nine Road. A 27-acre farmstead with Federal brick farmhouse built c.1837 and 3 late 19th-century dependencies. Cazenovia Town Multiple Resource Area. 11.02.1987

Shattuck House (Longshore House)
West Lake Road. A 15-acre property on Cazenovia Lake with Arts and Crafts/Colonial

Revival frame residence designed 1928 by Paul Hueber, Sr.; built as summer estate for Frank M. Shattuck, Syracuse restaurateur. Cazenovia Town Multiple Resource Area. 07.15.1991

Sweetland Farmhouse
Number Nine Road, north of Ballina Road. Small Federal frame farmhouse built c.1825. Cazenovia Town Multiple Resource Area. 11.02.1987

Tall Pines
Ridge Road, north of Hoffman Road. Federal frame farmhouse built 1835; additions in 1860 and 1920s. Adjacent guest house. Cazenovia Town Multiple Resource Area. 11.02.1987

Upenough
Rippleton Street. Dutch Colonial Revival frame residence built c.1910 as summer house of King family of Syracuse; design attributed to Melvin King. Adjacent outbuildings. Cazenovia Town Multiple Resource Area. 07.15.1991

Cottage Lawn, Oneida.

York Lodge (Bittersweet)
4448 East Lake Road. Eclectic frame residence with Jacobean Revival, Georgian Revival, and Shingle Style features; designed 1904 by George Bisham Page; built on Cazenovia Lake as summer house of Elizabeth Wharton McKean of Philadelphia. Includes several outbuildings. Cazenovia Town Multiple Resource Area. 07.15.1991

Cazenovia (Village)

Albany Street Historic District
Irregular pattern along Albany Street. Oldest portion of village, with approximately 80 commercial, civic, institutional, and residential buildings built 1795-1930s. Notable buildings include 5 adjoining limestone commercial buildings at 54-62 Albany Street (c.1830), 3-story brick commercial building at 57 Albany Street (c.1870), First Presbyterian Church (1805; enlarged 1860), Greek Revival

Lincklaen House Inn (c.1835), and Gothic Revival cottage at 7 Albany Street (1847). 10.10.1978 ILLUS. P. 79

Cazenovia Village Historic District
Roughly bounded by Union, Lincklaen, and Chenango streets, Rippleton Road, and Foreman Street. Village center with 360 commercial, institutional, and residential buildings dating from c.1795 to 1935, including notable examples of Federal, Greek Revival, Gothic Revival, and Victorian buildings. Also includes individually listed Lorenzo and Albany Street Historic District. Cazenovia Town Multiple Resource Area. 06.19.1986

The Hickories
47 Forman Street. Shingle Style/Georgian Revival frame residence and boathouse built 1897-1900 on Cazenovia Lake by carpenter Henry H. Potter and mason John D. Jones for Townsend and Sophia Jackson. Cazenovia Town Multiple Resource Area. 07.15.1991

Lehigh Valley Railroad Depot
25 William Street. Stick Style frame freight and passenger depot built c.1894. Cazenovia Town Multiple Resource Area. 07.15.1991

Lorenzo (State Historic Site)
Ledyard Street (US 20). An 86-acre estate with large Federal brick residence built 1807-09 for Colonel John Lincklaen, local agent of Holland Land Company and founder of Cazenovia; design attributed to John Hooker. 02.18.1971

Earlville

Earlville Historic District (see Chenango County)

Hamilton

Hamilton Village Historic District
Roughly Kendrick Avenue, and Broad, Payne, Hamilton, Madison, Pleasant, and Lebanon streets. Historic core of village, with approximately 150 properties, including early 19th-century residences of village founders, turn-of-the-century commercial district of brick buildings, several 19th-century churches, and village park. Notable buildings include Greek Revival Baptist Church (1843), Gothic Revival St. Thomas Church (1846, Richard Upjohn), Adon Smith House (individually listed), and Dutch Colonial Revival Colgate Inn (1925). Architects include A. W. Reynolds, Nichols & Beal, Orlando K. Foote, and F. H. George. 09.13.1984

Old Biology Hall
Colgate University. Richardsonian Romanesque building built 1884; 1906 addition. 09.20.1973

Adon Smith House
3 Broad Street. Italianate brick residence built 1850. 05.02.1974

United States Post Office–Hamilton
32 Broad Street. Colonial Revival brick post office built 1936-37. Interior sculptural relief (1938) by Humbert Albriszio. United States Post Offices in New York State, 1858-1943, Thematic Resources. 05.11.1989

Morrisville

First National Bank of Morrisville
Main Street. A 1-story Greek Revival/Italianate brick bank building with cast-iron decorative trim; built 1864. 09.12.1985

Old Madison County Courthouse
East Main Street. A 2-story Italianate frame courthouse with octagonal cupola; designed by J. K. Laas; built 1865; used as county courthouse until 1909 and now on campus of New York Agricultural School.
06.15.1978

Oneida

Cottage Lawn
435 Main Street. Gothic Revival stuccoed brick cottage designed by Alexander Jackson Davis; built 1849-50 for Miles Higinbotham. Headquarters of Madison County Historical Society.
11.06.1980

Main-Broad-Grove Streets Historic District
Roughly bounded by Main, Broad, East Grove, West Grove, Wilbur, Elizabeth, East Walnut, West Walnut, and Stone streets. Neighborhood of 197 residences built 1830-1930 including Federal, Greek Revival, Queen Anne, and Tudor Revival, among other styles.
09.15.1983

Oneida Community Mansion House
Sherrill Road. Massive, rambling U-shaped Victorian brick building built in several stages from early 1850s to 1914 as multipurpose principal building of radical communal society founded 1848 by John Humphrey Noyes; dissolved 1881. NHL 06.23.1965

United States Post Office–Oneida
133 Farrier Avenue. Colonial Revival brick post office built 1931-32. United States Post Offices in New York State, 1858-1943, Thematic Resources. 05.11.1989

Smithfield

Peterboro Land Office
Peterboro Road, Peterboro. Small Federal brick commercial building built 1804.
09.07.1984

MONROE COUNTY

Brighton

Stone-Tolan House
2370 East Avenue. Large Federal frame residence built 1805 by Orringh Stone; attached wing (original house) built 1792. Also includes 19th-century barn. Retains 4 acres of original 210-acre tract. Operated as house museum by Landmark Society of Western New York.
07.21.1983

Brockport

Morgan-Manning House
151 Main Street. Large Italianate brick residence built 1854. Home of Dayton S. Morgan, farm equipment manufacturer, in late 19th century. Headquarters of Western Monroe Historical Society. 04.25.1991

St. Luke's Episcopal Church
17 Main Street. Gothic Revival stone church built 1855; enlarged 1880s. Adjacent Romanesque Revival stone Cary Parish House built 1903. 04.26.1990

Chili

Chili Mills Conservation Area
Off Stuart Road, along Black Creek, one mile southwest of West Chili (also in town of Riga). A 50-acre property with buildings, structures, and sites related to 19th-century rural milling community developed by Joseph Sibley along Black Creek. Includes Federal cobblestone Sibley-Stuart House (c.1835), 2 Greek Revival residences, barn, icehouse, gristmill (1901), metal-truss bridge, millpond and dam, and historic archeological sites of log cabin and mills. 03.12.1975

East Rochester

United States Post Office–East Rochester
206 West Commercial Street. Colonial Revival brick post office built 1936-37. Interior mural (1938, now in storage) by Bernard Gussow. United States Post Offices in New York State, 1858-1943, Thematic Resources. 11.17.1988

Fairport

Henry Deland House (Green Lantern Inn)
99 South Main Street. Second Empire brick residence with 3-story tower and elaborate decorative features; built 1874 for prominent local businessman. 04.17.1980

Wilbur House
187 South Main Street. Second Empire brick residence built 1873 for local contractor and

Erie Canal superintendent. Includes carriage house and 7-acre parcel of original farm.
05.06.1980

Gates

Franklin Hinchey House
634 Hinchey Road. Large Italianate frame farmhouse built 1870 for farmer and railroad executive. Retains 3 acres of original farm, original wood fence, and 2 outbuildings.
11.10.1983

Greece

Our Mother of Sorrows Roman Catholic Church and Cemetery
1785 Latta Road, Paddy Hill. Early Romanesque Revival brick church built 1859-78 for Irish immigrant community. Now a public library. Adjacent 19th-century cemetery.
11.30.1989

Hamilton

Antoinette Louisa Brown Blackwell Childhood Home
1099 Pinnacle Road. Vernacular Federal stone farmhouse built 1830. Childhood home of prominent 19th-century women's rights activist and first ordained female minister in United States. Property retains 11 acres of original farm. 11.16.1989

Honeoye Falls

Lower Mill
61 North Main Street. A 3-story vernacular stone mill on Honeoye Creek; built c.1829 for Hiram Finch; late 19th-century alterations.
05.17.1973

St. John's Episcopal Church
11 Episcopal Avenue. Greek Revival stone church with Doric portico and Gothic-style windows; built 1841-42; Victorian interior and addition. 07.07.1988

United States Post Office–Honeoye Falls
West Main Street and Episcopal Avenue. Colonial Revival brick post office built 1940-41. Interior mural (1942) by Stuart Edie. United States Post Offices in New York State, 1858-1943, Thematic Resources.
05.11.1989

Mendon

Hiram Sibley Homestead
29 Sibley Road, Sibleyville. Federal frame residence built c.1827-32 for prominent financier, philanthropist, and founding partner in Western Union Telegraph Co.; modern additions. Retains 25-acre property including gristmill ruins. 09.12.1985

Totiakton Site
North of Honeoye Falls. A 38-acre arche-

ological site of Seneca Iroquois village occupied between c.1675-1687. Includes cemeteries and stockade site. 09.21.1978

Ogden

Adams-Ryan House
425 Washington Street, Adams Basin. A 2-story vernacular Federal frame inn built c.1825; mid- and late 19th-century alterations and additions. 09.05.1985

Penfield

Daisy Flour Mill
1880 Blossom Road. A 6-acre mill complex on Irondequoit Creek with 2 1/2-story frame flour mill built 1848 and three 19th-century frame mill workers' houses. Converted for use as restaurant. 06.26.1972

Mud House
1000 Whalen Road. Modest 1 1/2-story vernacular earthen farmhouse built 1835-36 by William Gors. 10.11.1978

Samuel Rich House
2204 Five Mile Line Road. Modest vernacular frame residence built 1816 for mill owner and farmer; large Federal frame addition in 1832 with arcaded facade. Includes smokehouse and 5-acre parcel of original 1,000-acre tract. 12.30.1987

Perinton

Richardson's Tavern
1474 Marsh Road, Bushnell's Basin. A 1 1/2-story Federal frame tavern built 1818; stone and frame enlargement c.1830s in Greek Revival style. Remains in use as restaurant. 05.06.1980

Pittsford (Town)

Spring House
3001 Monroe Avenue. A 3 1/2-story Federal brick building built 1832 for Joseph Towsey as health spa/hotel. Adjacent to former Erie Canal. 11.20.1975

Pittsford (Village)

Phoenix Building (Phoenix Hotel)
South Main and State streets. Large 3 1/2-story Federal brick former hotel with arcaded 1st story and 3rd-floor ballroom; built c.1820. 08.07.1974

Pittsford Village Historic District
Roughly bounded by Erie Canal, Jefferson Avenue, and Sutherland and South streets. Large residential district with 131 properties,

Phoenix Building, Village of Pittsford.

mostly 19th- and early 20th-century residences in Federal, Greek Revival, Gothic Revival, Italianate, Queen Anne, Eastlake, and Colonial Revival styles. Also includes 3 churches and 2 schools. Notable buildings include Federal Hargous-Briggs House (1812), Federal Little House (c.1819), Federal/Greek Revival Steele House (c.1810; enlarged c.1830s, home of landscape architect Fletcher Steele), Phoenix Building (individually listed), cobblestone District No. 6 Schoolhouse (1842), Gothic Revival Dr. Hartwell Carver House (c.1853), Early Romanesque Revival Presbyterian Church (c.1861), and High Victorian Gothic Christ Church (c.1868). Pittsford Village Multiple Resource Area. 09.07.1984

Riga

Chili Mills Conservation Area (see Chili)

Riga Academy
3 Riga-Mumford Road. A 2-story, 5-bay Federal brick building built 1811 as tavern by Joseph Thompson. Operated as academy 1847-61. 11.21.1980

Rochester

Andrews Street Bridge
Andrews Street over Genesee River. Quarry-faced stone bridge with 7 segmental arches; designed by J. Y. McClintock; built 1893. Inner Loop Multiple Resource Area: Stone Arch Bridge Thematic Resources. 10.11.1984

Susan B. Anthony House
17 Madison Street. Italianate brick residence built c.1860; home of suffragette Susan B. Anthony 1866-1906. Museum.
NHL 06.23.1965

Aquinas Institute
1127 Dewey Avenue. Large 3-story Jacobean Revival brick secondary school on 13-acre landscaped property; designed by J. Foster Warner; built 1923-24. 06.08.1989

Bevier Memorial Building
44 South Washington Street. A 3 1/2-story Italian Renaissance style eclectic brick building with variegated brick and ceramic tile decoration; designed by Claude F. Bragdon; built 1910 as Rochester Athenaeum and Mechanics Institute. 10.25.1973

Bridge Square Historic District
Roughly bounded by Inner Loop, Centre Park, Washington, and West Main streets. Low-scale commercial and industrial district with 24 mostly 2-, 3-, and 4-story late 19th-century brick buildings. Notable buildings include Federal United States Hotel (1826), and Italian Renaissance style Old City Morgue (1905). Inner Loop Multiple Resource Area. 10.11.1984

Adam Brown Block
480 East Main Street. A 4-story Romanesque Revival brick commercial/residential building with terra-cotta trim; designed by Harvey Ellis;

built 1885. Inner Loop Multiple Resource Area. 10.04.1985

Brown's Race Historic District
Roughly bounded by Genesee River and Mill, Platt, Commercial, and State streets. Group of 15 buildings, 2 structures, and 14 archeological sites related to 19th-century hydro-power industrial development along Genesee River gorge. Includes raceway and spillways (1818), Tripphammer Mill ruins (c.1818), Gothic Revival Rochester Water Works (1873, Andrew J. Warner), Rochester Button Factory (1905), stone Selye Fire Engine Factory (1826; enlarged 1868), lattice-truss Platt Street Bridge (1892), and Romanesque Revival brick Gorsline Building (1888). 03.02.1989

Campbell-Whittlesey House
123 South Fitzhugh Street. Large Greek Revival brick residence with Ionic portico; built 1835-36 for Benjamin Campbell, local merchant and miller. Notable interior finishes. Operated as house museum by Landmark Society of Western New York. 02.18.1971 ILLUS. P. 84

Chamber of Commerce
55 St. Paul Street. A 4-story Neoclassical limestone building designed by Claude F. Bragdon; built 1916-17; 1925 addition designed by Gordon & Kaelber. Inner Loop Multiple Resource Area. 10.04.1985

Jonathan Child House and Brewster-Burke House
37 South Washington Street and 130 Spring Street. Child House: large Greek Revival stuccoed residence with pedimented portico supported by Corinthian columns; built 1837-38 for first mayor of Rochester and son-in-law of city founder Nathaniel Rochester; design attributed to S. P. Hastings or Daniel Loomis. Brewster-Burke House: large Italianate brick villa with stone trim, cast-iron balconies, and Moorish-style porch; built 1849 for local banker and merchant. 02.18.1971 ILLUS. P. 85

City Hall Historic District
South Fitzhugh Street between Broad and West Main streets. Group of 4 buildings in 2-block area of downtown Rochester. St. Luke's Episcopal Church: early Gothic Revival stone church designed by Josiah R. Brady; built 1824. Rochester Free Academy: 3 1/2-story High Victorian Gothic brick academy designed by Andrew J. Warner; built 1872-73. Rochester City Hall: 3 1/2-story Victorian Gothic eclectic brick and limestone former city hall with corner tower; designed by Andrew J. Warner; built 1874-75. Monroe County Courthouse: Italian Renaissance style granite courthouse designed by J. Foster Warner; built 1894-96. 09.17.1974

H. C. Cohen Company Building
(Andrews Building)
400 Andrews Street. A 5-story Romanesque Revival brick industrial building built 1889 for garment manufacturer. Inner Loop Multiple Resource Area. 10.04.1985

Court Exchange Building
(National Casket Company)
142 Exchange Street. A 6-story Romanesque Revival brick commercial building designed by Harvey Ellis; built 1881 for Samuel Stein, casket manufacturer. Inner Loop Multiple Resource Area.   10.04.1985

Court Street Bridge
Court Street over Genesee River. Quarry-faced stone bridge with 6 segmental arches; designed by J. Y. McClintock; built 1893. Inner Loop Multiple Resource Area: Stone Arch Bridge Thematic Resources.   10.11.1984

Cox Building
36-48 St. Paul Street. A 7-story Romanesque Revival brick and brownstone commercial warehouse building built 1888. Inner Loop Multiple Resource Area: Department Store Thematic Group.   10.11.1984

Chester Dewey School No. 14
200 University Avenue. A 2-story Italian Renaissance style brick school with arcaded loggia; designed by Edwin S. Gordon; built 1915-16. Inner Loop Multiple Resource Area.   10.04.1985

East Avenue Historic District
Irregular pattern along East Avenue from Probert Street to Alexander Street. A 1 1/2-mile long residential neighborhood with approximately 700 buildings, including large mid-19th- to early 20th-century former estates on East Avenue, and late 19th- and early 20th-century detached brick and frame residences on cross streets. Also includes several churches. Notable buildings include Italianate Sibley House (1868; remodeled in Georgian Revival style), Greek Revival Pitkin-Powers House (1840), Greek Revival Woodside (1839-41; headquarters of Rochester Historical Society), Gothic Revival Bissell House (1852-54, Andrew J. Warner), George Eastman House

(individually listed), Italianate Bates-Ryder House (1856), Boynton House (1909, Frank Lloyd Wright), Federal Oliver Culver House (1816), and Atkinson Allen House (garden by Fletcher Steele, begun 1916).   04.17.1979

East High School
410 Alexander Street. Large 3-story Italian Renaissance style brick former school with paired towers and stone trim; designed by J. Foster Warner; built 1902-03.   06.30.1983

Eastman Dental Dispensary
800 East Main Street. Italian Renaissance style brick building with marble trim; designed by Gordon, Madden & Kaelber; built 1917. Established and endowed by George Eastman for low-cost dental treatment and education in dental hygiene.   04.28.1983

George Eastman House
900 East Avenue. Massive Georgian Revival brick residence designed by J. Foster Warner and McKim, Mead & White; completed 1905; since 1949 International Museum of Photography. Landscape and gardens designed by Claude F. Bragdon and Alling DeForest.   NHL 11.13.1966

Edwards Building
26-34 St. Paul Street. A 7-story Renaissance Revival Neoclassical terra-cotta-clad department store designed by Crandall & Strobel; built 1908. Inner Loop Multiple Resource Area: Department Store Thematic Group.   10.11.1984

Hervey Ely House
138 Troup Street. Greek Revival stuccoed brick residence with Doric portico and notable interior; built 1837 for mill owner. Owned by Irondequoit Chapter, Daughters of the American Revolution.   08.12.1971

Erie Canal: Second Genesee Aqueduct
Broad Street. An 800-foot limestone aqueduct designed by engineer Nathan Roberts; built 1836-42 to carry enlarged Erie Canal over Genesee River; concrete highway bridge built 1927 on top of aqueduct.   09.29.1976

Federal Building (New City Hall)
30 Church Street. Monumental Richardsonian Romanesque sandstone building with internal metal skeleton and large central atrium; designed by Mifflin E. Bell and Will A. Freret; built 1885-89 as federal courthouse and post office; now Rochester City Hall.   04.13.1972

First National Bank of Rochester
(Monroe County Savings Bank Building)
35 State Street. Classical Revival marble bank with Corinthian portico; designed by Mowbry & Uffinger; built 1924. Inner Loop Multiple Resource Area.   10.04.1985

First Presbyterian Church
(Central Church of Christ)
101 South Plymouth Avenue. Large Gothic Revival sandstone church designed 1871 by Andrew J. Warner.   10.25.1973

First Universalist Church
150 South Clinton Avenue. Arts and Crafts eclectic brick church designed by Claude F. Bragdon; built 1907-08.   05.27.1971

Gannett Building
55 Exchange Boulevard. A 5-story Neoclassical limestone industrial/commercial building designed by Howell & Thomas; built 1927 for Gannett Newspapers. Inner Loop Multiple Resource Area.   10.04.1985

Genesee Lighthouse
70 Lighthouse Street. An 80-foot-tall limestone octagonal lighthouse built 1822. Adjacent brick keeper's house built 1863.   08.13.1974

Granite Building
124 East Main Street. A 12-story Renaissance Revival/Beaux-Arts brick and granite retail and office building designed by J. Foster Warner; built 1893. Inner Loop Multiple Resource Area: Department Store Thematic Group.   10.11.1984

Grove Place Historic District
Gibbs, Selden, Grove, and Windsor streets. Small residential area with 28 small-scale late 19th-century Greek Revival, Italianate, Eastlake, Queen Anne, and Tudor Revival residences associated with Selden and Ward families. Inner Loop Multiple Resource Area.   10.11.1984

Jewish Young Men's and Women's Association
400 Andrews Street. Large complex of 3 Georgian Revival brick buildings designed by Siegmund Firestone; built 1931-34. Inner Loop Multiple Resource Area.   10.04.1985

Kirstein Building
242 Andrews Street. A 6-story Neoclassical brick industrial building built 1908 for eyeglass manufacturer. Inner Loop Multiple Resource Area.   10.04.1985

Lehigh Valley Railroad Station
99 Court Street. A 1 1/2-story brick railroad station with French Renaissance style decorative details; designed by F. D. Hyde; built 1905 on stone piers and iron girders above millrace on Genesee River. Inner Loop Multiple Resource Area.   10.04.1985

Leopold Street Shul
30 Leopold Street. Brick synagogue with eclectic Romanesque-style features; built 1886 for Eastern European Jewish community. Oldest surviving synagogue in city.   06.07.1974

Little Theatre
240 East Avenue. Art Deco terra-cotta-clad movie theater designed by Edgar Phillips; built 1923. Inner Loop Multiple Resource Area. 10.04.1985

Madison Square–West Main Street Historic District
Canal, King, Litchfield, South Madison, West Main, and Silver streets, Madison Park North and South, Spies Alley, and Susan B. Anthony Square. A 6-block neighborhood developed in early 19th-century. Includes 65 Greek Revival, Italianate, and Queen Anne brick and frame residences, approximately 30 late 19th-century commercial and industrial buildings, public park (1839, renamed Susan B. Anthony Square), and Susan B. Anthony House (individually listed).   11.03.1988

Main Street Bridge
Main Street over Genesee River. Limestone bridge with 5 segmental arches; designed by David Marsh with I. F. Quinby; built 1857. Inner Loop Multiple Resource Area: Stone Arch Bridge Thematic Resources.   10.11.1984

Michaels-Stern Building
87 North Clinton Avenue. A 7-story brick commercial/industrial building with Beaux-Arts and "Chicago School" design features; designed by Nolan, Nolan & Stern; built 1893 for garment manufacturer. Inner Loop Multiple Resource Area.   10.04.1985

Mt. Hope–Highland Historic District
Roughly bounded by Clarissa Street Bridge, Genesee River, and South and Mt. Hope avenues. A 200-acre district on east side of Genesee River. Includes Mt. Hope Cemetery (1838), Highland Park, and group of large- and small-scale early 20th-century residences. Much of area formerly part of Mt. Hope Botanic Gardens. Notable buildings include Italianate Patrick Barry House (1857, Gervase Wheeler), Gothic Revival Ellwanger & Barry Nursery Office (1854-55, Alexander Jackson Davis), Gothic Revival Warner Castle (1854, Andrew J. Warner), Gothic Revival cemetery chapel (1863, Andrew J. Warner), Lamberton Conservatory (1911), and elaborate mausoleums and monuments in cemetery. 01.21.1974

National Company Building
159 East Main Street. A 5-story Neoclassical stone department store designed by J. Foster Warner; built 1924. Inner Loop Multiple Resource Area: Department Store Thematic Group. 10.11.1984

Naval Armory–Convention Hall
(GeVa Theater)
75 Woodbury Boulevard. A 2-story Victorian building designed 1867 by Andrew J. Warner as armory; 1907 renovation and Neoclassical additions for use as convention hall. Now a theater. Inner Loop Multiple Resource Area. 10.04.1985

Nazareth House
94 Averill Avenue. A 3-story Italian Renaissance style brick institutional building built

1893 for educational and social programs; 1911 addition. 04.12.1984

Building at 551-555 North Goodman Street
A 3-story Queen Anne/eclectic commercial building built 1889. 03.20.1986

O'Kane Market and O'Kane Building
104-106 Bartlett Street and 239-255 Reynolds Street. O'Kane Market: Italianate brick commercial/residential building built 1878. O'Kane Building: Queen Anne brick commercial/residential building built 1889-90. 09.12.1985

Old Stone Warehouse
One Mt. Hope Avenue. Massive 4-story Medina sandstone warehouse built 1822 by Myron Holley and John Gilbert adjacent to Erie Canal; enlarged 1864. 10.15.1973

Powers Building
16 West Main Street. Massive 9-story Second Empire stone- and cast-iron-clad, metal-framed commercial building with 3-part mansard roof; designed by Andrew J. Warner; built 1869-70; later additions and renovations. 04.03.1973

Jonathan Child House, Rochester (p. 83).

Opposite: Campbell-Whittlesey House, Rochester (p. 83).

Reynolds Arcade
16 East Main Street. An 11-story Art Deco limestone commercial office building designed by Gordon & Kaelber; built 1932. Interior retail arcade. Inner Loop Multiple Resource Area. 10.04.1985

Residence at 235-237 Reynolds Street
Victorian Gothic brick double residence built c.1885 on speculation for John Abbs, local real estate broker. 09.12.1985

Rochester City School No. 24
(Ellwanger & Barry School)
900 Meigs Street. A 1-story Arts and Crafts Mission public school designed by Edwin S. Gordon; built 1913 with innovative design and safety features. 09.15.1983

Rochester Fire Department Headquarters and Shops
185 North Street. Two adjacent 2-story Art Deco brick buildings designed by Joseph F. Flynn; built 1936 with Public Works Administration funds. Inner Loop Multiple Resource Area. 10.21.1985

Rochester Savings Bank
40 Franklin Street. Large 4-story Italian Renaissance style stone bank designed by McKim, Mead & White with J. Foster Warner; built 1927. Elaborate eclectic main banking room with mosaic decoration by Ezra Winter. 03.16.1972

Rundel Memorial Library
115 South Avenue. Monumental 3-story Neoclassical/Art Deco limestone library designed by Gordon & Kaelber; built 1932-35. Inner Loop Multiple Resource Area. 10.04.1985

St. Joseph Roman Catholic Church and Rectory
108 Franklin Street. Large Greek Revival stone church built 1843-46 for German Catholic community; elaborate bell and clock tower added 1909; gutted by fire 1974. Stabilized walls and tower incorporated into city park. 05.29.1975

St. Paul–North Water Streets Historic District
St. Paul, North Water, and Andrews streets. A 4-block concentration of 17 masonry commercial warehouse and industrial buildings

built 1884-1928 as part of once large garment district. Inner Loop Multiple Resource Area. 10.11.1984

Shingleside
476 Beach Avenue. Large Colonial Revival/ Shingle Style frame residence and landscaped grounds designed by Claude F. Bragdon; built 1898-99 as summer residence for Rochester industrialist Nathan Stein. 09.13.1984

Sibley Triangle Building
20-30 East Avenue. A 5-story Italian Renaissance style/eclectic brick triangular commercial building with limestone and marble trim; designed by J. Foster Warner; built 1897 for realtor, banker, and philanthropist Hiram W. Sibley. Inner Loop Multiple Resource Area. 10.04.1985

State Street Historic District
109-173 State Street. Row of 12 commercial buildings, mostly 4-story mid-19th-century vernacular brick buildings constructed as part of downtown market area. Inner Loop Multiple Resource Area. 10.11.1984

Third Ward Historic District
Roughly bounded by Adams and Peach streets, US1490, and both sides of Troup and Fitzhugh streets. A 7-block residential neighborhood with approximately 125 small- to large-scale Greek Revival, Italianate, and Victorian residences, attached townhouses, and early 20th-century apartment houses. Includes individually listed Campbell-Whittlesey House and Henry Ely House and Greek Revival Hoyt Potter House (1840, headquarters of Landmark Society of Western New York). 07.12.1974

Times Square Building
45 Exchange Boulevard. A 12-story Art Deco limestone office building with distinctive signal tower decorated with aluminum stylized wings; designed by Voorhees, Gmelin & Walker; built 1929-30. 08.11.1982

University Club
26 Broadway. A 4-story Georgian Revival brick building with limestone trim; designed by Leon Stern; built 1930. Inner Loop Multiple Resource Area. 10.04.1985

Vanderbeck House
1295 Lake Avenue. Large Second Empire brick residence built 1874 for local developer Andrew W. Vanderbeck. 04.09.1984

H. H. Warner Building
72-82 St. Paul Street. A 7-story brick commercial building with Venetian Gothic style cast-iron facade; designed by Louis P. Rogers of Thomas & Rogers; cast iron produced by J. B. & J. M. Cornell Foundry; built 1883-84 as patent medicine laboratory and warehouse. Inner Loop Multiple Resource Area. 10.04.1985

Washington Street Rowhouses
30-32 North Washington Street. Pair of Greek Revival brick rowhouses built c.1840. Inner Loop Multiple Resource Area. 10.04.1985

Wilder Building
One East Main Street. An 11-story Romanesque Revival brick-clad commercial building designed by Andrew J. Warner and William Brockett; built 1887-88. Inner Loop Multiple Resource Area.   10.04.1985

Rush

Barber-Mulligan Farm (see Avon, Livingston County)

Scottsville

Rochester Street Historic District
Both sides of Rochester Street. Residential district with 41 buildings, mostly modest Greek Revival frame residences built 1830-50s
10.25.1973

Webster

Webster Baptist Church
59 South Avenue. Greek Revival cobblestone church with octagonal domed belfry; built 1856.   11.07.1991

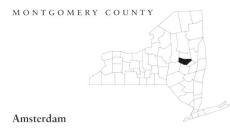

Amsterdam

Greene Mansion
92 Market Street. Large Queen Anne/eclectic brick residence built c.1881 for William K. Greene, carpet manufacturer.   12.31.1979

Guy Park
West Main Street. A 5-bay, 2-story Georgian stone residence on shore of Mohawk River; built 1773 for Guy Johnson, Superintendent of Indian Affairs in 1774 and son-in-law of Sir William Johnson; mid-19th-century alterations and flanking wings.   02.06.1973

Samuel Sweet Canal Store
65 Bridge Street. A 3-story vernacular limestone commercial building built c.1850 as Erie Canal store and warehouse in hamlet of Port Jackson.
09.19.1989

United States Post Office–Amsterdam
12-16 Church Street. Large Georgian Revival brick post office built 1935-36. Interior mural (1939) by Henry Schnakenberg. United States Post Offices in New York State, 1858-1943, Thematic Resources.   11.17.1988

Vrooman Avenue School
Vrooman Avenue. A 2-story Georgian Revival brick school built 1918.   06.30.1983

Canajoharie

United States Post Office–Canajoharie
50 West Main Street. Colonial Revival brick post office built 1937. Interior mural (1942) by Anatol Shulkin. United States Post Offices in New York State, 1858-1943, Thematic Resources.   11.17.1988

Van Alstyne House (Fort Rensselaer Club)
Moyer Street. Dutch Colonial stone residence with gambrel roof; purportedly built 1730 by early settlers and traders; later alterations and additions, including large 1915 rear addition designed by Bryant Fleming.   09.08.1983

Florida

Erie Canal (Schoharie Crossing State Historic Site)
NY 5S, 6 miles west of Amsterdam (also in town of Glen). A 3 1/2-mile section of Erie Canal. Includes original section of canal built 1817-19 and its crossing of Schoharie Creek, section of 1841 enlarged canal, Schoharie Aqueduct, 6 limestone locks, 5 canal-related buildings, and archeological sites of canal buildings and structures.   NHL 10.09.1960

Fonda

New Courthouse
Broadway. A 1-story Romanesque Revival brick courthouse with central tower; designed by Fuller & Wheeler; built 1892. Montgomery County Buildings Thematic Resources.
08.05.1982

Old Courthouse Complex
Railroad Street. Large 2-story Greek Revival brick courthouse with Ionic portico and dome; built 1836; 1910 additions and alterations. Adjacent Italianate Sheriff's Residence (1882, McIntyre Comrie), and jail (1912, William J. Beardsley). Montgomery County Buildings Thematic Resources.   08.05.1982

Schoharie Aqueduct over Erie Canal, Florida.

Opposite: Rochester Savings Bank, Rochester.

Sir William Johnson Residence, Fort Johnson.

Fort Johnson

Fort Johnson
Junction of NY 5 and 67. Large 2-story Georgian stone residence with intact interior; built 1748-49 as fortified home of Sir William Johnson and later his son, Sir John Johnson, Loyalist and soldier during American Revolution. Operated as house museum by Montgomery County Historical Society. NHL 11.28.1972

Fort Plain

Fort Plain Conservation Area (see Minden)

United States Post Office–Fort Plain
41 River Street. Georgian Revival brick post office built 1931-32. United States Post Offices in New York State, 1858-1943, Thematic Resources. 05.11.1989

Glen

Erie Canal (see Florida)

Minden

Fort Plain Conservation Area
Address restricted (also in village of Fort Plain). A 42-acre multicomponent area with prehistoric archeological sites of Mohawk Iroquois occupation 13th-17th century, historic archeological site of American fortification during American Revolution (1781-82), and Greek Revival stone Lipe Farmstead (1848). 11.15.1979

Mohawk

Walter Butler Homestead (Butlersbury)
Old Trail Road, northeast of Fonda. Large 1 1/2-story Colonial vernacular frame residence built 1742 for early settlers of Mohawk Valley who were active in French and Indian Wars and Loyalists during American Revolution. Once part of 4,000-acre land grant. 06.23.1976

Caughnawaga Indian Village Site
Address restricted. Archeological site of Mohawk Iroquois village occupied 1667-93. 08.28.1973

Nelliston

Ehle House Site
Address restricted. Archeological site and remains of early 18th-century vernacular stone residence built by Palatine German settler John Jacob Ehle. 06.14.1982

Peter Ehle House
East Main Street. A 5-acre farmstead with Federal stone farmhouse built 1826 and 19th-century barn complex. 09.27.1987

Lasher-Davis House
NY 5. Modest Italianate frame residence built 1865. 09.27.1980

Jacob Nellis Farmhouse
Nellis Street. A 29-acre farmstead with Greek Revival stone farmhouse built early 1830s and 2 barns. 09.27.1980

Nelliston Historic District
Prospect, River, Railroad, and Berthoud streets. Residential area developed 1860-90 with 57 buildings, including numerous large frame or brick Italianate residences overlooking Mohawk River. Also includes 1868 and 1879 freight houses, and 1902 stone railroad station. 09.27.1980

Walrath-Van Horne House
West Main Street. Greek Revival stone former farmhouse built 1842; frame 2nd story and mansard roof added 1895. Also includes 2 barns, well house, and early 19th-century stone kitchen/smokehouse. 09.27.1980

Waterman-Gramps House
School Street. Modest mid-19th-century Greek Revival stone residence. 09.27.1980

Palatine

County Farm
NY 5. A 352-acre property on north bank of Mohawk River settled in early 18th century and developed as county poor farm after 1899. Includes Federal Schenck Homestead (c.1820), Dutch barn, Colonial Revival inmate residences (c.1900, Lynn Kinne), numerous outbuildings, and potential prehistoric and historic archeological sites. Montgomery County Buildings Thematic Resources. 08.05.1982

Palatine Church
Mohawk Turnpike. Georgian vernacular stone church with gambrel roof and cupola; built 1770 for Palatine German settlement. Museum. 01.25.1973

Reformed Dutch Church of Stone Arabia
NY 10, east of Nelliston. Georgian/Federal stone church built 1787-89; octagonal frame belfry with bell cast roof possibly added later. Adjacent cemetery. 09.14.1977

Rice's Woods
Address restricted. Archeological site of large Mohawk Iroquois village occupied c.1590-1630. Includes prehistoric cemetery. 07.18.1980

Palatine Bridge

Palatine Bridge Freight House
NY 5. A 300-foot-long, 1-story vernacular limestone freight house built 1850s for New York Central Railroad. 03.07.1973

Webster Wagner House
East Grand Street. Large Second Empire frame residence with 3-story corner tower and elaborate decorative trim; designed by Horatio Nelson White; built 1876 as summer house for president of New York Central Sleeping Car Co. and politician. 03.07.1973

St. Johnsville (Town)

Fort Klock
NY 5, 2 miles east of St. Johnsville. A 1 1/2-story Colonial vernacular stone residence built 1750 by Johannes Klock as fortified frontier residence and fur-trading post on Mohawk River. Used as stronghold during American Revolution. Museum. NHL 11.28.1972

Nellis Tavern
NY 5. Colonial frame farmhouse built c.1750 by Palatine German settler Christian Nellis; enlarged c.1790 in Federal style and subsequently used as tavern. Interior finishes include early decorative stenciled walls. 05.10.1990

St. Johnsville (Village)

Bates-Englehardt Mansion
(St. Johnsville Community House)
19 Washington Street. Italianate brick residence built 1869 for local cheese merchant; additions and alterations 1909-34. 12.07.1989

United States Post Office–St. Johnsville
Main Street. Colonial Revival brick post office built 1937. Interior mural (1940) by Jirayr Zorthian. United States Post Offices in New York State, 1858-1943, Thematic Resources. 05.11.1989

Cove Neck

James Alfred Roosevelt Estate
(Yellow Banks)
360 Cove Neck Road. A 12-acre estate overlooking Oyster Bay Harbor with large Shingle Style main residence designed by Bruce Price; built 1881 as summer house for pioneer of cable communications.   05.17.1979

Sagamore Hill National Historic Site
End of Cove Neck Road. An 83-acre estate on Cold Spring Harbor with large, rambling Queen Anne frame residence designed by Lamb & Rich and landscaped grounds; built 1884-85 for Theodore Roosevelt; his home until his death in 1919. Contains original furnishings. Museum.   07.25.1962

East Hills

Mackay Estate Dairyman's Cottage
40 Elm Drive. Arts and Crafts brick and frame residence with Japanese-style decorative features; designed c.1902 by Warren & Wetmore; built as part of estate of Clarence H. Mackay, heir to Comstock lode silver fortune.   03.14.1991

Mackay Estate Gate Lodge
Harbor Hill and Roslyn roads. French Renaissance style stone building designed by Stanford White; built 1900-02 as part of estate of Clarence H. Mackay, heir to Comstock lode silver fortune.   03.14.1991

Mackay Estate Water Tower
Redwood Drive. Rustic-style circular stone structure containing metal water tower; designed by Stanford White; built 1900-02 as part of estate of Clarence H. Mackay, heir to Comstock lode silver fortune.   03.14.1991

East Williston

East Williston Village Historic District
Roughly bounded by East Williston Avenue, Roslyn Road, Atlanta Avenue, and Village Green. Small core of village with 19th- to early 20th-century properties, including 10 Italianate, Eastlake, late Gothic Revival, and Colonial frame residences, 2 commercial buildings, railroad station, village green, and Gothic Revival stone Community Church (1925, George W. Conable).   07.18.1985

Farmingdale

Farmingdale Railroad Station
Farmingdale Avenue. Queen Anne brick passenger station built 1896 for Long Island Railroad; enlarged 1910 with 2 1/2-story tower to accommodate electrical substation for cross-island trolley line.   11.13.1991

Flower Hill

George W. Denton House
West Shore Road. Italianate frame villa with 2 1/2-story tower; built c.1873 overlooking Hempstead Harbor for local attorney. Includes brick icehouse.   08.29.1985

Freeport

United States Post Office–Freeport
132 Merrick Road. Large Colonial Revival brick post office designed by Tachau & Vought; built 1932-33. Interior murals (1938) by William Gropper. United States Post Offices in New York State, 1858-1943, Thematic Resources.   05.11.1989

Garden City

Old Nassau County Courthouse
1550 Franklin Avenue. A 2-story Neoclassical reinforced-concrete courthouse with gilded dome; designed by William B. Tubby; built 1900; later additions.   02.17.1978

A. T. Stewart Era Buildings Thematic Group
Fourth, Fifth, and Sixth streets, and Cathedral and Cherry Valley avenues. Group of 50 residential, commercial, religious, and civic structures built 1871-93 as components of Garden City, an early planned suburban community; envisioned by A. T. Stewart as model country seat for employees of his New York City department store. Includes 44 Italianate and Second Empire frame and brick residences (1872-75, John Kellum), commercial block, waterworks, massive Gothic Revival Cathedral of the Incarnation (1885, Henry G. Harrison) and dependencies, Victorian Gothic St. Paul's School (1883, Henry G. Harrison), and Cathedral School of St. Mary (1893).   11.14.1978

United States Post Office–Garden City
600 Franklin Street. Neoclassical/Moderne brick post office designed by Walker & Gillette with Perry Duncan; built 1936. Interior mural (1937) by J. Theodore Johnson. United States Post Offices in New York State, 1858-1943, Thematic Resources.   05.11.1989

Glen Cove

Justice Court Building
Glen Cove Highway. A 3-story Flemish Revival brick building designed by Stephen F. Voorhees; built 1907-09.   04.26.1990

The Shell House
26 Westland Drive, East Island. Tudor Revival stuccoed and half-timbered residence built 1910 as dependency of former J. Pierpont Morgan, Jr. estate. Used as guest house and residence for captain of *Corsair*, financier J. Pierpont Morgan, Sr.'s yacht.   06.02.1988

United States Post Office–Glen Cove
2 Glen Cove Street. Colonial Revival brick post office with marble trim; designed by Delano & Aldrich; built 1932-33. United States Post Offices in New York State, 1858-1943, Thematic Resources.   05.11.1989

Woolworth Estate
77 Crescent Beach Road. A 16-acre estate with massive Italian Renaissance style marble-clad main house (Winfield Hall), garage, entrance arch, 2 greenhouses, balustraded terraces, ornamental walls, garden structures, and fountains; designed 1916 by C. P. H. Gilbert for Franklin W. Woolworth, developer of 5 & 10 Cent Stores.   05.17.1979 ILLUS. P. 90

Great Neck

United States Post Office–Great Neck
One Welwyn Road. Classical Revival Moderne limestone post office designed by William Dewey Foster; built 1939-40. Exterior relief sculpture (1940) by Gateano Cecere. United States Post Offices in New York State, 1858-1943, Thematic Resources.   05.11.1989

Great Neck Plaza

Grace and Thomaston Buildings
11 Middle Neck Road and 8 Bond Street. Two 3-story brick commercial buildings with restrained eclectic English features; designed by James W. O'Connor; built 1914 and 1926 for W. R. Grace & Co.   12.14.1978

Hempstead

Rectory of St. George's Episcopal Church
217 Peninsula Boulevard. A 2 1/2-story 5-bay Federal frame rectory with gambrel roof; designed by Timothy Clowes; built 1793.   05.03.1988

Detail of John E. Aldred Estate, Lattingtown (p. 90).

St. George's Church
319 Front Street. Federal frame church with octagonal belfry; designed by Timothy Clowes; built 1823.   03.07.1973

United States Post Office–Hempstead
200 Fulton Avenue. Neoclassical/Art Deco brick and limestone post office designed by Tooker & Marsh; built 1932-33. Interior murals (1936-37) by Peppino Mangravite. United States Post Offices in New York State, 1858-1943, Thematic Resources. 11.17.1988

Winfield Hall, Woolworth Estate, Glen Cove (p. 89).

Opposite: Farm Complex, Lillian Sefton Dodge Estate, Mill Neck.

Hicksville

Heitz Place Courthouse
(Hicksville Village Hall)
Modest Neoclassical frame building with octagonal cupola; built 1893-95 as village hall; 1915 brick jail addition. Museum.
07.30.1974

Lattingtown

John E. Aldred Estate (Ormston)
Lattingtown Road. A 117-acre estate on Long Island Sound with massive Tudor Revival limestone main residence, superintendent's house, stable, greenhouse, garage, gatehouses, and garden statues; designed 1916 by Bertram G. Goodhue. Formal gardens and landscape designed by Olmsted Brothers.
08.03.1979 ILLUS. P. 95

Lawrence

Rock Hall
199 Broadway. Large 2 1/2-story Georgian frame residence with gambrel roof and ornate Georgian and Federal exterior and interior features; built c.1767 for Josiah Martin, shipping merchant and Loyalist.
11.21.1976

Locust Valley

Matinecock Friends Meeting House
Piping Rock and Duck Pond roads. A 2 1/2-story

vernacular shingled Quaker meetinghouse with original austere interior features; built 1725. Also includes 2 frame privies, carriage house, shed, and cemetery; burned 1985 and reconstructed 1986. 07.19.1976

Long Beach

Granada Towers
310 Riverside Boulevard. A 7-story Spanish Colonial Revival brick apartment building with terra-cotta and stucco trim; designed by Lang & Rosenberg; built 1929.   05.31.1984

United States Post Office–Long Beach
101 East Park Avenue. Large Colonial Revival brick post office built 1936-37. Interior mural (1939) by Jon Corbino. United States Post Offices in New York State, 1858-1943, Thematic Resources.   05.11.1989

Manhasset

Horatio Gates Onderdonk House
1471 Northern Boulevard. Greek Revival frame residence with Doric portico; built 1836 for local attorney and judge.   04.16.1980

Massapequa

Old Grace Church Complex
Merrick and Dover roads. Small Gothic Revival frame church designed by Elbert Floyd-Jones; built 1844; remodeled 1905. Adjacent Colonial Revival Delancy Floyd-Jones Library (1895), Floyd-Jones family cemetery and lychgate, and early parish cemetery.
06.30.1983

Mill Neck

Lillian Sefton Dodge Estate (Sefton Manor–Mill Neck Manor School for the Deaf)
Frost Mill Road. An 86-acre estate with massive Tudor Revival stone main residence designed 1923 by Clinton & Russell; formal garden designed by Charles Leavitt. Includes Tudor Revival half-timbered farm complex.
07.22.1979

Mineola

United States Post Office–Mineola
Main and First streets. Colonial Revival/Moderne brick post office designed by Peabody, Wilson & Brown; built 1935-36. United States Post Offices in New York State, 1858-1943, Thematic Resources.
05.11.1989

Muttontown

Benjamin Moore Estate (Chelsea)
NY 25A, north of Muttontown. A 42-acre estate with large concrete main house with French Renaissance and Chinese features, gatehouse, garage, conservatory, gazebo, other out-

buildings, and landscape features; designed
1923-24 by William Adams Delano of Delano
& Aldrich. Grounds designed by Delano with
Alexandra Moore and Uberto Innocenti of
Innocenti & Webel. 05.14.1979

North Hempstead

East Toll Gate House
Northern Boulevard, Greenvale. Small Gothic
Revival frame residence built c.1860 as toll-
house on Flushing–North Hempstead turnpike.
Only surviving 19th-century tollhouse on Long
Island. 08.16.1977

Valley Road Historic District
South of Manhasset on Community Drive.
Small 5-acre archeological, structural, and
historic remains of hamlet of Success, a
community of free African-Americans, former
slaves, and Matinecock Indians established
1829. Includes vernacular Lakeville A.M.E.
Zion Church (1833) and cemetery, two 19th-
century residences, and archeological sites of
other buildings. 04.08.1977

Old Westbury

Old Westbury Gardens (John S. Phipps Estate)
71 Old Westbury Road. The 100-acre estate of
John S. Phipps, financier and philanthropist,
with imposing Georgian Revival brick residence
designed 1906 by George A. Crawley and
extensive landscaped grounds. Operated as
house museum. 11.08.1976

Oyster Bay

Adams-Derby House
166 Lexington Avenue. Large 2 1/2-story Queen
Anne frame residence designed by William A.
Potter and Robert H. Robertson; built 1878 for
Mrs. S. S. Adams. Longtime residence of Mrs.
Richard Derby, daughter of President Theodore
Roosevelt. 05.17.1979

James William Beekman House (The Cliffs)
West Shore Road. A 37-acre former estate with
large Gothic Revival frame residence designed
by Henry G. Harrison; built 1863-64 for
politician and civic leader. Also includes Spring
Lake Site, archeological site of Matinecock
Indian village or occupation in late 17th
century. 12.12.1973

Elmwood
East side of Cove Road. A 26-acre property
with large Greek Revival frame residence with
Ionic portico; built as country house for New
York City merchant Thomas F. Youngs. Outbuildings include gazebo, icehouse, greenhouse,
octagonal water tower, barns, and brick coach
house. Later owned by Charles L. Tiffany II.
04.03.1975

First Presbyterian Church of Oyster Bay
East Main Street. Stick Style frame church
designed by J. Cleveland Cady; built 1873; later

additions. Adjacent parsonage (1888).
12.12.1976

Raynham Hall
20 West Main Street. A 2 1/2-story Colonial
frame residence built c.1738 for local merchant
and politician Samuel Townsend; large mid-
19th-century additions; restored 1950s.
Museum. 06.05.1974

Seawanhaka Corinthian Yacht Club
Centre Island Road, Centre Island. A 12-acre
property overlooking Oyster Bay Harbor with

large Colonial Revival frame clubhouse
designed by Robert W. Gibson; built 1891-92
as headquarters for well-known small boat-
sailing club. 01.08.1974

Edward H. Swan House
Cove Neck Road. Large Second Empire brick
residence built 1853 for mercantile family.
05.24.1976

United States Post Office–Oyster Bay
Shore Avenue. Large Georgian Revival brick
post office designed by Bottomley, Wagner &
White; built 1935-36. Interior mural and
sculptural series by Abell Sturges, Ernest
Peixotto, and Leo Lentelli. United States Post
Offices in New York State, 1858-1943,
Thematic Resources. 05.11.1989

Port Washington

Thomas Dodge Homestead
58 Harbor Road. Modest Colonial frame
farmhouse built c.1721 for early settlers of Port
Washington; mid-18th-century and c.1903
additions. Includes 19th-century outbuildings.
06.26.1986

Main Street School
Main and South Washington streets. Large 3-
story Georgian Revival brick school with stone
trim; designed by Ralph Dusinberre and Frank
Cornell; built 1908-09. 02.10.1983

Monfort Cemetery
East of Main Street and Port Washington
Boulevard. Small cemetery with over 100

burials and gravestones from 1737 to 1892.
01.07.1988

Sands-Willets Homestead
336 Port Washington Boulevard. Small
Colonial vernacular frame residence built
c.1735 by Sands family; large mid-19th-
century Greek Revival addition by Willets
family. Also includes late 17th-century barn
moved to property in 1978. 09.19.1985

John Philip Sousa House (Wildbank)
14 Hicks Lane, Sands Point. A 2 1/2-story
eclectic stuccoed brick residence built c.1907.
Home of John Philip Sousa, conductor,
composer, and director of United States Marine
Corps Band. NHL 05.23.1966

Rockville Centre

United States Post Office–Rockville Centre
250 Merrick Road. Large Colonial Revival/
Moderne brick post office designed by William
Dewey Foster; built 1937-38. Interior murals
(1939) by Victor White. United States Post
Offices in New York State, 1858-1943,
Thematic Resources. 05.11.1989

Roslyn

Henry Western Eastman Cottage
130 Mott Avenue. Modest Victorian/
Picturesque frame residence built c.1870.
Multiple Resources of the Village of Roslyn.
10.02.1986

Hicks Lumber Company Store
1345 Old Northern Boulevard. A 2-story
Colonial Revival frame commercial building
with 2-story portico; designed by George R.
Thompson; built 1920. Multiple Resources of
the Village of Roslyn. 10.02.1986

Main Street Historic District
Main Street from North Hempstead Turnpike
to East Broadway, including Tower Street and
portions of Glen Avenue and Paper Mill Road.
Cluster of 50 buildings, mostly frame 19th-
century vernacular residential and commercial

buildings, and park. Notable buildings include Ellen E. Ward Memorial Clock Tower (1895, Lamb & Rich), Greek Revival Obadiah Washington Valentine House (c.1833-36), Second Empire Warren Wilkey House (c.1865), Colonial vernacular Van Nostrand-Starkins House (c.1680, museum), and Roslyn Park (c.1910; includes 18th-century millponds). 01.21.1974

Rescue Hook & Ladder Co. No. 1 Firehouse
School Street at Skillman Street. Colonial Revival brick firehouse designed by H. William Johnson; built 1937. 05.06.1991

Roslyn Cemetery
Northern Boulevard. A 13-acre cemetery containing graves of 8 people prominent in American arts and sciences in 19th and early 20th centuries, including poet and editor William Cullen Bryant, writer and editor Parke Goodwin, writer Frances Hodgson Burnett, writer and editor Christopher Morley, singer Bessie Abott, sculptor Thomas Waldo Story, scientist Frederic Anton Eilers, and health and criminal law writer John Ordronaux. 10.28.1991

Roslyn Gristmill
1347 Old Northern Boulevard. Colonial frame gristmill built 1715-41; converted for use as teahouse 1916. Multiple Resources of the Village of Roslyn. 10.02.1986

Roslyn National Bank & Trust Company
1432 Old Northern Boulevard. Neoclassical brick former bank with Tuscan portico; designed by William B. Tubby; built 1931. Multiple Resources of the Village of Roslyn. 10.02.1986

Roslyn Savings Bank
1400 Old Northern Boulevard. Georgian Revival brick bank designed by Alfred C. Shaknis; built 1932. Multiple Resources of the Village of Roslyn. 10.02.1986

Roslyn Village Historic District
(Main Street Historic District Expansion) Central historic core of village, with 81 buildings, mostly 19th-century residential and commercial structures including numerous Federal and Greek Revival frame buildings. Includes Main Street Historic District (individually listed). Notable properties include Georgian Revival Bryant Library (1920-21, Hoppin & Koen) and Georgian Revival Roslyn Presbyterian Church (1928, William B. Tubby). Multiple Resources of the Village of Roslyn. 04.15.1987

Willet Titus House
1441 Old Northern Boulevard. Italianate frame residence built c.1860 for local stove and metalware merchant. Multiple Resources of the Village of Roslyn. 10.02.1986

Trinity Church
Northern Boulevard and Church Street. Small brick church and parish house with eclectic English medieval features; designed by McKim,

Mead & White; built 1906-09. Multiple Resources of the Village of Roslyn. 10.02.1986

Samuel Adams Warner Estate Cottage
One Railroad Avenue. Victorian frame residence with Swiss Chalet style decorative features; designed by Samuel Adams Warner; built 1875 as part of the architect's estate. Now a restaurant. Multiple Resources of the Village of Roslyn. 10.02.1986

Roslyn Harbor

Cedarmere–Clayton Estates
Bryant Avenue and Northern Boulevard. Two contiguous estates on Hempstead Harbor. Cedarmere: 7-acre estate of poet and editor William Cullen Bryant with landscape designed by Frederick Law Olmsted in 1850s, 18th-century farmhouse enlarged in Colonial Revival style, and Gothic Revival mill (c.1850). Clayton: 165-acre estate of editor Lloyd Stephens Bryce and industrialist Henry Clay Frick with large Georgian Revival residence designed by Ogden Codman, Jr. (1899-1901; remodeled 1919 by Sir Charles Allom), formal and informal landscape features designed by Marian Coffin (1920s), large Neoclassical trellis designed by Milliken & Nevin, Gothic Revival Dewey Cottage (1860s, Frederick Copley), and several secondary buildings. Clayton now operated as art museum. 09.29.1986

Roslyn Heights

Roslyn House
Lincoln Avenue and Roslyn Road. A 2-story Italianate frame building built c.1870 as hotel; restored 1980s for commercial use. 06.07.1990

Saddle Rock

Saddle Rock Gristmill
Grist Mill Lane and Little Neck Bay. A 2 1/2-story timber-framed, shingled gristmill with gambrel roof; built 1715. Museum. Long Island Wind and Tide Mills Thematic Resources. 12.27.1978

Sea Cliff

House at 207 Carpenter Avenue
Queen Anne frame residence with 2-story porte cochere; built c.1885. Sea Cliff Summer Resort Thematic Resources. 02.18.1988

House at 115 Central Avenue
Large Stick Style frame residence with elaborate decorative trim; built 1890 by local butcher Oliver Combs as summer boardinghouse. Sea Cliff Summer Resort Thematic Resources. 02.18.1988

Central Hall
93 Central Avenue. A 2-story Victorian building designed 1894 by Fred Maidinent as dry goods

store and meeting hall. Sea Cliff Summer Resort Thematic Resources. 02.18.1988

Crowell House
375 Littleworth Lane. Second Empire concrete residence built 1871 as summer house. Sea Cliff Summer Resort Thematic Resources. 02.18.1988

House at 52 18th Avenue
Victorian frame residence built 1895 as summer house. Sea Cliff Summer Resort Thematic Resources. 02.18.1988

House at 58 18th Avenue
Victorian frame residence built 1893 as summer boardinghouse. Sea Cliff Summer Resort Thematic Resources. 02.18.1988

House at 290 Eighth Avenue
Victorian frame residence built c.1885 as summer boardinghouse. Sea Cliff Summer Resort Thematic Resources. 02.18.1988

House at 332 Franklin Avenue
Queen Anne frame residence built 1888 as summer boardinghouse. Sea Cliff Summer Resort Thematic Resources. 02.18.1988

House at 285 Glen Avenue
Large Second Empire frame residence with 3-story tower; designed by Theodore P. Edwards; built c.1885. Sea Cliff Summer Resort Thematic Resources. 02.18.1988

House at 378 Glen Avenue
Victorian frame residence with 2-story porch; built c.1886 as summer boardinghouse. Sea Cliff Summer Resort Thematic Resources. 02.18.1988

House at 9 Locust Place
Large Queen Anne frame residence built c.188o as summer house. Sea Cliff Summer Resort Thematic Resources. 02.18.1988

House at 19 Locust Place
Large Shingle Style/Queen Anne frame residence with 3-story corner tower; built 1893 as summer house. Sea Cliff Summer Resort Thematic Resources. 02.18.1988

House at 137 Prospect Avenue
Victorian frame residence with 3-story corner tower; built c.1870 as summer house. Sea Cliff Summer Resort Thematic Resources. 02.18.1988

House at 176 Prospect Avenue
Queen Anne frame residence with 3-story corner tower; built 1886. Sea Cliff Summer Resort Thematic Resources. 02.18.1988

House at 195 Prospect Avenue
Queen Anne frame residence built 1890 as summer house. Sea Cliff Summer Resort Thematic Resources. 02.18.1988

House at 199 Prospect Avenue
Queen Anne frame residence built 1890 as summer house. Sea Cliff Summer Resort Thematic Resources. 09.21.1988

93

Ansonia Hotel, New York (p. 94).

House at 103 Roslyn Avenue
Large Queen Anne frame residence built 1884
by local builder W. A. Smith as summer house.
Sea Cliff Summer Resort Thematic Resources.
02.18.1988

St. Luke's Episcopal Church
253 Glen Street. Victorian frame church
designed by Sibell & Miller; built 1892-94.
Sea Cliff Summer Resort Thematic Resources.
02.18.1988

House at 112 Sea Cliff Avenue
Queen Anne frame residence built 1884 as
parsonage; corner tower added 1887. Sea Cliff
Summer Resort Thematic Resources.
02.18.1988

House at 240 Sea Cliff Avenue
Victorian frame residence built 1888 as
parsonage. Sea Cliff Summer Resort Thematic
Resources. 02.18.1988

House at 285 Sea Cliff Avenue
Italianate residence designed 1884 by Richard
S. Pearsall as summer house. Sea Cliff Summer
Resort Thematic Resources. 02.18.1988

House at 362 Sea Cliff Avenue
Second Empire frame residence built c.1875
as summer boardinghouse. Sea Cliff Summer
Resort Thematic Resources.
02.18.1988

Sea Cliff Railroad Station
Sea Cliff Avenue, Glen Cove. Small Victorian
brick railroad passenger station built 1868.
Sea Cliff Summer Resort Thematic Resources.
02.18.1988

House at 18 17th Avenue
Queen Anne frame residence with 3-story
corner tower; designed by Richard S. Pearsall;
built 1890. Adjacent carriage house. Sea Cliff
Summer Resort Thematic Resources.
02.18.1988

House at 173 16th Avenue
Victorian frame residence built c.1880 as

summer house. Sea Cliff Summer Resort
Thematic Resources. 02.18.1988

House at 65 20th Avenue
Victorian frame residence built 1893 as carriage
house; converted to summer house c.1900. Sea
Cliff Summer Resort Thematic Resources.
02.18.1988

Upper Brookville

Planting Fields Arboretum (State Historic Park)
Planting Fields Road, west of Oyster Bay.
A 409-acre former estate with formal and
educational gardens, lawns with specimen trees,
winding roadways, open fields, woods, and
large residence and outbuildings. Structures
include Jacobean Revival stone residence
(1920, Walker & Gillette), greenhouse and
superintendent's house (Guy Lowell), Car-
shalton Gates (18th-century iron gates from
Sussex, England), stable complex, and other
outbuildings. Estate developed in early 20th
century for James Byrne family and expanded
after 1913 by investor William Robertson
Coe. Now a public/private arboretum.
01.25.1979

Valley Stream

Pagan-Fletcher House
17 Hendrickson Avenue. Vernacular frame
residence built c.1840; enlarged 1847 and
extensively remodeled c.1900-16 in Colonial
Revival style. 09.08.1983

Wantagh

Wantagh Railroad Complex
1700 Wantagh Avenue. Small Victorian frame
passenger station built 1885. Adjacent railroad
parlor car "Jamaica" built 1912 by
Pennsylvania Railroad for Long Island
Railroad. 06.30.1983

NEW YORK COUNTY

New York

Admiral's House
Governors Island. Large Greek Revival brick
residence with 2-story Doric porticoes; built
1840 as commanding general's quarters on
United States Army military fortification.
07.24.1972

Alwyn Court Apartments
180 West 58th Street. A 12-story French
Renaissance style building with elaborate terra-
cotta decoration; designed by Harde & Short;
built 1907-09 as luxury apartment building.
12.26.1976

Ambrose
Pier 16, East River. A 135-foot-long steel-
hulled lightship built 1907 by New York
Shipbuilding Corporation for United States
Lighthouse Service as floating navigational
guide in New York Harbor. 09.07.1984;
NHL 04.11.1989

American Fine Arts Society
215 West 57th Street. A 4-story French
Renaissance style limestone building designed
by Henry J. Hardenbergh with Walter C.
Hunting and John C. Jacobsen; built 1891-92
to provide facilities and exhibitions for Society
of American Artists, Architectural League, and
Art Students League. Now Art Students
League. 05.06.1980

American Museum of Natural History
Central Park West and 77th Street.
Monumental museum complex of 22
connected buildings on 23-acre parcel
overlooking Central Park. Includes Victorian
Gothic brick original building (1874-77, Vaux
& Mould), Romanesque Revival south wing

(1889-97, Cady, Berg & See), central core (1900, Cady, Berg & See), power station and west wing (1903 and 1908, Charles Volz), additions by Trowbridge & Livingston (1922, 1927, 1931-33), Classical Revival Roosevelt Memorial Hall (1929, John Russell Pope), and modern additions. Museum founded 1874; one of the world's outstanding repositories of natural and cultural artifacts. 06.24.1976

American Radiator Building
40-52 West 40th Street. A 23-story Gothic-inspired black brick skyscraper with gold terra-cotta trim; designed by Hood & Fouilhoux; built 1923-24; 5-story addition in 1936-37 designed by J. André Fouilhoux. 05.07.1980

American Stock Exchange
86 Trinity Place. Headquarters of second-largest United States securities exchange, begun as outdoor "Curb Exchange." Present building is 14-story Art Deco enlargement (1929-31, Starrett & Van Vleck) of building erected 1921. NHL 06.02.1978

Ansonia Hotel
2101-2119 Broadway. Massive 17-story Beaux-Arts limestone and terra-cotta apartment-hotel; designed by Paul E. M. Duboy; built 1899-1904 by capitalist William Earl Dodge Stokes. Well-known residence for musicians, authors, and theatrical performers. 01.10.1980 ILLUS. P. 93

Apartment Buildings at 131-135 East 66th Street and 130-134 East 67th Street
Two 11-story Italian Renaissance style luxury apartment buildings. 131-135 East 66th Street designed by Charles A. Platt; built 1905. 130-134 East 67th Street designed by Rossiter & Wright; built 1907. 08.11.1982

Apollo Theater
253 West 125th Street. Large theater with terra-cotta trim; designed by George Keister; built 1913-14 as burlesque house-theater; since 1934 one of the premier performance halls for African-American entertainers. 11.17.1983

Appellate Division Courthouse of New York State
27 Madison Avenue. Italian Renaissance style marble building with Corinthian portico; designed by James Brown Lord; built 1896-99. Significant exterior sculpture and interior murals. 07.26.1982

Apthorp Apartments
2201-2219 Broadway. Large 12-story Italian Renaissance style building with elaborate ornamentation and courtyard; designed by Clinton & Russell; built 1906-08. 01.30.1978

Chester A. Arthur House
123 Lexington Avenue. A 5-story Victorian brownstone townhouse built 1881-86; later altered. Home of President Chester A. Arthur and location of his 1881 swearing-in ceremony. NHL 01.12.1965

Association of the Bar of the City of New York
42 West 44th Street. A 5-story Neoclassical limestone clubhouse designed by Cyrus L. W. Eidlitz; built 1895. 01.03.1980

Association Residence Nursing Home
891 Amsterdam Avenue. Large 3-story French Renaissance style building designed by Richard Morris Hunt; built 1881-83 for Association for the Relief of Respectable Aged Indigent Females; 1907-08 addition designed by Charles A. Rich. Converted for use as American Youth Hostel. 02.20.1975

Astor Row Houses
8-62 West 130th Street. Group of 28 three-story Eastlake brick rowhouses designed by Charles Buek; built 1880-83. 08.11.1982

Audubon Terrace Historic District
Bounded by Broadway, Riverside Drive, and West 155th and 156th streets. Group of 8 3- and 4-story Italian Renaissance style stone institutional buildings and landscaped terrace mostly designed by Charles P. Huntington; built 1907-30 as center for specialized research by founder Archer M. Huntington. Includes Hispanic Society, American Geographical Society (former), Museum of the American Indian, and Church of Our Lady of Esperanza. Also includes American Academy of Arts and Letters, and National Institute of Arts and Letters; designed by William M. Kendall and Cass Gilbert. 05.30.1980

Bailey House
10 St. Nicholas Place. Large 3-story Queen Anne/Romanesque Revival stone residence designed by Samuel B. Reed; built 1886-88 for James Anthony Bailey of Barnum and Bailey Circus. 04.23.1980

George F. Baker, Sr. and Jr. Residences
67, 69, and 75 East 93rd Street. Three Federal Revival brick residences and courtyard designed by Delano & Aldrich. First residence built 1917-18 for Francis F. Palmer; later additions. Ballroom wing, garage apartment, and townhouse built 1928-31 for bankers George F. Baker, Sr. and Jr. Number 75 now Synod of the Bishops of the Russian Orthodox Church Outside of Russia. 06.03.1982

Barbizon Hotel for Women (Barbizon Hotel)
140 East 63rd Street. A 23-story brick hotel with sandstone and terra-cotta trim and eclectic blend of Italian Renaissance, Gothic, and Islamic-style decorative elements; designed by Murgatroyd & Ogden; built 1927 as residence for young women. 10.29.1982

Battery Park Control House
State Street and Battery Place. Small Italian Renaissance style/eclectic brick and limestone subway control house designed by Heins & LaFarge; completed 1905. Interborough Rapid Transit Subway Control Houses Thematic Resources. 05.06.1980

Bayard-Condict Building
65-69 Bleecker Street. A 12-story office building with elaborate terra-cotta facade; designed by Louis Sullivan; built 1897-99. NHL 12.08.1976

Beacon Theater and Hotel
2124 Broadway. Large brick and stone hotel/theater complex with 24-story and 15-story hotel blocks and 3-story theater block; lavish theater lobby, rotunda, and auditorium in eclectic Rococo, Renaissance, and Moorish styles; designed by Walter W. Ahlschlager; built 1927-28 by Chanin Construction Co. 11.04.1982

Bell Telephone Laboratories
463 West Street. A 13-story concrete and steel commercial building complex built 1896-98 to house laboratory facilities of Western Electric Co. From 1898 to 1966 home of Bell Telephone Laboratories, pioneer industrial research institute. Converted to apartments. NHL 05.15.1975

Bellevue Hospital, R & S Building
492 First Avenue. A 6-story Italian Renaissance style brick institutional building designed by Charles F. McKim of McKim, Mead & White; built 1903-12 as Pathological Department and Male Dormitory for Bellevue Hospital. 09.22.1986

Belnord Apartments
225 West 86th Street. Massive 13-story Italian Renaissance style brick and stone apartment building with central courtyard; designed 1908 by H. Hobart Weekes. 04.23.1980

Bialystoker Synagogue
7-13 Willett Street. Small late Federal masonry building built 1826 as Willett Street Methodist Episcopal Church; synagogue since 1905. 04.26.1972

Blackwell House
Roosevelt Island. Modest 2-story frame residence built c.1800 for Blackwell family, owners of Blackwell Island (later Welfare Island, now Roosevelt Island) from late 17th to early 19th century. 02.25.1972

The Block House
Governors Island. A 2-story, 5-bay Greek Revival residence designed by Martin E. Thompson; completed 1843 as quarters for commanding general of United States military fortification. 07.24.1972

Bouwerie Lane Theater
330 Bowery. A 5-story Second Empire cast-iron-front building designed 1874 by Henry Engelbert as Bond Street Bank. 04.23.1980

Bowery Savings Bank
130 Bowery. Large Neoclassical bank with Roman temple front; designed by McKim, Mead & White; built 1893. Sculpture in pediment by Frederick MacMonnies. Elaborate interior entrance hall and main banking room. 04.23.1980

Bowling Green Fence and Park
Broadway and Beaver Street. Elliptical park planned 1733 as bowling green; present iron fence installed 1770. Site of equestrian statue of George III which was pulled down in revolt against British on July 9, 1776. Numerous later alterations and restorations. 04.09.1980

Brooklyn Bridge (see Kings County)

Building at 361 Broadway
A 6-story Victorian cast-iron-front commercial building with columned bays and geometric and floral ornamentation; designed by W. Wheeler Smith; built 1881-82 for James L. Smith. 09.15.1983

James Brown House
326 Spring Street. Federal frame residence with gambrel roof, brick veneer facade, and ground-floor shop; built 1817; storefront remodeled early 20th century.   08.11.1983

Candler Building
220 West 42nd Street and 221 West 41st Street. A 24-story skyscraper with late Gothic and early Renaissance style white terra-cotta ornamentation; designed by Willauer, Shape & Bready; built 1912-14.   07.08.1982

Andrew Carnegie Mansion
(Cooper-Hewitt Museum)
2 East 91st Street. Monumental 3 1/2-story Beaux-Arts/Georgian Revival stone and brick residence designed by Babb, Cook & Willard; built 1900-01 for steel magnate and philanthropist. Adapted for use as Cooper-Hewitt Museum.   NHL 11.13.1966

Carnegie Hall
Seventh Avenue, 56th to 57th streets. A 6-story Second Renaissance Revival brick building containing one of America's premier concert halls; designed by William B. Tuthill; built 1889-91 with funds from Andrew Carnegie; several major additions and alterations. NHL 12.29.1962

Cary Building
105-107 Chambers Street. A 5-story Italianate building with identical cast-iron facades fronting 2 streets; designed by King & Kellum; facades fabricated by D. D. Badger's Architectural Iron Works; built 1856-57 as dry goods store of Cary, Howard & Sanger. One of the earliest and most important surviving cast-iron-front commercial buildings.   09.15.1983

Casa Italiana
1151-1161 Amsterdam Avenue. A 6-story Italian Renaissance style limestone building designed by William M. Kendall of McKim, Mead & White; built 1926-27 as center for Italian studies at Columbia University. 10.29.1982

Castle Clinton National Monument
Battery Park. Massive circular sandstone fort designed by Lieutenant Colonel Jonathan Williams with John McComb, Jr.; built 1808-11 on artificial island to defend New York Harbor; later converted for use as entertainment center (Castle Garden), immigration center, then aquarium, and most recently visitors center for National Park Service.   08.12.1946

Castle Williams
Governors Island. Massive 200-foot-diameter, 3-story circular sandstone military fortress designed by Lieutenant Colonel Jonathan Williams; built 1807-11 to defend waterway between Governors Island and New York City. 07.31.1972

Central Park
Bounded by Central Park South, Fifth Avenue, Central Park West, and 110th Street. An 840-acre park designed by Frederick Law Olmsted and Calvert Vaux; developed 1857-73. Considered one of America's premier naturalistic landscapes. Notable features from original design include Bethesda Fountain and Terrace, The Ramble, Belvedere Castle, Ladies Pavilion, the Mall, the Dairy, and numerous bridges, sculptures, entrance gates, and artificial lakes. NHL 05.23.1963

Central Park West Historic District
Central Park West between 61st and 97th streets. Linear district with approximately 40 late 19th- and early 20th-century luxury apartment buildings and other buildings overlooking Central Park. Notable buildings include Art Deco Century Apartments (1931, Irwin S. Chanin), Viennese Secession inspired New York Society for Ethical Culture (1910, Robert D. Kohn), Neoclassical Ethical Culture School (1902, Carrère & Hastings), Beaux-Arts Prasada Apartments (1907, Romeyn & Wynne), Gothic Revival Holy Trinity Lutheran Church (1903, Schickel & Ditmars), Art Deco 55 Central Park West apartments (1929, Schwartz & Cross), Neoclassical Second Church of Christ Scientist (1898, Frederick R. Comstock), Classical Revival Congregation Shearith Israel Synagogue (1892, Brunner & Tryon), Art Deco Majestic Apartments (1930, Irwin S. Chanin), Dakota Apartments (individually listed), Beaux-Arts Langham Apartments (1905, Clinton & Russell), Italian Renaissance style San Remo Apartments (1930, Emery Roth), Beaux-Arts Kenilworth Apartments (1908, Townsend, Sleinle & Hakell), Gothic Revival Universalist Church (1898, William A. Potter), Classical Revival New-York Historical Society (1908, York & Sawyer; 1938 addition, Walker & Gillette), American Museum of Natural History (individually listed), and Italian Renaissance style Beresford Apartments (1929, Emery Roth).   11.09.1982

Central Savings Bank
2100-2108 Broadway. Large 6-story Italian Renaissance style stone bank with elaborate exterior and interior ornamentation; designed by Benjamin Moscowitz of York & Sawyer; built 1926-28. Ironwork by Samuel Yellin. 09.08.1983

Central Synagogue
646-652 Lexington Avenue. Moorish-style eclectic stone synagogue with highly decorative exterior and interior finishes; designed by Henry Fernback; built 1871-72.   10.09.1970; NHL 05.15.1975

Century Association Building
5-7 West 43rd Street. A 4-story Italian Renaissance style building with ornate terra-cotta and brick facade; designed by McKim, Mead & White; built 1889-91.   07.15.1982

Chanin Building
122 East 42nd Street. A 56-story Art Deco brick skyscraper with limestone, terra cotta, and bronze ornamentation; designed by Irwin S. Chanin with Sloan & Robertson; sculptural decoration by René Chambellan with Jacques Delamarre; built 1927-29 by Chanin Construction Co. to serve as Chanin headquarters. 04.23.1980

Chapel of the Good Shepherd
Roosevelt Island. Victorian Gothic brick church designed by Frederick C. Withers; built 1888-89.   03.16.1972

Chapel of the Intercession Complex and Trinity Cemetery
550 West 155th Street. A 23-acre property with limestone church, cloister, parish house, and vicarage in English Gothic style (1910-14, Bertram G. Goodhue), and large cemetery with gates and walls (1881, Calvert Vaux). Cemetery includes graves of notable New Yorkers and distinctive monuments and mausoleums. 07.24.1980

House at 131 Charles Street
Late Federal brick townhouse built 1834 by builder and stonecutter David Christie. 11.03.1972

Charlton-King-Vandam Historic District
Roughly bounded by Varick, Vandam, MacDougal, and King streets. Small residential neighborhood of distinctive 2 1/2- to 3-story Federal and Greek Revival brick townhouses and rowhouses built from early 1820s to 1840s.   07.20.1973

Chelsea Historic District
Roughly bounded by West 19th and 23rd streets, and Eighth and Tenth avenues. Large residential neighborhood planned and developed on estate of Clement Clarke Moore 1835-65, with mostly 3-story Greek Revival and Italianate brick rowhouses with deep front gardens. Also includes Gothic

Central Synagogue, New York.

Revival St. Peter's Church (1836-38), and Gothic Revival West Hall (1836) and Collegiate Gothic main buildings (1883-1900, Charles C. Haight) of General Theological Seminary.   12.06.1977; BOUNDARY INCREASE 12.16.1982

Christodora House
147 Avenue B. A 16-story Art Deco.Colonial Revival brick building designed by Henry C. Pelton; built 1928 as settlement house. 03.20.1986

Chrysler Building
405 Lexington Avenue. A 77-story Art Deco skyscraper with enameled gray, white, and black brick exterior and trim of marble, granite, and steel; designed by William Van Alen; built 1928-30. Monument to the "Machine Age." NHL 12.08.1976

Church Missions House
281 Park Avenue South. A 6-story Flemish Revival limestone building designed by Robert W. Gibson and Edward J. Neville Stent; built 1892-94 to house Domestic and Foreign Missionary Society of Protestant Episcopal Church.   06.03.1982

Church of the Ascension
36-38 Fifth Avenue. Gothic Revival stone church designed by Richard Upjohn; built 1840-41; chancel designed 1888 by Stanford White; stained-glass windows and mural by John LaFarge; altar relief by Augustus Saint-Gaudens.   NHL 12.23.1987

Church of the Holy Apostles
300 Ninth Avenue. Gothic Revival/Italianate brick church with Italian Renaissance style interior; designed by Minard Lafever; built 1846-48; windows by William Jay Bolton; later alterations and additions, some designed by Richard Upjohn.   04.26.1972

Church of the Holy Communion and Buildings
656-662 Sixth Avenue. Gothic Revival brownstone church designed by Richard Upjohn; built 1844-46; chapel designed 1879 by Charles C. Haight or Richard M. Upjohn; adjacent Sister's House (1854), parish house (c.1853), and rectory (c.1853) designed by Richard Upjohn. No longer in use as church. 04.17.1980

Church of the Immaculate Conception and Clergy Houses
406-414 East 14th Street. A 3-story brick and stone church and clergy houses with French Gothic style features; designed 1894 by Barncy & Chapman; built as Grace Episcopal Chapel. 03.28.1980

Church of the Incarnation and Parish House
205-209 Madison Avenue. Gothic Revival brownstone church and rectory designed 1864 by Emlen T. Littell; church altered and enlarged 1882 by D. & J. Jardine; Jacobean Revival rectory facade designed 1905 by Edward P. Casey. Church interior contains Montgomery Memorial (1876, Henry Hobson Richardson

and Augustus Saint-Gaudens); stained-glass windows by John LaFarge, Louis Comfort Tiffany, and others; and murals by John LaFarge.   07.08.1982

Church of Notre Dame and Rectory
405 West 114th Street and 40 Morningside Drive. Stone church in French Classical style; designed by Daus & Otto; built 1909-10; enlargement and Italian Renaissance style rectory designed 1913-14 by Cross & Cross. 05.06.1980

Church of St. Ignatius Loyola Complex
Park Avenue, 83rd to 84th streets. Italian Renaissance style limestone church (1895-1900, William Schickel) with elaborately decorated interior, parish house (1882), St. Ignatius Loyola School (1908, Schickel & Ditmars), Regis High School (1913-17, Maginnis & Walsh), and Loyola School (1901). 07.24.1980

Church of St. Mary the Virgin Complex
145 West 46th Street. French Gothic style limestone-clad, steel-framed church and 3 dependencies; designed by Napoleon LeBrun & Sons; built 1894-95. Notable decorative features including exterior statuary by J. Massey Rhind.   04.16.1990

Church of St. Paul the Apostle
415 West 59th Street. Large granite church in French Gothic style designed by Jeremiah O'Rourke; built 1876-85. Interior features and windows designed by Stanford White, John LaFarge, Frederick MacMonnies, and others. 12.5.1991

Church of St. Vincent Ferrer and Priory
869 and 871 Lexington Avenue. Gothic Revival stone church designed by Bertram G. Goodhue; built 1914-18. Adjoining High Victorian Gothic brick priory designed by William Schickel; built 1880-81.   06.14.1984

Church of the Transfiguration
25 Mott Street. Georgian vernacular stone church built 1801 as English Zion Lutheran Church; Gothic windows added 1815; octagonal tower and cupola added c.1860. 04.16.1980

Church of the Transfiguration and Rectory
(The Little Church Around the Corner)
One East 29th Street. Gothic Revival brick church with sandstone trim; built 1849; later additions and alterations; Edwin Booth memorial window by John LaFarge; Otis Skinner memorial plaque by Paul Manship; lych-gate (1896) designed by Frederick C. Withers. Known as the Actor's Church. 06.04.1973

City and Suburban Homes Company's First Avenue Estate Historic District
First Avenue and East 64th and 65th streets. Block-long complex of thirteen 6-story brick apartment buildings designed by James E. Ware and Philip Ohm; built 1898-1915 as model tenements.   08.01.1986

City Hall
Broadway and Chambers Street. Monumental limestone building in Federal form with French Classical decorative detail and notable interior spaces including domed rotunda; designed by Joseph F. Mangin and John McComb, Jr.; built 1803-11; interior restored early 20th century by Grosvenor Atterbury; exterior marble facades replaced 1950s with limestone. NHL 12.19.1960

City Hospital
Roosevelt Island. Large 4 1/2-story Second Empire granite building designed by James Renwick, Jr.; built 1858-70.   03.16.1972

City Pier A
South end of Battery Place at Hudson River. A 285-foot-long 2- to 3-story brick and iron-clad pier with 4-story clock tower; designed by G. S. Greene, Jr., Engineer-in-Chief, New York City Department of Docks; built 1885-86 as headquarters of agencies regulating New York City waterfront; extended early 20th century. 06.27.1975

Civic Club
243 East 34th Street. A 3 1/2-story Beaux-Arts limestone and brick building designed by Thomas A. Gray; commissioned by social reformer Frederick Norton Goddard; built 1898-99.   09.16.1982

Claremont Stable
(Claremont Riding Academy)
173-177 West 89th Street. A 4-story masonry building with Romanesque and Flemish-style decorative features; designed by Frank A. Rooke; built 1892 to house carriages and horses of nearby residents. Remains in use as stables.   04.16.1980

College of the City of New York
Bounded by Amsterdam Avenue, St. Nicholas Terrace, and West 138th and 140th streets. An 8-acre landscaped campus with complex of 6 Collegiate Gothic stone buildings with terra cotta decorative features; designed by George B. Post & Sons; original 5 buildings, elaborate entrance gates, and landscape features built 1898-1908; School of Technology building built 1929-30.   09.07.1984

Congregation B'nai Jeshurun and Community House
257 West 88th Street and 270 West 89th Street. Granite synagogue with Middle Eastern and Moorish-style decorative features and ornate auditorium; designed by Walter S. Schneider and Henry B. Herts; built 1916-18. Adjacent Community House designed 1926 by Henry I. Herts and Louis Allen Abramson.   06.02.198

Control House on 72nd Street
West 72nd Street and Broadway. Italian Renaissance style/eclectic brick and limestone subway control house designed by Heins & LaFarge; completed 1904. Interborough Rapid Transit Subway Control Houses Thematic Resources.   05.06.1980

Chrysler Building (center), New York.

Will Marion Cook House
221 West 138th Street. A 3-story Georgian Revival brick townhouse built 1891. Residence of African-American musician, composer, and conductor Will Marion Cook from 1918 until his death in 1944.   NHL 05.11.1976

Cooper Union
Cooper Square, Seventh Street, and Fourth Avenue. A 7-story Italianate brownstone building designed by Frederick A. Peterson; built 1859 for Peter Cooper as school offering free education in manual arts. First building in United States to use rolled steel beams. Site of 1860 speech by Abraham Lincoln on slavery issue that brought him national attention. NHL 07.04.1961

Croton Aqueduct Gate House
135th Street and Convent Avenue. A 2-story Romanesque Revival stone building designed by Frederick S. Cook; built 1884-90 to regulate water flow into New York City from New Croton Aqueduct.   09.22.1983

Lucy Drexel Dahlgren Residence
15 East 96th Street. A 5 1/2-story Classical Revival limestone townhouse with French Renaissance decorative details; designed by Ogden Codman, Jr.; built 1915-16. 07.20.1989

Daily News Building
220 East 42nd Street. A 36-story Art Deco white and black brick skyscraper and attached 9-story printing plant designed by Raymond Hood; built 1929-30.   11.14.1982; NHL 06.29.1989

Dakota Apartments
One West 72nd Street. A 10-story Renaissance Revival brick apartment building with elaborate stone and terra-cotta decorative ornamentation; designed by Henry J. Hardenbergh; built 1880-84. One of the earliest large-scale apartment houses.   04.26.1972; NHL 12.08.1976

DeLamar Mansion (Polish Consulate General)
233 Madison Avenue. Large 4-story Beaux-Arts limestone residence designed by C. P. H. Gilbert; built 1902-05 for mining magnate Joseph R. DeLamar. Later headquarters of National Democratic Club. 08.25.1983

DeVinne Press Building
393-399 Lafayette Street. A 7-story Romanesque Revival brick commercial building designed by Babb, Cook & Willard; built 1885. 09.14.1977

Dorilton
171 West 71st Street. A 10-story Beaux-Arts brick luxury apartment building with elaborate limestone and terra-cotta ornamentation; designed by Janes & Leo; built 1900-02. 09.08.1983

Adelaide L. T. Douglas House
57 Park Avenue. A 6-story Beaux-Arts granite and limestone townhouse in Louis XVI style; designed by Horace Trumbauer; built 1909-11. 07.15.1982

James B. Duke Mansion
(New York University Institute of Fine Arts) One East 78th Street. A 3-story limestone townhouse in Louis XVI style; designed by Horace Trumbauer; built 1909-12 for president of American Tobacco Co.   11.10.1977

Duke Residence
1009 Fifth Avenue. A 6-story Beaux-Arts brick and limestone townhouse designed by Alexander M. Welch of Welch, Smith & Provot; built 1899-1901 on speculation by builders W. W. and T. H. Hall. Home of Duke family of American Tobacco Co.   12.07.1989

Dunbar Apartments
Bounded by Seventh and Eighth avenues and West 149th and 150th streets. A 1-block complex of six 5- and 6-story brick apartment buildings clustered around interior courtyard; designed by Andrew J. Thomas; built 1926-28; financed by John D. Rockefeller, Jr. as first cooperative apartments for African-Americans. Contains Matthew Henson Residence (individually listed). 03.29.1979

William Dyckman House
4881 Broadway. A 1 1/2-story Dutch Colonial stone and brick residence with gambrel roof; built 1783 by William Dyckman. Only remaining 18th-century farmhouse in Manhattan. Museum.   NHL 12.24.1967

House at 37 East Fourth Street
Greek Revival brick townhouse built 1845 for businessman Samuel Treadwell Skidmore. 01.03.1980

Houses at 326, 328, and 330 East 18th Street
Group of 3 modest Italianate brick rowhouses with elaborate 1st-story cast-iron verandas and entrance canopies; built 1853. 09.30.1982

House at 203 East 29th Street
Modest 3 1/2-story vernacular frame residence with gambrel roof; built c.1790. Adjacent late 19th-century brick carriage house. 07.08.1982

Houses at 311 and 313 East 58th Street
Two modest Italianate brick residences built c.1857.   11.14.1982

Building at 45 East 66th Street
A 10-story brick luxury apartment building with elaborate French Renaissance and Gothic-style terra-cotta ornamentation; designed by Harde & Short; built 1906-08.   05.06.1980

Rowhouses at 322-344 East 69th Street
Group of twelve 3-story Victorian brownstone rowhouses with Neo-Grec decoration; designed by Jacob Valentine and William R. Smith; built 1879-80. 09.07.1984

East 73rd Street Historic District
161-179 and 166-182 East 73rd Street. Group of eleven 2- to 3-story eclectic brick carriage houses built late 19th to early 20th centuries for owners of nearby mansions. Architects include William Schickel, Charles W. Romeyn, Richard Morris Hunt, and Hobart Walker. Also includes 2 Italianate rowhouses, commercial stable, and Beaux-Arts commercial garage (1906). 07.22.1982

Houses at 157, 159, 161, and 163-165 East 78th Street
Row of 5 modest 2-story Italianate brick rowhouses built 1861; stoops removed and other alterations in early-20th century. 03.25.1980

Houses at 208-218 East 78th Street
Group of six 3-story Italianate brick rowhouses built 1861-65 by Warren and Ransom Beman and John Buckley. 06.30.1983

Houses at 116-130 East 80th Street
Row of 4 large 4-story Georgian Revival/Federal Revival brick and stone townhouses built for prominent New Yorkers, including Lewis Spencer Morris, George Whitney, Clarence Dillon, and Vincent Astor. Numbers 116 (1922-23) and 120 (1929-30) designed by Cross & Cross. Numbers 124 (1930) and 130 (1927-28) designed by Mott B. Schmidt. 03.26.1980

Houses at 146-156 East 89th Street
Row of 6 Queen Anne brick townhouses designed by Hubert, Pirsson & Co.; built 1886-87. 06.03.1982

Houses at 120 and 122 East 92nd Street
Two 3-story Italianate frame townhouses. Number 120 built 1859. Number 122 built 1871. 10.29.1982

Eldridge Street Synagogue (Congregation K'hal Adath Jeshurun with Anshe Lubtz)
12-16 Eldridge Street. Imposing synagogue with ornate Romanesque, Gothic, and Moorish-style brick and terra-cotta facade and elaborate interior; designed by Herter Brothers, architects; built 1886-87. Headquarters of the Eldridge Street Project. 03.28.1980

Edward Kennedy "Duke" Ellington Residence
935 St. Nicholas Avenue, Apartment 4A. A 6-story early 20th-century brick apartment building with Gothic-style ornamentation. Apartment 4A home to composer and musician Duke Ellington 1939-61.   NHL 05.11.1976

Emigrant Industrial Savings Bank
51 Chambers Street. A 14-story Beaux-Arts limestone former bank building with twin towers and exuberant exterior and interior decorative features; designed by Raymond F. Almirall; built 1909-12. 02.25.1982

Empire State Building
350 Fifth Avenue. Monumental 102-story Art Deco limestone skyscraper with tall aluminum, chrome-nickel-steel, and glass mast; designed by Shreve, Lamb & Harmon; built 1930-31 on speculation for General Motors executive John J. Raskob. Final and most celebrated product of the skyscraper building boom of the 1920s. 11.17.1982; NHL 06.24.1986

Equitable Building
120 Broadway. A 40-story full-block

Renaissance Revival skyscraper faced with brick, limestone, granite, and terra-cotta; designed by Ernest R. Graham of Daniel H. Burnham & Co.; built 1914-15; served 1915-24 as home office of nationally important insurance company, Equitable Life Assurance Society.   NHL 06.02.1978

Federal Hall National Memorial
Wall and Nassau streets. Large Greek Revival stone temple-form building with Doric portico; originally designed by Town & Davis with major redesign by Samuel Thomson, John Frazee, and others; completed 1842 as United States Custom House; converted 1862 as Subtreasury Building. Statue of George Washington in front of building by John Q. A. Ward; dedicated 1883. Site of original Federal Hall, nation's first capital, and location of 1789 inauguration of George Washington as first president. Museum.   05.26.1939

Federal Office Building
641 Washington Street. Massive 10-story Romanesque Revival brick warehouse with elements of "Chicago School"; designed by Willoughby J. Edbrooke, William Martin Aiken, and James Knox Taylor; built 1892-99 as United States Appraisers' Warehouse; remodeled 1938 and now apartments.
08.30.1974

Federal Reserve Bank of New York
33 Liberty Street. Massive 14-story Italian Renaissance style limestone and sandstone bank building designed by York & Sawyer; built 1919-24; exterior metalwork by Samuel Yellin.   05.06.1980

Houses at 647, 651-653 Fifth Avenue, and House at 4 East 52nd Street
Three large Beaux-Arts stone townhouses. Number 647 Fifth Avenue designed by Hunt & Hunt; built 1902-05 for George W. Vanderbilt. Number 651-653 Fifth Avenue designed by Robert W. Gibson; built 1903-05 for railroad magnate Morton E. Plant; 1917 alterations by William Welles Bosworth for conversion into Cartier jewelry store. Number 4 East 52nd Street designed by C. P. H. Gilbert for Edward Holbrook; built 1904-05; altered 1929 for commercial use.   09.08.1983

Film Center Building
630 Ninth Avenue. A 13-story Art Deco brick office building designed by Ely Jacques Kahn; built 1928-29. Elaborate Art Deco lobby.
09.07.1984

Firehouse, Engine Company 31
87 Lafayette Street. A 3 1/2-story stone and brick firehouse with elaborate French Renaissance style decorative features; designed by Napoleon LeBrun & Sons; built 1895.
01.20.1972

Firehouse, Engine Company 33
44 Great Jones Street. A 4-story Beaux-Arts brick and stone firehouse designed by Ernest Flagg with Walter B. Chambers; built 1898-99.
03.16.1972

First Houses
East Third Street and Avenue A. Complex of eight 4- and 5-story brick apartment buildings grouped around landscaped courtyard; designed by Frederick L. Ackerman; built 1935-36. First public low-income housing project in the United States, financed in part by Federal Emergency Relief Administration.
12.18.1979

First National City Bank
55 Wall Street. Large 8-story granite building built in 2 sections. Four-story Greek Revival original section with imposing Ionic columns; designed by Isaiah Rogers; completed 1842 as Merchants' Exchange; later used as United States Custom House. Second 4-story tier with Corinthian columns and interior renovation designed by Charles F. McKim of McKim, Mead & White; completed 1910 for major banking firm.   08.18.1972; NHL 06.02.1978

First Police Precinct Station House
South Street and Old Slip. A 4-story Italian Renaissance style limestone building designed by Hunt & Hunt; built 1909-11.   10.29.1982

First Shearith Israel Graveyard
55-57 St. James Place. Small cemetery used by Jewish community in New York City 1683-1831 with approximately 100 burials of early settlers and prominent citizens.   04.17.1980

Hamilton Fish House (Stuyvesant-Fish House)
21 Stuyvesant Street. A 3 1/2-story Federal brick rowhouse built 1803-04. Birthplace and long-time residence of Hamilton Fish, Governor of New York and Secretary of State under Ulysses S. Grant.   07.31.1972; NHL 05.15.1975

Flatiron Building
Fifth Avenue and Broadway. Triangular 21-story Beaux-Arts brick, stone, and terra-cotta office building designed by Daniel H. Burnham & Co.; built 1902. Renowned New York City landmark.   11.20.1979; NHL 06.29.1989

Fort Jay
Governors Island. Large pentagonal masonry fortification originally built 1797-98 to defend New York City; rebuilt 1806-08 with Federal stone entrance gate, dry moat, and brick officers' quarters.   03.27.1974

Fort Tryon Park and The Cloisters
Broadway and Dyckman Street. A 66-acre park designed 1920s-30s by Olmsted Brothers on prehistoric occupational site and site of British Fort Tryon. The Cloisters developed 1934-39 by John D. Rockefeller, Jr. as branch of Metropolitan Museum of Art devoted to arts of the Middle Ages; museum designed by Charles Collins incorporating elements of medieval European monasteries.   12.19.1978

Fort Washington Site
Address restricted. Archeological site of fortifications built 1776 for American defense of New York City by General George Washington during American Revolution.
12.06.1978

Founder's Hall, Rockefeller University
(Rockefeller Institute for Medical Research) 66th Street and York Avenue. A 5-story brick and limestone building built 1905-06 as laboratory. Founded 1901 by John D. Rockefeller as scientific research foundation.   NHL 05.30.1974

Fourteenth Ward Industrial School
(Astor Memorial School) 256-258 Mott Street. A 4-story Queen Anne brick school with sandstone and terra-cotta trim; designed by Calvert Vaux of Vaux & Radford; built 1888-89 for Children's Aid Society.   01.27.1983

Fraunces Tavern Block
Bounded by Pearl, Water, and Broad streets, and Coenties Slip. Group of sixteen 2- to 6-story Georgian, Federal, Greek Revival, and Victorian masonry residential and commercial buildings. One of the few surviving sections of 19th-century New York City waterfront. Includes reconstructed Fraunces Tavern (1907, museum).   04.28.1977

General Grant National Memorial
Riverside Drive and West 122nd Street. Monumental Classical Revival granite building with Doric portico, colonnaded drum, and marble interior with tombs of President Ulysses S. Grant and wife; designed by John H. Duncan; completed 1897.   05.01.1959

Gilsey Hotel
1200 Broadway. An 8-story Second Empire former hotel with cast-iron facades and 3-story mansard roof; designed by Stephen D. Hatch; cast iron fabricated by D. D. Badger's Architectural Iron Works; built 1869-71.
12.14.1978

Gouverneur Hospital
621 Water Street. A 5-story Renaissance Revival brick hospital designed by John R. Thomas; built 1897-1901 to serve poor immigrants of Lower East Side; west wing built 1904-07.   10.29.1982

Governor's House
Governors Island. A 2-story Georgian brick residence possibly built c.1702 as residence of Governor Lord Cornbury; later additions.
04.26.1973

Governors Island
Strategic island component of New York Harbor defense system since late 18th century and major United States Army administrative center. Operated by United States Coast Guard since 1966. Notable structures include Gothic Revival Chapel of St. Cornelius the Centurion (1905, Charles C. Haight), and individually listed Castle Williams, Fort Jay, Admiral's House, Governor's House, and Block House.   NHL 02.04.1985

Grace Church and Dependencies
Broadway, Tenth Street, and Fourth Avenue. Gothic Revival complex with elaborately decorated marble church and rectory designed by James Renwick, Jr.; built 1843-46. Other buildings include Chantry (1877-79, James

Harlem Fire Watchtower, New York.

Opposite: High Bridge Water Tower, New York.

Renwick, Jr.), Grace Memorial House (1882-83, James Renwick, Jr.), Clergy House and Choir School (1902, Heins & LaFarge), Neighborhood House (1907, Renwick, Aspinwall & Tucker), and 84 and 86 Fourth Avenue (1911, Renwick, Aspinwall & Tucker). 06.28.1974; NHL 12.22.1977

Archibald Gracie Mansion
East End Avenue at 88th Street. A 2-acre property with large Federal frame residence built 1799 for merchant Archibald Gracie; doubled in size 1811; restored 1936 and 1985. Official residence of mayor of New York City since 1943. 05.12.1975

Gramercy Park Historic District
Roughly bounded by Third Avenue, Park Avenue South, and East 18th and 22nd streets. Residential neighborhood with Greek Revival, Gothic Revival, and Italianate townhouses surrounding large rectangular landscaped private square. Park developed 1830s by

Samuel B. Ruggles; first buildings constructed 1840s. Notable buildings include individually listed Samuel J. Tilden House and The Players Club, Italianate Friends Meeting House (1859, King & Kellum, now Brotherhood Synagogue), Gothic Revival Calvary Church (1846, James Renwick, Jr.), and Greek Revival 3 and 4 Gramercy Park West (c.1846, attributed to Alexander Jackson Davis). 01.23.1980

Grand Central Terminal
71-105 East 42nd Street. Monumental Beaux-Arts stone railroad passenger terminal designed by Reed & Stem and Warren & Wetmore; built 1903-13. Park Avenue Viaduct designed by Warren & Wetmore; built 1917-19. 01.17.1975; NHL 12.08.1976; BOUNDARY INCREASE 08.11.1983

Grand Hotel
1232-1238 Broadway. A 7-story Second Empire marble hotel designed 1868 by Henry Engelbert. 09.15.1983

Greenwich Village Historic District
Roughly bounded by West 13th Street, St. Luke's Place, University Place, and Washington Street. A 100-block residential neighborhood with hundreds of 19th-century rowhouses and townhouses, and later apartment buildings, located on irregular street grid pattern. Numerous distinctive examples of Federal, Greek Revival, Gothic Revival, and Italianate townhouses. Notable properties include row of Greek Revival townhouses on Washington Square North (c.1831), Washington Square Park, row of Italianate townhouses on West Tenth Street (1856-58), row of Greek Revival townhouses on West 11th Street (1844-45), Church of the Ascension (individually listed), Gothic Revival First Presbyterian Church (1845, Joseph C. Wells), and Third Judicial District Courthouse (individually listed). Area known historically as place of residence or work for famous artists and writers such as Thomas Paine, Edgar Allan Poe, Henry Jarvis Raymond, Richard Watson Gilder, Henry James, Mark Twain, Edna St. Vincent Millay, Theodore Dreiser, Richard Morris Hunt, Albert Pinkham Ryder, Eastman Johnson, William Merritt Chase, Sanford Gifford, John F. Kensett, Frederic Church, Augustus Saint-Gaudens, and Allen Ginsberg. 06.19.1979 ILLUS. P. 102

Hamilton Grange National Memorial
287 Convent Avenue. A 2-story Federal frame residence built 1801. Country home of statesman Alexander Hamilton until his death in 1804. Museum. NHL 12.19.1960

Hamilton Heights Historic District
Roughly bounded by St. Nicholas and Amsterdam avenues and West 145th and 140th streets. A 12-block residential neighborhood with rows of 2- and 3-story Queen Anne, Romanesque Revival, Flemish Revival, Renaissance Revival, Beaux-Arts, Georgian Revival, and Federal Revival brick and stone rowhouses built 1886-1906. Architects of residences include Neville & Bagge, William E. Mowbray, Adolph Hoak, and Henri Fouchaux. Notable structures include Hamilton Grange

(individually listed), St. Luke's Episcopal Church (1892-95, Robert H. Robertson), Convent Avenue Baptist Church (1897-99, Lamb & Rich), and St. James Presbyterian Church (1904, Ludlow & Valentine). 09.30.1983

Harlem Courthouse

170 East 121st Street. A 4 1/2-story Romanesque Revival brick courthouse with stone and terra-cotta trim and rounded corner tower; designed by Thom & Wilson; built 1891-93. 04.16.1980

Harlem Fire Watchtower

Garvey Park at East 122nd Street. Octagonal cast-iron fire lookout tower designed by James Bogardus and engineer Julius Krochl; built 1856. 06.21.1976

Harlem River Houses

West 151st to 153rd street, Macombs Place, and Harlem River Drive. Apartment complex of 4- and 5-story brick buildings grouped around courtyards and plazas; designed by Archibald Manning Brown, chief architect, with Charles F. Fuller, Horace Ginsbern, Frank J. Forster, Will Rice Amon, and Richard W. Buckley, and landscape architect Michael Rapuano; built 1936-37. First federally funded, built, and owned housing project in New York City. 12.18.1979

Harvard Club of New York City

27 West 44th Street. A 3-story Georgian Revival brick club designed by McKim, Mead & White; built 1894 with large additions in 1900-05 and 1913-16. Notable principal rooms. 03.28.1980

Barbara Rutherford Hatch House

153 East 63rd Street. A 3-story Spanish Colonial Revival stuccoed townhouse designed by Frederick J. Sterner; built 1917-19. Later home of entertainer Gypsy Rose Lee. 06.09.1983

E. V. Haughwout Building

488-492 Broadway. A 5-story cast-iron-front building with Palladian-inspired facades; built 1856-57 by J. P. Gaynor for china, glass, and silver merchant. Contained first practical passenger cable elevator with safety devices. 08.28.1973

Henderson Place Historic District

Henderson Place. Group of 24 Queen Anne brick townhouses designed by Lamb & Rich; built 1880-82. 06.20.1974

Henry Street Settlement and Neighborhood Playhouse

263-267 Henry Street and 466 Grand Street. Group of 3 early 19th-century Federal townhouses and nearby Georgian Revival Neighborhood Playhouse (1915). Founded 1895 as private social agency by Lillian D. Wald and Mary M. Brewster to provide social, educational, and recreational programs for poor immigrant families on Lower East Side. NHL 05.30.1974

Matthew Henson Residence

Dunbar Apartments, 246 West 150th Street, Apartment 3F. Latter-day home of African-American explorer who was assistant to Robert E. Perry and first man to reach North Pole (1909). See entry for Dunbar Apartments. NHL 05.15.1975

High Bridge Aqueduct and Water Tower

Harlem River at West 170th Street and High Bridge Park (also in Bronx County). A 1,420-foot-long and 138-foot-high stone-arched bridge designed by engineer John B. Jervis; built 1839-48 to carry water across Harlem River as part of Old Croton Aqueduct system; center arches replaced 1937 with larger steel arch. Octagonal stone water tower built 1872 to increase gravity pressure in aqueduct. 12.04.1972

Holy Trinity Church, St. Christopher House and Parsonage

312-316 and 332 East 88th Street. French Gothic style brick church complex with terra-cotta trim and 150-foot-high bell tower; designed by Barney & Chapman; completed 1897 as memorial to Rhinelander family. 05.30.1980

Isaac T. Hopper House

(Women's Prison Association Building) 110 Second Avenue. A 3 1/2-story Greek Revival brick townhouse built c.1840. Home since 1874 of early and innovative association devoted to rehabilitation of female prisoners. 05.22.1986

Hotel Chelsea

222 West 23rd Street. An 11-story Queen Anne brick cooperative apartment building with prominent iron balconies on 2nd through 8th stories; designed by Hubert, Pirsson & Co.; built 1883 and later converted to hotel. Residence of well-known artists including Mark Twain, Sarah Bernhardt, John Sloan, Eugene O'Neill, Thomas Wolfe, Dylan Thomas, Virgil Thomson, and William Burroughs. 12.27.1977

Hotel Gerard

123 West 44th Street. A 13-story brick building with German Renaissance and Northern Gothic decorative features; designed by George Keister; built 1893-94 as apartment-hotel. 02.10.1983

Langston Hughes House

20 East 127th Street. Italianate brownstone rowhouse designed by Alexander Wilson; built 1869. Home of Langston Hughes, African-American author, poet, and one of the foremost figures of the Harlem Renaissance, from 1947 until his death in 1967. 10.29.1982

International Mercantile Marine Company Building

1 Broadway. A 12-story Neoclassical limestone office building originally built 1882; completely redesigned 1919-21 by Walter B. Chambers. 03.02.1991

IRT Broadway Line Viaduct

(Manhattan Valley Viaduct) Broadway from West 122nd to 135th Street. A 2,147-foot-long steel-framed elevated viaduct designed by engineer William B. Parsons; built 1900-04 as component of first subway system in New York City. 09.15.1983

Jeffrey's Hook Lighthouse

Fort Washington Park. A 40-foot-conical steel plate lighthouse built 1920. Hudson River Lighthouses Thematic Group. 05.29.1979

John A. Lynch

Pier 15, East River. A 151-foot-long steel-hulled, double-ended, steam-powered New York Harbor ferryboat built 1925 by Staten Island Shipbuilding Co. Last of 16 vessels of its class remaining afloat. 09.07.1984

Building at 170-176 John Street

A 5-story Greek Revival commercial building with granite front; built c.1840. 05.13.1971

John Street Methodist Church

44 John Street. Federal/Greek Revival stuccoed brick church built 1841. 06.04.1973

James Weldon Johnson House

187 West 135th Street. A 5-story early 20th-century Renaissance Revival brick apartment building. Residence of author, musician, educator, and African-American leader James Weldon Johnson from 1925 until his death in 1938. NHL 05.11.1976

Houses at 26, 28, and 30 Jones Street

Row of 3 Greek Revival brick rowhouses built 1844. 06.03.1982

Judson Memorial Church, Campanile, and Judson Hall

Washington Square at Thompson Street. Italian Renaissance style brick church complex with terra-cotta trim and 10-story tower; designed by McKim, Mead & White; built 1888-96; tower and hall now college dormitories. 10.16.1974

Jumel Terrace Historic District
West 160th and 162nd streets between St. Nicholas and Edgecombe avenues. Small residential neighborhood with approximately 50 Italianate, Queen Anne, Romanesque Revival, Renaissance Revival, and Classical Revival rowhouses and 1 apartment building; built 1882-1909. Includes Morris-Jumel Mansion (individually listed).   04.03.1973

Knickerbocker Hotel
142 West 42nd Street. A 12-story Beaux-Arts brick building with 3-story mansard roof and ornate facades trimmed with limestone and terra-cotta; designed by Marvin & Davis with Bruce Price; built 1901-06 as luxury hotel. 04.11.1980

Knox Building
(Republic National Bank Building)
452 Fifth Avenue. A 10-story Beaux-Arts limestone commercial building designed by John H. Duncan; built 1901-02 as headquarters of Knox Hat Co.   06.03.1982

Building at 376-380 Lafayette Street
Large 6-story Romanesque Revival brick industrial/commercial building designed by Henry J. Hardenbergh; built 1888-89. 12.28.1979

Lagrange Terrace (Colonnade Row)
428-434 Lafayette Street. Group of four of original nine 3-story Greek Revival rowhouses unified by rusticated ground floor and 2-story Corinthian colonnade above; built 1832-33 by Seth Geer.   12.12.1976

Lamb's Club (Church of the Nazarene)
128 West 44th Street. A 6-story Colonial Revival brick building with marble and terra-cotta trim; designed by McKim, Mead & White; built 1904-05 as theatrical club; 1915 addition by George Freeman.   06.03.1982

James F. D. Lanier Residence
123 East 35th Street. A 5-story Beaux-Arts brick and stone townhouse designed by Hoppin & Koen; built 1901-03.   06.03.1982

Building at 85 Leonard Street
A 5-story cast-iron-front commercial building with upper facade composed of 2 tiers of elongated columns; designed and built 1861 by James Bogardus, pioneer of cast-iron construction.   04.23.1980

Daniel LeRoy House
20 St. Mark's Place. Large late Federal brick rowhouse with limestone trim; built 1832. 10.29.1982

Lescaze House
211 East 48th Street. International style stucco and glass brick townhouse designed by William Lescaze; built 1933-34 as his home and office using structure of earlier townhouse. 05.19.1980

Lettie G. Howard (*Mystic C*)
Pier 16, East River. A 75-foot-long wood-hulled, 2-masted fishing schooner built 1893 by Arthur D. Story at Essex, Massachusetts; rebuilt 1923. Last remaining substantially intact surviving example of "Fredonia" class fishing schooner. On exhibit at South Street Seaport Museum.   09.07.1984; NHL 04.11.1989

Level Club
253 West 73rd Street. A 15-story brick, stone, and terra-cotta building in Italian Romanesque style with Masonic decorative features; designed by Clinton & Russell with Wells, Holton & George; built 1925-27 as club and hotel for local Masonic organization. 04.09.1984

Lever House
390 Park Avenue. A 24-story International style steel and glass office building with ground-floor open plaza; designed by Skidmore, Owings & Merrill with Gordon Bunshaft, partner-in-charge; built 1950-52 as headquarters of Lever Brothers Co. One of the first corporate expressions of the International Style after World War II; considered a milestone in American architectural development.   10.02.1983

Liberty Tower
55 Liberty Street. A 33-story skyscraper with terra-cotta facades and Gothic-style decorations; designed by Henry Ives Cobb; built 1909-10.   09.15.1983

Lighthouse
Roosevelt Island. A 50-foot-tall octagonal granite lighthouse built c.1842.   03.16.1972

Lincoln Building
One Union Square West. A 9-story Romanesque Revival limestone and brick office building designed by Robert H. Robertson; built 1887-88.   09.08.1983

William Goadby Loew House
56 East 93rd Street. Large 4-story limestone townhouse with English Regency features; designed by Walker & Gillette; built 1930-31 for prominent stockbroker. Later home of showman Billy Rose.   07.15.1982

Low Memorial Library, Columbia University
Columbia University. Monumental Classical

Revival stone building with Ionic portico and imposing dome; designed by Charles F. McKim of McKim, Mead & White; built 1895-98 as centerpiece of campus with funds donated by Seth Low. Octagonal central hall with 105-foot-high inner dome. Seated statue of "Alma Mater" by Daniel Chester French located on front approach stairs.   NHL 12.23.1987

MacDougal-Sullivan Gardens Historic District
74-76 MacDougal Street and 170-188 Sullivan Street. Two rows of mid-19th-century Greek Revival brick townhouses remodeled 1920 in Federal Revival style by Francis Y. Joannes and Maxwell Hyde for Hearth & Home Real Estate Co. to provide duplexes, apartments, and interior communal garden.   06.30.1983

R. H. Macy and Company Store
151 West 34th Street. Block-long multistoried eclectically styled department store with 9-story original section designed by DeLemos & Cordes; built 1901-02; 20-story and other 1920s additions designed by Robert D. Kohn. Some notable remaining original entrances and interior features.   NHL 06.02.1978

Madison Avenue Facade of the Squadron A Armory
Madison Avenue between East 94th and 95th streets. Remains of facade of armory with large multistoried medieval-inspired corner towers and crenellations; designed by John R. Thomas; completed 1895; main section demolished 1966.   03.24.1972

Apartment at 1261 Madison Avenue
A 7-story Beaux-Arts limestone luxury apartment building with Baroque decorative elements; designed by Buchman & Fox; built 1900-01.   10.29.1982

Manhattan Bridge (see Kings County)

Marble Collegiate Reformed Church
275 Fifth Avenue. Early Romanesque Revival Gothic Revival marble church designed by Samuel A. Warner; built 1851-54. 04.09.1980

Mariner's Temple
12 Oliver Street. Greek Revival brownstone church with temple-form facade and Ionic columns; built and designed c.1844 by Isaac Lucas as Oliver Street Baptist Church. 04.16.1980

House at 51 Market Street
Late Federal brick rowhouse built 1824-25. 07.29.1977

McGraw-Hill Building
326 West 42nd Street. A 33-story Art Deco/Moderne skyscraper with horizontally massed facades clad with blue-green terra-cotta; designed by Raymond Hood; built 1930-31 for publishing company.   03.28.1980; NHL 06.29.1989

Claude McKay Residence
180 West 135th Street. A 14-story brick Young Men's Christian Association building built 1931-32. Home of African-American poet,

novelist, and lecturer Claude McKay 1942-46.
NHL 12.08.1976

Mecca Temple
(City Center of Music and Drama)
131 West 55th Street. Large masonry building
with 12-story tower and domed theater
embellished with ornate polychromatic terra-
cotta in Moorish-inspired motifs; designed by
Harry P. Knowles; built 1922-24 as Shriners
temple. 09.07.1984

Merchants Refrigerating Company Warehouse
501 West 16th Street. A 12-story brick cold
storage building with minimal fenestration and
simple Renaissance-style terra-cotta and cast-
stone trim; designed by John B. Snook & Sons;
built 1916-18. 05.31.1985

Metropolitan Life Insurance Tower
One Madison Avenue. A 700-foot-tall, 49-story
marble office building with Renaissance Revival
decorative details patterned after bell tower of
St. Mark's Cathedral in Venice; designed by
Pierre and Michel LeBrun; completed 1909,
when it was the world's tallest masonry
structure. NHL 06.02.1978

Metropolitan Museum of Art
Fifth Avenue at 82nd Street. Monumental
4-block-long masonry museum built in several
stages over period of more than 100 years:

Victorian Gothic original building (1874-80,
Vaux & Mould), south wing (1888, Theodore
Weston), north wing (1894, Arthur L. T.
Tuckerman), Beaux-Arts/Neoclassical Fifth
Avenue facade (1895-1902, Richard Morris
Hunt), north and south wings (1904-26,
McKim, Mead & White), American wing
(1924, Grosvenor Atterbury), and numerous
later and recent alterations and additions by
Kevin Roche and others. One of the world's
most prestigious museums for its buildings
and collections. NHL 06.24.1986

Metropolitan Savings Bank
9 East Seventh Street. Second Empire stone
building designed by Carl Pfeiffer; built 1867 as
bank. Now a church. 12.12.1976

Florence Mills House
220 West 135th Street. A 4-story Neo-Grec
brick rowhouse built 1886. Residence of famed
African-American actress, singer, dancer, and
entertainer Florence Mills from 1910 until her
death in 1927. NHL 12.08.1976

Minton's Playhouse
206-210 West 118th Street. Former dining
room of Cecil Hotel (1895), converted 1939 for
use as nightclub. Known as one of the foremost
jam session nightclubs in the United States,
particularly as site of 1940s bebop revolution.
09.18.1985

Metropolitan Museum of Art, New York.

*Opposite: Doorway, Morton Street, Greenwich
Village Historic District, New York (p. 100).*

Edward Mooney House
18 Bowery. A 3 1/2-story Georgian Federal rowhouse with gambrel roof; built 1785-89 for meat wholesaler.   12.12.1976

William H. Moore House
(American-Israel Cultural Foundation)
4 East 54th Street. A 5-story Classical Revival stone residence designed by McKim, Mead & White; built 1898-1900 for Chicago industrialist.   03.16.1972

J. P. Morgan & Co. Building
(Morgan Guaranty Trust Company)
23 Wall Street. A 4-story Neoclassical marble bank designed by Trowbridge & Livingston; built 1913-14.   06.19.1972

J. Pierpont Morgan Library
33 East 36th Street. A 2-story Renaissance-inspired limestone building with elaborate interior; designed by McKim, Mead & White; built 1902-07 to house personal library of major American financier; 1928 addition designed by Benjamin W. Morris. Operated as museum/library.   NHL 11.13.1966

Lewis G. Morris House
100 East 85th Street. Large 3 1/2-story Federal Revival brick townhouse designed by Ernest Flagg; built 1914 for stockbroker.
02.12.1977

Morris-Jumel Mansion
160th Street and Edgecombe Avenue. Large 2 1/2-story Georgian frame residence with Tuscan portico and octagonal drawing room; built 1765 as country house for British Colonel Roger Morris and wife Mary Philipse. Used as George Washington's headquarters during American Revolution. Remodeled c.1810 by Stephen and Eliza Jumel. Museum.
NHL 01.20.1961

Mount Morris Bank
East 125th Street and Park Avenue. A 5-story Queen Anne/Romanesque Revival brick former bank and apartment building designed by Lamb & Rich; built 1883; enlarged 1897.
12.07.1989

Mount Morris Park Historic District
Bounded roughly by Lenox Avenue, Mount Morris Park West, and West 119th and 124th streets. Small residential neighborhood adjacent to park, with rows of 3- and 4-story Queen Anne, Neo-Grec, Romanesque Revival, and Renaissance Revival brick and brownstone townhouses built 1878 to early 20th century. Also includes several churches and apartment buildings. Architects include Arnold W. Brenner, Lamb & Rich, George F. Pelham, William A. Potter, John R. Thomas, Thom & Wilson, James E. Ware, and McKim, Mead & White.   02.06.1973

Municipal Asphalt Plant
Between East 90th and 91st streets along FDR Drive. An 85-foot-tall reinforced-concrete building in form of parabolic arch; designed by Ely Jacques Kahn and Robert Allan Jacobs;

built 1941-44. Unusual and innovative use of concrete for industrial building. Adapted 1984 as George & Annette Murphy (recreation) Center.   05.23.1980

Municipal Building
Chambers at Centre Street. A 25-story C-shaped granite skyscraper with multistoried central tower, barrel-vaulted vehicular passageway, and ornamentation derived from Roman antique and Italian Renaissance sources; designed by William M. Kendall; built 1912-14.   10.18.1972

Municipal Ferry Pier
(Battery Maritime Building)
11 South Street. Massive structural-steel building with unusual Beaux-Arts decorative elements; designed by Morris & Walker; completed 1909 as ferry terminal for line connecting Manhattan with South Brooklyn.
12.12.1976

Building at 75 Murray Street
A 5-story Italianate cast-iron-front commercial building built 1865.   04.03.1973

New Amsterdam Theater
214 West 42nd Street. An 11-story limestone office tower with main auditorium behind and second smaller theater atop auditorium; exterior and elaborate interior decoration in Art Nouveau style; designed 1902 by Herts & Tallant as performance showplace for theatrical production team of Marc Klaw and Abraham Erlanger. Innovative design, theater plan, and mechanical systems.   01.10.1980

New York Amsterdam News Building
2293 Seventh Avenue. A 4-story late 19th-century brownstone rowhouse. Home of nationally prominent African-American newspaper 1916-38, during its years of greatest growth.   NHL 05.11.1976

New York Cancer Hospital
2 West 106th Street. A 3 1/2-half-story brick building with sandstone trim and circular corner towers in style of French chateau with Gothic details; designed by Charles C. Haight; built in 3 sections 1884-90. First hospital built in United States solely for treatment of cancer.
04.29.1977

New York Chamber of Commerce Building
65 Liberty Street. A 4 1/2-story Beaux-Arts marble building with elaborate exterior and interior ornamentation; designed by James B. Baker; built 1901-02. First organization in America for promotion of trade and commerce; founded 1768.   02.06.1973; NHL 12.27.1977

New York City Marble Cemetery
52-74 East Second Street. Small cemetery with 254 marble underground burial vaults, tombstones, and monuments, and original iron fence. Second nonsectarian burial ground in Manhattan; begun 1831.   09.17.1980

New York Cotton Exchange (India House)
One Hanover Square. A 3-story Italian Renaissance style brownstone building built 1852-53 for Hanover Bank. Headquarters of

New York Cotton Exchange, 1872-85, and W. R. Grace & Co., 1885-1913; expanded 19th and 20th centuries to include adjacent buildings; remodeled 1914 by Delano & Aldrich as clubhouse for India House.   01.07.1972; NHL 12.27.1977

New York County Lawyers Association Building
14 Vesey Street. A 4-story Georgian Revival limestone clubhouse designed by Cass Gilbert; built 1928-30. Notable interior.   10.29.1982

New York Life Building
51 Madison Avenue. Massive 34-story granite and limestone skyscraper with Gothic-style decorative trim; designed by Cass Gilbert; completed 1928 for major life insurance company founded 1841.   NHL 06.02.1978

New York Life Insurance Company Building (former)
346 Broadway. Long, narrow 12- to 13-story Italian Renaissance style marble office building with clock tower; eastern section (1894-96) designed by Stephen D. Hatch; western section (1896-98) designed by McKim, Mead & White.   06.28.82

New York Marble Cemetery
Between East Second and Third streets, Second Avenue, and Bowery. Small cemetery with 156 marble underground burial vaults and grave markers affixed to stone wall. First nonsectarian burial ground in Manhattan; begun 1830.   09.17.1980

New York Presbyterian Church
(Metropolitan Baptist Church)
151 West 128th Street. Gothic/Romanesque Revival limestone church with notable stained glass and carved oak interior; designed by John R. Thomas; built 1884-85; auditorium addition designed by Richard R. Davis; built 1889-90.   06.03.1982

New York Public Library, 115th Street Branch
203 West 115th Street. A 3-story Italian Renaissance style limestone library designed by McKim, Mead & White; built 1907-09.
05.06.1980

New York Public Library and Bryant Park
Avenue of the Americas, Fifth Avenue, and 40th and 42nd streets. Monumental 3-story Beaux-Arts stone library with Corinthian portico and notable interior spaces; designed by Carrère & Hastings; built 1902-11; restored 1980s. Large formal park at rear designed 1934 by Lusby Simpson. Includes Josephine Shaw Lowell Memorial Fountain (1912, Charles A. Platt) and statue of William Cullen Bryant by Henry Adams.   NHL 12.21.65; BOUNDARY INCREASE 05.06.80

New York Public Library, Hamilton Grange Branch
503 and 505 West 145th Street. A 3-story Italian Renaissance style stone library designed by McKim, Mead & White; built 1905-06.
07.23.1981

New York Public Library, Ottendorfer Branch, and Stuyvesant Polyclinic Hospital
135 and 137 Second Avenue. Adjacent 3-story Italian Renaissance style/eclectic brick buildings with terra-cotta trim; designed by William Schickel; built 1883-84 as gifts of Anna and Oswald Ottendorfer to New York German community. 07.22.1979

New York Public Library, Yorkville Branch
222 East 79th Street. A 3-story Italian Renaissance style limestone library designed by James Brown Lord; built 1902. 07.15.1982

New York School of Applied Design
160 Lexington Avenue. A 5-story Classical Revival stone, brick, and terra-cotta building designed by Harvey Wiley Corbett; built 1908-09 to house New York School of Applied Design for Women. 12.16.1982

New York Shakespeare Festival Public Theater
(Astor Library)
425 Lafayette Street. Large 4-story Italianate/eclectic brick building built as library in 3 stages: south wing (1849-53, Alexander Saeltzer), central section (1856-59, Griffith Thomas), north wing (1879-81, Thomas Stent). Remodeled 1960s as theater. 12.02.1970

New York Stock Exchange
18 Broad Street and 11 Wall Street. 18 Broad Street: 10-story Beaux-Arts marble building with Corinthian colonnade; designed by George B. Post; completed 1903; exterior sculpture by John Q. A. Ward. 11 Wall Street: 23-story Neoclassical marble building designed by Trowbridge & Livingston; completed 1923. Home of principal securities market in United States. NHL 06.02.1978

New York Yacht Club
37 West 44th Street. A 7-story Beaux-Arts stone building with fanciful bay windows carved to resemble sterns of waterborne Baroque-style sailing vessels; designed by Whitney Warren of Warren & Wetmore; built 1899-1900 as clubhouse of America's oldest yachting organization (founded 1844). 10.29.1982; NHL 05.28.1987

Andrew S. Norwood House
241 West 14th Street. A 4-story Greek Revival/Italianate brick townhouse built 1845-47. 07.09.1979

The Octagon
Roosevelt Island. A 3-story Greek Revival octagonal granite building with octagonal lantern, dome (1878), and hollow circular core with cantilevered iron staircase; designed by Alexander Jackson Davis; built 1835-39 as New York Insane Asylum. 03.16.1972

Odd Fellows Hall
165-171 Grand Street. A 4-story Italianate brownstone building designed by Trench & Snook; built 1847-48; 2 additional floors (1881-82) in Queen Anne style designed by John Buckingham. 09.22.1983

Old Colony Club
(American Academy of Dramatic Arts)
120 Madison Avenue. A 3 1/2-story Georgian Revival brick building with elaborate facade; designed by McKim, Mead & White; built 1905-08 for women's club. Interior decoration by Elsie deWolfe. 04.23.1980

Old Grolier Club
29 East 32nd Street. Small 3-story Romanesque Revival brick and stone building designed by Charles W. Romeyn; built 1890. 04.23.1980

Old Merchant's House
(Seabury Tredwell House)
29 East Fourth Street. A 3 1/2-story late Federal brick townhouse with Greek Revival interiors; built 1831-32. Home of Seabury Tredwell family 1835-1933. Retains original decorations and family furnishings. Museum. NHL 06.23.1965

Old New York County Courthouse
(Tweed Courthouse)
52 Chambers Street. Large 2-story Italianate marble building with tetrastyle Corinthian portico; designed 1861 by John Kellum; completed 1881 by Leopold Eidlitz. Excess in construction costs of building linked with notorious graft of Tweed Ring. 09.25.1974; NHL 05.11.1976

Old New York Evening Post Building
20 Vesey Street. A 13-story stone commercial building designed by Robert D. Kohn in style of Viennese Secession; built 1906-07 as publishing office for famous newspaper; exterior sculptures by Gutzon Borglum and Estelle Rombold Kohn. 08.16.1977

Old St. Patrick's Cathedral Complex
Mott and Prince streets. Georgian/Gothic Revival stone church designed by Joseph F. Mangin; built 1809-15; interior rebuilt in Gothic Revival style after 1866 fire; Cathedral Church of the See of New York until 1879. Also includes Gothic Revival St. Michael's Chapel (1859, Renwick & Rodrigue), Greek Revival rectory (1828), and Federal orphanage (1825-26, now convent and girls' school). 08.29.1977

Houses at 680, 684, 686, and 690 Park Avenue
Row of 4 similar large 4-story Georgian Revival brick townhouses with limestone trim. Number 680 designed by McKim, Mead & White; built 1906 for Percy R. Pyne. Number 684 designed by McKim, Mead & White; built 1925-26 for Oliver D. Filley. Number 686 designed by Delano & Aldrich; built 1916-19 for William Sloane. Number 690 designed by Walker & Gillette; built 1916-17 for H. P. Davison, a partner of J. P. Morgan. 01.03.1980

Park East Synagogue, Congregation Zichron Ephraim
163 East 67th Street. Brick synagogue with exuberant Moorish and Byzantine-style decorative features; designed by Schneider & Herter; built 1889-90. Associated with Rabbi Bernard Drachmar and Jonas Weil, pioneers in the effort to adapt Orthodox practice to contemporary American life. 08.18.1983

The Players Club
16 Gramercy Park. Gothic Revival stone rowhouse built 1845; converted 1888-89 to theatrical club by Stanford White of McKim, Mead & White for actor Edwin Booth. NHL 12.29.1962

Plaza Hotel and Grand Army Plaza
Fifth Avenue and 59th Street. Massive 18-story French Renaissance style brick and marble hotel designed by Henry J. Hardenbergh; built 1905-07; additions and alterations 1921 and later. One of America's most celebrated luxury hotels. 11.29.1978; NHL 06.24.1986

Police Headquarters Building
240 Centre Street. Monumental 5-story Beaux-Arts granite and limestone building with elaborate Baroque dome and decorative features; designed by Hoppin & Koen; built 1905-09. Redeveloped as condominiums. 03.28.1980

Pomander Walk District
261-267 West 94th Street, 260-274 West 95th Street, and Pomander Walk. Small planned residential area of 16 two-story Tudor Revival attached houses on private, pedestrian walk and 11 adjacent residences; designed by King & Campbell; commissioned 1921 by theater devotee Thomas Healy and inspired by set design for Broadway play *Pomander Walk*. 09.08.1983

House at 203 Prince Street
Late Federal brick townhouse built 1833-34 for John P. Haff, a leather inspector. 05.26.1983

Public Baths
Asser Levy Place and East 23rd Street. Beaux-Arts brick and limestone bathhouse designed by Brunner & Aiken; built 1904-06. 04.23.1980

Public School 9 (Livingston School)
466 West End Avenue. A 5-story Flemish Revival brick school with limestone trim; designed by C. B. J. Snyder; built 1892-95. 08.03.1987

Public School 35
(East Side International Community Center)
931 First Avenue. A 4-story Romanesque Revival brick school with brownstone trim; designed by George W. Debevoise; built 1890-92. 10.27.1980

Public School 157
327 St. Nicholas Avenue. Large 4 1/2-story Renaissance Revival brick school with sandstone trim; designed by C. B. J. Snyder; built 1898. 10.27.1980

Puck Building
295-309 Lafayette Street. Composite 7- and 9-story Romanesque Revival brick industrial building designed by Albert and Herman Wagner; built in 3 stages 1885-99 for humor magazine *Puck* and J. Ottman Lithography Co. Cast-metal statue of Puck by Casper Buberl located on corner. 07.21.1983

Pupin Physics Laboratories, Columbia University
Broadway and West 120th Street. A 10-story brick laboratory building. Location of cyclotron magnet which first split uranium atom in New York on January 25, 1939, ten days after world's first atom-splitting in Copenhagen, Denmark. NHL 12.21.1965

Queensboro Bridge
59th Street, spanning East River (also in Queens County). A 4,168-foot-long double-span, through-cantilever truss bridge of steel frame on masonry piers with Beaux-Arts stone approaches; designed by engineer Gustav Lindenthal and architect Henry Hornbostel; public market beneath Manhattan approaches with vaults designed by Raphael Guastavino. 12.20.1978

Racquet and Tennis Club Building
370 Park Avenue. Large 4-story Italian Renaissance style brick building designed by McKim, Mead & White; built 1916-18. 07.13.1983

Radio City Music Hall
1260 Avenue of the Americas. Art Deco limestone theater with bronze trim, 6,200-seat auditorium, and notable Art Deco foyer and secondary spaces; designed as integral part of Rockefeller Center (individually listed) by Reinhard & Hofmeister; Hood, Godley & Fouilhoux; and Corbett, Harrison & MacMurray working in association with Samuel "Roxy" Rothafel; built 1931-32. Retains most of original interior finishes and decoration. 05.08.1978

Red House
350 West 85th Street. A 6-story brick apartment building with extensive terra-cotta decoration in François I style; designed by Harde & Short; built 1903-04. 09.08.1983

Isaac L. Rice Mansion
(Villa Julia–Yeshiva Chofetz)
346 West 89th Street. Large 3-story Beaux-Arts Georgian Revival brick residence on landscaped lot; designed by Herts & Tallant; built 1901-03 for lawyer, financier, and inventor, and wife, Julia Barnett Rice, founder of Society for the Suppression of Noise; 1908 additions and alterations by C. P. H. Gilbert for Solomon Schinasi. 06.25.1980

Riverside Drive West 80th-81st Streets Historic District
Small residential neighborhood with 32 rowhouses and 3 small apartment buildings built 1892-98. Includes 21 five-story Beaux-Arts brick and limestone rowhouses designed by Clarence True and three six-story Beaux-Arts brick apartment buildings designed by Janes & Leo, James E. Ware & Son, and Townsend & Harde. 05.10.1984

Riverside Park and Drive
From West 72nd to 129th Street. A 57-block-long linear park along Hudson River varying in width from 100 to 500 feet; organized on 4 levels, with Riverside Drive at highest point, then promenade, landscaped steep hill, plateau with recreational areas, and Henry Hudson Parkway. Original landscape designed by Frederick Law Olmsted and Calvert Vaux beginning in 1874; major alterations and addition of acreage and recreational facilities under direction of Robert Moses 1934-37 with architects Gilmore D. Clarke and Clinton Lloyd. Includes numerous early 20th-century monuments such as General Grant National Memorial (individually listed) and Soldier's and Sailor's Monument (1900-02, Arthur A. and Charles W. Stoughton with Paul E. M. Duboy). 09.02.1983

Riverside–West 105th Street Historic District
Roughly bounded by West End Avenue, Riverside Drive, West 104th and 106th streets. Small residential neighborhood with 30 buildings built 1899-1902, mostly 4-story Beaux-Arts limestone rowhouses. Architects of buildings include Janes & Leo, William E. Mowbray, Hoppin & Koen, and Robert D. Kohn. 08.19.1980

Robbins & Appleton Building
1-5 Bond Street. A 6-story Second Empire cast-iron-front commercial building designed by Stephen D. Hatch; built 1879-80 for watch factory and publishing firm. 10.29.1982

Paul Robeson Home
555 Edgecombe Avenue. A 13-story Beaux-Arts brick apartment building built 1916. Residence of famous African-American concert artist, actor, and scholar Paul Robeson 1939-41. NHL 12.08.1976

Rockefeller Center
Bounded by Fifth Avenue, West 48th Street, Seventh Avenue, and West 51st Street. Massive planned urban complex integrating architecture, city planning, landscape architecture, and sculpture. Original 3-block complex of 14 multistoried Art Deco limestone skyscrapers developed by John D. Rockefeller, Jr. 1930-39 with associated architects Corbett, Harrison & MacMurray; Hood, Godley & Fouilhoux; and Reinhard & Hofmeister. Buildings in original scheme include 1270 Avenue of the Americas, Radio City Music Hall (individually listed), Associated Press Building, International Buildings, RCA Buildings, Simon & Schuster Building, and buildings at 1 and 10 Rockefeller Plaza. Also includes gardens and walkways, underground connecting corridors and shops, ice-skating rink, and numerous works of art, sculpture, and sculptural relief. Known as one of the most successful urban planning projects in the history of American architecture. NHL 12.23.1987

John S. Rogers House
(New York Society Library)
53 East 79th Street. A 5-story Italian Renaissance style limestone townhouse designed by Trowbridge & Livingston; built 1917; home of New York Society Library since 1937. 06.30.1983

Sara Delano Roosevelt Memorial House
47 and 49 East 65th Street. A 5-story Georgian Revival brick double house with limestone trim; designed by Charles A. Platt; built 1907-08. Commissioned by Sara Delano Roosevelt and used as city residence by her and her son, Franklin D. Roosevelt, and her daughter-in-law, Eleanor Roosevelt. Occupied by Hunter College Student Social and Religious Club Association since 1943. 03.28.1980

Theodore Roosevelt Birthplace National Historic Site
28 East 20th Street. A 3-story brownstone rowhouse designed by Theodate Pope Riddle; built 1923 for Womens Roosevelt Memorial Association as replica of 1848 house that was birthplace of President Theodore Roosevelt. Museum. 07.25.1962

St. Andrew's Episcopal Church
2067 Fifth Avenue. High Victorian Gothic granite church with 125-foot-high clock tower designed by Henry M. Congdon; built 1872-73 on East 127th Street; moved 3 blocks and reconstructed and enlarged 1889 on present site. 03.18.1980

St. Augustine's Chapel
290 Henry Street. Georgian/Gothic Revival stone church built 1829 as All Saints Free Church; design attributed to John Heath. 05.06.1980

St. Bartholomew's Church and Community House
109 East 50th Street at Park Avenue. Large brick church with Romanesque and Byzantine style brick features and limestone, marble, and tile trim; designed by Bertram G. Goodhue; built 1917-19; elaborate main portal salvaged from previous church (1901-03; McKim, Mead & White); lavish interior and octagonal dome (1930). Community House designed by Goodhue's successors, Mayers, Murray & Phillip; built 1926-28. 04.16.1980

St. Cecilia's Church and Convent
112-120 East 106th Street. Romanesque Revival/Italian Renaissance style brick and terra-cotta church designed by Napoleon

LeBrun & Sons; built 1883-87. Adjoining convent designed 1907 in similar style by Neville & Bagge. 02.02.1984

St. George's Episcopal Church
Third Avenue and East 16th Street. Early Romanesque Revival brownstone church designed by Blesch & Eidlitz; built 1846-56. Also includes chapel and parsonage. Harry T. Burleigh, famous African-American songwriter, held position of soloist at church 1908-1948. NHL 12.08.1976

St. James Church
32 James Street. Greek Revival stuccoed brick church with Doric columns; built 1837. Notable interior cast-iron gallery ornament. 07.24.1972

St. Jean Baptiste Church and Rectory
1067-1071 Lexington Avenue. Large French Neoclassical style masonry church with twin towers, dome, and elaborate interior; designed by Nicholas Serracino; built 1910-13. Adjacent rectory. 04.23.1980

St. Mark's Historic District
Roughly bounded by Second and Third avenues, and East Ninth and 11th streets. Small residential neighborhood with 35 townhouses, including Hamilton Fish House (individually listed), Federal townhouse at 21 Stuyvesant Street (1795, built for Nicholas William Stuyvesant III), and mid-19th-century Greek Revival and Italianate brick rowhouses. Also includes St. Mark's-Church-In-The-Bowery (individually listed). 11.13.1974

St. Marks-Church-In-The-Bowery
East Tenth Street and Second Avenue. Georgian stone church built 1795-99; Greek Revival steeple (1828, Ithiel Town); remodeling and cast-iron porch (1854, George Platt). Parish hall designed 1861 by James Renwick, Jr. and rectory designed 1900 by Ernest Flagg. Adjacent cemetery with burials of Stuyvesant family and other prominent New Yorkers. 06.19.1972

St. Nicholas Historic District
West 138th and 139th streets between Seventh and Eighth avenues. Residential neighborhood with approximately 150 large Georgian Revival and Italian Renaissance style brick and stone rowhouses designed by James Brown Lord, Bruce Price, Clarence S. Luce, and McKim, Mead & White; built 1891 by developer David H. King. Later importance for emergence of Harlem as major African-American community in early 20th century. Includes Will Marion Cook House (individually listed). 10.29.1975

St. Patrick's Cathedral
Bounded by Fifth and Madison avenues, and East 50th and 51st streets. Large-scale Gothic Revival marble church with features

Opposite: Queensboro Bridge, New York.

Rockefeller Center, New York.

derived from English, French, and German sources; designed by James Renwick, Jr; built 1858-79; 330-foot-high spires completed 1888. Includes Lady Chapel (1906, Charles T. Mathews), rectory, and cardinal's residence. NHL 12.08.1976

St. Paul's Chapel
Broadway between Fulton and Vesey streets. Georgian fieldstone church with brownstone trim and finely crafted exterior and interior decorative features; built 1764-66; design attributed to Thomas McBean and influenced by St. Martin-in-the-Fields, London. Tower and multitiered spire designed by James C. Lawrence; added 1794. Place of worship for both American and British military officers during American Revolution. Adjacent early cemetery. NHL 10.09.1960

St. Peter's Roman Catholic Church
22 Barclay Street. Greek Revival granite church with Ionic portico; designed by John R. Haggerty and Thomas Thomas; built 1836-40. Notable interior. 04.23.1980

St. Thomas Church and Parish House
1-3 West 53rd Street. Gothic Revival limestone church with French Gothic features; designed by Cram, Goodhue & Ferguson; built 1909-13. Notable interior with clerestory windows by Whitefriars and reredos sculpted by Lee Lawrie. 04.09.1980

Salmagundi Club
47 Fifth Avenue. A 4-story Italianate brownstone townhouse built 1852-53. Home since 1917 of Salmagundi Club, established 1871 as private artists' club whose membership has included John LaFarge, Howard Pyle, Louis Comfort Tiffany, George Inness, Stanford White, and other well-known artists. 07.25.1974

Schermerhorn Row Block
Block bounded by Front, Fulton, and South streets, and Burling Slip. Group of approximately 12 Federal brick commercial buildings built 1811-12 for Peter Schermerhorn on New York waterfront; later alterations. Also includes several similar buildings built 1830s and 1840s. Sections of buildings incorporated into South Street Seaport Museum. 02.18.1971

Schinasi Residence (The Children's Mansion)
351 Riverside Drive. A 2 1/2-story French Renaissance style freestanding marble residence designed by William B. Tuthill; built 1907-09 for tobacco manufacturer Morris Schinasi. 04.23.1980

Schomburg Center for Research in Black Culture
103 West 135th Street. A 3-story Italian Renaissance style stone library designed by McKim, Mead & White; built 1905 as branch of New York Public Library. Since World War I a major resource center for African-American history, art, and literature. 09.21.1978

General Winfield Scott House
24 West 12th Street. Italianate brownstone townhouse built 1851-52. Residence of War of 1812 and Mexican War military leader. NHL 11.07.1973

Scribner Building
153-157 Fifth Avenue. A 6-story Beaux-Arts limestone commercial building designed by Ernest Flagg; built 1893-94 for publishing firm. 05.06.1980

Sea and Land Church
61 Henry Street. Georgian/Gothic Revival stone church built 1819 as Northeast Dutch Reformed Church. Now First Chinese Presbyterian Church. 04.09.1980

Seventh Regiment Armory
643 Park Avenue. Massive block-long armory with granite trim and Gothic-style ornamentation and crenellations; designed by Charles W. Clinton; built 1877-80. Elaborate interior designed 1881 by Associated Artists, with Louis Comfort Tiffany, Stanford White, Augustus Saint-Gaudens, Samuel Coleman, Lockwood deForest, and Candace Wheeler. 04.14.1975; NHL 02.24.1986

Sidewalk Clock at 200 Fifth Avenue
Freestanding cast-iron sidewalk clock manufactured 1909 by Helca Iron Works. Sidewalk Clocks of New York City Thematic Resources. 04.18.1985

Sidewalk Clock at 522 Fifth Avenue
Freestanding cast-iron sidewalk clock manufactured 1907 by Seth Thomas Co. Sidewalk Clocks of New York City Thematic Resources. 04.18.1985

Sidewalk Clock at 783 Fifth Avenue
Freestanding cast-iron sidewalk clock manufactured c.1927 by E. Howard Clock Co. Sidewalk Clocks of New York City Thematic Resources. 04.18.1985

Sidewalk Clock at 519 Third Avenue
Freestanding cast-iron sidewalk clock manufactured c.1880-1930. Sidewalk Clocks of New York City Thematic Resources. 04.18.1985

Sidewalk Clock at 1501 Third Avenue
Freestanding cast-iron sidewalk clock manufactured c.1880-1930 by E. Howard Clock Co. Sidewalk Clocks of New York City Thematic Resources. 04.18.1985

Harry F. Sinclair House
(Ukranian Institute of America)
2 East 79th Street. Large 3 1/2-story French Renaissance style limestone residence designed 1899 by C. P. H. Gilbert for Isaac D. Fletcher. Residence of Harry F. Sinclair, oil magnate and principal figure in Teapot Dome scandal, 1918-30. NHL 06.02.1978

Smallpox Hospital
Roosevelt Island. A 3-story Gothic Revival granite hospital built 1854-56; design attributed to James Renwick, Jr.; early 20th-century additions designed by York & Sawyer and Renwick, Aspinwall & Owen. 03.16.1972

Abigail Adams Smith Museum
421 East 61st Street. Large Federal stone carriage house built 1799 on riverfront estate of Colonel William Stephen and Abigail Adams Smith. Converted 1826 to residence and 1924 headquarters of Colonial Dames of America. 01.12.1973

Alfred E. Smith House
25 Oliver Street. Italianate brick rowhouse built c.1870. Residence of popular politician and New York governor 1907-24. NHL 11.28.1972

Fleming Smith Warehouse
451-453 Washington Street. A 6-story Flemish Revival brick and stone commercial building designed by Stephen D. Hatch; built 1891-92. 05.26.1983

Sniffen Court Historic District
East 36th Street between Lexington and Third avenues. Group of 10 Early Romanesque Revival brick residences built c.1860 as carriage houses. 11.28.1973

Society for the Lying-In Hospital
(Bernstein Institute, Beth Israel Hospital)
305 Second Avenue. A 7-story Classical Revival hospital with 3-story central attic; designed 1899 by Robert H. Robertson as hospital for poor and immigrant population of Lower East Side. Converted to apartments. 09.01.1983

Sofia Warehouse
43 West 61st Street. A 27-story Art Deco brick skyscraper with terra-cotta trim; designed by Jardine, Hill & Murdock; built 1929-30 as Kent Columbus Circle garage. Converted to apartments. 09.27.1984

SoHo Cast-Iron Historic District
Roughly bounded by West Broadway, Houston, Crosby, and Canal streets. A 26-block industrial, commercial, and residential district containing probably the world's largest existing group of cast-iron facades in broad range of styles, built mostly in second half of 19th century. Also includes many mid-19th-century masonry commercial buildings and later high-rise lofts. Principal architects include Isaac Duckworth, Henry Fernbach, John Kellum, J. Morgan Slade, John B. Snook, Griffith Thomas, Samuel A. Warner, and Alfred Zucker. Includes E. V. Haughwout Building (individually listed). NHL 06.29.1978

South Street Seaport Historic District
Bounded by East River, Brooklyn Bridge, Fletcher Alley, and Pearl and South streets. A 12-block waterfront commercial area with numerous, mostly 3- to 6-story, late 18th- to mid-19th-century buildings related to maritime commercial trade. Includes Schermerhorn Row (individually listed), 170-176 John Street (individually listed), Joseph Rose House (c.1773, oldest commercial building in Manhattan), 18th-century archeological sites, and 4 piers. 10.18.1972; BOUNDARY INCREASE 12.12.1978

Statue of Liberty National Monument
Liberty and Ellis islands, New York Harbor (also in New Jersey). Statue of Liberty: 152-foot-tall copper statue conceived and designed by sculptor Frederic Auguste Bartholdi; constructed 1875-84 in France; steel framework designed by Alexandre Gustave Eiffel; mounted 1885-86 on 89-foot-tall granite pedestal (Richard Morris Hunt) in center of early 19th-century Fort Hood. World monument to freedom and opportunity in America for newcomers to United States. Museum. Ellis Island: 27-acre island site of major immigration station to United States, 1892-1954, with large

donated 1836 to city by Peter G. Stuyvesant and redesigned 1936. Includes St. George's Church (individually listed) and Greek Revival Friends Meeting House and Seminary (1860-61).   11.21.1980

Houses at 83 and 85 Sullivan Street
Two Federal brick townhouses built 1819.   11.17.1980

Surrogate's Court (Hall of Records)
31 Chambers Street. An 8-story Beaux-Arts/ French Renaissance style granite building with elaborate ornamentation; designed by John R. Thomas and Horgan & Slattery; built 1899-1907.   01.29.1972; NHL 12.22.1977

complex of buildings. Main building designed by Boring & Tilton; completed 1900; restored and opened 1990 as museum.   10.15.1924; Ellis Island added 1965

A. T. Stewart Company Store
280 Broadway. A 7-story commercial building; original 5-story Italian Renaissance style marble section designed by Trench & Snook; built 1845-46 for A. T. Stewart. Known as America's first department store.
NHL 06.02.1978

Strecker Memorial Laboratory
Roosevelt Island. Granite and brick building designed by Withers & Dickson; built 1892.   03.16.1972

Studio Apartments
44 West 77th Street. A 14-story brick apartment building with elaborate Gothic-style trim and artist's studio floor plan; designed by Harde & Short; built 1907-09.   05.19.1983

Stuyvesant Square Historic District
Roughly bounded by Nathan D. Perleman Place, Third Avenue, and East 18th and 15th streets. Group of approximately 50 Greek Revival, Italianate, and Romanesque Revival rowhouses clustered around southern and western edge of Stuyvesant Square Park,

Sutton Place Historic District
1-21 Sutton Place and 4-16 Sutton Square. Group of 12 late 19th-century rowhouses; redesigned early 1920s in Georgian Revival and Italian Renaissance styles as residential enclave grouped around communal garden overlooking East River. Architects include Mott B. Schmidt, Polhemus & Coffin, Read & Everett, James Casale, William Lescaze, Carl Volmer, Murphy & Dann, Delano & Aldrich, and Henry O. Milliken. Original residents included Anne Vanderbilt, Anne Morgan, and Elsie deWolfe.   09.12.1985

Third Judicial District Courthouse (Jefferson Market Branch, New York Public Library)
425 Avenue of the Americas. Large Victorian Gothic brick building with elaborate polychromatic trim and tall clock tower; designed by Vaux & Withers; built 1875-77 as courthouse. Renovated 1967 as library.   11.09.1972; NHL 12.22.1977 ILLUS. P. 111

Building at 8 Thomas Street
A 5-story High Victorian Gothic cast-iron- and brick-front commercial building designed by J. Morgan Slade; built 1875-76.   04.30.1980

Tiffany and Company Building
401 Fifth Avenue. A 7-story marble and terra-cotta building closely modeled on 16th-century

Ellis Island, Statue of Liberty National Monument, New York.

Palazzo Grimani in Venice; designed by McKim, Mead & White; completed 1906 and home of famous jewelry store until 1940. NHL 06.02.1978

Samuel J. Tilden House (National Arts Club)
14-15 Gramercy Park South. A 4-story Victorian Gothic sandstone double house; originally built mid-19th century; remodeled 1881-84 by Calvert Vaux for Samuel J. Tilden, Governor of New York State and principal reform campaigner against Tammany Hall. Notable interior. NHL 05.11.1976

Town Hall
113-123 West 43rd Street. A 4-story Georgian Revival brick building with limestone trim and Neoclassical auditorium; designed by McKim, Mead & White; built 1919-21 for League for Political Education as meeting and concert hall. Well-known forum for internationally prominent speakers and performers. 04.23.1980

Triangle Shirtwaist Factory Building (Brown Building)
23-29 Washington Place. A 10-story Italian Renaissance style masonry commercial building designed by John Woolsey; built 1901. Site of disastrous fire on March 25, 1911, in which 146 garment workers, mostly young women, died, leading to important progressive factory legislation. NHL 07.17.1991

Trinity Chapel Complex (Serbian Orthodox Cathedral of St. Sava Complex)
15 West 25th Street. Gothic Revival brownstone church and clergy house designed by Richard Upjohn; built 1850-55. Notable interior. Adjacent Victorian Gothic parish house (1860, Jacob Wrey Mould). 12.16.1982

Trinity Church and Graveyard
Broadway and Wall Street. Gothic Revival brownstone church designed by Richard Upjohn based on English precedents; built 1841-46. Notable interior. Adjacent cemetery oldest in Manhattan with graves of many prominent New Yorkers, including Alexander Hamilton, Robert Fulton, and William Bradford. NHL 12.08.1976

Tudor City Historic District
Bounded by East 40th and 44th streets and First and Second avenues. Planned residential complex of 14 Tudor Revival brick apartments, apartment-hotel, and hotel buildings clustered around private parks; developed 1925-30 by Fred F. French Co. with H. Douglas Ives, principal architect. Buildings range from 6 to 36 stories in height, with elaborate terra-cotta and cast-stone trim. 09.11.1986

Turtle Bay Gardens Historic District
226-246 East 49th Street and 227-245 East 48th Street. Two rows of 20 brownstone rowhouses built 1860s and redesigned 1921-23 in Neoclassical style by Clarence Dean around landscaped interior courtyard. Longtime residence of theatrical and literary notables. 07.21.1983

Union Theological Seminary
West 120th Street and Broadway. A 2-block campus with 8 connected Collegiate Gothic stone buildings grouped around landscaped quadrangle; designed by Allen & Collens; built 1908-10. 04.23.1980

United Charities Building Complex
105 East 22nd Street, 289 Park Avenue South, and 111-113 East 22nd Street. Group of 3 Romanesque Revival/Renaissance Revival limestone, brick, and terra-cotta buildings. Nine-story United Charities and Kennedy buildings designed by Robert H. Robertson; built 1892. Four-story Dockbuilders Building designed by James B. Baker; built 1915. Buildings served as headquarters for several charities. 03.28.1985; NHL 07.17.1991

United States Courthouse
Foley Square. Monumental 31-story Classical Revival granite skyscraper with Corinthian colonnade and gilt pyramidal roof; designed by Cass Gilbert and Cass Gilbert, Jr.; built 1933-36. 09.02.1987

United States Custom House
Bowling Green. Monumental 7-story Beaux-Arts masonry building with elaborate decoration; designed by Cass Gilbert; built 1900-07. Exterior sculpture by Daniel Chester French. Interior rotunda with frescoes (1937) by Reginald Marsh and others. NHL 12.08.1976

United States General Post Office
Eighth Avenue between West 31st and 33rd streets. Monumental Classical Revival granite building with colonnade of 31 Corinthian columns; designed by McKim, Mead & White; built 1910-13; massive rear addition c.1930. 01.29.1973

United States Post Office–Canal Street Station
350 Canal Street. Moderne terra-cotta post office designed by Alan Balch Mills; built 1937-39. Interior sculpture (1938) by Wheeler Williams. United States Post Offices in New York State, 1858-1943, Thematic Resources. 05.11.1989

United States Post Office and Federal Office Building–Church Street Station
90 Church Street. A 15-story Classical Revival/Art Deco limestone building designed by Cross & Cross and Pennington, Lewis & Mills; built 1934-38. Exterior sculptural reliefs (1937) by Carl Paul Jennewein. United States Post Offices in New York State, 1858-1943, Thematic Resources. 05.11.1989

United States Post Office–Cooper Station
96 Fourth Street. Classical Revival brick and limestone post office designed by William Dewey Foster; built 1936-37. United States Post Offices in New York State, 1858-1943, Thematic Resources. 05.11.1989

United States Post Office–Inwood Station
90 Vermilyea Avenue. Colonial Revival brick post office designed by Carroll H. Pratt; built 1935-37. United States Post Offices in New York State, 1858-1943, Thematic Resources. 05.11.1989

United States Post Office–Knickerbocker Station
130 East Broadway. Colonial Revival brick post office designed by William Dewey Foster; built 1936-37. United States Post Offices in New York State, 1858-1943, Thematic Resources. 05.11.1989

United States Post Office–Lenox Hill Station
221 East 70th Street. A 3-story Colonial Revival brick and limestone post office designed by Eric Kebbon; built 1935. United States Post Offices in New York State, 1858-1943, Thematic Resources. 05.11.1989

United States Post Office–Madison Square Station
149-153 East 23rd Street. Classical Revival/Moderne granite post office designed by Lorimer Rich; built 1935-37. Exterior sculpture (1937) by Edmond Amateis. Interior mural series (1939) by Louis Slobodkin and Kindrid McLeary. United States Post Offices in New York State, 1858-1943, Thematic Resources. 05.11.1989

United States Post Office–Old Chelsea Station
217 West 18th Street. Colonial Revival brick post office designed by Eric Kebbon; built 1935-37. Interior sculptural relief (1938) by Paul Fiene. United States Post Offices in New York State, 1858-1943, Thematic Resources. 05.11.1989

University Club
One West 54th Street. A 6-story granite building modeled after Italian Renaissance palazzo; designed by McKim, Mead & White; built 1897-1900. Notable interior. 04.16.1980

University Settlement House
184 Eldridge Street. A 6-story Georgian Revival brick building. Original 4-story section designed by Harry Fischel; built 1898 for University Settlement Society. Top stories designed by Harry Baum; added 1904. 09.11.1986

Upper East Side Historic District
Roughly bounded by Third and Fifth avenues, and East 59th and 79th streets. A 57-block residential and commercial neighborhood with approximately 1,000 buildings built 1860s-1930's. Primary building types include late 19th-century Victorian rowhouses on east-west cross streets; tall apartment buildings, institutions, and commercial buildings on north-south avenues; Beaux-Arts and Georgian Revival mansions throughout. Individually listed buildings include Gertrude Rhinelander Waldo Mansion, Sara Delano Roosevelt Memorial House, and Seventh Regiment Armory. Architects include McKim, Mead, & White, Carrère & Hastings, Warren & Wetmore, Peabody & Stearns, Horace Trumbauer, Ernest Flagg, and many others. 09.07.1984

USS Edson
Intrepid Square, foot of 46th Street. A 418-foot-long Forrest Sherman class welded-steel destroyer built 1956-58 by Bath Iron Works

shipyard, Bath, Maine. Decommissioned 1989 and on exhibit at Intrepid Air-Sea-Space Museum.   NHL 06.21.1990

USS *Intrepid* (CV-11)
Intrepid Square, foot of 46th Street. An 856-foot-long Essex class steel aircraft carrier built 1943 by Newport News Shipbuilding & Drydock Co. for United States Navy. Served in World War II, Vietnam War, and as recovery ship for astronaut splashdowns. Decommissioned 1981 and on exhibit at Intrepid Air-Sea-Space Museum.   NHL 01.14.1986

Mrs. Graham Fair Vanderbilt Residence
(Lycée Français de New York)
60 East 93rd Street. A 3-story limestone townhouse in French Neoclassical style; designed by John Russell Pope; built 1930-31.
10.29.1982

Stephen Van Rensselaer House
149 Mulberry Street. A 2 1/2-story Federal brick townhouse with gambrel roof; built 1816 for Stephen Van Rensselaer III.   06.16.1983

Giuseppe Verdi Monument
Verdi Square Park (Broadway and Amsterdam Avenue). Triangular park with 25-foot-tall Neoclassical granite and marble sculpture consisting of statues of 4 operatic characters surmounted by heroic statue of Italian composer Giuseppe Verdi; designed and executed 1906 by Pasquale Civiletti.   10.04.1990

Villard Houses
29 1/2 50th Street, 24-26 East 51st Street, and 451, 453, 455, and 457 Madison Avenue. Group of five 3-story brownstone residences clustered in U-shape around courtyard and unified in form of Italian Renaissance palazzo; designed by McKim, Mead & White; built 1882-85; now partially incorporated into Helmsley Palace Hotel. Northern section serves as The Urban Center. Notable interiors.
09.02.1975

Gertrude Rhinelander Waldo Mansion
867 Madison Avenue. Large 4 1/2-story French Renaissance style limestone residence with elaborate ornamentation; designed by Kimball & Thompson; built 1895-98 for, but never occupied by, leading society matron; commercial use since 1921.   05.06.1980

Felix M. Warburg Mansion
(The Jewish Museum)
1109 Fifth Avenue. A 5-story limestone residence with elaborate ornamentation in François I style; designed by C. P. H. Gilbert; built 1906-08 for banking and philanthropic family. Donated 1944 by family to Jewish Museum.   10.29.1982

Washington Bridge (see Bronx County)

James Watson House
(Shrine of the Blessed Elizabeth Seton)
7 State Street. A 3-story Federal brick townhouse. East section built 1793; design attributed to John McComb, Jr. West section, with distinctive curved Ionic portico, built 1806.
07.24.1972

Wavertree
Pier 17, foot of Fulton Street. A 279-foot-long 3-masted iron-hulled sailing ship built 1885 by Oswald, Mordaunt & Co. of Southampton, England, to transport jute from India to Europe. On exhibit at South Street Seaport Museum.   06.13.1978

Webster Hotel
40 West 45th Street. A 12-story Classical Revival brick and limestone former hotel designed 1902 by Tracy & Swartwout.
09.07.1984

House at 17 West 16th Street
Greek Revival brick townhouse with bow front; built c.1846. Housed Margaret Sanger's Birth Control Clinic Research Bureau 1930-73.
05.26.1983

Houses at 437-459 West 24th Street
Group of 12 three-story Greek Revival/Italianate brick townhouses with deep front yards; built 1849-50 by Phil V. Beebe.
10.29.1982

5-15 West 54th Street Residences
Group of 5 large limestone and brick townhouses, including Italian Renaissance style Dr. Moses Allen Starr Residence (1897, Robert H. Robertson), Beaux-Arts Philip Lehman Residence (1899-1900, John H. Duncan), Colonial Revival James J. Goodwin Residence (1896, McKim, Mead & White), and French Renaissance style 13 and 15 West 54th Street residences (1897, Henry J. Hardenbergh; later home, office, and museum of politician and patron Nelson A. Rockefeller).   01.04.1990

**West 67th Street Artists' Colony
Historic District**
1-41 and 40-50 West 67th Street. Group of 7 multistoried brick and limestone apartment buildings and 1 institution (Swiss House) with Gothic-style decorative features; built 1901-29 primarily as cooperative artists' studio apartments. Includes Hotel des Artistes (1915-18, George Mort Pollard), Central Park Studios (1904-05, Simonson, Pollard & Steinham), 67th Street Studios (1901-03, Sturgis & Simonson), Atelier Building (1903-05, Simonson, Pollard & Steinham), Swiss House (1904-05, John E. Scharsmith), Colonial Studios (1906-07, Rosario Candela), and Number 50 (1916-17, Shape & Bready). Residence of numerous renowned American artists.   07.11.1985

West 73rd-74th Street Historic District
West 73rd and 74th streets between Central Park West and Columbus Avenue. A 2-block residential neighborhood with 42 late 19th- to early 20th-century rowhouses, 2 apartments, and 1 commercial building. Notable buildings include 2 rows of Renaissance Revival rowhouses designed 1882 by Henry J. Hardenbergh and row of 18 Georgian Revival rowhouses designed 1902 by Percy Griffin.
09.08.1983

West 76th Street Historic District
West 76th Street between Central Park West and Columbus Avenue. Group of 44 Beaux-Arts, French and Italian Renaissance style, and Romanesque Revival stone and brick rowhouses built 1887 to 1900. Architects include John H. Duncan, Cleverdon & Putzel, Schickel & Ditmars, G. A. Schillinger, and George M. Walgrove.   07.24.1980

Stables at 167, 169, and 171 West 89th Street
Group of three 2-story Romanesque Revival brick former stables designed by Frank A. Rooke; built 1892.   08.25.1983

**West End Collegiate Church
and Collegiate School**
West End Avenue and West 77th Street. Dutch Flemish Revival brick church and school with stepped-gable ends and terra-cotta trim; designed by Robert W. Gibson; built 1892-93.
05.06.1980

Westchester House (Pioneer Hotel)
541-551 Broome Street. A 4-story Greek Revival brick hotel built c.1835; enlarged and altered c.1867 and later. Headquarters of Tammany Hall boss "Big Tim" Sullivan in early 20th century.   03.20.1986

Woolworth Building
233 Broadway. A 60-story skyscraper with Gothic-style terra-cotta facades and elaborate interior lobby; designed by Cass Gilbert; built 1913 as corporate headquarters for variety store chain. World's tallest building until 1930.
NHL 11.13.1966

Yiddish Art Theatre
189 Second Avenue. Brick and cast-stone former theater with Moorish-style exterior and interior decoration; designed by Harrison G. Wiseman; built 1926 for Yiddish theater group.
09.19.1985

Third Judicial District Courthouse, New York (p. 109).

Lewiston

Frontier House
460 Center Street. A 3 1/2-story Federal stone inn built 1824 for Benjamin and Samuel Barton. 07.08.1974

Lewiston Mound
Lewiston State Park. Native American burial mound, approximately 60 feet by 70 feet, dating from 2nd century A.D. and attributed to Squawkie Hill phase of Hopewell culture. 01.21.1974

Lewiston Portage Landing Site
Address restricted. Archeological site of human activity from Archaic-period settlement through late 18th century. Artifacts recovered include stone tools, pottery, and also materials related to British occupation.   07.18.1974

Lockport

Lockport Industrial District
Bounded roughly by Erie Canal, Gooding, Clinton, and Water streets. Historic industrial center of city, including double flight of locks of Erie-Barge Canal, remains of hydraulic raceway, 3-story factory, and ruins of several other 19th-century industrial buildings. 11.11.1975

Lowertown Historic District
Roughly bounded by Erie Canal and New York Central Railroad. Historic commercial and residential center of city, with approximately 110 buildings dating to era of Lockport's canal-related development, 1830-60. Includes numerous stone and brick residences, commercial blocks, warehouses, and churches in variety of architectural styles. 06.04.1973

Benjamin C. Moore Mill (Lockport City Hall)
Pine Street on the Erie Canal. A 2 1/2-story stone flour mill built 1864; later converted to one of the nation's first water-pumping plants; 2-story rear wing added 1893 when converted to city hall.   06.19.1973

United States Post Office–Lockport
One East Avenue. A 3-story Beaux-Arts brick and limestone post office and courthouse designed by James Knox Taylor; built 1902-04. United States Post Offices in New York State, 1858-1943, Thematic Resources.   05.11.1989

Union Station
95 Union Avenue. Romanesque Revival brick railroad station built 1889; all but exterior walls destroyed by fire 1974.   12.02.1977

Middleport

United States Post Office–Middleport
42 Main Street. Colonial Revival/Moderne post office built 1940-41. Interior mural (1941) by Marianne Appel. United States Post Offices in New York State, 1858-1943, Thematic Resources.   05.11.1989

Newfane

Van Horn Mansion
2165 Lockport-Olcott Road. Federal brick residence built 1826 for James Van Horn, local businessman and politician; remodeled c.1860 for U.S. Congressman Burt Van Horn; remodeled c.1900 in Colonial Revival style as summer house for Van Horn family. 09.09.1991

Niagara Falls

Adams Power Plant Transformer House
Buffalo Avenue near Portage Road. Large 1-story stone building in which alternating-current system was first developed. Only remaining structure in complex designed 1895 by McKim, Mead & White.   06.11.1975; NHL 05.04.1983

Deveaux School Historic District
2900 Lewiston Road. Orphanage and boys' prep school with 4 buildings: Gothic Revival stone Van Rensselaer Hall (1855, with later additions); stone barn (1863); shop (1869, originally gymnasium); and frame residence. 06.05.1974

Holley-Rankine House
525 Riverside Drive. A 2 1/2-story stone Gothic Revival residence built late 1850s or 1860s for state assemblyman George Washington Holley. Later owned by William B. Rankine, who was largely responsible for establishment of Niagara Falls Power Co. 10.04.1979

Niagara Falls Public Library
1022 Main Street. Beaux-Arts brick and stone library with oak and marble interior; endowed by Andrew Carnegie and completed 1904. 06.05.1974

Niagara Reservation
(Niagara Reservation State Park)
A 435-acre property adjacent to Niagara Falls; original portion acquired 1885 by New York State, in first use of eminent domain powers for creation of scenic park. Landscape plan (1887) by Olmsted & Vaux.   NHL 05.23.1963

United States Customhouse
2245 Whirlpool Street. A 2 1/2-story stone building built 1863; substantially renovated after 1920s fire.   07.16.1973

United States Post Office–Niagara Falls
Main and Walnut streets. Large Beaux-Arts marble and granite post office designed by James Knox Taylor; built 1904-07. United States Post Offices in New York State, 1858-1943, Thematic Resources.   05.11.1989

Whitney Mansion
335 Buffalo Avenue. Greek Revival residence with monumental Ionic portico; built 1849 for Solon Whitney; substantially enlarged late 19th century.   01.17.1974

Johann Williams Farm
10831 Cayuga Drive. A 10-acre farmstead with farmhouse built 1840s (late 19th- and early 20th-century additions) and several barns and outbuildings.   01.10.1980

North Tonawanda

Allan Herschell Carousel Factory
180 Thompson Street. Group of several interconnected frame buildings built 1910-30. Includes 40-foot-diameter carousel building built 1916.   04.18.1985

Riviera Theatre
27 Webster Street. Movie palace with 1,100-seat auditorium; built 1926. Interior decoration by Willard M. Lusk.   03.20.1980

United States Post Office–North Tonawanda
141 Goundry Street. Large Neoclassical brick post office with limestone Corinthian portico and wood cupola; designed by Oscar Wenderoth; built 1912-14. United States Post Offices in New York State, 1858-1943, Thematic Resources.   05.11.1989

Porter

Fort Niagara Light
Niagara River, Youngstown. A 50-foot-high octagonal limestone lighthouse built 1871-72; raised 11 feet in 1900. United States Coast Guard Lighthouses and Light Stations on the Great Lakes Thematic Resources.   07.19.1984

Old Fort Niagara (State Historic Site)
Fort Niagara State Park. A 30-acre area on Lake Ontario at mouth of Niagara River encompassing fortifications, buildings, cemetery, and archeological sites of structures associated with defense of Great Lakes by French, British, and Americans. Developed by French beginning 1726, captured 1759 by British, surrendered to United States after American Revolution, and recaptured 1813 by British. Includes stone chateau (1726-27, Chaussegros de Lery) and 5 other 18th-century stone buildings. Operated as museum by Old Fort Niagara Association.   NHL 10.09.1960

Somerset

Thirty Mile Point Light
A 60-foot-high square limestone lighthouse and attached keeper's dwelling built 1875-76. United States Coast Guard Lighthouses and Light Stations on the Great Lakes Thematic Resources.   07.19.1984

Youngstown

St. John's Episcopal Church
117 Main Street. Gothic Revival frame church built 1878.   05.10.1990

Mappa Hall, Barneveld.

Opposite: Erie Canal Locks, Lockport Industrial District.

Barneveld

Mappa Hall
Mappa Avenue. A 2 1/2-story Federal stone mansion built c.1801-09 for prominent Dutch settler Adam Gerard Mappa.   05.12.1982

Boonville (Town)

Five Lock Combine and Locks 37 and 38, Black River Canal (Boonville Gorge Park)
NY 46. Remaining features of abandoned Black River Canal including stone locks 37 and 38 (1896) and stone and concrete combined locks (1890s-early 1900s).   03.20.1973

Boonville (Village)

Boonville Historic District
Schuyler, Post, West Main, and Summit streets. Historic core of village, with approximately seventy 19th-century residential and commercial buildings in variety of architectural styles. Notable buildings include Federal/Greek Revival Hulbert House (1812, enlarged 1839), Second Empire First National Bank (1866, A. J. Lathrop; now village offices), late 19th-century octagonal bandstand, Federal residence at 106 West Street (c.1820), several Gothic Revival and Italianate frame residences, and Erwin

Library and Pratt House (individually listed).
11.16.1979

Erwin Library and Pratt House
104-106 Schuyler Street. Romanesque Revival
stone library (1890, C. L. Vivian) and ornate
Second Empire brick mansion (1875, J. B.
Lathrop).   08.14.1973

United States Post Office–Boonville
101 Main Street. Colonial Revival brick post
office built 1937-38. Interior mural (1939) by
Suzanne and Lucerne McCullough. United
States Post Offices in New York State, 1858-
1943, Thematic Resources.   11.17.1988

Clinton

Clinton Village Historic District
North, South, East, and West Park rows, and
Marvin, Williams, Chestnut, Fountain, College,
and Utica streets. Historic center of village, with
approximately 200 buildings, including village
green (1794), 19th-century commercial and
civic buildings surrounding green, and 19th-
and early 20th-century residences and churches
on side streets. Notable buildings include
Federal Williams House (c.1820, now a restaurant), Federal Clinton Grammar School and
lawyers' offices (c.1795), Early Romanesque
Revival Presbyterian Church (1878, Horatio
Nelson White), Georgian Revival Lumbard
Town Hall (1926, Arthur L. Easingwood), and
Greek Revival Methodist Church (1841, now
Kirkland Art Center).   06.14.1982

Holland Patent

Holland Patent Stone Churches
Historic District
Group of 4 Greek Revival limestone churches
sited around village green laid out in 1798.
Includes First Presbyterian Church (1843),
former Baptist Church (1844), former Welsh
Congregational Church (early 19th century;
remodeled 1858), and former Unitarian Church
(1842).   11.21.1991

Kirkland

Hamilton College Chapel
Hamilton College campus. A 3-story Federal
stone chapel and classroom building with
classical trim and wood steeple; designed by
Philip Hooker; completed 1827.   11.03.1975

Norton Farm
Norton Road. An 8-acre farmstead with
vernacular frame farmhouse built c.1798, barn,
and chicken coop. Home of Reverend Asahel
Norton, one of the town's original settlers and
founder of Hamilton College.   07.11.1985

Elihu Root House
101 College Hill Road. Federal frame residence
built 1817. Home of early 20th-century
statesman Elihu Root during most of his adult
life. NHL 11.28.1972

New York Mills

Middle Mills Historic District
NY 5A. Textile mill complex with 3-story
Federal limestone mill (1827, enlarged
throughout 19th century), adjoining 19th-
century mill buildings, 2 churches, and rows
of worker housing. Original mill demolished
1970s.   05.28.1976

Oriskany Falls

First Congregational Free Church
177 North Main Street. Federal limestone
church begun 1833 and completed 1845; spire
added 1886 and stained-glass windows added
1902-03.   11.19.1979

Remsen

Welsh Calvinistic Methodist Church
Prospect Street. A 2-story vernacular limestone
meetinghouse built 1831. Associated with
county's Welsh immigrant settlement.
01.13.1988

Rome

Arsenal House
514 West Dominick Street. Imposing Federal
brick residence built 1813 by federal government for commandant of arsenal formerly
located on site.   07.18.1974

Fort Stanwix National Monument
Bounded by Dominick, Spring, Liberty, and
James streets. Site of 1758 fort which was
location of major treaty with Iroquois Indians
in 1768 and figured prominently in American
Revolution under control of Continental Army.
Current fort is 1970s reconstruction. Museum.
NHL 11.23.1962

Gansevort-Bellamy Historic District
Roughly bounded by Liberty, Steuben,
Huntington, and Bissel streets. Two adjacent
half-acre parks and 10 surrounding buildings,
including Greek Revival Oneida County
Courthouse (1849-50; reconstructed 1902),
post office, City Hall (1894), Justice Building,
2 churches, and 4 residences.   11.12.1975

Jervis Public Library
613 North Washington Street. Large Greek
Revival/Italianate former residence with Doric
portico; built 1858; designed and occupied by
prominent 19th-century engineer John B. Jervis.
11.04.1982

Oriskany Battlefield (State Historic Site)
NY 69 (also in town of Whitestown). A 70-acre
archeological site of American Revolutionary
Battle of Oriskany, August 6, 1777, between
American militiamen under command of
General Nicholas Herkimer and British and
Indians under command of Lieutenant Barry
St. Leger. NHL 11.23.1962

Utica

Roscoe Conkling House
3 Rutger Street. Large Federal/Greek Revival
stuccoed brick residence designed by Philip
Hooker; completed 1830. Home of prominent
United States senator and political boss.
NHL 05.15.1975

First Baptist Church of Deerfield
Herkimer Road. Federal vernacular frame
church with attached tower; built 1811.
Interior retains original features. Adjacent
cemetery.   07.11.1985

First Presbyterian Church
1605 Genesee Street. Large Georgian Revival
brick church designed 1920 by Ralph Adams
Cram. Adjacent Beaux-Arts Robert McKinnon
House designed 1899 by C. Edward Vosbury.
11.03.1988

Fountain Elms
318 Genesee Street. Large Italianate brick villa
designed by William L. Woollett; built 1850-
52; later additions. Notable interior with
reconstructed "period" rooms. Operated as
museum as part of Munson-Williams-Proctor
Institute complex.   11.03.1972

Lower Genesee Street Historic District
Bounded by Seneca, Water, West Genesee,
Division, and Liberty streets. Commercial and
industrial area with approximately 40 Federal,
Greek Revival, Italianate, Romanesque
Revival, and Neoclassical 3- and 4-story
masonry buildings built 1830-1929.
10.29.1982

New Century Club
253 Genesee Street. Large Federal brick
residence built 1826; enlarged c.1840;
Italianate cornice and portico added c.1860;
large brick wing built 1897. Home of one of
New York State's earliest women's civic
organizations.   09.12.1985

Rutger-Steuben Park Historic District
Rutger Street from Steuben Park to Taylor
Avenue. Group of 64 Italianate villas and other
residences dating from 1830. Includes resi-
dence designed by Alexander Jackson Davis
and another derived from Andrew Jackson
Downing designs. Also includes Roscoe
Conkling House (individually listed) and
Rutger B. Miller House (c.1823-30, Philip
Hooker).   09.19.1973

St. Joseph's Church
704-708 Columbia Street. Romanesque
Revival brick and limestone church built 1871
for German congregation; some windows
executed by Tyrolese Art Glass Works in
Innsbruck, Austria. Also includes brick school
(1885), residence (1906), and convent (1891).
08.22.1977

Stanley Theater
259 Genesee Street. A 3,500-seat theater with
French-inspired Renaissance and Baroque-style
details; includes street-level shops and intact
interior; designed by Thomas W. Lamb, built
1928.   08.13.1976

Union Station
Main Street between John and First streets. Monumental 3-story Beaux-Arts granite and brick railroad station designed by Stem & Fellheimer; built 1914. Notable barrel-vaulted waiting room. 04.28.1975

Utica Public Library
303 Genesee Street. A 5-story Neoclassical brick library with limestone trim; designed by Alexander C. Jackson of Carrère & Hastings; built 1903. 10.29.1982

Utica State Hospital
1213 Court Street. Massive 550-foot-long Greek Revival limestone building with monumental Doric portico; designed by William Clark; built 1837-43. One of the largest Greek Revival buildings in the United States. Wings threatened with demolition. Original landscaping by Andrew Jackson Downing. 10.26.1971; NHL 07.18.1989

General John G. Weaver House
711 Herkimer Road. Imposing Federal brick residence built 1815 with elaborate detailing thought to be influenced by work of Philip Hooker. 12.07.1989

Vernon

Vernon Center Green Historic District
Vernon Center. Small park laid out 1798 with c.1900 gazebo and 2 adjacent 19th-century churches complexes. 09.19.1985

Waterville

Tower Homestead and Masonic Temple
210 Tower Street and Sanger Street. Group of 9 buildings. Includes Tower Homestead, built in 3 sections: Federal portion c.1800, pedimented Greek Revival center section c.1830, and west wing c.1910. Masonic Temple built 1896 as residence. 10.05.1977

Waterville Triangle Historic District
East Main, West Main, and White streets, and Stafford Avenue. Central 19th-century core of village, with Italianate brick commercial buildings, frame churches, civic buildings, and residences. Notable buildings include Italianate Richards Residence (1858, A. B. Cady), Victorian Gothic First Presbyterian Church (1873, Archimedes Russell), Federal Locke House (c.1820), Gothic Revival Grace Episcopal Church (1854, Thomas S. Jackson), High Victorian Gothic George Putnam House (c.1880, adapted for use as nursing home), and Italianate Candee-Harris Residence (c.1850). 04.04.1978

Union Station, Utica.

Western

General William Floyd House
Main Street opposite Gilford Hill Road, Westernville. Large Georgian frame residence built 1803 by signer of Declaration of Independence. NHL 07.17.1971

Whitesboro

Whitestown Town Hall
(Oneida County Courthouse)
8 Park Avenue. Federal brick building built 1807 as county courthouse in half-shired county. 11.26.1973

Whitestown

Oriskany Battlefield (see Rome)

Baldwinsville

Oswego-Oneida Streets Historic District
Oswego, East, and West streets, and Sunset
Terrace. A 3-block residential neighborhood
with thirty-four 19th- and early 20th-century
residences, mostly in Greek Revival, Italianate,
Queen Anne, Shingle, and Arts and Crafts
styles. Architects include H. M. Stephenson and
Ward Wellington Ward. Also includes Gothic
Revival First Presbyterian Church (1865,
Horatio Nelson White). 07.29.1982

Camillus

Camillus Union Free School
First and LeRoy streets. A 2-story Colonial
Revival brick school designed by Eugene
H. Sacket of Sacket & Park; built 1912-13;
gymnasium addition 1928. 05.28.1991

Hall of Languages, Syracuse University.

Nine Mile Creek Aqueduct
Thompson Road, northeast of Camillus.
A 144-foot-long, 4-span arched stone Erie
Canal aqueduct built 1841-44, during first
enlargement of canal; design attributed to
engineer Frederick C. Mills. 05.17.1976

Wilcox Octagon House
5420 West Genesee Street. Victorian octagonal
residence constructed of stuccoed cobblestone
aggregate and cement; built 1856 by Isaiah
Wilcox following principles of Orson Fowler.
07.28.1983

Cicero

Robinson Site
Address restricted. Prehistoric archeological
occupational site from Brewerton Phase of
Laurentian Tradition, c.2000 B.C., containing
features such as pits, hearths, and burials.
07.29.1985

DeWitt

Dr. John Ives House
6575 East Seneca Turnpike, Jamesville. Large
Federal frame residence with hipped roof and
modillioned cornice; built c.1812-15 for
dentist. Intact interior. Adjacent early 19th-
century carriage house and brick smokehouse.
08.29.1985

Elbridge

**Elbridge Hydraulic Industry Archeological
District**
Address restricted. A 16-acre parcel encompassing archeological sites and ruins of several
mid-19th- to early 20th-century water-powered
mill complexes, including chair factory, paper
mill, hydroelectric facility, pail factory, and
sawmill. 06.15.1982

Fayetteville

**Genesee Street Hill–Limestone Plaza
Historic District**
Roughly both sides of Genesee Street from
Chapel Street to Limestone Plaza. A 3-block
central section of village, with 42 buildings
built 1820-85, including Federal, Greek Revival, Gothic Revival, and Stick Style residences,
2 churches, and small row of Greek Revival
commercial buildings. Includes boyhood home
of President Grover Cleveland. 07.29.1982

Levi Snell House
416 Brooklea Drive. Large Greek Revival/
Italianate brick residence with Doric porch;
built c.1855 for merchant and investor.
08.20.1987

Jordan

Jordan Village Historic District
Roughly bounded by North Main, South Main,
Elbridge, Clinton, Hamilton, Lawrence, and
Mechanic streets. Central core of village on
former Erie Canal, with 73 commercial,
residential, and religious buildings built from
1820 to early 20th century in wide range of
styles. Notable structures include Erie Canal
aqueduct and canal park, White Mill (c.1810),
Jordan Hotel (1820; enlarged 1870), and
Romanesque Revival Hendricks Block
(c.1876). 09.15.1983

Liverpool

Lucius Gleason House (Liverpool Village Hall)
314 Second Street. Large Italianate stuccoed

brick residence built c.1860 for industrialist. Acquired 1938 by village.　05.10.1990

Lysander

Whig Hill and Dependencies
West Genesee and Gates roads. A 25-acre property with large Federal/Greek Revival brick residence with decorative stone lintels and urn-shaped iron newel posts at entrance; built 1833 for prominent farmer James L. Voohrees. Outbuildings include 2 early 19th-century Dutch barns and tenant house. Once center of vast land holdings of Voorhees, who was later involved in state politics and commercial enterprises in Brooklyn and Syracuse. 05.12.1975

Manlius (Town)

Mycenae Schoolhouse
NY5. Greek Revival 1-room limestone schoolhouse built c.1850.　08.11.1983

Manlius (Village)

Manlius Village Historic District
Pleasant, Franklin, North, Clinton, and East Seneca streets. A 3-block section of village with approximately 45 buildings, including large group of Federal and Greek Revival brick and frame detached residences, commercial block, 4 churches, and late 19th-century bandstand in Academy Park.　11.06.1973

Marcellus

Dan Bradley House
59 South Street. Federal frame residence built c.1804-12 for local judge and leading citizen of village; his son, Dr. Dan Beech Bradley, was early medical and religious missionary to Siam. 12.12.1978

Onondaga

General Orrin Hutchinson House
4311 West Seneca Turnpike. Large Federal brick residence with stepped gable ends and elaborate interior woodwork; built 1812. 04.13.1973

Pompey

Delphi Baptist Church
Oran-Delphi Road, Delphi Falls. Federal frame church with engaged tower and octagonal belfry; built 1815-18. Adjacent cemetery. 08.24.1979

Delphi Village School
East Road, Delphi Falls. Greek Revival 2-room schoolhouse built c.1854-60.　05.22.1986

Salina

Alvord House
Berwick Road, north of Syracuse. Large Federal stone residence built c.1835 for Dioclesian Alvord.　08.27.1976

Skaneateles (Town)

Community Place
725 Sheldon Road, south of Skaneateles. A 5-acre section of former farmstead with Late Federal/Greek Revival limestone residence built 1830, massive stuccoed masonry carriage house, stuccoed shed, and frame barn. Occupied by Fourierist commune 1843-46. 04.20.1979

Kelsey-Davey Farm
Old Seneca Turnpike, northeast of Skaneateles. A 79-acre farmstead with Federal frame farmhouse built c.1810 and 19th-century outbuildings including shop, privy, and barns. 04.16.1980

Skaneateles (Village)

Skaneateles Historic District
Jordan, Fennell, and East and West Genesee streets. Central commercial and residential core of village, with fifty-nine 19th-century buildings, including several rows of 3-story Federal and Greek Revival brick commercial buildings, stone mill (1842), Romanesque Revival library, Victorian commercial buildings, and several Federal, Greek Revival, and Italianate residences. Also includes Shingle Style Willetts House (Stanford White), Gothic Revival St. James Episcopal Church (1873, Horatio Nelson White), and park.　05.10.1984

Reuel E. Smith House
28 West Lake Street. Large Gothic Revival stuccoed brick villa overlooking Skaneateles Lake; designed by Alexander Jackson Davis; built 1849-52 as summer house for New York City merchant.　07.27.1979

Syracuse

Amos Block
210-216 West Water Street. Large 4-story Romanesque Revival/eclectic brick commercial building with polychromatic decoration; designed by Joseph Lyman Silsbee; built 1878 adjacent to Erie Canal.　11.16.1978

Armory Square Historic District
South Clinton, South Franklin, Walton, West Fayette, and West Jefferson streets. A 5-block area adjacent to and including Armory Park in central business district of city, with 46 buildings, including Italianate, Second Empire, Queen Anne, Romanesque Revival, and Moderne warehouses, factories, hotels, and armory built late 19th to early 20th century. Architects include Archimedes Russell, Charles E. Colton, Gustavas A. Young, and Asa Merrick. Includes Loew's State Theater (individually listed).　09.07.1984

Alexander Brown House
726 West Onondaga Street. Large Richardsonian Romanesque limestone residence designed by Gordon Wright; built 1895 for inventor and manufacturer. Adjacent frame carriage house.　11.03.1983

Central New York Telephone and Telegraph Building
311 Montgomery Street. A 5-story Italian Renaissance style brick commercial building with terra-cotta trim; designed by Henry W. Wilkinson; built 1895-96. Headquarters of Onondaga Historical Association. 04.03.1973

Central Technical High School
South Warren Street at Adams Street. Massive 3-story Neoclassical brick school with limestone trim and 2-story Ionic pedimented portico; designed by Archimedes Russell; built 1900-03; 1931 addition designed by Albert Brisbane.　04.09.1981

Crouse College
Syracuse University campus. Monumental 3-story Romanesque Revival sandstone building with corner tower and elaborate decoration; designed by Archimedes Russell; built 1881-84 as school of music with funds donated by banker John Crouse. Notable 2-story auditorium with open timber roof. 07.30.1974

Gere Bank Building
121 East Water Street. A 5-story Romanesque Revival brick commercial building with granite and terra-cotta trim; designed by Charles E. Colton; built 1894 for James J. Belden. 03.16.1972

William J. Gillett House
515 West Onondaga Street. Second Empire frame residence with brick veneered exterior and elaborate wood ornamentation; designed by contractor William J. Gillett and built 1871 as his home.　05.06.1982

Grace Episcopal Church
819 Madison Street. Victorian Gothic limestone church designed by Horatio Nelson White; built 1876-77.　03.20.1973

John Gridley House
205 East Seneca Turnpike. Federal 4-bay limestone residence with stepped gable ends; built c.1812.　08.16.1977

Hall of Languages, Syracuse University
Syracuse University campus. Massive Second Empire limestone building designed by Horatio Nelson White; built 1871-73. First building on Syracuse University campus.　09.20.1973

Hanover Square Historic District
101-203 East Water Street, 120-200 East Genesee Street, 113 Salina Street, and 109-114 South Warren Street. Group of seventeen 19th- and early 20th-century commercial buildings sited around triangular square. Includes Federal Phoenix Buildings (built 1834 as Erie Canal lofts), Second Empire buildings, 22-story Art Deco State Tower Building (1927,

Thompson & Churchill), Neoclasical former Bank of Syracuse (1896, Albert L. Brockway), Neoclassical Onondaga Savings Bank Building (1896, Robert W. Gibson), and individually listed Gridley Building and Gere Bank Building. 06.22.1976

Hawley-Green Street Historic District
Green Street and Hawley Avenue. A 19th-century neighborhood with approximately 50 buildings, ranging from modest Greek Revival to large Queen Anne residences. Includes Second Empire Greenway Place and row of 14 rowhouses built 1882 and later remodeled in Tudor Revival style. 05.02.1979

Polaski King House
2270 Valley Drive. Federal brick residence built c.1810. 04.20.1979; DEMOLISHED

Loew's State Theater
362-374 South Salina Street. An 8-story Neoclassical stone commercial building with storefronts on 1st floor, offices on upper floors, and massive 3,000-seat auditorium and lobbies elaborately decorated in Oriental and Moorish motifs; designed by Thomas W. Lamb; built 1927-28. 05.02.1977

Montgomery Street–Columbus Circle Historic District
East Jefferson, East Onondaga, Montgomery, and East Fayette streets. Downtown district with 16 principal civic, religious, and cultural properties, including individually listed City Hall, St. Paul's Cathedral and Parish House, and Central New York Telephone and Telegraph Building. Other notable buildings include Hills Building (1928, Melvin King), Renaissance Revival New York Telephone Building (1906), Beaux-Arts Syracuse Public Library (1901-02, James Randall), Greek Revival First Gospel Church (1846), Beaux-Arts Fourth Onondaga County Courthouse (1904-06, Archimedes Russell and Melvin King), Romanesque Revival St. Mary's Cathedral and Rectory (1913, Archimedes Russell), Gothic Revival First Baptist Church (1912, Gordon Wright), and statue of Christopher Columbus in Columbus Square (c.1930). 02.19.1980

North Salina Street Historic District
517-951 and 522-854 North Salina Street, 1121 North Townsend Street, and 504-518 Prospect Avenue. Commercial district with 98 properties, mostly late 19th- to early 20th-century Italianate brick attached buildings. Mercantile center of German community in late 19th century and Italian community in early 20th century. 09.19.1985

Oakwood Cemetery
940 Comstock Avenue. A 160-acre rural cemetery originally designed 1859 by landscape architect Howard Daniels; expanded throughout late 19th century. Contains large collection of tombs and monuments, mausoleums designed by well-known architects such as Horatio Nelson White and Archimedes Russell, and graves of prominent citizens. Victorian

Gothic chapel and receiving vault designed c.1880 by Joseph L. Silsbee. Romanesque Revival railroad bridge and old office building designed c.1902 by H. Q. French & Co. 05.09.1991

Onondaga County Savings Bank
(Gridley Building)
101 South Salina Street. Large 3 1/2-story Second Empire limestone building with corner clock tower; designed by Horatio Nelson White; built 1867-69 adjacent to Erie Canal. 02.24.1971

Onondaga County War Memorial
200 Madison Street. Massive limestone-clad building with innovative concrete barrel-vaulted auditorium; designed by Edgarton & Edgarton with structural design by Ammann & Whitney; built 1949-51 as commemorative memorial to World War I and World War II veterans and casualties. 12.19.1988

Pi Chapter House of Psi Upsilon Fraternity
101 College Place. Large Neoclassical frame fraternity house with Ionic portico and octagonal cupola; designed by W. W. Taber; built 1898. 05.16.1985

St. Paul's Cathedral and Parish House
310 Montgomery Street. Large Gothic Revival limestone church with 225-foot-tall tower; designed by Henry Dudley; built 1884. Attached parish house designed by Alfred Taylor; built 1909. 12.01.1978

South Salina Street Historic District
1555-1829 and 1606-1830 South Salina Street and 111 West Kennedy Street. The 3-block core of former village of Danforth, with 27 mid-19th- to early 20th-century buildings, including Gothic Revival, Italianate, and Colonial Revival residences, 1 commercial building, and 2 churches. 03.27.1986

Gustav Stickley House
438 Columbus Avenue. Queen Anne frame residence built 1900; significant Arts and Crafts interior alterations in 1903 by Gustav Stickley as his own residence. 08.23.1984

Syracuse City Hall
233 East Washington Street. Massive 5-story Romanesque Revival limestone building with tall bell tower; designed by Charles E. Colton; built 1889-93. 08.27.1976

Syracuse Savings Bank
102 North Salina Street. Large 5 1/2-story High Victorian Gothic polychromatic sandstone building with 171-foot central tower; designed by Joseph Lyman Silsbee; built 1876. 02.18.1971

Syracuse University–Comstock Tract Buildings
Syracuse University campus. Group of 15 brick and stone buildings at core of original campus built 1873-1937 in variety of styles, including Second Empire, Romanesque Revival, Beaux-Arts, Neoclassical, and Italian Renaissance. Architects include Dwight James Baum, John Russell Pope, Archimedes Russell, E. W. and E. H. Gaggin, Revels & Hallenbeck, and

Syracuse City Hall.

Opposite: Lobby, Loew's State Theater, Syracuse.

Horatio Nelson White. Includes individually listed Crouse College and Hall of Languages. 07.22.1980

Oliver Teall House
105 South Beech Street. Federal frame residence with arcaded facade; built 1819 by superintendent of construction for Erie Canal. 03.16.1972; DEMOLISHED 1990

Third National Bank
107 James Street at Salina Street. A 5 1/2-story Queen Anne brick and sandstone building designed by Archimedes Russell; built 1885; rebuilt and enlarged early 20th century. 09.22.1972

Walnut Park Historic District
Walnut Place and Walnut Avenue. Residential neighborhood surrounding park, with 17 large Georgian Revival, Colonial Revival, Tudor Revival, Jacobean Revival, and Chateauesque-style brick, frame, and stone residences built 1897-1930. 09.15.1983

Weighlock Building
Erie Boulevard East at Montgomery Street. Large 2-story Greek Revival/Italianate brick building built 1849-50 for collection of tolls and barge inspection at junction of Erie and Oswego canals. Erie Canal Museum. 02.18.1971

White Memorial Building
106 East Washington Street. Massive 5-story High Victorian Gothic brick commercial building with elaborate polychromatic brick and stone trim; designed by Joseph Lyman Silsbee; built 1876. 02.06.1973

Hamilton White House
307 South Townsend Street. Large Greek Revival brick residence with Ionic porch and cupola; built c.1842. 07.20.1973

Canandaigua

Adelaide Avenue School
108-116 Adelaide Avenue. Small Queen Anne brick school designed by Orlando K. Foote; built c.1890. Converted to apartments. Canandaigua Multiple Resource Area. 04.26.1984

Benham House
280-282 South Main Street. A 2-story Italianate brick residence with ornate cast-iron-front fence and cresting on cupola; built c.1876. Canandaigua Multiple Resource Area. 04.26.1984

Brigham Hall (Grace Home)
229 Bristol Street. Complex of 11 buildings on 16-acre site with picturesque landscaping, originally built for care of mentally ill. Includes Gothic Revival main building (c.1855) and Tudor Revival Cook Memorial Building (1920s). Canandaigua Multiple Resource Area. 09.29.1984

Canandaigua Historic District
Roughly Main Street from Chapel to Saltonstall streets; Howell, Gibson, Gorham, Bristol, Bemis, and Center streets. Historic core of city, with approximately 300 buildings in variety of 19th- and early 20th-century architectural styles. Includes North Main Street Historic District (individually listed), commercial blocks, and several residential blocks. Canandaigua Multiple Resource Area. 04.26.1984

Thaddeus Chapin House
128 Thad Chapin Street. Large Federal brick residence with stepped gable ends; built 1820s. Includes late 19th-century barn. Canandaigua Multiple Resource Area. 04.26.1984

Cobblestone Manor
495 North Main Street. Greek Revival cobblestone residence built late 1830s; early 20th-century Colonial Revival additions and alterations. Canandaigua Multiple Resource Area. 04.26.1984

Granger Cottage
60 Granger Street. Gothic Revival frame residence built 1850s; Colonial Revival front porch added early 20th century. Associated with prominent Granger family. Canandaigua Multiple Resource Area. 04.26.1984

Francis Granger House
426 North Main Street. Federal frame residence built c.1817 with later alterations. Home of prominent Whig politician. Canandaigua Multiple Resource Area. 04.26.1984

Marshall House
274 Bristol Street. Federal brick residence built 1844; later modifications include Italianate porch and eave brackets. Canandaigua Multiple Resource Area. 04.26.1984

North Main Street Historic District
Between railroad tracks and Buffalo-Chapel Street. Nearly mile-long section of North Main Street, with 86 residential, religious, and civic buildings. Notable buildings include Federal Granger Homestead (1816; museum), Federal First Congregational Church (1812), Late Federal City Hall (built 1824 as county courthouse), Ontario County Courthouse (1857-59, Henry Searl; reconstructed and enlarged 1908-09 by J. Foster Warner), Victorian Gothic St. John's Episcopal Church (1871-73, Emlen T. Littell), and United States Post Office (individually listed). 07.20.1973

Saltonstall Street School
47 Saltonstall Street. Brick school built 1875, with Queen Anne front section added 1890. Canandaigua Multiple Resource Area. 04.26.1984

Sonnenberg Gardens
151 Charlotte Street. A 40-acre estate with 8 distinct formal gardens designed c.1900 by landscape architect Ernest Bowditch. Includes large Queen Anne residence built 1887; enlarged early 20th century for philanthropists Frederick Ferris Thompson and Mary Clark Thompson. 09.28.1973

Building at 426 South Main Street
Imposing 2-story Italianate brick residence built c.1880. Canandaigua Multiple Resource Area. 04.26.1984

United States Post Office–Canandaigua
28 North Main Street. Classical Revival stone post office with 2-story portico; designed by Allen & Collens; built 1910-12. United States Post Offices in New York State, 1858-1943, Thematic Resources. 11.17.1988

Clifton Springs

Clifton Springs Sanitarium
9 and 11 East Main Street. Water curative facility developed c.1850-c.1926 by Dr. Henry Foster. Buildings include 5-story brick main building (1896, Pierce & Bickford) and Gothic Revival Foster Cottage (1854). 04.06.1979; BOUNDARY INCREASE 05.24.1990

East Bloomfield

East Bloomfield Historic District
State, Main, South, and Park streets. Historic core of small village, with 49 residential, religious, commercial, and civic properties. Notable properties include Elton Park (1847, with 1866 Civil War Monument), Greek Revival frame First Congregational Church (c.1837), Federal brick East Bloomfield Academy (c.1838), East Bloomfield Cemetery (begun 1838), 2 Federal taverns, 2 Federal stores, and numerous Federal and Greek Revival residences. 11.13.1989

Geneva (Town)

Belhurst Castle
Lochland Road. A 23-acre estate with large Romanesque Revival residence designed by Albert W. Fuller; built 1888-91 for socialite Carrie Young Harron Collins. Notable interior. Converted to restaurant/inn. 01.29.1987

Geneva (City)

Ashcroft
112 Jay Street. A 5-acre property with ornate 2½-story High Victorian Gothic brick residence designed 1862 by Calvert Vaux for Amon Langdon. Landscaped grounds. 11.20.1975

Geneva Hall and Trinity Hall, Hobart & William Smith College
South Main Street. Two 3-story Federal stone buildings, both originally dormitories. Geneva Hall built 1822, Trinity Hall built 1837. Oldest buildings of original Hobart College campus. 07.16.1973

Nester House
1001 Lochland Road. A 3-story Italian Renaissance style stuccoed residence designed by Albro & Lindeberg; modeled after Villa Lancellotti near Rome, Italy; built 1911; later additions and conversion to apartments. Formal gardens designed by Pitkin & Weinrichter. 04.09.1984

Parrott Hall
West North Street. A 3-story Italianate brick villa with ornate cast-iron veranda; built early 1850s for Nehemiah Denton. Used since 1882 as headquarters for state's agricultural experiment station. 08.12.1971

Smith's Opera House
82 Seneca Street. Renaissance Revival brick and stone theater designed by Pierce & Bickford; built 1894. Interior renovations 1929-31 in Baroque motif. 10.10.1979

South Main Street Historic District
Irregular pattern along South Main Street. Mile-long district with 140 structures, Poultney Park, and original quadrangle of Hobart College. Numerous 19th-century residences include Federal Williamson, Truslow, and Prouty-Chew houses (Prouty-Chew House, headquarters of Geneva Historical Society), and Greek Revival Watson-Chew and Clark houses. Includes St. John's Chapel (1852, Richard Upjohn) and individually listed Geneva and Trinity halls. 12.31.1974

United States Post Office–Geneva
67 Castle Street. Colonial Revival brick and stone post office with Roman Doric portico; designed by James Knox Taylor; built 1905-06. Interior mural (1938) by T. Barbarossa and exterior sculptural relief (1942) by Peter Blume. United States Post Offices in New York State, 1858-1943, Thematic Resources. 05.11.1989

Hopewell

Oliver Warner Farmstead
NY88, near Clifton Springs (also in town of Phelps). A 203-acre farmstead with Federal/Greek Revival cobblestone farmhouse built c.1840, barn, and wagon shed. 11.17.1988

Phelps (Town)

Oliver Warner Farmstead (see Hopewell)

Phelps (Village)

St. John's Episcopal Church
Church Street. Gothic Revival stone church designed by Major David B. Douglass; completed 1850. Interior features Kingpost truss roof framing; apse added 1897 and tower added 1905. 11.07.1978

Sonnenberg Gardens, Canandaigua

Opposite: Francis Granger House, Canandaigua.

Seneca

Thomas Barron House
1160 Canandaigua Road. Large Greek Revival cobblestone residence with Ionic portico; built 1848. 10.06.1988

Seneca Presbyterian Church
Off NY245 on Number Nine Road, east of Stanley. Greek Revival frame church built 1838; enlarged 1863; bell tower added 1873. 05.25.1973

Victor (Town)

Boughton Hill (Ganondagan State Historic Site)
Boughton Hill Road. Archeological site of "great town" of Seneca tribe which was destroyed 1687 by the French. NHL 07.19.1964

Victor (Village)

Osborne House
146 Maple Avenue. Italianate brick residence designed by Austin & Warner; built c.1855-58. 07.11.1980

Chester

Yelverton Inn and Store
112-116 Main Street. Large Colonial frame
inn built c.1765 with later additions and
alterations. Adjacent Greek Revival frame
commercial building, barn, and shed built
1841-43. 03.28.1980

Cornwall (Town)

Cornwall Friend's Meeting House
275 Quaker Avenue (NY107 off US9W). A 5-
acre property with 2-story frame Quaker
meetinghouse built c.1790, carriage shed, and
cemetery. Cornwall Multiple Resource Area.
12.07.1988

Knox Headquarters (see New Windsor)

Storm King Highway
NY218 (also in town of Highlands). A 4-mile-
long scenic, winding highway along Hudson
River between Cornwall Landing and West
Point; designed by engineer T. Fenner of New
York State Department of Transportation; built
1916-22 by John L. Hayes Construction Co.
Hudson Highlands Multiple Resource Area.
11.23.1982

Cornwall (Village)

Amelia Barr House
Mountain Road. Large Victorian frame resi-
dence built c.1881. Onetime residence of
Anglo-American author Amelia Barr. Hudson
Highlands Multiple Resource Area.
11.23.1982

Camp Olmsted
114 Bayview Avenue. A 21-acre property with
large Victorian main residence, caretaker's
residence, annex, entrance gate, pool, dining
hall, changing houses, and gazebo; former
estate developed after 1901 as fresh air camp
for city children. Hudson Highlands Multiple
Resource Area. 11.23.1982

Deer Hill
58 Deerhill Road. A 12-acre property with large
Italianate frame residence built c.1875, barn,
shed, and garage. Hudson Highlands Multiple
Resource Area. 11.23.1982

Gatehouse on Deerhill Road
Deerhill Road. A 30-acre property with large
Norman style stuccoed residence with circular
tower; built c.1885 as gatehouse of unbuilt
estate. Hudson Highlands Multiple Resource
Area. 11.23.1982

LeDoux-Healey House
60 Deerhill Road. A 5-acre property with large

Shingle Style frame and stone residence and
carriage barn built c.1890. Hudson Highlands
Multiple Resource Area. 11.23.1982

River View House
146 Bayview Avenue. A 9-acre property with
large Italianate/Gothic Revival frame residence
and cottage built c.1860. Hudson Highlands
Multiple Resource Area. 11.23.1982

Deerpark

**Delaware and Hudson Canal,
Cuddebackville Section**
Cuddebackville. Intact section of canal com-
pleted 1828 between Honesdale, Pennsylvania,
and Kingston, New York, to transport coal to
furnaces in New York. Includes canal basin,
Neversink Feeder, remains of Neversink
Aqueduct, and several associated buildings.
Museum. Delaware and Hudson Canal
Thematic Resources. NHL 11.24.1968

Goshen (Town)

District School No. 9 (Old Stone Schoolhouse)
NY17A. Vernacular stone 1-room schoolhouse
built c.1820. 09.15.1988

Dutchess Quarry Cave Site
Address restricted. Large cave in limestone cliff
with archeological evidence of inhabitation
from Paleo-Indian to Late Woodland stages.
01.18.1974

Goshen (Village)

Church Park Historic District
Park Place, Main and Webster streets. Resi-
dential and commercial neighborhood focused
on triangular Church Park, with approximately
70 properties, including late Federal, Greek
Revival, and Victorian commercial buildings
and residences. Notable properties include
Elizabethan Revival Goshen Inn (1912, Walker
& Gillette), E. H. Harriman Memorial
Fountain (1911), Charles Everett Bandstand
(1917), Gothic Revival stone St. James
Episcopal Church (1853, Richard Upjohn),
Federal brick Lawyers' Row (c.1820), Orange
Inn (c.1790), Goshen Library (1918, Huse
Templeton Blanchard), Federal Maplewood
(c.1800), and individually listed 1841 Goshen
Courthouse and Historic Track. 11.17.1980

1841 Goshen Courthouse
101 Main Street. Greek Revival stuccoed brick
building with Doric pedimented portico and
Ionic cupola; designed by Thornton M. Niven;
built 1841 as courthouse in half-shired county.
Adjacent Victorian annex built 1874.
03.04.1975

Historic Track (Goshen Historic Track)
Main Street. Horse-racing complex with half-
mile-long oval dirt trotting track and associated
buildings; established 1838 and improved late
19th and early 20th centuries. One of the oldest
active trotting courses in America.
NHL 05.23.1966

United States Post Office–Goshen
Grand Street. Colonial Revival brick post office
designed by E. P. Valkenburgh; built 1935.
Interior mural (1937) by Georgina Klitgaard.
United States Post Offices in New York State,
1858-1943, Thematic Resources. 05.11.1989

Hamptonburgh

Bull Stone House
Hamptonburgh Road, Campbell Hall. A 9-acre
property with large Colonial vernacular stone
residence built 1722-27 by English-born stone
mason William Bull as his residence. Adjacent
Dutch barn. 07.18.1974

Bull-Jackson House (Hill-Hold)
NY416, northwest of Campbell Hall. A 189-
acre farmstead with large Georgian stone
residence built 1769 by Thomas Bull; Greek
Revival alterations. Property includes several
19th-century farm outbuildings. Operated as
agricultural museum by Orange County.
05.17.1974

Harriman

Arden (see Woodbury)

Highland Falls

House at 37 Center Street
Greek Revival frame residence built c.1850.
Hudson Highlands Multiple Resource Area.
11.23.1982

Church of the Holy Innocents and Rectory
112 Main Street. Gothic Revival stone church
designed by artist Robert Walter Weir; built
1846-47; extensive additions and alterations
1887. Adjacent Tudor Revival rectory built
c.1900. Hudson Highlands Multiple Resource
Area. 11.23.1982

First Presbyterian Church of Highland Falls
140 Main Street. Gothic/Romanesque Revival
granite church designed by Frederick C.
Withers; built 1868. Hudson Highlands
Multiple Resource Area. 11.23.1982

Highland Falls Railroad Depot
Dock Road. A 2-story Victorian shingled
railroad station with elaborate decorative
details; built c.1882. Hudson Highlands
Multiple Resource Area. 11.23.1982

Highland Falls Village Hall
Main Street. Large 3-story Victorian brick
commercial building built c.1894. Hudson
Highlands Multiple Resource Area.
11.23.1982

House at 116 Main Street
Italianate/Picturesque frame villa with 3-story
corner tower; built c.1865. Hudson Highland
Multiple Resource Area. 11.23.1982

Parry House
Michel Road. Modest Second Empire frame
residence built c.1860-70 for owner of flour

mill. Hudson Highlands Multiple Resource
Area.   11.23.1982

Pine Terrace
Main Street. Large Second Empire brick
residence with 3-story tower; built 1865 for
Major General Charles Roe; large modern
additions. Now apartments. Hudson Highlands
Multiple Resource Area.   11.23.1982

The Squirrels
225 Main Street. A 12-acre Hudson River estate
with mid-19th-century frame farmhouse
significantly enlarged and remodeled 1856 in
Picturesque style by architect Calvert Vaux for
noted journalist and author John Bigelow.
Large gatehouse (1856) and shed in similar
style. Hudson Highlands Multiple Resource
Area.   11.23.1982

Stonihurst
NY218. A 27-acre Hudson River estate with
large Gothic Revival/eclectic frame residence
built c.1880 for New York City lawyer Charles
Tracy. Property includes rustic pavilion, gatehouse, and barn complex. Hudson Highlands
Multiple Resource Area.   11.23.1982

Storm King Highway (see town of Cornwall)

Webb Lane House
Webb Lane. Large Arts and Crafts stone and
stuccoed residence with 3-story corner tower;
built c.1903. Hudson Highlands Multiple
Resource Area.   11.23.1982

Highlands

Cragston Dependencies
NY218, near Highland Falls. Gothic Revival
frame residence, carriage house, barn, and
stable built c.1860 as dependencies of J.
Pierpont Morgan estate (main house demolished). Hudson Highlands Multiple Resource
Area.   11.23.1982

Fort Montgomery Site
South of Fort Montgomery, on shore of Hudson
River, north of Popolopen Creek. Archeological
site of American earthen fortification and
associated structures constructed 1776-77 to
defend against British advance up Hudson
River during American Revolution.
NHL 11.28.1972

St. Mark's Episcopal Church
Canterbury Road and US9W, Fort Montgomery. Small Arts and Crafts/eclectic stone
church built 1923. Hudson Highlands Multiple
Resource Area.   11.23.1982

Storm King Highway (see town of Cornwall)

United States Bullion Depository
United States Military Academy. Massive
1-story utilitarian reinforced-concrete building
built 1938 by federal government to house
stock of silver bullion.   12.02.1987

United States Military Academy
NY218, West Point (also in town of Philipstown, Putnam County). The 2,500-acre historic
core of military academy established 1802 on
commanding site overlooking Hudson River
which was American military post and fortification during American Revolution. Includes
hundreds of historic buildings relating to all
periods of growth and several monuments and
archeological sites. Significant buildings include
Federal Superintendent's Quarters (1820),
Commandant's Quarters (1821), and Professors
Row (1821-28); Greek Revival Old Cadet
Chapel (1834-36); Gothic Revival Quarters
102 (1856-57, Q. A. Gillmore); series of
Collegiate Gothic buildings designed by Cram,
Goodhue & Ferguson, including Administration Building (1905-10), Thayer Hall (1908-
11), Cadet Chapel (1906-10), and Gymnasium
(1906-10); Neoclassical Cullem Hall (1895-98,
McKim, Mead & White); and buildings
designed by Arnold W. Brunner, Assoc.,
Richard Morris Hunt, and Gehron & Ross.
NHL 12.19.1960

Maybrook

John Blake House
924 Homestead Avenue. Federal vernacular
brick farmhouse built 1794 by farmer and
politician; rear kitchen wing built 1842.
Property includes historic shed and privy.
12.20.1984

Middletown

Webb Horton House (Morrison Hall)
115 South Street. Large Queen Anne/Chateau-
esque rock-faced marble residence with
elaborate exterior and interior decorative
features; designed by Frank Lindsay; built
1902-08 for retired industrialist. Property
includes garage/stable complex and portion of
original landscaped grounds. In use by Orange
County Community College since 1950.
04.26.1990

Oliver Avenue Bridge
Oliver Avenue over former Erie-Lackawanna
Railroad. A 105-foot-long, single-span, metal
through Pratt truss bridge built 1895 as trolly
bridge by Havana Bridge Works.
07.19.1984

Montgomery (Town)

Nathaniel Hill Brick House
NY17K, east of Montgomery. A 37-acre
property with large Georgian brick residence
built 1768 for whiskey merchant; rear wing
built 1774. Property includes stone smoke
house, hay barn, shed, and carriage house.
Operated as museum by Orange County.
01.05.1978

Montgomery (Village)

Bridge Street Historic District
Small residential neighborhood with 28

*Judges' Stand, Historic Track, Village of
Goshen.*

buildings, mostly small Federal and Greek
Revival vernacular frame residences built
1790s-1840s. Montgomery Village Multiple
Resource Area.   11.21.1980

Johannes Miller Farmhouse
272 Union Street. Colonial frame farmhouse
built 1771; large Federal frame addition
c.1790; remodeled 1835 in Greek Revival style.
Property includes formal gardens, pond, and
stone springhouse. Montgomery Village
Multiple Resource Area.   11.21.1980

Montgomery Worsted Mills
Factory Street. A 20-acre property on Wallkill
River with 3-story brick mill, 90-foot smoke-
stack, hydro plant, and water tower; built 1892
for Englishman William Crabtree and Arthur
Patchett on site of early 19th-century mills.
Montgomery Village Multiple Resource Area.
11.21.1980

Patchett-Crabtree House
232 Ward Street. Large Federal brick residence
built c.1812 as inn; purchased 1880s by
Patchett family and remodeled in Victorian
style, then Colonial Revival style. Montgomery
Village Multiple Resource Area.
11.21.1980

Union Street–Academy Hill Historic District
Roughly bounded by Ward Street, Wallkill
Avenue, and Sears and Hanover streets. Central
residential, civic, and commercial core of
village, with approximately 80 buildings,
mostly 19th-century residences in variety of
architectural styles. Also includes 4 churches,
several inns, municipal buildings, and commercial structures. Notable buildings include
Federal Montgomery Academy (1818; altered
late 19th century; now village hall), Greek
Revival First Presbyterian Church (1830), and
group of 12 late 19th-century Victorian
residences built by developer Chauncy Brooks.
Montgomery Village Multiple Resource Area.
11.21.1980

New Windsor

Edmonston House
NY94, Vails Gate. Colonial stone residence built 1755 by Eilliam Edmonston; doubled in size late 18th century. Served as staff quarters and hospital storage for Continental Army during American Revolution. Operated as museum by National Temple Hill Association. 03.02.1979

Haskell House
Off NY32, west of New Windsor. A 2-story vernacular residence with 1st story built of squared logs and frame 2nd story; built c.1729 by John Haskell as homestead on large land patent; burned early 1980s. 06.04.1973

Knox Headquarters (John Ellison House–Knox Headquarters State Historic Site)
Quassaick Avenue and Forge Hill Road, Vails Gate (also in town of Cornwall). A 50-acre property with large Georgian/Colonial stone residence built 1754 for John Ellison by local mason William Bull; 1799 frame addition. Served as headquarters of Major Generals Henry Knox, Nathanial Greene, Fredrich Von Steuben, and Horatio Gates 1779-83, during encampments of Continental Army at nearby New Windsor during American Revolution. NHL 11.28.1972

New Windsor Cantonment (State Historic Site)
Temple Hill Road, New Windsor. A 2,200-acre property encompassing archeological sites of 3 large permanent encampments of Continental Army during American Revolution 1775-83. 07.31.1972

Newburgh (Town)

Silas Gardner House
1141 Union Avenue, Gardnertown. Small 18th-century Colonial stone residence. Home of Silas Gardner, Loyalist during American Revolution. 03.28.1980

Maple Lawn
24 Downing Street, Balmville. Large Gothic Revival/Picturesque brick villa designed by Frederick C. Withers; built 1859 for Walter S. Vail. 06.28.1984

Mill House (Gomez the Jew House)
Mill House Road. A 10-acre property with large Colonial stone and brick residence; original 1-story stone section built c.1714-20 by Jewish merchant Daniel Gomez; brick 2nd story added c.1772; later owned by novelist Henry Armstrong and papermaker Dard Hunter. Property includes outbuildings and ornamental half-timbered early 20th-century mill. Operated as museum by Gomez House Association. 01.29.1973

Newburgh (City)

David Crawford House
189 Montgomery Street. Large Federal frame residence with pedimented Ionic portico and elaborate decorative trim; built 1829-31 for steamboat owner and shipper. Notable interior. Headquarters of Historical Society of Newburgh Bay and the Highlands. 09.27.1972

Dutch Reformed Church
Grand and Third streets. Monumental Greek Revival stuccoed stone church with pedimented Ionic portico; designed by Alexander Jackson Davis with superintendent of construction Russell Warren; built 1835-37; extended at rear 1867-68. Deteriorated condition. 12.18.1970

East End Historic District
Roughly bounded by Robinson Avenue, LeRoy Place, Water Street, Bay View Terrace, and Monument and Renwick streets. Central core of city, with approximately 2,400 residential, commercial, civic, institutional, and religious buildings built mid-18th to early 20th century. Includes civic and institutional area with large Neoclassical and Beaux-Arts stone buildings, small 19th-century industrial area, St. George's Cemetery, commercial district on Broadway with 3-story 19th-century brick commercial buildings, Downing Park (1887, Frederick Law Olmsted and Calvert Vaux; constructed as memorial to Andrew Jackson Downing), and several residential neighborhoods with mix of Federal, Greek Revival, Italianate, Tuscan Villa, Victorian Gothic, and Second Empire brick and frame rowhouses, townhouses, and villas. Also includes early 20th-century suburban neighborhood with Queen Anne, Shingle Style, and Colonial Revival residences. Individually listed properties include Montgomery-Grand-Liberty Streets Historic District, New York State Armory, and Washington's Headquarters. 09.12.1985

Montgomery-Grand-Liberty Streets Historic District
Montgomery, Grand, and Liberty streets. Several-block-long residential neighborhood with approximately 250 buildings, including numerous Federal, Greek Revival, Italianate, Tuscan Villa, Second Empire, and Victorian Gothic brick and frame rowhouses, townhouses, and villas. Also includes 9 churches and several public buildings. Notable buildings include Victorian Gothic Newburgh Free Library (1876, John Wood), Greek Revival Courthouse (1842, Thornton M. Niven), Greek Revival Quality Row (1837, Thornton M. Niven), Gothic Revival First Presbyterian Church (1858, Frederick C. Withers), and individually listed David Crawford House and Dutch Reformed Church. 07.16.1973

New York State Armory
Broadway and Johnson Street. Massive Victorian Gothic brick armory with 3-story crenellated tower and parapets; designed by John A. Wood; built 1879. 06.18.1981

United States Post Office–Newburgh
215-217 Liberty Street. Monumental Colonial Revival brick post office with gambrel roof; built 1931-32. United States Post Offices in New York State, 1858-1943, Thematic Resources. 05.11.1989

Washington's Headquarters (State Historic Site)
Liberty and Washington streets. A 7-acre property with 1 1/2-story Dutch Colonial stone residence built in sections 1750-70 for Jonathan Hasbrouck. Served as military headquarters of General George Washington during American Revolution in 1782-83. State historic site since 1850. NHL 01.20.1961

Port Jervis

Erie Railroad Station
Jersey Avenue and Fowler Street. Large Queen Anne brick passenger station and adjacent railway express building designed and built 1892 by Grattan & Jennings. 04.11.1980

Fort Decker
127 West Main Street. A 1 1/2-story vernacular stone residence built 1793 incorporating foundation of fort or blockhouse built before American Revolution. Used as store and later for workers constructing Delaware and Hudson Canal. Museum. 06.13.1974

United States Post Office–Port Jervis
20 Sussex Street. Colonial Revival brick post office with terra-cotta trim; built 1914-16. United States Post Offices in New York State, 1858-1943, Thematic Resources. 05.11.1989

Tuxedo

Southfield Furnace Ruin
Off NY17, south of Monroe. Standing ruins of stone and brick iron blast furnace complex, including furnace stack, charging bridge, remains of water race, casting room, and foundry building or stamping mill; built c.1804 by Peter Townsend family; abandoned 1887. 11.02.1973

Tuxedo Park

Tuxedo Park Historic District
Tuxedo Lake and environs. A 2,300-acre area planned as resort community around large lake

beginning in 1886 by Pierre Lorillard V with landscape engineer Ernest Bowditch and architect Bruce Price. Includes approximately 200 large-scale residences and associated stables and outbuildings designed in Tudor Revival, Mission, Georgian Revival, Jacobean Revival, Elizabethan Revival, Romanesque Revival, Queen Anne, Shingle Style, and Colonial Revival styles from 1886 to 1930s. Architects include Bruce Price, William A. Bates, James Brown Lord, Russell Sturgis, Wilson Eyre, William Lescaze, James Renwick, Jr., and McKim, Mead & White. 03.13.1980

Wallkill

William Bull III House
Bart Bull Road. A 113-acre farmstead with large Federal vernacular brick residence built 1780; remodeled c.1830 in Greek Revival style. Property includes Victorian frame carriage barn and well house. 10.24.1986

Warwick

Warwick Village Historic District
Roughly bounded by NY17A, High and South streets, and Oakland, Maple, and Colonial avenues. Historic core of village, with approximately 200 buildings, including late 18th- and early 19th- century brick commercial buildings, and group of 30 large-scale early 20th-century residences built during period of resort development. Notable buildings include Colonial Shingle House (1764; museum), Smith-Welling House (1830s), Colonial stone Baird's Tavern (1766), and eclectic stone former railroad station (1893). Architects of Queen Anne, Shingle Style, Tudor Revival, and Colonial Revival summer residences include Ernest G. W. Dietrich and Clinton Wheeler Wisner. 09.07.1984

Wawayanda

Primitive Baptist Church of Brookfield
NY6, Slate Hill. A 2-story vernacular frame church built 1792; attached 4-story tower and belfry added 1828. Intact interior with exposed framing. Adjacent cemetery. 11.13.1976

Woodbury

Arden (E. H. Harriman Estate)
NY17 (also in village of Harriman). A 472-acre former estate with massive stone main residence in style of French chateau, carriage shed, remnants of cable car complex, and stable complex; designed by Carrère & Hastings; completed 1909 for railroad organizer and builder Edward Henry Harriman. Now part of Columbia University. NHL 11.13.1966

Smith Clove Meetinghouse
Quaker Road. A 11/2-story vernacular frame Quaker meetinghouse built 1803. Intact interior. 01.11.1974

Opposite: Doorway, David Crawford House, City of Newburgh.

Residence, Tuxedo Park Historic District.

ORLEANS COUNTY

Albion (Town)

Mount Albion Cemetery
NY31. A 70-acre landscaped rural cemetery; original section designed 1842 by Marvin Potter; enlarged late 19th century in several stages. Extensive use of local Medina sandstone in tombs and buildings. Notable structures include Civil War Monument (1874; Field & Diem), offices and barn (1889; Warner & Brockett), and Gothic Revival chapel (1875) and entrance gate (1881). 09.27.1976

Albion (Village)

William V. N. Barlow House
223 South Clinton Street. Second Empire brick residence designed by William V. N. Barlow; built c.1875 as his residence. Adjacent frame carriage house. 09.08.1983

Orleans County Courthouse Historic District
Courthouse Square and environs. Civic, religious, and residential core of village, with 33 19th- to early 20th-century buildings on and adjacent to Courthouse Square, including 7

churches, 18 residences, and 8 public and institutional buildings. Notable buildings include Greek Revival Orleans County Courthouse (1857-58, William V. N. Barlow), Victorian Gothic First Presbyterian Church (1874; Andrew J. Warner), Romanesque Revival Pullman Memorial Universalist Church (1894; Simon Soloman Beman), Italianate St. Joseph's Rectory (c.1875; William V. N. Barlow), Italianate Swan Library (1840s; William V. N. Barlow), and Victorian Surrogate's Building (1888; Harvey and Charles Ellis). 08.31.1979

United States Post Office–Albion
Main Street. Colonial Revival brick post office built 1937-38. Interior mural (1939) by Judson Smith. United States Post Offices in New York State, 1858-1943, Thematic Resources. 11.17.1988

Clarendon

Gifford-Walker Farm (see Bergen, Genesee County)

Medina

United States Post Office–Medina
128 West Center Street. Colonial Revival brick post office built 1932. United States Post Offices in New York State, 1858-1943, Thematic Resources. 05.11.1989

Hastings

Fort Brewerton
State and Lansing streets, Brewerton. Archeological site of 8-pointed fort built 1759 to protect Mohawk-Oneida-Oswego waterways during French and Indian Wars. 03.07.1973

Lacona

Smith H. Barlow House
Harwood Drive. Queen Anne frame residence built 1898 for owner of sash and door factory. Adjacent late 19th-century carriage house. Sandy Creek Multiple Resource Area. 11.15.1988

First National Bank of Lacona
Harwood Drive and Salina Street. Neoclassical brick commercial building with multilevel parapet roof and brick and limestone trim; built 1922-23. Sandy Creek Multiple Resource Area. 11.15.1988

David Van Buren House, Volney (p. 128).

Constantia

Trinity Church
NY 49. Federal frame church with Gothic features; built 1831. Adjacent 19th-century cemetery. 10.29.1982

Fulton

United States Post Office–Fulton
214 South First Street. Neoclassical limestone post office with Doric colonnade; designed by James Knox Taylor; built 1912-15. Interior mural (1944) by Caroline S. Rohland. United States Post Offices in New York State, 1858-1943, Thematic Resources. 05.11.1989

Lacona Clock Tower
Harwood Drive. Freestanding square, 3-tiered red brick tower with pyramidal roof; built 1925 as gift to village by local civic club. Sandy Creek Multiple Resource Area. 11.15.1988

Charles M. Salisbury House
9089 Church Street. Modest Queen Anne/ Colonial Revival frame residence built 1908 for businessman and civic leader. Adjacent small bungalow and carriage house. Sandy Creek Multiple Resource Area. 11.15.1988

Matthew Shoecroft House
Ridge Road at Smartville Road. Large Italianate frame residence built c.1867 for attorney. Sandy Creek Multiple Resource Area. 11.15.1988

Fred Smart House
Salina Street. Queen Anne frame residence with pressed metal and shingle siding; designed and built 1900 for wood craftsman and merchant. Adjacent carriage house. Sandy Creek Multiple Resource Area. 11.15.1988

Newman Tuttle House
Harwood Drive and Ridge Road. Italianate frame residence built 1871. Sandy Creek Multiple Resource Area. 11.15.1988

Mexico (Town)

Arthur Tavern
Clarke Road and County 16. A 2-story late Federal stone building built 1838 by William S. Carpenter as tavern and residence of Alexander I. Danby. Mexico Multiple Property Submission. 11.14.1991

Mexico Octagon Barn
5276 Ames Street. Small octagonal frame barn built c.1880. Mexico Multiple Property Submission. 06.20.1991

Red Mill Farm
7177 Red Mill Road. A 175-acre farmstead with Federal/Greek Revival frame farmhouse built c.1832 and several outbuildings, including shop, granary, horse barn, silo, garage, milk-house, and windmill. Mexico Multiple Property Submission. 11.14.1991

Slack Farmstead
5174 Row Road. A 38-acre farmstead with 1 1/2-story vernacular frame farmhouse built c.1838, 19th-century granary, dairy barn, and henhouse. Mexico Multiple Property Submission. 11.14.1991

Stillman Farmstead
NY 104. A 92-acre farmstead with large Queen Anne farmhouse built 1889, early 19th-century barn, and early 20th-century garage. Mexico Multiple Property Submission. 06.20.1991

Thayer Farmstead
5933 Church Street. A 13-acre farmstead with Federal/Greek Revival frame farmhouse built c.1836 and adjacent barn. Mexico Multiple Property Submission. 11.14.1991

Mexico (Village)

Leonard Ames Farmhouse
5707 Main Street. A 2-story late Federal stone farmhouse built 1835; small frame wing was original house, c.1815. Mexico Multiple Property Submission. 11.14.1991

Peter Chandler House
5897 Main Street. A 2-story Greek Revival stone residence built 1838 for local merchant and philanthropist. Mexico Multiple Property Submission. 11.14.1991

Phineas Davis Farmstead
5422 North Road. A 64-acre farmstead with large Italianate brick farmhouse built 1870-73. Mexico Multiple Property Submission. 06.20.1991

Fowler-Loomis House
6022 Main Street. Greek Revival frame residence with portico; built c.1847 by LeRoy L. Fowler. Adjacent carriage house. Mexico Multiple Property Submission. 11.14.1991

Hamilton Farmstead

5644 Hamilton Street. A 16-acre property with Greek Revival cobblestone farmhouse built 1848 by David Wilcox. Adjacent outbuildings. Mexico Multiple Property Submission. 11.14.1991

Mexico Academy and Central School

5805 Main Street. Large Georgian Revival brick school designed by Harold O. Fullerton; built 1928-37. Interior scenic wallpaper mural "La Guerre d'Indépendance" by Zuber & Cie., c.1930. Mexico Multiple Property Submission. 11.14.1991

Mexico Railroad Depot

5530 Scenic Avenue. Stick Style frame railroad passenger and freight depot built 1905. Adjacent privy. Mexico Multiple Property Submission. 06.20.1991

Mexico Village Historic District

Commercial and residential core of small 19th-century village with approximately 56 buildings, including frame residences in broad range of styles, several mid- to late 19th-century Italianate brick commercial blocks, 1 hotel and 4 churches. Mexico Multiple Property Submission. 06.20.1991

Timothy Skinner House

5355 Scenic Avenue. Italianate brick residence built c.1865 for local attorney. Mexico Multiple Property Submission. 06.20.1991

Oswego

Fort Ontario (State Historic Site)

East Seventh Street at Lake Ontario. Pentagonal fort with 5 arrowhead-shaped bastions; stone walls built 1860; earth, stone, and wood powder magazine built 1839-44. Site of military occupation beginning in mid-18th century. Served as European refugee camp 1944-46. 12.18.1970

Franklin Square Historic District

Roughly bounded by Third, Sixth, Van Buren, and Bridge streets. Group of 91 residences built 1825-1900 surrounding landscaped park; includes all major 19th-century architectural styles. Architects include Claude F. Bragdon and W. B. Reid. Park designed 1797 by Simeon DeWitt. 08.04.1982

Market House

Water Street. Massive 3-story Federal brick and stone market building designed and built 1836-37 by Jacob Bonesteel as market, village (and later city) offices, and meeting rooms. 06.20.1974

Oswego Armory

265 West First Street. Massive castellated brick and sandstone armory with large drill hall and steel-truss roof; designed by George L. Heins; built 1906. 05.19.1988

Oswego City Hall

West Oneida Street. Massive Second Empire limestone building with central clock tower; designed by Horatio Nelson White; built 1870. 02.20.1973

Oswego City Library

120 East Second Street. A 2-story Early Romanesque Revival brick building with castellated parapet and tower; designed and built 1855-56 by Hewes & Rose. 09.22.1971

Oswego Theater

138 West Second Street. Art Deco brick theater with geometric patterned brick exterior and elaborate interior; designed by John Eberson; built 1940-41. 01.19.1988

Pontiac Hotel

West First Street. A 4-story Classical Revival/Mission-style brick building designed by George B. Post & Sons; built 1912. Distinctive interior rotunda. 07.21.1983

Richardson-Bates House

135 East Third Street. Massive Italianate brick residence with 4-story tower; designed by Andrew J. Warner; built 1867-71 for Maxwell B. Richardson; large 1887 addition. Elaborate interior decoration and original furnishings. Operated as museum by Oswego County Historical Society. 09.05.1975

Sheldon Hall

State University at Oswego. Large Neoclassical academic building with terra-cotta ornamentation; built 1911. 05.13.1980

George B. Sloan Estate

107 West Van Buren Street. Massive Italianate limestone villa and frame carriage barn built 1866-70. Lavish interior attributed to Herter Brothers. 08.11.1988

Tugboat *Nash*

A 114-foot-long steel harbor tug built 1943 by Jakobson Shipyard, Oyster Bay, New York, to handle U.S. sealift to Europe during WWII; sailed to Normandy as part of D-Day invasion force and shot down Focke-Wulf fighter. NHL 12.04.1991

United States Custom House (and Post Office)

West Oneida Street between First and Second streets. A 3-story Italianate stone custom house and post office designed by Ammi B. Young; built 1858; flanking wings built 1935. 11.21.1976

Walton And Willett Stone Store

One Seneca Street. A 3-story Federal limestone building built 1828 as ship chandlery. 05.24.1976

Phoenix

Sweet Memorial Building

821 Main Street. A 2-story Neoclassical brick municipal building with cast-stone trim and portico; designed by Albert L. Brockway; built 1929 as memorial to prominent citizen Thaddeus C. Sweet. 04.26.1990

Pulaski

Pulaski Village Historic District

Jefferson, Broad, Bridge, Hubbel, and Lake streets. Commercial, civic, and residential core of village, with approximately 35 properties including 2 parks and 2 churches. Notable buildings include Federal Macy House (c. 1830), Federal Oswego County Courthouse (1819; enlarged 1859 by Zina Stevens), Masonic Temple (1892), former Pulaski National Bank (1882; Archimedes Russell), and commerical rows built 1882-1901. 09.08.1983

Richland

Selkirk Lighthouse

Lake Road, west of Pulaski. A 2-story stone keeper's dwelling with octagonal tower; built 1838. 03.30.1979

Sandy Creek (Town)

Holyoke Cottage

Seber Shore Road. A 19-acre property on Lake Ontario with Arts and Crafts summer cottage built 1905. Sandy Creek Multiple Resource Area. 11.15.1988

Sandy Creek (Village)

First Baptist Church

Harwood Drive. Queen Anne octagonal frame church designed by Charles M. Salisbury; built 1917-18. Sandy Creek Multiple Resource Area. 11.15.1988

Methodist Church

Harwood Drive. High Victorian Gothic polychromatic brick church designed 1878 by Winslow Tucker. Sandy Creek Multiple Resource Area. 11.15.1988

Pitt M. Newton House

8114 Harwood Drive. Greek Revival frame residence with Ionic portico; designed and built 1851 by William E. Howlett for merchant and civic leader. Property includes late 19th-century carriage house. Sandy Creek Multiple Resource Area. 11.15.1988

Samuel Sadler House

9278 North Main Street. Italianate brick residence built c.1870 by owner and master mason Samuel Sadler. Sandy Creek Multiple Resource Area. 11.15.1988

Sandy Creek Historic District

Lake Road and US 11. Commercial and civic core of village, with 14 historic buildings built 1834-1928 and small park. Includes 2-story frame Greek Revival and Italianate commercial buildings, 2 Greek Revival residences, and Arnsworth Memorial Library (1928). Sandy Creek Multiple Resource Area. 11.15.1988

Schroeppel

Schroeppel House
Morgan Road. Large Federal/Greek Revival frame residence built 1818; later enlarged. 09.09.1982

Volney

David Van Buren House
Van Buren Drive at Oswego River, near Fulton. Greek Revival brick residence built 1847. 06.09.1988 ILLUS. P. 126

John Van Buren Tavern
NY 57 and Van Buren Drive, near Fulton. Large Federal brick tavern and residence built 1800-21. 11.03.1988

Volkert Van Buren House
NY 57 and Distin Road, near Fulton. Federal brick residence built c.1832. 10.07.1988

OTSEGO COUNTY

Butternuts

Otsdawa Creek Site
Address restricted. Large prehistoric village site associated with Early Owasco settlement, c.1100 A.D. 07.22.1980

Cherry Valley

Cherry Valley Historic District
Roughly bounded by Alden and Montgomery streets, Maple Avenue, and Elm and Main streets. Historic core of small village, with approximately 140 properties, mostly residential and commercial buildings built late 18th to early 20th centuries. Many notable Federal buildings, including frame Morse House (c.1790), frame Dr. Delos White House (c.1812), stone Cherry Valley National Bank (1815), and brick Campbell House (1800). Later buildings include Gothic Revival Episcopal Church (1846), Italianate limestone commercial blocks (1862 and c.1870), and Second Empire residences. Also includes Cherry Valley Cemetery (begun c.1750). 04.28.1988

Cooperstown

Cooperstown Historic District
NY 28, NY 80, and Main Street (also in town of Middlefield). Major section of village, with over 500 residential, commercial, public, and religious buildings built 1786-1930s. Includes many notable Federal, Greek Revival, and Italianate frame and masonry residences. Other notable buildings include Colonial Revival Fenimore House (1932, headquarters of New York State Historical Association), Greek Revival Otsego County Bank (1831), Iron-clad Building (1862, James Bogardus), Georgian Revival Otesaga Hotel (1909), Shingle Style McKim House (1884; Babb, Cook & Willard), Neoclassical Racing Stables (1900), Colonial Revival Baseball Hall of Fame (1939, Henry St. Clair Zogbaum) and Doubleday Field, Classical Revival Municipal Building (1896-98, Ernest Flagg), and Otsego County Courthouse (individually listed). 11.18.1980

Otsego County Courthouse
193 Main Street. Victorian Gothic brick and stone courthouse designed by Archimedes Russell; built 1880. 06.20.1972

United States Post Office–Cooperstown
28-40 Main Street. Colonial Revival brick post office built 1935-36. Interior sculpture (1938) by Bela Janowsky. United States Post Offices in New York State, 1858-1943. Thematic Resources. 11.17.1988

Gilbertsville

Gilbertsville Historic District
Roughly bounded by incorporated village boundary. Small 19th-century village with many Greek Revival and Italianate houses, as well as later houses, commercial buildings, churches, and parks. Includes stone-arch and lenticular-truss bridges, and individually listed Major's Inn, Gilbert Block, and Tianderah. 05.17.1974; BOUNDARY INCREASE 11.04.1982

Major's Inn and Gilbert Block
Both sides of Commercial Street near NY 51. A 2-story commercial block and 3 1/2-story inn, both Tudor Revival and of brick with half-timbering and stone trim; built 1893-97. 04.11.1973

Tianderah
Off NY 51. A 33-acre property with 2 1/2-story Queen Anne stone and frame residence with

gambrel roof; designed 1885 by William Ralph Emerson. Property includes Shingle Style stables. 11.02.1978

Middlefield

Cooperstown Historic District
(see Cooperstown)

Middlefield District No. 1 School
County 35. A 2-story Italianate frame school built 1875; 1-story rear wing added 1930. 08.13.1987

Middlefield Hamlet Historic District
County 35, and Rezen, Whiteman, and Long Patent roads. A 19th-century hamlet with 24 buildings, primarily residential. Notable buildings include Federal Pinney Tavern (c.1795), former Central Hotel (c.1800), numerous Greek Revival residences, and Gothic Revival cottage (c.1850). 07.11.1985

Benjamin D. North House
NY 166, The Plank Road. A 15-acre property with 2-story Federal brick residence built 1799-1802; frame wing added 1840s. Includes 19th-century outbuildings. 07.11.1985

Morris

The Grove
Off NY 51. A 20-acre estate with 2-story Greek Revival stone residence with imposing Doric portico and notable interior; built c.1833. Property includes Federal frame gatehouse and other outbuildings. Associated with prominent Rotch family. 07.10.1980

New Lisbon

Lunn-Musser Octagon Barn
South of Garrattsville. A 60-foot-diameter stone and frame octagonal barn built 1885; mid-20th-century concrete-block additions. Central Plan Dairy Barns of New York State Thematic Resources. 09.29.1984

Oneonta (Town)

Fortin Site
Address restricted. Multicomponent stratified prehistoric archeological site with evidence of occupation from Late Archaic to Late Woodland stages. 11.28.1980

Stonehouse Farm
NY 7, east of Oneonta. An 11-acre farmstead with 2 1/2-story Federal stone residence with 1 1/2-story flanking wings; built 1817-23; front portico added c.1950. Property includes c.189_ barn. 11.19.1980

Oneonta (City)

Bresee Hall
Hartwick Drive. A 3-story Colonial Revival brick classroom building on Hartwick Colleg_

campus; designed 1928 by John Russell Pope
and Dwight James Baum.   04.12.1984

Fairchild Mansion
318 Main Street. Italianate brick residence built
1867; enlarged and remodeled 1897 in Queen
Anne style for politician and businessman
George W. Fairchild. Adapted for use as
Masonic lodge.   02.12.1974

Ford Block
188-202 Main Street. A 3-story Queen Anne
brick commercial block built 1882.
09.07.1984

Municipal Building
238-242 Main Street. A 3-story Beaux-Arts
brick and terra-cotta building designed 1906 by
Linn Kinne; originally housed city hall and
firehouse.   10.29.1982

Old Post Office–Oneonta
Main Street. A 2-story Neoclassical limestone
and granite post office designed 1915 by Oscar
Wenderoth; rear wing added 1950s. Adapted
for use as City Hall.   11.17.1978

Oneonta State Normal School
A 3 1/2-story Romanesque Revival limestone
and brick school designed by Fuller & Wheeler;
built 1894.   12.16.1976; DEMOLISHED

Swart-Wilcox House
Wilcox Avenue. A 14-acre property with small
1 1/2-story frame residence reflecting German

vernacular building traditions; built c.1807 by
Lawrence Swart.   05.24.1990

Walnut Street Historic District
Ford Avenue, and Walnut, Dietz, Elm, and
Maple streets. Residential street with 46
buildings built 1850-1915. Includes several
notable Queen Anne residences, as well as
examples of Greek Revival, Second Empire,
Chateauesque, and Classical Revival styles.
07.30.1980

Richfield

Baker Octagon Barn
NY28. A 60-foot-diameter stone and frame
octagonal barn with hipped roof and cupola;
built 1882. Central Plan Dairy Barns of New
York State Thematic Resources.   09.29.1984

Richfield Springs

Sunnyside
72 East Main Street. A 2-story Queen Anne
frame residence built 1890; 1909 addition.
Includes shingled carriage house.   03.10.1988

United States Post Office–Richfield Springs
12 East Main Street. Colonial Revival brick
post office built 1941-42. Interior mural (1942)
by John W. Taylor. United States Post Offices in
New York State, 1858-1943. Thematic
Resources.   05.11.1989

Hyde Hall, Springfield (p. 130).

Opposite: Cooperstown Historic District.

PUTNAM COUNTY

Springfield

Hyde Hall (State Historic Site)
Glimmerglass State Park, south of Springfield Center. Monumental 2-story limestone residence with Doric portico, extensive wings, open paved interior courtyard, and elaborate interior finishes; designed by Philip Hooker and George Clarke as country seat of Clarke family; built 1817-35. Contains original furnishings. Property includes carriage house, domed gate lodge, Clarke family tomb, and gardener's cottage. Operated as museum by Friends of Hyde Hall. 10.07.1971; NHL 06.24.1986 ILLUS. P. 129

Unadilla (Town)

Andrew Mann Inn
33 Riverside Road. A 2-story Federal frame inn built c.1795; later wing and outbuildings. 01.10.1980

Russ-Johnsen Site
Address restricted. Prehistoric archeological site containing evidence of settlement from Early Archaic to Late Woodland periods. 07.22.1980

Unadilla (Village)

Roswell Wright House
25 Main Street. A 2-story Greek Revival frame residence with pedimented portico; built 1823; later rear additions. 09.01.1988

Worcester

Worcester Historic District
Both sides of Main Street (NY7) between Decatur and Cook streets. Commercial center of village, with 24 buildings, mostly 2-story Victorian commercial buildings built late 19th century. 06.10.1975

Brewster

Walter Brewster House
Oak Street. Large Greek Revival frame residence with 2-story Ionic colonnade; built c.1850 by Walter F. Brewster, who was primarily responsible for early development of village. Headquarters of Landmarks Preservation Society of Southeast. 10.04.1978

First National Bank of Brewster
(Southeast Town Hall)
Main Street. A 1-story Queen Anne brick building with decorative features in stone, brick, and slate shingles; built 1886 as bank. 01.07.1988

Old Southeast Town Hall
Main Street. A 3-story Colonial Revival/eclectic brick building with elaborate decorative features; designed by Child & deGoll; built 1896; rear addition c.1900. 07.24.1979

Carmel

Gilead Cemetery
Mechanic Street. A 1-acre cemetery with approximately 300 burials and wide range of grave markers from 1766 through early 20th century. 12.01.1988

Putnam County Courthouse
NY52 and NY301. A 2-story Federal frame courthouse built 1814 by local builder James Townsend; rebuilt 1847 with monumental pedimented Corinthian portico and cupola. 08.11.1976

Reed Memorial Library
2 Brewster Avenue. A 1-story trapezoidal Tudor Revival stone library designed by Gaylor &

Pryor; built 1913-14 by Miller-Reed Construction Co. 03.28.1980

Cold Spring

Cold Spring Historic District
Roughly Main, Fair, and Chestnut streets, and Paulding Avenue. The 8-block commercial core and adjacent residential block of village on Hudson River, with approximately 220 buildings, including early to late 19th-century frame and brick residences and commercial buildings in variety of styles. Hudson Highlands Multiple Resource Area. 11.23.1982

West Point Foundry
Foundry Cove, between NY90 and New York Central Railroad tracks (also in town of Philipstown). A 93-acre area with archeological site, structural remains, and remaining buildings associated with major iron- and brass- manufacturing complex; established 1816-17 by Gouvernor Kemble. Major supplier of wide variety of products to federal government and private contracts, including Parrott Gun for use in Civil War. 04.11.1973

Nelsonville

H. D. Champlin & Son Horseshoeing and Wagonmaking
286 Main Street. Small 1 1/2-story vernacular brick commercial building built c.1858; 1-story addition c.1880. Hudson Highlands Multiple Resource Area. 11.23.1982

Cold Spring Cemetery Gatehouse
Peekskill Road. Gothic Revival granite gatehouse residence and adjacent structure built 1862-65; design attributed to George E. Harvey. Hudson Highlands Multiple Resource Area. 11.23.1982

House at 3 Crown Street
Large Italianate brick residence built c.1868. Hudson Highlands Multiple Resource Area. 11.23.1982

J. Y. Dykman Flour and Feed Store
289 Main Street. A 2-story Victorian brick commercial/residential building built c.1860. Hudson Highlands Multiple Resource Area. 11.23.1982

J. Y. Dykman Store
255 Main Street. Modest 1-story Victorian commercial building built c.1890. Hudson Highlands Multiple Resource Area. 11.23.1982

First Baptist Church of Cold Spring
Main Street. Frame church built 1831-33; later Italianate alterations and decorative details. Hudson Highlands Multiple Resource Area. 11.23.1982

Fish and Fur Club (Nelsonville Justice Court)
258 Main Street. Modest 1-story frame building with Rustic-style decorative porch; built 1905. Hudson Highlands Multiple Resource Area. 11.23.1982

Hustis House
328 Main Street. Modest vernacular frame residence built c.1840. Hudson Highlands Multiple Resource Area.   11.23.1982

House at 249 Main Street
Victorian frame residence built c.1880. Hudson Highlands Multiple Resource Area. 07.31.1989

Philipstown

The Birches
Cat Rock Road. Queen Anne/Stick Style stone and frame residence with gambrel roof; design attributed to Ralph Adams Cram; built 1882 for William H. Osborn. Adjacent carriage house. Hudson Highlands Multiple Resource Area.   11.23.1982

Boscobel
NY9D, north of Garrison. Large Federal frame residence with 2-story recessed pedimented portico and refined Adamesque decorative detail; designed by William Vermilye; built 1804-06 for States Morris Dyckman in Montrose, 15 miles south of present location; reconstructed 1950s on present site overlooking Hudson River. Notable Neoclassical interior. Operated as museum by Boscobel Restorations. 11.07.1977

Castle Rock
NY9D, near Garrison. A 128-acre estate with massive Queen Anne/Chateauesque stone mountaintop residence designed by J. Morgan Slade; built 1881 for William H. Osborn, president of Illinois Central Railroad; enlarged 1906 for prominent paleontologist Henry Fairfield Osborn. Property includes rustic lodge (c.1900), Victorian Lilac Cottage (1850s), large Victorian residence, stone and frame barn complex, stone gatehouse, and other residences. 12.12.1977

DeRham Farm
Indian Brook Road, north of Garrison. A 19-acre farm/estate on Hudson River with Federal frame residence built c.1810 by Philipse family; enlarged in Greek Revival style and later in Second Empire style as summer residence for New York City merchant and banker Henry Casimir DeRham. Property includes fourteen 19th-century dependencies, including caretaker's cottage, Gothic Revival cottage, Romanesque Revival carriage house, and farm buildings. 03.28.1980

Eagle's Rest (Jacob Rupert Estate)
NY9D. A 214-acre estate overlooking Hudson River with massive rambling Tudor Revival stone residence and numerous associated outbuildings, including garage/servants' quarters, water tower, several masonry birdhouses, horse and cow barn, monkey house, gazebo, windmills, stone cottages, and other buildings; built 1920s-30s for Jacob Rupert, president of New York City brewery. Now a school. Hudson Highlands Multiple Resource Area. 11.23.1982

Fair Lawn
NY9D. A 68-acre estate overlooking Hudson River with large 3-story Italianate residence designed by painter Thomas P. Rossiter as his residence; built c.1860; Colonial Revival modifications. Hudson Highlands Multiple Resource Area. 11.23.1982

Garrison Landing Historic District
Bounded by Hudson River and New York Central Railroad tracks. Small hamlet with 17 buildings, mostly small mid-19th-century frame residences designed and built as tenant properties by Henry White Belcher, owner of Garrison and West Point Ferry Co. Also includes brick Golden Eagle Hotel, stone railroad station (1892), Italianate/Gothic Revival former railroad station (c.1848), and Ferry House. Hudson Highlands Multiple Resource Area. 11.23.1982

Garrison Union Free School
NY9D, Garrison. A 1-story Arts and Crafts stone school built 1908. Hudson Highlands Multiple Resource Area. 11.23.1982

Glenfields
Old Manitou Road. Modest Victorian frame residence designed by Mead & Taft; built c.1870 for quarry owner Archibald Gracie King. Hudson Highlands Multiple Resource Area. 11.23.1982

Hurst-Pierrepont Estate
NY9D, Garrison. A 12-acre property with large Gothic Revival brick villa designed by Alexander Jackson Davis; built 1867 for lawyer Edwards Pierrepont; 1912-13 alterations by Cross & Cross. Adjacent carriage house and cow barn. Hudson Highlands Multiple Resource Area. 11.23.1982

Mandeville House
Lower Station Hill Road. A 1 1/2-story Dutch Colonial vernacular frame residence built 1735 by Jacob Mandeville; altered numerous times from 18th through early 20th centuries,

Castle Rock, Philipstown.

Opposite: Boscobel, Philipstown.

retaining original and later Colonial Revival features. Headquarters of General Israel Putnam during American Revolution. Hudson Highlands Multiple Resource Area. 11.23.1982

Montrest
Late Gate Road. Large estate with massive, rambling Victorian frame residence built c.1868 for leather dealer Aaron Healey; original house designed by William H. LaDue; substantially enlarged late 19th century by architect Alfred Raymond. Property includes Gothic Revival farm cottage, greenhouse, carriage house and barn complex, and tenant house. Hudson Highlands Multiple Resource Area. 11.23.1982

Moore House
Nelson Lane, Garrison. Modest 2-family vernacular frame residence built c.1860 as farmworkers' housing. Hudson Highlands Multiple Resource Area. 11.23.1982

Normandy Grange
NY9D. A 43-acre property with group of several stuccoed and stone buildings in Norman style built c.1905 as support buildings for nearby Dick's Castle, unfinished estate of Evans Dick. Hudson Highlands Multiple Resource Area. 11.23.1982

Old Albany Post Road
Near US9. A 6.6-mile-long dirt and paved road north from Continental Village to US9 above Nelson Corners. Section of original land route between New York City and Albany; developed 1669 and improved throughout 18th century. Retains 6 milestones (1797-98). 07.08.1982

Oulagisket
NY9D. Several-acre estate with Italianate stuccoed masonry main residence and carriage

house built c.1864 for Samuel Sloan, president of Hudson River Railroad. Includes late 19th- to early 20th-century superintendent's house, dairy barn/stable complex, and other dependencies. Hudson Highlands Multiple Resource Area.   11.23.1982

Rock Lawn and Carriage House
NY9D, Garrison. A 12-acre estate with large Italianate brick villa designed by Richard Upjohn; built 1852-53 for ferry operator Henry White Belcher; late 19th-century Shingle Style addition and carriage house built for Hamilton Fish II. Hudson Highlands Multiple Resource Area.   11.23.1982

Walter Thompson House and Carriage House
Philipsebrook Road. A 29-acre estate with large Tudor Revival stuccoed and half-timbered residence and carriage house built c.1883-90 for local minister. Hudson Highlands Multiple Resource Area.   11.23.1982

Walker House
Cat Rock Road, Garrison. Large Queen Anne frame residence built c.1890. Hudson Highlands Multiple Resource Area.   11.23.1982

United States Military Academy (see Highlands, Orange County)

West Point Foundry (see Cold Spring)

Wilson House
Lower Station Hill Road, Garrison. Gothic Revival frame cottage built c.1854. Hudson Highlands Multiple Resource Area. 11.23.1982

Woodlawn (Malcolm Gordon School)
NY9D, Garrison. A 42-acre former estate on Hudson River with large Gothic Revival brick villa designed by Richard Upjohn; built 1854 for William Moore and Margaret Philipse; converted and altered for use as school after 1927. Includes three 19th-century outbuildings. Hudson Highlands Multiple Resource Area.   11.23.1982

Putnam Valley

Tompkins Corners United Methodist Church
Peekskill Hollow Road. Modest Victorian vernacular frame church and Sunday school designed by Robert Baker; built 1891. Adjacent early 19th-century carriage house.   03.31.1983

Southeast

Old Southeast Church
NY22, off Putnam Lake Road, north of Brewster. A 2-story vernacular frame church built 1794; remodeled and belfry added 1830. Adjacent early 19th-century vernacular 1-room schoolhouse.   07.24.1972

Queens

Allen-Beville House
29 Center Drive, Douglaston. Large Greek Revival/Italianate frame former farmhouse built c.1848-50.   09.22.1983

Louis Armstrong House
3456 107th Street, Corona. A 2-story brick detached rowhouse built c.1910. Residence of African-American musician and composer Louis "Satchmo" Armstrong from 1943 until his death in 1971.   NHL 05.11.1976

John Bowne House
37-01 Bowne Street, Flushing. A 1 1/2-story Colonial frame residence begun 1661 by John Bowne; main section added 1680-96; addition c.1830. Oldest structure in Queens County; associated with fight for religious freedom in American colonies for role played by its owner, a Quaker, in Flushing Remonstrance. Museum. 09.13.1977

Ralph Bunche House
115-25 Grosvenor Road, Kew Gardens. Early 20th-century Tudor Revival stuccoed wood and brick residence. Residence of African-American diplomat and scholar Ralph Johnson Bunche from 1952 until his death in 1971. NHL 05.11.1976

Central Avenue Historic District
Roughly bounded by Myrtle and 70th avenues, and 65th and 66th streets, Ridgewood. A 5-block residential neighborhood with 104 3-story Romanesque and Renaissance Revival brick tenements imitating "Mathews Flats" model tenements; designed by Louis Berger & Co.; built 1916 by Henry W. Meyer. Ridgewood Multiple Resource Area.   09.30.1983

Central Ridgewood Historic District
Roughly bounded by Fresh Pond Road and Putnam, 68th, Forest, Catalpa, Onderdonk, and 71st avenues, Ridgewood. A 23-block residential neighborhood with 782 buildings, mostly 2-story Renaissance and Romanesque Revival brick rowhouses with rounded or squared bay fronts; designed by Louis Berger & Co.; built in unified rows 1895-1927. Also includes Gothic Revival brick Covenant Lutheran Church (1914, Carl L. Otto). Ridgewood Multiple Resource Area.   09.30.1983

Cooper Avenue Row Historic District
6434-6446 Cooper Avenue, Ridgewood. Row of seven 2-story Romanesque and Renaissance Revival brick rowhouses designed by Louis Berger & Co.; built 1915 by Albin Wagner. Ridgewood Multiple Resource Area. 09.30.1983

Cornelia-Putnam Historic District
Roughly bounded by Jefferson Street and

Putnam, Wyckoff, and Myrtle avenues, Ridgewood. A 1 1/2-block residential neighborhood with 87 Renaissance and Romanesque Revival 2-story brick rowhouses and 3-story brick tenements designed by Louis Berger & Co.; built in several individual rows 1907-22. Ridgewood Multiple Resource Area. 09.30.1983

Cornell (Creedmoor) Farmhouse
(Jacob Adriance Farmhouse)
73-50 Little Neck Parkway, Bellerose. A 7-acre former farmstead with Dutch Colonial vernacular frame residence built 1772; enlarged c.1835 and later alterations. Farm museum. 07.24.1979

Cypress Avenue East Historic District
Roughly bounded by Linden and Cornelia streets, and Seneca and St. Nicholas avenues, Ridgewood. A 10-block residential neighborhood with 247 buildings, mostly 3-story Romanesque and Renaissance Revival brick tenements, similar to well-known "Mathews Flats" model tenements; most designed by Louis Berger & Co.; built 1900-14 by Bauer & Stier, and Spaeth, Hempleman & Rodler. Ridgewood Multiple Resource Area. 09.30.1983

Cypress Avenue West Historic District
Roughly bounded by St. Nicholas and Seneca avenues, and Linden and Stockholm streets, Ridgewood (also in Kings County). A 16-block residential neighborhood with 440 buildings (6 blocks in Brooklyn), mostly 2- and 3-story Renaissance and Romanesque Revival brick rowhouses and tenements built 1888-1906. Architects and builders include John Maske, Louis Berger & Co., and G. X. Mathews Co. Also includes Georgian Revival brick Public School 81 (1902), and Gothic Revival brick St. John's Ridgewood United Methodist Church (1905-10, Carl L. Otto). Ridgewood Multiple Resource Area. 09.30.1983

First Reformed Church
153 Jamaica Avenue, Jamaica. Early Romanesque Revival brick church designed and built 1858-59 by master carpenter Sidney J. Young; renovated 1902, including stained-glass windows by Emil Zundel and Frederick S. Lamb.   04.16.1980

Flushing Town Hall
137-35 Northern Boulevard, Flushing. A 2-story Early Romanesque Revival brick building built 1862. Served as town hall until 1900.   03.16.1972

Forest-Norman Historic District
Forest Avenue from Summerfield to Stephen Street, and Norman Street to Myrtle Avenue, Ridgewood. A 4-block residential neighborhood with 37 buildings, mostly 2-story Romanesque and Renaissance Revival brick rowhouses and tenements built 1908-10; many designed by Louis Berger & Co. and built by Henn & Ballweg or J. and G. Burkardt. Ridgewood Multiple Resource Area. 09.30.1983

Fort Tilden Historic District
Rockaway Beach Boulevard, Breezy Point. A 98-acre property developed by United States Army from 1917 on as part of defensive network for New York Harbor. Includes Battery Harris Casemates, magazines, and support buildings associated with technological developments in military history during first half of 20th century. Part of Gateway National Recreation Area.   04.20.1984

Fort Totten Officers' Club
Totten and Murray avenues, Bayside. Large Gothic Revival frame building with crenellated 3-story towers and parapets; built c.1870; substantially enlarged 1887.   03.17.1986

Fresh Pond-Traffic Historic District
Roughly bounded by Fresh Pond Road, Traffic Avenue, and Woodbine and Linden streets, Ridgewood. A 7-block residential neighborhood with 197 buildings, mostly 2-story Romanesque and Renaissance Revival rowhouses constructed of cream-colored, iron-spot brick, imitating rusticated stone; designed by Louis Berger & Co.; built 1914-21 by Bauer & Stier. Ridgewood Multiple Resource Area. 09.30.1983

Grace Episcopal Church Complex
15515 Jamaica Avenue, Jamaica. Gothic Revival sandstone church designed by Dudley Field; built 1861-62; chancel designed 1901 by Cady, Berg & See. Adjacent Tudor Revival parish house (1912) and cemetery (established 1734).   09.08.1983

Grove–Linden–St. John's Historic District
Fairview Avenue, St. John's Road, and Linden and Grove streets, Ridgewood. A 4-block neighborhood with fifty-one 2- and 3-story brick rowhouses and tenements distinguished by unusual window keystones of cast-stone mascarons; designed by Louis Berger & Co.; built 1908-10 by Spaeth & Senger. Ridgewood Multiple Resource Area.   09.30.1983

Hunters Point Historic District
45th Avenue between 21st and 23rd streets. A 1-block area with stone rowhouses built 1870s in Italianate, Second Empire, and other styles.   09.19.1973

Jamaica Chamber of Commerce Building
8931 161st Street, Jamaica. A 10-story Colonial Revival brick building with stone and terra-cotta decorative trim; designed by George W. Conable; built 1928-29.   09.08.1983

Jamaica Savings Bank
161-02 Jamaica Avenue, Jamaica. A 4-story Beaux-Arts limestone building with elaborate decorative details; designed by Hough & Deuell; built 1897-98.   05.19.1983

King Manor (Rufus King House)
150th Street and Jamaica Avenue, Jamaica. Large Georgian Federal frame residence of Rufus King, member of Continental Congress, signer of Constitution, United States senator, and minister to Great Britain. Original rear section built c.1730; part of main gambrel-roofed section built c.1750; both incorporated c.1806 by King into present house. Notable interior. Museum.   NHL 12.02.1974

Kingsland Homestead
37th Street and Parsons Boulevard, Flushing. Georgian/Dutch Colonial shingled residence with gambrel roof; built 1785 for Charles Doughty; moved twice, second time in 1968 to present site. Headquarters of Queens Historical Society.   05.31.1972

J. Kurtz & Sons Store Building
162-24 Jamaica Avenue, Jamaica. A 6-story Art Deco building with facades decorated with black tile, black brick, terra-cotta, and aluminum; designed by Allmendinger & Schlendorf; built 1931 as furniture store. 09.08.1983

La Casina (Polyform Bra Company–Roxanne Swimsuit Company)
90-33 160th Street, Jamaica. A 1-story commercial building built c.1907; remodeled c.1936 in streamlined Art Deco style for use as nightclub.   03.01.1990

Lent Homestead and Cemetery
78-03 19th Road, Steinway. Dutch Colonial stone and frame farmhouse; original 1-room stone section built 1729 by Abraham Lent; enlarged late 18th-century and again c.1800 with clapboard sheathing. Adjacent 18th-century Riker and Lent families cemetery. 02.02.1984

Madison–Putnam–60th Place Historic District
Roughly bounded by Woodbine Street, 60th Place, and 67th and Forest avenues, Ridgewood. A 7-block residential neighborhood with 145 buildings, mostly 2-story Romanesque and Renaissance Revival brick rowhouses; designed by Louis Berger & Co.; built by Henn & Ballweg, Ignatz Martin, and Anton Kluepfel and John Eisenhouer. Ridgewood Multiple Resource Area.   09.30.1983

Marine Air Terminal
La Guardia Airport. Large 2-story circular Art Deco brick building with terra-cotta frieze of flying fish; designed by William Adams Delano of Delano & Aldrich; built 1939-40 as waterfront passenger terminal for transoceanic flights. Notable interior waiting room with encircling mural "Flight" (1940, James Brooks).   07.09.1982

Office of the Register (Jamaica Arts Center)
161-04 Jamaica Avenue, Jamaica. A 3-story Italian Renaissance style limestone building designed by A. S. Macgregor; built c.1898. 01.03.1980

Old Quaker Meetinghouse
South side of Northern Boulevard, Flushing. A 2-story vernacular shingled meetinghouse built 1695; additions 1716-19. Used continuously as meetinghouse since it was built, except when used by British as prison and hospital during American Revolution.   NHL 12.24.1967

Queensboro Bridge (see New York County)

Long Island City Courthouse Complex
25-10 Court Square, Long Island City. A 4-story Renaissance Revival/Beaux Arts brick and stone building with elaborate decorative trim; designed by Peter M. Coco; built 1904-08 incorporating walls of original building (1876), which burned 1904. Attached jail (c.1915) and jail annex (c.1925), both demolished after 1983. Now New York State Supreme Court. 09.26.1983

Paramount Studios Complex, Astoria (p. 134).

Paramount Studios Complex
35th Avenue, and 35th, 36th, and 37th streets, Astoria. A 5-acre complex of 9 concrete buildings built 1918-66. Original buildings built as eastern film distribution center for Famous Players Lasky Corporation with one of the world's largest sound studios. More than 110 feature silent films produced at studio 1921-27, and later major sound movies. After 1942 used by United States Army for production of military films; since 1988 home of American Museum of the Moving Image. 11.14.1978 ILLUS. P. 133

Poppenhusen Institute
114-04 14th Road, College Point. A 3-story Second Empire brick institutional building designed by Mundell & Teckritz; built 1868 for philanthropist Conrad Poppenhusen as civic center and vocational school.   08.18.1977

Reformed Church of Newtown Complex
8515 Broadway, Elmhurst. Federal/Greek Revival frame church built 1831 and attached Fellowship Hall (1854). Adjacent cemetery. 04.23.1980

Jacob Riis Park Historic District
Rockaway Beach Boulevard, Rockaway. A 160-acre municipal bathing beach and recreational park developed 1920s and completed 1932-37 through Works Progress Administration; designed by Julius Burgevin, Stoughton & Plonck, and Aymar Embury. Notable features include Art Deco Main Bathhouse and 14,000-car parking lot.   06.17.1981

RKO Keith's Theater
129-143 Northern Boulevard, Flushing. Massive movie theater with atmospheric interior, lobby, and auditorium in Spanish Baroque style; designed by Thomas W. Lamb; built 1928. Auditorium altered.   10.29.1982

Russell Sage Memorial Church
(First Presbyterian Church of Far Rockaway) Beach 12th Street, Far Rockaway. Massive Gothic Revival brick church with concrete trim; designed by Cram, Goodhue & Ferguson; built 1908-10 as memorial to business tycoon Russell Sage by his wife Margaret Olivia Slocum Sage. Notable interior with windows by Mary Tillinghast, Tiffany Glass & Decoration Co., and the architect. A 3-acre parcel with grounds designed by Olmsted Brothers.   09.22.1986

St. Monica's Church
9420 160th Street, Jamaica. Early Romanesque Revival brick church built 1856-57 by Mason Anders Peterson.   04.09.1980

Seneca Avenue East Historic District
Roughly Seneca Avenue East between Hancock and Summerfield streets, Ridgewood. A 9-block residential neighborhood with 120 buildings, mostly 2- and 3-story Romanesque and Renaissance Revival brick rowhouses and tenements, including 2 rows of "Mathews Flats" model tenements; built 1905-15. Ridgewood Multiple Resource Area. 09.30.1983

Seneca-Onderdonk-Woodward Historic District
Roughly bounded by Woodward, Seneca, and Catalpa avenues, and Woodbine Street, Ridgewood. A 10-block residential neighborhood with 211 buildings, mostly 3-story Romanesque and Renaissance Revival brick "Mathews Flats" model tenements designed by Louis Allmendinger; built 1911-12 by G. X. Mathews Co. Ridgewood Multiple Resource Area.   09.30.1983

75th Avenue–61st Street Historic District
Roughly bounded by St. Felix Avenue, 60th Lane, and 60th and 62nd streets, Ridgewood. A 6-block residential neighborhood with 183 buildings, mostly 2-story Romanesque Revival, Renaissance Revival, and Arts and Crafts brick rowhouses designed by Louis Berger & Co.; built 1910-25 by Charles Fritz. Ridgewood Multiple Resource Area.   09.30.1983

Sidewalk Clock at 161-11 Jamaica Avenue
Freestanding cast-iron sidewalk clock manufactured c.1900. Sidewalk Clocks of New York City Thematic Resources.   04.18.1985

68th Avenue–64th Place Historic District
Roughly 64th Place from Catalpa Avenue to 68th Avenue and from 64th to 65th Street, Ridgewood. A 4-block residential neighborhood with 46 buildings, mostly 2-story Romanesque and Renaissance Revival brick rowhouses designed by Louis Berger & Co.; built 1909-13 by Charles Groesch. Ridgewood Multiple Resource Area. 09.30.1983

Steinway House
18-22 41st Street, Steinway. Large Italianate brick villa with 4-story tower and cast-iron decorative trim; built c.1858 for Benjamin Pike, Jr. Later residence of piano manufacturer William Steinway.   09.08.1983

Stockholm-DeKalb-Hart Historic District
Stockholm Street, DeKalb Avenue, and Hart Street, between Onderdonk and Woodward avenues, Ridgewood. A 2 1/2-block residential neighborhood with seventy-nine 2-story Romanesque and Renaissance Revival brick rowhouses designed by Louis Berger & Co.; built 1905-21. Ridgewood Multiple Resource Area.   09.30.1983

Summerfield Street Row Historic District
5912-5948 Summerfield Street, Ridgewood. Row of nineteen 2-story Romanesque and Renaissance Revival brick rowhouses with 2-story rounded bays; designed by Louis Berger & Co.; built 1912 by Jacob Erbach. Ridgewood Multiple Resource Area. 09.30.1983

Sunnyside Gardens Historic District
Roughly bounded by Queens Boulevard, 43rd and 52nd streets, and Barnett and Skillman avenues. A 16-block planned residential garden community with 562 2-story brick 1-, 2-, and 3-family rowhouses surrounding landscaped courtyards, 10 apartment buildings, playground, 2 parks, and 84 garages; designed by Henry Wright and Clarence Stein; built in sections 1924-35 by City Housing Corporation using standard city grid.   09.07.1984

United States Post Office–Far Rockaway
18-36 Mott Avenue. Colonial Revival brick post office with domed polygonal central pavilion; designed by Eric Kebbon; built 1935-36. United States Post Offices in New York State, 1858-1943, Thematic Resources. 11.17.1988

United States Post Office–Flushing
41-65 Main Street. Monumental Colonial Revival brick post office with marble Ionic portico; designed by Dwight James Baum and William W. Knowles; built 1932-34. Interior mural series (1933-34) by Vincent Aderente. United States Post Offices in New York State, 1858-1943, Thematic Resources. 11.17.1988

United States Post Office–Forest Hills Station
106-28 Queens Boulevard. International style terra-cotta-clad post office designed by Lorimer Rich; built 1937-38. Exterior terra-cotta relief sculpture by Sten Jacobson. United States Post Offices in New York State, 1858-1943, Thematic Resources.   11.17.1988

United States Post Office–Jackson Heights Station
78-02 37th Avenue. Colonial Revival brick post office designed by Benjamin C. Flournoy; built 1936-37. Interior mural (1940) by Peppino Mangravite. United States Post Offices in New York State, 1858-1943, Thematic Resources.   11.17.1988

United States Post Office–Jamaica
88-40 164th Street. Imposing Colonial Revival brick post office with marble Ionic portico; designed by Cross & Cross; built 1932-34. United States Post Offices in New York State, 1858-1943, Thematic Resources.   11.17.198?

United States Post Office–Long Island City
46-02 21st Street. Monumental Colonial Revival brick post office built 1928-29. United States Post Offices in New York State, 1858-1943, Thematic Resources.   05.11.1989

Cornelius Van Wyck House
126 West Drive, Douglaston. Modest Dutch Colonial frame residence built 1735; enlarged in Georgian style c.1750-70.   10.06.1983

Vander Ende-Onderdonk House Site
1820 Flushing Avenue, Ridgewood. A 2-acre archeological site and remains of early 18th-century Dutch Colonial stone farmhouse and associated features.   01.31.1977

Woodbine-Palmetto-Gates Historic District
Roughly bounded by Forest and Fairview avenues, and Woodbine and Linden streets, Ridgewood. A 3 1/2-block residential neighborhood with 91 buildings, mostly 3-story Romanesque and Renaissance Revival brick "Mathews Flats" model tenements designed by Louis Allmendinger; built 1908-11 by G. X. Mathews Co. Ridgewood Multiple Resource Area.   09.30.1983

Brunswick

Garfield School
NY 2 and Moonlawn Road, Eagle Mills. Stick Style frame 2-room rural schoolhouse designed by Nicholas Pawley; built 1881. Headquarters of Brunswick Historical Society.   06.09.1988

Hoosick .

Bennington Battlefield (State Historic Site)
NY67, on Vermont state line (also in Vermont). Archeological site of American Revolutionary War battle on August 16, 1777, between British forces and American militiamen (under command of General John Stark). American victory helped lead to surrender of British at Saratoga soon after.   NHL 01.20.1961

Buskirk Covered Bridge
(see Cambridge, Washington County)

David Mathews House (State Line House)
NY67 and VT67. Large 3-story Federal brick residence built c.1800 straddling border of New York and Vermont.   09.10.1979

Tibbits House
NY22 and NY7. Large Gothic Revival sandstone residence designed by Henry Dudley; built 1860 for major landowner and agriculturist George Mortimer Tibbits. Now part of Hoosac School.   05.22.1978

Hoosick Falls

Estabrook Octagon House
8 River Street. Victorian octagonal residence constructed of stuccoed Rosendale cement; built 1853-54 by Ezra Estabrook.
02.08.1980

Hoosick Falls Historic District
Central Avenue and Main Street. Central commercial and residential core of village, with 40 buildings, mostly Italianate, Second Empire, Eastlake, and Georgian Revival commercial buildings with residential upper floors; built late 19th to early 20th centuries during period of industrial growth.   12.03.1980

United States Post Office–Hoosick Falls
35 Main Street. Colonial Revival post office built 1923-25. United States Post Offices in New York State, 1858-1943, Thematic Resources.   11.17.1988

Nassau (Town)

Henry Tunis Smith Farm
NY203, south of Nassau. A 157-acre farmstead with late 18th-century Federal frame farmhouse

built in 3 stages. Property includes several 19th-century outbuildings.   09.18.1975

Nassau (Village)

Albany Avenue Historic District
Group of ten 19th-century residences on large lots at edge of village, including 7 Federal frame residences (1 former academy), 1 Greek Revival frame temple-front residence, and 2 early 20th-century residences.   11.21.1978

Chatham Street Row
Group of five 19th-century buildings, including 2 Victorian residences, Victorian commercial building, and 2 Federal residences.
12.01.1978

Church Street Historic District
Linear district of 36 residences, churches, and commercial buildings. Notable buildings include 10 late 18th-century and early 19th-century brick and frame Federal residences and stores, Victorian residences, and Romanesque Revival frame Nassau Reformed Church (1901).   11.21.1978

North Greenbush

DeFreest Homesteads
US4 and Jordan Road, south of Troy. Two similar Dutch Colonial brick farmhouses with gambrel roofs. Philip DeFreest House built c.1760; David DeFreest House built c.1770.
08.02.1977

Rensselaer

Aikin House
Broadway and Aikin Avenue. Large Federal brick townhouse with high stepped gable ends and refined exterior and interior decorative features; design attributed to Philip Hooker; built 1818 for William Aikin, founder of City of Rensselaer.   12.31.1974

Beverwyck Manor
(St. Anthony-on-Hudson Seminary)
Washington Avenue. Imposing 3-story Greek Revival stuccoed brick residence designed by Frederick Diaper; built 1839-42 for William P. Van Rensselaer, son of last patroon of Manor of Rensselaerswyck. Notable interior includes cantilevered marble staircase with bronzed cast-iron balusters and music room with frescoed ceiling.   08.03.1979

Fort Crailo (Crailo State Historic Site)
9 1/2 Riverside Avenue. Large Dutch Colonial brick residence built early 18th century as manor house for Van Rensselaer family; mid-19th-century addition. Legendary site of composition of ballad "Yankee Doodle."
NHL 11.05.1961

Patroon Agent's House and Office
15 Forbes Avenue. Large Greek Revival brick residence and attached brick office completed 1839 for Caspar W. Pruyn, rent collection agent for William P. Van Rensselaer.   08.03.1979

Schaghticoke

Knickerbocker Mansion
Knickerbocker Road. Large Georgian residence with wood structural system and brick-veneer exterior walls; completed c.1788 for Johannes Knickerbocker II, prominent landowner.
12.11.1972

Schodack

Muitzeskill Historic District
Schodack Landing and Muitzeskill roads. Small rural hamlet with approximately 22 Federal, Greek Revival, and Italianate vernacular farmhouses, residences, and commercial buildings. Also includes cemetery and Italianate Reformed Dutch Church of Schodack (1876).   07.24.1974

Schodack Landing Historic District
NY9J. An 18th- and 19th-century Hudson River trading hamlet with approximately 85 buildings, mostly residences. Includes several Dutch Colonial and Colonial brick and frame residences, Dutch barn, Federal and Victorian frame residences, 2 churches, 3 commercial buildings, and cemetery.   09.15.1977

Joachim Staats House and Gerrit Staats Ruin
Staats Road, Papscanee Island. A 27-acre property on Hudson River with Dutch Colonial vernacular stone Joachim Staats House (c.1700; brick and later frame additions c.1790), ruins of Dutch Colonial Gerrit Staats house (1758), family cemetery, smokehouse, and archeological sites of sloop landing and Native American occupation.   12.15.1978

Troy

Burden Iron Works Office Building
Polk Street. Large 1-story Romanesque Revival brick office building designed by Robert H. Robertson; built c.1881-86 as office building for massive ironworks. Museum and headquarters of Hudson-Mohawk Industrial Gateway.   03.16.1972

Burden Iron Works Site
East of Burden Avenue. A 50-acre property with archeological sites, buildings, structures, and ruins associated with ironworks complex on Wynantskill Creek; developed 1813-98. Sites and ruins include Troy Iron and Nail Factory (1813), Burden horseshoe-making shop (c.1851), Burden Upper Works and 60-foot-diameter water wheel (1851), Burden mansions, and dams and sluices. Buildings include Gothic Revival stone Woodside Presbyterian Church (1867) and Chapel.
11.10.1977

Esek Bussey Firehouse
302 Tenth Street. Romanesque Revival brick firehouse designed by H. P. Fielding; built 1891-92.   07.16.1973

Cannon Building (Cannon Place)
One Broadway. Large 4 1/2-story Greek Revival commercial building designed by Alexander

Jackson Davis; built 1835; mansard roof added 1870s and other 19th- and 20th-century alterations. 03.05.1970

Central Troy Historic District
Roughly bounded by Grand Street, Fifth Avenue, and Third, Adams, First, River, and Fulton streets. Large 25-block district encompassing commercial and residential core of city, with approximately 650 buildings. Includes numerous Federal, Greek Revival, Gothic Revival, and Italianate brick townhouses, commercial and civic buildings, and many Romanesque Revival, Neoclassical, and Georgian Revival commercial and civic buildings. Includes individually listed Cannon Building, Fifth Avenue–Fulton Street Historic District, Grand Street Historic District, Hart-Cluett Mansion, Ilium Building, McCarthy Building, National State Bank Building, Proctor's Theater, River Street Historic District, St. Paul's Episcopal Church Complex, Second Street Historic District, Troy Music Hall, Troy Public Library, and Washington Park Historic District. Other notable buildings include Federal Vail House (1818), Greek Revival First Presbyterian Church (1835, James H. Dakin; now Bush Memorial), Greek Revival Atheneum Building (1846; demolished 1991), Gothic Revival St. John's Episcopal Church (1856, Henry Dudley), Victorian Gothic Rice Building (1871, Frederick C. Withers), Victorian Congregation Berith Sholom Temple (1870), Beaux-Arts Frear's Troy Cash Bazaar (1897-1900, Mortimer L. Smith & Son), Arts and Crafts former Young Men's Christian Association Building (1905, W. L. & J. W. Woollett; demolished 1991), and Colonial Revival Hendrick Hudson Hotel (1926). 07.15.1986

Church of the Holy Cross
136 Eighth Street. Gothic Revival stone church designed 1843 by Alexander Jackson Davis for Mary B. Warren as free church; enlarged 1848 by Richard Upjohn; tower and ante-chapel designed 1859 by Henry Dudley. Adjoining rectory (1857) and Mary Warren Free Institute Building (1863). 06.04.1973

Fifth Avenue–Fulton Street Historic District
Bounded by Grand, William, and Union streets, and Broadway. A 2-block residential area with 37 buildings, mostly 3-story Italianate brick and brownstone rowhouses built late 19th century. Also includes W. & L. E. Gurley Company (individually listed) and Second Presbyterian Church (1864-65, Marcus F. Cummings). 03.05.1970

Gasholder House
Jefferson Street. Large Victorian circular brick building designed by engineer Frederick A. Sabbaton; built 1873 for storage of illuminating gas. 02.18.1971

Glenwood (Titus Eddy Mansion)
Eddy's Lane. Large Greek Revival brick residence with Ionic portico; built 1840s for printing-ink manufacturer. 05.25.1973

Grand Street Historic District
Grand Street between Fifth and Sixth avenues. A 1-block residential area with 2- and 3-story Italianate brick rowhouses built 1860s-70s, including row of 5 identical rowhouses designed by Marcus F. Cummings (from Cummings' *Modern American Architecture*, 1868). 02.27.1973

W. & L. E. Gurley Building
514 Fulton Street. A 4-story Early Romanesque Revival brick industrial building built 1862 for one of the world's oldest manufacturers of surveying instruments. 03.05.1970; NHL 05.04.1983

Hart-Cluett Mansion
59 Second Street. Large Federal townhouse with marble front and elaborate interior decoration; built 1827 by New York City merchant William Howard for daughter Betsey and her husband Richard P. Hart. Later owned by Cluett family, shirt and collar manufacturers. Operated as museum by Rensselaer County Historical Society. 04.11.1973

Ilium Building
Fulton and Fourth streets. A 5-story Beaux-Arts brick commercial building with terra-cotta and stone trim; designed by M. F. Cummings & Son; built 1904. 12.18.1970

Lansingburgh Academy
Fourth and 114th streets, Lansingburgh. A 2-story Federal brick school built 1820; 1902 addition designed by Edward W. Loth. Adapted for use as library. 10.14.1976

McCarthy Building
255-257 River Street. A 5-story Beaux-Arts commercial building with elaborate terra-cotta facade; built 1904. 03.05.1970

National State Bank Building
297 River Street. A 5-story Beaux-Arts brick commercial building with stone and terra-cotta trim; designed by M. F. Cummings & Son; built 1904. 12.29.1970

Northern River Street Historic District
403-429 and 420-430 River Street. A 1-block area with 13 multistoried brick commercial and industrial buildings built mid-19th to early 20th centuries as warehouses, salesrooms, and collar factories. 05.19.1988

Oakwood Cemetery
101st Street. A 325-acre rural cemetery founded 1848; landscape designed by John C. Sidney. Includes numerous Greek Revival, Gothic Revival, Egyptian Revival, Romanesque Revival, and Neoclassical monuments and mausoleums by well-known sculptors, including Robert E. Launitz, William Rinehart, and J. Massey Rhind. Notable buildings include Gothic Revival Warren Family Vault and Chapel (1860, Henry Dudley), Romanesque Revival Gardner Earl Memorial Chapel and Crematorium (1887-89, Fuller & Wheeler), Queen Anne Office and Lodge (1884, Fuller & Wheeler), and Gothic Revival Keeper's House (1861). Contains graves of prominent citizens, including "Uncle Sam" Wilson, Emma

Willard, Russell Sage, and Generals John E. Wool and George E. Thomas. 10.04.1984

Old Troy Hospital
Eighth Street. Large 3-story Second Empire brick building built 1868; additions in 1870s and c.1900; design attributed to Marcus F. Cummings. Adapted for use by Rensselaer Polytechnic Institute. 10.25.1973

Poestenkill Gorge Historic District
Between Spring Avenue and NY2. A 37-acre area along steep gorge of Poestenkill Creek with ruins and archeological sites of large complex of 19th-century water-powered mills and mill housing. Includes remains of major hydraulic power system developed 1840 by Benjamin Marshall. 03.08.1978

Powers Home
819 Third Avenue, Lansingburgh. Greek Revival frame residence with Ionic portico; built c.1846; large additions in 1883-84 when converted for use as old age home founded by Deborah Powers. 04.16.1974

Proctor's Theater
82 Fourth Street. A 5-story commercial building with Gothic-style terra-cotta decoration and large vaudeville auditorium; designed by Arland Johnson; built 1914. Movie Palaces of the Tri-Cities Thematic Resources. 10.04.1979

River Street Historic District
River Street from Congress Street to First Street. A 2-block area with mostly 4-story brick commercial buildings built early to late 19th century as warehouses and salesrooms during development of city as shipping and industrial center. 06.03.1976

St. Paul's Episcopal Church Complex
58 Third Street. Gothic Revival stone church built 1826-28; interior remodeled 1890s by Tiffany Glass & Decoration Co. Adjoining Victorian Gothic Martha Memorial House (1881; 1887 addition) and adjacent Gothic Revival Guild House (1869). 09.07.1979

Second Street Historic District
Second Street between Washington Street and Broadway. A 6-block residential, commercial, civic, and institutional district with mostly 19th-century Federal, Greek Revival, and Italianate brick townhouses. Individually listed buildings include Troy Public Library, Hart-Cluett Mansion, Cannon Building, and Troy Savings Bank and Music Hall. Buildings designed by M. F. Cummings & Son include Young Women's Association Building, Neoclassical Rensselaer County Courthouse, and 3 buildings of Russell Sage College. Also includes Arts and Crafts Caldwell Apartments (1907, W. L. & J. W. Woollett). 08.07.1974

Troy Savings Bank and Music Hall
32 Second Street. Massive Second Empire granite building with elaborate French Renaissance style decorative features and large audi-

Opposite: Hart-Cluett Mansion, Troy.

torium on upper floors; designed by George B. Post; built 1871-75. Known for its outstanding acoustics; one of the finest 19th-century music halls in the United States.   NHL 04.11.1989

Emma Willard School, Troy.

Opposite: Elizabeth Alice Austen House, Staten Island.

Troy Public Library
100 Second Street. Italian Renaissance style marble library designed by Barney & Chapman; built 1896-97. Notable interior.   01.17.1973

United States Post Office–Troy
400 Broadway. Large Classical Revival stone post office built 1936-38. Interior murals (1939) by Waldo Pierce. United States Post Offices in New York State, 1858-1943, Thematic Resources.   05.11.1989

Washington Park Historic District
Washington Park and adjacent properties on Second, Third, and Washington streets and Washington Place. Residential neighborhood with large Greek Revival, Gothic Revival, and Italianate brick townhouses, 1 church, and former school facing large private square; established c.1838. Notable buildings include monumental block-long terrace of 10 Greek Revival townhouses (1838-42).   05.25.1973

Emma Willard School
Pawling and Elmgrove avenues. Secondary school for women on 55-acre property with 18 historic buildings. Original campus of 3 Jacobean Revival stone buildings designed by M. F. Cummings & Son; built 1910. Other notable buildings include Tudor Revival E. Harold Cluett Residence (1910, Marcus T. Reynolds), Georgian Revival George Cluett Residence (1911; Marcus T. Reynolds), and several school buildings built 1920s-30s in similar style to original buildings.
08.30.1979

Staten Island

House at 5910 Amboy Road
Greek Revival frame former farmhouse built c.1840 for Abraham J. Wood.   12.16.1982

Elizabeth Alice Austen House
(Clear Comfort)
2 Hylan Boulevard. Vernacular frame and stone residence built in sections during 18th century; enlarged and remodeled in Gothic Revival/Picturesque style c.1845 for John H. Austen. Residence of photographer Alice Austen 1867-1945. Museum.   7.28.1970

Battery Weed (Fort Richmond)
Fort Wadsworth Reservation. Massive 3-story, 3-sided granite fort overlooking The Narrows; built 1845-61 as major United States military fortification on site of Dutch, British, and American fortifications.   01.20.1972

Billou-Stillwell-Perine House
1476 Richmond Road. Modest Colonial vernacular residence built in several stages with 2 contiguous stone sections (c.1680 and c.1700), and 3 stone and frame additions (c.1749, c.1760-90, and c.1830). Museum.
01.01.1976

Brighton Heights Reformed Church
320 St. Mark's Place. Gothic Revival frame church designed by John Correja; built 1863-64.   06.03.1982

Conference House
Hylan Boulevard. Large Colonial vernacular stone residence built c.1680 by Christopher Billop; enlarged 1720. Site of unsuccessful peace conference between British, represented by Lord Richard Howe, and Americans, represented by John Adams, Benjamin Franklin, and Edward Rutledge, on September 11, 1776. Museum.   NHL 05.23.1966

Edgewater Village Hall and Tappen Park
Bounded by Wright, Water, Bay, and Canal streets. Romanesque Revival brick building designed by Paul Kuhne; built 1889. Situated in small late 19th-century park.   05.19.1980

Dr. Samuel MacKenzie Elliott House
69 Delafield Place. Modest Gothic Revival stone cottage built c.1850 for local doctor, developer, member of literary community, and anti-slavery activist.   03.28.1980

Fire Fighter
St. George Ferry Terminal. A 129-foot steel fireboat built 1938 by United Shipyards, Staten Island, for Fire Department of New York. One of 10 surviving historic fireboats in United States.   NHL 06.30.1989

Fort Tompkins Quadrangle
Building 137, Fort Wadsworth. Massive 250-by-500-foot granite, brick, and earthen fortification built 1858-76 by federal government as fortified barracks in support of adjacent Battery Weed and other batteries.   07.30.1974

Gardiner-Tyler House
27 Tyler Street. Large Greek Revival frame residence with Corinthian portico; built c.1835. Later home of Julia Gardner Tyler, widow of President John Tyler.   11.23.1984

Garibaldi Memorial
420 Tompkins Avenue. Modest Gothic Revival frame cottage built c.1845. Home of Italian liberator Giuseppe Garibaldi for 18-month exile in 1850-51. Also home of Anthony Meucci, credited with early development of telephone. Museum.   04.17.1980

Hamilton Park Community Houses
105 Franklin Avenue, 66 Harvard Avenue, and 32 Park Place. Group of 3 residences built as part of planned suburban residential park developed early 1850s by Charles K. Hamilton. Includes Italianate Pritchard House (c.1853), Second Empire 32 Park Place (c.1865), and Italianate Hamilton Park Cottage (c.1860).   09.29.1983

Peter Houseman House
308 St. John Avenue. A 1-room Colonial stone residence built c.1730; larger frame section added c.1760 by millwright Peter Housman. Became part of summer resort "Prohibition Park" in late 19th century.   10.29.1982

Kreischer House
4500 Arthur Kill Road. Large Stick Style frame residence built c.1885 for brick manufacturer.   10.29.1982

Kreuzer-Pelton House
1262 Richmond Terrace. Residence with 3 connected sections, including 1-room Dutch Colonial section (1722, built by Cornelius Van Santvoord), central Colonial frame section (1770, built by Cornelius Kreuzer; headquarters of American Loyalists during American Revolution under command of General Cortlandt Skinner), and 2-story brick section built 1836 for Daniel Pelton, Sr.   01.29.1973

LaTourette House
Richmond Hill Road. Large Greek Revival former farmhouse built c.1836 for prosperous farmer David LaTourette; large 1-story porch added 1936 when converted to clubhouse for golf course.   03.05.1982

McFarlane-Bredt House
30 Hylan Boulevard. A 3-acre property overlooking The Narrows, with large Italianate/Picturesque frame villa built in stages 1840s-90s. Home of New York Yacht Club 1868-71. Now part of public park with adjacent Elizabeth Alice Austen House (individually listed).   09.08.1983

Miller Army Air Field Historic District
New Dorp Lane. Two remaining intact structures of former Army air base established 1919-21 as part of aerial coastal defense system: steel-framed and stuccoed Seaplane Hangar, and octagonal concrete Elm Tree Light beacon tower.   04.11.1980

Moore-McMillen House
3531 Richmond Road. Federal shingled residence with gambrel roof; built 1818 as rectory of Church of St. Andrew.   04.23.1980

Neville House
806 Richmond Terrace. Large Colonial sandstone residence with 2-story veranda; built c.1770 for Captain John Neville, retired naval officer. Later a tavern.   07.28.1977

New Brighton Village Hall
66 Lafayette Avenue. A 3-story Second Empire brick former village hall designed by James Whitford; built 1868-71.   12.15.1978

New Dorp Light
Altamont Avenue, New Dorp Heights. Vernacular frame residence with central square light tower; built c.1854 as navigational beacon for The Narrows and New York Bay.   08.28.1973

Office Building and United States Light-House Depot Complex
One Bay Street. Large Second Empire brick and stone former administration building (1868-71, Alfred B. Mullett) and associated buildings used as experimental station in development of lighthouse technology.   09.15.1983

Poillon-Seguine-Britton House
360 Great Kills Road. Colonial stone residence built c.1695 by French Huguenot Jacques Poillon; frame enlargement c.1730 and large Greek Revival enlargement and alterations c.1845 by Seguine family; last major alterations c.1930.   02.02.1984

Sailors' Snug Harbor
Richmond Terrace. Large complex of buildings on extensive grounds developed from 1831 on as home for aged seamen. Includes monumental group of 5 Greek Revival dormitory and administration buildings. Central building designed by Minard Lafever; built 1831-33 by Samuel Thomson; interior redecorated 1884. Flanking buildings designed by Minard Lafever; built 1839-41. End buildings designed in same style by Richard Smyth; built 1879-81. Property also includes chapel, gatehouses, and several other buildings. Under development as Snug Harbor Cultural Center.   03.16.1972; NHL 12.08.1976   ILLUS. P. 140

St. Alban's Episcopal Church
76 St. Alban's Place. Victorian Gothic frame church designed by Richard M. Upjohn; built in 2 stages, 1865 and 1869-73, as Church of the Holy Comforter. Adjacent rectory.   10.29.1982

St. Paul's Memorial Church and Rectory
225 St. Paul's Avenue. High Victorian Gothic stone church and rectory designed by Edward Tuckerman Potter of Potter & Clinton; built 1866-70. Chapel addition built 1889.   11.21.1980

Sandy Ground Historic Archeological District
Address restricted. A 158-acre area encompassing archeological site, structural remains, intact residence, and cemetery of 19th-century free African-American oystering community of Sandy Ground.   09.23.1982

Scott-Edwards House
752 Delafield Avenue. A 1 1/2-story Dutch Colonial stone residence with roof ending in spring eaves; built c.1730; Greek Revival veranda and other alterations c.1840; later rear addition.   02.11.1983

Seguine House
440 Seguine Avenue. Large Greek Revival frame residence with monumental pedimented portico supported by square columns; built c.1840 for businessman Joseph H. Seguine.   05.06.1980

*Pavilion, Sailors' Snug Harbor, Staten Island
(p. 139).*

Staten Island Borough Hall and Richmond County Courthouse
Richmond Terrace. A 5-acre civic complex with 2 buildings and formal gardens. Monumental 3-story French Renaissance style brick and limestone borough hall (1903) in Louis XIII style with tall clock tower. Monumental Italian Renaissance style Neoclassical limestone courthouse (1913) with Corinthian portico. Both buildings designed by Carrère & Hastings. 10.06.1983

Houses at 364 and 390 Van Duzer Street
Two similar Greek Revival frame townhouses with 2-story porticoes, 1 with Doric columns and 1 with Corinthian columns; built c.1835 in village of Stapleton. 11.14.1982

Voorlezer's House
Arthur Kill Road, opposite Center Street. A 2½-story Dutch Colonial frame building built c.1695 as meeting house and school; restored 1939. Part of Richmondtown Restoration museum village. NHL 11.05.1961

Ward's Point Conservation Area
Southwest of Tottenville at Arthur Kill and Hylan Boulevard. A 33-acre area overlooking confluence of Raritan River, Arthur Kill, and Raritan Bay, with substantial prehistoric archeological components relating to Early Archaic stage, and historic archeological features relating to Conference House (individually listed) and Colonial inhabitation from c.1675. 09.29.1982

Caleb T. Ward Mansion
141 Nixon Avenue. Imposing 3-story Greek Revival stuccoed brick residence with Ionic portico and large cupola; built c.1835 by George B. Davis for locally prominent family; design features derived from builders' handbooks of Minard Lafever. Converted 1923 into apartments. 07.26.1982

Woodrow Methodist Church
1109 Woodrow Road. Greek Revival frame church with Doric portico; built 1842; Italianate bell tower added 1876. Adjacent mid-19th-century vernacular frame parsonage and large 18th- to 19th- century cemetery. 10.29.1982

Clarkstown

Blauvelt House
Zukor Road, New City. Federal vernacular brick farmhouse with gambrel roof, flared eaves, and clapboard ends; built 1834 incorporating 18th-century brick smokehouse and small late 18th-century brick farmhouse as wings. Adjacent late 18th-century barn and privy, and 19th-century woodshed. Museum and cultural center. 03.28.1985

English Church and Schoolhouse
(New Hempstead Presbyterian Church) 484 New Hempstead Road. Federal vernacular frame church built 1827 on site of 1734 meetinghouse. Adjacent Queen Anne frame manse (1905) and vernacular frame 1-room schoolhouse (1867; enlarged 1891). 11.23.1977

Rockland County Courthouse and Dutch Gardens
South Main Street, New City. Large Art Deco limestone courthouse with elaborate ornamentation; designed by Dennison & Hirons; built 1928. Adjacent 3-acre park and gardens with decorative brick structures; designed by Mary Mobray Clarke; constructed 1934-36 as Works Progess Administration project. 01.03.1991

Terneur-Hutton House
160 Sickelton Road, West Nyack. A 1½-story Dutch Colonial stone house built in 2 phases, 1731 and built c.1753. 04.23.1973

Haverstraw (Town)

M/V Commander
Haverstraw Marina. A 60-foot-long 275-passenger wooden excursion boat built 1917 by Beele Wallace Co. Operated 1919-81 between Sheepshead Bay, Brooklyn, and Far Rockaway, Queens. 09.27.1984

Haverstraw (Village)

The Homestead
143 Hudson Avenue. Vernacular frame former farmhouse built c.1800 for DeNoyelles family; mid-19th-century Victorian modifications. Owned 1850s by Edward Pye, first village president. 11.10.1983

King's Daughters Public Library
Main and Allison streets. A 2-story Classical Revival/Renaissance Revival brick library designed by William H. Parkton; built 1903. 08.09.1991

United States Post Office–Haverstraw
86 Main Street. Colonial Revival brick post

office with limestone and terra-cotta trim; built 1935-36. United States Post Offices in New York State, 1858-1943, Thematic Resources. 11.17.1988

Nyack

Tappan Zee Playhouse (Broadway Theater) 20 South Broadway. Neoclassical brick building with 2-story main facade and large classically decorated auditorium; built 1911 as vaudeville house. 07.21.1983

United States Post Office–Nyack 48 South Broadway. Classical Revival brick post office built 1932. Interior mural series (1936) by Jacob Getlar. United States Post Offices in New York State, 1858-1943, Thematic Resources. 05.11.1989

Orangetown

The Big House US9W, near Closter Road, Palisades. Dutch Colonial stone residence built c.1735; enlarged c.1750, c.1770, and 1826; central section altered in Picturesque style 1867. Palisades Multiple Resource Area. 07.12.1990

Cliffside (Henry E. Lawrence Estate) Lawrence Lane, Palisades. A 4-acre estate overlooking Hudson River with large Victorian stone residence designed by J. Cleveland Cady; built 1876 as summer house of Lawrence family. Adjacent carriage house. Palisades Multiple Resource Area. 07.12.1990

Closter Road–Oak Tree Road Historic District Palisades. Group of 16 residential, commercial, religious, and civic properties at historic core of hamlet. Includes 3 Italianate frame residences, several Greek Revival frame residences, Gothic Revival Palisades Community Center (c.1870), Greek Revival Palisades Country Store (c.1840), Palisades Cemetery, Greek Revival Methodist Episcopal Church (1859), and Georgian vernacular Trenchard House (c.1780). Palisades Multiple Resource Area. 07.12.1990

Abner Concklin House (Old Yellow House) Closter Road, Palisades. Modest Italianate vernacular frame residence built c.1859; enlarged late 19th and early 20th century. Palisades Multiple Resource Area. 08.06.1987

De Wint House (De Clark-De Wint House) Livingston Avenue and Oak Tree Road, Tappan. A 1 1/2-story Dutch Colonial brick and stone residence built 1700; remodeled mid-19th century. Headquarters of General George Washington 4 times during American Revolution. Museum. NHL 05.23.1966

Haring-Eberle House US9W, near Oak Tree Road, Palisades. Modest frame residence with Gothic Revival alterations and enlargement c.1865. Property includes late

19th-century barn. Palisades Multiple Resource Area. 07.12.1990

The Little House US9W, near Oak Tree Road, Palisades. Modest Federal frame residence built c.1820 with later additions. Palisades Multiple Resource Area. 07.12.1990

Neiderhurst (Winthrop S. Gilman, Jr. Estate) Ludlow Lane, Palisades. A 14-acre estate overlooking Hudson River with large High Victorian Gothic brick main residence designed by Winthrop S. Gilman, Jr.; built 1872-74. Outbuildings include observatory (1869), Gothic Revival Fern Lodge (1866), and barn (1872). Landscaped grounds by Gilman and daughter Anna G. Hill. Palisades Multiple Resource Area. 07.12.1990

Palisades Interstate Park West bank of Hudson River (also in New Jersey). A 14-mile stretch of Palisades along Hudson River from Fort Lee, New Jersey, to Piermont, New York, including (in New York) half-mile section of present Palisades State Park and Tallman Mountain State Park. Early conservation effort of New York and New Jersey to protect scenic beauty of lower west bank of Hudson River with formation of Palisades Interstate Park Commission in 1900. NHL 01.12.1965

Edward Salyer House 241 South Middletown Road, Pearl River. Dutch Colonial frame former farmhouse with gambrel roof and flared eaves; built c.1765; early 19th-century alterations. 09.04.1986

Seven Oaks Estate End of Ludlow Lane, Palisades. A 15-acre estate with large Gothic Revival frame residence designed by George E. & F. W. Woodward; built 1862 as summer house for Charles F. Park. Former estate outbuildings include Gothic Revival coachman's house, barn, laundry, summer kitchen, and machine shop. Palisades Multiple Resource Area. 07.12.1990

Tappan Historic District Main Street and Kings Highway. Historic commercial and residential core of hamlet, with approximately 30 buildings, 2 cemeteries, and village green. Notable buildings include Colonial '76 House (1753-55), Federal Tappan Reformed Church (1835), vernacular Tappan Reformed Church Manse (1797), Federal Dr. Morris Bartow House (1835), Greek Revival Rockland Academy (1843), Greek Revival Blauvelt House (1835-36), and several Victorian-period buildings. 04.26.1990

United States Post Office–Pearl River Franklin and Main streets, Pearl River. Colonial Revival/Moderne brick post office built 1935-36. United States Post Offices in New York State, 1858-1943, Thematic Resources. 11.17.1988

Washington Spring Road–Woods Road Historic District Palisades. Residential neighborhood of 34 properties with eclectic mix of vernacular

Dutch Colonial, Federal, Greek Revival, Picturesque, Gothic Revival, Second Empire, Colonial Revival, and Arts and Crafts residences built late 18th to early 20th centuries. Developed as Hudson River landing in 18th century (Snedens Landing), country retreat for New Yorkers in late 19th century, and enclave for cultural and artistic leaders in early 20th century. Notable buildings include William Sneden House (c.1700; a.k.a. Cheer Hall), Mollie Sneden House (c.1750, enlarged c.1874), Captain John Willsey House (c.1830), Candine Heider House (c.1790), The Log Cabin (c.1850, enlarged c.1930), Peggy Parcell House (c.1810), United Presbyterian Church (1863), Coles House (c.1864), Cedar Grove (c.1862), Watson House (c.1750, enlarged c.1859), and Captain Larry Sneden House (c.1780). Palisades Multiple Resource Area. 07.12.1990 ILLUS P. 143

Piermont

Haddock's Hall 300 Ferdon Avenue. A 2-story Victorian brick building with 3-story tower; designed and built 1875-76 by William Hand for Roger Haddock as store and public hall. Served as village hall and library in late 19th century. Later used as textile mill. 06.20.1991

Sparkill Creek Drawbridge Bridge Street over Sparkill Creek. Single-leaf, metal, hand-operated mechanical drawbridge with Pratt Pony truss deck; built 1880 by King Iron Bridge Co. 03.28.1985

Ramapo

Brick Church Complex Brick Church Road and NY306, West New Hempstead. Greek Revival brick church with Doric columns; built 1856; late 19th-century Renaissance Revival wood tower. Includes mid-18th-century vernacular frame superintendent's house, late 19th-century Victorian parish school, and large late 18th- to 19th-century cemetery on 4-acre parcel. 09.07.1984

Torne Brook Farm Torne Brook Road. A 12-acre estate with large High Victorian Gothic frame residence, related outbuildings, and landscaped grounds built early 1870s for industrialist Charles T. Pierson; early 20th-century additions and alterations to main residence and grounds for Mapes family and Alfred E. Clegg. 05.19.1988

Sloatsburg

Sloat House 19 Orange Turnpike. Large Federal stone and brick residence built c.1813-14 incorporating modest vernacular stone and frame residence (c.1755) as rear wing; Greek Revival porch and trim added to main section in mid-19th century. Property includes barn, carriage house, and well house. Associated with locally prominent family of Stephen Sloat. 11.05.1974

South Nyack

Ross-Hand Mansion
122 South Franklin Street. A 4-acre estate overlooking Hudson River with large Gothic Revival brick villa designed and built c.1860 by stone contractor Azariah Ross as his summer house; interior remodeled 1880s. Property includes summer kitchen, carriage house, and brick smokehouse. 09.08.1983

Spring Valley

United States Post Office–Spring Valley
7 North Madison Avenue. Colonial Revival brick post office built 1936-37. Interior mural (1938) by Stephen Elnier. United States Post Offices in New York State, 1858-1943, Thematic Resources. 05.11.1989

Stony Point

Bear Mountain Bridge and Toll House
NY6, 202 across Hudson River (also in Cortlandt, Westchester County). A 2,257-foot-long steel suspension bridge with 2 towers; built 1923-24 by Harriman family through Bear Mountain Hudson River Bridge Co. with architect Howard C. Baird, Terry & Trench Construction Co., and Carey Construction Co. Includes Tudor Revival/eclectic stone tollhouse. Hudson Highlands Multiple Resource Area. 11.23.1982

Stony Point Battlefield (State Historic Site)
Off US9W and 202, north of Stony Point. Archeological site of British-held fort captured July 16, 1779, during American Revolution by American Light Infantrymen led by General "Mad" Anthony Wayne. Capture ensured control of Hudson River by General George Washington. NHL 01.20.1961

Stony Point Lighthouse
Stony Point Battlefield. A 2-story octagonal stone lighthouse built 1825. Hudson River Lighthouses Thematic Group. 05.29.1979

Suffern

United States Post Office–Suffern
15 Chestnut Street. Colonial Revival/Moderne brick post office built 1935-36. Interior sculptural relief (1937) by Elliott Means. United States Post Offices in New York State, 1858-1943, Thematic Resources. 05.11.1989

Upper Nyack

Upper Nyack Firehouse
330 North Broadway. Queen Anne brick firehouse with 3-story bell tower; designed by G. W. Knapp; built 1887. 09.23.1982

West Haverstraw

Fraser-Hoyer House
Treason Hill off US9W. A 9-acre estate with large Federal frame residence built c.1810 on site of 18th-century residence of William Smith, Loyalist during American Revolution. 04.22.1976

Henry Garner Mansion
18 Railroad Avenue. Imposing Greek Revival brick residence with Corinthian portico and octagonal tower; built c.1845 for manufacturer Henry Garner. 08.14.1973; DEMOLISHED 1976

Adirondack State Forest Preserve
(see Clinton County)

Brasher

Dr. Buck-Stevens House
West Main Street, Brasher Falls. A 2-story Italianate octagonal residence built 1855-57 with stucco over concrete exterior walls, scored to give appearance of stone. 05.20.1982

Canton (Town)

Harrison Gristmill
NY345, Morley. A 3-story Federal stone mill on Grasse River; built 1840. 09.16.1982

Trinity Episcopal Church
County 65, Morley. Gothic Revival fieldstone chapel designed by Charles C. Haight; built c.1870. Adjacent 19th-century cemetery. 02.19.1990

Canton (Village)

Herring-Cole Hall
Saint Lawrence University. Italianate stone library built 1869. Reading room addition designed by Huberty & Hudswell; built 1902. Notable interior. 05.01.1974

Richardson Hall
Saint Lawrence University. A 3-story Italianate brick classroom building built 1855-56. Interior rebuilt 1962. 05.01.1974

Saint Lawrence University–Old Campus Historic District
Park Street. A 23-acre campus with 10 buildings, 8 built 1905-26 in variety of revival styles. Includes Dean-Eaton Residence Hall (1926-27, Bertram G. Goodhue) and individually listed Herring-Cole Hall and Richardson Hall. 09.15.1983

United States Post Office–Canton
Park Street. Colonial Revival brick post office built 1936-37. Interior sculptural relief (1939) by Berta Margoulies. United States Post Offices in New York State, 1858-1943, Thematic Resources. 11.17.1988

Village Park Historic District
Both sides of Main and Park streets, and Park Place. Residential, commercial, and civic district with 19th- and early 20th-century buildings around and near village park. Notable buildings include Greek Revival Silas Wright House (1834), Victorian Gothic Presbyterian Church (1876, Lawrence B. Valk), and United States Post Office (individually listed). 05.06.1975; BOUNDARY INCREASE 09.29.198?

Gouverneur

United States Post Office–Gouverneur
35 Grove Street. Classical Revival brick post office built 1915-17. United States Post Offices in New York State, 1858-1943, Thematic Resources.   05.11.1989

Lisbon

Lisbon Town Hall
Church and Main streets. Queen Anne frame building with gambrel roof; built 1889. Elaborate interior Stick Style auditorium. 09.04.1980

Massena

Robinson Bay Archeological District
North of Massena. A 100-acre property along shore of St. Lawrence River with cluster of 6 prehistoric archeological sites containing artifacts from Late Archaic and Middle Woodland stages.   09.13.1977

Morristown

Jacob Ford House
Northumberland Street. A 2 1/2-story Federal stone residence built 1837; classical portico added c.1890. Summer home and studio of painter Charles S. Chapman. Morristown Village Multiple Resource Area.   09.02.1982

Land Office
Main Street. Small Greek Revival stone office built 1821. Now village library. Morristown Village Multiple Resource Area.   09.02.1982

Paschal Miller House
Main and Gouverneur streets. A 1 1/2-story Greek Revival frame residence built c.1838-43. Morristown Village Multiple Resource Area. 09.02.1982

Morristown Schoolhouse
Columbia Street. Small vernacular stone school built c.1824. Morristown Village Multiple Resource Area.   09.02.1982

Samuel Stocking House
83 Gouverneur Street. Large Federal/Greek Revival stone residence built 1821; Victorian modifications. Morristown Village Multiple Resource Area. 09.02.1982

Stone Windmill
Morris Street. A 40-foot-high stone windmill built 1825; vanes and gears removed and new roof added 1940s. Morristown Village Multiple Resource Area.   09.02.1982

United Methodist Church
Gouverneur Street. Small vernacular frame church with Doric portico and Gothic windows; built c.1838. Interior with pressed tin walls and ceilings. Morristown Village Multiple Resource Area.   09.02.1982

Wright's Stone Store
Main Street. A 2 1/2-story Federal vernacular stone store built c.1821. Morristown Village Multiple Resource Area.   09.02.1982

Norfolk

Raymondville Parabolic Bridge
Grant Road over Raquette River, Raymondville. A 288-foot, single-span, lenticular-truss metal bridge built 1886 by Berlin Iron Bridge Co. of Connecticut.   09.07.1984

Ogdensburg

Acker and Evans Law Office
315 State Street. A 1-story Greek Revival office with marble facade and limestone side and rear walls; built 1830 as Ogdensburg Bank. 09.15.1983

Judge John Fine House
422 State Street. Greek Revival stone residence built 1849-51 incorporating rear wing built c.1823. Home of prominent politician and jurist. 01.09.1986

Library Park Historic District
303-323 Washington Street, 100-112 Carolina Street, and Library Park. Group of 7 buildings in and adjacent to Library Park, including Federal brick Remington Art Museum (1809-10), Classical Revival library (1888, remodeled

East entrance, Herring-Cole Hall, Village of Canton.

Opposite: Bruere House, Washington Spring Road–Woods Road Historic District, Orangetown (p. 141).

1921), and 5 residences in Italianate and Queen Anne styles (c.1880-91).   11.04.1982

New York State Armory
100 Lafayette Street. A 2-story castellated Gothic Revival stone armory designed by Horatio Nelson White; built 1858.   12.12.1976

Oswegatchie Pumping Station
Mechanic Street. A 2-story Victorian limestone building built 1868 to supply water and power to city; enlarged 1897. Adjacent trash racks, headgates, tailrace, and concrete dam across Oswegatchie River.   06.11.1990

United States Custom House
127 North Water Street. Large 3 1/2-story Federal stone commercial building built 1809-10 as warehouse, store, and shipping base for David Parish. Used as United States Custom House since 1938.   10.09.1974

United States Post Office–Ogdensburg
431 State Street. Large Italianate stone post office designed by Alfred B. Mullett; built 1867-70. Octagonal dome removed 1906.   08.16.1977

Pierrepont

Gardner Cox House
Main Street, Hannawa Falls. Large late Federal stone residence built 1838. Home of prominent early settler and industrialist.   03.20.1986

Pierrepont Town Buildings
Main Street, Pierrepont Center. Three adjacent buildings: vernacular frame schoolhouse (1826), Greek Revival frame town hall (1847, altered 1901), and Queen Anne frame Union Church (1885).   11.04.1982

Potsdam (Town)

French Family Farm
US 11, southwest of Potsdam. A 9-acre farmstead with large Federal frame residence built 1815; enlarged c.1820. Includes c.1900 barn.   11.04.1982

Potsdam (Village)

Market Street Historic District
Market and Raymond streets. Commercial center of village, with 27 buildings built 1820-1900. Includes notable examples of Federal, Italianate, Romanesque Revival, and Classical Revival brick and stone commercial buildings.   11.16.1979

United States Post Office–Potsdam
21 Elm Street. Large Classical Revival brick post office with Doric portico; built 1932-33. United States Post Offices in New York State, 1858-1943, Thematic Resources.   05.11.1989

Stockholm

West Stockholm Historic District
West Stockholm and Livingston roads. Early 19th-century hamlet comprising 28 buildings, mostly residences. Includes examples of Federal, Greek Revival, and Italianate styles, as well as vernacular structures.   11.20.1979

Waddington

Chase Mills Inn
Mein and Townline roads, Chase Mills. A 2-story Italianate frame inn built c.1865.   11.29.1978

SARATOGA COUNTY

Ballston Spa

Brookside
Charlton Street. Large Federal frame building built 1793 by Benajah Douglas as hotel adjacent to mineral springs; 2-story Greek Revival front piazza. Headquarters of Saratoga County Historical Society.   05.21.1975

Saratoga County Courthouse Complex
Group of 3 buildings, including Victorian County Clerk's Office (1866) and Romanesque Revival brick Courthouse and Jail (1889), all designed by Marcus F. Cummings; 1902-03 enlargements designed by R. Newton Brezee.   03.18.1971; DEMOLISHED

Union Mill Complex
NY 50, Milton Avenue. A 4-acre mill complex on Kayederosseras Creek built in stages 1850-86 for paper manufacturer George West. Includes 4-story Second Empire brick Union Mill (1879), office building (1884), West Bag Factory (c.1850), and mill dam.   06.17.1982

United States Post Office–Ballston Spa
One Front Street. Colonial Revival brick post office built 1935-36. United States Post Offices in New York State, 1858-1943, Thematic Resources.   11.17.1988

Verbeck House
20 Church Avenue. Large Queen Anne frame residence designed by Marcus F. Cummings; built 1889 for attorney James Verbeck. Adapted for use as National Bottle Museum.   04.07.1983

Charlton

Charlton Historic District
Main Street (NY 51). Rural hamlet with 49 buildings, mostly early to mid-19th-century vernacular frame residences and farmhouses.

Notable buildings include Greek Revival frame Freehold Presbyterian Church (1852), Federal frame former St. Paul's Episcopal Church (1804), schoolhouse (1859), store (c.1829), and Federal Charlton House (c.1791).   01.01.1976

Clifton Park

Vischer Ferry Historic District
Junction of River View, Vischer Ferry, and Crescent roads. Rural hamlet on Mohawk River with 64 buildings, including numerous Greek Revival frame residences built mid-19th century during heyday of community as canal town on Erie Canal. Also includes Colonial Nicholas Vischer Homestead (c.1730; 1800 addition) and several late 19th-century residences and church.   10.15.1975

Hadley

Hadley Parabolic Bridge
County 1. A 181-foot-long, double-span, semi deck lenticular iron-truss bridge built 1895 by Berlin Iron Bridge Co. of Connecticut.   03.25.1977

Half Moon

Mechanicville Hydroelectric Plant
NY 32 (also in Schaghticoke, Rensselaer County). Hydroelectric plant complex spanning Hudson River; built 1897-98 by Hudson River Power Transmission Co. to designs of architect and engineer A. C. Rice. Includes 257-foot-long brick powerhouse (original generators and exciters; turbines and governors replaced 1902-03), earthen embankment, concrete non-overflow dam, and 700-foot-long concrete gravity overflow dam.   11.13.1989

Old Champlain Canal
(see village of Waterford)

Malta

Ruhle Road Stone Arch Bridge
Ruhle Road. Single-arch stone vehicular bridge built c.1873 by Elbin Miller.   09.29.1988

Mechanicville

Colonel Elmer E. Ellsworth Monument and Grave
Hudson View Cemetery. A 25-foot-tall granite monument marking grave of first Northern casualty of Civil War; erected 1874.   11.13.1976

Moreau

Grant Cottage (State Historic Site)
County 101, north of NY 9, Mount McGregor Victorian frame residence on mountaintop setting; built 1872. Retreat of General Ulysse

S. Grant for 5 weeks until his death on July 23, 1885; interior unchanged since that time. 02.18.1971

Northumberland

Gansevoort Mansion
Off NY32, Gansevoort. Large Federal vernacular frame residence built 1813 for Herman Gansevoort to manage large landholdings and mills of his father, General Peter Gansevoort; Greek Revival modifications.   06.23.1976

Old Champlain Canal (see village of Waterford)

Round Lake

Round Lake Historic District
US9. Residential community established 1860s as religious campground, with approximately 250 modest Victorian/Picturesque cottages on streets laid out in wheel design. Includes Stick Style open-air auditorium (1884) with Ferris organ (1847-48) from Calvary Episcopal Church in New York City.   04.24.1975

Saratoga

Old Champlain Canal (see village of Waterford)

Broadway Historic District
Broadway and Washington, Phila, Caroline, Byron, and Rock streets, and Maple and Woodlawn avenues. Central commercial and residential core of mid-19th-century resort community, with approximately 135 buildings, including large Italianate brick commercial blocks, residences, and hotels.   09.12.1979; BOUNDARY INCREASE 04.15.1983

Canfield Casino and Congress Park
Bounded by Broadway, and Spring and Circular streets. A 33-acre landscaped park with formal gardens, fountains, sculpture of "Spirit of Life" (Daniel Chester French), vases representing "Day" and "Night," and Italianate Canfield Casino (1867-69; massive classical dining room added 1902-03). Park designed by Frederick Law Olmsted (1875), and Charles Leavitt and Henry Bacon (1914). Casino associated with careers of famous gamblers John Morrissey and Richard Canfield. NHL 02.27.1987

Casino–Congress Park–Circular Street Historic District
Bounded by Broadway, and Spring and Circular streets. Includes Canfield Casino and Congress Park (individually listed) and group of 10 large Victorian residences on edge of park. 06.19.1972

The Drinkhall
297 Broadway. Neoclassical/eclectic stuccoed

Canfield Casino, Saratoga Springs.

building designed by Ludlow & Peabody; built 1915 as trolley station on Hudson Valley Railroad. Used after 1941 as public mineral dispensary. Converted for use as offices and headquarters of Saratoga Urban Cultural Park. 11.20.1974

East Side Historic District
Roughly bounded by George, Henry, East, and North streets. Large 19th- and early 20th-century neighborhood with approximately 350 buildings, mostly detached residences in full range of sizes and architectural styles. Architects include Gilbert Cross, Rufus H. Dorn, J. D. Stevens, Frelïn G. Vaughan, S. Gifford Slocum, R. Newton Brezee, Isaac G. Perry, Alfred Hopkins, Ludlow & Peabody, Vaughan & LaFarge, and Warren & Clark. Also includes original 1915 campus of Skidmore College.   10.29.1982

Franklin Square Historic District
Irregular pattern from Beekman Street along Grand Avenue, and Franklin and Clinton streets to Van Dam Street. Residential neighborhood with approximately 50 small- to large-scale 19th-century residences in variety of styles, including notable group of temple-front Greek Revival residences. Includes Hiram Charles Todd House (individually listed) and Queen Anne/Rustic-style former Adirondack Railroad Station (1884).   10.09.1973

Pure Oil Gas Station
65 Spring Street. Modest brick gas station in style of English cottage; built 1933; moved 1978 from nearby to present site.   10.18.1978

Saratoga Spa State Park District
US 9 and NY 50. A 970-acre section of state park established 1909 as state reservation to conserve and develop mineral springs; developed 1909-35 as major spa and recreational park. Georgian Revival spa complex includes Simon Baruch Research Institute (1932-34, Joseph H. Freedlander), Hall of Springs (1934-35, Joseph H. Freedlander), Roosevelt Bathhouse (1934-35, Joseph H. Freedlander), Victoria Pool complex (1934-35, Dwight James Baum), Gideon Putnam Hotel (1935, Marcus T. Reynolds), and State Seal Bottling Plant (1934, Dwight James Baum). Golf course and significant landscape features designed by Arthur F. Brinckerhoff. Other buildings include Arts and Crafts Washington Bathhouse (built c.1903 as carbonic gas plant; converted 1918-20 to bathhouse by architect Lewis W. Pilcher), Neo-

classical Lincoln Bathhouse (1928-30), and Greek Revival Latour House (1835, pre-park). 09.12.1985; NHL 02.27.1987

Hiram Charles Todd House
4 Franklin Square. Massive, rambling Greek Revival frame residence with Doric portico and cupola; built c.1837 for Thomas Marvin, hotel proprietor. Later owned by New York City lawyer Hiram Charles Todd.   05.31.1972

United States Post Office–Saratoga Springs
475 Broadway. Italian Renaissance style. Neoclassical brick post office with limestone and marble trim; designed by James Knox Taylor; built 1909-11. Interior murals (1936-37) by Guy Pène Du Bois. United States Post Offices in New York State, 1858-1943, Thematic Resources.   05.11.1989

Union Avenue Historic District
Large district encompassing 3 distinct property types, including Saratoga Race Track, Yaddo estate, and large residences along Union Avenue. Saratoga Race Track: 350-acre property includes massive Victorian grandstand (1865), 2 racetracks, clubhouse (1920s), and approximately 200 associated structures such as stables, shops, and living quarters. Yaddo: 245-acre estate includes large Queen Anne stone residence, formal gardens, 5 lakes, and 13 dependencies (1892, William Halsey Wood; built for New York financier Spencer Trask and wife Katrina; well-known retreat for artists and writers since 1901). Union Avenue includes approximately 30 large Victorian, Queen Anne, and Colonial Revival residences.   04.04.1978

Schuylerville

Old Champlain Canal (see village of Waterford)

Stillwater   (Town)

Old Champlain Canal (see village of Waterford)

Saratoga National Historical Park
US 4 and NY 32. A 3,000-acre area with archeological site of American victory over British in 1777 which was turning point of American Revolution.   06.01.1938

Stillwater (Village)

Old Champlain Canal (see village of Waterford)

Waterford (Town)

Peebles (Peobles) Island (State Park)
At junction of Mohawk and Hudson rivers. A 132-acre island with archeological sites of Native American habitation, American fortifications during American Revolution made under direction of Thaddeus Kosciuszko, and farm sites. Includes early 20th-century bleachery complex developed by Cluett-Peabody Co. Headquarters of New York State Bureau of Historic Sites and Division for Historic Preservation.   10.02.1973

Waterford (Village)

Northside Historic District
Saratoga Avenue (NY 32) from Maple Avenue to Roosevelt Bridge. A 19th-century residential neighborhood with approximately 120 buildings, ranging from modest Greek Revival cottages built for factory and canal workers to large-scale Victorian residences built for mill owners. Includes Greek Revival Hugh White Mansion (c.1830, museum).   12.04.1975

Old Champlain Canal
Extends north from Waterford to Whitehall (also in towns of Waterford, Halfmoon, Stillwater, Saratoga, and Northumberland; villages of Stillwater and Schuylerville; and Washington County). A 73-mile-long canal completed 1823 between Cohoes, Albany County, and Lake Champlain at Whitehall, Washington County. Major impetus for development of northern New York State. Extant features include large sections of canal bed, Waterford sidecut locks, aqueducts at Stillwater and Schuylerville, and several other stone locks and culverts.   09.01.1976

Ormsby-Laughlin Textile Companies Mill
31 Mohawk Avenue. Large 4 1/2-story Romanesque Revival brick industrial building with 6 1/2-story tower; built 1894 as part of industrial community known as Dial City. 03.20.1986

Waterford Village Historic District
Roughly bounded by Hudson River, Erie Canal, and State Street. Large portion of village at junction of Mohawk and Hudson rivers and junction of Old Champlain and Erie canals, with approximately 200 buildings, mostly residences, including notable examples of Federal brick townhouses, temple-form Greek Revival residences, and large Victorian residences.   07.14.1977

Delanson

Delanson Historic District
Main Street. Residential area of rural hamlet, with 17 Victorian frame residences and out-buildings, 1 church, and 1 former commercial building; built c.1860-90. Duanesburg Multiple Resource Area.   10.11.1984

Jenkins House
57 Main Street. Large Victorian frame residence with 2 1/2-story central tower; built c.1876. Duanesburg Multiple Resource Area. 10.11.1984

Duanesburg

Abrahams Farmhouse
Hardin Road. Greek Revival frame farmhouse built c.1839. Duanesburg Multiple Resource Area.   10.11.1984

Avery Farmhouse
NY 30. A 203-acre farmstead with Greek Revival frame farmhouse with portico supported by square columns; designed and built c.1850 by master carpenter Alexander Delos "Boss" Jones. Property includes large 19th-century barn complex and 5 silos. Duanesburg Multiple Resource Area. 10.11.1984

Becker Farmhouse
Creek Road. A 113-acre farmstead with Greek Revival/Italianate farmhouse with cupola; built c.1850. Property includes six 19th-century outbuildings and farm pond. Duanesburg Multiple Resource Area.   10.11.1984

Joseph Braman House
Braman's Corners. Greek Revival frame residence with flanking wings; built c.1850 for local physician. Includes original carriage house. Duanesburg Multiple Resource Area. 04.24.1987

Chadwick Farmhouse
Schoharie Turnpike. A 10-acre property with large Victorian frame farmhouse built c.1870, dairy building, and springhouse. Duanesburg Multiple Resource Area.   10.11.1984

Chapman Farmhouse
Miller's Corners Road. A 131-acre farmstead with late Federal Greek Revival vernacular frame farmhouse built c.1832 and 19th-century barn. Duanesburg Multiple Resource Area. 10.11.1984

Christ Episcopal Church
US20. A 2-story Federal frame church with meetinghouse plan; built 1793 with funds from James Duane and Trinity Episcopal Church, New York City; tower and belfry added 1811.

Intact interior with Duane family crypt. Adjacent carriage shed and cemetery on 5-acre parcel. Duanesburg Multiple Resource Area. 04.24.1987

Christman Bird and Wildlife Sanctuary
Schoharie Turnpike. A 105-acre rural and largely wooded property including mid-19th-century farmstead and waterfalls of Bosenkill; established 1888 by writer W. W. Christman as bird and wildlife sanctuary.   08.25.1970

Duane Mansion
Off US20. A 30-acre property with large Federal frame residence with 2-story piazza supported by Doric columns; built 1812-16 as country seat of Catherine Livingston Duane, daughter of James Duane, founder of town. Landscape plan designed by Joseph Jaques Ramee. Notable interior. Property includes original barn complex. Duanesburg Multiple Resource Area.   04.24.1987

Duanesburg-Florida Baptist Church
NY 30. Greek Revival frame church built c.1868; Queen Anne main facade and tower designed by A. Wilmot; added 1891. Adjacent church hall/parsonage built 1913. Duanesburg Multiple Resource Area.   10.11.1984

Stockade Historic District, Schenectady (p. 149).

Opposite: Hall of Springs, Saratoga Spa State Park District, Saratoga Springs.

Mabee House, Rotterdam.

Eatons Corners Historic District
Eatons Corners Road. Group of 3 remaining buildings of small rural hamlet, including Federal frame Eaton Homestead (c.1800), Federal frame Barlow Tavern (1820s), and Greek Revival Brumley Homestead (1840s). Duanesburg Multiple Resource Area. 10.11.1984

Ferguson Farm Complex
US20. Farm complex with Greek Revival frame farmhouse built c.1848, large c.1800 hay/dairy barn, and 2 mid-19th-century outbuildings. Duanesburg Multiple Resource Area. 04.24.1987

Gaige Homestead
Weaver Road. A 71-acre farmstead with large Federal vernacular frame farmhouse built c.1830 and four 19th-century frame outbuildings. Duanesburg Multiple Resource Area. 10.11.1984

Gilbert Farmhouse
Thousand Acre Road. A 6-acre property with Victorian frame farmhouse built c.1860 and four 19th-century outbuildings. Duanesburg Multiple Resource Area. 10.11.1984

Joseph Green Farmhouse
NY159. A 30-acre farmstead with Greek Revival frame farmhouse built c.1857 and four 19th-century frame outbuildings. Duanesburg Multiple Resource Area. 10.11.1984

Halladay Farmhouse
US20. A 92-acre farmstead with late 18th-century frame farmhouse remodeled and expanded 1830s in Greek Revival style, and six 19th-century frame outbuildings. Duanesburg Multiple Resource Area. 10.11.1984

Hawes Homestead
Herrick Road. An 88-acre farmstead with Greek Revival frame farmhouse built 1830s and five 19th-century outbuildings, including stone smokehouse. Duanesburg Multiple Resource Area. 10.11.1984

Howard Homestead
McGuire School Road. A 114-acre farmstead with late Federal/Greek Revival frame farmhouse built c.1830. Duanesburg Multiple Resource Area. 10.11.1984

Jenkins Octagon House
NY395. A 151-acre farmstead with Greek Revival frame octagonal farmhouse designed and built c.1850 by master carpenter Alexander Delos "Boss" Jones. Property includes four 19th-century outbuildings. Duanesburg Multiple Resource Area. 10.11.1984

A. D. "Boss" Jones House
McGuire School Road. A 104-acre farmstead with large Greek Revival frame farmhouse designed and built c.1860 by and for master carpenter Alexander Delos "Boss" Jones. Property includes 2 large 19th-century barns and shed. Duanesburg Multiple Resource Area. 10.11.1984

Ladd Farmhouse
Dare Road. A 137-acre farmstead with Greek Revival frame farmhouse designed and built c.1850 by master carpenter Alexander Delos "Boss" Jones. Property includes three 19th-century and one 20th-century outbuildings. Duanesburg Multiple Resource Area. 10.11.1984

George Lasher House (Rainbow Hill)
Levey Road. A 183-acre farmstead with large Federal frame farmhouse built c.1800 and ten 19th-century frame outbuildings. Duanesburg Multiple Resource Area. 10.11.1984

Alexander Liddle Farmhouse
Gamsey Road. A 122-acre farmstead with Greek Revival frame farmhouse designed and built c.1850 by master carpenter Alexander Delos "Boss" Jones. Property includes 19th-century barn, early 20th-century garage, and 4 other outbuildings. Duanesburg Multiple Resource Area. 10.11.1984

Robert Liddle Farmhouse
Little Dale Farm Road. A 111-acre farmstead with Greek Revival frame farmhouse designed and built c.1850 by master carpenter Alexander Delos "Boss" Jones. Duanesburg Multiple Resource Area. 10.11.1984

Thomas Liddle Farm Complex
Eatons Corners Road. A 177-acre farmstead with Greek Revival frame farmhouse built c.1850, incorporating small late 18th-century farmhouse as rear wing. Property includes barn complex and tenant house. Duanesburg Multiple Resource Area. 10.11.1984

Macomber Stone House
Barton Hill Road. A 99-acre farmstead with large Federal limestone farmhouse built c.1836 and three 19th-century frame barns. Duanesburg Multiple Resource Area. 10.11.1984

Mariaville Historic District
NY159. Core of early 19th-century commercial and industrial hamlet, with 7 frame buildings built c.1830-50, including 5 Greek Revival frame residences, Greek Revival Silas Marsh General Store, and Greek Revival First Presbyterian Church of Duanesburg. Duanesburg Multiple Resource Area. 10.11.1984

North Mansion and Tenant House
North Mansion Road. A 6-acre property with large Georgian frame residence built c.1795 for General William North, politician, entrepreneur, and estate manager and son-in-law of James Duane. Vernacular frame tenant house built 1780s. Once part of 1,000-acre estate. Duanesburg Multiple Resource Area. 04.24.1987

Quaker Street Historic District
Schoharie Turnpike, and Gallupville and Darby Hill roads. Rural hamlet with 43 properties, mostly Federal, Greek Revival, and Victorian frame residences and outbuildings. Also includes Quaker Meetinghouse and cemetery (c.1807), McDonald Shoe Factory (c.1850), and Darius Gorge Store (1830s). Duanesburg Multiple Resource Area. 10.11.1984

Reformed Presbyterian Church Parsonage
Duanesburg Churches Road. A six-acre property with large Federal vernacular frame residence built c.1829 and large barn. Duanesburg Multiple Resource Area. 10.11.1984

Sheldon Farmhouse
NY7. A 41-acre farmstead with large Federal vernacular frame farmhouse built c.1795 and 19th-century barn complex. Duanesburg Multiple Resource Area. 10.11.1984

Shute Octagon House
McGuire School Road. A 41-acre farmstead with Greek Revival frame octagonal farmhouse designed and built c.1850 by master carpenter Alexander Delos "Boss" Jones, and seven 19th-century outbuildings, including large barns and brick smokehouse. Duanesburg Multiple Resource Area. 10.11.1984

Joseph Wing Farm Complex
NY30. A 106-acre farmstead with Federal frame farmhouse and seven 19th-century outbuildings, including 4 large barns. Duanesburg Multiple Resource Area. 10.11.1984

William R. Wing Farm Complex
US20. A 96-acre farm complex with large late Federal/Greek Revival frame farmhouse and 2 barns. Duanesburg Multiple Resource Area. 10.11.1984

Glenville

Seeley Farmhouse
2 Freemans Bridge Road. Greek Revival frame former farmhouse with narrow pedimented central pavilion; built c.1850; large rear addition. 05.23.1978

Niskayuna

General Electric Research Laboratory
(see Schenectady)

Niskayuna Reformed Church
3041 Troy Road. Greek Revival brick church with octagonal belfry; built 1852. Adjacent 18th- to 19th-century cemetery. 04.18.1979

Rotterdam

Dellemont-Wemple Farm
Wemple Road, west of Schenectady. A 90-acre farmstead with large Dutch Colonial vernacular brick residence built c.1790 and Dutch barn built c.1770. 10.25.1973

Mabee House
NY5S, south of Rotterdam Junction. A 10-acre property on Mohawk River with modest Dutch Colonial stone residence distinguished by steeply pitched gable roof; built c.1700; 18th-century frame addition. Adjacent modest 18th-century vernacular brick residence and family cemetery. 05.22.1978

Schenectady

H. S. Barney Building
217-229 State Street. Large 2- to 5-story masonry commercial building composed of 6 connected sections built or acquired, and altered for large department store 1873-1923; Neoclassical principal facade completed 1923. 07.19.1984

Central Fire Station
Erie Boulevard. Large 3-story Georgian Revival brick firehouse built 1924-29. 04.11.1985

Foster Building (Foster Hotel)
508 State Street. A 6-story Beaux-Arts terra-cotta-clad building designed by Penn Varney; built 1907 as commercial building and hotel. 06.03.1991

Franklin School
Avenue B and Mason Street. Large 2-story Georgian Revival brick school built 1907. 06.30.1983

General Electric Research Laboratory
General Electric main plant and in town of Niskayuna. World-renowned industrial research laboratory established 1900 by Willis R. Whitney for General Electric Co. Located in 2 buildings at main plant and 1 in Niskayuna. NHL 05.15.1975

General Electric Realty Plot
Roughly bounded by Oxford Place, Union Avenue, Nott Street, and Lenox and Lowell roads. A 9-block planned suburban residential neighborhood with approximately 100 large early 20th-century Queen Anne, Shingle Style, Arts and Crafts, and Georgian and Colonial Revival residences on landscaped lots; begun 1899 to house top scientists and engineers working at nearby General Electric Co. Includes Irving Langmuir House (individually listed). Architects include Russell & Rice, Oren Finch, W. T. B. Mynderse, C. G. Van Rensselaer, Walter P. Crabtree, A.G. Lindley Co., E. Atkinson, and Thomas Harlan Ellett. 11.18.1980

Hotel Van Curler
78 Washington Avenue. Massive 6-story rambling Georgian Revival brick former hotel designed by H. L. Stevens & Co.; built 1925. Converted for use as Schenectady County Community College. 09.12.1985

Irving Langmuir House
1176 Stratford Road. Colonial Revival brick residence built 1906. Home of Irving Langmuir, distinguished chemist, inventor, and winner of 1934 Nobel Prize in chemistry, 1919-57. NHL 01.07.1976

Nott Memorial Hall
Union College. Monumental Victorian Gothic 16-sided stone building with polychromatic walls and decorative slate dome with inset colored-glass "illuminators"; originally conceived by Joseph Jacques Ramee as centerpiece of 1813 plan for campus; designed by Edward Tuckerman Potter; begun 1858 and completed 1872-76. Interior cast-iron structural system. 05.05.1972; NHL 06.24.1986

F. F. Proctor Theatre and Arcade
432 State Street. A 2-story through-block shopping and office arcade with massive attached auditorium in Adamesque style; designed by Thomas W. Lamb; built 1926. Movie Palaces of the Tri-Cities Thematic Resources. 10.04.1979

Schenectady City Hall and Post Office
Jay Street. Monumental Georgian Revival brick city hall with elaborate marble trim, tall cupola, and interior rotunda; designed by McKim, Mead & White; built 1930-31. Adjacent United States Post Office (individually listed). 10.11.1978

Stockade Historic District
Roughly bounded by Mohawk River, railroad tracks, and Union Street. A 15-block residential neighborhood with approximately 380 buildings. Site of stockaded village established 1664 and burned by French in 1690. Includes several 18th-century Dutch Colonial frame and brick residences and numerous Federal, Greek Revival, Gothic Revival, and Italianate brick and frame rowhouses and townhouses. Also includes small-scale commercial buildings, several churches, and several public buildings. 04.03.1973; BOUNDARY INCREASE 09.07.1984 ILLUS. P. 147

Union Street Historic District
Union Street from Hudson River to Phoenix Avenue. An 18-block-long district with 190 buildings, mostly detached 19th- and early 20th-century residences in wide range of styles. Notable buildings include Second Empire John C. Ellis Mansion (1878), Queen Anne Willis T. Hanson Estate (1888), massive St. John the Evangelist Church (1898-99, John L. Reilly and Edward P. Loth), and numerous large Queen Anne and Colonial Revival residences. 11.17.1982

United States Post Office–Schenectady
Jay and Liberty streets. Monumental Neoclassical stone post office with Corinthian and Ionic colonnades; designed by James Knox Taylor; built 1911-13; substantially enlarged 1934-35. United States Post Offices in New York State, 1858-1943, Thematic Resources. 05.11.1989

Scotia

United States Post Office–Scotia Station
224 Mohawk Avenue. Colonial Revival brick post office built 1939-40. Interior mural (1941) by Amy Jones. United States Post Offices in New York State, 1858-1943, Thematic Resources. 05.11.1989

Blenheim

Lansing Manor House

NY 30, two miles south of North Blenheim. Farmstead with large Federal frame residence built c.1818 for Jacob Sutherland, son-in-law of owner, John Lansing, to manage Lansing landholdings. Includes numerous 19th-century outbuildings. Operated as museum by New York Power Authority.   05.25.1973

Lansing Manor House, Blenheim.

Opposite: Schuyler County Courthouse, Watkins Glen.

North Blenheim Historic District

NY 30. Small rural hamlet on Schoharie Creek with approximately 20 buildings, mostly Greek Revival frame residences built 1830-60.   12.31.1974

Old Blenheim Bridge

NY 30 over Schoharie Creek, North Blenheim. A 210-foot-long single-span covered wooden bridge with single center arch; built 1855 by entrepreneur Nicholas M. Powers; used until 1932. One of the world's longest single-span wooden covered bridges.   NHL 01.29.1964

Cobleskill (Town)

Bramanville Mill (Chickering Gristmill)

East of Cobleskill on Caverns Road. A 2 1/2-story frame gristmill with intact machinery; built 1816 by Nelson Eckerson. Property

includes millrace, dam and pond, tailrace, and barn.   08.27.1976

Cobleskill (Village)

Cobleskill Historic District

Irregular pattern along Washington Avenue, and Main, Grand, and Elm streets. A 10-block core of village, with approximately 180 buildings, mostly late 19th-century residences and commercial buildings in variety of Victorian styles. Also includes churches, school, railroad depot, and fairgrounds. Notable buildings include Italianate brick former Hotel Augustan (1874) and Federal Bull's Head Inn (1802).   09.18.1978

Fulton

Breakabeen Historic District

Roughly bounded by River Street, NY 30, and Main Street to Bush Road. Small hamlet on Schoharie Creek with approximately 30 buildings, mostly Greek Revival frame residences built 1830-60. Also includes church, store, and Victorian hotel.   12.31.1974

Shafer Site

Address restricted. Multicomponent prehistoric archeological site with features spanning Middle Archaic (c.4000 B.C.) to Late Woodland (c.1000 A.D.) stages.   11.28.1980

Jefferson

Parker 13-Sided Barn

NY 10. A 60-foot-diameter 13-sided frame barn with double-hipped roof and 13-sided cupola; built 1896. Central Plan Dairy Barns of New York State Thematic Resources.   09.29.1984

Middleburgh

United States Post Office–Middleburgh

162 Main Street. Colonial Revival brick post office built 1939-40. United States Post Offices in New York State, 1858-1943, Thematic Resources.   05.11.1989

Schoharie (Town)

Sternbergh House

Oak Hill Road. A 14-acre rural property with large Federal frame vernacular farmhouse built c.1825. Property includes 1813 grave of Abraham Sternbergh.   03.21.1985

Westheimer Site

Address restricted. A 13-acre parcel encompassing multicomponent prehistoric archeological site with features ranging from 570 B.C. to Late Woodland Owasco occupation, 1300 A.D.   07.22.1980

George Westinghouse, Jr., Birthplace and Boyhood Home

Westinghouse Road, Central Bridge. A 3-acre

property with two 19th-century vernacular frame residences, 2 small barns, and privy. Birthplace (1846) and boyhood home of inventor and industrialist George Westinghouse, Jr. 03.20.1986

Schoharie (Village)

Old Lutheran Parsonage
Adjacent to Spring Street in Lutheran Cemetery. Modest Colonial frame residence built 1743 for minister of German Lutheran Church; used as meetinghouse until construction of main church in 1750. 06.19.1972

Schoharie Valley Railroad Complex
Depot Lane. Railroad depot complex with 2-story brick passenger station, freight and locomotive house, office with weighing scales, coal silos, and outbuildings, all built c.1875. 04.26.1972

Sharon Springs

American Hotel
Main Street. Large 3 1/2-story Greek Revival frame hotel with 2-story colonnade; built 1847-51 as resort hotel near mineral springs. 09.09.1975

Summit

Bute-Warner-Truax Farm
Truax Road. A 103-acre farmstead established c.1853 by Jedediah Bute. Includes Greek Revival frame farmhouse, outbuildings, and family cemetery. 07.25.1985

Wright

Becker Stone House
Murphy Road, east of Schoharie. A 4-acre property along Fox Creek with Colonial stone residence built c.1772-75 by Joseph Becker, son of Palatine German immigrant Johannes Becker. Site of raid by British and Mohawk Indians in 1782. Also includes site of 18th-century mill. 11.20.1979

Becker-Westfall House
NY443, east of Schoharie. A 4-acre property with Georgian/Federal brick residence built c.1784; mid-19th-century addition and conversion for use as tavern and post office. Includes brick smokehouse and frame outbuildings. 11.20.1979

Gallupville House
Main Street, Gallupville. Large 2 1/2-story Victorian frame commercial building built 1872 as hotel in small hamlet. 09.07.1979

Catharine

Lattin-Crandall Octagon Barn
County 14, east of Catharine. A 55-foot-diameter octagonal frame barn built 1893 by George Stewart; large 2-story rectangular addition. Central Plan Dairy Barns of New York State Thematic Resources. 09.29.1984

Montour Falls

Montour Falls Historic District
Main and Genesee streets. Historic core of village, with twenty-four 19th-century residential and civic buildings dramatically sited at base of waterfalls. Greek Revival civic group includes Sheriff's and County Clerk's offices, Village Hall (all 1854), and Library (1864). Notable residences include Greek Revival Ashton House and Italianate villa at 203 South Genesee Street. 08.31.1978

Tyrone

Lamoka
Address restricted. Large prehistoric archeological site associated with Lamoka phase of Archaic stage (c.3000 B.C.). NHL 01.20.1961

Watkins Glen

Schuyler County Courthouse Complex
Franklin Street. Group of 3 Italianate brick buildings: County Courthouse (1855), County Clerk's Office, and Sheriff's Office and jail; 1953 addition connects courthouse and clerk's office. 06.05.1974

United States Post Office–Watkins Glen
600 North Franklin Street. Colonial Revival brick post office built 1934-35. United States Post Offices in New York State, 1858-1943, Thematic Resources. 05.11.1989

Covert

Covert Historic District
NY96. Small hamlet with 20 buildings and 1 cemetery developed early 19th to early 20th century. Includes primarily Greek Revival residences, also Gothic Revival Fenn House (c.1860) and Greek Revival Covert Baptist Church (1850). 11.21.1980

Fayette

Christ Evangelical and Reformed Church
Main Street. Small Federal stone church built 1823; Romanesque Revival remodeling and bell tower addition in 1882. 12.08.1989

Rose Hill
NY96A, west of Fayette, near Geneva. Monumental Greek Revival frame residence with imposing Ionic portico, cupola, and flanking wings; built 1837-39 overlooking Seneca Lake for merchant and broker William K. Strong. Later owned by agriculturist Robert J. Swan. Notable interior. Operated as house museum by Geneva Historical Society. 02.06.1973; NHL 06.24.1986 ILLUS. P. 152

Lodi

Lodi Methodist Church
South Main and Grove streets. Victorian Gothic brick church designed by Warren H. Hayes; built 1880-81. 05.06.1982

Ovid (Town)

Willard Asylum for the Chronic Insane
Willard State Psychiatric Center, Willard (also in town of Romulus). Massive Second Empire brick asylum; built 1869 and enlarged in 1870s. Significant in the history of Victorian-era mental health care. 03.07.1975; DEMOLISHED

Ovid (Village)

Seneca County Courthouse Complex at Ovid (The Three Bears)
NY414. Group of 3 adjacent Greek Revival brick buildings: 2-story Courthouse and 1 1/2-story Clerk's Office built 1845 by O. B. and O. S. Latham; 1-story New Clerk's Office built 1860 by Horace H. Bennett. 12.12.1976

Romulus

Willard Asylum for the Chronic Insane (see town of Ovid)

Seneca Falls

Fall Street–Trinity Lane Historic District
Off NY414 at Van Cleef Lake. Archeological site and ruins of 19th-century industrial complex flooded c.1914. Also includes Gothic Revival stone Trinity Church (1886, Brown & Dawson), Mission-style Mynderse Library (1916), locks of Cayuga & Seneca Canal, and several other buildings and structures. 02.25.1974

Fourth Ward School
8 Washington Street. A 2-story Italianate brick school built c.1869; 1-story wings added 1896-1904. 03.19.1986

Mumford House (Amelia Bloomer House)
53 East Bayard Street. A 2-story Italianate frame residence built c.1850. Reputed home of prominent women's rights activist Amelia Bloomer. Women's Rights Historic Sites Thematic Resources. 08.29.1980

Seneca Falls Village Historic District
North and South Park streets, Trinity Lane, Beryl Avenue, and parts of Fall, State, Cayuga Johnston, and Water steets. Commercial core and adjoining residential areas of village, with approximately 175 mid-19th- to early 20th-century buildings. Includes Italianate brick commercial blocks, 4 churches, 2 railroad stations, 2 schools, 2 bridges, and residences in variety of styles. Notable buildings include Seneca Falls Knitting Mills Complex (1844), Victorian Gothic Presbyterian Church (1873, Archimedes Russell), New York State Electric & Gas hydroelectric complex and Barge Canal locks, and outstanding Gothic Revival and Second Empire residences. Also includes individually listed Fall Street–Trinity Lane Historic District, United States Post Office, and Wesleyan Methodist Church. 04.05.1991

Elizabeth Cady Stanton House
32 Washington Street. A 2-story vernacular frame residence built c.1835. Home of prominent women's rights activist. Women's Rights Historic Sites Thematic Resources. NHL 06.23.1965

United States Post Office–Seneca Falls
34-42 State Street. Large Classical Revival/Art Deco brick and limestone post office built 1932-34. United States Post Offices in New York State, 1858-1943, Thematic Resources. 05.11.1989

Wesleyan Methodist Church
(Wesleyan Chapel)
126 Fall Street. A 2-story brick church built 1843; extensively altered in 20th century. Site of 1848 Women's Rights Convention. Women's Rights Historic Sites Thematic Resources. 08.29.1980

Front Porch, Rose Hill, Fayette (p. 151).

Women's Rights National Historical Park
Commemorative park encompassing sites related to early women's rights activist, including individually listed Wesleyan Methodist Church and Elizabeth Cady Stanton House. 12.08.1980

Waterloo

Hunt House
401 East Main Street. A 2 1/2-story Greek Revival brick residence built c.1830 with front portico added 1920. Home of prominent women's rights activist Jane Hunt. Women's Rights Historic Sites Thematic Resources. 08.29.1980

McClintock House
14 East Williams Street. A 2-story Federal brick residence built 1833-36. Home of prominent women's rights activist Mary Ann McClintock. Women's Rights Historic Sites Thematic Resources. 08.29.1980

United States Post Office–Waterloo
2 East Main Street. Georgian Revival brick post office built 1924-25. United States Post Offices in New York State, 1858-1943, Thematic Resources. 05.11.1989

STEUBEN COUNTY

Addison

Addison Village Hall
Tuscarora and South streets. A 4-story Italian Renaissance-style/eclectic brick building containing village offices, opera house, and Odd Fellows hall, built 1906-07. 04.23.1980

Bath

Campbell-Rumsey House
225 East Steuben Street. A 2-story Italianate brick residence built c.1855. Home of prominent politician Robert Campbell, Jr. and Judge David Rumsey. Bath Village Multiple Resource Area. 09.30.1983

Cobblestone House
120 West Washington Street. A 2-story Greek Revival cobblestone residence built c.1851; Colonial Revival porch added c.1920. Bath Village Multiple Resource Area. 09.30.1983

Davenport Library
West Morris Street. A 2-story Greek Revival brick residence built 1830; remodeled 1850s in Italianate style; converted to library between 1893 and 1915. Bath Village Multiple Resource Area. 09.30.1983

Erie Freight House Historic District
Cohocton Street and Railroad Avenue. Group of 6 commercial buildings built for storage, transfer, and manufacture of goods for distribution on Erie Railroad. Includes Erie Freight House (c.1852), G. L. F. Service Building (c.1920), G. L. F. Farm Machinery Storage Building, E. H. Dudley Warehouse (c.1905), Bath Harness Company (1906), and produce warehouse. 03.18.1991

Gansevoort-East Steuben Streets Historic District
Group of 22 residences, including examples of Greek Revival, Italianate, Queen Anne, and Colonial Revival styles; built c.1830-1908. Bath Village Multiple Resource Area. 09.30.1983

Haverling Farm House
313 Haverling Street. A 1 1/2-story Greek Revival frame residence built c.1838. Bath Village Multiple Resource Area. 09.30.1983

Liberty Street Historic District
Roughly Liberty Street from East Morris Street to Haverling Street. Historic core of village, with 76 buildings centered on 3-acre village green (Pultney Square, 1793) and built c.1819-c.1930. Notable buildings include Greek Revival County Courthouse (c.1860), Italianate Howell Building with cast-iron facade (c.1862), Second Empire Opera House (c.1872), High Victorian Gothic First Presbyterian Church (c.1876, Jacob Wrey Mould), and Gothic Revival St. Thomas Episcopal Church (c.1870, Henry Dudley). Bath Village Multiple Resource Area. 09.30.1983

McMaster House
207 East Washington Street. A 1 1/2-story vernacular Greek Revival frame residence built c.1830. Bath Village Multiple Resource Area. 09.30.1983

Potter-Van Camp House
4 West Washington Street. A 1 1/2-story Gothic Revival frame residence built c.1845; porch and dormers added early 20th century. Bath Village Multiple Resource Area. 09.30.1983

Reuben Robie House
16 West Washington Street. A 2-story Greek Revival brick residence built 1847; entry portico added c.1900. Bath Village Multiple Resource Area. 09.30.1983

Sedgwick House
101 Haverling Street. A 2 1/2-story Italianate stuccoed brick residence built c.1850. Bath Village Multiple Resource Area. 09.30.1983

William Shepherd House
110 West Washington Street. A 2-story Italianate brick villa built 1873. Bath Village Multiple Resource Area. 09.30.1983

United States Post Office–Bath
101 Liberty Street. Colonial Revival brick post office built 1931-32. United States Post Offices in New York State, 1858-1943, Thematic Resources. 11.17.1988

M. J. Ward Feed Mill Complex
1-9 Cameron Street. A 3-story frame and brick feed mill (1909) and associated barn and residence; built for transfer of agricultural goods to Erie Railroad. 03.18.1991

Cohocton

The Larrowe House
(Cohocton Town and Village Hall)
South Main Street. A 2-story Italianate frame residence built 1856 with stuccoed exterior scored to imitate stone. 12.07.1989

Corning

Jenning's Tavern (Patterson Inn)
59 West Pulteney Street. A 2-story Federal frame inn built 1796. 09.20.1973

Market Street Historic District
Market Street from Chestnut Street to Wall Street. Historic commercial center of city, with approximately 130 mostly 2- and 3-story brick buildings built 1830-1900, many with brick and terra-cotta trim made by Corning Brick & Terra Cotta Works. Notable buildings include Cain's-Brown's Store with cast-iron storefront (1859), Romanesque Revival City Hall (1892, Andrew J. Warner), Hyat's Mill (1879), Bain's Furniture Store (1887), Classical Revival Baron Steuben Place (built 1929 as hotel, now offices and Rockwell Museum), and clock tower in Centerway Square (1883). Numerous restored facades. 03.01.1974

United States Post Office–Corning
129 Walnut Street. Large Neoclassical brick post office with elaborate terra-cotta trim; designed by James Knox Taylor; built 1908-09. United States Post Offices in New York State, 1858-1943, Thematic Resources. 11.17.1988

Hornell

Hornell Armory
100 Seneca Street. A 3-story Romanesque Revival castellated brick and stone armory designed by Isaac G. Perry; built 1894-96. 05.06.1980

Hornell Public Library
64 Genesee Street. Beaux-Arts brick library with stone trim; designed by Edward L. Tilton; built 1911. 02.24.1975

Painted Post

Delaware, Lackawanna & Western Railroad Station
Steuben Street. Small Gothic Revival frame passenger depot built c.1881. 11.21.1991

United States Post Office–Painted Post
135 North Hamilton Street. Colonial Revival brick post office built 1937-38. Interior mural

(1939) by Amy Jones. United States Post Offices in New York State, 1858-1943, Thematic Resources. 05.11.1989

Riverside

William Erwin House
508 Water Street. Large Greek Revival brick residence with porticoes on 3 sides; built 1850-52. Ornamental features based on published drawings of Minard Lafever. 04.11.1980; DEMOLISHED

Urbana

Pleasant Valley Wine Company
NY88. Historic portion of winery comprising 9 Italianate and later vernacular stone buildings; built 1860-1911. 11.18.1980

SUFFOLK COUNTY

Asharoken

Delamater-Bevin Mansion
Bevin Lane. Large Second Empire frame residence built 1867 for Cornelius Delamater, owner of Brooklyn iron foundry. Huntington Town Multiple Resource Area. 09.26.1985

N. J. Felix House
235 Asharoken Avenue. Queen Anne/Colonial Revival shingled and clapboarded residence built 1900 for watch inventor. Located on large landscaped lot overlooking Northport Harbor. Huntington Town Multiple Resource Area. 09.26.1985

Babylon

Nathaniel Conklin House
280 Deer Park Avenue. Federal shingled residence built c.1803 for local tanner; moved and remodeled c.1871. 12.08.1988

Brookhaven

Bald Hill Schoolhouse
Horseblock Road (Route 16), Farmingville. Greek Revival shingled 1-room schoolhouse built 1850 and 2 privies. 07.21.1988

Caroline Church and Cemetery
Dyke Road, Setauket. Colonial shingled church built 1729 by John Sears; 1905 parish hall addition; restored 1937. Adjacent cemetery established 1734. 09.09.1991

William Floyd Estate (Old Mastic House)
20 Washington Avenue, Mastic. A 611-acre property on Moriches Bay, with large 2 1/2-story 7-bay Georgian residence; original section built c.1729. Associated with prominent Floyd family and William Floyd, signer of the Declaration of Independence. Museum. 04.21.1971

Hawkins Homestead
165 Christian Avenue, near Stony Brook. Small Colonial shingled farmhouse built c.1660 by Zachariah Hawkins; enlarged c.1720, c.1750, and c.1812. 06.09.1988

Robert Hawkins Homestead
Yaphank Avenue, Yaphank. Large Italianate frame residence with cupola; built c.1855 for locally prominent Hawkins family. Headquarters of Yaphank Historical Society. 04.10.1986

Homan-Gerard House and Mills
Yaphank Road, Yaphank. A 6-acre property with large Federal shingled, gambrel-roofed residence built c.1790, late 19th-century barn and sheds, family cemetery, and archeological remains of two 18th-century mills and 19th-century store. 12.16.1988

Nathaniel Longbotham House
1541 Stony Brook Road, Stony Brook. A 1 1/2-story vernacular frame residence in half-house plan; built c.1740; attached 1-story wing built as residence late 17th or early 18th century. 11.16.1989

Masury Estate Ballroom
Old Neck Road, Center Moriches. Long, rambling Colonial Revival/Shingle Style frame building with elaborately decorated domed ballroom; designed by William Lambert; built 1898 as adjunct to waterfront mansion of Grace Harkins Masury. 09.11.1986

Miller Place Historic District
North Country Road, Miller Place. Central core of hamlet, with 27 buildings, mostly vernacular frame residences and outbuildings built mid-18th to mid-19th centuries. Notable buildings include Greek Revival Reverend Ezra King House (c.1840), Federal Miller Place

Academy (1834), and Georgian William Miller House (c.1720, with later additions). 06.17.1976

William Sidney Mount House
Stony Brook Road and NY25A, Stony Brook. A vernacular shingled early 18th-century residence enlarged in 19th century. Longtime residence of genre painter William Sidney Mount. NHL 12.21.1965

Radio Central Complex
South of Rocky Point on Rocky Point-Yaphank Road. Remaining structures and features of world's first commercial overseas radio-transmitting station established 1921 by Radio Corporation of America and once a vast 5,000-acre complex. Includes Building 1 (1921; later additions), principal access road, and Building 9 (1931). 06.27.1980

St. Andrew's Episcopal Church
East Main Street, Yaphank. Greek Revival/ Gothic Revival frame church built c.1853 for James H. Weeks family by builder Edmund Petty. Adjacent cemetery. 09.15.1988

Smith Estate
Longwood and Smith roads, north of Brookhaven. A 35-acre former farm complex and estate with vernacular frame main residence built c.1790; enlarged and altered several times with Federal, Greek Revival, Gothic Revival, and Colonial Revival features. Also includes late 18th- to early 20th-century complex of farm outbuildings, Smith family cemetery, and 1-room schoolhouse moved to site in 1977. Property is part of original Manor of St. George purchased 1693 by William Smith; occupied by family until 1967. 12.10.1981

Smith-Rourke House
350 South Country Road, East Patchogue. Large 2-story Greek Revival frame residence with elaborate exterior ornamentation including cupola and porch with Corinthian columns; built 1837 for sea captain William Smith, Jr. Adjacent mid-19th-century carriage house. 11.28.1989

Stony Brook Gristmill (see Head of the Harbor)

Suffolk County Almshouse Barn
Yaphank Avenue, Yaphank. Large shingled frame barn with decorative cupolas; built 1871 as hay and livestock barn for no longer extant almshouse. 09.11.1986

Thompson House
North Country Road, Setauket. A 2-story Colonial vernacular frame farmhouse in salt-box form sheathed with shingles and clap-boards; built c.1709; restored c.1950. Includes small family cemetery. Operated as museum by Society for the Preservation of Long Island Antiquities. 01.07.1988

East Hampton (Town)

Caleb Bragg Estate
Star Island Road, Montauk. A 4-acre estate on Star Island in Lake Montauk, with group of 7 Picturesque stuccoed cottages grouped around circular drive; designed by Walker & Gillette; built 1929 for resort developer. 11.02.1987

HMS *Culloden* Shipwreck Site
Off Culloden Point. Archeological site of wreck of 74-gun British frigate; launched 1776; sunk 1783 while in service during American Revolution. 03.05.1979

Gardiners Island Windmill
Octagonal shingled smock mill built 1795 by Nathaniel Dominy V; rebuilt 1815. Long Island Wind and Tide Mills Thematic Resources. 12.27.1978

Montauk Association Historic District
DeForest Road, off NY27. A 100-acre summer colony on Atlantic Ocean with 7 rambling Shingle Style frame residences. Site plan designed 1881 by Frederick Law Olmsted. Houses designed by McKim, Mead & White; built 1881-84 for wealthy New Yorkers. 10.22.1976

Opposite: Cain's-Brown's Store, Market Street Historic District, Corning.

Thompson House, Brookhaven.

Montauk Manor
Fairmont Avenue, Montauk. A 12-acre property with monumental 3 1/2-story Tudor Revival brick and stuccoed former resort hotel designed by Schultze & Weaver; built 1926 as part of extensive development scheme of Carl G. Fisher (see also Montauk Tennis Auditorium). 08.23.1984

Montauk Point Lighthouse
Montauk Point State Boulevard. A 108-foot-tall octagonal stone lighthouse designed by John McComb, Jr.; built 1796-97; rebuilt and enlarged 1860. 07.07.1969

Montauk Tennis Auditorium
(Montauk Playhouse)
Flamingo Avenue and Edgemere Street, Montauk. Large-scale Tudor Revival stuccoed indoor tennis auditorium built 1928-29 as part of Montauk Manor resort complex (individually listed). 02.08.1988

Pleasants House
NY27, Amagansett. Italianate frame residence built c.1860 for stagecoach operator Jeremiah Baker; design attributed to local builder George Eldridge. 02.02.1984

Wainscott Windmill
Georgica Association grounds, Wainscott.
Octagonal shingled smock mill built 1813;
attributed to Samuel Schellinger; moved 1922
to present site. Long Island Wind and Tide Mills
Thematic Resources.   12.27.1978

East Hampton (Village)

Briar Patch Road Historic District
End of Briar Patch Road along Georgica Pond.
Group of 6 Shingle Style and Colonial Revival
shingled residences built 1897-1932 as summer
houses and studios for members of East
Hampton's art community, including Augustus
Thomas, Lawrence Aspinwall, and John
Heywood Roudebush. East Hampton Village
Multiple Resource Area.   07.21.1988

Buell's Lane Historic District
47-114 Buell's Lane. Small residential area with
group of 18 mostly late 19th- to early 20th-
century Victorian shingled residences, 1 church,
and 1 wagon shop. East Hampton Village
Multiple Resource Area.   07.21.1988

East Hampton Village Historic District
Main Street to Newton Lane, Ocean and Lee
avenues, and Pond Lane to Hedges Lane. Large
residential and commercial central core of
village, with approximately 230 buildings
ranging from small late 17th and 18th-century
vernacular shingled residences built during
settlement as agricultural community to
numerous large Shingle Style and Colonial
Revival summer houses built at height of
village's development as summer resort.
Notable properties include mid-17th-century
Village Green and South End Burial Ground,
Mulford House (c. 1680), Thomas Moran
House (individually listed), Panitgo Windmill
(1804), Gardiner Windmill (1804), row of early
20th-century commercial buildings, English
Gothic style St. Luke's Episcopal Church (1909-
10, Thomas Nash), Elizabethan Revival East
Hampton Free Library (1911, Aymar Embury
II), and Maidstone Arms Hotel (19th century).
Architects of late 19th- and early 20th-century
summer residences include Isaac H. Green, Jr.,
J. C. Lawrence, J. G. Thorp, George A.
Eldredge, Albro & Lindeberg, Sport Ward, and
Grosvenor Atterbury. East Hampton Village
Multiple Resource Area.   05.02.1974;
BOUNDARY INCREASE 05.09.1988

Egypt Lane Historic District
111, 117, and 129 Egypt Lane. Group of 3
18th- and early 19th-century vernacular
shingled residences moved to present site and
renovated in early 20th century as summer
residences. East Hampton Village Multiple
Resource Area.   07.21.1988

Hayground Windmill
Windmill Lane. Octagonal shingled smock mill
built 1801; moved 1950 to present site. Long
Island Wind and Tide Mills Thematic
Resources.   12.27.1978

Hook Windmill
North Main Street. Octagonal shingled smock
mill built 1806 by Nathaniel Dominy V. Long
Island Wind and Tide Mills Thematic
Resources.   12.27.1978

Jericho Historic District
Montauk Highway. Group of 3 modest early
19th-century Federal shingled residences built
by and for Jones family, local builders. East
Hampton Village Multiple Resource Area.
07.21.1988

Jones Road Historic District
Jones Road from Apaquogue Road to Lily
Pond Lane. Group of 10 residential properties
with 18th- and 19th-century vernacular frame
former farmhouses converted to summer
houses, and Shingle Style and Colonial Revival
residences. Notable buildings include 4
Colonial Revival residences designed by and
for Mary Talmage, Miller House (c.1750),
and Spendthrift (1921, Lewis Colt Albro).
East Hampton Village Multiple Resource Area.
07.21.1988

Thomas Moran House
229 Main Street. A 2-story Victorian shingled
residence built 1884. Long-time residence and
studio of artist Thomas Moran.
NHL 12.21.1965

North Main Street Historic District
Group of 12 Federal, Greek Revival, and
Victorian vernacular shingled residences and
Gothic Revival shingled church grouped
around North End Cemetery (1770), and Hook
Windmill (individually listed). East Hampton
Village Multiple Resource Area.
07.21.1988

Pantigo Road Historic District
Pantigo Road from Egypt Lane and Accabonac
Road to Amy's Lane. Small residential area with
27 buildings, including Colonial shingled
Dayton-Stratton House (c.1715), 19th-century
former farmhouses, Victorian shingled
residences, and modest Colonial Revival
residences. East Hampton Village Multiple
Resource Area.   07.21.1988

Greenport

Greenport Railroad Station Complex
Third and Wiggins streets. A 1-story brick
passenger station built 1892 at eastern terminus
of Long Island Railroad. Complex includes
freight depot, turntable, and railroad tracks.
Greenport Village Multiple Resource Area.
07.20.1989

Greenport Village Historic District
Roughly bounded by Stirling Basin, and Main,
Monsell, Second, and Front streets. Large
concentration of approximately 250 buildings
comprising older commercial and residential
core of village, including waterfront business
district and large residential areas. Includes
vernacular frame 18th-century residences,
19th-century commercial buildings, numerous
19th- and early 20th-century residences, and
several churches and institutional buildings.

Greenport Village Multiple Resource Area.
09.13.1984

Head of the Harbor

Box Hill Estate
Moriches Road, northwest of St. James.
A 20-acre estate overlooking Stony Brook
Harbor with rambling Colonial Revival/
eclectic main residence surfaced in pebble-
dashed stucco; originally built as farmhouse
and enlarged late 19th century by architect
Stanford White and son Lawrence Grant White
as White family summer residence. Notable
interior by Stanford White with innovative
materials and finishes. Property includes formal
gardens, farm complex, and octagonal water
tower, all designed or modified by Stanford and
Lawrence Grant White. Lawn features
"Diana" sculpture by Augustus Saint-Gaudens.
12.04.1973

Stony Brook Gristmill
Harbor Road (also in town of Brookhaven).
A 2 1/2-story shingled gristmill built c.1750;
enlarged 19th and early 20th century. Adjacent
sluice, weir, dam, and millpond.
08.03.1990

Huntington

M. Baylis House
530 Sweet Hollow Road, Melville. Vernacular
shingled frame residence built c.1820.
Huntington Town Multiple Resource Area.
09.26.1985

Bethel A.M.E Church and Manse
291 Park Avenue. Small vernacular frame
church built 1840s; used since 1860 by local
African-American congregation. Adjacent
manse built 1915. Huntington Town Multiple
Resource Area.   09.26.1985

George McKesson Brown Estate
(Coindre Hall)
Brown's Road (also in village of Lloyd Harbor).
A 13-acre estate on Huntington Harbor with
large, rambling Chateauesque stuccoed main
residence with circular towers and tile roof;
designed by Clarence Luce; built 1910 for
owner of McKesson Chemical Co. Includes
original boathouse and garage. Huntington
Town Multiple Resource Area.
09.26.1985

Brush Farmstead
344 Greenlawn Road, Greenlawn. Second
Empire frame farmhouse built c.1873 and
caretaker's cottage, barns, and other
outbuildings. Huntington Town Multiple
Resource Area.   09.26.1985

Eliphas Buffett House
159 West Rogues Path, Cold Spring Harbor.
A 3-acre property with vernacular shingled
frame residence built c.1800; Greek Revival
addition c.1835. Property includes 2 late 19th-
century outbuildings and family cemetery.
Huntington Town Multiple Resource Area.
09.26.1985

Joseph Buffett House
169 West Rogues Path, Cold Spring Harbor.
Small Colonial shingled residence built c.1750;
larger main section built c.1830. Huntington
Town Multiple Resource Area.
09.26.1985

John Bumpstead House
473 Woodbury Road, Cold Spring Harbor.
Small vernacular frame former farmhouse built
c.1835 and 2 late 19th-century outbuildings.
Huntington Town Multiple Resource Area.
09.26.1985

Carll Burr, Jr., House
293 Burr Road, Commack. Victorian frame
residence with shingle and clapboard siding and
3-story corner tower; built c.1895 for state
assemblyman and senator. Huntington Town
Multiple Resource Area.   09.26.1985

Carll S. Burr Mansion
304 Burr Road, Commack. Large Second
Empire shingled frame residence with belvedere; original section built c.1830; greatly
enlarged and remodeled c.1885. Includes late
19th-century barn and early 20th-century
cottage. Huntington Town Multiple Resource
Area.   09.26.1985

Carll House
79 Wall Street, Cold Spring Harbor. Vernacular
shingled residence built c.1820; c.1840 wing
moved to present site in mid-19th century.
Huntington Town Multiple Resource Area.
09.26.1985

Carll House
380 Deer Park Road, Dix Hills. A 15-acre
property with large vernacular shingled former
farmhouse built c.1750; remodeled early 19th
century in Federal style. Includes mid-19th-
century cottage and 3 early 19th-century barns
around small pond. Huntington Town Multiple
Resource Area.   09.26.1985

Ezra Carll Homestead
49 Melville Road, Huntington Station. Small
Colonial shingled residence built c.1700; large
main section built c.1740. Huntington Town
Multiple Resource Area.   09.26.1985

Marion Carll Farm
475 Commack Road, Commack. A 9-acre
farmstead with Italianate frame farmhouse built
c.1860. Numerous 18th- to 20th-century
outbuildings including privy, garage, smokehouse, milkhouse, horse/carriage barn, sheep
barn, and several other barns. Occupied
continuously by Carll family since 1701.
06.26.1979

Chichester's Inn
97 Chichester Road, West Hills. A 1 1/2-story,
11-bay Colonial frame building; original
section built c.1680 as inn; several later
additions. Huntington Town Multiple Resource
Area.   09.26.1985

Cold Spring Harbor Library
One Shore Road, Cold Spring Harbor. A

1-story Neoclassical brick library with
octagonal cupola and Doric portico; designed
by Julian Peabody; built 1913. Adapted for use
as gallery by Society for the Preservation of
Long Island Antiquities. Huntington Town
Multiple Resource Area.   09.26.1985

Commack Methodist Church and Cemetery
486 Townline Road, Commack. Vernacular
shingled church built 1789. Large adjacent
18th- and 19th-century cemetery. Huntington
Town Multiple Resource Area.   09.26.1985

David Conklin House
2 High Street, Cold Spring Harbor. A 2 1/2-story
Colonial frame former farmhouse built c.1750;
additions c.1810 and 1920s. Operated as
museum by Huntington Historical Society.
Huntington Town Multiple Resource Area.
09.26.1985

Harry E. Donnell House
71 Locust Lane, Eatons Neck. Large Tudor
Revival shingled, stuccoed, and half-timbered
residence with 2 outbuildings on large landscaped lot; designed by Harry E. Donnell; built
1902-03. Huntington Town Multiple Resource
Area.   09.26.1985

Dowden Tannery
210 West Rogues Path, Cold Spring Harbor.
A 2-story brick industrial building built c.1840;
early 20th-century additions. Huntington Town
Multiple Resource Area.   09.26.1985

East Shore Road Historic District
Halesite. Residential area on Huntington
Harbor with 3 early 19th-century residences,
site of mid-18th-century pottery works,
approximately 10 Victorian working-class
residences (c.1860-1900), and mid-18th-
century town park. Huntington Town Multiple
Resource Area.   09.26.1985

Eatons Neck Light
Eatons Neck Point at Huntington Bay and Long
Island Sound off NY25A. A 50-foot-high
octagonal stone lighthouse designed by John
McComb, Jr.; built 1798.   04.03.1973

John Everit House
130 Old Country Road, West Hills. Vernacular
shingled farmhouse built c.1830 and 3 late
19th-century outbuildings. Huntington Town
Multiple Resource Area.   09.26.1985

**Fort Golgotha and the
Old Burial Hill Cemetery**
Main Street and Nassau Road. A 3-acre
cemetery begun mid-17th century. Includes
archeological site of British fort built 1782.
03.02.1981

Gilsey Mansion
36 Browns Road. Large Colonial Revival frame
residence with Doric portico and porte cochere;
built 1900. Huntington Town Multiple
Resource Area.   09.26.1985

Goose Hill Road Historic District
Cold Spring Harbor. Small former agrarian
community with 5 Federal and Greek Revival
frame farmhouses and 1 Victorian farmhouse.

Huntington Town Multiple Resource Area.
09.26.1985

Halsey Estate (Tallwood)
Sweet Hollow Road, West Hills. A 12-acre
estate with large Colonial Revival shingled
residence built c.1925 as replica of Prince
House (c.1750) in Flushing, New York; built
for R. T. H. Halsey, first curator of American
Wing at Metropolitan Museum of Art. Now
a day camp. Huntington Town Multiple
Resource Area.   09.26.1985

Harbor Road Historic District
Cold Spring Harbor. Large residential neighborhood with archeological site of mill (1791)
and 14 Federal, Greek Revival, and Italianate
residences built 1791-1869 during settlement
period and later development as resort
community. Huntington Town Multiple
Resource Area.   09.26.1985

John Harned House
26 Little Neck Road, Centerport. Vernacular
frame residence built c.1850 and late 19th-
century barn. Huntington Town Multiple
Resource Area.   09.26.1985

Wallace K. Harrison Estate
140 Round Swamp Road, West Hills. An
11-acre estate with International Style concrete
main residence designed by Wallace K. Harrison; built 1929-31 as his residence. One of
the earliest examples of the International Style
to be built in America. Huntington Town
Multiple Resource Area.   09.26.1985

Heckscher Park
Bounded by Madison Street, Sabbath Day
Path, Main Street, and Prince Avenue, Huntington. An 18-acre landscaped park established
1920 with funds from industrialist and
financier August Heckscher. Includes
Renaissance Revival Heckscher Museum of
Art, cobblestone cottage, and octagonal
cobblestone gazebo (all built 1920s).
Huntington Town Multiple Resource Area.
09.26.1985

Hook Windmill, Village of East Hampton.

Bell Tower, William K. Vanderbilt Estate, Huntington.

Hewlett House
559 Woodbury Road, Cold Spring Harbor. A 6-acre former farmstead with vernacular frame farmhouse built c.1815; enlarged 1870s. Huntington Town Multiple Resource Area. 09.26.1985

Ireland-Gardiner Farm
863 Lake Road, Greenlawn. A 24-acre farmstead with Colonial vernacular shingled farmhouse built c.1750 (addition c.1775) and 4 early 19th-century outbuildings. Huntington Town Multiple Resource Area. 09.26.1985

Jarvis-Fleet House
138 Cove Road, Huntington Beach. A 2 1/2-story, 7-bay Colonial shingled residence built c.1700; enlarged c.1750; Victorian alterations. Huntington Town Multiple Resource Area. 09.26.1985

B. Ketchum House
237 Middleville Road, Middleville. A 1 1/2-story, 6-bay vernacular shingled residence built c.1765. Huntington Town Multiple Resource Area. 09.26.1985

Little Jennie
Centerport Harbor, Centerport. An 86-foot-long plank-on-frame, 2-masted Chesapeake bay bugeye built 1884 by James T. Marsh; used until 1930 on Chesapeake Bay as oyster boat and sailing freighter; converted 1930 to pleasure yacht. 05.12.1986

Lloyd Harbor Lighthouse
Entrance to Lloyd Harbor. A 2-story square reinforced-concrete lighthouse with octagonal lantern and attached keeper's dwelling supported by concrete foundation and riprap; built 1912 by Charles Mead & Co. 05.31.1989

Isaac Losee House
269 Park Avenue, Huntington. A 1 1/2-story vernacular frame residence built c.1750; remodeled mid-19th century. Huntington Town Multiple Resource Area. 09.26.1985

Main Street Historic District
Cold Spring Harbor. Residential and commercial neighborhood at historic core of community, with 27 buildings in variety of styles from development as seaport/whaling center in early 19th century to summer resort in late 19th century and affluent residential neighborhood in 20th century. Notable buildings include large Victorian residences on "Ship Captain's Row" (1860s-70s), Shingle Style Queen Anne Reque House (1907, Brown & Von Beren), Greek/Gothic Revival Methodist Episcopal Church (1842), and Greek Revival Baptist Chapel (1844). Huntington Town Multiple Resource Area. 09.26.1985

John Oakley House
Sweet Hollow Road, West Hills. An 18-acre former farmstead with small Colonial shingled residence built c.1720; addition built c.1780 and moved to present site c.1850. Huntington Town Multiple Resource Area. 11.06.1985

Old First Church
125 Main Street, Huntington. Federal frame church with octagonal bell tower; built 1794. Huntington Town Multiple Resource Area. 11.06.1985

Old Town Green Historic District
Park Avenue, Huntington. Small residential area with seven 17th- to 19th-century buildings, archeological site, and village green; core of original settlement of hamlet in 1653. Notable properties include Colonial frame Jarvis-Fleet House (1653; c.1702 addition), Colonial Arsenal (c.1745; later addition and recent restoration), and site of Platt's Tavern (c.1650). Huntington Town Multiple Resource Area. 09.26.1985

Old Town Hall Historic District
Main Street and Nassau Road, Huntington. Small group of mostly late 19th- and early 20th-century civic and residential buildings near commercial core of community. Includes Tudor Revival Soldiers and Sailors Memorial Building (1892, Cady, Berg & See), Neo-classical former Town Hall (1910, Julian Peabody), Tudor Revival Sewing and Trade School (c.1900, Cady & See), 3 large Queen Anne residences, Greek Revival Universalist Church (1837), and Fort Golgotha and Old Burial Hill Cemetery (individually listed). Huntington Town Multiple Resource Area. 09.26.1985

House at 244 Park Avenue
Huntington. A 4-bay vernacular frame residence with saltbox profile; built c.1830. Huntington Town Multiple Resource Area. 09.26.1985

Potter-Williams House
165 Wall Street, Huntington. Vernacular frame residence built 1827 for silversmith and politician Nathaniel Potter; Victorian porch added c.1870. Includes mid-19th-century springhouse. Huntington Town Multiple Resource Area. 09.26.1985

Prime House
35 Prime Avenue, Huntington. Vernacular

frame 2-family residence built c.1855 as workers' housing for adjacent thimble factory. Huntington Town Multiple Resource Area. 09.26.1985

Prime-Octagon House
41 Prime Avenue, Huntington. A 2-story Victorian stuccoed concrete and brick octagonal residence built c.1859. Huntington Town Multiple Resource Area. 09.26.1985

Michael Remp House
42 Godfrey Lane, Greenlawn. A 32-acre farmstead with small vernacular shingled residence built c.1770; enlarged c.1830 with Greek Revival features. Includes 3 mid-19th and early 20th-century barns. Huntington Town Multiple Resource Area. 09.26.1985

Rogers House
136 Spring Road, Huntington. Vernacular shingled residence built c.1820. Huntington Town Multiple Resource Area. 09.26.1985

John Rogers House
627 Half Hollow Road, Half Hollow Hills. Vernacular shingled residence built 1732; alterations in Federal style Huntington Town Multiple Resource Area. 09.26.1985

Silas Sammis House
302 West Neck Road, Huntington. Small vernacular shingled residence built c.1730; larger main section added c.1800. Huntington Town Multiple Resource Area. 09.26.1985

Seaman Farm
1378 Carlls Straight Path, Dix Hills. A 16-acre farmstead with vernacular shingled farmhouse built c.1805. Includes early 19th-century barn and early 20th-century outbuildings sited around large pond. Huntington Town Multiple Resource Area. 09.26.1985

Shore Road Historic District
Cold Spring Harbor and vicinity. Residential neighborhood with 6 early to mid-19th-century Federal and Greek Revival farmhouses and residences, Victorian residence, and estate. Includes Wawapek Estate (1898-1900, Grosvenor Atterbury; built for Robert DeForest), and Federal Henry Titus Farmstead (c.1790; several outbuildings). Huntington Town Multiple Resource Area. 09.26.1985

Daniel Smith House
117 West Shore Road, Huntington Beach. Greek Revival frame residence built c.1855 for mill operator; incorporates c.1830 frame residence as wing. Huntington Town Multiple Resource Area. 09.26.1985

Henry Smith Farmstead
900 Park Avenue, Huntington Station. A 3-acre former farmstead with Colonial frame farmstead built c.1750 and remodeled c.1860. Includes 5 mid-19th-century outbuildings. Huntington Town Multiple Resource Area. 09.26.1985

Jacob Smith House
High Hold Drive, West Hills. A 2-acre parcel within large county park, with small Colonial shingled farmhouse built c.1740; Greek Revival main section built c.1830. Huntington Town Multiple Resource Area. 09.26.1985

Suydam House
One Fort Salonga Road, Centerport. A 1 1/2-story Colonial shingled residence with saltbox form; built c.1730. Huntington Multiple Resource Area. 10.27.1988

Sweet Hollow Presbyterian Church Parsonage
152 Old Country Road, Melville. Greek Revival frame residence built c.1830. Huntington Town Multiple Resource Area. 09.26.1985

Titus-Bunce House
7 Goose Hill Road, Cold Spring Harbor. Greek Revival frame residence built c.1820 with mid-19th-century Italianate decorative details. Huntington Town Multiple Resource Area. 09.26.1985

Henry Townsend House
231 West Neck Road, Huntington. Vernacular frame residence built c.1830; remodeled c.1850 in Picturesque style. Includes 5 mid- to late 19th-century outbuildings. Huntington Town Multiple Resource Area. 09.26.1985

Charles Van Iderstine Mansion
Idle Day Drive, Little Neck. Large, rambling Queen Anne/eclectic residence with clapboard and shingle siding and 3-story octagonal corner tower; built 1897 for businessman and civic leader. Huntington Town Multiple Resource Area. 09.26.1985

William K. Vanderbilt Estate (Eagles Nest)
Little Neck Road, Little Neck. A 43-acre estate on Northport Harbor begun 1907 by philanthropist and civic leader William K. Vanderbilt, Jr., as retreat and private marine museum; enlarged and remodeled in Spanish Baroque style by Warren & Wetmore; completed 1928. Includes large 3-story stuccoed main residence with 4-story bell tower and polychromatic ornament, wrought-iron entrance gates, elaborate formal gardens, marine museum, garage/servants' quarters, boathouse, airplane hangar, powerhouse garage complex, and caretaker's cottage. Museum. Huntington Town Multiple Resource Area. 09.26.1985

N. Velzer House and Caretaker's Cottage
22 Fort Salonga Road, Centerport. Greek Revival frame residence built c.1830. Adjacent caretaker's cottage built c.1858. Huntington Town Multiple Resource Area. 09.26.1985

Charles M. Weeks House
76 Mill Lane, Huntington. Second Empire frame residence built c.1860. Huntington Town Multiple Resource Area. 09.26.1985

West Neck Road Historic District
Huntington. Residential neighborhood with 23 buildings, mostly Victorian frame residences built 1860-1900 adjacent to commercial core of

community. Huntington Town Multiple Resource Area. 09.26.1985

Joseph Whitman House
365 West Hills Road, West Hills. A 1 1/2-story Colonial shingled residence built c.1692; later additions and alterations; moved to present site 1913. Property includes early 19th-century barn and site of 17th-century fort. Huntington Town Multiple Resource Area. 09.26.1985

Walt Whitman House (State Historic Site)
246 Walt Whitman Road, West Hills. Vernacular shingled residence built c.1815 by Walter Whitman. Birthplace of great American poet Walt Whitman. Includes early 19th-century barn. Huntington Town Multiple Resource Area. 09.26.1985

Whitman-Place House
69 Chichester Road, West Hills. A 5-acre property with shingled former farmhouse built c.1810, barn (built as house in late 17th century), and early 20th-century springhouse. Huntington Town Multiple Resource Area. 09.26.1985

Wiggins-Rolph House
518 Park Avenue, Huntington. Large Greek Revival frame residence built 1848 incorporating mid-18th-century residence as rear wing. Huntington Town Multiple Resource Area. 09.26.1985

Henry Williams House
43 Mill Lane, Huntington. Picturesque frame residence built c.1850. Huntington Town Multiple Resource Area. 09.26.1985

Harry Wood House
481 West Main Street, Huntington. Vernacular frame residence built c.1853. Huntington Town Multiple Resource Area. 09.26.1985

John Wood House
121 McKay Road, Huntington Station. A 1-story Colonial frame residence built c.1704; c.1800 and later additions. Huntington Town Multiple Resource Area. 09.26.1985

William Wooden Wood House
90 Preston Street, Huntington Beach. Large Picturesque frame residence with elaborate decorative trim; built 1868-69. Huntington Town Multiple Resource Area. 09.26.1985

Charles Woodhull House
70 Main Street, Huntington. Italianate frame residence with cupola; built c.1870. **Huntington Town Multiple Resource Area.** 09.26.1985

Huntington Bay

House at 200 Bay Avenue
Large Tudor Revival shingled, stuccoed, and half-timbered residence built c.1890. Huntington Town Multiple Resource Area. 09.26.1985

Bay Crest Historic District

Beech Avenue, Valley Road, and Woodside and Valley drives. Small residential neighborhood with 12 large Stick Style, Queen Anne, Shingle Style, and Colonial Revival residences built c.1890-1905 as summer enclave. Huntington Town Multiple Resource Area. 09.26.1985

Beaux Arts Park Historic District

Locust Lane, and Upper and Lower drives. Group of 5 large Tudor Revival and Spanish Colonial Revival stuccoed residences built c.1905-15. Huntington Town Multiple Resource Area. 09.26.1985

Bowes House

15 Harbor Hill Drive. Large Shingle Style frame residence built 1899. Huntington Town Multiple Resource Area. 09.26.1985

Charles Geoghegan House

9 Harbor Hill Drive. Large Queen Anne/Shingle Style frame residence and garage on landscaped lot; built c.1915. Huntington Town Multiple Resource Area. 09.26.1985

John Green House

167 East Shore Road. Large, rambling Colonial Revival shingled residence on landscaped lot overlooking Huntington Harbor; built c.1900. Huntington Town Multiple Resource Area. 09.26.1985

John P. Kane Mansion

37 Kanes Lane. Large Italianate frame residence built c.1850; early 20th-century additions and alterations. Huntington Town Multiple Resource Area. 09.26.1985

A. P. W. Kennan House

Sydney Road. Large, rambling Colonial Revival shingled residence on landscaped waterfront lot; built c.1900. Huntington Town Multiple Resource Area. 11.06.1985

C. A. O'Donohue House

158 Shore Road. Large Colonial Revival shingled residence on large landscaped lot overlooking Huntington Harbor; built 1917. Huntington Town Multiple Resource Area. 09.26.1985

Islip

Bayard Cutting Estate

(Bayard Cutting Arboretum State Park)
NY 27, north of Great River. A 750-acre former estate with massive, rambling Tudor Revival shingled and half-timbered main residence, gatehouse, and carriage house; designed 1886 by Charles C. Haight for wealthy entrepreneur W. Bayard Cutting. Landscaped grounds designed by Frederick Law Olmsted. Includes large farm complex known as Westbrook Farms. 10.02.1973

Fire Island Light Station

Robert Moses Causeway, near Bay Shore. A 140-foot-high conical stuccoed brick lighthouse completed 1858. Adjacent keeper's house completed 1859. 09.11.1981

John Ellis Roosevelt Estate (Meadowcroft)

Middle Road, Sayville. An 86-acre estate with large Colonial Revival frame residence designed by Isaac H. Green, Jr.; built 1891-92 as summer residence for New York City banker; incorporates mid-19th-century farmhouse as wing. Includes several original outbuildings. Now part of Suffolk County's Sans Souci Nature Preserve. 11.05.1987

Sagtikos Manor

Montauk Highway (NY 27A), West Bay Shore. A 10-acre property with large, rambling frame residence; original section built late 17th century; gambrel-roofed addition by Isaac Thompson family; extensively enlarged and remodeled in Colonial Revival style c.1902 by Isaac H. Green, Jr. for philanthropist Frederick Diodati Thompson. Includes brick buttery, carriage house, small cemetery, and landscaped grounds. Museum. 11.21.1976

Southside Sportsmens Club District

(Connetquot River State Park)
Off NY 27, northeast of Great River. A 3,528-acre property begun 1866 as game preserve and sporting club by group of prominent New York City business families. Buildings grouped at southernmost end of property include large clubhouse originally built early 19th century as inn and substantially enlarged in late 19th century, mid-18th-century gristmill, 2 clubhouse annexes, and outbuildings. 07.23.1973

United States Post Office–Bay Shore

10 Bay Shore Avenue, Bay Shore. Colonial Revival brick post office built 1933-35. Interior sculptural relief (1936) by Wheeler Williams. United States Post Offices in New York State, 1858-1943, Thematic Resources. 11.17.1988

Lloyd Harbor

George McKesson Brown Estate

(see Huntington)

Marshall Field III Estate (Caumsett State Park)

Lloyd Harbor Road. A 1,400-acre former estate property between Long Island Sound and Lloyd Harbor with diverse landscape, main house, and numerous dependencies designed by John Russell Pope; completed 1925 for grandson of Chicago department store pioneer as home, hunting preserve, cattle-breeding farm, and dairy. Includes Georgian Revival main residence, cottages, stables, greenhouses, and massive farm complex. Also includes Colonial Henry Lloyd House (1711; museum), and historic and prehistoric archeological features. Became state park 1961. 04.30.1979

Fort Hill Estate

Fort Hill Drive. A 23-acre estate on Cold Spring Harbor with monumental Tudor Revival brick and limestone residence designed 1900 by Boring & Tilton for chemist and business leader William John Matheson; incorporates earlier building designed by McKim, Mead & Bigelow. Includes water tower, outbuildings, and formal garden. 06.02.1988

Joseph Lloyd Manor House

Lloyd Harbor Road, northwest of Huntington. Large 2 1/2-story Colonial shingled residence built c.1766-67 as second manor house of Manor of Queen Village; notable interior woodwork fabricated by Abner Osborn; 19th- and 20th-century alterations. Operated as museum by Society for the Preservation of Long Island Antiquities. 11.07.1976

Van Wyck-Lefferts Tide Mill

Two miles northeast of Mill and Southdown roads. A 3 1/2-story frame tide mill with original machinery; built 1793-97. Long Island Wind and Tide Mills Thematic Resources. 06.02.1978

Northport

United States Post Office–Northport

244 Main Street. Colonial Revival brick post office built 1936. United States Post Offices in New York State, 1858-1943, Thematic Resources. 05.11.1989

Patchogue

United States Post Office–Patchogue

170 East Main Street. Large Art Deco limestone post office designed by John V. Van Pelt; built 1932-33. United States Post Offices in New York State, 1858-1943, Thematic Resources. 05.11.1989

United Methodist Church

South Ocean Avenue and Church Street. Large Romanesque Revival brick church and chapel designed by Oscar S. Teale; built 1889. Stained-glass rose windows by Tiffany Brothers Studios. 04.19.1984

Riverhead

Hallock Homestead

163 Sound Avenue, Northville. Large vernacular shingled farmhouse built 1845 incorporating original house of c.1765. Includes late 18th-century shoemaker's shop, early 18th-century shop/wood house, early 19th-century barn, and privy. 06.07.1984

United States Post Office–Riverhead

23 West Second Street. Colonial Revival brick post office built 1935. United States Post Offices in New York State, 1858-1943, Thematic Resources. 05.11.1989

Vail-Leavitt Music Hall

Peconic Avenue. A 2 1/2-story Victorian brick building with commercial storefronts on 1st floor and classically decorated auditorium on 2nd floor; built 1881 as theater and public meeting space. 08.25.1983

Sag Harbor

Sag Harbor Village District
Roughly bounded by Sag Harbor, Rysam, Hamilton, Marsden, and Main streets, and Long Island Avenue. Central commercial and residential core of early 19th-century whaling village, with large concentration of Federal and Greek Revival vernacular shingled and clapboarded residences. Notable buildings include Federal Jared Wade House (c.1797), Federal Custom House (1789), Greek Revival Benjamin Huntting House and L'Hommedieu House, Egyptian Revival Whalers Presbyterian Church (1843-44, attributed to Minard Lafever), and Italianate Hannibal-French House (early 19th century, remodeled 1860s). 07.20.1973

Shelter Island

James Havens Homestead
NY114. Vernacular shingled residence built c.1750 for James Havens, prominent settler appointed to New York State Provincial Congress in 1776; enlarged early and mid-19th century. 04.10.1986

Shelter Island Windmill
North of Manwaring Road. Octagonal shingled smock mill built 1810 by Nathaniel Dominy V; moved 1926 to present site. Long Island Wind and Tide Mills Thematic Resources. 12.27.1978

Union Chapel
The Grove, Shelter Island Heights. Victorian shingled church built 1875 as focal point of Methodist camp. 11.23.1984

Smithtown

Blydenburgh Park Historic District
Blydenburgh County Park. A 10-acre area encompassing remaining 9 structures of early 19th-century settlement of Bushy Neck. Includes 2-story New Mill (c.1800), Federal Miller's Cottage (c.1802), Isaac Blydenburgh House (1821), Gothic Revival Blydenburgh Cottage (c.1850), and dependencies. Now part of 600-acre county park. 08.11.1983

First Presbyterian Church
175 East Main Street. Federal shingled church with tiered, balustraded belfry; built 1823-25 by local carpenter/housewright George Curtiss. 12.23.1977

Fort Salonga
Address restricted. Archeological site of square earthen fortification erected 1776-81 as British military outpost during American Revolution. 05.21.1982

Mills Pond District
North Country Road (NY25A). A 200-acre area with several buildings at heart of small 18th- to 19th-century farming hamlet founded by Mills family; dominated by Greek Revival Mills Homestead (1837, Calvin Pollard) and dependencies. 08.01.1973

St. James Historic District
North Country Road (NY25A). A 90-acre corridor centered around nucleus of 3 properties: Federal shingled Timothy Smith House and dependencies (c.1800; moved and enlarged c.1906 by architect/owner Lawrence Smith Butler); Greek Revival frame Deepwells Estate (1845-47; built by artisan/builder George Curtiss for Joel L. G. Smith); and Gothic Revival frame St. James Episcopal Church, rectory, and cemetery (1853; windows by Louis Comfort Tiffany and John LaFarge; grave of Stanford White). Also includes St. James Railroad Station, St. James General Store, and other 19th-century buildings. 07.20.1973

Wyandanch Club Historic District
(Caleb Smith State Park)
Jericho Turnpike. A 518-acre property developed late 19th and early 20th century as hunting and fishing club. Includes undeveloped woodland, open space, natural waterways, and several buildings predating club development and altered for use by club: Vail House (c.1810-20) and outbuildings, Chipman House (late 18th century) and Gristmill (1795), Caleb Smith I House (c.1751, enlarged late 19th century for use as clubhouse), and Whitman Farmhouse (early 19th century) and outbuildings. Acquired 1963 by State of New York. 08.03.1990

Southampton (Town)

Beebe Windmill
Ocean Road and Hildreth Avenue, Bridgehampton. Octagonal shingled smock mill built 1820 by Pardon T. Tabor; moved 1915 to present site. Long Island Wind and Tide Mills Thematic Resources. 12.27.1978

James Benjamin Homestead
1182 Flanders Road, Flanders. Vernacular shingled farmhouse on Reeves Bay; built c.1785; later additions and alterations. Includes 19th-century barn. 08.13.1986

William Merritt Chase Homestead
Canoe Place Road, Shinnecock Hills. Shingle Style/eclectic residence designed by McKim, Mead & White; built 1892 as summer house and studio of painter William Merritt Chase, who taught at nearby Shinnecock Summer School of Art. 06.16.1983

Stephen Jagger House
Old Montauk Highway, Westhampton. Small 1 1/2-story Colonial shingled residence with gambrel roof; built c.1748; large early 19th-century addition. 12.12.1978; DEMOLISHED

Water Mill
Old Mill Road, Water Mill. A 2-story shingled gristmill built 1644 by Edward Howell; moved in 18th century to present site and refitted for textile and later paper manufacturing. Now a museum. 10.13.1983

Windmill at Water Mill
NY27 and Halsey Lane, Water Mill. Octagonal shingled smock mill built 1800; moved 1813 to present site. Long Island Wind and Tide Mills Thematic Resources. 12.27.1978

Southampton (Village)

Balcastle
Herrick and Little Plains roads. Large brick residence with castellated Gothic-style towers and decorative features; built 1909-10 by local builder Edward Elliston as summer residence for prosperous Russian immigrant. Southampton Village Multiple Resource Area. 10.02.1986

Beach Road Historic District
Group of 7 large early 20th-century oceanfront summer estates in variety of eclectic styles, including Spanish Colonial Revival, Georgian Revival, and Tudor Revival. Architects includes Edward P. Mellon, Cross & Cross, and Peabody, Wilson & Brown. Southampton Village Multiple Resource Area. 10.02.1986

Dr. Wesley Bowers House
Beach Road. A 7-acre oceanfront estate with large Spanish Colonial Revival stuccoed residence and garden pavilion designed by LeRoy P. Ward; built c.1930 as summer house for New York City doctor. Southampton Village Multiple Resource Area. 10.02.1986

James L. Breese House
155 Hill Street. Large Colonial Revival shingled residence designed by McKim, Mead & White incorporating earlier farmhouse; built 1897-98 as summer house; music room, conservatory, and formal gardens designed 1906 by Stanford White. Notable interior. 04.18.1980

Captain C. Goodale House
300 Hampton Road. Large Second Empire frame residence built 1875 for ship captain. Southampton Village Multiple Resource Area. 10.02.1986

North Main Street Historic District
Small concentration of 20 residential and commercial buildings, including three 18th-century vernacular frame residences, several late 19th- and early 20th-century Victorian and Colonial Revival residences, eclectic stone and oyster shell railroad station (1902) with landscaped plaza, and brick warehouse (1900). Southampton Village Multiple Resource Area. 10.02.1986

Southampton Village Historic District
Roughly bounded by Hill and Main streets, Old Town Road, Atlantic Ocean, and Coopers Neck. Large section of village with approximately 350 buildings, including small number of 17th- and 18th-century vernacular frame settlement period homesteads, section of business district with late 19th- and early 20th-century commercial buildings, and large concentration of Queen Anne, Shingle Style, and Colonial Revival summer estates built during development as resort community in

late 19th and early 20th centuries. Notable properties include 2 settlement-era cemeteries, Colonial frame Thomas Halsey Homestead (1662), Federal and Greek Revival residences, Italianate Leon D. DeBoot House (1875), Queen Anne Nelson cottages (c.1887), Shingle Style Aspegren House (c.1895), Colonial Revival Kiser Estate (1927), Colonial Revival Parrish commercial buildings (1928), Spanish Colonial Revival Parrish Art Museum (1898, Grosvenor Atterbury), Southampton Club (1899, Grosvenor Atterbury), Meadow Club (1902, James Brown Lord), and James L. Breese

The Old House, Southold.

Opposite: Roebling Aqueduct, Highland.

House (individually listed). Architects of summer estates include McKim, Mead & White, Robert H. Robertson, Bruce Price, John Russell Pope, Carrère & Hastings, and Walker & Gillette. Southampton Village Multiple Resource Area.   04.25.1988

Wickapogue Road Historic District
Small agrarian district with 6 farmsteads containing late 17th- to early 20th-century vernacular shingled farmhouses and outbuildings. Southampton Village Multiple Resource Area.   07.10.1987

Southold

Richard Cox House
Mill Road, Mattituck. Large Italianate frame residence built c.1870, incorporating early 19th-century residence. Notable Arts and Crafts entrance hall. Adjacent Stick Style carriage house.   08.21.1986

Fort Corchaug Site
Address restricted. A 25-acre archeological site of mid-17th-century log defensive fort and village site built by Corchaug Indians.   01.18.1974

Andrew Gildersleeve Octagonal Building
Main Road and Love Lane, Mattituck. Large 2-story Italianate frame octagonal building with side wing; built 1854 by Andrew Gildersleeve as combination residence/store.   08.19.1976

The Old House
NY25, Cutchogue. A 2-story Colonial frame residence with some original features including casement window frames; built 1649 by John Budd; moved 1659 to present location. Museum.   NHL 11.05.1961

Orient Historic District
NY25, Orient. Central core of small agricultural and seafaring hamlet, with approximately 120 buildings, mostly late 18th- to late 19th-century vernacular frame residences. Notable structures include Colonial Richard Shaw House (c.1730),

Orient Wharf (1839; enlarged 1848), Federal residence on Village Lane (1790; operated as museum), Greek Revival George Vail House (1833), Poquatuck Hall (1870), and Italianate Richard House (c.1850).   05.21.1976

Terry-Mulford House
NY25, Orient. Colonial shingled residence with saltbox profile; built late 17th century; c.1700 rear lean-to and other additions and alterations in 19th and early 20th centuries. Includes well cover and small shed on 6-acre property.   02.07.1984

David Tuthill Farmstead
New Suffolk Lane, Cutchogue. Farm complex with frame farmhouse built 1798 (1880 addition) and 5 outbuildings.   11.23.1984

Village of the Branch

Branch Historic District
Middle Country Road, NY25 and 25A, and Judges Lane. Group of 15 residences, 1 church, and 1 library built from early 18th to early 20th century.   09.11.1986

Halliock Inn
263 East Main Street. Large vernacular frame former inn; original section built 18th century; enlarged c.1800.   08.07.1974

Westhampton Beach

Crowther House
97 Beach Lane. Large Shingle Style frame residence with notable Arts and Crafts interior; built 1910 as summer house.   03.21.1985

United States Post Office–Westhampton Beach
Main Street. Colonial Revival brick post office built 1940-41. Interior mural (1942) by Sol Wilson. United States Post Offices in New York State, 1858-1943, Thematic Resources.   05.11.1989

Bloomingburg

Bloomingburg Reformed Protestant Dutch Church
NY17M. Federal frame church with 80-foot-tall staged tower and octagonal belfry; built 1821-22 by Peter Weller and George Miller.   01.10.1980

Cochecten

Millanville–Skinners Falls Bridge
Delaware River (also in Pennsylvania). A 2-span metal-truss vehicular bridge built 1902

by American Bridge Co. Highway Bridges Owned by the Commonwealth of Pennsylvania, Department of Transportation Thematic Resources.   11.14.1988

Delaware

Stone Arch Bridge
NY 52, north of Kenoza Lake. A 3-arch stone bridge built c.1873 by German immigrant masons Henry and Philip Hembolt. 12.12.1976

Fallsburgh

Glen Wild Methodist Church
Old Glen Wild Road. Gothic Revival frame church with board-and-batten siding; built 1867. Intact interior and adjacent privy. 05.10.1984

Highland

Delaware and Hudson Canal, Roebling Aqueduct
Spans Delaware River between Minisink Ford and Lackawaxen, Pennsylvania. A 600-foot-long, 4-span wood suspension bridge supported by wire rope hangers and resting on stone piers; designed and built 1847-48 as canal aqueduct by John A. Roebling; converted to vehicular traffic 1898; acquired 1980 by National Park Service and reconstructed 1987-88 as vehicular bridge. Delaware and Hudson Canal Thematic Resources.   NHL 11.24.1968

Jeffersonville

Jeffersonville School
Terrace Avenue. Monumental Colonial Revival brick school with elaborate decorative features; designed by Harold O. Fullerton; built 1938-39 as Public Works Administration project. 04.28.1988

Liberty

Liberty Village Historic District
North Main, Academy, and Law streets. A 2-block area near central business district, with twelve 19th- and early 20th-century buildings. Notable buildings include Hillig Photo Studio complex (1914 and 1922), Gothic Revival Keller House (mid-19th century), Greek Revival United Methodist Church (altered 1890s), and Romanesque Revival Sullivan County National Bank (1898). 04.11.1978

Lumberland

Pond Eddy Bridge
Delaware River (also in Pennsylvania). A 2-span metal-truss vehicular bridge built 1905 by Oswego Bridge Co. Highway Bridges Owned by the Commonwealth of Pennsylvania, Department of Transportation Thematic Resources.   11.14.1988

Neversink

Grahamsville Historic District
NY 55. Group of 6 properties, including Greek Revival Marenius Dayton House, Gothic Revival 1857 House, Italianate Southwick House (1880s), Greek Revival former commercial building, Grahamsville Rural Cemetery (1874), vernacular Grahamsville Reformed Church (1882), and Memorial Hall (1935).   12.06.1979

Rockland

Rockland Mill Complex
Palen Place. An 18-acre property on east bank of Beaver Kill, with buildings and remains of water-powered facility, including 2 1/2-story gristmill (c.1850), tenant house (c.1850), proprietor's house (1867), small icehouse, power canal, millpond, tailrace, and retaining wall.   08.23.1984

Tusten

Arlington Hotel
Main Street, Narrowsburg. A 4-story Victorian frame hotel built 1894. Headquarters of Delaware Valley Arts Alliance.   03.31.1983

Kirk House
Kirk's Road, Narrowsburg. A 2-story frame residence built c.1840 as 1-story schoolhouse; enlarged and moved c.1865; exterior stuccoed c.1920 by German immigrant, Karl Paul, with unusual classical decorative details. 05.10.1984

Berkshire

Lyman P. Akins House
West Creek Road. Greek Revival frame residence with pedimented portico and symmetrical wings; built c.1850. Berkshire Town Multiple Resource Area. 07.02.1984

Robert Akins House
Main Street. Federal brick residence built c.1830; later additions. Berkshire Town Multiple Resource Area. 07.02.1984

J. Ball House
NY38. Greek Revival frame residence built c.1850 and late 19th-century dairy barn. Berkshire Town Multiple Resource Area. 07.02.1984

Levi Ball House
NY38. A 12-acre property with large Federal/Greek Revival frame residence built c.1850; late 19th-century front porch. Includes 4 historic farm buildings. Berkshire Town Multiple Resource Area. 07.02.1984

Stephen Ball House
Main Street. Greek Revival frame residence with square-columned, pedimented portico; built c.1849. Berkshire Town Multiple Resource Area. 07.02.1984

Belcher Family Homestead and Farm
NY38. A 199-acre farmstead with Victorian vernacular frame residence built 1850s, 19th-century barns, and c.1815 Federal house now used as storage shed. Berkshire Town Multiple Resource Area. 07.02.1984

Berkshire Village Historic District
Main Street and Leonard Avenue. Historic core of hamlet, with 13 residences, church, and community buildings, built c.1820-1932 in variety of styles. Includes Queen Anne United Methodist Church (1889; Pierce & Dockstader). Berkshire Town Multiple Resource Area. 07.02.1984

Calvin A. Buffington House
Depot Street and Railroad Avenue. Large Queen Anne frame residence built 1909. Home of inventor and manufacturer. Berkshire Town Multiple Resource Area. 07.02.1984

Nathaniel Bishop Collins House
NY38. Large Federal brick residence built c.1830. Property includes 3 historic farm buildings. Berkshire Town Multiple Resource Area. 07.02.1984

East Berkshire United Methodist Church
East Berkshire Road. Queen Anne frame church built 1888. Berkshire Town Multiple Resource Area. 07.02.1984

First Congregational Church
Main Street. Victorian Gothic/Queen Anne brick church designed by Pierce & Dockstader; built 1889. Berkshire Town Multiple Resource Area. 07.02.1984

Lebbeus Ford House
Jewett Hill Road. Large Federal brick residence built c.1830. Berkshire Town Multiple Resource Area. 07.02.1984

Deodatus Royce House
NY38. A 2-story Federal brick residence built c.1830. Berkshire Town Multiple Resource Area. 07.02.1984

J. B. Royce House and Farm Complex
NY38. A 50-acre farmstead with vernacular frame residence built c.1829; Gothic Revival alterations c.1850. Property includes historic garage, barn, and shed. Berkshire Town Multiple Resource Area. 07.02.1984

Newark Valley

Bement-Billings House
NY38. A 5-acre property with 1 1/2-story vernacular frame farmhouse; original section built c.1796 by Asa Bement; additions c.1816-32, 1840, and 1880. Adjacent privy. Headquarters of Newark Valley Historical Society. 02.19.1990

Nichols

Platt-Cady Mansion
(George P. and Susan Platt-Cady Library) 18 River Street. Large Federal brick residence built c.1830 by Nehemiah Platt; Greek Revival portico with Egyptian Revival capitals added to facade. Library since 1935. 08.13.1976

Owego

Owego Central Historic District
North Avenue and Park, Main, Lake, Court, and Front streets. Historic center of village on Susquehanna River with approximately 90 buildings, mostly Greek Revival and Italianate brick commercial buildings. Notable structures

include Federal Owego Academy (1828), Early Romanesque Revival Presbyterian Church and Chapel (1854-59, Gervase Wheeler and Chauncey Hungerford), Queen Anne Sheriff's Office (1882), Beaux-Arts Owego National Bank (1913, J. Mills Platt), Beaux-Arts County Clerk's Office (1906, Pierce & Bickford), individually listed Tioga County Courthouse and United States Post Office, Georgian Revival Owego Village Firehouse (1911), and Court Street Bridge (1893). 12.03.1980

Tioga County Courthouse
Village Park. Victorian Gothic Second Empire brick courthouse designed by Miles F. Howe, built 1871-73. 12.26.1972

United States Post Office–Owego
6 Lake Street. Colonial Revival brick post office built 1919-20. United States Post Offices in New York State, 1858-1943, Thematic Resources. 05.11.1989

Waverly

United States Post Office–Waverly
434-438 Waverly Street. Colonial Revival Moderne post office built 1836-37. Interior mural (1939) by Musa McKim. United States Post Offices in New York State, 1858-1943, Thematic Resources. 05.11.1989

Cayuga Heights

Cornell Heights Historic District
(see city of Ithaca)

Dryden (Town)

West Dryden Methodist Episcopal Church
West Dryden Road at Sheldon Road, West Dryden. Federal frame church built 1832 by Peter Conover; remodeled c.1880. Community center since 1966. 08.09.1991

Dryden (Village)

Luther Clarke House
39 West Main Street. Federal frame residence built c.1820-30. Dryden Village Multiple Resource Area. 06.08.1984

Dryden Village Historic District
Roughly bounded by East Main, James, Lake, and South streets. Historic section of village, with 44 properties, mostly residential, built 1800-1905. Includes notable examples of Greek Revival, Victorian Gothic, Second Empire, and Queen Anne styles. Dryden Village Multiple Resource Area. 06.15.1984

Jennings-Marvin House
9 Library Street. Shingle Style frame residence with 3-story octagonal tower; built 1897. Dryden Village Multiple Resource Area. 06.08.1984

Lacy-Van Vleet House
45 West Main Street. Large Greek Revival frame residence with pedimented central gable ends; built 1845. Dryden Village Multiple Resource Area. 06.08.1984

Methodist Episcopal Church
2 North Street. Romanesque Revival/Italianate frame church built 1874. Dryden Village Multiple Resource Area. 06.08.1984

Rockwell House
52 West Main Street. Italianate frame residence built c.1860-66 by Darius Givens. Dryden Village Multiple Resource Area. 06.08.1984

Southworth House
14 North Street. Federal brick residence with frame wing and original scenic wallpapers in parlor; built 1836; porches added late 1920s. Property includes barn. Dryden Village Multiple Resource Area. 06.08.1984

Southworth Library
24 West Main Street. Small Romanesque Revival stone library designed by William H. Miller; built 1894. Dryden Village Multiple Resource Area. 06.08.1984

Enfield

Enfield Falls Mill and Miller's House
Robert H. Treman State Park. A 3-story Greek Revival vernacular frame mill and residence, both built late 1830s. Used as museum, meeting space, and comfort station. 02.05.1979

Ithaca (Town)

Rice Hall
Cornell University. A 3-story Neoclassical brick classroom building designed by Martin, Hebrard & Young; built 1911-12 as Poultry Husbandry Building. New York State College of Agriculture Thematic Resources. 09.24.1984

Wing Hall
Cornell University. A 3-story Neoclassical brick classroom building designed by Green & Wicks; built 1912-14 as Animal Husbandry Building. New York State College of Agriculture Thematic Resources. 09.24.1984

Ithaca (City)

Bailey Hall
Cornell University. Neoclassical stone auditorium building with Ionic colonnades on 3 sides; designed by Green & Wicks; built 1912-13. New York State College of Agriculture Thematic Resources. 09.24.1984

Boardman House
120 East Buffalo Street. Large Italianate brick residence with cupola; built 1867. Home of Judge Douglas Boardman. Now offices. 05.10.1971

Caldwell Hall
Cornell University. A 4-story Neoclassical brick classroom building designed by Green & Wicks; built 1914. New York State College of Agriculture Thematic Resources. 09.24.1984

Rockwell House, Village of Dryden.

Opposite: Tioga County Courthouse, Owego.

Cascadilla School Boathouse
Stewart Park. Large Shingle Style frame boathouse designed by Vivian & Gibb; built 1894-96 on Cayuga Lake for rowing team of Cascadilla College Preparatory School. 10.04.1991

Clinton Hall
108-114 North Cayuga Street. A 3-story Greek Revival brick commercial block with cast-iron storefront and 2nd-story cast-iron balcony; built 1847-51. 07.07.1988

Clinton House
116 North Cayuga Street. A 3-story Greek Revival hotel with full-height Ionic portico; built 1828-30; design attributed to Ira Tillotson; remodeled 1872 (William H. Miller) and 1901 (Clinton Vivian). 08.12.1971

Comstock Hall
Cornell University. A 4-story Neoclassical brick classroom building designed by Martin, Hebrard & Young; built 1911-12 as Home Economics Building. New York State College of Agriculture Thematic Resources. 09.24.1984

Cornell Heights Historic District
Roughly bounded by Kline Road, Highland Avenue, Brock Lane, Triphammer Road, Fall Creek, Stewart Avenue, and Needham Place (also in village of Cayuga Heights). Residential

subdivision developed 1896-1915 by Cornell Heights Land Co.; William Webster, landscape architect. Includes approximately 150 residences, mostly built 1898-1935 in Colonial Revival, Tudor Revival, Arts and Crafts, and other styles. Architects include William H. Miller, Clarence Martin, and Clinton Vivian. 09.14.1989

Deke House
13 South Avenue. Richardsonian Romanesque stone residence designed by William H. Miller; built 1893 as lodge for Cornell University chapter of Delta Kappa Epsilon fraternity; large 1910 addition designed by Arthur Norman Gibb. 01.11.1991

DeWitt Park Historic District
Square roughly bounded by properties fronting on East Buffalo, East Court, North Cayuga, and North Tioga streets. Historic residential, civic, scholastic, and religious buildings surrounding park, designed in a variety of 19th- and early 20th-century styles. Includes individually listed Boardman House and Second Tompkins County Courthouse. 10.26.1971

East Hill Historic District
Roughly bounded by Cascadilla Creek, Eddy Street, Six Mile Creek, and Aurora Street. A 29-block neighborhood with 250 buildings, mostly residences built c.1830-1930s. Includes notable examples of Greek Revival, Gothic Revival, Italianate, Queen Anne, Colonial Revival, and Arts and Crafts styles. 08.14.1986

East Roberts Hall
Cornell University. A 3-story Neoclassical brick classroom building designed by George L. Heins; built 1905-07 as Dairy Building. New York State College of Agriculture Thematic Resources. 09.24.1984; DEMOLISHED 1990

Fernow Hall
Cornell University. A 2 1/2-story Neoclassical brick classroom building designed by Green & Wicks; built 1912-14 as Forestry Building. New York State College of Agriculture Thematic Resources. 09.24.1984

Ithaca Pottery Site
Address restricted. Vernacular frame pottery shop and warehouse built late 1830s. Converted to apartments. Includes associated archeological site. 07.17.1979

Lehigh Valley Railroad Station
West Buffalo Street and Taughannock Boulevard. Colonial Revival brick passenger station and frame freight station built 1898. 12.31.1974

Llenroc
100 Cornell Avenue. Massive, rambling Gothic Revival stone residence designed by Nichols & Brown with Thomas Fuller; built 1865-75 for university founder Ezra Cornell. Now a fraternity. 04.16.1980

Morrill Hall
Cornell University. A 4-story Second Empire stone building, the university's first, designed by Henry W. Wilcox; built 1866-68. NHL 12.21.1965

Roberts Hall
Cornell University. A 4-story Neoclassical brick classroom building designed by George L. Heins; built 1905-07. New York State College of Agriculture Thematic Resources. 09.24.1984; DEMOLISHED 1990

St. James A.M.E. Zion Church
116-118 Cleveland Avenue. Vernacular frame church begun c.1836 and enlarged late 19th century in Victorian style. Center of anti-slavery activity in 19th century. 07.22.1982

Second Tompkins County Courthouse
121 East Court Street. Gothic Revival stuccoed brick courthouse designed by John F. Maurice; built 1854. Interior features open timber roof in 2nd-story courtroom, intact but obscured by 1974-75 modifications. 03.18.1971

Stone Hall
Cornell University. A 3-story Neoclassical brick classroom building designed by George L. Heins; built 1905-07 as Agronomy Building. New York State College of Agriculture Thematic Resources. 09.24.1984; DEMOLISHED 1986

Strand Theatre
310 East State Street. Tudor Revival brick and limestone theater with Adamesque lobby and auditorium; designed and built 1916-17 as movie and vaudeville house by Driscoll Brothers and Co.; used for stage productions 1920s-40s. 02.22.1979

United States Post Office–Ithaca
213 North Tioga Street. Large Beaux-Arts limestone post office designed by James Knox Taylor; built 1909-10; enlarged 1936. United States Post Offices in New York State, 1858-1943, Thematic Resources. 05.11.1989

Andrew Dickson White House
27 East Avenue. Large Victorian Gothic brick residence designed by George Hawthorne with William H. Miller and Charles Babcock; built 1871-73 as residence for president of Cornell University. Now in academic use. 12.04.1973

Trumansburg

Hermon Camp House
Camp Street. Imposing Greek Revival brick residence with 2-story Doric portico; designed by Thomas Judd; built 1845. Adjacent garden pavilion and 4-acre property once planted with formal gardens. 12.04.1973

Ulysses

Indian Fort Road Site
Address restricted. Site of Cayuga Iroquois village believed to date to 16th century. 09.30.1983

Ellenville

United States Post Office–Ellenville
Liberty Place. Colonial Revival stone post office designed by R. Stanley-Brown (with advice from President Franklin D. Roosevelt) to evoke 18th-century regional vernacular residence; built 1940. Interior mural (1942) by Louis Bouche. United States Post Offices in New York State, 1858-1943, Thematic Resources. 11.17.1988

Esopus

John Burroughs Riverby Study
Between US9W and Hudson River, West Park. Small 1-story bark-covered frame building overlooking Hudson River; built 1881 by writer and naturalist John Burroughs as secluded study on his estate Riverby. NHL 11.24.1968

Esopus Meadows Lighthouse
Hudson River. Second Empire frame keeper's dwelling with integral light tower, situated on stone riprap; built 1871. Hudson River Lighthouses Thematic Group. 05.29.1979

Kingston–Port Ewen Suspension Bridge
US9W across Rondout Creek (also in Kingston). A 1,145-foot-long steel single-span suspension bridge built 1919-22 by Terry & Trench Construction Co. 04.30.1980

Perrine's Bridge
Off US87 over Wallkill River (also in town of Rosendale). A 21-acre property with 138-foot-long, single-span, Burr Arch covered wooden bridge built 1844. 04.13.1973

Poppletown Farm House
Old Post Road and Swarte Kill Road. A 1 1/2-story Federal stone farmhouse built c.1802. 11.07.1991

Slabsides (John Burroughs Cabin)
West of West Park. A 16-acre property with rustic bark-covered cabin built 1895 by writer and naturalist John Burroughs as summer wilderness retreat. NHL 11.24.1968

Gardiner

Peter Aldrich Homestead
168 Decker Road. A 15-acre property with Colonial frame former farmhouse built c.1750 incorporated as wing into Federal addition c.1794. Notable interior Federal woodwork. Shawangunk Valley Multiple Resource Area. 09.26.1983

Bevier House
Bevier Road, Tuthilltown. A 42-acre property

Esopus Meadows Lighthouse, Esopus.

with large Victorian frame farmhouse built c.1850; early 20th-century kitchen wing. Property includes barn and sheds. Shawangunk Valley Multiple Resource Area. 09.26.1983

Brykill
Bruynswick Road. A 180-acre rural estate with large rambling stone residence built in several stages; original vernacular section built c.1720; enlarged 1736; substantially enlarged 1927 in Dutch Colonial Revival style by architect Myron Teller for William C. Bruyn. Includes early 20th-century caretaker's house, stables, carriage house, and gazebo. Shawangunk Valley Multiple Resource Area. 09.26.1983

Hendrikus DuBois House
600 Albany Post Road, near Libertyville. Small 1 1/2-story Colonial stone farmhouse built c.1730; incorporated as kitchen wing for 2-story Federal brick and stone residence built c.1820. 07.08.1982

Lake Mohonk Mountain House
(see Marbletown)

Locust Lawn Estate
NY 32, southeast of Gardiner. An 18-acre estate with Colonial stone residence built 1738 by Evert Terwilliger, large 3-story Federal frame residence built 1814 for Colonel Josiah Hasbrouck, and 19th-century outbuildings including slaughterhouse, carriage house, smokehouse, and shed. Now operated as museum by Huguenot Historical Society. 05.17.1974

Tuthilltown Gristmill
Albany Post Road. A 3-story frame water-powered grain mill on Shawangunk Kill; built 1788 by Selah Tuthill; later additions and alterations including late 19th-century processing machinery. Includes 2,500-foot millrace. 06.14.1982

Van Vleck House
Bruynswick Road. A 21-acre property with Federal frame residence built c.1800 and sheds. Shawangunk Valley Multiple Resource Area. 09.26.1983

Hardenbergh

Beaverkill Valley Inn
Beaverkill Road, near Lew Beach. A 60-acre property along Beaverkill River with large 2-story Victorian frame inn built 1895 to lodge sport fisherman. 09.12.1985

Hurley

Hurley Historic District
Main Street, Hurley Mountain Road, and Schoonmaker Lane. Central core of hamlet founded 1662 by Dutch and Huguenot settlers, with 10 Dutch Colonial stone residences, mostly built early to mid-18th century. Also includes early 18th-century Old Hurley Cemetery, Greek Revival frame Reformed Church of Hurley (1853), and 2 non-contiguous properties near hamlet: Colonial vernacular stone Hardenburgh House (c.1750) and Matthias Ten Eyck House (early 18th century; enlarged late 18th century). NHL 11.05.1961

Kingston

Chestnut Street Historic District
Roughly bounded by West Chestnut Street, Broadway, and East Chestnut, Livingston, and Stuyvesant streets. Small residential neighborhood with approximately 40 large Italianate, Second Empire, Queen Anne, Colonial Revival, and Italian Renaissance style frame and masonry residences on landscaped hillside lots; built c.1855-1919. Also includes Victorian Immanuel Lutheran Church (c.1880). 09.19.1985

Clinton Avenue Historic District
Clinton Avenue and Fair Street. Group of 13 late 18th- to early 20th-century frame and masonry residences adjacent to Senate House (individually listed). 02.05.1970

Community Theatre
(Ulster Performing Arts Center)
601 Broadway. A 2-story Neoclassical brick commercial building with Corinthian portico and elaborate classically decorated semicircular domed auditorium; designed by George E. Lowe and builders Skinner & Cook; completed 1927. 07.22.1979

Kingston City Hall
408 Broadway. Large 3-story Second Empire brick building with central bell tower and decorative stone and brick trim; designed by Arthur Crooks; built 1872-73; roof and tower redesigned after 1927 fire. Abandoned since 1971. 12.09.1971

Kingston–Port Ewen Suspension Bridge
(see Esopus)

Kingston Stockade District
Area bounded by both sides of Clinton Avenue, and Main, Green, and Front streets. Central 8-block core of original 17th-century stockaded settlement of Kingston, with commercial and residential areas. Includes eight late 17th-century and approximately twelve 18th- and early 19th-century stone vernacular residences. Also includes Federal, Greek Revival, Italianate, and Second Empire brick and frame residences, 19th-century brick commercial buildings, and individually listed Clinton Avenue Historic District. Notable buildings include Greek Revival stone First Reformed Dutch Church (1852; Minard Lafever) and cemetery, Federal stone Ulster County Courthouse (1818), Greek Revival Kingston Trust Company, and Senate House (individually listed). 06.13.1975

Kingston–Rondout 2 Lighthouse
Hudson River and Rondout Creek. A 2-story Classical Revival brick keeper's dwelling with attached light tower; built 1913. Hudson River Lighthouses Thematic Group. 05.29.1979

Ponckhockie Union Chapel
91 Abruyn Street. Gothic Revival church constructed of poured concrete, stuccoed to resemble ashlar stone; built 1870 by Newark Lime & Cement Co. for families of local cement industry workers. 04.23.1980

Rondout–West Strand Historic District
Roughly bounded by Broadway, Rondout Creek, and Ravine, Hone, and McEntee streets. Large district incorporating major remaining portion of 19th-century Hudson River port village of Rondout, with approximately 275 buildings, including Federal, Greek Revival, Italianate, Second Empire, Queen Anne, and Colonial Revival rowhouses and detached houses, several rows of Italianate brick commercial buildings with cast-iron storefronts, 3 Romanesque Revival churches, and 2 Gothic Revival churches. 08.24.1979

Senate House (State Historic Site)
Clinton Avenue near North Front Street. A 1 1/2-story Colonial stone and brick residence purportedly built late 17th century with major mid-18th-century and later alterations. Used as temporary headquarters for first New York State Senate in 1777. 08.21.1971

West Strand Historic District
West Strand and Broadway. Group of nine 4-story Italianate brick commercial buildings built c.1850-60. 06.28.1974

Lloyd

Anthony Yelverton House
39 Maple Avenue, Highland. Modest 1 1/2-story Colonial frame residence built c.1754; interior remodeled c.1810 in Federal style. 09.22.1983

Poughkeepsie Railroad Bridge
(see Poughkeepsie, Dutchess County)

Marbletown

Delaware and Hudson Canal, Locks at High Falls
NY 213, High Falls. Remains of stone Locks 15 through 20 of canal; built 1852. Also includes abutment of aqueduct built 1849 by John A. Roebling and large vernacular stone DePuy Canal House (1797). Delaware and Hudson Canal Thematic Resources. NHL 11.24.1968

Lake Mohonk Mountain House
Northwest of New Paltz, between Wallkill Valley on east and Rondout Valley on west (also in towns of New Paltz, Rochester, Gardiner, and Rosendale). A 7,500-acre resort complex and nature preserve in Shawangunk Mountains developed late 19th century by Smiley family as healthful retreat and site of numerous humanitarian conferences. 770-foot-long main hotel complex in variety of eclectic styles; built in 9 stages 1879-1910 and ranging from 3 to 7 stories; several sections designed

by Napoleon LeBrun & Sons and James F. Ware. Complex includes gardens, golf course, rustic pavilions, stone towers, and numerous summer cottages and dependencies. 07.16.1973; NHL 06.24.1986

Main Street Historic District, Stone Ridge
US 209, Stone Ridge. Residential core of hamlet, with 36 properties, including large group of 18th-century Dutch Colonial stone residences and outbuildings, numerous Greek Revival frame residences, 3 mid-19th-century commercial buildings, Greek Revival Dutch Reformed Church (1851), and group of early 20th-century Arts and Crafts bungalows. 06.07.1988

New Paltz (Town)

Josiah DuBois Farm
Libertyville Road. A 28-acre farmstead with large Federal brick farmhouse built 1822 and 19th-century frame dependencies including wagon barn, granary, shop, smokehouse, henhouse, privy, well house, and Greek Revival tenant house.   02.18.1988

Lake Mohonk Mountain House
(see Marbletown)

New Paltz (Village)

Jean Hasbrouck House
Huguenot and North Front streets. A 1 1/2-story Colonial stone residence with distinctive high, steep gable roof; built c.1712 by French Huguenot settler. Notable interior includes jambless fireplace. Museum.
NHL 12.24.1967

Huguenot Street Historic District
A 3-block residential area with 5 late 17th- to early 18th-century Colonial stone houses built by French Huguenot settlers. Includes Jean Hasbrouck House (individually listed), DuBois Fort (1705), Bevier-Elting House (1694; enlarged 1724), Abraham Hasbrouck House (1692; pre-1712 additions), and Hugo Freer House (pre-1709; later addition). Also includes altered late 17th-century stone house, 2 late 18th-century houses, Greek Revival brick Reformed Church of New Paltz (1839), and reconstructed French Church. Several residences operated as museums.
NHL 10.09.1960

Plattekill

Thaddeus Hait Farm
75 Allhusen Road, Modena. A 142-acre farm complex with Federal frame and stone farmhouse built c.1825, late 18th-century stone smokehouse and stone barn, c.1800 Dutch barn, early 19th-century granary, and several other outbuildings.   12.29.1988

Reformed Dutch Church of New Hurley
NY 208, north of Wallkill. Greek Revival frame church with Doric portico; built 1835. Adjacent cemetery.   11.29.1982

Rochester

Common School No. 10
Upper Cherrytown Road (Palentown Road), Palentown. Vernacular frame 1-room schoolhouse built c.1870 by Horace Dymond. 09.15.1988

Delaware and Hudson Canal, Alligerville Section
North side of County 27. A 2-mile-long intact section of canal completed 1828 between Honesdale, Pennsylvania, and Kingston, New York, to bring anthracite coal to furnaces in New York. Delaware and Hudson Canal Thematic Resources.   NHL 11.24.1968

Lake Mohonk Mountain House
(see Marbletown)

Rosendale (Town)

Binnewater Historic District
Sawdust Avenue, and Breezy Hill and Binnewater roads. Group of 9 late 19th- and early 20th-century frame buildings associated with Keater family and development of local cement industry. Includes railroad station, privy, store, boarding house, livery stable, cottage, and outbuildings.   11.04.1982

Lake Mohonk Mountain House
(see Marbletown)

Perrine's Bridge (see Esopus)

Rosendale (Village)

All Saints' Chapel (Rosendale Library)
Main Street. Small Gothic Revival church constructed of Rosendale cement, natural cement rock, and brick; built 1870. Converted 1959 for use as library.   09.11.1986

Saugerties (Town)

Trumpbour Homestead Farm
1789 Old Kings Highway, Asbury. An 81-acre farmstead with 1 1/2-story Colonial stone farmhouse built c.1732 by Palatine German immigrants; enlarged c.1760. Also includes mid-19th-century brick tenant house, barn, and early 19th-century residence. 09.19.1985

Wynkoop House
NY 32. A 1 1/2-story Dutch Colonial stone residence in linear form with original 1-room section built c.1740 and large 5-bay adjacent section built c.1760.   09.07.1984

Saugerties (Village)

Loerzel Beer Hall
213 Partition Street. Large 3-story Italianate brick commercial building with interior ballroom; built c.1873 by Lorenz Loerzel. 09.07.1984

Opposite: Lake Mohonk Mountain House, Marbletown.

Abraham Hasbrouck House, Huguenot Street Historic District, Village of New Paltz.

Main-Partition Streets Historic District
Roughly bounded by Main, Partition, Market, and Jane streets. The 8-block commercial core of village, with approximately 80 buildings, mostly 2- and 3-story mid- to late 19th-century brick buildings with 1st-story storefronts. Also includes 2 churches, 3 residences, and 3 brick barns.   07.08.1982

Saugerties Lighthouse
Hudson River at Esopus Creek. A 2-story Italianate brick keeper's dwelling and attached light tower; built 1869. Hudson River Lighthouses Thematic Group.   05.29.1979

Shawangunk

J. B. Crowell & Son Brick Mould Mill Complex
Lippencott Road, near Wallkill. A 13-acre property on Dwaarkill Creek with group of 19 industrial, residential, and agricultural buildings; established 1868 as manufacturing complex. Includes 3-story frame Crowell Mill (1915) and associated structures, Federal frame James B. Crowell III House (c.1800-30) and dependencies, Federal frame Bate House (c.1800), and late 18th- to early 19th-century agricultural complex.   06.30.1983

Johannes Decker Farm
Red Mill Road and Shawangunk Kill. A 65-acre farmstead with 1 1/2-story Dutch Colonial stone residence built c.1720; additions c.1750, 1784, and 1787. Property includes Dutch barn (c.1750) and 18th-century carriage house and icehouse.   03.05.1974

William Decker House
New Prospect Road. A 9-acre property with 1 1/2-story Dutch Colonial stone residence in linear form; original section built c.1730; large 5-bay adjacent section built 1776; 20th-century addition when converted for use as restaurant. Shawangunk Valley Multiple Resource Area.   09.26.1983

Dill Farm
Off Goebel Road. A 23-acre farmstead with Colonial frame residence with steeply pitched overhanging roof; built c.1760; addition and alterations c.1800. Property includes Greek Revival tenant house, barns, milkhouse, and icehouse. Shawangunk Valley Multiple Resource Area.   09.26.1983

Johannes Jansen House and Dutch Barn
Decker Road. A 40-acre farmstead with small 1-story Colonial stone residence built c.1750; large Federal stone addition c.1800. Property includes Dutch barn (c.1760) and corn crib (c.1800). Shawangunk Valley Multiple Resource Area.   09.26.1983

Thomas Jansen House
Jansen Road. A 38-acre property with 1-story Dutch Colonial stone residence built c.1727; Federal stone main section added c.1790. Property includes barn, springhouse, and shed. Shawangunk Valley Multiple Resource Area.   09.26.1983

Miller's House at Red Mills
Red Mills Road and Wallkill Avenue. Greek Revival frame residence with 2-story veranda; built c.1835 for Roe and Arminda Coleman, owners of adjacent mills on Shawangunk Kill. Shawangunk Valley Multiple Resource Area.   09.26.1983

Pearl Street Schoolhouse
Awosting and Decker roads. Vernacular frame 1-room schoolhouse built c.1850; altered and enlarged as residence. Shawangunk Valley Multiple Resource Area.   09.26.1983

Reformed Church of Shawangunk Complex
Hoagerburgh Road, near Bruynswick. Dutch Colonial stone church built 1755; renovated 1794-97; Greek Revival portico and tower added c.1830. Adjacent vernacular stone parsonage (1751, enlarged late 18th century), Colonial Revival frame assembly hall (1916), 19th-century carriage house, and cemetery.   06.03.1982

Terwilliger House
Hoagerburgh Road, east of Bruynswick. A 68-acre farmstead with Colonial frame residence built c.1766; remodeled c.1800 in Federal style. Property includes barn, garage, and shed. Shawangunk Valley Multiple Resource Area.   09.26.1983

Wawarsing

Chetolah
Vista Maria Road, south of Cragsmoor. A 115-acre mountainside estate with large, rambling Queen Anne/eclectic shingled and stuccoed main residence with classical detailing and 10 support structures, including green-house, studio, tennis house, log cabin, stone tower, gatehouse, and secondary residences; designed by landscape painter George Inness, Jr. with architect Howard Greenley as summer house of Inness near Cragsmoor art colony.   10.21.1980

Hoornbeek Store Complex
Main Street, Napanoch. Complex of early 19th-century frame buildings, including Federal William H. Doll House (c.1810), attached Greek Revival Hoornbeek Store (c.1833), vernacular Napanoch Female Seminary (c.1841), and 5 outbuildings.   02.09.1984

Woodstock

Byrdcliffe Historic District
Glasco Turnpike and Larks Nest Road, west of Woodstock. The 190-acre core of rural arts and crafts colony founded 1902-03 by Anglo-American Ralph Radcliffe Whitehead. Includes approximately 40 original buildings built as cottages and studios with design features derived from Stick Style and Swiss chalets. Home of numerous well-known artists, writers, and social theorists including John Dewey, Bolton C. Brown, Charlotte Perkins Gilman, Clarence Darrow, Eva Watson, Edward Thatcher, and Bob Dylan.   05.07.1979

Adirondack State Forest Preserve
(see Clinton County)

Bolton

Sagamore Hotel Complex
Green Island and Federal Hill, Bolton Landing. Resort complex consisting of 36-acre hotel complex on Green Island in Lake George and nearby 266-acre golf course; developed in phases 1883-1930. Principal buildings include rambling Colonial Revival frame main hotel (1922-30, Harold Field Kellog), Tudor Revival golf course clubhouse, Tudor Revival E. B. Warren Cottage (1886, Wilson Brothers), Queen Anne J. B. Simpson House (1886, Wilson Brothers), and several 19th- and early 20th-century support buildings. Golf course designed by Donald J. Ross; constructed 1927.   07.21.1983

Chester

Chestertown Historic District
Canada Drive (US9), Chestertown. Group of 3 buildings at core of hamlet: Greek Revival frame Fowler House (1840s), Victorian Gothic frame Church of the Good Shepherd (1884), and Colonial Revival frame Chester Town Hall (1913, built as high school). Also includes outbuildings and Fowler family cemetery.   08.22.1977

Glens Falls

Argent Apartments
17-18 Sherman Avenue. Large 3-story Second Empire/Queen Anne frame apartment building designed by William E. Lawrence; built 1895. Glens Falls Multiple Resource Area.   09.29.1984

Bemis Eye Sanitarium Complex
Glen Street. Two separate clusters of 4 buildings each, all remodeled or built c.1895 for controversial medical institution. Includes 5 Second Empire/eclectic patient residence halls (c.1895, Ephraim B. Potter), 2 residences, carriage house converted for use by sanitarium and Sherman House (individually listed). Glens Falls Multiple Resource Area.   09.29.1984

Stephen T. Birdsall House
186-192 Ridge Street. Large Queen Anne stone and shingled residence and carriage house built 1884-85 for local physician. Glens Falls Multiple Resource Area.   09.29.1984

Thomas Burnham House
195 Ridge Street. Massive Queen Anne/Colonial Revival frame residence designed by Ephraim B. Potter; built 1897 for local

businessman. Glens Falls Multiple Resource Area: Buildings of Ephraim B. Potter Thematic Resources.   09.29.1984

Addison B. Colvin House
453-455 Glen Street. Large, rambling Queen Anne frame residence built c.1890 for newspaper editor, publisher, and civic leader. Glens Falls Multiple Resource Area.   09.29.1984

W. T. Cowles House
43-47 William Street. Queen Anne/Colonial Revival frame residence designed by Ephraim B. Potter; built 1897 for banker. Glens Falls Multiple Resource Area: Buildings of Ephraim B. Potter Thematic Resources. 09.29.1984

Cunningham House
169 Warren Street. A 2-story eclectic stuccoed residence with Flemish-inspired stepped gables and 2-story enclosed center court; designed by Henry Forbes Bigelow; built 1910-11 as pottery studio for Nell Pruyn; 1919 kitchen service wing designed by Charles A. Platt. Part of Hyde Museum complex. Glens Falls Multiple Resource Area: Buildings of Henry Forbes Bigelow Thematic Resources.   09.29.1984

Zopher Delong House
(Chapman Historical Museum)
348 Glen Street. Large Italianate/Second Empire brick residence and carriage house built c.1870 for hardware merchant; design attributed to Marcus F. Cummings. Notable interior. Operated as museum by Glens Falls–Queensbury Historical Association. Glens Falls Multiple Resource Area.   09.29.1984

James L. Dix House
191 Ridge Street. Italianate brick residence built c.1866 for prominent industrialist; remodeled early 20th century in Colonial Revival style. Glens Falls Multiple Resource Area. 09.29.1984

18th Separate Company Armory
143-149 Warren Street. Monumental Romanesque Revival brick and stone armory with crenellated tower; built 1895; design attributed to Isaac G. Perry. Glens Falls Multiple Resource Area.   09.29.1984

Dr. James Ferguson Office
5 Culvert Street. Small Second Empire brick building built c.1870 as physician's office. Glens Falls Multiple Resource Area.   09.29.1984

First Presbyterian Church
402-410 Glen Street. Imposing Gothic Revival granite and limestone church designed by Ralph Adams Cram; built 1927. Glens Falls Multiple Resource Area.   09.29.1984

Dr. Charles A. Foster House
162-164 Warren Street. Large Queen Anne stone and shingled residence with 3-story circular corner tower; built 1889 for physician. Glens Falls Multiple Resource Area. 09.29.1984

Fredella Avenue Historic District
15-21R Fredella Avenue. Group of 8 modest Colonial Revival residences constructed of molded concrete block; built 1914-18 by Fredella Co. builders as speculative housing. Glens Falls Multiple Resource Area: Fredella Concrete Block Structures Thematic Resources. 09.29.1984

Joseph J. Fredella House and Garage
15-17 Mohican Street. Colonial Revival residence and garage constructed of rusticated molded concrete block; built 1912 by Fredella Co. builders as residence for head of company. Glens Falls Multiple Resource Area: Fredella Concrete Block Structures Thematic Resources. 09.29.1984

Glens Falls Feeder Canal
Roughly between Richardson Street and Old Champlain Canal (also in Queensbury and Washington County). A 7-mile-long hydraulic and former transportation canal parallel to Hudson River between Glens Falls and Champlain Canal in Fort Edward, Washington County, with total descent of 130 feet; completed 1829 under supervision of engineer James Walker to supply water to Champlain Canal; altered to navigable waterway 1830s and closed to traffic 1928. Includes 13 bluestone locks (1873-75) and other features. Remains in use as feeder to Champlain Barge Canal. Glens Falls Multiple Resource Area. 10.25.1985

Glens Falls High School
421-433 Glen Street. Massive 4-story Neoclassical/Georgian Revival brick school with cast-stone trim; designed by Ephraim B. Potter; built 1905; enlarged 1925; modern additions. Glens Falls Multiple Resource Area: Buildings of Ephraim B. Potter Thematic Resources. 09.29.1984

Glens Falls Home for Aged Women
178-186 Warren Street. Massive Colonial Revival brick residence with gambrel roof and elaborate stone and wood decorative features; built 1903. Glens Falls Multiple Resource Area. 09.29.1984

Stephen L. Goodman House
65-67 Park Street. Large Greek Revival/Italianate vernacular brick residence built c.1860 for prominent industrialist family overlooking their limestone processing works. Glens Falls Multiple Resource Area. 09.29.1984

Hoopes House
153 Warren Street. Large Colonial Revival stuccoed residence designed by Henry Forbes Bigelow; built 1904 for engineer Maurice Hoopes and Mary Pruyn Hoopes. Glens Falls Multiple Resource Area: Buildings of Henry Forbes Bigelow Thematic Resources. 09.29.1984

Hyde House
161 Warren Street. Large 2-story stuccoed residence in style of Italian Renaissance palazzo with enclosed central court; designed by Henry Forbes Bigelow; built 1910-11 for Louis Fiske

and Charlotte Pruyn Hyde as residence and art gallery. Operated as museum by The Hyde Collection Trust. Glens Falls Multiple Resource Area: Buildings of Henry Forbes Bigelow Thematic Resources.   09.29.1984

Joubert and White Building
79 Warren Street. Large 3-story brick factory/warehouse building with restrained Neoclassical decorative features; built 1905 as factory and salesroom for prominent carriage manufacturer; used after 1911 as garage and automobile showroom. Glens Falls Multiple Resource Area.   09.29.1984

Hiram Krum House
133 Warren Street. Large Italianate/Second Empire brick residence built c.1865 by local contractor as his own residence; design derived from pattern book *Architecture* (1865), by Marcus F. Cummings. Glens Falls Multiple Resource Area.   09.29.1984

Russell M. Little House
17 Center Street. Victorian frame residence with elaborate carpenter Gothic trim; built 1876 for founder of Glens Falls Insurance Co. Glens Falls Multiple Resource Area. 09.29.1984

William McEchron House
65 Ridge Street. Massive Queen Anne/Shingle Style stone and shingled residence built 1891 for lumber merchant. Glens Falls Multiple Resource Area.   09.29.1984

Jones Ordway House
142 Warren Street. Vernacular brick residence built c.1850; altered c.1885 in Queen Anne style for owner of lumber company. Glens Falls Multiple Resource Area.   09.29.1984

George H. Parks House
444 Glen Street. Large Queen Anne frame residence with massive 3-story cylindrical corner tower and decorative shingles; built c.1900 for son of local paper manufacturer. Glens Falls Multiple Resource Area. 09.29.1984

John E. Parry House
146 Warren Street. Large Queen Anne/Colonial Revival frame residence designed by Ephraim B. Potter; built 1890-91 for banker. Glens Falls Multiple Resource Area: Buildings of Ephraim B. Potter Thematic Resources.   09.29.1984

Peyser and Morrison Shirt Company Building
211-217 Warren Street. Block-long, 2-story Romanesque/Classical Revival brick industrial building with highly embellished principal facade; designed by Ephraim B. Potter; built c.1893 as shirt factory. Glens Falls Multiple Resource Area: Buildings of Ephraim B. Potter Thematic Resources.   09.29.1984

Ephraim B. Potter House
15 Sherman Avenue. Queen Anne/Colonial Revival frame residence designed by and built for architect Ephraim B. Potter; built 1900. Glens Falls Multiple Resource Area: Buildings of Ephraim B. Potter Thematic Resources. 09.29.1984

Enoch Rosekrans House
62 Warren Street. Large Italianate/Greek Revival brick residence built c.1855 by contractor Lindsey Pike for local attorney and civic leader. Glens Falls Multiple Resource Area. 09.29.1984

A. S. Rugge House
428 Glen Street. Italianate brick residence built c.1880 for shirt, collar, and cuff manufacturer. Glens Falls Multiple Resource Area. 09.29.1984

St. Mary's Academy
10-12 Church Street. Monumental 3-story Gothic Revival sandstone school with tall central entrance/carillon tower; designed by Ralph Adams Cram; built 1930. Glens Falls Multiple Resource Area. 09.29.1984

Sherman House
380 Glen Street. Imposing Italianate brick residence with large octagonal cupola; built 1850s for businessman Augustus Sherman; altered c.1897 as part of Bemis Eye Sanitarium. 11.07.1977

Smith Flats
53-61 Bay Street. Large 3-story Victorian frame apartment building with 3-story porches; designed by William E. Lawrence; built c.1895. Glens Falls Multiple Resource Area. 09.29.1984

Society of Friends Hall
172-174 Ridge Street. A 2-story Italianate brick building built 1875 as Quaker meeting hall; design attributed to Marcus F. Cummings. Converted for commercial use. Glens Falls Multiple Resource Area. 09.29.1984

Thomas Stilwell House
134 Maple Street. Italianate/Eastlake frame residence built c.1876 for hardware merchant. Glens Falls Multiple Resource Area. 09.29.1984

Three Squares Historic District
Roughly South, Glen, Maple, and Ridge streets. Commercial and civic core of city, with 77 buildings, mostly 2- to 5-story Italianate, Romanesque Revival, Queen Anne, Beaux-Arts, Neoclassical, and Colonial Revival brick buildings built late 19th to early 20th century. Notable buildings include Italianate brick Cowles Block (c.1865, Marcus F. Cummings), Neoclassical Rogers Building (1926), Colonial Revival brick Crandall Library (1930, Charles A. Platt), Beaux-Arts terra-cotta Saunders Building (1907), Neoclassical brick City Hall (1900, Fuller & Pitcher), and Beaux-Arts Empire Theater (1899, J. B. McElphatrick). Glens Falls Multiple Resource Area. 09.29.1984

F. W. Wait House
173-175 Ridge Street. Large Italianate/Second Empire brick residence built c.1876 for local lime manufacturer; design derived from pattern book *Architectural Details*, by Marcus F. Cummings. Glens Falls Multiple Resource Area. 09.29.1984

House at 216 Warren Street
Second Empire frame residence built c.1875; design inspired by pattern book of architect Gilbert B. Croff. Glens Falls Multiple Resource Area. 09.29.1984

Martin L. C. Wilmarth House
528 Glen Street. Colonial Revival frame residence with elaborate decorative trim; designed by Ephraim B. Potter; built c.1910-11 for furniture and wallpaper manufacturer. Adjacent original carriage house. Glens Falls Multiple Resource Area: Buildings of Ephraim B. Potter Thematic Resources. 09.29.1984

Helen Wing House
126 Warren Street. Large Queen Anne/Colonial Revival residence designed by Ephraim B. Potter; built c.1893 for widow of prosperous grocer. Glens Falls Multiple Resource Area: Buildings of Ephraim B. Potter Thematic Resources. 09.29.1984

Hague

Grace Memorial Union Chapel
Sabbath Day Point Road. Queen Anne eclectic stone church with Rustic and Picturesque decorative elements; designed by William B. Tuthill; built 1885 for summer residents of Lake George. 08.11.1982

Silver Bay Association Complex
NY9N, Silver Bay. A 97-acre summer resort on Lake George, with 32 historic buildings, including massive Silver Bay Inn, Rustic-style auditorium, chapel, and numerous guest cottages, dormitories, and service and recreational buildings; developed 1880 to 1925, originally as hotel; since 1902 training and conference center for Young Men's Christian Association personnel. 03.20.1980

Johnsburg

North Creek Railroad Station Complex
Railroad Place, North Creek. A 6-acre complex of buildings and structures, including Stick Style passenger station, old station, horse barn, roundhouse, toolhouse, turntable, and freight house; built 1871-74 at northern terminus of Adirondack Railroad. Associated with recreational and industrial development of Adirondacks. 08.27.1976

Lake George (Town)

Royal C. Peabody Estate (Wikiosco)
Lake Shore Drive. A 5-acre section of summer estate on Lake George with massive rambling Tudor Revival stone and half-timbered residence designed by Charles S. Peabody for his father; built c.1905. 06.21.1984

Lake George (Village)

Old Warren County Courthouse Complex
Canada and Amherst streets. Complex of 5 attached Victorian brick buildings built in 4 stages: Courthouse (1845), towered Courthouse facade and judges chamber (1878), and jail and addition (1890s). Adapted for use as museum and civic center. 06.19.1973

United States Post Office–Lake George
Canada and James streets. Colonial Revival/Moderne brick post office built 1940-41. Interior mural (1942) by Judson Smith. United States Post Offices in New York State, 1858-1943, Thematic Resources. 05.11.1989

Queensbury

Owl's Nest (Edward Eggleston Estate)
NY9L, Joshua's Rock, Lake George. A 10-acre estate on Lake George with complex of rustic stone and frame residences and library built c.1879-90. Principal residence of novelist Edward Eggleston from 1881 until his death in 1902. NHL 11.11.1971

Warrensburg

Merrill MaGee House
2 Hudson Street. Greek Revival frame residence built c.1833; large addition with pedimented portico added for industrialist Stephen Griffin II. Property developed in early 20th century as country retreat. Includes 19th- and early 20th-century outbuildings and significant landscape features.   04.11.1985

Warrensburg Mills Historic District
Roughly bounded by Osborne and Woolen Mill bridges, Schroon River, and railroad right of way. A 40-acre 19th- and early 20th-century industrial and residential district along Schroon River with mills, farm-supply store, grain warehouses, 2 bridges, and approximately 50 vernacular and frame residences built for mill workers.   09.18.1975

WASHINGTON COUNTY

Cambridge (Town)

Buskirk Covered Bridge
Buskirk, over Hoosic River (also in town of Hoosick, Rensselaer County). A 160-foot-long, single-span Howe patent truss covered wooden bridge built c.1850. Covered Bridges of Washington County Thematic Resources. 03.08.1978

Cambridge (Village)

Cambridge Historic District
Irregular pattern along Main and South Union streets. Principal core of village, with approximately 240 buildings built late 18th to early 20th centuries, including residential and commercial buildings, 4 churches, printing industry, railroad station, hotel, former school, and 2 mills. Notable buildings include Georgian Federal Dorr-Randall residence (1779), numerous Federal and Greek Revival residences, Italianate Cambridge Hotel, Rice Seed Company complex, and Second Empire Opera House (1878).   11.15.1978

Easton

Coffin Site
Address restricted. Stratified multicomponent prehistoric archeological site with evidence of Late Archaic, Transitional, and Woodland stage Native-American occupation.   07.22.1980

DeRidder Homestead
Off NY29, east of Schuylerville. A 7-acre farmstead on Hudson River with Federal brick residence built 1792, incorporating earlier

residence as wing. Includes outbuildings. 03.22.1974

Fort Edward (Town)

Glens Falls Feeder Canal
(see Glens Falls, Warren County)

Old Champlain Canal
(see Waterford, Saratoga County)

Fort Edward (Village)

Old Champlain Canal
(see Waterford, Saratoga County)

Old Fort House
29 Lower Broadway. Large Colonial frame residence with gambrel roof; built 1772-73 by Patrick Smyth; extensively remodeled 1839 in Federal/Greek Revival style. Served as Charlotte County Courthouse (1773-75) and military headquarters during American Revolution. Museum.   09.15.1983

Rogers Island
Hudson River, west of Fort Edward. A 40-acre section of island with prehistoric and historic archeological sites from Woodland stage occupations through American Revolution. Key strategic site during French and Indian Wars and American Revolution.   07.24.1973

Granville

Lemuel Haynes House
NY149, South Granville. Vernacular frame farmhouse built 1793. Residence of Lemuel Haynes, first ordained African-American minister in United States and first African-American minister to white congregation, 1822-33.   NHL 05.15.1975

Opposite: Grace Memorial Union Chapel, Hague.

Village Park, Hudson Falls Historic District (p. 174).

United States Post Office–Granville
41 Main Street. Colonial Revival brick post office built 1935-36. United States Post Offices in New York State, 1858-1943, Thematic Resources. 05.11.1989

Greenwich

Old Champlain Canal
(see Waterford, Saratoga County)

Hampton

William Miller Chapel and Ascension Rock
County 11, west of Fair Haven, Vermont. Modest Greek Revival frame church (1848) and large rock outcropping associated with beginning of Advent Christian movement in the United States. 07.17.1975

Hudson Falls

Glens Falls Feeder Canal
(see Glens Falls, Warren County)

Hudson Falls Historic District
Roughly bounded by Oak, Mechanic, River, Maple, and Main streets. Central core of village, with approximately 150 buildings, including 19th-century commercial and civic buildings surrounding village park and numerous residential buildings, built throughout 19th century and early 20th century. Notable buildings include Italianate Washington County Courthouse (1873, Marcus F. Cummings), Italianate and Romanesque Revival commercial blocks on Main Street, and numerous Federal, Greek Revival, Italianate, Second Empire, Queen Anne, and Colonial Revival residences. 09.15.1983 ILLUS. P. 173

United States Post Office–Hudson Falls
114 Main Street. Colonial Revival brick post office built 1935-36. Interior mural (1937) by George Picken. United States Post Offices in New York State, 1858-1943, Thematic Resources. 05.11.1989

Jackson

Eagleville Covered Bridge
Eagleville Road, over Batten Kill (also in town of Salem). A 100-foot-long, single-span Town patent truss covered wooden bridge built 1858 by Ephraim Clapp. Covered Bridges of Washington County Thematic Resources. 03.08.1978

Rexleigh Covered Bridge
Rexleigh Road, over Batten Kill (also in town of Salem). A 107-foot-long single-span Howe patent truss covered wooden bridge built 1874. Covered Bridges of Washington County Thematic Resources. 03.08.1978

Shushan Covered Bridge
Shushan hamlet, over Batten Kill (also in town of Salem). A 161-foot-long, double-span (continuous) Town patent truss covered wooden bridge built 1858 by Milton Stevens. Museum. Covered Bridges of Washington County Thematic Resources. 03.08.1978

Kingsbury

Glens Falls Feeder Canal
(see Glens Falls, Warren County)

Old Champlain Canal
(see Waterford, Saratoga County)

Salem

Eagleville Covered Bridge (see Jackson)

Rexleigh Covered Bridge (see Jackson)

Salem Historic District
Broadway and Main Street. Cross-shaped section of village core, with 79 residences, commercial buildings, and churches, mostly built second half of 19th century. Notable buildings include Georgian Judge Blanchard House (1790), Federal Judge John McLean House, Greek Revival First Presbyterian Church, Proudfit-Sherman House, Victorian Proudfit Building (1890), and Italianate Washington County Courthouse (1869, Marcus F. Cummings). 05.28.1975

Shushan Covered Bridge (see Jackson)

White Creek

White Creek Historic District
NY 68, Byars and Niles roads. Hamlet settled by Quakers in late 18th century, with 22 properties, mostly frame Federal, Greek Revival, and Victorian residences. Notable buildings include 3 Georgian frame residences built 1770-72 and 3 Greek Revival commercial buildings built c.1840. 04.26.1979

Whitehall (Town)

Old Champlain Canal
(see Waterford, Saratoga County)

Whitehall (Village)

Main Street Historic District
Williams Street and both sides of Main Street Bridge. A 3-block-long row of 40 mostly 2- and 3-story brick commercial buildings facing Champlain Canal; built late 19th century in variety of styles. 04.24.1975

Old Champlain Canal
(see Waterford, Saratoga County)

Judge Joseph Potter House (Skene Manor)
Mountain Terrace. Massive Victorian Gothic stone residence designed by Almon Chandler Hopson; built 1874 for well-known lawyer and judge. 05.02.1974

United States Post Office–Whitehall
88 Broadway. Colonial Revival brick post office built 1938. Interior mural (1940) by Axel Horn. United States Post Offices in New York State, 1858-1943, Thematic Resources. 05.11.1989

WAYNE COUNTY

Clyde

United States Post Office–Clyde
26 South Park Street. Colonial Revival brick post office built 1940-41. Interior mural (1941) by Thomas Donnelly. United States Post Offices in New York State, 1858-1943, Thematic Resources. 11.17.1988

Lyons

Broad Street–Water Street Historic District
Commercial core of village with 28 buildings, mostly built 1830-90 during development as Erie Canal town. Notable buildings include Knowles Block (1852, cast-iron storefront), and Greek Revival Exchange Buildings (1835). 08.14.1973

Hotchkiss Essential Oil Company Plant
93-95 Water Street. A 2-story vernacular frame commercial/industrial building built c.1885. Site of development of essential oil industry (peppermint, spearmint, etc.) in America. 11.02.1987

United States Post Office–Lyons
1-5 Pearl Street. Colonial Revival brick post office built 1931-32. United States Post Offices in New York State, 1858-1943, Thematic Resources. 05.11.1989

Macedon

Charles Bullis House
1727 Canandaigua Road. A 6-acre property with 2-story Federal/Greek Revival cobblestone residence built 1839; frame rear wing built 1845 (rebuilt 1983). 03.20.1986

Newark

United States Post Office–Newark
Maple Court and South Main Street. Neoclassical stuccoed masonry post office designed by James Knox Taylor; built 1912-13. United States Post Offices in New York State, 1858-1943, Thematic Resources. 05.11.1989

Detail of Charles Bullis House, Macedon.

Ontario

Brick Church Corners
Junction of Brick Church and Ontario Center roads. Rural crossroads with vernacular buildings, including brick church (1866), frame residence (late 1830s), 1-room brick schoolhouse (1869), and log cabin (relocated and reconstructed 1972). 06.05.1974

Palmyra

East Main Street Commercial Historic District
Between Clinton and William-Cuyler streets. A 2-block area with 19th-century 2- and 3-story Italianate brick commercial blocks, many with cast-iron storefronts. Includes Greek Revival Palmyra Hotel (1835-37). 11.21.1974

Market Street Historic District
Market Street between Canal and Main streets. A 1-block section of commercial street with 14 buildings, mostly built 1830s-80s during development as Erie Canal town. Notable buildings include cobblestone building at 105 Market Street (c.1830), Old Ritter Store (c.1830), Federal Cole-Johncox House (c.1830), and Sybil Phelps House with cast-iron storefront (c.1845). 12.08.1972

Sodus Point

Customs House
Sentell Street. A 2-story Italianate brick commercial building built 1874 as bank; used as custom house after 1885. 05.06.1980

Lotus
A 47-foot-long plank-on-frame auxiliary schooner designed 1916 by William H. Hand, Jr.; built 1917-18 by Rocky River Drydock Co., Ohio, as yacht *Miss Glouster* for T. B. Van Dorn. 05.10.1990

Sodus Point Lighthouse
Off NY14 at Lake Ontario. A 45-foot-tall stone lighthouse and attached 2-story stone

residence built 1871; frame addition in 1892. 10.08.1976

Williamson

Pultneyville Historic District
Sections of Lake Road and Jay Street, Pultneyville. Historic residential core of hamlet, with 33 buildings built c.1810-90s. Includes many examples of Federal and Greek Revival styles and some late 19th-century residences, including prominent Second Empire mansion at 4138 Lake Road (c.1865). 09.11.1985

WESTCHESTER COUNTY

Bedford

Bedford Village Historic District
Roughly bounded by Court, Seminary, Pound Ridge, and Greenwich roads. Historic core of original hamlet founded 1680 by settlers from Connecticut, with several public and commercial buildings, cemetery, and late 18th- to mid-19th-century residences on large lots surrounding village green. Notable buildings include vernacular frame County Courthouse (1787), Historical Hall (1806), library (1807), stone schoolhouse (1829), Greek Revival post office (1838), and Gothic Revival frame Presbyterian Church (1872). 10.02.1973

John Jay Homestead (State Historic Site)
Jay Street, Katonah. A 60-acre property with 2 1/2-story Federal frame residence with gambrel roof; built 1787 as country seat of John Jay, major American political figure from American Revolution to end of 18th century; enlarged 1800-02, 1818, and later; extensive mid-20th-century restoration. Outbuildings include brick farm manager's house (1798-1800), schoolhouse (1824-28), several early 19th-century barns and sheds, and later buildings. 07.24.1972; NHL 05.29.1981

Katonah Village Historic District
Parkway, Valleyedge, Edgemont, and Bedford roads, Katonah. Small residential neighborhood with approximately 35 buildings on grid plan and landscaped parkway designed 1895 by Olmsted Brothers. Includes concentration of large Queen Anne residences, several 19th-century buildings moved from old village, 3 churches, and Colonial Revival stone Katonah Village Library (1928, Kerr Rainsford). 09.15.1983

Merestead (Sloane Estate)
Byram Lake Road (also in town of New Castle). A 136-acre estate with large Georgian Revival brick residence, several support buildings, and formal and informal landscaping; designed by Delano & Aldrich; built 1906-07 for William Sloane, president of New York City furniture

manufacturing company. Includes farm buildings predating estate. 09.27.1984

Briarcliff Manor

Old Croton Aqueduct (see Yonkers)

Bronxville

Bronx River Parkway Reservation
From Sprain Brook Parkway to Kensico Dam Plaza (also in towns of East Chester, Scarsdale, Greenburgh, Mount Pleasant, North Castle; cities of Yonkers and White Plains; and village of Tuckahoe). A 10-mile-long section of landscaped automobile parkway along Bronx River, ranging in width from 200 to 1,200 feet; planned and built 1906-25. Includes numerous landscape features, 32 bridges, and 2 service stations. Principal designers include landscape architects Hermann Merkel and Gilmore D. Clarke, and engineers Jay Downer, Leslie Holleran, and Arthur Hayden. Consulting architects include Charles W. Stoughton, Carrère & Hastings, Delano & Aldrich, Palmer & Hornbostel, Bowdoin & Webster, and Penrose V. Stout. Reservation also includes Art Deco Westchester County Center (c.1927-30, Walker & Gillette). 01.11.1991

Lawrence Park Historic District
Roughly bounded by Side Hill, Prescott, Kensington, Garden, and Chestnut avenues, Maidens Lane, and Valley and Pondfield roads. A 20-acre suburban residential neighborhood developed 1888 to early 20th century by William Van Duzer Lawrence, with approximately 98 large Tudor Revival, Shingle Style, Colonial Revival, and eclectic residences on large, irregular lots; many designed by William A. Bates. Home of many prominent artists and writers of the period. 01.23.1980

Masterton-Dusenberry House
90 White Plains Road. Greek Revival frame residence with Doric porch; built early 1830s as summer residence for Alexander Masterton, prosperous marble quarry owner. 04.16.1980

United States Post Office–Bronxville
Pondfield Road. Colonial Revival brick post office designed by Eric Kebbon; built 1937-38. Interior mural (1939) by John Sloan. United States Post Offices in New York State, 1858-1943, Thematic Resources. 11.17.1988

Cortlandt

Bear Mountain Bridge
(see Stony Point, Rockland County)

Bear Mountain Bridge Road
NY6 and 202. A 3-mile-long, 2-lane scenic highway built 1923-24 by Terry & Trench Construction Co. and Carey Construction Co as toll road for Bear Mountain–Hudson River Bridge Co. Includes Tudor Revival toll house. Hudson Highlands Multiple Resource Area. 11.23.1982

John Jones Homestead
Oregon Road and Durrin Avenue, Van
Cortlandtville. Large Federal frame residence
with gambrel roof; built c.1790; possibly
incorporates mid-18th-century building.
05.25.1989

Old Croton Aqueduct (see Yonkers)

Old St. Peter's Church
Oregon Road and Locust Avenue, Van
Cortlandtville. Modest Colonial frame church
built 1766-67.   03.07.1973

Site of Old Croton Dam; New Croton Dam
NY129, north of Ossining (site of Old Croton
Dam located in town of Yorktown; New
Croton Dam located in town of Cortlandt). Old
Croton Dam: 670-foot-long, 57-foot-high
rubble and granite dam designed by engineer-in-
charge John B. Jervis; built 1837-42 for New
York City water supply system; now submerged
in New Croton Reservoir. New Croton Dam:
1,168-foot-long, 291-foot-high rubble and
granite dam designed by engineers Alphonse
Fteley, William R. Hill, J. Waldo Smith, and
Walter H. Sears; built 1893-1906 for New York
City water supply system. 06.19.1973

Van Cortlandt Upper Manor House
Oregon Road. Large Colonial brick residence
built 1770s by prominent Van Cortlandt family;
remodeled c.1850 in Picturesque style and used
as country estate by New York City businessman James Robertson; large additions c.1820
and later.   04.02.1981

Van Cortlandtville School
(Common District School No. 10)
297 Locust Avenue, Van Cortlandtville. Gothic
Revival frame 1-room schoolhouse built
c.1850.   04.07.1989

Croton-on-Hudson

Croton North Railroad Station
Albany Post Road (US9). A 1-story eclectic
brick suburban passenger station built c.1890
by New York Central Railroad. Includes 2
Pullman-Standard coach cars built 1930.
08.27.1987

Van Cortlandt Manor
US9, north of junction with US9A. A 2 1/2-story
Dutch Colonial/Georgian stone residence with
2-story wood porch; built c.1748-49 incorporating earlier residence as manor house of
Cortlandt Manor. Extensive mid-20th-century
restoration of house and reconstruction of
outbuildings. Operated as house museum by
Historic Hudson Valley.   NHL 11.05.1961

Dobbs Ferry

Estherwood and Carriage House
Clinton Avenue. A 10-acre former estate with
massive Chateauesque/French Renaissance style
brick residence with granite and terra-cotta
trim, and elaborate exterior and interior

decorative features; designed by Buchman &
Deisler; built 1894-95 for inventor James
Jennings McComb. Acquired 1910 by Masters
School for Girls. Includes large carriage house.
11.20.1979

Hyatt-Livingston House
152 Broadway. Large Colonial frame residence
built 18th century incorporating small c.1698
residence; large Georgian/Federal addition
c.1779-1810 for Philip Livingston, merchant
and politician.   10.05.1972; DEMOLISHED
1983

Old Croton Aqueduct (see Yonkers)

United States Post Office–Dobbs Ferry
Main Street. Colonial Revival brick post office
built 1935-36. United States Post Offices in
New York State, 1858-1943, Thematic
Resources.   11.17.1988

East Chester

Bronx River Parkway Reservation
(see Bronxville)

Armour-Stiner House, Irvington (p. 178).

Opposite: Schooner Lotus, *Sodus Point.*

Elmsford

Elmsford Reformed Church and Cemetery
30 South Central Avenue. A 2-story vernacular shingled church built 1793. Adjacent 18th-century cemetery.   09.15.1983

Greenburgh

Bronx River Parkway Reservation
(see Bronxville)

East Irvington School
Taxter Road, East Irvington. A 2-story Romanesque Revival/eclectic school built 1891; 2nd story added 1925.   10.06.1983

Odell House (Rochambeau Headquarters)
425 Ridge Road. A 1 1/2-story vernacular shingled residence built 1732 by John Tompkins as farmhouse on Philipsburg Manor; additions in 1765, 1785, 1853-55, and 1900. Headquarters of Count de Rochambeau and campsite of French forces in 1781 during American Revolution.   03.28.1973

Harrison

Reid Hall, Manhattanville College
Purchase Street, Purchase. Large 3-story Romanesque Revival former residence with crenellated tower and parapets; designed by Stanford White; completed 1892 for publisher Whitelaw Reid; massive addition designed 1912 by McKim, Mead & White. Notable interior.   03.22.1974

United States Post Office–Harrison
258 Halstead Avenue. Colonial Revival stone post office built 1938-39. Interior mural (1941) by Harold Goodwin. United States Post Offices in New York State, 1858-1943, Thematic Resources.   05.11.1989

Hastings-on-Hudson

Jasper F. Cropsey House and Studio
49 Washington Avenue. A 4-acre property overlooking Hudson River with Gothic Revival frame residence originally built c.1832, enlarged c.1885 by Hudson River School painter Jasper F. Cropsey as his country house and studio; occupied by him until his death in 1900.   05.17.1973

John W. Draper House
407 Broadway. Picturesque frame residence built c.1840. Home of John W. Draper, renowned for research in photochemistry, chemistry, physiology, and history; occupied by him until his death in 1882.   NHL 05.15.1975

Hastings Prototype House
546 Farragut Parkway. Modest 2-story Moderne residence constructed of prefabricated concrete; designed by Charles A. Horn; built 1936 by Louis Gelbman.   12.19.1991

Old Croton Aqueduct (see Yonkers)

Irvington

Armour-Stiner House
45 West Clinton Avenue. Large Second Empire/eclectic octagonal frame residence with domed roof, cupola, and elaborate wood and cast-iron decorative details; built 1859-60 for New York City financier Paul J. Armour; enlarged and present dome added c.1876 for tea importer Joseph Stiner; later residence of historian Carl Carmer. Notable interior with 4-story central hall and staircase.   12.18.1975; NHL 12.08.1976 ILLUS. P. 177

Irvington Town Hall
85 Main Street. Large 2-story Colonial Revival brick building with stone and terra-cotta trim and ornate clock tower; designed by Alfred J. Manning; built 1901-02. Interior theater and library with decorative features by Tiffany Glass & Decoration Co.   11.01.1984

Nuits (Cottenet-Brown House)
Hudson Road and Clifton Place, Ardsley-on-Hudson. A 4-acre estate overlooking Hudson River with large Italianate stone villa designed by Detlef Lienau; built 1852 for New York City merchant Francis Cottenet; enlarged 1858-59 and interiors modified late 19th and early 20th century. Landscaped grounds.   04.18.1977

Old Croton Aqueduct (see Yonkers)

Villa Lewaro
North Broadway. A 5-acre estate overlooking Hudson River, with Italian Renaissance style residence and grounds; designed by Vertner W. Tandy, first African-American architect registered in New York State; completed 1918 for African-American entrepreneur Madame C. J. Walker.   NHL 05.11.1976

Larchmont

United States Post Office–Larchmont
One Chatsworth Avenue. Classical Revival brick post office designed by William Dewey Foster; built 1937-38. United States Post Offices in New York State, 1858-1943, Thematic Resources.   5.11.1989

Lewisboro

Bridge L-158
West of Goldens Bridge at Croton River (also in town of Somers). A 163-foot-long double intersection Whipple through truss cast- and wrought-iron bridge manufactured 1883 by Clarke, Reeves & Co. as 1 of 3 spans to carry New York, West Shore, and Buffalo Railroad over Rondout Creek near Kingston; moved 1904 to present location.   11.29.1978

Mount Kisco

St. Mark's Cemetery
East Main Street and St. Mark's Place. A 1-acre cemetery established 1761; served as burial ground for 2 churches, veterans of American Revolution, and local citizens.   06.23.1988

St. Mark's Episcopal Church
North Bedford Road and East Main Street. Gothic Revival stone church designed by Bertram G. Goodhue; built 1909-13; tower added 1919-20; side aisle and parish hall built 1927-28.   11.21.1991

United Methodist Church and Parsonage
300 East Main Street and 31 Smith Avenue. Victorian Gothic frame church with elaborate decorative trim; designed by J. King; built 1866-68 by local builder Edward Dauchey; 20th-century additions.   11.04.1982

Mount Pleasant

Bronx River Parkway Reservation
(see Bronxville)

Hammond House
South of Hawthorne on Grasslands Road. A 1 1/2-story Colonial farmhouse built c.1719 by William Hammond on Philipsburg Manor; enlarged 1835 and 1860. Museum.   05.06.1980

John A. Hartford House
NY100, southwest of Valhalla. A 10-acre former estate with massive Tudor Revival stone residence completed 1932 for John A. Hartford, pioneer merchandising genius of the Great Atlantic and Pacific Tea Co. (A & P). Now part of Westchester Community College.   NHL 12.22.1977

John D. Rockefeller Estate (Kykuit)
Pocantico Hills. A 250-acre estate developed 1890s-1930s by oil magnate and philanthropist John D. Rockefeller and family. Includes massive Georgian Revival stone main residence (1907-09, Delano & Aldrich; enlarged 1911-13), elaborate formal and informal gardens (William Welles Bosworth), Japanese Gardens (1908-09, Uyeda & Takahashi), 20th-century sculpture collected by Nelson A. Rockefeller, Orangerie (1907, William Welles Bosworth), carriage house, stables (1907-08, William Welles Bosworth; enlarged 1915 as garage), and other dependencies.   NHL 05.11.1976

Mount Vernon

St. Paul's Church National Historic Site
897 South Columbus Avenue. Georgian stone church begun 1765; completed 1805. Associated with John Peter Zenger trial regarding freedom of the press. Bill of Rights museum occupies parish hall.   07.05.1943

John Stevens House
29 West Fourth Street. Large Greek Revival frame residence with Doric porch; built 1849-51. Home of founder of Mount Vernon.   04.26.1972

United States Post Office–Mount Vernon
15 South First Street. Large Neoclassical limestone post office designed by Oscar Wenderoth; built 1915-17; side wings added 1936. United States Post Offices in New York State, 1858-1943, Thematic Resources. 05.11.1989

New Castle

Chappaqua Railroad Depot and Depot Plaza
200 South Greeley Avenue, Chappaqua. A 1-story eclectic stone passenger station and entrance plaza built 1901-02. Horace Greeley Thematic Resources. 04.19.1979

Church of St. Mary the Virgin and Greeley Grove
191 South Greeley Avenue, Chappaqua. Gothic Revival stone church modeled after English church; designed by Morgan M. O'Brien; built 1904-05 for Gabrielle Greeley Clendenin, only surviving child of Horace Greeley, and her husband. Horace Greeley Thematic Resources. 04.19.1979

Greeley House
100 King Street, Chappaqua. Vernacular frame residence built c.1820 and later altered. Residence of Horace Greeley family 1864-72. Horace Greeley Thematic Resources. 04.19.1979

Merestead (see Bedford)

Old Chappaqua Historic District
Quaker Road, Chappaqua. Formerly rural Quaker hamlet with early 19th-century frame farmhouses and Friend's Meeting House (1753; enlarged 1778-80 and 1961). 07.15.1974

Old Croton Aqueduct (see Yonkers)

Rehoboth
33 Aldrige Road, Chappaqua. Large 3-story concrete barn designed and built 1856 by Horace Greeley; converted 1892 into residence for Greeley's daughter by architect Ralph Adams Cram. Horace Greeley Thematic Resources. 04.19.1979

Sarles' Tavern–Granite House
NY100, Millwood. A 2-story, 8-bay vernacular granite building purportedly built 1814-17 by David G. Crasto as tavern/stagecoach stop. 12.31.1979

Williams-DuBois House
Pinesbridge Road. Large Federal frame farmhouse with gambrel roof; built c.1780. 05.25.1989

New Rochelle

Davenport House
157 Davenport Road. Large rambling Gothic Revival stone residence; central portion designed by Alexander Jackson Davis; built 1858-59 for Lawrence Montgomery Davenport. Additions include south wing (1871, Alexander Jackson Davis), north wing (c.1875, Frederick H. Coles), wing enlargements (late 19th century, Snelling & Potter), and north wing enlargement (c.1912, Parish & Schroeper). Additional remodeling c.1920. 04.30.1980

First Presbyterian Church and Lewis Pintard House
Pintard Avenue. Large Colonial Revival stone church with tall corner steeple and Ionic portico; designed by John Russell Pope; built 1926-29; attached stuccoed administration and classroom building. Arcaded walkway connects church to rectory; original portion built early 18th century by French Huguenot settler. 09.07.1979

Leland Castle (Castleview)
29 Castle Place. Large Gothic Revival stone residence with crenellated towers; designed by William Thomas Beers; built 1855-59 for hotel entrepreneur Simeon Leland; late 19th- and early 20th-century additions. Part of College of New Rochelle. 08.27.1976

Lispenard-Rodman-Davenport House
180 Davenport Avenue. Large, rambling Victorian/Colonial Revival stone, brick, and frame residence built in several stages; original stone section built c.1708 by Huguenot settler; enlarged and altered c.1732, c.1800, c.1860, and c.1920. 09.22.1986

Thomas Paine Cottage
20 Sicard Avenue. A 2-story vernacular frame residence built c.1800; porch added 1804; moved to present site 1908. Home and burial place of author and patriot Thomas Paine. NHL 11.28.1972

Pioneer Building
14 Lawton Street. A 2-story Victorian brick commercial building built 1892 by local builders John New & Son for headquarters of city's first newspaper, *The Pioneer*. 12.29.1983

United States Post Office–New Rochelle
255 North Avenue. Large Moderne post office designed by Frost, Hart & Shape; built 1937-38; significantly altered. Interior mural series (1940) by David Hutchinson. United States Post Offices in New York State, 1858-1943, Thematic Resources. 05.11.1989

North Castle

Bedford Road Historic District
12-44 Bedford Road, Armonk. Group of 7 properties including Greek Revival St. Stephen's Church (1842) and Cemetery, 5 Federal/Greek Revival frame residences built 1842-c.1850, and Victorian frame residence built c.1880. 11.21.1985

Bronx River Parkway Reservation
(see Bronxville)

Miller House
Virginia Road, North White Plains. A 1 1/2-story Colonial farmhouse built 1738; enlarged 1770. Used as George Washington's headquarters during Battle of White Plains in October 1776, during American Revolution. Museum since 1917. 09.29.1976

Smith Tavern
440 Bedford Road, Armonk. Vernacular frame farmhouse built mid-18th century; enlarged late 18th century as tavern; enlarged and remodeled 1898. 09.15.1983

North Salem

North Salem Town Hall
Titicus Road, Salem Center. Large Georgian frame building with gambrel roof; built 1770-73 for DeLancey family, Tory sympathizers. Confiscated during American Revolution and later converted for use as academy. 09.04.1980

Joseph Purdy Homestead
Junction of NY22 and 116, Purdys. Large Colonial shingled residence built 1776; bracketed cornice and porch added c.1870. 01.25.1973

Union Hall
NY116 and Keeler Lane. A 3-story Italianate frame commercial building and adjacent carriage house built 1865 as store, meeting hall, stagecoach stop, and residence. 08.28.1986

North Tarrytown

Dutch Reformed (Sleepy Hollow) Church
US9, north edge of Tarrytown. A 1-story Dutch Colonial stone church with gambrel roof and octagonal belfry; built c.1697 for proprietors and tenants of Philipsburg Manor; achieved fame as Sleepy Hollow Church in Washington Irving's *The Legend of Sleepy Hollow*. Adjacent cemetery. NHL 11.05.1961

Old Croton Aqueduct (see Yonkers)

Patriots' Park (see Tarrytown)

Philipsburg Manor
381 Bellwood Avenue. A 20-acre property with 2-story Colonial stone residence built c.1690 as first manor house of Philipsburg Manor; enlarged before 1749 and substantially altered under ownership of Beekman family after American Revolution; restored 1941-42. Property includes Dutch barn moved to site from Hurley, Ulster County, and reconstructed mill, granary, and dam. Operated as museum by Historic Hudson Valley. NHL 11.05.1961

Philipse Manor Railroad Station
Riverside Drive. Tudor Revival stone passenger station built c.1910 for suburban commuters to New York City on New York Central Railroad. 03.14.1991

Tarrytown Lighthouse
Hudson River, near Kingsland Point Park. A 5-story conical steel lighthouse built 1882-83. Hudson River Lighthouses Thematic Group. 05.29.1979

Ossining (Town)

Jug Tavern
Revolutionary Road and Rockledge Avenue. Vernacular stone and frame residence built 3rd quarter of 18th century; used as tavern in late 18th century; 19th-century alterations. 06.07.1976

Scarborough Historic District
US9, Scarborough (also in town of Mount Pleasant). Group of 7 properties, including mid-18th-century cemetery, 3 estates, school complex, and 2 church complexes. Churches include Gothic Revival stone St. Mary's Church (1850-51; windows by William Bolton) and Parish Hall (1897), and Renaissance-inspired Scarborough Presbyterian Church (1895, Haydel & Shepard). Estates include Renaissance Revival Woodlea (1892-95, McKim, Mead & White; now Sleepy Hollow Country Club), Greek Revival Rosemont (c.1840, demolished 1990), and Federal Beechwood (late 18th century; major additions c.1900 by Robert H. Robertson; further additions and formal landscape elements c.1906 by William Welles Bosworth). Neoclassical Scarborough School (now Clear View School) main building designed by William Welles Bosworth; completed 1917. 09.07.1984

Ossining (Village)

Richard Austin House
196 Croton Avenue. Italianate frame residence built 1878-79 for lawyer. Museum. 09.20.1988

Brandreth Pill Factory
Water Street. A 5-acre industrial complex on Hudson River, with large Second Empire brick main factory (1872; several additions), office (1886), shop, Greek Revival storage building (1836; attributed to Calvin Pollard), and several other late 19th-century brick and frame buildings. Complex developed 1836-1907 for Dr. Benjamin Brandreth, important figure in patent medicine industry. 01.10.1980

Downtown Ossining Historic District
US9, Main Street, and Croton Avenue. Central core of village, with 35 mid-19th- to early 20th-century commercial, religious, and civic buildings. Notable buildings include large group of 3-story Victorian brick commercial buildings, Art Deco former National Bank and Trust Company (1930), Classical Revival Municipal Building (1913-14, Donn Barber), Gothic Revival Trinity Episcopal Church (1891, Robert W. Gibson), Collegiate Gothic Ossining High School (c.1929, James Gamble Rogers), Victorian Gothic United Methodist Church (1877, E. L. Roberts and Lawrence B. Valk), First Baptist Church (individually listed), section of Old Croton Aqueduct (individually listed), and Greek Revival commercial building at 155 Main Street (1845). 08.09.1989

First Baptist Church of Ossining
South Highland Avenue and Main Street. Victorian Gothic brick church designed by J. Walsh; completed 1874. 01.12.1973

Highland Cottage (Squire House)
36 South Highland Avenue. Large Second Empire/eclectic rubble concrete residence with elaborate exterior and interior decorative trim; built 1872 for Henry J. Baker. Headquarters of Westchester Preservation League. 07.22.1982

Old Croton Aqueduct (see Yonkers)

George Rohr Saloon and Boardinghouse
1-3 Highland Avenue. Large 3 1/2-story Second Empire brick commercial building built c.1860. 07.21.1981; DEMOLISHED

St. Paul's Episcopal Church and Rectory
(Calvary Baptist Church and Annex) St. Paul's Place. Gothic Revival marble church designed by Calvin Pollard; built 1835. Gothic Revival stone rectory built 1864. 12.06.1978

Washington School
81 Croton Avenue. Large 3-story Beaux-Arts brick and terra-cotta school designed by Wilson Potter; built 1907. 02.12.1987

Peekskill

Beecher-McFadden Estate
Main Street (Route 6). A 4-acre estate with landscaped grounds developed 1860s-70s by well-known clergyman and lecturer Henry Ward Beecher. Main residence built 1875 for Beecher and extensively remodeled in Jacobean Revival style c.1925 for William T. McFadden family. Includes large carriage house. 11.02.1987

Drum Hill High School
Ringgold Street. Large 3-story Neoclassical brick school with stone trim; designed by Edward E. Joralemon; built 1909-11. Notable interior atrium. 12.31.1979

United States Post Office–Peekskill
738 South Street. Georgian Revival brick post office built 1930-31. United States Post Offices in New York State, 1858-1943, Thematic Resources. 05.11.1989

Villa Loretto
Crompond Road. An 18-acre property with monumental 4-story H-shaped Colonial Revival brick institutional building designed by architect-builder Frank J. Murphy; completed 1928 for innovative rehabilitation program for young women established by Sisters of the Good Shepherd. 04.27.1989

Pelham

Bolton Priory
7 Priory Lane. Large Gothic Revival Elizabethan Revival stone residence with crenellated towers; built 1838 for Robert Bolton family; design of house and formal gardens attributed to Robert Bolton and Washington Irving; interior finishes by Bolton's sons, including stained glass by William Jay Bolton. 06.28.1974

Edgewood House
(Pelham Hall, Mrs. Hazen's School) 908 Edgewood Avenue. Large 4-story Colonial Revival frame institutional building built 1893 as part of private girls day and boarding school. 06.26.1986

Pelhamdale
45 Iden Avenue. Mid-18th-century stone residence greatly enlarged and remodeled c.1830 in Greek Revival style. Associated with Pell family. 11.04.1982

Port Chester

Bush-Lyon Homestead
John Lyon Park, King Street. A 1 1/2-story Colonial shingled former farmhouse built c.1720; enlarged late 18th and early 19th centuries. Property includes carriage house and other outbuildings. Museum. 04.22.1982

Capitol Theater
147-151 Westchester Avenue. A 2-story Italian Renaissance style brick and terra-cotta commercial building and adjoining auditorium with Byzantine-style interior; designed by Thomas W. Lamb; built 1926.
06.07.1984

Life Savers Building
North Main Street. Large 5-story concrete, brick, and terra-cotta industrial building with decorative details derived from classical sources and images of product; designed and built 1920 by engineering firm of Lockwood, Green & Co. for manufacture of Life Savers candy.
07.11.1985

Putnam and Mellor Engine and Hose Company Firehouse
46 South Main Street. A 3-story Queen Anne brick and terra-cotta firehouse designed by Howard G. Slater; built 1888.
09.15.1983

United States Post Office–Port Chester
245 Westchester Avenue. Large Colonial Revival brick post office with limestone Corinthian portico; designed by Zoller & Muller; built 1932-36. Interior mural series (1936) by Domenico Mortellito. United States Post Offices in New York State, 1858-1943, Thematic Resources. 05.11.1989

Pound Ridge

Pound Ridge Historic District
Roughly bounded by Pound Ridge, Old Stone Hill, and Salem roads, Trinity Pass, and Westchester Avenue. Small rural hamlet with approximately 26 buildings, mostly late 18th- to early 19th-century vernacular frame residences built by settlers from Connecticut. Many residences altered mid-19th century and early 20th century during development of community as suburb of New York City. Includes school, store, mill, library, and 2 churches.
12.30.1985

Rye (Town)

William E. Ward House
Comly Avenue, Rye Brook. An 8-acre property with large Second Empire/eclectic reinforced-concrete residence with crenellated towers; built 1873-76 by mechanical engineer William E. Ward in collaboration with architect Robert Mook. Prototypic use of concrete in United States. 11.07.1976

Rye (City)

Boston Post Road Historic District
Roughly bounded by Boston Post Road and Milton Harbor. A 300-acre area on Long Island Sound with three 19th-century former estates, cemetery, and archeological sites associated with John Jay family, and prehistoric archeological sites and nature conservation area. Large main houses of estates include Greek Revival Alansten (built 1838 for Peter Jay), Greek Revival Lounsberry (built 1838 for Edward Lamb Parsons), and Gothic Revival Whitby (1852-54, Alexander Jackson Davis; built for William P. Chapman). 10.29.1982

Opposite: Entrance Gates, Beechwood, Scarborough Historic District, Town of Ossining.

Lyndhurst, Tarrytown (p. 183).

Widow Haviland's Tavern (The Square House)
Purchase Street. Colonial shingled residence with gambrel roof; built mid-18th century. Operated as tavern in late 18th century by Haviland family. Museum. 04.16.1974

Timothy Knapp House and Milton Cemetery
265 Rye Beach Avenue and Milton Road. Knapp House: large Colonial shingled residence; original section built c.1670; additions in late 17th, mid-18th, and early 20th centuries. Milton Cemetery: 1-acre cemetery founded in 18th century as Rye's first public burying ground. 06.14.1982

Playland Amusement Park
Playland Parkway and Forest Avenue. A 280-acre recreational complex with amusement rides, concessions, water-oriented facilities, man-made lake, and nature preserve. First totally planned amusement park in America; developed 1920s by Westchester County Park Commission with architects Walker & Gillette and landscape architect Gilmore D. Clarke; opened 1928. Includes 3 original rides and numerous buildings in Art Deco and Spanish Colonial Revival styles. 07.04.1980; NHL 02.27.1987

United States Post Office–Rye
41 Purdy Avenue. Classical Revival brick post office built 1935-36. Interior mural (1938) by Guy Pène Du Bois. United States Post Offices in New York State, 1858-1943, Thematic Resources. 05.11.1989

Scarsdale

Bronx River Parkway Reservation
(see Bronxville)

Caleb Hyatt House (Cudner-Hyatt House)
937 Post Road. Vernacular frame farmhouse; small original section built mid-18th century as tenant house on Manor of Scarsdale; raised to 2 stories c.1836; addition built prior to 1830. Operated as museum by Scarsdale Historical Society. 01.22.1973

United States Post Office–Scarsdale
Chase Road. Neoclassical brick post office designed by Schultze & Weaver; built 1937-38. Interior murals (1940) by Gordon Samstag. United States Post Offices in New York State, 1858-1943, Thematic Resources. 05.11.1989

Wayside Cottage
1039 Post Road. A 1 1/2-story Colonial shingled residence built c.1720; large central section added 1828 and additional wing added late 19th century. Associated with locally promi-

nent Varian family, patriots during American Revolution. Owned by village since 1919. 05.01.1981

Somers

Gerard Crane House
Old Croton Falls Road. A 30-acre estate with large Greek Revival granite residence built 1849 for circus entrepreneur. Notable interior. Property also includes 5 original outbuildings, stone bridge, and section of early 19th-century Somertown Turnpike. 09.05.1985

Mt. Zion Methodist Church
Primrose Street. A 2 1/2-story vernacular frame church built 1794 by Micajah Wright; remodeled c.1860. Adjacent cemetery begun late 18th century. 05.10.1990

Somers Town House (Elephant Hotel)
Junction of US202 and NY100. Large 3-story Federal brick hotel built 1820-25 by Hachaliah Bailey, known as "Father of the American Circus." Statue of "Old Bet" elephant (1827) in front of hotel. Center of circus industry in 19th century. Headquarters of Somers Historical Society and town offices. 08.07.1974

Tarrytown

Christ Episcopal Church
Broadway and Elizabeth Street. Gothic Revival brick church built 1836-37; enlarged 1857; renovated 1868 and 1896. Attached rectory (1875) and adjacent parish hall (1898). Associated with writer Washington Irving, local resident and church member. 04.23.1987

First Baptist Church and Rectory
56 South Broadway. High Victorian Gothic bluestone church with brownstone trim; designed by Russell Sturgis; built 1875-76. Notable interior. Adjacent Classical Revival brick rectory built 1896. 07.21.1983

Foster Memorial A.M.E. Zion Church
90 Wildey Street. A 2-story vernacular brick church with Gothic-style decorative details; built 1865 by architect-builder James Bird. Oldest African-American church in continuous use in Westchester County. 06.03.1982

Washington Irving High School
18 North Broadway. Large 2 1/2-story Elizabethan Revival brick school with elaborate terra-cotta trim; designed by Alfred J. Manning; built 1897. Converted to apartments. 04.26.1984

Lyndhurst (Jay Gould Estate)
635 South Broadway. A 70-acre estate on Hudson River with massive Gothic Revival marble residence distinguished by 4-story tower, crenellations, buttresses, and finials, and notable interior decorations and furniture;

Staircase, Mt. Zion Methodist Church, Somers.

original section designed 1838 by Alexander Jackson Davis for former mayor of New York City William Paulding; substantially enlarged 1864-65 by Davis for New York City merchant George Merritt; summer residence 1880-92 for financier Jay Gould. Property includes landscaped grounds, massive greenhouse (1881, Lord & Burnham), stable complex, stone gardener's cottage and gatehouse, laundry/guest cottage, bowling alley, bridge over railroad tracks to yacht dock, and other outbuildings. Operated as museum by National Trust for Historic Preservation. NHL 11.13.1966 ILLUS. P. 181

Music Hall
11 Main Street. Large 2 1/2-story Queen Anne brick, stuccoed, and half-timbered commercial building with corner towers, decorative brick and terra-cotta trim, and interior auditorium space; designed by Philip Edmunds; built 1885. 02.12.1980

North Grove Street Historic District
1, 2, 8, 15, and 19 North Grove Street. Group of 5 large Gothic Revival, Italianate, and Second Empire brick and frame residences and 1 carriage house; built 1848-68. No. 1 headquarters of Historical Society of the Tarrytowns. 03.13.1979

Old Croton Aqueduct (see Yonkers)

Patriots' Park
US9 (also in North Tarrytown). A 4-acre park designed 1892 by Carrère & Hastings as part of small Beaux-Arts residential neighborhood. Includes stone gatehouse, bridges, landscape features, and Captors' Monument (1853; redesigned 1880). 06.14.1982

Sunnyside (Washington Irving House)
Sunnyside Lane. Estate overlooking Hudson River with eclectic stuccoed stone residence built 17th century; enlarged and extensively remodeled 1830s and 1840s for renowned writer Washington Irving. Features high stepped "Dutch" gables, tower wing, and naturalistic landscaped grounds. Restored 1950s. Operated as museum by Historic Hudson Valley. NHL 12.29.1962

Tuckahoe

Bronx River Parkway Reservation
(see Bronxville)

White Plains

Bronx River Parkway Reservation
(see Bronxville)

Leo Friedlander Studio
825 West Hartsdale Road. A 2 1/2-story stuccoed concrete block building with classical decorative details; built 1908 as studio residence by Mr. Bertelli of Roman Bronze Co. Studio and residence for 30 years of well-known sculptor Leo Friedlander. 07.29.1982

Mapleton
(Alumnae House, College of White Plains)
52 North Broadway. Large Italianate/Second Empire frame residence and gazebo built c.1864 for carriage manufacturer William Franklin Dusenburg. 09.28.1976

Jacob Purdy House
60 Park Avenue. A 1 1/2-story Colonial shingled residence built c.1721; enlarged c.1750; moved to present site 1973. Washington's headquarters in 1776 and 1778 during American Revolution. 08.31.1979

White Plains–Westchester County Courthouse Complex
Main Street. Complex of 6 attached court buildings, including wing of Italianate stone courthouse (1857), stone Hall of Records (1893), Neoclassical granite Hall of Records addition and Supreme Court Building (1904 and 1907, Lord & Hewlitt), and large Neoclassical granite courthouse addition (1915-17, Benjamin W. Morris). 01.17.1975; DEMOLISHED

White Plains Armory
35 South Broadway. Massive Romanesque Revival/eclectic brick and sandstone armory with 4-story central tower and crenellated parapets; designed by Franklin B. Ware; built 1909. Converted to senior citizens housing. 04.16.1980

Yonkers

Bronx River Parkway Reservation
(see Bronxville)

Edwin H. Armstrong House
1032 Warburton Avenue. Queen Anne residence built 1902 for Armstrong family. Residence from 1902 to 1923 of Edwin H. Armstrong, important contributor to development of radio. NHL 01.07.1976; DEMOLISHED NOVEMBER 1982

Bell Place–Locust Avenue Historic District
Roughly bounded by Bell Place, Cromwell Place, Locust Hill Avenue, Baldwin Place, and North Broadway. Small residential neighborhood with 8 Italianate, Second Empire, Victorian Gothic, and Queen Anne brick and frame residences and carriage houses. 08.29.1985

John Copcutt Mansion
239 Nepperhan Avenue. Large Italianate stone villa with 3-story central tower; built 1854 for owner of wood veneer mill. Notable interior. 09.12.1985

Delavan Terrace Historic District
Roughly bounded by Delavan Terrace, and Palisade and Park avenues. Group of 11 large 19th- and 20th-century Victorian Gothic, Queen Anne, Shingle Style, bungalow, Tudor Revival, and Spanish Colonial Revival stuccoed, shingled, and brick residences. 09.15.1983

Halcyon Place Historic District
Cul-de-sac of 12 Queen Anne, Shingle Style, Mission, and Colonial Revival frame and masonry residences built 1901-24 by carpenter and builder Harry Woodhouse as suburban development.   01.11.1991

Eleazer Hart House
243 Bronxville Road. Vernacular frame residence built pre-1783 as tenant house on Philipsburg Manor; incorporated into rear section of Federal shingled residence built c.1788.   07.29.1982

Old Croton Aqueduct
(Old Croton Trailway State Park)
Runs north from Yonkers to New Croton Dam (also in Hastings-on-Hudson, Dobbs Ferry, Irvington, Tarrytown, North Tarrytown, Mount Pleasant, Briarcliff Manor, Ossining, New Castle, and Cortlandt). A 26-mile-long mostly underground stone and brick aqueduct constructed 1837-42 as first major water supply system for New York City; John B. Jervis, chief engineer. Structures included ventilator shafts, gatehouses, viaducts, culverts, and maintenance building.   12.02.1974

Philipse Manor Hall (State Historic Site)
Warburton Avenue and Dock Street. Large 2 1/2-story Georgian brick residence built in stages 1682-1758; social and administrative center of Philipsburg Manor. Notable decorative interior plasterwork (c.1745).
NHL 11.05.1961

Public Bath House No. 2
27 Vineyard Avenue. Romanesque Revival brick bath house built 1898. Public Bath Houses of Yonkers Thematic Resources.
10.21.1985

Public Bath House No. 3
48 Yonkers Avenue. Second Renaissance Revival brick bath house with ornamental polychromatic tile and brickwork; designed by George S. Cowles; built 1909. Public Bath Houses of Yonkers Thematic Resources.
10.21.1985

Public Bath House No. 4
138 Linden Street. Large stuccoed masonry bath house with eclectic features blending classical detailing with Spanish Mission style; designed by O. J. Gette; built 1925. Public Bath Houses of Yonkers Thematic Resources.
10.21.1985

St. John's Protestant Episcopal Church
One Hudson Street. Victorian Gothic stone and brick church designed by Edward Tuckerman Potter; completed 1874 incorporating part of original mid-18th-century stone church. Notable interior. Attached stone rectory, chapel, and parish house designed by Robert H. Robertson; built 1890-91.
07.29.1982

Sherwood House
340 Tuckahoe Road. Small Colonial frame residence built c.1740 as tenant house of Manor

of Philipsburg; enlarged c.1810 and c.1850. Property includes mid-19th-century caretaker's house and former barn.   05.10.1984

Alexander Smith Carpet Mills Historic District
Roughly bounded by Saw Mill River Road, Orchard Street, and Lake and Ashburton avenues. A 38-acre property with 15 industrial buildings and 6 rows of workers' housing built 1871-1930 as major carpet-manufacturing complex. Includes massive 3-story Second Empire brick building built 1871 as worsted yarn mill (enlarged 1876-83) and numerous related buildings.   08.11.1983

W. B. Thompson Mansion
1061 North Broadway. Large Italian Renaissance style limestone residence and formal garden designed by Carrère & Hastings; built 1912 for financier, mining engineer, and philanthropist W. B. Thompson. Notable design features include components from Italian Renaissance buildings and elaborate interior decoration. Now part of Elizabeth Seton College.   10.29.1982

John Bond Trevor House (Glenview)
511 Warburton Avenue. Large Victorian stone residence with 84-foot tower; designed by Charles W. Clinton of Clinton & Russell; built 1876-77 for financier and philanthropist. Notable Eastlake interior. Now part of Hudson River Museum.   06.19.1972

United States Post Office–Yonkers
79-81 Main Street. Monumental 2-story Classical Revival limestone post office built 1927. United States Post Offices in New York State, 1858-1943, Thematic Resources.
05.11.1989

Untermyer Park
Warburton Avenue and North Broadway, south of Odell Avenue. A 16-acre municipal park overlooking Hudson River with formal Grecian garden, Grecian amphitheater, classical pavilion, pergola, rock garden, and statuary; developed early 20th century as part of estate of lawyer Samuel Untermyer. Much of garden designed by William Welles Bosworth. Sculptures by Paul Manship.   05.31.1974

Yonkers Water Works
Roughly bounded by Saw Mill River and Grassy Sprain roads, and Gilmare Drive. Complex of 3 Victorian brick and stone buildings including Tuckahoe Road Pump House, Grassy Sprain Reservoir Gatehouse, and Tubewell Station; pump house and gate house built 1876; station built 1898 with early 20th-century additions.   07.21.1982

Yorktown

Amawalk Friends Meeting House
Quaker Church Road, Amawalk. A 2-story vernacular shingled meetinghouse with intact meeting room; built 1831 for Hicksite sect of Quakers. Adjacent cemetery.   11.16.1989

Site of Old Croton Dam; New Croton Dam
(see Cortlandt)

Yorktown Heights Railroad Station
Commerce Street, Yorktown Heights. Modest 1-story Stick Style frame passenger station built c.1877-86 for New Central Railroad's Putnam Division. Museum.   03.19.1981

WYOMING COUNTY

Arcade

Arcade and Attica Railroad
Railroad right-of-way from Arcade to North Java (in town and village of Arcade and town of Java). A 15-mile-long railroad built 1880 with 3 small frame passenger stations (Arcade Depot, c.1830 with c.1900 addition; Curriers and Java Center depots, both c.1900) and wrought-iron Beaver Meadow Trestle (1895). Includes 2 locomotives and 6 passenger cars manufactured 1914-20. One of the last operational independent short lines in New York State.   11.17.1980

Attica

United States Post Office–Attica
76 Main Street. Colonial Revival brick post office built 1936-37. Interior mural (1941) by Thomas Donnelly. United States Post Offices in New York State, 1858-1943, Thematic Resources.   11.17.1988

Java

Arcade and Attica Railroad (see Arcade)

Silver Lake

Silver Lake Institute Historic District
Roughly bounded by Wesley, Embury, Thompson, Haven, Lakeside, and Lakeview avenues. Methodist camp established 1873 with 70 cottages and 2 institutional buildings built 1873-1930. Frame cottages include many notable examples of Eastlake, Queen Anne, and Colonial Revival styles.
09.19.1985

Warsaw

Trinity Church
West Buffalo Street. Small Gothic Revival frame church designed by Richard Upjohn; built 1853-54. Parish house built 1925.
03.18.1980

Opposite: Number 14, Arcade and Attica Railroad, Arcade.

United States Post Office–Warsaw

35 South Main Street. Georgian Revival brick post office built 1934-35. United States Post Offices in New York State, 1858-1943, Thematic Resources. 05.11.1989

Warsaw Academy

73 South Main Street. A 2-story Greek Revival cobblestone school built 1846; brick rear wing added 1854. 01.03.1980

Wyoming

Middlebury Academy

22 South Academy Street. A 2-story Federal brick school built 1817; pedimented Doric portico added c.1840. 01.17.1973

Wyoming Village Historic District

NY19. Historic core of village centered on small triangular green, with approximately 70 19th- and early 20th-century buildings. Notable buildings include Federal Presbyterian Church (1830), Greek Revival Ferris-Arnold House with formal gardens, Carpenter Gothic board-and-batten Warren-Main House, and Middlebury Academy (individually listed). 12.27.1974

YATES COUNTY

Dresden

Robert Ingersoll Birthplace

61 Main Street. Early 19th-century Federal frame residence composed of 2 sections built separately and joined before 1833. Birthplace of well-known orator in 1833. 02.11.1988

Penn Yan

Penn Yan Historic District

Roughly bounded by Water, Seneca, Elm, Wagener, Court, Clinton, North, and Main streets. Historic core of regional center of commerce, agriculture, and industry in 19th and early 20th century, with approximately 210 civic, religious, commercial, industrial, and residential buildings in wide range of styles including 4 churches, mill complex, and library.

Notable buildings include Greek Revival William Oliver House (c.1825), Birkett Mills (1824-1915), Victorian Chronicle Building (c.1889), Second Empire Knapp Hotel (c.1877-87), numerous Federal, Greek Revival, and Italianate brick and frame residences and commercial buildings, and Yates County Courthouse Park District (individually listed). 03.14.1985

United States Post Office–Penn Yan

159 Main Street. Colonial Revival brick post office designed by James Knox Taylor; built 1912-13. United States Post Offices in New York State, 1858-1943, Thematic Resources. 05.11.1989

Yates County Courthouse Park District

Main, Court, and Liberty streets. Group of 4 buildings focused around or adjacent to landscaped park: Greek Revival brick County Courthouse (1835), Romanesque Revival brick County Office Building (1889), Early Romanesque Revival brick First Baptist Church (1870-71), and Georgian Revival brick Old County Jail (1904, William J. Beardsley). 06.19.1979

Properties described elsewhere in this book were listed in the National Register before the end of 1991. Those named below were added before the end of 1992. The 1992 properties are not included in subsequent appendixes or in the indexes.

Broome County
Highland Park Carousel, Union 01.25.1992
C. Fred Johnson Park Carousel, Johnson City 01.25.1992
George F. Johnson Recreation Park Carousel, Binghamton 01.25.1992
George W. Johnson Park Carousel, Endicott 01.25.1992
Ross Park Carousel, Binghamton 01.25.1992
West Endicott Park Carousel, West Endicott 01.25.1992

Chautauqua County
School No. 7, Dunkirk 03.05.1992

Chemung County
St. Patrick's Parochial Residence, Convent and School, Elmira 11.05.1992

Cortland County
Peck Memorial Library, Marathon 05.19.1992

Erie County
Warren Hull House, Lancaster 05.11.1992

Essex County
Adsit Log House, Willsboro 05.11.1992
Barngalow, Saranac Lake 11.06.1992
Bogie Cottage, Saranac Lake 11.06.1992
Peyton Clark Cottage, Saranac Lake 11.06.1992
Coulter Cottage, Saranac Lake 11.06.1992
Denny Cottage, Saranac Lake 11.06.1992
Fallon Cottage Annex, Saranac Lake 11.06.1992
Highland Park Historic District, Saranac Lake 11.06.1992
Kennedy Cottage, Saranac Lake 11.06.1992
Lane Cottage, Saranac Lake 11.06.1992
Larom-Welles Cottage, Saranac Lake 11.06.1992
Dr. Henry Leetch House, Saranac Lake 11.06.1992
Lent Cottage, Saranac Lake 11.06.1992
Marquay Cottage, Saranac Lake 11.06.1992
Marvin Cottage, Saranac Lake 11.06.1992
Morgan Cottage, Saranac Lake 11.06.1992
Partridge Cottage, Saranac Lake 11.06.1992
Pittenger Cottage, Saranac Lake 11.06.1992
State Theater, Ticonderoga 04.30.1992
Stevenson Cottage, Saranac Lake 11.06.1992

Franklin County
Dr. A. H. Allen Cottage, Saranac Lake 11.06.1992
Ames Cottage, Saranac Lake 11.06.1992
Baird Cottage, Saranac Lake 11.06.1992
Camp Intermission, Saranac Lake 11.06.1992
Church Street Historic District, Saranac Lake 11.06.1992
Colbath Cottage, Saranac Lake 11.06.1992
Cottage Row Historic District, Saranac Lake 11.06.1992
Distin Cottage, Saranac Lake 11.06.1992
Drury Cottage, Saranac Lake 11.06.1992
Ellenberger Cottage, Saranac Lake 11.06.1992
Feisthamel-Edelberg Cottage, Saranac Lake 11.06.1992
Feustmann Cottage, Saranac Lake 11.06.1992
Freer Cottage, Saranac Lake 11.06.1992
E. L. Gray House, Saranac Lake 11.06.1992
Hathaway Cottage, Saranac Lake 11.06.1992
Hill Cottage, Saranac Lake 11.06.1992
Hillside Lodge, Saranac Lake 11.06.1992
The Homestead, Saranac Lake 11.06.1992
Hooey Cottage, Saranac Lake 11.06.1992
Hopkins Cottage, Saranac Lake 11.06.1992
Jennings Cottage, Saranac Lake 11.06.1992
Johnson Cottage, Saranac Lake 11.06.1992
Larom Cottage, Saranac Lake 11.06.1992
Leis Block, Saranac Lake 11.06.1992
Little Red, Saranac Lake 11.06.1992
Magill Cottage, Saranac Lake 11.06.1992
McBean Cottage, Saranac Lake 11.06.1992
Musselman Cottage, Saranac Lake 11.06.1992
Noyes Cottage, Saranac Lake 11.06.1992
Pomeroy Cottage, Saranac Lake 11.06.1992
Radwell Cottage, Saranac Lake 11.06.1992

Ryan Cottage, Saranac Lake 11.06.1992
Sarbanes Cottage, Saranac Lake 11.06.1992
Orin Savage Cottage, Saranac Lake 11.06.1992
Schrader-Griswold Cottage, Saranac Lake 11.06.1992
Seeley Cottage, Saranac Lake 11.06.1992
Sloan Cottage, Saranac Lake 11.06.1992
Smith Cottage, Saranac Lake 11.06.1992
Stonaker Cottage, Saranac Lake 11.06.1992
Stuckman Cottage, Saranac Lake 11.06.1992
Walker Cottage, Saranac Lake 11.06.1992
Wilson Cottage, Saranac Lake 11.06.1992
Witherspoon Cottage, Saranac Lake 11.06.1992

Greene County
Pratt Rock Park, Prattsville 12.10.1992

Hamilton County
Hamilton County Courthouse Complex, Lake Pleasant 09.24.1992

Herkimer County
Newport Stone Arch Bridge, Newport 02.10.1992

Kings County
Andrews United Methodist Church, Brooklyn 01.22.1992
Lefferts Manor Historic District, Brooklyn 05.18.1992

Madison County
Chittenango Landing Dry Dock Complex, Sullivan 04.30.1992

Monroe County
Brick Presbyterian Church Complex, Rochester 03.12.1992
English Evangelical Church of the Reformation and Parish House, Rochester 03.12.1992
Immaculate Conception Roman Catholic Church Complex, Rochester 03.12.1992
Our Lady of Victory Roman Catholic Church, Rochester 03.12.1992
St. Mary's Roman Catholic Church and Rectory, Rochester 03.12.1992

Montgomery County
Temple of Israel, Amsterdam 08.27.1992

Nassau County
Sands Family Cemetery, Sands Point 03.12.1992

New York County
Machigonne Ferryboat, Manhattan NHL 12.03.1992
Manhattan Avenue–West 120th-123rd Streets Historic District, Manhattan 01.17.1992
Tenement Building at 97 Orchard Street, Manhattan 05.19.1992

Oneida County
Ava Town Hall 05.18.1992

Ontario County
Cobblestone Railroad Pumphouse, Victor 05.22.1992
Felt Cobblestone General Store, Victor 05.22.1992
First Baptist Church of Phelps 05.22.1992
Harmon Cobblestone Farmhouse and Cobblestone Smokehouse, Phelps 05.22.1992
Rippey Cobblestone Farmhouse, Seneca 10.06.1992
St. Bridget's Roman Catholic Church Complex, Bloomfield 08.28.1992

Otsego County
South Worcester Historic District 11.05.1992
Unadilla Village Historic District 09.04.1992
Unadilla Waterworks 09.04.1992

Putnam County
Plumbush, Philipstown 01.30.1992

Queens County
Flushing High School 02.10.1992

Rensselaer County
Melville, Herman, House, Lansingburgh 08.21.1992

Rockland County
Hopson-Swan Estate, Sparkill 11.23.1992

St. Lawrence County
Waddington Historic District 05.18.1992

Steuben County
Church of the Redeemer, Addison 11.12.1992

Suffolk County
Jacob Ockers House, Oakdale 07.10.1992

Sullivan County
Ellery Calkins House, Cochecton 11.27.1992
Cochecton Presbyterian Church 11.27.1992
Old Cochecton Cemetery 11.27.1992
Page House, Cochecton 11.27.1992
Parsonage Road Historic District, Cochecton 11.27.1992
Reilly's Store, Cochecton 11.27.1992
Valleau Tavern, Cochecton 11.27.1992

Tompkins County
Groton High School 07.24.1992

Ulster County
National Youth Adminstration Woodstock Resident Work Center, Woodstock 04.30.1992
Snyder Estate Natural Cement Historic District, Rosendale 06.09.1992

Warren County
Wiawaka Bateaux Site, Lake George 06.14.1992

Wayne County
Smith-Ely Mansion, Clyde 02.10.1992

Westchester County
Mamaroneck Methodist Church 10.02.1992
Old Croton Aqueduct (also in Bronx County) NHL 04.27.1992
The Woodpile, Mt. Kisco 02.10.1992

Wyoming County
Seth M. Gates House, Warsaw 02.21.1992
Monument Circle Historic District, Warsaw 05.11.1992

Yates County
Angus Cobblestone Farmhouse and Barn Complex, Benton 05.11.1992
Barden Cobblestone Farmhouse, Benton 05.11.1992
Bates Cobblestone Farmhouse, Middlesex 05.11.1992
Jephtha Earl Cobblestone Farmhouse, Benton 05.11.1992
William Nichols Cobblestone Farmhouse, Benton 05.11.1992
Dr. Henry Spence Cobblestone Farmhouse and Barn Complex, Starkey 05.11.1992
Daniel Supplee Cobblestone Farmhouse, Starkey 05.11.1992
Young-Leech Cobblestone Farmhouse and Barn Complex, Torrey 05.11.1992

The 1966 legislation enacting the National Register made specific provision for the nomination of districts comprising a significant concentration of properties linked geographically or historically. There were more than 400 of these historic districts listed in the National Register in New York State by the end of 1992.

Albany County
Alcove Historic District
Altamont Historic District
Arbor Hill Historic District–Ten Broeck Triangle, Albany
Broadway–Livingston Avenue Historic District, Albany
Buildings at 744, 746, 748, 750 Broadway, Albany
Center Square–Hudson Park Historic District, Albany
Clinton Avenue Historic District, Albany
Downtown Albany Historic District
Downtown Cohoes Historic District
Harmony Mill Historic District, Cohoes
Lafayette Park Historic District, Albany
Loudon Road Historic District, Loudonville
Mansion Historic District, Albany
Menand Park Historic District, Menands
Olmstead Street Historic District, Cohoes
Onesquethaw Valley Historic District, New Scotland
Pastures Historic District, Albany
Rensselaerville Historic District
South End–Groesbeckville Historic District, Albany
Washington Park Historic District, Albany
Watervliet Shaker Historic District, Colonie

Allegany County
Alfred Village Historic District
Angelica Park Circle Historic District
South Street Historic District, Cuba

Bronx County
Grand Concourse Historic District, Bronx
Longwood Historic District, Bronx
Morris High School Historic District, Bronx
Mott Haven Historic District, Bronx

Broome County
Court Street Historic District, Binghamton
Railroad Terminal Historic District, Binghamton
State Street–Henry Street Historic District, Binghamton
Windsor Village Historic District

Cattaraugus County
Ellicottville Historic District
Gowanda Historic District
Park Square Historic District, Franklinville

Cayuga County
Aurora Village–Wells College Historic District
South Street Area Historic District, Auburn

Chautauqua County
Chautauqua Institution Historic District
East Main Street Historic District, Westfield
Fredonia Commons Historic District
French Portage Road Historic District, Westfield

Chemung County
Elmira Civic Historic District
Elmira College Old Campus
Hanover Square Historic District, Horseheads
Horseheads 1855 Extension Historic District
Near Westside Historic District, Elmira

Chenango County
Bainbridge Historic District
Chenango County Courthouse District, Norwich
Earlville Historic District
Greene Historic District
Main Street Historic District, Afton
New Berlin Historic District
North Broad Street Historic District, Norwich
Oxford Village Historic District
Sherburne Historic District
South Otselic Historic District

Clinton County
Brinkerhoff Street Historic District, Plattsburgh

Court Street Historic District, Plattsburgh
Keeseville Historic District
The Point Historic District, Plattsburgh
United States Oval Historic District, Plattsburgh

Columbia County
Clermont Estates Historic District
Front Street–Parade Hill–Lower Warren Street Historic District, Hudson
Hudson Historic District
Hudson River Historic District
Kinderhook Village Historic District
Rossman–Prospect Avenue Historic District, Hudson
Sixteen Mile District
Stuyvesant Falls Mill District

Cortland County
Cincinnatus Historic District
Main Street Historic District, McGraw
Old Homer Village Historic District, Homer
Tompkins Street–Main Street Historic District, Cortland

Delaware County
Andes Historic District
Churchill Park Historic District, Stamford
Delaware County Courthouse Square District, Delhi
Franklin Village Historic District
Gardiner Place Historic District, Walton
Main Street Historic District, Roxbury
Pakatakan Artist Colony Historic District, Middletown

Dutchess County
Academy Street Historic District, Poughkeepsie
Balding Avenue Historic District, Poughkeepsie
Bloomvale Historic District
Church Street Row, Poughkeepsie
Dwight Street–Hooker Avenue Historic District, Poughkeepsie
Eastman Terrace, Poughkeepsie
Fishkill Village Historic District
Garfield Place Historic District, Poughkeepsie
Harlow Row, Poughkeepsie
Lower Main Street Historic District, Beacon
Main Mall Row, Poughkeepsie
Main Street Historic District, New Hamburg
Market Street Row, Poughkeepsie
Mill Street–North Clover Street Historic District, Poughkeepsie
Rhinebeck Village Historic District
South Hamilton Street Row, Poughkeepsie
Stone Street Historic District, New Hamburg
Union Street Historic District, Poughkeepsie
Upper-Mill Street Historic District, Poughkeepsie
Vassar-Warner Row, Poughkeepsie
Wappingers Falls Historic District
Wheeler Hill Historic District, Wappinger

Erie County
Allentown Historic District, Buffalo
Cazenovia Park–South Park System, Buffalo
Delaware Avenue Historic District, Buffalo
Delaware Park–Front Park System, Buffalo
Laurel and Michigan Avenues Row, Buffalo
Parkside East Historic District, Buffalo
Parkside West Historic District, Buffalo
Row at 17-21 Emerson Place, Buffalo
Row at 33-61 Emerson Place, Buffalo
West Village Historic District, Buffalo
Woodlawn Avenue Row, Buffalo

Essex County
Amherst Avenue Historic District, Ticonderoga
Essex Village Historic District
Hand-Hale Historic District, Elizabethtown
Ironville Historic District, Crown Point
Lake George Avenue Historic District, Ticonderoga

Franklin County
Berkeley Square Historic District, Saranac Lake

Fulton County
Downtown Gloversville Historic District
Kingsboro Historic District, Gloversville

Genesee County
Genesee County Courthouse Historic District, Batavia

Lake Street Historic District, Bergen
Stafford Village Four Corners Historic District

Greene County
Athens Lower Village Historic District
Brick Row Historic District, Athens
East Side Historic District, Catskill
Reed Street Historic District, Coxsackie

Jefferson County
Broadway Historic District, Cape Vincent
Chaumont Historic District
Clayton Historic District
Point Salubrious Historic District, Lyme
Public Square Historic District, Watertown
The Row Historic District, Lyme
Sackets Harbor Village Historic District
State Street Historic District, Carthage
Thousand Island Park Historic District, Orleans
Three Mile Bay Historic District, Lyme

Kings County
Albemarle-Kenmore Terraces Historic District, Brooklyn
Floyd Bennett Field Historic District, Brooklyn
Boerum Hill Historic District, Brooklyn
Brooklyn Heights Historic District
Carroll Gardens Historic District, Brooklyn
Clinton Hill Historic District, Brooklyn
Clinton Hill South Historic District, Brooklyn
Cobble Hill Historic District, Brooklyn
Ditmas Park Historic District, Brooklyn
Fort Greene Historic District, Brooklyn
Fulton Ferry Historic District, Brooklyn
Greenpoint Historic District, Brooklyn
Houses at 291-299 and 290-324 State Street, Brooklyn
Houses on Hunterfly Road Historic District, Brooklyn
Park Slope Historic District, Brooklyn
Prospect Heights Historic District, Brooklyn
Prospect Park South Historic District, Brooklyn
Rockwood Chocolate Factory Historic District, Brooklyn
Stuyvesant Heights Historic District, Brooklyn
Sunset Park Historic District, Brooklyn
Willoughby-Suydem Historic District, Brooklyn

Lewis County
Constableville Village Historic District

Livingston County
Geneseo Historic District
Lima Village Historic District

Madison County
Albany Street Historic District, Cazenovia
Cazenovia Village Historic District
Hamilton Village Historic District
Main-Broad-Grove Streets Historic District, Oneida
South Peterboro Street Commercial Historic District, Canastota
South Peterboro Street Residential Historic District, Canastota

Monroe County
Bridge Square Historic District, Rochester
Brown's Race Historic District, Rochester
City Hall Historic District, Rochester
East Avenue Historic District, Rochester
Grove Place Historic District, Rochester
Madison Square–West Main Street Historic District, Rochester
Mt. Hope–Highland Historic District, Rochester
Pittsford Village Historic District
Rochester Street Historic District, Scottsville
St. Paul–North Water Streets Historic District, Rochester
State Street Historic District, Rochester
Third Ward Historic District, Rochester
Washington Street Rowhouses, Rochester

Montgomery County
Nelliston Historic District

Nassau County
East Williston Village Historic District
Main Street Historic District, Roslyn
Roslyn Village Historic District
Valley Road Historic District, North Hempstead

APPENDIX II (CONT.)
Historic Districts

New York County
Astor Rowhouses
Audubon Terrace Historic District
Central Park West Historic District
Charlton-King-Vandam Historic District
Chelsea Historic District
City and Suburban Homes Company's First Avenue Estate
  Historic District
Rowhouses at 322-344 East 69th Street
East 73rd Street Historic District
Houses at 157, 159, 161, and 163-165 East 78th Street
Houses at 208-218 East 78th Street
Houses at 116-130 East 80th Street
Houses at 146-156 East 89th Street
First Houses
Fraunces Tavern Block
Gramercy Park Historic District
Greenwich Village Historic District
Hamilton Heights Historic District
Harlem River Houses
Henderson Place Historic District
Jumel Terrace Historic District
Lagrange Terrace
MacDougal–Sullivan Gardens Historic District
Mount Morris Park Historic District
Park Avenue, Houses at 680, 684, 686, and 690
Pomander Walk District
Riverside Drive West 80th-81st Streets Historic District
Riverside–West 105th Street Historic District
St. Mark's Historic District
St. Nicholas Historic District
Rockefeller Center
Schermerhorn Row Block
Sniffen Court Historic District
SoHo Cast-Iron Historic District
South Street Seaport Historic District
Stuyvesant Square Historic District
Sutton Place Historic District
Tudor City Historic District
Turtle Bay Gardens Historic District
Upper East Side Historic District
Villard Houses
Houses at 437-459 West 24th Street
5-15 West 54th Street Residences
West 67th Street Artists' Colony Historic District
West 73rd-74th Street Historic District
West 76th Street Historic District

Niagara County
Deveaux School Historic District, Niagara Falls
Lockport Industrial District
Lowertown Historic District, Lockport

Oneida County
Boonville Historic District
Clinton Village Historic District
Gansevort-Bellamy Historic District, Rome
Holland Patent Stone Churches Historic District
Lower Genesee Street Historic District, Utica
Middle Mills Historic District, New York Mills
Rutger-Steuben Park Historic District, Utica
Vernon Center Green Historic District, Vernon
Waterville Triangle Historic District

Onondaga County
Armory Square Historic District, Syracuse
Genesee Street Hill–Limestone Plaza Historic District,
  Fayetteville
Hanover Square Historic District, Syracuse
Hawley-Green Street Historic District, Syracuse
Jordan Village Historic District
Manlius Village Historic District
Montgomery Street–Columbus Circle Historic District,
  Syracuse
North Salina Street Historic District, Syracuse
Oswego-Oneida Streets Historic District, Baldwinsville
Skaneateles Historic District
South Salina Street Historic District, Syracuse
Syracuse University–Comstock Tract Buildings
Walnut Park Historic District, Syracuse

Ontario County
Canandaigua Historic District
East Bloomfield Historic District
North Main Street Historic District, Canandaigua
South Main Street Historic District, Geneva

Orange County
Bridge Street Historic District, Montgomery
Church Park Historic District, Goshen
East End Historic District, Newburgh
Montgomery-Grand-Liberty Streets Historic District,
  Newburgh
Tuxedo Park Historic District
Union Street–Academy Hill Historic District,
  Montgomery
Warwick Village Historic District

Orleans County
Orleans County Courthouse Historic District, Albion

Oswego County
Franklin Square Historic District, Oswego
Mexico Village Historic District
Pulaski Village Historic District
Sandy Creek Historic District

Otsego County
Cherry Valley Historic District
Cooperstown Historic District
Gilbertsville Historic District
Middlefield Hamlet Historic District
Walnut Street Historic District, Oneonta
Worcester Historic District

Putnam County
Cold Spring Historic District
Garrison Landing Historic District, Philipstown

Queens County
Central Avenue Historic District, Ridgewood
Central Ridgewood Historic District
Cooper Avenue Row Historic District, Ridgewood
Cornelia-Putnam Historic District, Ridgewood
Cypress Avenue East Historic District, Ridgewood
Cypress Avenue West Historic District, Ridgewood
Forest-Norman Historic District, Ridgewood
Fort Tilden Historic District, Breezy Point
Fresh Pond–Traffic Historic District, Ridgewood
Grove-–Linden–St. John's Historic District, Ridgewood
Hunters Point Historic District, Queens
Madison–Putnam–60th Place Historic District,
  Ridgewood
Riis, Jacob, Park Historic District, Rockaway
Seneca Avenue East Historic District, Ridgewood
Seneca-Onderdonk-Woodward Historic District,
  Ridgewood
75th Avenue–61st Street Historic District, Ridgewood
68th Avenue–64th Place Historic District, Ridgewood
Stockholm-DeKalb-Hart Historic District, Ridgewood
Summerfield Street Row Historic District, Ridgewood
Sunnyside Gardens Historic District, Queens
Woodbine-Palmetto-Gates Historic District, Ridgewood

Rensselaer County
Albany Avenue Historic District, Nassau
Central Troy Historic District
Chatham Street Row, Nassau
Church Street Historic District, Nassau
Fifth Avenue–Fulton Street Historic District, Troy
Grand Street Historic District, Troy
Hoosick Falls Historic District
Muitzeskill Historic District, Schodack
Northern River Street Historic District, Troy
Poestenkill Gorge Historic District, Troy
River Street Historic District, Troy
Schodack Landing Historic District
Second Street Historic District, Troy
Washington Park Historic District, Troy

Richmond County
Miller Army Air Field Historic District, Staten Island, 145
Sailors' Snug Harbor, Staten Island, 145

Rockland County
Closter Road–Oak Tree Road Historic District,
  Orangetown
Tappan Historic District
Washington Spring Road–Woods Road Historic District,
  Orangetown

St. Lawrence County
Library Park Historic District, Ogdensburg
Market Street Historic District, Potsdam
Robinson Bay Archeologial District
Saint Lawrence University–Old Campus Historic District,
  Canton
Village Park Historic District, Canton
West Stockholm Historic District

Saratoga County
Broadway Historic District, Saratoga Springs
Casino–Congress Park–Circular Street Historic District,
  Saratoga Springs
Charlton Historic District
East Side Historic District, Saratoga Springs
Franklin Square Historic District, Saratoga Springs
Northside Historic District, Waterford
Round Lake Historic District
Saratoga Spa State Park District
Union Avenue Historic District, Saratoga Springs
Vischer Ferry Historic District, Clifton Park
Waterford Village Historic District

Schenectady County
Delanson Historic District
Eatons Corners Historic District, Duanesburg
General Electric Realty Plot, Schenectady
Mariaville Historic District, Duanesburg
Quaker Street Historic District, Duanesburg
Stockade Historic District, Schenectady
Union Street Historic District, Schenectady

Schoharie County
Breakabeen Historic District, Fulton
Cobleskill Historic District
North Blenheim Historic District

Schuyler County
Montour Falls Historic District

Seneca County
Covert Historic District
Fall Street–Trinity Lane Historic District, Seneca Falls
Seneca Falls Village Historic District

Steuben County
Erie Freight House Historic District, Bath
Gansevoort–East Steuben Streets Historic District, Bath
Liberty Street Historic District, Bath
Market Street Historic District, Corning

Suffolk County
Bay Crest Historic District, Huntington Bay
Beach Road Historic District, Southampton
Beaux Arts Park Historic District, Huntington Bay
Blydenburgh Park Historic District, Smithtown
Branch Historic District, Village of the Branch
Briar Patch Road Historic District, East Hampton
Buell's Lane Historic District, East Hampton
East Hampton Village Historic District
East Shore Road Historic District, Huntington
Egypt Lane Historic District, East Hampton
Goose Hill Road Historic District, Huntington
Greenport Village Historic District
Harbor Road Historic District, Huntington
Jericho Historic District, East Hampton
Jones Road Historic District, East Hampton
Main Street Historic District, Huntington
Miller Place Historic District, Brookhaven
Mills Pond District, Smithtown
Montauk Association Historic District, East Hampton
North Main Street Historic District, East Hampton
North Main Street Historic District, Southampton
Old Town Green Historic District, Huntington
Old Town Hall Historic District, Huntington
Orient Historic District, Southold
Pantigo Road Historic District, East Hampton
Sag Harbor Village District
Shore Road Historic District, Huntington

Southampton Village Historic District
Southside Sportsmens Club District, Islip
St. James Historic District, Smithtown
West Neck Road Historic District, Huntington
Wickapogue Road Historic District, Southampton
Wyandanch Club Historic District, Smithtown

Sullivan County
Grahamsville Historic District, Neversink
Liberty Village Historic District

Tioga County
Berkshire Village Historic District
Owego Central Historic District

Tompkins County
Cornell Heights Historic District, Ithaca
De Witt Park Historic District, Ithaca
Dryden Village Historic District
East Hill Historic District, Ithaca

Ulster County
Binnewater Historic District, Rosendale
Byrdcliffe Historic District, Woodstock
Chestnut Street Historic District, Kingston
Clinton Avenue Historic District, Kingston
Huguenot Street Historic District, New Paltz
Hurley Historic District
Kingston Stockade District
Main Street Historic District, Stone Ridge
Main-Partition Streets Historic District, Saugerties
Rondout–West Strand Historic District, Kingston
West Strand Historic District, Kingston

Warren County
Chestertown Historic District
Fredella Avenue Historic District, Glens Falls
Three Squares Historic District, Glens Falls
Warrensburg Mills Historic District

Washington County
Cambridge Historic District
Hudson Falls Historic District
Main Street Historic District, Whitehall
Salem Historic District
White Creek Historic District

Wayne County
Broad Street–Water Street Historic District, Lyons
East Main Street Commercial Historic District, Palmyra
Market Street Historic District, Palmyra
Pultneyville Historic District, Williamson

Westchester County
Bedford Road Historic District, North Castle
Bedford Village Historic District
Bell Place–Locust Avenue Historic District, Yonkers
Boston Post Road Historic District, Rye
Delavan Terrace Historic District, Yonkers
Downtown Ossining Historic District
Halcyon Place Historic District, Yonkers
Katonah Village Historic District, Bedford
Lawrence Park Historic District, Bronxville
North Grove Street Historic District, Tarrytown
Old Chappaqua Historic District, New Castle
Pound Ridge Historic District
Scarborough Historic District, Ossining
Smith, Alexander, Carpet Mills Historic District, Yonkers

Wyoming County
Silver Lake Institute Historic District
Wyoming Village Historic District

Yates County
Penn Yan Historic District
Yates County Courthouse Park District, Penn Yan

Since 1977, the National Park Service has encouraged the nomination of groups of noncontiguous properties linked geographically or thematically, both locally and statewide, in order for communities to identify and evaluate their historic resources in a more comprehensive manner. Originally called Multiple Resource Area and Thematic Resource nominations (and identified as such in this book), they are now known as Multiple Property Submissions. They are listed below — with the exception of one thematic group, United States Post Offices, which is treated separately in Appendix IV.

Albany County

Colonie Town Multiple Resource Area
Bacon-Stickney House
Senator William T. Byrne House
Frederick Cramer House
Martin Dunsbach House
Royal K. Fuller House
Isaac M. Haswell House
Hedge Lawn
Henry-Remsen House
Ebenezer Hills, Jr. Farmhouse
Friend Humphrey House
John Wolf Kemp House
John V. A. Lansing Farmhouse, Billsen Cemetery, and
    Archeological Site
George H. Lawton House
Louis Menand House
Menand Park Historic District
Menands Manor
Casparus F. Pruyn House
Reformed Dutch Church of Rensselaer in Watervliet
Alfred H. Renshaw House
Simmons Stone House
Jedediah Strong House
Treemont Manor
George Trimble House
Van Denbergh-Simmons House
Verdoy School

Guilderland Town Multiple Resource Area
Altamont Historic District
Apple Tavern
Aumic House
Chapel House
Coppola House
Frederick Crounse House
Jacob Crounse Inn
John and Henry Crounse Farm Complex
Freeman House
Fuller's Tavern
Gardner House
Gifford Grange Hall
Gillespie House
Guilderland Cemetery Vault
Hamilton Union Church Rectory
Hamilton Union Presbyterian Church
Helderberg Reformed Church
Adam Hilton House
Houck Farmhouse
Knower House
McNiven Farm Complex
Mynderse-Frederick House
Stephen Pangburn House
Charles Parker House
Prospect Hill Cemetery Building
Rose Hill
St. Mark's Lutheran Church
John Schoolcraft House
Schoolhouse No. 6
Sharp Brothers House
Sharp Farmhouse
Van Patten Barn Complex
Vanderpool Farm Complex
Veeder Farmhouse No. 1
Veeder Farmhouse No. 2

Historic Resources of U.S. Route 9, Town of Colonie
Bryan's Store
Godfrey Farmhouse
Gorham House

Hughson Mansion
Loudon Road Historic District
D. D. T. Moore Farmhouse
Springwood Manor
Wheeler Home
Whitney Mansion

Movie Palaces of the Tri-Cities Thematic Resources
Palace Theatre

Bronx County

Interborough Rapid Transit Control House Thematic Resources
Mott Avenue Control House

Chautauqua County

United States Coast Guard Lighthouses and Light Stations of the Great Lakes Thematic Resources
Point Gratiot Lighthouse Complex

Westfield Village Multiple Resource Area
Atwater-Stone House
L. Bliss House
Harriet Campbell-Taylor House
East Main Street Historic District
Fay-Usborne Mill
French Portage Road Historic District
Frank A. Hall House
Lake Shore & Michigan Southern Freight Depot
Lake Shore & Michigan Southern Railroad Station
Gerald Mack House
McMahan Homestead
Nixon Homestead
Rorig Bridge
Henry Dwight Thompson House
Ward House
Welch Factory Building No. 1
Reuben Gridley Wright Farm Complex
Reuben Wright House
York-Skinner House

Chemung County

Zim Thematic Resources
Teal Park
Zimmerman House

Chenango County

Central Plan Dairy Barns of New York State Thematic Resources
Bates Round Barn
Young Round Barn

Clinton County

Keeseville Village Multiple Resource Area
Double-Span Metal Pratt Truss Bridge
Keeseville Historic District

Plattsburgh City Multiple Resource Area
William Bailey House
Brinkerhoff Street Historic District
John B. Carpenter House
Clinton County Courthouse Complex
House at 56 Cornelia Street
Court Street Historic District
Delaware & Hudson Railroad Complex
D'Youville Academy
First Presbyterian Church
W. W. Hartwell House & Dependencies
Hawkins Hall
Paul Marshall House
Charles C. Platt Homestead
The Point Historic District
Z. Ritchie House
St. John the Baptist Roman Catholic Church and Rectory
S. F. Vilas Home for Aged & Infirmed Ladies
W. G. Wilcox House
Winslow-Turner Carriage House

Columbia County

Clermont Town Multiple Resource Area
Bouwerie
Thomas Brodhead House
Clarkson Chapel
Clermont Academy
Coons House
Hickory Hill
Old Parsonage
St. Luke's Church

Hudson Multiple Resource Area
Hudson Historic District
Rossman-Prospect Avenue Historic District

Delaware County

Central Plan Dairy Barns of New York State Thematic Resources
McArthur-Martin Hexadecagon Barn
Kelly Round Barn

Dutchess County

Chelsea Multiple Resource Area
Cornelius Carman House
Chelsea Grammar School
Captain Moses W. Collyer House
St. Mark's Episcopal Church

Dutchess County Quaker Meeting Houses Thematic Resources
Beekman Meeting House and Friends' Cemetery
Clinton Corners Friends Church
Creek Meeting House and Friends' Cemetery
Crum Elbow Meeting House and Cemetery
Montgomery Street Meeting House and Cemetery
Nine Partners Meeting House and Cemetery
Oswego Meeting House and Cemetery
Poughkeepsie Meeting House

Hudson Highlands Multiple Resource Area
Mount Beacon Incline Railway and Power House
Bannerman's Island Arsenal
Dutchess Manor

New Hamburg Multiple Resource Area
Abraham Brower House
Adolph Brower House
Main Street Historic District
St. Nicholas-on-the-Hudson Church
William Shay Double House
Shay's Warehouse and Stable
Stone Street Historic District
Union Free School

Poughkeepsie Multiple Resource Area
Academy Street Historic District
Adriance Memorial Library
Amrita Club
Balding Avenue Historic District
Barrett House
O. H. Booth Hose Company
Boughton-Haight House
Cedarcliff Gatehouse
Church Street Row
Clark House
Clinton House
Dixon House
Dutchess County Court House
Dwight Street–Hooker Avenue Historic District
Eastman Terrace
Ethol House
Farmer's and Manufacturer's Bank
First Presbyterian Church
First Presbyterian Church Rectory
Freer House
Glebe House
Gregory House
Grey Hook
Harlow Row
Hasbrouck House
Hershkind House
Lady Washington Hose Company
Luckey, Platt & Company Department Store

Mader House
Main Mall Row
Market Street Row
Moore House
Mulrien House
New York State Armory
Niagara Engine House
Pelton Mill
Phillips House
Post-Williams House
Poughkeepsie Trust Company
Poughkeepsie Underwear Factory
Reynolds House
Rombout House
Sague House
St. Paul's Episcopal Church
South Hamilton Street Row
Thompson House
Travis House
Trinity Methodist Episcopal Church and Rectory
Upper-Mill Street Historic District
Vassar-Warner Row
Young Men's Christian Association (Old)

Rhinebeck Town Multiple Resource Area
Astor Home for Children
Barringer Farmhouse
Benner House
Cox Farmhouse
Evergreen Lands
Fredenburg House
Free Church Parsonage
Grasmere
The Grove
Heermance House and Law Office
Hillside Methodist Church
Kip-Beekman-Heermance Site
Mansakenning
The Maples
Marquardt Farm
J. W. Moore House
Morton Memorial Library
O'Brien General Store and Post Office
Jan Pier House
Pilgrim's Progress Road Bridge
Progue House
Pultz Farmhouse
Rhinecliff Hotel
Riverside Methodist Church and Parsonage
Rock Ledge
St. Paul's Lutheran Church, Parsonage, and Cemetery
Salisbury Turnpike Bridge
Sipperly-Lown Farmhouse
Slate Quarry Road Dutch Barn
Steenburg Tavern
Stonecrest
Strawberry Hill
Traver House
J. E. Traver Farm
John H. Traver Farm
Van Vredenberg Farm
Williams Farm

Wappingers Falls Multiple Resource Area
Bain Commercial Building
Duchess Company Superintendent's House
Mulhern House
Wappingers Falls Historic District

Erie County

**Central Plan Dairy Barns of New York State
Thematic Resources**
Gamel Hexadecagon Barn

Masten Neighborhood Rows Thematic Resources
Row at 17-21 Emerson Place
Row at 33-61 Emerson Place
Laurel and Michigan Avenues Row
Woodlawn Avenue Row

Olmsted Parks and Parkways Thematic Resources
Cazenovia Park–South Park System
Martin Luther King, Jr., Park
Parkside East Historic District
Parkside West Historic District
Riverside Park

**United States Coast Guard Lighthouses and Light Stations
of the Great Lakes Thematic Resources**
Buffalo Main Light
Buffalo North Breakwater South End Light
South Buffalo North Side Light

Essex County

Great Camps of the Adirondacks Thematic Resources
Camp Santanoni

Keeseville Village Multiple Resource Area
Rembrandt Hall
Tomlinson House

Ticonderoga Multiple Resource Area
Black Watch Library
H. G. Burleigh House
Central School
Clark House
Community Building
Clayton H. Delano House
Ferris House
Gilligan and Stevens Block
Hancock House
Lake George Avenue Historic District
Liberty Monument
Silas B. Moore Gristmill
New York State Armory
The PAD Factory
Ticonderoga High School
Ticonderoga National Bank
Ticonderoga Pulp and Paper Company Office

Franklin County

Great Camps of the Adirondacks Thematic Resources
Camp Topridge
Camp Wild Air
Eagle Island Camp
Moss Ledge
Prospect Point Camp

Saranac Lake Multiple Resource Area
Berkeley Square Historic District
Paul Smith's Electric Light and Power and Railroad
    Company Complex

Greene County

Athens Village Multiple Resource Area
Athens Lower Village Historic District
Brick Row Historic District
Stranahan-DelVecchio House
Albertus Van Loon House
Zion Lutheran Church

Hudson River Lighthouses Thematic Group
Hudson-Athens Lighthouse

**Central Plan Dairy Barns of New York State
Thematic Resources**
Bronck Farm 13-Sided Barn

Hamilton County

Great Camps of the Adirondacks Thematic Resources
Camp Pine Knot
Camp Uncas
Echo Camp
Sagamore

Herkimer County

**Central Plan Dairy Barns of New York State
Thematic Resources**
Zoller-Frasier Round Barn

Jefferson County

Cape Vincent Multiple Resource Area
Levi Anthony Building
Aubertine Building
John Borland House
Broadway Historic District
James Buckley House
E. K. Burnham House
Xavier Chevalier House
Nicholas Cocaigne House
Remy Dezengremel House
Joseph Docteur House
Duvillard Mill
Reuter Dyer House
Jean Philippe Galband du Fort House
Glen Building
Johnson House
Lewis House
Captain Louis Peugnet House
George Reynolds House
Roxy Hotel
Cornelius Sacket House
General Sacket House
St. John's Episcopal Church
St. Vincent of Paul Catholic Church
Otis Starkey House
Union Meeting House
Claude Vautrin House
Warren Wilson House

Lyme Multiple Resource Area
Cedar Grove Cemetery
Chaumont Grange Hall and Dairymen's League Building
Chaumont Historic District
Chaumont House
Chaumont Railroad Station
Evans-Gaige-Dillenback House
George Brothers Building
George House
District School No. 3
Getman Farmhouse
Lance Farm
Old Stone Shop
Point Salubrious Historic District
The Row Historic District
Taft House
Taylor Boathouse
Three Mile Bay Historic District
United Methodist Church
Menzo Wheeler House
Wilcox Farmhouse

Hounsfield Multiple Resource Area
Bedford Creek Bridge
Conklin Farm
District School No. 19
District School No. 20
East Hounsfield Christian Church
Dr. Samuel Guthrie House
Resseguie Farm
Shore Farm
Stephen Simmons Farmhouse
Star Grange No. 9
Stephenson-Frink Farm
Sulphur Springs Cemetery

Stone Houses of Brownville Thematic Resources
William Archer House
General Jacob Brown Mansion
Brownville Hotel
Vogt House
Arthur Walrath House

**United States Coast Guard Lighthouses and Light Station
of the Great Lakes Thematic Resources**
Tibbetts Point Light
Galloo Island Light

Kings County

**Interborough Rapid Transit Control House
Thematic Resources**
Atlantic Avenue Control House

Ridgewood Multiple Resource Area
Willoughby-Suydem Historic District

Livingston County

Lima Town Multiple Resource Area
Alverson-Copeland House
Barnard Cobblestone House
Bristol House
Cargill House
Clark Farm Complex
Dayton House
Draper House
William DePuy House
Ganoung Cobblestone Farmhouse
Godfrey House and Barn Complex
Harden House
William Harmon House
Leech-Lloyd Farmhouse
Leech-Lloyd Farmhouse: Barn Complex
Leech-Parker Farmhouse
Markham Cobblestone Farmhouse
Martin Farm Complex
Morgan Cobblestone Farmhouse
Ogilvie Moses Farmhouse
Zebulon Moses Farmhouse
Franklin J. Peck House
Thomas Peck Farmhouse
School No. 6
Spencer House
Stanley House
William L. Vary House
Asahel Warner House
Matthew Warner House

Madison County

Canastota Multiple Resource Area
Canal Town Museum
Canastota Methodist Church
Canastota Public Library
House at 233 James Street
House at 205 North Main Street
House at 313 North Main Street
House at 326 North Peterboro Street
House at 328 North Peterboro Street
Peterboro Street Elementary School
Judge Nathan S. Roberts House
House at 115 South Main Street
South Peterboro Street Commercial Historic District
South Peterboro Street Residential Historic District
House at 107 Stroud Street
United Church of Canastota

Cazenovia Town Multiple Resource Area
Abell Farmhouse and Barn
Annas Farmhouse
Beckwith Farmhouse
Brick House
Cazenovia Village Historic District
Cedar Cove
Chappell Farmhouse
Cobblestone House
Zephinia Comstock Farmhouse
Crandall Farm Complex
Evergreen Acres
The Hickories
Hillcrest
Lehigh Valley Railroad Depot
The Maples
The Meadows Farm Complex
Middle Farmhouse
Niles Farmhouse
Notleymere
Old Trees
Ormonde
Parker Farmhouse
Rolling Ridge Farm
Shattuck House
Sweetland Farmhouse
Tall Pines

Upenough
York Lodge

Monroe County

Inner Loop Multiple Resource Area
Bridge Square Historic District
Adam Brown Block
Chamber of Commerce
H. C. Cohen Company Building
Court Exchange Building
Chester Dewey School No. 14
First National Bank of Rochester
Gannett Building
Grove Place Historic District
Jewish Young Men's and Women's Association
Kirstein Building
Lehigh Valley Railroad Station
Little Theatre
Michaels-Stern Building
Naval Armory–Convention Hall
Reynolds Arcade
Rochester Fire Department
Rundel Memorial Library
St. Paul–North Water Streets Historic District
Sibley Triangle Building
State Street Historic District
University Club
H. H. Warner Building
Washington Street Rowhouses
Wilder Building

Inner Loop Multiple Resource Area: Department Store Thematic Group
Cox Building
Edwards Building
Granite Building
National Company Building

Inner Loop Multiple Resource Area: Stone Arch Bridge Thematic Resources
Andrews Street Bridge
Court Street Bridge
Main Street Bridge

Pittsford Village Multiple Resource Area
Pittsford Village Historic District

Montgomery County

Montgomery County Buildings Thematic Resources
County Farm
New Courthouse
Old Courthouse Complex

Nassau County

Long Island Wind and Tide Mills Thematic Resources
Saddle Rock Grist Mill

Multiple Resources of the Village of Roslyn
Henry Western Eastman Cottage
Hicks Lumber Company Store
Roslyn Grist Mill
Roslyn National Bank & Trust Company
Roslyn Savings Bank
Roslyn Village Historic District
Willet Titus House
Trinity Church
Samuel Adams Warner Estate Cottage

Sea Cliff Summer Resort Thematic Resources
House at 207 Carpenter Avenue
House at 115 Central Avenue
Central Hall
Crowell House
House at 52 18th Avenue
House at 58 18th Avenue
House at 290 Eighth Avenue
House at 332 Franklin Avenue
House at 285 Glen Avenue
House at 378 Glen Avenue
House at 9 Locust Place
House at 19 Locust Place
House at 137 Prospect Avenue

House at 176 Prospect Avenue
House at 195 Prospect Avenue
House at 199 Prospect Avenue
House at 103 Roslyn Avenue
St. Luke's Episcopal Church
House at 112 Sea Cliff Avenue
House at 240 Sea Cliff Avenue
House at 285 Sea Cliff Avenue
House at 362 Sea Cliff Avenue
Sea Cliff Railroad Station
House at 18 17th Avenue
House at 173 16th Avenue
House at 65 20th Avenue

New York County

Interborough Rapid Transit Subway Control Houses Thematic Resources
Battery Park Control House
Control House on 72nd Street

Sidewalk Clocks of New York City Thematic Resources
Sidewalk Clock at 200 Fifth Avenue
Sidewalk Clock at 522 Fifth Avenue
Sidewalk Clock at 783 Fifth Avenue
Sidewalk Clock at 519 Third Avenue
Sidewalk Clock at 1501 Third Avenue

Niagara County

United States Coast Guard Lighthouses and Light Stations on the Great Lakes Thematic Resources
Fort Niagara Light
Thirty Mile Point Light

Orange County

Cornwall Multiple Resource Area
Cornwall Friend's Meeting House

Delaware and Hudson Canal Thematic Resources
Delaware and Hudson Canal, Cuddebackville Section

Hudson Highlands Multiple Resource Area
Storm King Highway
Amelia Barr House
Camp Olmsted
Deer Hill
Gatehouse on Deerhill Road
LeDoux/Healey House
River View House
House at 37 Center Street
Church of the Holy Innocents and Rectory
First Presbyterian Church of Highland Falls
Highland Falls Railroad Depot
Highland Falls Village Hall
House at 116 Main Street
Parry House
Pine Terrace
The Squirrels
Stonihurst
Webb Lane House
Cragston Dependencies
St. Mark's Episcopal Church

Montgomery Village Multiple Resource Area
Bridge Street Historic District
Johannes Miller Farmhouse
Montgomery Worsted Mills
Patchett-Crabtree House
Union Street–Academy Hill Historic District

Oswego County

Mexico Multiple Property Submission
Leonard Ames Farmhouse
Arthur Tavern
Peter Chandler House
Phineas Davis Farmstead
Fowler-Loomis House
Hamilton Farmstead
Mexico Academy and Central School
Mexico Octagon Barn
Mexico Village Historic District
Red Mill Farm

Timothy Skinner House
Slack Farmstead
Stillman Farmstead
Thayer Farmstead

Sandy Creek Multiple Resource Area
Smith H. Barlow House
First Baptist Church
First National Bank of Lacona
Holyoke Cottage
Lacona Clock Tower
Methodist Church
Pitt M. Newton House
Samuel Sadler House
Charles M. Salisbury House
Sandy Creek Historic District
Matthew Shoecroft House
Fred Smart House
Newman Tuttle House

Otsego County

Central Plan Dairy Barns of New York State Thematic Resources
Lunn-Musser Octagon Barn
Baker Octagon Barn

Putnam County

Hudson Highlands Multiple Resource Area
The Birches
Cold Spring Historic District
H. D. Champlin & Son Horseshoeing and Wagonmaking
Cold Spring Cemetery Gatehouse
House at 3 Crown Street
J. Y. Dykman Flour and Feed Store
J. Y. Dykman Store
Eagle's Rest
Fair Lawn
First Baptist Church of Cold Spring
Fish and Fur Club
Garrison Landing Historic District
Garrison Union Free School
Glenfields
Hurst-Pierrepont Estate
Hustis House
House at 249 Main Street
Mandeville House
Montrest
Moore House
Normandy Grange
Oulagisket
Rock Lawn and Carriage House
Walter Thompson House and Carriage House
Walker House
Wilson House
Woodlawn

Queens County

Ridgewood Multiple Resource Area
Central Avenue Historic District
Central Ridgewood Historic District
Cooper Avenue Row Historic District
Cornelia-Putnam Historic District
Cypress Avenue East Historic District
Cypress Avenue West Historic District
Forest-Norman Historic District
Fresh Pond–Traffic Historic District
Grove-Linden-St. John's Historic District
Madison–Putnam–60th Place Historic District
Seneca Avenue East Historic District
Seneca-Onderdonk-Woodward Historic District
75th Avenue–61st Street Historic District
68th Avenue–64th Place Historic District
Stockholm-DeKalb-Hart Historic District
Summerfield Street Row Historic District
Woodbine-Palmetto-Gates Historic District

Sidewalk Clocks of New York City Thematic Resources
Sidewalk Clock at 161-11 Jamaica Avenue

Rensselaer County

Movie Palaces of the Tri-Cities Thematic Resources
Proctor's Theater

Rockland County

Hudson River Lighthouses Thematic Group
Stony Point Lighthouse

Palisades Multiple Resource Area
The Big House
Cliffside
Closter Road–Oak Tree Road Historic District
Abner Concklin House
Haring-Eberle House
The Little House
Neiderhurst
Seven Oaks Estate
Washington Spring Road–Woods Road Historic District

Hudson Highlands Multiple Resource Area
Bear Mountain Bridge and Toll House

St. Lawrence County

Morristown Village Multiple Resource Area
Jacob Ford House
Land Office
Paschal Miller House
Morristown Schoolhouse
Samuel Stocking House
Stone Windmill
United Methodist Church
Wright's Stone Store

Schenectady County

Duanesburg Multiple Resource Area
Abrahams Farmhouse
Avery Farmhouse
Becker Farmhouse
Joseph Braman House
Chadwick Farmhouse
Chapman Farmhouse
Christ Episcopal Church
Delanson Historic District
Duane Mansion
Duanesburg-Florida Baptist Church
Eatons Corners Historic District
Ferguson Farm Complex
Gaige Homestead
Gilbert Farmhouse
Joseph Green Farmhouse
Halladay Farmhouse
Hawes Homestead
Howard Homestead
Jenkins House
Jenkins Octagon House
A. D. "Boss" Jones House
Ladd Farmhouse
George Lasher House
Alexander Liddle Farmhouse
Robert Liddle Farmhouse
Thomas Liddle Farm Complex
Macomber Stone House
Mariaville Historic District
North Mansion and Tenant House
Quaker Street Historic District
Reformed Presbyterian Church Parsonage
Sheldon Farmhouse
Shute Octagon House
Joseph Wing Farm Complex
William R. Wing Farm Complex

Movie Palaces of the Tri-Cities Thematic Resources
F. F. Proctor Theater and Arcade

Schoharie County

Central Plan Dairy Barns of New York State Thematic Resources
Parker 13-Sided Barn

Schuyler County

Central Plan Dairy Barns of New York State Thematic Resources
Lattin -Crandall Octagon Barn

Seneca County

Women's Rights Historic Sites Thematic Resources
Hunt House
McClintock House
Mumford House
Elizabeth Cady Stanton House
Wesleyan Methodist Church

Steuben County

Bath Village Multiple Resource Area
Campbell-Rumsey House
Cobblestone House
Davenport Library
Gansevoort–East Steuben Streets Historic District
Haverling Farm House
Liberty Street Historic District
McMaster House
Potter-Van Camp House
Reuben Robie House
Sedgwick House
William Shepherd House

Suffolk County

East Hampton Village Multiple Resource Area
Briar Patch Road Historic District
Buell's Lane Historic District
Egypt Lane Historic District
Jericho Historic District
Jones Road Historic District
North Main Street Historic District
Pantigo Road Historic District

Greenport Village Multiple Resource Area
Greenport Railroad Station Complex
Greenport Village Historic District

Huntington Town Multiple Resource Area
House at 200 Bay Avenue
Bay Crest Historic District
M. Baylis House
Beaux Arts Park Historic District
Bethel A.M.E. Church and Manse
Bowes House
George McKesson Brown Estate
Brush Farmstead
Eliphas Buffett House
Joseph Buffett House
John Bumpstead House
Carll Burr, Jr., House
Carll S. Burr Mansion
Carll House (Cold Spring Harbor)
Carll House (Dix Hills)
Ezra Carll Homestead
Chichester's Inn
Cold Spring Harbor Library
Commack Methodist Church and Cemetery
David Conklin House
Delamater-Bevin Mansion
Harry E. Donnell House
Dowden Tannery
East Shore Road Historic District
John Everit House
N. J. Felix House
Charles Geoghegan House
Gilsey Mansion
Goose Hill Road Historic District
John Green House
Halsey Estate
Harbor Road Historic District
John Harned House
Wallace K. Harrison Estate
Heckscher Park
Hewlett House
Ireland-Gardiner Farm
Jarvis-Fleet House
John P. Kane Mansion

A. P. W. Kennan House
B. Ketchum House
Isaac Losee House
Main Street Historic District
John Oakley House
C. A. O'Donohue House
Old First Church
Old Town Green Historic District
Old Town Hall Historic District
House at 244 Park Avenue
Potter-Williams House
Prime House
Prime-Octagon House
Michael Remp House
Rogers House
John Rogers House
Silas Sammis House
Seaman Farm
Shore Road Historic District
Daniel Smith House
Henry Smith Farmstead
Jacob Smith House
Suydam House
Sweet Hollow Presbyterian Church Parsonage
Titus-Bunce House
Henry Townsend House
Charles Van Iderstine Mansion
William K. Vanderbilt Estate
N. Velzer House and Caretaker's Cottage
Charles M. Weeks House
West Neck Road Historic District
Joseph Whitman House
Walt Whitman House
Whitman-Place House
Wiggins-Rolph House
Henry Williams House
Harry Wood House
John Wood House
William Wooden Wood House
Charles Woodhull House

Long Island Wind and Tide Mills Thematic Resources
Beebe Windmill
Gardiners Island Windmill
Hayground Windmill
Hook Windmill
Shelter Island Windmill
Van Wyck–Lefferts Tide Mill
Wainscott Windmill
Windmill at Water Mill

Southampton Village Multiple Resource Area
Balcastle
Beach Road Historic District
Dr. Wesley Bowers House
Captain C. Goodale House
North Main Street Historic District
Southampton Village Historic District
Wickapogue Road Historic District

Sullivan County

**Highway Bridges Owned by the Commonwealth
of Pennsylvania, Department of Transportation
Thematic Resources**
Millanville–Skinners Falls Bridge
Pond Eddy Bridge

Delaware and Hudson Canal Thematic Resources
Delaware and Hudson Canal, Roebling Aqueduct

Tioga County

Berkshire Town Multiple Resource Area
Lyman P. Akins House
Robert Akins House
J. Ball House
Levi Ball House
Stephen Ball House
Belcher Family Homestead and Farm
Berkshire Village Historic District
Calvin A. Buffington House

Nathaniel Bishop Collins House
East Berkshire United Methodist Church
First Congregational Church
Lebbeus Ford House
Deodatus Royce House
J. B. Royce House and Farm Complex

Tompkins County

Dryden Village Multiple Resource Area
Luther Clarke House
Dryden Village Historic District
Jennings-Marvin House
Lacy-Van Vleet House
Methodist Episcopal Church
Rockwell House
Southworth House
Southworth Library

**New York State College of Agriculture
Thematic Resources**
Bailey Hall
Caldwell Hall
Comstock Hall
East Roberts Hall
Fernow Hall
Rice Hall
Roberts Hall
Stone Hall
Wing Hall

Ulster County

Hudson River Lighthouses Thematic Group
Esopus Meadows Lighthouse
Kingston/Rondout 2 Lighthouse
Saugerties Lighthouse

Delaware and Hudson Canal Thematic Resources
Delaware and Hudson Canal, Alligerville Section
Delaware and Hudson Canal, Locks at High Falls

Shawangunk Valley Multiple Resource Area
Peter Aldrich Homestead
Bevier House
Brykill
William Decker House
Dill Farm
Johannes Jansen House and Dutch Barn
Thomas Jansen House
Miller's House at Red Mills
Pearl Street Schoolhouse
Terwilliger House
Van Vleck House

Warren County

Glens Falls Multiple Resource Area
Argent Apartments
Bemis Eye Sanitarium Complex
Stephen T. Birdsall House
Addison B. Colvin House
Zopher Delong House
James L. Dix House
18th Separate Company Armory
Dr. James Ferguson Office
First Presbyterian Church
Dr. Charles A. Foster House
Glens Falls Feeder Canal
Glens Falls Home for Aged Women
Stephen L. Goodman House
Joubert and White Building
Hiram Krum House
Russell M. Little House
William McEchron House
Jones Ordway House
George H. Parks House
Enoch Rosekrans House
A. S. Rugge House
St. Mary's Academy
Smith Flats
Society of Friends Hall
Thomas Stilwell House
Three Squares Historic District

F. W. Wait House
House at 216 Warren Street

**Glens Falls Multiple Resource Area: Buildings of
Ephraim B. Potter Thematic Resources**
Thomas Burnham House
W. T. Cowles House
Glens Falls High School
John E. Parry House
Peyser and Morrison Shirt Company Building
Ephraim B. Potter House
Martin L. C. Wilmarth House
Helen Wing House

**Glens Falls Multiple Resource Area: Buildings of
Henry Forbes Bigelow Thematic Resources**
Cunningham House
Hoopes House
Hyde House

**Glens Falls Multiple Resource Area: Fredella Concrete
Block Structures Thematic Resources**
Fredella Avenue Historic District
Joseph J. Fredella House and Garage

Washington County

**Covered Bridges of Washington County
Thematic Resources**
Buskirk Covered Bridge
Eagleville Covered Bridge
Rexleigh Covered Bridge
Shushan Covered Bridge

Westchester County

Horace Greeley Thematic Resources
Chappaqua Railroad Depot and Depot Plaza
Church of Saint Mary the Virgin and Greeley Grove
Greeley House
Rehoboth

Hudson Highlands Multiple Resource Area
Bear Mountain Bridge Road

Public Bath Houses of Yonkers Thematic Resources
Public Bath House No. 2
Public Bath House No. 3
Public Bath House No. 4

United States Post Offices in New York State, 1858-1943, Thematic Resources

The largest thematic group listed in the National Register comprises 141 post offices located in 53 different counties. These have been separated from Appendix II to clarify their identity as a single cohesive group.

Albany County
Delmar

Allegany County
Wellsville

Bronx County
Morrisania Station

Broome County
Endicott
Johnson City

Cattaraugus County
Little Valley
Olean

Chautauqua County
Dunkirk
Fredonia

Chenango County
Norwich
Oxford

Columbia County
Hudson

Cortland County
Cortland
Homer

Delaware County
Delhi
Walton

Dutchess County
Beacon
Hyde Park
Poughkeepsie
Rhinebeck
Wappingers Falls

Erie County
Akron
Angola
Buffalo
Depew
Lancaster
Springville
Tonawanda

Essex County
Lake Placid
Ticonderoga

Franklin County
Malone

Fulton County
Johnstown

Genesee County
LeRoy

Greene County
Catskill

Herkimer County
Dolgeville
Frankfort
Herkimer

Ilion
Little Falls

Jefferson County
Carthage

Kings County
Flatbush Station
Kensington Station
Metropolitan Station
Parkville Station

Livingston County
Dansville

Madison County
Canastota
Hamilton
Oneida

Monroe County
East Rochester
Honeoye Falls

Montgomery County
Amsterdam
Canajoharie
Fort Plain
St. Johnsville

Nassau County
Freeport
Garden City
Glen Cove
Great Neck
Hempstead
Long Beach
Mineola
Oyster Bay
Rockville Centre

New York County
Canal Street Station
Church Street Station
Cooper Station
Inwood Station
Knickerbocker Station
Lenox Hill Station
Madison Square Station
Old Chelsea Station

Niagara County
Lockport
Middleport
Niagara Falls
North Tonawanda

Oneida County
Boonville

Ontario County
Canandaigua
Geneva

Orange County
Goshen
Newburgh
Port Jervis

Orleans County
Albion
Medina

Oswego County
Fulton

Otsego County
Cooperstown
Richfield Springs

Queens County
Far Rockaway
Flushing
Forest Hills Station
Jackson Heights Station

Jamaica
Long Island City

Rensselaer County
Hoosick Falls
Troy

Rockland County
Haverstraw
Nyack
Pearl River
Spring Valley
Suffern

St. Lawrence County
Canton
Gouverneur
Potsdam

Saratoga County
Ballston Spa
Saratoga Springs

Schenectady County
Schenectady
Scotia Station

Schoharie County
Middleburgh

Schuyler County
Watkins Glen

Seneca County
Seneca Falls
Waterloo

Steuben County
Bath
Corning
Painted Post

Suffolk County
Bay Shore
Northport
Patchogue
Riverhead
Westhampton Beach

Tioga County
Owego
Waverly

Tompkins County
Ithaca

Ulster County
Ellenville

Warren County
Lake George

Washington County
Granville
Hudson Falls
Whitehall

Wayne County
Clyde
Lyons
Newark

Westchester County
Bronxville
Dobbs Ferry
Harrison
Mount Vernon
New Rochelle
Peekskill
Port Chester
Rye
Scarsdale
Yonkers

Wyoming County
Attica
Warsaw

Yates County
Penn Yan

APPENDIX V
National Historic Landmarks

Under the Historic Sites Act of 1935, the National Park Service started research of nationally important historic properties, later recognized as National Historic Landmarks by the Secretary of the Interior. All properties so designated were subsequently listed in the National Register of Historic Places as of October 15, 1966. Properties designated as National Historic Landmarks since that time are automatically entered in the National Register. The date of listing is preceded by the letters NHL in the property descriptions.

Albany County
James Hall Office
New York State Capitol
St. Peter's Church
Philip Schuyler Mansion
Watervliet Arsenal

Bronx County
Bartow-Pell Mansion and Carriage House
Lorillard Snuff Mill
New York Botanical Garden
Frederick Van Cortlandt House

Cayuga County
William H. Seward House
Harriet Tubman Home for the Aged
Jethro Wood House

Chautauqua County
Lewis Miller Cottage
Chautauqua Institution Historic District

Chemung County
Newtown Battlefield

Clinton County
Adirondack State Forest Preserve
Plattsburgh Bay
Valcour Bay

Columbia County
Olana
Clermont
Lindenwald
Mount Lebanon Shaker Society
Steepletop
Lucas Van Alen House

Delaware County
Woodchuck Lodge

Dutchess County
Hudson River State Hospital, Main Building
Locust Grove
Vassar College, Main Building
Matthew Vassar Estate

Erie County
Buffalo and Erie County Historical Society
Buffalo State Hospital
Millard Fillmore House
Kleinhans Music Hall
Darwin D. Martin House
Guaranty Building
Roycroft Campus
St. Paul's Episcopal Cathedral
USS *The Sullivans* (DD-537)

Essex County
Adirondack State Forest Preserve
Fort Crown Point
Fort St. Frederick
Fort Ticonderoga
Elkanah Watson House

Franklin County
Adirondack State Forest Preserve

Fulton County
Adirondack State Forest Preserve
Johnson Hall

Genesee County
Holland Land Office

Greene County
Pieter Bronck House
Thomas Cole House

Hamilton County
Adirondack State Forest Preserve

Herkimer County
Adirondack State Forest Preserve

Kings County
Brooklyn Bridge
Brooklyn Heights Historic District
Brooklyn Historical Society Building
Church of St. Ann and the Holy Trinity
Plymouth Church of the Pilgrims Quarters A
John Roosevelt "Jackie" Robinson Residence
Wyckoff-Bennett Homestead
Pieter Claesen Wyckoff House

Lewis County
Franklin B. Hough House

Livingston County
Geneseo Historic District

Madison County
Oneida Community Mansion House

Monroe County
Susan B. Anthony House
George Eastman House

Montgomery County
Erie Canal
Fort Johnson
Fort Klock

Nassau County
John Philip Sousa House

New York County
Ambrose
American Stock Exchange
Chester A. Arthur House
Bayard-Condict Building
Bell Telephone Laboratories
Andrew Carnegie Mansion
Carnegie Hall
Central Park
Central Synagogue
Church of the Ascension
Chrysler Building
City Hall
Will Marion Cook House
Cooper Union
Daily News Building
Dakota Apartments
William Dyckman House
Edward Kennedy "Duke" Ellington Residence
Empire State Building
Equitable Building
First National City Bank
Hamilton Fish House
Flatiron Building
Founder's Hall, Rockefeller University
Governors Island
Grace Church and Dependencies
Grand Central Terminal
Hamilton Grange National Memorial
Henry Street Settlement and Neighborhood Playhouse
Matthew Henson Residence
James Weldon Johnson House
Lettie G. Howard (*Mystic C*)
Low Memorial Library, Columbia University
R. H. Macy and Company Store
McGraw-Hill Building
Claude McKay Residence
Metropolitan Life Insurance Tower
Metropolitan Museum of Art
Florence Mills House
J. Pierpont Morgan Library
Morris-Jumel Mansion
New York Amsterdam News Building
New York Chamber of Commerce Building
New York Cotton Exchange
New York Life Building
New York Public Library and Bryant Park
New York Stock Exchange
New York Yacht Club
Old Merchant's House
Old New York County Courthouse
The Players Club
Plaza Hotel and Grand Army Plaza
Pupin Physics Laboratories, Columbia University
Paul Robeson Home
Rockefeller Center
St. George's Episcopal Church
St. Patrick's Cathedral
St. Paul's Chapel
General Winfield Scott House
Seventh Regiment Armory
Harry F. Sinclair House
Alfred E. Smith House
Soho Cast-Iron Historic District
A. T. Stewart Company Store
Surrogate's Court
Third Judicial District Courthouse
Tiffany and Company Building
Samuel J. Tilden House
Triangle Shirtwaist Factory Building
Trinity Church and Graveyard
United Charities Building Complex
United States Custom House
USS *Edson*
USS *Intrepid* (CV-11)
Woolworth Building

Niagara County
Adams Power Plant Transformer House
Niagara Reservation
Old Fort Niagara

Oneida County
Roscoe Conkling House
General William Floyd House
Oriskany Battlefield
Elihu Root House
Utica State Hospital

Ontario County
Boughton Hill

Orange County
Delaware and Hudson Canal, Cuddebackville Section
Fort Montgomery Site
Arden
Historic Track
Knox Headquarters
United States Military Academy
Washington's Headquarters

Oswego County
Tugboat *Nash*

Otsego County
Hyde Hall

Queens County
Louis Armstrong House
Ralph Bunche House
King Manor
Old Quaker Meetinghouse

Rensselaer County
Bennington Battlefield
Fort Crailo
W. & L. E. Gurley Building
Troy Savings Bank and Music Hall

Richmond County
Conference House
Fire Fighter
Sailors' Snug Harbor
Voorlezer's House

Rockland County
De Wint House
Palisades Interstate Park
Stony Point Battlefield

St. Lawrence County
Adirondack State Forest Preserve

Saratoga County
Canfield Casino and Congress Park
Saratoga Spa State Park District

Schenectady County
General Electric Research Laboratory
Irving Langmuir House
Nott Memorial Hall

Schoharie County
Old Blenheim Bridge

Schuyler County
Lamoka

Seneca County
Rose Hill
Elizabeth Cady Stanton House

Suffolk County
Thomas Moran House
William Sidney Mount House
The Old House

Sullivan County
Delaware and Hudson Canal, Roebling Aqueduct

Tompkins County
Morrill Hall

Ulster County
John Burroughs Riverby Study
Delaware and Hudson Canal, Alligerville Section
Delaware and Hudson Canal, Locks at High Falls
Jean Hasbrouck House
Huguenot Street Historic District
Hurley Historic District

Lake Mohonk Mountain House Complex
Slabsides

Warren County
Adirondack State Forest Preserve
Owl's Nest

Washington County
Lemuel Haynes House

Westchester County
Armour-Stiner House
Edwin H. Armstrong House
John W. Draper House
Dutch Reformed (Sleepy Hollow) Church
Lyndhurst
John A. Hartford House
John Jay Homestead
Thomas Paine Cottage
Philipsburg Manor
Philipse Manor Hall
Playland Amusement Park
John D. Rockefeller Estate
Sunnyside
Van Cortlandt Manor
Villa Lewaro

APPENDIX VI
Architects, Landscape Architects, Builders, and Engineers

A total of 948 individuals and firms responsible for the design and construction of National Register properties in New York State are named in the property descriptions. Index 1 provides page references to specific examples of their work.

Abramson, Louis Allen
Ackerman, Frederick L.
Adams & Prentice
Ahlschlager, Walter W.
Aiken, William Martin
Albro & Lindeberg
Albro, Lewis Colt
Allen & Collens
Allmendinger & Schlendorf
Allmendinger, Louis
Allom, Sir Charles
Almirall, Raymond F.
Ammann & Whitney
Amon, Will Rice
Arnold, James B.
Arnold, Silas
Atkinson, E.
Atterbury, Grosvenor
Auchmuty, Richard T.
Austin & Warner
Babb, Cook & Willard
Babcock, Charles
Backus, Frederick
Bacon, Henry
Baird, Howard C.
Baker, James B.
Baker, Robert
Barber, Donn
Barber, E. L.
Barlow, William V. N.
Barnes, Edward Larrabee
Barney & Chapman
Bartholdi, Frederic Auguste
Batcheller, Zephaniah
Bates, William A.
Baum, Dwight James
Baum, Harry
Beard, William
Beardsley, William J.
Beebe, H. L.
Beebe, Phil V.
Beers, William Thomas
Belcher, Henry White
Bell, Mifflin E.
Beman, Simon Soloman
Beman, Warren and Ransom
Bennett, Horace H.
Berger, Louis, & Co.
Bigelow, Henry Forbes
Bird, James
Birdsall, George W.
Blake, Theodore
Blanchard, Huse Templeton
Blesch & Eidlitz
Bley & Lyman
Bluemiser, Oscar
Bogardus, James
Bohacket & Brew
Bolton, Robert
Bonesteel, Jacob
Borgeau, Victor
Boring & Tilton
Bosworth, William Welles
Bottomley, Wagner & White
Bowditch, Ernest
Bowdoin & Webster
Brady, Josiah R.
Bragdon, Claude F.
Brenner, Arnold W.
Brisbane, Albert
Brockett, William
Brockway, Albert L.
Brown & Dawson

Brown & Von Beren
Brown, Archibald Manning
Brown, Frederick W.
Brunner & Aiken
Brunner & Tryon
Buchman & Deisler
Buchman & Fox
Buck, J. J.
Buckingham, John
Buckley, John
Buckley, Richard W.
Buek, Charles
Bunshaft, Gordon
Bunting, Charles T.
Burgevin, Julius
Burnham, Daniel H., & Co.
Bushnell, Raymond H.
Bussell, Alfred
Butler, Frederic
Butler, Lawrence Smith
Cady & See
Cady, A. B.
Cady, Berg & See
Cady, J. Cleveland
Candela, Rosario
Cannon, Arnout, Jr.
Carpenter & Blair
Carpenter, Charles A.
Carpenter, DuBois
Carpenter, William S.
Carrere & Hastings
Cary, George
Casale, James
Casey, Edward P.
Chambers, Walter B.
Chanin, Irwin S.
Chappell, George P.
Child & deGoll
Christie, David
Church, Frederic E.
Churchill, John
Civiletti, Pasquale
Clapp, Ephraim
Clark, Carl W.
Clark, Frank
Clark, Mary Mobray
Clark, William
Clarke, Charles E.
Clarke, George
Clarke, Gilmore D.
Clarkson, Robert L.
Cleverdon & Putzel
Clinton & Russell
Clinton, Charles W.
Clowes, Timothy
Cobb, Henry Ives
Cobb, William R.
Codman, Ogden, Jr.
Coffin, Marian
Cogden, Henry M.
Coles, Frederick H.
Collins, Charles
Colton, Charles (and Charles E.)
Comrie, McIntyre
Comstock, Frederick L. (and
     Frederick R.)
Conable, George W.
Congdon, Henry M.
Conover, Peter
Conrad & Cummings
Considine, Joseph
Cook, Frederick S.
Cook, William M.
Cooley, Elihu
Coolidge, Shepley, Bulfinch &
     Abbot
Copley, Frederick
Corbett, Harrison & MacMurray
Corbett, Harvey Wiley
Cornell, Frank
Coulter, William L.
Cowles, George S.
Crabtree, Walter P.
Cram, Goodhue & Ferguson
Cram, Ralph Adams
Crandall & Strobel

Crawley, George A.
Croff, Gilbert B.
Crooks, Arthur
Cropsey, Jasper F.
Cross & Cross
Cross, Gilbert
Cummings, Frederick
Cummings, M. F., & Son
Cummings, Marcus F.
Curtis, Enoch
Curtis, George (and
     Curtiss, George)
Cutler, James G.
Cutter, Manly N.
Cuyler, John Y.
Daniels, Howard
Daus & Otto
Daus, Rudolph L.
Davis, Alexander Jackson
Davis, Richard R.
de Lery, Chaussegros
Dean, Clarence
Debevoise, George W.
Delano & Aldrich
Delano, William Adams
DeLemos & Cordes
Dennison & Hirons
Dewey, Charles E.
DeWitt, Simeon
Diaper, Frederick
Dickenson, Warren C.
Dietrich, Ernest G. W.
Distin, William, Jr.
Dixon, Robert
Dockstader & Considine
Dockstader, Otis
Dominy, Nathaniel, V
Donnell, Harry E.
Dorn, Rufus H.
Douglas, William O.
Douglass, Major David B.
Downer, Jay
Downing, Andrew Jackson
Driesler, Benjamin
Duboy, Paul E. M.
Duckworth, Isaac
Dudley, Henry
Dudley, John
Duncan, John (and John H.)
Duncan, Perry
Durant, William West
Dusinberre, Ralph
Dymond, Horace
Earnshaw, Joseph
Easingwood, Arthur L.
Eberson, John
Edbrooke, Willoughby J.
Edgarton & Edgarton
Edmunds, Philip
Edwards, Theodore P.
Eidlitz, Cyrus L.W.
Eidlitz, Leopold
Eiffel, Alexandre Gustave
Eldredge, George (and Eldridge,
     George)
Eldredge, Hezekiah
Ellett, Thomas Harlan
Ellis, Charles
Ellis, Harvey
Elliston, Edward
Embury, Aymar
Embury, Aymar, II
Embury, Aymar, III
Emerson, William Ralph
Engelbert, Henry
Esenwein & Johnson
Eyre, Wilson
Fardon, Thomas
Farrar, Charles S.
Fellheimer & Long
Fellheimer & Wagner
Felson, Jacob M.
Fenner, T.
Fernback, Henry
Field & Diem
Field, Dudley

Field, William, & Son
Fielding, H. P.
Finch, Oren
Fine, Marvin
Firestone, Siegmund
Fischel, Harry
Fischer, Adam E.
Flagg, Ernest
Fleming, Bryant
Flournoy, Benjamin C.
Floyd-Jones, Elbert
Flynn, Joseph F.
Foit & Baschnagel
Foote, Orlando K.
Forster, Frank J.
Foster, William Dewey
Fouchaux, Henri
Fouilhoux, J. Andre
Fowler & Hough
Fowler, Halstead P.
Frazee, John
Fredella Company
Freeburg, Raymond
Freedlander, Joseph H.
Freeman, Frank
French, H. Q., & Co.
Freret, Will A.
Frost, Hart & Shape
Fteley, Alphonse
Fuller & Pitcher
Fuller & Robinson
Fuller & Wheeler
Fuller, Albert W.
Fuller, Charles F.
Fuller, Samuel
Fuller, Thomas
Fullerton, Harold O.
Gaborial, John
Gaggin, E. W. and E. H.
Gale, William A.
Gamble & Sons
Gander, Gander & Gander
Garvin, Michael J.
Gaylor & Pryor
Gaynor, J. P.
Geer, Seth
George, F. H.
Gette, O. J.
Gibb, Arthur Norman
Gibson, Robert W.
Gilbert, C. P. H.
Gilbert, Cass
Gilbert, Cass, Jr.
Gilchrist, Edmund
Gillespie, G. Curtis
Gillett, William J.
Gilman, Winthrop S., Jr.
Ginsbern, Horace
Givens, Darius
Glover, J. G.
Goodhue, Bertram G.
Gordon & Kaelber
Gordon, Edwin S.
Gordon, James Riley
Gordon, Madden & Kaelber
Graham, Ernest R.
Grattan & Jennings
Gray, Thomas A.
Green & Wicks
Green, Edward B.
Green, Isaac H., Jr.
Greene, G. S., Jr.
Greenley, Howard
Greenstein, Louis
Griffin, Percy
Griffin, Tristram
Griffing, J. W.
Gruwe, Emile M.
Hagaman, John I.
Haggerty, John R.
Haight, Charles C.
Halcott, J. B.
Hall, Aaron
Hallenbeck, Earl
Hamlin, W.
Hand, William H., Jr.

Harde & Short
Hardenbergh, Henry J.
Harrison, Henry G.
Harrison, Wallace K.
Harvey, George E.
Hastings, S. P.
Hatch, Stephen D.
Hatheway, Charles
Haugaard, William E.
Hausle, Max
Haydel & Shepard
Hayden, Arthur
Hayes, Warren H.
Heath, John
Hedman, Axel S.
Heins & LaFarge
Heins, George L.
Helmle & Huberty
Helmle, Frank J.
Helmle, Huberty & Hudswell
Hembolt, Henry and Philip
Herter Brothers
Herts & Tallant
Herts, Henry B.
Hewes & Rose
Hewitt & Hewitt
Hildenbrand, Wilhelm
Hill, Amzi
Hill, Anna G.
Hill, James G.
Hill, William R.
Hillger, Samuel
Hinman, Colonel Walker
Hoak, Adolph
Hoffman, Ernest
Holland, Henry Osgood
Holland, J. C.
Holleran, Leslie
Hood & Fouilhoux
Hood, Godley & Fouilhoux
Hood, Raymond
Hooker, John
Hooker, Philip
Hopkins, Alfred
Hoppin & Koen
Hoppin, Francis L. V.
Hoppin, Koen & Huntington
Hopson, Almon Chandler
Horgan & Slattery
Horn, Charles A.
Hornbostel, Henry
Hose & Kieff
Hose, John
Hough & Deuell
Howe, August
Howe, Miles F.
Howell & Thomas
Howlett, William E.
Hubbard, Melvin H.
Hubert, Pirsson & Co.
Huberty & Hudswell
Huckel, Samuel, Jr.
Hueber, Paul, Sr.
Hungerford, Chauncey
Hunt & Hunt
Hunt, R. H.
Hunt, Richard Morris
Hunting, Walter C.
Huntington, Charles P.
Huntington, Robert Palmer
Hyde, F. D.
Hyde, Maxwell
Inness, George, Jr.
Innocenti & Webel
Innocenti, Uberto
Irving, Washington
Isham, Arlington D.
Ives, H. Douglas
Jackson & Rosencrans
Jackson, Alexander C.
Jackson, Thomas S.
Jacobs, Robert Allan
Jacobsen, John C.
Janes & Leo
Jardine, D. & J.
Jardine, Hill & Murdock

The index has been divided into two sections. Index I includes such entries as name of property, location, architect, builder, historic owner, and historical association. Index II lists properties according to style, function, and some particularly significant materials (cast iron, cobblestone). It isolates such National Register listings as archeological sites, battlefields, parks, parkways and roads, and village greens and provides a listing of demolished National Register listings. The properties named and briefly described as components of historic districts are referenced after "see also" at the end of each categorical grouping.

229

Zion Episcopal Church, Greene, 37

Zion Lutheran Church, Athens, 63

see also:

Pierrepont Manor Complex, Ellisburg, 67; Sunnyslope, Bronx, 31

City Halls

Albany, 21

Batavia, 62

Binghamton, 31

Buffalo, 54

Canandaigua, 120

Cohoes, 24

Corning, 154

Elmira, 35

Glens Falls, 172

Gloversville, 61

Kingston, 168

New York, 96

Norwich, 37

Oneonta, 129

Oswego, 157

Plattsburgh, 38

Poughkeepsie (Old), 50

Rochester, 83, 84

Rome, 114

Schenectady, 149

Syracuse, 119

Classical Revival Style (see also **French Neoclassical, Greek Revival,** and **Neoclassical**)

Albany Institute of History and Art, 21

Baron Steuben Place, Corning, 154

Blithewood, Red Hook, 41

Chapel of Our Lady Help of Christians, Cheektowaga, 56

Chemung County Courthouse Complex, Elmira, 35

Congregation Shearith Israel, New York, 95

County Building, Batavia, 62

Dahlgren, Lucy Drexel, Residence, 98

Federal Building, Binghamton, 31

First Baptist Church and Rectory, Tarrytown, 183

First National Bank of Rochester, 84

Flatlands Dutch Reformed Church, Brooklyn, 72

Friends Meetinghouse and School, Brooklyn, 72

Glove Theater, Gloversville, 61

Grant, General, National Memorial, New York, 99

Hill, The, Livingston, 42

King's Daughters Public Library, Haverstraw, 140

Kingston-Rondout 2 Lighthouse, 168

Library, Ogdensburg, 143

Low Memorial Library, Columbia University, New York, 102

Luckey, Platt & Company Department Store, Poughkeepsie, 49

Montgomery Place, Red Hook, 50

Moore, William H., House, New York, 104

Municipal Building, Cooperstown, 128; Ossining, 180

New York School of Applied Design, 105

New-York Historical Society, 95

Peyser and Morrison Shirt Company Building, Glens Falls, 171

Pontiac Hotel, Oswego, 127

Roosevelt Memorial Hall, New York, 94

Society for the Lying-In Hospital, New York, 108

Sylvania, Red Hook, 41

United States Courthouse, New York, 110

United States General Post Office, New York, 110

United States Post Office, Canandaigua, 120; Cooper Station, 110; Gouverneur, 143; Great Neck, 89; Larchmont, 178; Madison Square Station, New York, 110; Malone, 60; Nyack, 141; Potsdam, 144; Rye, 181; Seneca Falls, 153; Troy, 138; Yonkers, 184

United States Post Office and Federal Office Building–Church Street Station, New York, 110

Webster Hotel, New York, 111

Williamsburgh Savings Bank, Brooklyn, 74

see also:

Jumel Terrace Historic District, New York, 102; Market Street Historic District, Potsdam, 144; Morris High School Historic District, Bronx, 29; Park Slope Historic District, Brooklyn, 73; Walnut Street Historic District, Oneonta, 129; Willoughby-Suydem Historic District, Brooklyn, 74

Clubs

Amrita Club, Poughkeepsie, 48

Batavia Club, 62

Black River Valley Club, Watertown, 69

Civic Club, New York, 96

Eccentric Club, Gloversville, 61

Fish and Fur Club, Nelsonville, 131

Fort Totten Officers' Club, Bayside, 133

Harvard Club of New York City, 101

Knickerbocker Field Club, Brooklyn, 72

Lamb's Club, New York, 102

Level Club, New York, 102

Lincoln Club, Brooklyn, 72

Meadow Club, Southampton, 162

Montauk Club, Brooklyn, 73

National Arts Club, 110

New Century Club, Utica, 114

New York Yacht Club, 105

Old Colony Club, New York, 105

Old Grolier Club, New York, 105

Players Club, The, New York, 105

Racquet and Tennis Club Building, New York, 106

Salmagundi Club, New York, 108

Seawanhaka Corinthian Yacht Club, Oyster Bay, 91

Southampton Club, Southampton, 162

University Club, New York, 110; Rochester, 86

Cobblestone Buildings

Alexander Classical School, 62

Barber-Mulligan Farm, Avon, 76

Barnard Cobblestone House, Lima, 77

Barron, Thomas, House, Seneca, 121

Bullis, Charles, House, Macedon, 174

Cobblestone House, Bath, 153; Cazenovia, 79

Cobblestone Manor, Canandaigua, 120

District No. 6 Schoolhouse, Pittsford, 83

Ganoung Cobblestone Farmhouse, Lima, 77

Guilderland Cemetery Vault, 26

Hamilton Farmstead, Mexico, 127

Markham Cobblestone Farmhouse and Barn Complex, Lima, 77

Morgan Cobblestone Farmhouse, Lima, 77

Prospect Hill Cemetery Building, Guilderland, 26

School No. 6, Lima, 77

Schoolhouse No. 6, Guilderland Center, 27

Sibley-Stuart House, Chili, 81

Warner, Oliver, Farmstead, Hopewell, 121

Warsaw Academy, 185

Webster Baptist Church, 87

see also:

Crandall Farm Complex, Cazenovia, 79; Market Street Historic District, Palmyra, 176

Colleges and Universities

Albany Business College, 21

Alfred University, 27

Bard College, Red Hook, 41

Bronx Community College, 29

Colgate University, Hamilton, 80

College of Mount St. Vincent, Bronx, 29

College of New Rochelle, 179

College of the City of New York, 96

College of White Plains, 183

Columbia University, New York, 95, 102, 106

Cooper Union, New York, 98

Cornell University, Ithaca, 165, 166

Crouse College, Syracuse University, 117

Elizabeth Seton College, Yonkers, 184

Elmira College Old Campus, 35

Erie County Community College, Buffalo, 56

Genesee College, Lima, 77

Hamilton College, Kirkland, 114

Hartwick College, Oneonta, 128

Hobart & William Smith College, Geneva, 120

Hunter College, New York, 106

Manhattanville College, Harrison, 178

Marist College, Poughkeepsie, 48

New York University, 98, 101

Rensselaer Polytechnic Institute, Troy, 137

Rockefeller University, New York, 99

Russell Sage College, Troy, 137

Saint Lawrence University, Canton, 142

Schenectady County Community College, Schenectady, 149

Skidmore College, Saratoga Springs, 146

State University of New York at Oswego, 127

State University of New York at Plattsburgh, 38

State University of New York Maritime College, Bronx, 29

Syracuse University, 117, 119

Vassar College, Poughkeepsie, 48

Wells College, Aurora, 33

Westchester Community College, Mount Pleasant, 178

Collegiate Gothic Style

College of the City of New York, 96

General Theological Seminary, New York, 96

Hamilton Hall, Elmira, 35

Hawkins Hall, Plattsburgh, 38

Ossining High School, 180

Peterboro Street Elementary School, Canastota, 78

Sherburne High School, 37

Tompkins Hall, Elmira, 35

Union Theological Seminary, New York, 110

see also:

United States Military Academy, West Point, 123

Colonial Style (see also **Colonial Revival** and **Dutch Colonial**)

Aldrich, Peter, Homestead, Gardiner, 166

Apple Tavern, Guilderland, 26

Arsenal, Huntington, 158

Baird's Tavern, Warwick, 125

Becker Stone House, Wright, 151

Benner House, Rhinebeck, 53

Bethlehem House, 23

Billou-Stillwell-Perine House, Staten Island, 138

Bowne, John, House, Flushing, 132

Buffett, Joseph, House, Huntington, 157

Bull Stone House, Hamptonburgh, 122

Bush-Lyon Homestead, Port Chester, 181

Butler, Walter, Homestead, Mohawk, 88

Carll, Ezra, Homestead, Huntington, 157

Caroline Church and Cemetery, Setauket, 154

Chichester's Inn, Huntington, 157

Conference House, Staten Island, 138

Conklin, David, House, Huntington, 157

Cox Farmhouse, Rhinebeck, 51

Dayton-Stratton House, East Hampton, 156

Dill Farm, Shawangunk, 170

Dodge, Thomas, Homestead, Port Washington, 91

DuBois, Hendrikus, House, Gardiner, 167

Dutch Reformed Church, Fishkill, 46

Edmonston House, New Windsor, 124

Elmendorph Inn, Red Hook, 50

Fort Herkimer Church, German Flatts, 65

Fort Klock, St. Johnsville, 88

Fredenburg House, Rhinebeck, 51

Freeman House, Guilderland Center, 26

Freer House, Poughkeepsie, 49

Gardner, Silas, House, Newburgh, 124

Halsey, Thomas, Homestead, Southampton, 162

Hammond House, Mount Pleasant, 178

Hardenburgh House, Hurley, 167

Hasbrouck, Jean, House, New Paltz, 169

Hawkins Homestead, Brookhaven, 154

Houseman, Peter, House, Staten Island, 139

Huguenot Street Historic District, New Paltz, 169

Hyatt-Livingston House, Dobbs Ferry, 177

Ireland-Gardiner Farm, Huntington, 158

Jagger, Stephen, House, Southampton, 161

Jansen, Johannes, House and Dutch Barn, Shawangunk, 170

Jarvis-Fleet House, Huntington, 158

Kane, John, House, Pawling, 47

Knapp, Timothy, House and Milton Cemetery, Rye, 181

Knox Headquarters, New Windsor, 124

Kreuzer-Pelton House, Staten Island, 139

Lloyd, Henry, House, Lloyd Harbor, 160

Lloyd, Joseph, Manor House, Huntington, 158

Locust Lawn Estate, Gardiner, 167

Melius-Bentley House, Pine Plains, 47

Mesier Homestead, Wappingers Falls, 53

Mill House, Newburgh, 124

Miller, Johannes, Farmhouse, Montgomery, 123

Miller, House, North White Plains, 179

Nellis Tavern, St. Johnsville, 88

Neville House, Staten Island, 139

Oakley, John, House, Huntington, 158

Oblong Friends Meetinghouse, Pawling, 47

Old Fort House, Fort Edward, 173

Old House, The, Southold, 162

Old Lutheran Parsonage, Schoharie, 151

Old St. Peter's Church, Cortlandt, 177

Philipsburg Manor, North Tarrytown, 179

Pier, Jan, House, Rhinebeck, 51

Poillon-Seguine-Britton House, Staten Island, 139

Purdy, Jacob, House, White Plains, 183

Purdy, Joseph, Homestead, North Salem, 179

Raynham Hall, Oyster Bay, 91

Roslyn Gristmill, Roslyn, 92

Sands-Willets Homestead, Port Washington, 91

Senate House, Kingston, 168

'76 House, Tappan, 141

Shaw, Richard, House, Southold, 162

Sherwood House, Yonkers, 184

Shingle House, Warwick, 125

Smith, Henry, Farmstead, Huntington, 159

Smith, Jacob, House, Huntington, 159

Stoothoff-Baxter-Kouwenhaven House, Brooklyn, 74

Stoutenburgh, William, House, East Park, 47

Suydam House, Huntington, 159

Sylvan Cottage, Clermont, 41

Ten Eyck, Matthias, House, Hurley, 167

Terry-Mulford House, Southold, 162

Jacobean Revival Style

Jails

Laboratories

Libraries

Lighthouses

Masonic Halls and Temples

Meetinghouses: see Quaker Meetinghouses

Memorials and Monuments